HISTORY OF THE
ENGLISH-SPEAKING PEOPLES

HISTORY *of the*

ENGLISH-SPEAKING

∘ ∘ PEOPLES ∘ ∘

BY

R. B. MOWAT, Late Professor of History,
University of Bristol

AND

PRESTON SLOSSON, Professor of History,
University of Michigan

NEW YORK   ∘   LONDON   ∘   TORONTO

OXFORD UNIVERSITY PRESS

1943

Printed in the United States of America

THIS BOOK is something of an experiment and an adventure. There have been many histories of the British people and of their Empire-Commonwealth; many also of the American people and their Republic. There have been works on British-American relations, ranging from detailed studies of parliamentary law or of diplomatic controversies to propagandist pleas for Anglo-Saxon solidarity. But there have been very few attempts, such as this, to tell in one narrative the story of all the English-speaking peoples.

The successive parts of the book are designed to show the separate stages in the differentiation of the civilization which began in Britain and has since extended so widely. Part I, 'The Growth of the English Tradition,' deals with origins and carries the story down to the time when a New World was discovered overseas. Part II, 'Britain in the Days of Empire,' covers the evolution of British institutions during the period when colonization was proceeding. Part III, 'The First British Empire,' takes up the transit of civilization from the British Isles to the British colonies in America, and shows the modification of that civilization under the changed conditions presented by a new environment. Part IV, 'The United States of America,' tells the story of the young Republic, with emphasis on the points at which it diverged from British origins and on the new sectional variations between East and West, North and South. Part V, 'The Development of Modern Britain,' deals with British political, social and economic development from the time of the American Revolution to the First World War. Part VI, 'The Second British Empire,' is the story of those overseas possessions which have remained within the Empire: India, the Dominions, the Crown Colonies. Part VII, 'The English-Speaking Peoples between Two Wars,' covers the history of Great Britain, the British Empire-Commonwealth and the United States of America from 1914 to the date of publication of this book.

In this manner, blending the topical method with the chrono-

v

logical, we hoped in some degree to have escaped the Athanasian curse which befalls the historian who either 'confounds the persons' or 'divides the substance' of the proud and distinct American, British, Irish, Canadian, Australian, and South African nations, which nevertheless have so much in common. The authors believed themselves able to make these distinctions, since one was a British historian who had taught in the United States and the other an American who had taught in England, Scotland, and Wales. They did not think it necessary to include many details of national history which, if not actually familiar to 'every schoolboy,' can be found in almost every textbook. Rather the effort has been to emphasize the development of institutions and traditions in the different parts of the English-speaking world, and to make comparisons which will express American facts in terms familiar to British readers and British facts in terms familiar to American readers. Even kinsfolk often need to be introduced to each other!

The tragic death of Professor R. B. Mowat of the University of Bristol deprived me of a dear friend and an invaluable collaborator. The final form of the book shows only too plainly the loss of his skill in giving it finishing touches and a final polish. Fortunately, the main body of the manuscript had been completed some time before he left America, his well-loved 'second fatherland,' for the disastrous airplane voyage across the Atlantic; in substance, the book is as much his as mine, even if in form it may of necessity be too much my own.

PRESTON SLOSSON.

Ann Arbor, Michigan
September, 1942

○ CONTENTS ○

CONTENTS

PART IV

THE UNITED STATES OF AMERICA

PART V

THE DEVELOPMENT OF MODERN BRITAIN

PART VI

THE SECOND BRITISH EMPIRE

PART VII

THE ENGLISH-SPEAKING PEOPLES BETWEEN TWO WARS

◦ LIST OF MAPS ◦

LIST OF MAPS

PART I

THE GROWTH OF THE ENGLISH TRADITION

THE ISLANDERS

THE fact that English is the everyday language of the two greatest units in the modern world, the British Commonwealth of Nations and the United States of America, is commonly taken for granted, without reflection, and yet it is the most important political fact of our time. As every traveler knows, a common language is a convenience; but it is much more than that. So potent, so subtle, so pervasive is the influence of language on mind and character that community of language transcends difference of race. Without destroying the individuality of peoples, community of speech makes them mutually intelligible and—though less certainly—mutually sympathetic.

An American commentator has noted: 'One can hint at, not outline, in the space of a few pages, the greatness and immense power of the group of small islands in the North Sea, which, although territorially only about a third of the area of the state of Texas, have sent out their tentacles to every part of the globe.'[1] The accidents of history have brought about an extraordinary spread for the English language. It extends, though not to the exclusion of other tongues (such as French in Quebec and Dutch in South Africa), over all the British Dominions; it is spoken as a convenient *lingua franca* in nearly all the seaports of Asia; it covers North America from the Rio Grande to the Arctic Ocean; it is a second tongue to many continental Europeans and Latin Americans. At the time of the Norman conquest of England in the eleventh century less than a million persons used it, in its old Anglo-Saxon form; today it is the native tongue of some two hundred millions, and is understood and familiarly used by at least fifty millions more. Chinese alone is spoken by more people, but it is practically confined to one country, whereas

[1] Albert Citon, *Great Britain, An Empire in Transition* (1940), p. 4.

3

English has traveled around the globe in the wake of British and American trade.

But the wide distribution of English is not its only cosmopolitan quality. It has, so lexicographers say, the largest vocabulary of any language, living or dead. It is also the most composite of all languages; it has gathered tribute from every people that Englishmen have encountered, whether in war or trade. In talking English we are constantly speaking also, whether we realize it or not, in French, Latin, Greek, Spanish, Hebrew, and Arabic. For almost every word of pure Anglo-Saxon origin there is at least one synonym taken from the Norman French, and very often others from the Danish, the Latin, or the Greek. But the new words are seldom used in quite the same way as the old; they permit of subtle distinctions of atmosphere if not of definition. One can be both 'fatherly' and 'paternal,' 'hearty' and 'cordial.' This has given English writers a choice of idiom such as the authors of no other language enjoy. In the same age and the same Puritan environment, Milton could use a largely Latin vocabulary while Bunyan rarely stepped outside the Anglo-Saxon.

So great has been the expansion and alteration of the English tongue, in grammatical forms as well as in vocabulary, that the modern Englishman must study Anglo-Saxon as a foreign language and a rather difficult one at that, harder than French, Spanish, or Italian. Anglo-Saxon was as highly inflected as modern German; today English is the least inflected of all the Aryan languages. The nearest kindred to English, Frisian and *Platt-deutsch*, are languages of the misty shores of the North Sea. In origin English, in its old Anglo-Saxon form, was but a Low German dialect, a branch of the great Teutonic tree, which at some unknown time in the past became differentiated from other Aryan tongues.

The Anglo-Saxon homeland has been vividly described for us in the opening words of John Richard Green's *Short History of the English People:*

For the fatherland of the English race we must look far away from England itself. In the fifth century after the birth of Christ, the one country which bore the name of England was what we now call Sleswick [Schleswig], a district in the heart of the peninsula which parts the Baltic from the Northern Seas. Its pleasant pastures, its black-timbered homesteads, its prim little townships looking down on inlets of purple water, were then but a wild waste of heather and sand, girt along the coast with sunless woodland, broken only on the westernside by meadows which crept down to the marshes and the sea. The dwellers in this district were one out of three tribes, all belonging to the same Low German branch of the Teutonic family, who at the moment when history discovers them were bound together into a confederacy by the ties of a common blood and a common speech. To the north of the English lay the tribe of the Jutes, whose name is still preserved in their district of Jutland. To the south of them the tribe of the Saxons wandered over the sand-flats of Holstein, and along the marshes of Friesland and the Elbe.

Bede, who wrote his history in the eighth century, is the authority for the division of the Germanic invaders of Britain into Angles, Saxons, and Jutes. Later authorities, however, have questioned whether there were Jutes among the invaders, and the so-called Jutes may really have come from the middle Rhine.[2] Doubtless there were also some Frisians among the invaders, already much mixed with Angles and Saxons in their homeland. The tribal distribution of peoples so closely kindred, however, matters little. Like other north Germans, the Angles and Saxons were markedly tall and fair, of the type which is now conventionally called 'Nordic.'

All these ancestors of the English were pagan. They were 'free' in the sense that they governed themselves by tribal councils under their chiefs. These chiefs may have been hereditary, but the heads of wartime confederacies of several tribes were not so. Bede tells us that 'These old Saxons have no king, but several satraps set over their own tribes, who at the coming of war draw lots and, whomever the lot falls on, him all follow as leader for the time of war.' This is similar to the custom of other German tribes as described by Caesar, Tacitus, and other early historians.

But Angles, Saxons, and Jutes (if there were Jutes) made up only a part of the population of England before the Norman Conquest. We must reckon also with the native inhabitants of Britain whom they conquered but did not wholly exterminate. The Britons were a Celtic-speaking people, already very mixed in racial origin. Among them were dark Iberians, fair Celts, and no doubt some de-

---

[2] See the discussion of this point in R. H. Hodgkin, *History of the Anglo-Saxons* (1935), I, 89-95.

scendants of Roman legionaries, Phoenician merchants, and other immigrants.

The Roman conquest of Britain had a less permanent effect than the conquest of Spain and of Gaul. Julius Caesar twice raided the country, in 55 and 54 B.C., but it was not until A.D. 43, in the time of the Emperor Claudius, that the Roman occupation was continuous. Britain in time became a fruitful province of the Roman Empire, with walled towns and pleasant country villas, although the climate may have been wetter and colder than it is today.[3] By the end of the Roman occupation, which may be dated either A.D. 417 or in 428,[4] much woodland had been cleared and some marshland drained. The Romans occupied the island as far north as the Forth and the Clyde, where they built the Antonine Wall, 37 miles in length, in A.D. 143. Their permanent settlement, however, extended only as far north as Hadrian's Wall, constructed in A.D. 126, from Bowness on Solway to Wallsend on Tyne, a length of about 73 miles.

The population of Roman Britain has been estimated at half a million. The richest and most populous town was London, a Celtic name but a Roman foundation; 'there were probably more buildings of stone and brick than at any subsequent period until after the great fire of 1666.'[5] As everyone knows, the Romans were masters of highway engineering. Six main roads converged at London: Watling Street, between Chester and the Channel ports; Stane Street, which came from Chichester; Ermine Street from York; and roads from Silchester and Colchester. The Fosse Way, from the mouth of the Axe (at Seaton in Devonshire), through Bath, Cirencester, and Leicester to Lincoln, is the only great Roman road which did not lead to London. The Icknield Way, from Salisbury Plain over the Berkshire Downs and Chilterns to the Wash, was an ancient 'Ridgeway,' dating from the bronze age, perhaps as much as fifteen centuries before the coming of the Romans.

Very little was left of the Roman-British civilization after the de-

[3] E. W. Gilbert, 'The Human Geography of Roman Britain,' in H. C. Darby, *An Historical Geography of England* (1936), p. 31.

[4] Collingwood and Myres, *Roman Britain and the English Settlements* (1936), p. 301.

[5] R. E. M. Wheeler, 'London in Roman Times' (1930), pp. 156-7, in Darby, op. cit. p. 63.

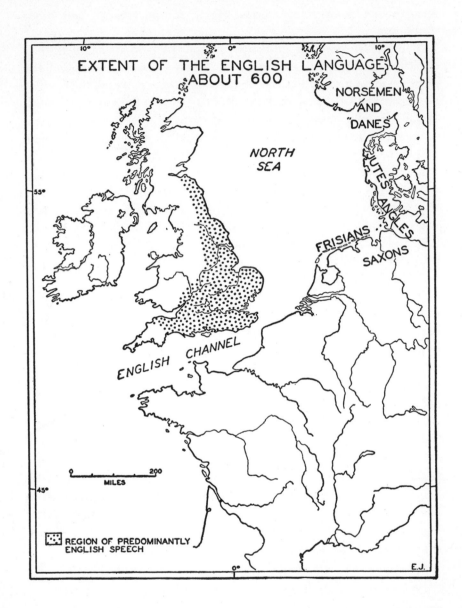

EXTENT OF THE ENGLISH LANGUAGE
ABOUT 600

NORSEMEN AND DANES

JUTES

ANGLES

NORTH SEA

FRISIANS

SAXONS

ENGLISH CHANNEL

0   200
MILES

REGION OF PREDOMINANTLY
ENGLISH SPEECH

E.J.

parture of the legions and the incursions of the Teutonic barbarians. The Angles and Saxons were pagan, and their England was pagan until it had been converted by missionaries from Ireland and from Rome; Christianity retreated to the 'Celtic fringe' of the British Isles—Scotland, Wales, and Ireland. Patrick, the son of a Roman-British family, had been captured by Irish pirates about A.D. 400. After six years of captivity he escaped from Ireland, studied to be a monk under St. Germanus at Tours, returned to Ireland in 432, and began the conversion of the Irish. A Roman-British monk called Ninian Christianized Galloway in southwestern Scotland; another, St. Illtyd, Wales.

The fierce Teutonic invaders had little use for the abandoned Roman towns. All that is meant by 'city life' disappeared for a time. A curious fact is that certain towns (Verulamium, Silchester, Wroxeter, and Caister) were not sacked by the invaders but were peacefully deserted by the inhabitants. 'Where did all these people go? That most of them went to Wales, already densely inhabited, is inconceivable. Some of them may have swelled the emigration to Brittany . . . On the whole it is probable that the greater part of them were absorbed by degrees into the population of the English settlements, and that in this way a stream of Romano-Celtic history and tradition mingled with the life of England.'[6] The assimilation was the more easy since the blond Celts (as distinguished from the dark pre-Celtic Iberian strain) were racially akin to the Teutonic Angles and Saxons; they differed in language and customs rather than in physical type. Hence it is impossible, by mapping the distribution of long heads and short, or blue eyes and brown, in different districts, to settle the much-debated question whether the average modern Englishman is really an 'Anglo-Saxon' or is a Briton who adopted the English tongue!

Some light is thrown on the question, however, by the fact that at the time of the Norman Conquest there were about 600,000 people in England, excluding Wales. It is unlikely that more than 100,000 Angles and Saxons landed in Britain in the fifth century. Danish and Norwegian invasions of the ninth and tenth centuries may have added another 50,000 to the population. Making every allowance for pos-

[6] Collingwood and Myres, op. cit. p. 319.

sible increase in the population—and the age was not favorable to any rapid increase—it seems probable that much of the difference may be accounted for by the presence of Britons, who had neither fled to Wales and Brittany nor died of war and famine, but who, in the phrase of Bede, 'submitted themselves to the enemy for food.'

But the Englishman is more than a blend of Anglo-Saxon and Celtic Briton. The Danes made a deep mark on the country. 'In the northern Danelaw there is no doubt that more than half the native personal names which survived the Norman Conquest are definitely Scandinavian.'[7] After the Danes came the Normans, Scandinavian in origin but French in culture, whose influence on English history was great but whose contribution to English blood was relatively slight.[8] This was the last of the conquests of Britain, but the English stock has been slowly modified by peaceful immigration along the ways of trade by French Huguenot refugees, Flemish weavers, and others.

It is obvious that one must not speak of the English-speaking peoples of today as constituting an Anglo-Saxon *race*. Probably the Angles, Saxons, and Jutes who invaded Britain have contributed less than half of the blood of the modern Englishman, and the mixed English stock in turn makes up at most scarcely two-fifths of the population of the contemporary United States. Moreover, the early Anglo-Saxons were in no discernible respect different from their neighbors in other parts of northern Europe; if 'Anglo-Saxon blood' is blue blood, so equally is Dutch and Danish. The most that can be racially claimed for the English-speaking peoples is that they have a large number of the tall, robust, and energetic North European types, and this is an advantage shared by many other nations including some whose institutions are almost at the opposite pole from the British or the American.

Defoe in his *True Born Englishman* came close to the truth, though he forgot the Celts:

> Your Roman-Saxon-Danish-Norman-English . . .
> A True Born Englishman's a contradiction!
> In speech an irony, in fact a fiction! . . .

[7] F. M. Stenton, *The Danes in England* (Proceedings of the British Academy, 1927), p. 29.
[8] See Chapter III.

A metaphor invented to express
A man akin to all the universe!

Still there is something to be said in favor of a 'man akin to all the universe.' The mixture of strains in the British Isles was, in the main, a good one. All the invaders—Celts, Romans, Saxons, Danes, Normans, and the rest—were physically vigorous, and they were not too different to blend easily into a common national stock. They found a group of islands close enough to the continent for trade and far enough from it for defense, with a mild and yet stimulating climate that both encouraged hard work and permitted it the year round. Great opportunities lay before them; what they did with these opportunities is the subject of this book.

◦ II ◦

THE ANGLO-SAXON POLITY

WHATEVER may be the true proportion of the conquering Angles and Saxons to the conquered Britons, there is no doubt that English life followed in the main the traditions of the former. Aside from place names, there are astonishingly few Celtic words, dating back before the Norman Conquest, in the English language. The laws and customs of the Anglo-Saxon kingdoms were distinctly of Teutonic origin, showing little Celtic or Roman influence. Except in the far-western parts of England, in Wales, and in northwestern Scotland, Great Britain became almost completely Anglicized.

Though the Angles and Saxons long retained differences of dialect, they became 'so intimately linked to one another that in our own island the Angles were called Saxons by strangers and the Saxons were content to call themselves Angles and to speak of their language as English.'[1] This fusion of the tribes was made easier by the gradual process of the conquest. Instead of moving over as units, the Angles and Saxons came as small groups, occupying the land in isolated spots. 'We might as well criticize the positions held, let us say, by early American farmers filtering out into the west of their continent, as apply principles of scientific warfare to the Anglo-Saxon migration to Britain.'[2] This haphazard colonization and settlement of Britain by the Anglo-Saxons occupied about a hundred and fifty years, longer than the 'winning of the West' took the Americans. No doubt it was more destructive, since the land was settled by more or less civilized Celtic peasants instead of being merely a hunting ground for wandering tribes of savages; but it was none the less essentially rather a colonization than a conquest.

The first invasion, that of the so-called Jutes (who may have been

[1] R. H. Hodgkin, *History of the Anglo-Saxons* (1935), I, 6.
[2] Ibid. I, 154.

10

Saxons), was obviously made by a mercenary war band, like one of the Free Companies of the Middle Ages, who would fight with equal zeal for any employer. They were hired by a petty British prince named Vortigern to fight against the Picts, wild inhabitants of northern Britain who had troubled the Romans for centuries and who may have come to southeastern Britain by sea. The names of the Jutish leaders are given by Bede as Hengist and his brother Horsa. They landed at Thanet, then an island, in A.D. 449. Apparently they kept their bargain and defeated the Picts, but they then turned their spears against their paymasters and conquered Kent. They were still pagans, but well advanced beyond barbarism because of their long contact in their homeland with the civilization of the Gauls and of the Franks. Kentish jewelry in the next century was as beautiful as any produced at that period in western Europe.

The next invader whose name has come down to us was Aelle, whose South Saxons have left their name on Sussex, and who landed in 477. The third was Cerdic, who with his son Cymric founded Wessex, the Kingdom of the West Saxons, in 495. About the same period nameless Angles penetrated from the Wash on the east coast into the Midlands, where pagan cemeteries show Angle settlements around the Trent valley and the upper Ouse. The Humber gave a route to Angles who colonized Northumbria. North of the River Tees no pagan cemeteries have been discovered, and it is probable that this region represents a later settlement by Angles from the south of that river.

The long period of colonization drew to an end in the last years of the sixth century and the early years of the seventh. The southern tribes formed a confederacy south of the Thames under the energetic West Saxon House of Cerdic. North of the Trent the Kingdom of Northumbria was formed. In the center, probably younger than either, was the Kingdom of the Borderers or 'Marchmen' (Mercians), Mercia. Little enclaves of native Britons were first surrounded by and then slowly submerged in the advancing flood of Anglo-Saxon invasion. It appears true that the Angles and Saxons did not occupy British villages that were on high ground. They preferred the valleys and lowland plains. Gradually the British hill villages were abandoned, but their site and their fields can still be picked out by air photography.

By the end of the sixth century there were three main kingdoms in England: Northumbria, Mercia, and Wessex; and a fourth, which did not long maintain an independent existence, Kent. All these kingdoms were heathen, though Christianity survived in Wales. The Welsh priests, however, would have nothing to do with their barbarian foes, the English. The conversion of England came from two sources, Ireland and Rome.

Patrick, the Roman-British boy who had been taken prisoner by Irish pirates, became a monk in Gaul and went to Ireland as a missionary in 432. Rather more than a century later, about 550, an Irish missionary, Columba, crossed to the little island of Iona, established a monastery there, and converted the western Scots. In 597, St. Augustine and forty other monks, sent by Pope Gregory the Great, came to Canterbury, the court of King Ethelbert of Kent. By the middle of the seventh century 'Celtic' Christianity had been introduced from Ireland and Scotland into Northumbria; but in 664 the Synod of Whitby decided to follow the Roman rule for all England. The Church in England retained its connection with Rome until 1534, since when it has continued as an independent institution under royal authority.

Northumbria played a brilliant part in the period immediately following the conversion of the Anglo-Saxons. King Edwin of Northumbria (617-33) founded Edinburgh, which still bears his name. Although Northumbrian rule in southeastern Scotland was very brief, the Angles settled the region so thoroughly that some scholars consider it the most Anglian part of Britain, and there the English tongue was spoken with greatest purity. The Northumbrian kings warred successfully with the Mercians and claimed the title of Bretwalda or *Rex Angliae* or *Rex Britonniae*, as if they ruled all the English, or even all Britain. Their power, however, did not extend south of the Thames.

Mercian supremacy was practically limited to the reign of two kings, Ethelbald (716-57) and his cousin Offa (757-96). Little is known of these kings, who must have been men of considerable force of character, to judge from their achievements. Offa called himself *Rex Anglorum*, induced the Pope to make the Mercian bishopric of Lichfield into an archbishopric,[3] and maintained trade

---

[3] This lasted, however, only to the year 802.

with the continent and diplomatic correspondence with Charlemagne, King of the Franks. In the ninth century, however, the West Saxon dynasty increased its influence. Against the Danes they championed all England, and in the end became lords of the whole country.

It was in 850 and 851 that the Northmen, pagan Danes and Norwegians, who had for some fifty years raided and harried the English coasts, first wintered at Thanet, where pagan Jutes or Saxons had preceded them almost exactly four centuries earlier. The partial Danish conquest of England is but one phase of the great expansion of the Scandinavian peoples who, within a few generations, raided Scotland, plundered Ireland, founded a colony in France (Normandy, the Duchy of the Northmen), established their rule in Sicily, settled Iceland, explored Greenland and, probably, the Atlantic coast of Canada, founded a dynasty in Russia, and sent mercenary recruits to the Eastern Roman Emperor at Constantinople! Their settlements in northeastern England, called the 'Danelaw' or region subject to the law of the Danes, formed a kind of 'Normandy in England,' just as the Danish settlements around Dublin formed a short-lived 'Normandy in Ireland.' Except that they were still pagan, the Northmen were not essentially different from the Angles and Saxons. All alike spoke Teutonic languages; all alike were of the tall, fair, North European physical type. Once they had received Christianity they were easily assimilated into the general mass of English population.

The Norse invasions attained their height in the reign of King Alfred of Wessex. All Northumbria and Mercia fell into the hands of the Northmen, and of Wessex only the extreme western portion around Cornwall, Devonshire, and Somerset, a region still partly Celtic, held out against the invaders. King Alfred's sojourn in this West country, his adventures around Athelney,[4] his brilliant victory over King Guthrum and his Danes at Ethandun in 878 are among the favorite tales of English history and legend. Guthrum not only relinquished Wessex but accepted Christianity. A treaty in 886 secured London and all England west and south of the Roman

---

[4] Such as his legendary visit to the Danish camp disguised as a harper, and his finding shelter in a peasant cottage, where he was set to mind the cakes by a busy housewife who took him for a beggar.

road of Watling Street to Wessex; the rest of England was the Danelaw. As the poet Chesterton put it in his *Ballad of the White Horse:*

> A line was drawn north-westerly,
> That set King Egbert's empire free,
> Giving all lands by the northern sea,
> To the sons of the northern star.

King Alfred of Wessex became to the English the ideal of Christian kingship, very much as did Saint Louis, four centuries later, to the French. He was not a legendary figure in the sense in which we can use the word of King Arthur, for we know many indisputable facts about him, but he is legendary in the sense that popular tradition loved to invent stories about him. He was called the father of the jury system and of Oxford University, though both came into existence long after his time. But his fame can rest securely enough on his real work. He collected and selected from the precedents of previous reigns, neglected during the chaos of the Danish wars, the best laws for his subjects. He reformed discipline among the clergy and devoted himself to education. He translated and edited Latin books for popular use. Noting the great military advantage which the Danes possessed in their ability to raid any portion of the English coast, Alfred built a small defensive fleet. His sailors explored the Arctic wastes and his envoys visited distant courts.

After Alfred's time Anglo-Saxon England entered its golden age. Under the warrior kings Edward the Elder (901-25) and Athelstan (925-40), the Danelaw was reconquered. Edgar 'the Peaceful' reigned over a united England from 959 to 975. But the conquest of the Danelaw did not end the Danish peril. In the late tenth and early eleventh centuries there was a new series of invasions, and King Canute (1017-35) ruled all England as part of a great Anglo-Scandinavian Empire. He ruled, however, as an enlightened and Christian monarch, and a few years after his death the old Saxon line was restored in the person of Edward the Confessor (1042-66), a sovereign renowned for piety rather than for wisdom. During his reign the Normans acquired great influence in England, and within a few months of his death England passed under Norman rule, thus ending the Anglo-Saxon period of England's national history.

Though English institutions underwent profound changes under Norman influence, enough remained of their Anglo-Saxon origins to make a study of them useful to all who are interested in any period of English history. In many an English church today the visitor sees first the Gothic towers and spires of its outer shell; then he enters, and sees the round, heavy arches of a Norman nave; then he is shown to the crypt, and down at the very base of the whole edifice are rough-hewn stones that date back to Saxon times. Thus it is with the British constitution. Outwardly it wears a 'late Gothic' form, partly Plantagenet and partly Tudor, but research will reveal the contributions of the Norman and the still earlier Anglo-Saxon foundations.

Among the early Anglo-Saxons kinship was the primary social and political bond. Members of each tribe assumed that they had community of descent. Kinsmen had to answer for each other before the law: they produced the offender and were collectively responsible for his fine; they swore to the character of the accused; they undertook a feud to avenge a slain man of their blood, unless they accepted lawful compensation. Even murder could be condoned for money payment, and the kindred of the victim received and distributed the 'wergild.' The freemen of tribe or village assembled in 'moot' were the court and its judges. Every freeman acknowledged the duty of loyalty to his kindred, to his tribe, and to the chief. He had a share in the village land, and he might have land given or lent him by his chief. People were noblemen, common freemen, or slaves as they were born. If a nobleman were killed the compensation due for his death, his wergild, was higher than that for a commoner.

The head of a tribe or league of tribes was the king. If permanent kingship were not an original Saxon institution, it became so in the course of the conquest of Britain. 'War begat the king.' The number of kingdoms in England varied with the fortunes of war. Sometimes there were more than the seven kingdoms implied in the common phrase 'the Heptarchy'; sometimes the whole land was under a single ruler.

Under the king were the nobles. Nobility by birth conferred social consideration and a high wergild, but it gave no direct political authority. It was soon overshadowed by 'lordship,' for as the lesser kingdoms were drawn together into a common nation, the tie of tribal kindred weakened. Lordship became a substitute for kinship: Athelstan, son of Alfred, ordained in 930 that if the kindred were not sufficient surety for a man, they must 'find him a lord in the folk moot.' In bad times every small man was glad to have a lord and to 'commend' himself by oath. The oath of commendation ran: 'By the Lord before whom this relic is holy, I will be to N. faithful and true, and love all that he loves, and shun all that he shuns, according to God's law . . . on condition that he me keep as I am willing to deserve, and all that fulfil that our agreement was, when I to him submitted and chose his will.' This form seems to date from the time of the early Danish invasions, when the small man had to take a lord as a refuge.

Obviously we have here the beginnings of a feudal relationship, but full-blown feudalism never existed in England until after the Norman Conquest. The basis of feudalism is a permanent tie, based on the tenure of land, and involving service from the tenant to his landlord from generation to generation. In England a Ceorl or common freeman did not lose consideration by commending himself to a lord. His wergild remained the same as before. Evidence from William the Conqueror's Domesday Book proves that a man could undo the tie of commendation, provided that he had discharged all his duties to his lord and so had a clear bill. Such a man could lease his land, could sell it (*potuit recedere, potuit vendere*), and could go where he would (*ire quo vellet*). A great man like Bishop Oswald of Worcester about the year 900 might 'lend' land to the 'thegns' (gentry serving the ruler) and take an oath of obedience from them; but this was not a 'fief' granted in perpetuity; it extended to three or five lives.

The unit of society was the village community, the township or *tun*. In this every free family had the right to land for cultivation and to a share in the common pasturage and woodland. The village might have no overlord; even if it did, the freemen of the village still held their own village moot. In many ways the villagers were better off among the 'barbarous' Anglo-Saxons than had been the provincials of 'civilized' Rome; 'the entry of the Germans into the Roman system brought with it very important innovations and changes which must have considerably improved the position of the small free farmers and especially of the tenants on the large estates.'[5]

The Anglo-Saxons also escaped to a great extent the impositions of the tax gatherer. It was heavy taxation, the grinding impositions, and exactions of the Roman *fisc*, which had ruined the free cultivators of the Roman Empire. In Anglo-Saxon polity there were some, but few and small, dues exacted by the Crown. The king practically 'lived of his own'; and, throughout the whole period, except when 'Danegeld' was levied to buy off the Danish pirates (and Danegeld did not begin until 994), the English had the benefit of little or no taxation.

Everything was regulated by custom. The people of every community knew what was the custom or law of the folk, its 'folk-right.' Every village had its local assembly or 'tunmoot'; every kingdom its 'folkmoot.' The whole folk, however, could not attend the king's court, especially when kingdoms had grown to cover a third or a half of England. Usually for declaration of laws or judgments the king relied on the experienced elders of rank and consideration, the 'wise men' or 'Witan' of the folk. In the larger kingdoms, and the kingdom of all England after Alfred's time, the highest court and legislative assembly was the meeting of the Witan. The Witan were wise men chosen by the king; the device of election was not used by the Anglo-Saxons, 'but the witan of the English were not essentially different from those of the smallest folkmoot in the eyes of Saxon England.'[6]

The term 'legislative assembly' does not, of course, accurately describe the Witan. Medieval Europeans generally thought of law as a permanent tradition, which had rather to be discovered and declared than enacted. Laws were customs. King Alfred went about his business of making laws rather in the spirit of a codifier than in that of a legislator. 'I, then, Alfred, king, gathered these laws together, and commended many of them to be written which our forefathers held, those which seemed to me good: and many of those which seemed to me not good I rejected, by the counsel of my Witan . . . I, then, Alfred, king of the West Saxons, shewed these all to my

[5] A. Dopsch, *The Economic and Social Foundations of European Civilization* (trans. 1937), p. 160.

[6] J. E. A. Jolliffe, *The Constitutional History of Mediaeval England* (1937), p. 25.

Witan, and they then said that it seemed good to them all to be holden.' Sometimes the Witan seems to have taken the initiative, with the concurrence of the king: 'These are the dooms which the witan instituted at Exeter by the counsel of King Athelstan.' If law were the old custom of the folk, the king himself was subject to it. The Bishop of Worcester brought suit against King Berhtwulf at the Mercian Witan, sitting at Tamworth, and obtained judgment for the restoration of certain lands taken by the king.

Between the village or tun and the kingdom stood the shire or county. In Wessex the shires were as old as the first Saxon settlements; Somerset, Wiltshire, Dorset, and Devonshire were the regions of the Sumorsaetas, Wiltsaetas, Dortsaetas, Devonsaetas, and the rest. Elsewhere in England the shire seems to have been a later creation, and to have been grouped around certain fortified towns. In Wessex and Mercia another unit, the 'hundred,' was intermediate between tun and shire. The first mention of it is in the Ordinance of the Hundred, made by King Edgar about 960. The Hundred Moot became an important court, attended by the freemen of the hundred, just as the freemen of the tun attended the Tunmoot. The shire-reeve, or sheriff, was the king's representative in each shire almost from the beginning.

Even in a rude economy like that of the Angles and Saxons, where men lived on the produce of their own fields, the king as much as the rest, and where the folk of each village passed judgment according to local custom, there was still some need of administration. The king had no feudal claim on the services of the 'dear-born' nobles, so he created a sort of knighthood, men who served the king and carried out his instructions. They were commonly called the king's thegns. Some lived in the king's house and looked after his food and drink—the 'cup-thegns' and 'disc-thegns.' The 'hoarders' or 'hoard thegns' kept the king's treasury. The thegns in the shires were landed gentry, who often held land by charter or 'boc' (book), but their boc-land was not dependent on the service they owed the king, and they owed him personal service whether they held land or not; so their position was only remotely analogous to that of the later feudal knighthood.

A freeman with five hides of land—perhaps about 600 acres in all—was certain of being recognized as a thegn if he performed cer-

tain duties for the king; noble birth was no prerequisite. *Peoples'*
Ranks and Laws, a tenth-century compilation, says: 'If a ceorl [com-
mon freeman] throve so that he had fully five hides of his own land,
church and kitchen, bell-house and burh-gate, seat and special duty
in the king's hall, then he was thenceforth of thegn-right worthy.'
The country gentleman, active in the affairs of local government and
occasionally also in national affairs, is already becoming a feature of
the English polity!

As compared with the Roman Law, or the Norman system of administration later introduced, or indeed most of the continental European legal systems, the Anglo-Saxon polity was extraordinarily
informal and flexible. Custom governed nearly everything; there
were few written laws. Thus the monarchy was, in a sense, hereditary, for it was usually kept within the same dynasty and no one but
a prince of the blood, or at least a high noble, would be considered
for the kingship; yet the consent of the Witan seems to have given
the king his legal position, and the nearest heir by blood was sometimes set aside as too young, or otherwise unfit. The powers and
duties, even the composition, of the Witan itself were never precisely
defined. All over England there was a network of feudal contracts,
and yet no precisely organized 'feudal *system*.' Many slaves had risen
to serfdom; many freemen had sunk into the same rank. The old
nobility of blood and the new nobility of royal service overlapped
and confused each other. Even after the kingdom had become united
in name, it was parcelled out among great earls who enjoyed almost
royal privileges within their own domains; in a sense, the England
of Edward the Confessor might be called a federal state. Yet England had more real national unity than the Kingdom of France or
the Holy Roman Empire could boast at the same period, and feudal
fragmentation of royal authority never went quite so far in England
as it frequently did on the continent.

A few generations ago there was a tendency among historians to
read modern conceptions into the old Anglo-Saxon institutions. Thus
the popular 'moots' which arranged fines, determined land titles, and
decided whether accused criminals must undergo an 'ordeal' were
called 'juries'; the Witan was considered a law-making, tax-granting
Parliament; a direct, lineal connection was traced from German tribal
institutions described by Tacitus to the New England town meeting.

In the seventeenth and eighteenth centuries some radical reformers even contended that the Norman conquest had ended a liberal democracy, and that 'our ancient constitution' was based on the 'right to every freeman' to an equal share in the government.

Against this idealization of the Anglo-Saxons there came a reaction. A new generation of historians pointed out that the Witan was merely an advisory assembly of dignitaries and not an elected parliament; that the jury was a French institution imported into England by Norman kings; and that, in general, the origins of the 'British constitution' were Norman and feudal rather than Saxon and popular. All this may be conceded, without denying importance to early English institutions. After all, the Angles and Saxons at least drew the map of England; their 'shires' are still its major divisions. An American county still has its sheriff and an American town its board of aldermen, though their functions are no longer those of the old 'shire-reeve' and 'ealdormen.' The tradition of local self-government, zealously preserved in all countries of English speech, is a continuous one from the times of the Heptarchy to our own.

There were also stubborn, deep-rooted political habits, whether one call them principles or prejudices, which have been championed in each generation against the arbitrary power of feudal lords or ambitious monarchs. Though they were not peculiar to the Anglo-Saxons, being found with minor variations in most Teutonic countries, they were better preserved in England than elsewhere, and they have influenced all lands where the English tongue is spoken.

One of these principles is the personal liberty of the freeman. Each common man, if he were not of the small class of slaves, had certain rights guaranteed by custom or contract or tribal law. Even though he commended himself to a lord, his freedom was limited only by the terms of the agreement; to his neighbors, to strangers, and to all men but his feudal superior he was still a freeman. The harsher Norman conceptions of feudal status lessened this freedom, and yet within a few centuries it reappeared more clearly defined than before. England was almost the first country in Europe to witness the disappearance of serfdom within its bounds.

Another principle was the supremacy of law over mere executive power. The Anglo-Saxon kings were codifiers rather than legislators; their 'wise men' professed (almost in the spirit of a modern American

Supreme Court) to interpret old law and custom rather than to make new laws. No doubt this reverence for mere custom and tradition, this readiness to warp an old law out of its original meaning to meet a new situation rather than frankly to innovate, had its unfortunate side. But it contained the useful idea of a Common Law, more fully developed in later centuries,[7] which is handed down from age to age by judicial decisions on cases actually arising; a law flexible and adaptable to new conditions, and yet never tearing itself loose from its first roots. In this way freedom has been able to 'broaden down from precedent to precedent' where a fixed code might have required a revolution to alter it.

[7] See Chapter IV.

III

THE NORMAN CONTRIBUTION

THE Norman Conquest of England was on a much smaller scale than the earlier Danish invasions. Perhaps not more than 5,000 warriors followed the banner of William the Conqueror when he landed on English soil in 1066. Even if we double or treble this figure to allow for later French and Norman immigration following in the wake of the successful army, it remains true that the Normans were a mere garrison in the conquered land, like the Romans in early Britain or the modern British in India.

The real importance of the Conquest was of quite another sort. As the historian Stubbs remarks, it gave a Norman superstructure to the Anglo-Saxon substructure. In Anglo-Saxon institutions there was more freedom than authority; in Norman institutions more authority than freedom. The Normans brought in strong kingship, a military aristocracy, a fully developed feudal system under which every man owed service to his special 'lord.' There was sharper definition in the laws, and stricter discipline in the Church. Under the harsh but salutary rule of the Normans, England became for centuries the most centralized, the best-administered, and possibly the most truly national state in all Catholic Christendom. In the long run this was an advantage even to freedom, since England, having early attained national unity, was not forced, like most of the nations of the continent, to struggle through centuries of anarchy to win it, and hence escaped the temptation to overvalue mere 'strong government.' William the Conqueror performed his task so thoroughly at the start that England in later years had no need to develop a Richelieu, a Peter the Great, or a Mussolini.

The Normans, as their name implies, were the Northmen. They were a mixed group of Scandinavians, probably in most part from Norway, but certainly with many Danes and Swedes among them.

Driven from their homes by pressure of population, by dislike of the stricter royal rule which the early Scandinavian kings were beginning to impose, or by sheer love of plunder and adventure, they became the terror of all the European coasts. They were pagans whose religion was war, whose virtues were valor and military loyalty, who could gain heaven only by dying bravely in battle. Arrogant and oppressive as they were, they had a fierce love of freedom among themselves, and the man who led them into battle must have uncommon qualities if he could secure any kind of obedience when the campaign was over. Paradoxically enough, they were also eager litigants, fond of the ritual and formalities of law, competent administrators, as ready to engage in trade as in battle. The Icelandic sagas, such as the *Saga of Burnt Njal*, are full at the same time of lawless violence and of pedantic insistence on legal technicalities.

In the course of their raids the Northmen visited the shores of France. According to an old tradition Charlemagne is said to have wept over the fate of his successors when he saw the long viking ships on the sea. He did not live to experience their invasions, but a few generations later France had been shaken almost to atoms. In 911 the hard-pressed King Charles 'the Simple' granted a large province to the Norse chief Rollo (or Hrolf) to hold from him in feudal dependence. A few years later neighboring districts in the north of France were added, and thus grew the Duchy of Normandy. From 911 to 1204, when Philip Augustus made the French monarchy the real, not merely the nominal, overlord of Normandy, the Duchy continued to play a remarkable part in European history. The lords of Normandy became Christians, even particularly devout ones; they accepted with singular readiness the French language, laws, and customs; they intermarried with Frenchmen of suitable rank; but they retained all their old love of war and adventure, their haughty spirit of domination, and their remarkable capacity for law and government.

The institutions of Normandy, like those of most parts of France, were thoroughly feudal; indeed in no part of the world were feudal institutions more systematically organized. Every man, unless he were a king (sometimes even in that case), must have an overlord. To this overlord he owed service; from him he held his lands or other property. Among men of good birth this service was usually military, save in the special case of the clergy. Among the humble, service was in labor or in a share of the crops. All tenants owed not service only, but obedience; the 'vassal' must carry his legal business to his lord's court. (By refusing to do this, in a later generation, King Balliol lost Scotland to Edward of England; and King John of England lost Normandy to Philip Augustus of France.) A lord on his travels was usually entertained at the cost of his tenants, and he often had the right to demand special fees on grand occasions, such as the knighting of his son, the marriage of his daughter, the payment of ransom in war, or the transfer of a tenancy to a new heir. Even the Church came into the feudal system; the lands of a bishopric or abbey had to pay feudal fees and provide knights for the king's service, but the terms of tenure were often lighter than for lay vassals.

The greatest of the Dukes of Normandy, and perhaps the most remarkable ruler of any eleventh-century state, was William, the illegitimate son of Duke Robert. Because of the shadow on his birth he had to fight for recognition in his native duchy. Even after he had made his authority good, he had many wearisome wars with his subordinates, the rebellious barons; with his equals, such as the Counts of Anjou; and with his superior, the King of France. Long before he invaded England he was one of the great captains of the age. 'Only because the duke was strong at home could he hope to be strong abroad, only because he was master of an extraordinarily vigorous, coherent and well-organized state in Normandy could he attempt the . . . task of conquering a kingdom and the still greater task of organizing it under a firm government.'[1]

It is no disparagement of his ability to say that William was greatly favored by circumstances. The death of Edward the Confessor left the succession to the throne of England uncertain. Harold, son of Earl Godwin, was chosen by the Witan. He was a public-spirited noble and a competent soldier; had he survived he might have become a memorable king. But he was not of the old royal house, and he had many enemies among his jealous fellow nobles. Even his own brother Tostig rebelled against him and leagued with a foreign monarch, King Harold Haardraade of Norway. Against him Duke William advanced a fourfold claim: he was kinsman to the late

---

[1] C. H. Haskins, *The Normans in European History* (1915), p. 72.

King Edward; he had Edward's favor as a candidate to the throne; Harold had once given him an oath of allegiance (apparently to redeem himself from captivity); and the Pope had consecrated his banner on the ground that Harold was forsworn and because the Archbishop of Canterbury, Stigand, was regarded as schismatic. It was characteristic of the legalistic Norman temper to find so many ingenious pretexts and justifications for what was essentially a war of conquest.

Harold defeated the Norwegian invasion at Stamford Bridge, and then marched south in great haste to fight the Normans under William. A single battle (Hastings or Senlac) crushed the English army and left the English king dead on the field. William secured the submission of London and southern England, but he had to carry fire and sword through the northern shires before the land was quiet under his rule. Though, from his own standpoint of legal right, William had merely enforced his claim to the throne against a usurper, he proceeded to deal with England as a conquered land. Not by any one definite act, but by piecemeal confiscation as the country was conquered after the battle of Hastings, the estates of the vanquished were parcelled out among the four or five thousand Normans who became lords of manors. Some of the English, that is of the Angles, Saxons, and Danes, retained their status as freemen; the rest became villeins. Hardly any were left among the landowning aristocracy.

'No land without a lord' was the principle on which William's lawyers worked, so a chain of lordship was set up, with everyone below the king a tenant of someone above him, and even King William still held Normandy and Maine as vassal of the King of France, though he refused to accept any superior for England itself. Tenants-in-chief, called the Major (great) Barons, held their land directly from the king. They attended the Council (*Concilium* or *Curia Regis*), which took the place of the old Saxon Witan. Like its predecessor, this was not really a Parliament but an advisory council; it had, however, a more definite structure and was more closely tied to the feudal system and the holding of land. The tenants-in-chief had tenants of their own, from whom they exacted dues of the same nature that they paid to their own overlord the king; but King William wisely made all the landowners, great and small, 'whosoever men they were,' swear allegiance directly to himself. Allegiance to the king was to be their primary obligation.

English feudalism, as organized by King William, thus differed from the type prevailing generally on the continent in that loyalty to the king was every man's first obligation; loyalty to his immediate landlord came second. This helped prevent successful rebellions by ambitious nobles. Though there was no standing army, the king had a double recourse in time of war. He could call on his great barons in the name of their feudal obligations to supply and equip a fixed number of cavalrymen from among their own knightly tenants, and of infantry from among their retainers of humbler birth. He could also, following the old Saxon law, summon the Fyrd or militia of every able-bodied freeman.

To keep the conquered English in awe, the Normans built many castles. Some of these, such as the Tower of London, were of stone, but many of the earliest ones were merely wooden towers protected by stockades and earthworks (not unlike the early forts erected in frontier days against the American Indians). As military architecture improved, these early wooden 'keeps' were replaced by stone, longer walls were built around ample courtyards, the simple ditch became a moat filled with water and crossed by a drawbridge, the living quarters within the castle were made more comfortable; and at last, by the time of the first Edward, we have the lovely English castles which stand today, with their quiet courts and grassy lawns, looking like abodes of ancient peace rather than grim fortresses for war. Some of the castles, such as the Tower, were garrisoned directly by the king; but most of them were baronial, defended by the men-at-arms of the nobleman who held the manor. They were particularly numerous on the Welsh and Scottish borders. It is a testimony to the strong and efficient central government of England, or perhaps to the protection of the sea, that but few English cities found it necessary to have the elaborate walled fortifications so general in Germany, France, and Italy.

The lords held their land in manors; that is to say, the estate of each lord was either a single manor or comprised several of them. In many cases a manor was identical in extent with a parish, whose boundaries were often very old, and would have its village church as well as its manor house where the lord resided. A typical manor would have its mill stream and fishpond, its pasture and woodlot, its mill and forge, its row of cottages and its arable fields. The land was divided into strips, so arranged that each holder had some of the better and some of the poorer land, and some of the strips would be reserved as 'demesne land' for the lord and some as 'glebe land' for the Church. Usually a third of the cultivated land was allowed to lie fallow each season so as to recover its fertility—the 'three field system' of agriculture (though in some places there was a two-field system). The 'waste' would be common [2] to all the inhabitants of the manor for pasturage, and each tenant would have certain rights to cut wood. Plowing was done by oxen.

A main source of our knowledge of rural England in early Norman times and earlier is the *Domesday Book,* or census of persons and property which King William caused to be levied in order that the feudal dues which were his right might be accurately assessed. His census takers were asked to report the name of each manor, its owner in the time of King Edward the Confessor, the number of 'hides,' [3] the number of plows, the number of farmers and laborers of different classes, the value in King Edward's time and in King William's. Social classes were still in a confused state of transition between Saxon informality and Norman legalism. There were free peasants and 'socmen,' who had to attend the manor court but were in no way bound to the soil; 'villeins,' or common peasants of the estate or 'vil'; 'cottars' and 'bordars,' peasants or laborers of the poorer sort; even a few slaves. Slavery and the slave trade existed in Anglo-Saxon times, though slaves never made up more than a small minority of the population. The tendency of Norman law in the long run was to obliterate all these fine social distinctions, and simultaneously raise the slave and lower the free peasant until the great majority were in a common class of 'serfs.'

King William was careful and correct in his relations with the Church. His Norman Archbishop of Canterbury, Lanfranc, saw to it

---

[2] The village 'common' of modern times still carries the old idea of a reserve of land held in common by all the villagers, though it has now a more restricted meaning, since in the eighteenth and early nineteenth century most of the good common land was 'enclosed' into individual farms.

[3] The exact extent of this measure of land is still a subject of debate by antiquaries, but an average 'hide' was 120 acres.

that every diocese had a Norman bishop. From this time onward parish churches of stone began to replace the wooden ones which had often sufficed the Anglo-Saxons. Though King William jealously maintained his own royal rights, even against the Pope, he perhaps erred in setting up special courts for the clergy, in which clergymen alone might be judges; for this concession, though it relieved the shire courts of clerical business, made trouble for his successors.

One noteworthy result of Norman rule was Forest Law. Certain royal forests were set apart, and in some cases villages were demolished to make way for them. In these forests only the king and his guests might hunt, and poachers were liable to lose a hand or a foot if they were caught killing the king's deer. The writer of the *Anglo-Saxon Chronicle* tells us that King William, 'As he forbade killing the deer, so also the boars; and he loved the tall stags as if he were their father. He also appointed concerning the hares, that they should go free. The rich complained and the poor murmured, but he was so sturdy that he recked nought of them.' Strict rules for the preservation of game and severe punishments for poaching remained a notable feature of British law well into the nineteenth century.

Several features of Norman law show the watchfulness of a ruling, but hated, minority. Such was the 'curfew' (cover-fire), which forbade people to wander abroad late at night. Such also was the 'presentment of Englishry,' which placed the burden of proof on any locality that a slain man was 'merely' an Englishman; if he proved to be a Norman a special fine was levied on the whole district. The law of England is rich to this day in terms of Norman French and Norman Latin origin. Yet the old local Saxon courts did not speedily disappear; 'hundred moot' and 'shire-moot' long continued to do local business after the central government had become completely Norman. The shire-moot was attended by the freemen of the county and by the 'four best men and the reeve' from every manor.

In 1087 King William died while on a campaign in France. His eldest son, Robert, became Duke of Normandy (his second son, Richard, had been killed while hunting); his third son, William II or 'Rufus' (the 'Red'), became King of England. Thus Normandy and England were separated, and it would undoubtedly have been well if they had so remained. To the kings of that age, however, neither English nor Normans constituted a nation; England and

Normandy were pieces of feudal property which might or might not happen to belong to the same ruler. In 1100 William Rufus died, slain by an arrow in the New Forest where he hunted the deer. He was an unpopular ruler, having all the harshness of his father without his genius. He did, however, do much to consolidate the feudal system (especially the military side of it) and to extend royal authority over 'Strathclyde,' the half-Celtic region of Lancashire, Westmoreland, and Cumberland.

Henry I (1100-1135), the fourth son of William the Conqueror, was a well-educated man who deserved the title of 'beauclerk' popularly given him.[4] Like all the English kings from William I down to and including Edward III he spoke, wrote, and thought in French. He defeated and imprisoned his elder brother Robert of Normandy and thus once more united Normandy and England under a single ruler.

As the barons, who were all of Norman blood, preferred the easy-going Robert, King Henry relied for support on the English, and to win their good will restored the 'Law of Edward.' No one knew exactly what the Law of Edward was; but it was taken to mean the old English customs, as known in every village or manor, and also the old shire-moots and hundred moots, as they existed before the Conquest. The English were immensely pleased, and when rebellion broke out in Normandy they followed Henry and fought as the old popular Saxon militia, the Fyrd, at Tinchebrai in 1106, where the rebel Normans were completely defeated. Further to conciliate the English, Henry married Matilda, a princess of the old Saxon line. The monkish chronicler, William of Malmesbury, says that the Norman nobles laughed at Henry and his English queen and nicknamed them 'Godric and Godgifu.'

There was far more method in medieval administration than is generally understood. William I had largely relied on his feudal retainers for administration, but Henry I began to enroll the lesser gentry into his 'household,' and thus form a sort of royal civil service. Many of these were laymen; for although the clergy were the best-educated men of the age, and freely employed for diplo-

---

[4] He was wont to say that an ignorant king was but *un âne couronné* (a crowned ass).

matic services, they had a double allegiance, to the Pope as well as to the king. In the reign of Henry I there was a serious dispute in England, analogous to disputes in France and in the Holy Roman Empire, about the investiture of the clergy with land. To the king a bishop or abbot holding lands was simply a feudal dependent who ought, like other tenants, to give an oath of allegiance to his land-lord. But the Pope and the clergy objected that this would, in effect, amount to royal appointment of church officials. The peaceful resist-ance of the English clergy to the king's demands was led by the scholarly and saintly Anselm, Archbishop of Canterbury. Fortu-nately, both king and archbishop kept their tempers, and in 1107, in the Concordat of Bec, they agreed that bishops and abbots should be elected (but in the presence of the king) by the chapters of their cathedrals or monasteries; and that after election they should be in-vested by the king with their lands, and so, in a strictly temporal way, should do him homage. Election in the presence of the king really meant that the king's nominee would be chosen.

The last of the direct line of Norman kings was Stephen, Count of Blois, whose mother was a daughter of William the Conqueror. Matilda, daughter of Henry I, also claimed the throne, and received a good deal of popular support, particularly in the West Country around Bristol. The result of the civil war was anarchy, for between two rival monarchs the lawless barons could do very much as they pleased. They struck their own coins, raised their own soldiers, cap-tured and held for ransom wealthy commoners. In short, during Stephen's reign (1135-54) England had a brief experience of the uncontrolled tyranny of a feudal nobility which was the rule rather than the exception on the continent. The last continuer of the Anglo-Saxon Chronicle, a monk of Peterborough, wrote that cultivation was no longer worth undertaking, 'You might as well have tilled the sea,' and added that the harassed common people openly said that 'Christ and his saints slept.' On Stephen's death the throne passed to Henry, son of Matilda and of Geoffrey of Anjou. A new line of French princes was to rule over England.

Nigel, Bishop of Ely, tells in his *Dialogue of the Exchequer*, written some eighty years after Henry I came to the throne, how the amalgamation of Norman and Saxon proceeded apace. 'The two peoples are now so intermixed that it is scarcely possible to discern who is English, who Norman.' He added, 'I am speaking of free-men,' for in England only English were villeins; the Normans were gentry. When villeinage, however, began to decay, there was only one people. Particularly after the loss of Normandy in 1204, the Anglo-Normans gave up calling themselves 'Normans.'

Though the direct Norman line had failed, Normandy still re-mained an essential and central part of the Angevin Empire of Henry II and his sons. Norman nobles were still the aristocracy of England. Norman institutions continued to modify English law. Norman bishops governed the English Church. As Henry Adams put it, the Normans 'were a part, and a great part, of the Church, of France, and of Europe . . . Norman Dukes cast the Kings of France into the shade . . . Normans were everywhere in 1066, and everywhere in the lead of their age.' [5] The Norman kingdom of Sicily, a by-product of the expanding energies of that remarkable people, was as distinctive a political achievement in its own way as the Norman kingdom of England. But both instances show the most remarkable characteristic of the Normans, the ease with which they became assimilated to their environment. Just as the Sicilian Norman became an Italian, and the Norman of Rouen a Frenchman, so did the Norman conqueror of the English become in time an Eng-lishman. Like water in thirsty soil, the Normans enriched at the same time that they disappeared. The English language was remade by its contact with a French-speaking Norman ruling class, but it was English and not French which prevailed. Only the French form of some English family names (usually pronounced in a thoroughly unGallic fashion) testifies to the days of the Conquest.

[5] Henry Adams, *Mont Saint Michel and Chartres* (1933 edition), p. 4.

IV

ENGLAND AS PART OF THE ANGEVIN EMPIRE

THE accession of Henry II (1154-89) made England part of a great empire. A man of the twelfth century might, indeed, quarrel with the term 'empire,' since to him there were at most two Emperors in the world—the Basileus of the Eastern Roman Empire at Constantinople, and the Kaiser of the Holy Roman Empire in Central Europe, the two claimants to the mantle of ancient Rome. But in the looser modern sense of 'empire,' a state made up of many states, King Henry ruled an empire indeed. Besides being King of England directly and in his own right, he was also by various feudal tenures ruler of half of France—Normandy, Maine, Anjou through inheritance, and Poitou, Guienne, Gascony and the disputed County of Toulouse by his marriage with Eleanor of Aquitaine. He also claimed suzerainty over Celtic Wales in Britain and Celtic Brittany in France, and he was the first English sovereign seriously to undertake the conquest of Celtic Ireland.

It is not, however, the extent of Henry's Angevin Empire that is the notable fact, but the means which he adopted to govern it. This is shown, for example, in his handling of the military problem. He began to accept money in lieu of personal military service from his barons; this was called *scutage*, or shield-money, and he employed it to raise a hired army of mercenaries. These soldiers might be Englishmen, but equally they might be Welshmen, Flemings, Frenchmen, or of any other nationality, and at the end of each campaign they were paid off and were free to enlist under any other banner. This manner of raising troops was everywhere common till the eighteenth century; there was a touch of it even later in the French 'Foreign Legion.'

Far more important than King Henry's military innovations were his legal reforms. It was he who did most to make the king's justice

THE ANGEVIN EMPIRE

NORTH
SEA

SCOTLAND

IRELAND

YORK

CHESTER

WALES

SEVERN

CAMBRIDGE

OXFORD
LONDONS
BRISTOL
R. THAMES
CANTERBURY
WINCHESTER

ENGLISH CHANNEL

ROUEN
R. SEINE
NORMANDY

BRITTANY MAINE

ANJOU
R. LOIRE

POITOU

MILES 200

AUVERGNE

BORDEAUX
DORDOGNE R.
TOULOUSE
GARONNE R.
GASCONY

DOMINIONS DIRECTLY
GOVERNED BY HENRY II
DOMINIONS DEPENDENT
ON HENRY II

E.J

supersede that of feudal lords and of local courts. He did not abolish these by any sweeping decree but put them out of existence by persuading as many persons as possible to take their legal business into the king's courts and by devising writs to bring all manner of cases to them. He did not do this solely from love of justice, but partly to increase the royal power and also to increase the royal revenues. King's justice was not free. But, as a biographer of Henry II has remarked, 'if the commodity was expensive it was at least the best of its kind, and there is a profound difference between the selling of justice and of injustice.'[1] The royal judges were usually preferred by honest litigants, because they were more impartial than local judges subject to all the prejudices and self-interest of the neighborhood.

The king was an incessant traveler, for he had to superintend territories stretching from the Scottish border to the Bay of Biscay and almost to the Mediterranean. He was also the 'fountain of justice,' and it was not always easy to keep up with a stream which ran so rapidly! A certain Richard of Annesty followed the king about for seven years before gaining a judgment. This must, however, have been an exceptional episode, for King Henry, aware that even he could not be everywhere at once, organized a very efficient system of circuit courts and appointed judges, 'justices in eyre,' to superintend them. This is the origin of the Assizes which take place three times a year in all county towns. The justices in eyre were—and still are—the High Court come down into the counties. The judge on circuit is always received in state, lives in a noble house, and entertains the gentry royally.

The judges' chief business was the repression of crime. Henry II was familiar with the workings of the jury system in French and Norman law. This was not the modern institution of trial by jury, but rather the investigation of a case with the aid of independent witnesses of repute, sworn (*juré*) to aid the judge in ascertaining facts. The Norman kings had used this method in England on occasion. Henry II made it a common and accepted routine. In every hundred, twelve reputable men were named to 'present' to the justice in eyre any person accused of serious crime. This 'jury of presentment' was called in modern times the Grand Jury and existed in England until

[1] L. F. Salzmann, *Henry II* (1915), p. 176.

its abolition in 1932. The Grand Jury still exists in some American states.

When the jury of presentment put before the judge a reputed robber or murderer, the judge still might use the ancient Saxon 'ordeal' as a test of the validity of the accused man's oath. Henry II evidently doubted the efficacy of the ordeal or the honesty of those who administered it, for he ordained that men of bad reputation, even if acquitted by the ordeal, must leave the country. In the next generation the ordeal was generally abandoned, partly because of the growing disapproval of the clergy,[2] partly also because a new and better method of trying cases was beginning to be used. This was trial by a second jury, a 'petty jury,' of twelve men. It soon replaced not only the ordeal, but also the Saxon custom of 'compurgation' or acquittal by the solemn oath of the accused, supported by a legally fixed number of independent 'oath helpers' who were willing to peril their souls to testify to their belief in his oath. The Norman 'trial by battle' also gradually fell into disuse. It is an amusing evidence of English conservatism that neither compurgation nor trial by combat, though long obsolete, was formally abolished by statute till the nineteenth century.

Henry II also applied the jury method to the determination of civil causes. Hitherto persons disputing land titles had often settled the matter by a formal duel or trial by combat. Henry II ordained, about 1170, that the defendant in a property dispute, instead of submitting to the 'dilatory and uncertain' verdict of the duel, could 'put himself on the Assize,' which would give him a jury of twelve men to try the case. Possession as distinct from property (or 'ownership') could also be decided through a jury. This was ordained by Henry II in three 'possessing assizes'—*mort d'ancestor, darrien presentment* (dealing with presentations to clerical benefices), and *novel disseisin.*

By a curious paradox which almost every historian has noted, trial by jury, one of the bulwarks of English liberty, had thus a foreign and royal origin. A Frankish institution, it had been carried to England by the Normans and developed on English soil by Norman and Angevin kings. Still more curiously, it died out in the land of

---

[2] Pope Innocent III in the Lateran Council in 1216 forbade the clergy to take part in the ordeal.

its origin. The Roman law, with its emphasis on the judge instead of the juryman, influenced all the countries of Roman Catholic Christendom in the later Middle Ages, but of all those countries it seems to have influenced England least.

Except in the ecclesiastical and chancery courts, it never obtained any considerable hold in England. It is due to the work of Henry II that it did not, for, while in other countries no single system existed able to dispute the superior claims of the intrusive guest, Henry II so simplified and unified divergent practices that by the time the Roman law was in a position to make itself felt in the Island, the common law was too widespread and too firmly founded to be supplanted by an alien rival.[3]

Henry II practically completed the 'rule of law' by one of the clauses in his Assize of Clarendon: 'Let there be no one in a city or town or in a castle or outside a castle, not even in the honour of Wallingford, who shall forbid the sheriff from entering his land.' The sheriff was a royal officer, dating from Anglo-Saxon times. Cities and towns, and still more the privileged lords of castles, 'honours,' and 'socs,' claimed to be areas of private jurisdiction where 'the king's writ did not run.' Henry now ordained that his officers could not be excluded from private jurisdictions. It seems a little humorous, however, that as an example of a grand honor which could not exclude a royal officer he should have selected Wallingford (on the Thames below Oxford), which already belonged to the Crown!

This great king was checked in one direction in his attempts to make the king's law uniform throughout the land, and the man who checked him was no great baron or distant Pope but one of his own chosen officials, Thomas Becket. Almost the first act of the young king on coming into power was to appoint an energetic young Englishman of the middle class, the son of a London merchant, to be his highest official, the Chancellor. Thomas Becket, full of the joy of life and eagerness for work, ably seconded the king in war and peace. In 1159 when King Henry led an army against the Count of Toulouse and the King of France, Becket led a company of knights. He is still remembered in Cahors; it is told of him that he would scour the country not only for the enemies of his master but for manu-

[3] A. L. Cross, *A Shorter History of England and Greater Britain* (1929), p. 77.

scripts in monastic libraries. Many an hour he spent reading, and admiring the beautiful illuminations, the painting, and gold work of the monks. When he returned to England he brought some of the manuscripts with him. He was a clerk in minor orders. Pleased to find a candidate at once so competent, so learned, so devout, and (as Henry thought) so compliant with royal wishes, the king secured his appointment as Archbishop of Canterbury, the highest office in the English Church.

But Thomas Becket considered the new office as the beginning of a new career and the service of a new master. To the king's displeasure he resigned the Chancellorship and devoted himself wholly to the interests of the clergy. He opposed the methods or irregularities of the collection of the tax called 'Danegeld.' [4] But open quarrel broke out only when King Henry proposed to extend the jurisdiction of the king's courts and laws to the clergy.

In nothing is the age of Henry II more unlike our own than in the position of the Church. In modern times there are many churches, sects, and denominations; liberty is accorded to all, and none, even if established by law, has a very privileged position. In medieval Christendom there was but one Church. All believed its creed and were subject to its authority, and not in spiritual matters only but in many others which today are left to secular authorities. Bishoprics, abbeys, and other clerical foundations held from a third to a fifth of all the lands in western and central Europe.[5] This wealth was never scattered among different heirs, since the clergy were celibate; or subject to ordinary taxation, or quite so liable as secular property to the hazards of war and confiscation. By tithing the laity the Church had revenues over and above its heavy endowments in productive land. From those revenues, the clergy carried on almost the whole work of education and philanthropy: the schools, the hospitals, the payment of alms and doles to the poor, which now fall so largely on the taxpayer.

Having a great sense of their corporate unity, the clergy claimed to be, if not above, at all events *outside* the law of the land. William

[4] When Danegeld was discontinued, Henry found new sources of revenue, for example the 'Saladin tithe,' levied for a crusade against the Saracen monarch of that name.

[5] Estimated at that time to be about a fourth of the property in England.

the Conqueror had recognized this by permitting the establishment of separate courts for the clergy. These courts administered the 'canon law,' that is, law according to the canons or decrees of the Church, which were the same throughout Catholic Christendom. Punishments under canon law were milder than those of secular law, there were no executions, no mutilations. 'Criminous clerks' (clergy guilty of crimes) were at most degraded, 'unpriested'; their necks were safe until their next offense, when, being no longer entitled to 'benefit of clergy,' they could be punished like other laymen.

To Henry's logical mind this special legal position of the clergy, their exemption from the common law, was unreasonable and inacceptable. He demanded that 'benefit of clergy' should be restricted and that a criminous clerk, tried, convicted and unfrocked by a clerical court, should then be turned over to the secular court for punishment. Archbishop Thomas Becket objected; he urged that this would be a double punishment for a single offense. In 1164 King Henry induced Becket to accept a series of regulations of this and other legal matters affecting the clergy by the so-called 'Constitutions of Clarendon.' Almost at once, however, Becket raised difficulties and repudiated the agreement. Henry prosecuted him, and he fled into exile. In 1170 there was a temporary reconciliation, but quarrels flared forth once more. The king in a moment of impatience, scarce meaning what he said, cried out for friends to rid him of this pestilent and ungrateful priest. Four knights took him at his word and slew Becket before the altar of his own cathedral, thus adding sacrilege to murder.

This horrible crime ruined the king's plans. He had to submit to a flogging from monks by way of personal penance, and to rescind his ordinances restricting the privileges of the clergy. Becket became St. Thomas, and his shrine in Canterbury was a Mecca for pilgrims from every part of Europe. The greatest English poem of the Middle Ages, Chaucer's *Canterbury Tales*, tells of such a pilgrimage, from the point of view of two centuries after Becket's martyrdom. In the long run, however, and especially after the Protestant Reformation, the objects of Henry's legislation were attained.

Another grievous failure of Henry's reign was within his family. He who ruled all England and half France with marked success could not rule his intriguing, ambitious wife, Eleanor of Aquitaine, or his rebellious, ungrateful sons. Henry, the eldest, crowned during his father's lifetime to secure the succession but dying too soon to come to the throne; Richard 'of the Lion's Heart' (*Coeur-de-Lion*); Geoffrey of Brittany, and John 'Lackland,' so called because he had been assigned no territory of his own; all schemed for power during their father's lifetime, and thus carried out the tradition of their Plantagenet dynasty [6] that filial piety was as nothing compared with personal ambition. With a breaking heart King Henry learned of one treason after another, and when he was told that even his favorite John had joined the rebels he had no more will to live, and died murmuring 'Shame, shame on a conquered king!'

King Richard I (1189-99) is one of the most famous and attractive royal figures in all history, and he carried the English name to glory in the most distant lands then known, but for England he was only an absentee landlord and he cared little about the country except to draw from it revenues for his crusades. His romantic career is no part of the history of England, and he personally contributed nothing to the development of English institutions save to permit the reforms of his father to be continued and consolidated. If his contemporaries, dazzled by his brilliant feats of arms in the Holy Land, did him too much favor, perhaps we, prejudiced by the strongly national feeling of our own age, do him too little justice. After all, he may have been right in thinking that to champion all Christendom against the 'paynim' was more important than to sit at home and rule a single land; certainly his own century thought so. He was much more than a mere bold knight; he was a brilliant general and a man of culture, a poet and a musician of some talent himself and a great admirer of the minstrel's art in others. Proud, wrathful, greedy, and ambitious, like nearly all of his family, he was none the less sincerely devout and capable of splendid outbursts of generosity, as when he forgave his brother John for conspiring against him, and again when, on his deathbed, he forgave the man who slew him.

From 1096 to 1280 there were several great crusades against the Mohammedans in the Near East. The First Crusade, 1096, established the Latin Kingdom of Jerusalem. It was mainly a French

---

[6] The Angevin monarchs had as their family badge the broom plant (*planta genêt*).

affair, though a few Englishmen followed Robert of Normandy. The Second Crusade, in 1148, was largely French and German; it aimed to strengthen the Latin Kingdom but had little success. The Third Crusade, in 1189, had for its object the recapture of Jerusalem from the Saracen Emperor Saladin, who had taken it in 1188. Three great sovereigns started in this campaign—Frederick Barbarossa, Holy Roman Emperor; Philip II, called 'Augustus,' of France; and Richard I of England. Frederick was drowned on his way; Philip returned to France as soon as he could in decency do so; Richard and his own army proved unable to do more than secure a temporary respite for a portion of the Latin Kingdom, but without Jerusalem.

On his return Richard was kidnapped by the Archduke of Austria and detained until a huge ransom had been paid. His brother John usurped his power during his absence. Richard returned to England, but after only a few months spent in that country went to France to look after his possessions there, endangered by the ambitious plans of his nominal overlord, King Philip II of France. He died in this campaign and the throne was taken by his brother John (1199-1216).

John is commonly considered the worst of all English kings. Perhaps the hostility of his chroniclers has painted his character in darker colors than need be, as when Roger Hoveden wrote that Hell was made blacker by his presence. At the very outset of his reign he got rid of a troublesome rival, his nephew Arthur, who as the son of his late elder brother Geoffrey had a better claim than his own to the throne by strict hereditary right. King Philip used Arthur's cause to stir up opposition to John in his French possessions. John was a fairly capable general, but no match for the persistent policy and cool wisdom of King Philip, and the upshot of the war was that John lost Normandy and part of Aquitaine. This was a blessing in disguise to England, since it forced the Norman nobility to identify their interests with England instead of with the continent; but the men of that time could see only that their king's blunders had cost the Crown some of its most valuable provinces.

King John further estranged public opinion by a quarrel with the Church. He refused for years to accept Stephen Langton, the able papal nominee for the post of Archbishop of Canterbury. As a champion of national, or at least royal, rights against ecclesiastical meddling, he might have had some popular support had it not been for the general suspicion that his motives were selfish rather than patriotic. Pope Innocent III imposed an interdict on England, suspending all the usual services of the Church. John being still obdurate, the Pope threatened him with deposition, with the King of France to execute the sentence. Thoroughly frightened at last, John made submission in 1213, agreed to accept Langton as archbishop, to restore to their offices the clergy whom he had driven into exile, and— the crowning humiliation of all—to make England legally a feudal dependency, or fief, of the Papacy.

The new archbishop, however, found John, as usual, false to his promises. He took advantage of the existing revolutionary discontent among the oppressed commons and defrauded barons to give the sanction of the Church to the whole reform movement. On Runnymede island in the Thames, on 15 June 1215, John was forced to sign a Great Charter (Magna Carta) embodying the demands of his discontented subjects. It is true that he seized the first opportunity to repudiate his pledges, persuaded the Pope to absolve him from his oath, and waged war with some success against the French and against the English barons who sided with them. But he died in 1216, and the Charter which he had signed survived him by many centuries. Indeed, Magna Carta has often been considered the very cornerstone of that structure of charters, statutes, and political usages which we call the British constitution.

What was the Great Charter and what was its real importance? It was certainly not a revolutionary or innovating document, like the American Declaration of Independence, or a philosophical statement of the rights of a common humanity, like the French Declaration of the Rights of Man and of the Citizen. It was a conservative charter, reaffirming existing rights rather than asking for new ones; a feudal charter, taking for granted the division of society into a hierarchy of classes, each with its own special privileges; a national charter, applying only to the country of England and making no appeal to 'natural law' or the 'rights of humanity'; a concrete and practical charter, listing abuses by name and remedying them by specific provisions, without attempting to lay down general principles.

The Church was to have her traditional rights guaranteed and reaffirmed. The king, in particular, was not to interfere, as John had done, with the election of church officials. The nobles, direct tenants of the Crown, were to pay only those feudal dues for which there existed old authority.[7] Heirs under age, who were under the guardianship of the king, were not to have their estates exploited for his benefit. Tenants-in-chief were to extend similar rights to their own vassals. The City of London was to have its lawful rights and freedom of carrying on commerce. Even the villeins were not entirely overlooked, for by the twentieth article 'a villein is only to be amerced, saving his plow team'; in other words, the means of getting a living must not on any pretext be taken from him.

More interest today attaches to the general provisions of the Charter, and about them the greatest controversy has arisen. Vast constitutional issues depended on the exact meaning of single Latin words and phrases. Thus, in several places, rights are granted to every 'free man' (*liber homo*). Today, that would mean every man in the country; in the thirteenth century it may have meant everyone except the serfs, but some historians contend that it had an even more restricted meaning and applied only to those of gentle birth. In this light we must consider the famous thirty-ninth article:

No freeman is to be taken, or deprived of his property, or outlawed, or in any way destroyed, nor will we go against him or send against him, except by the judgment of his equals or the law of the land [*nisi per judicium parium suorum vel per legem terrae*].

This clause did not, as was once thought, guarantee trial by jury, which, as we have seen, was only beginning to come into operation. The fortieth article, it is true, is not limited to freemen, but it is very general in its terms:

To no one will we sell, to no one will we deny or delay right or Justice.

Again, in the twelfth article, King John agreed to levy no 'scutage or aid' except with the consent of the Great Council. This sounds like parliamentary control over taxation, but it should be noted that it applied only to certain classes of feudal dues, and that the Great Council itself was then an advisory body of nobles and of the higher

---

[7] Thus a special 'aid' for ransom in battle, or for marrying off a daughter, or knighting a son, and a 'relief' when land changed tenants, were consecrated by custom.

clergy; its development into the modern type of Parliament had still to come. A special committee of barons was to oversee the enforcement of the provisions of the Charter, and the king (a curious provision to modern though not to medieval ears) had to authorize in advance their right to wage war against him if he broke his word.

With all deductions, Magna Carta remains indeed great. It brought together clergy, barons, and townsmen in a joint resistance to royal tyranny; it defined and asserted the privileges of each class; it acquired new meaning in the course of time, and was appealed to as a standard of liberty by each successive generation. Often violated, it was never wholly set aside; and though some of its provisions have become obsolete with the disappearance of feudalism, other clauses have taken on increasing significance and underlie the modern political institutions alike of the British Commonwealth of Nations and of the United States of America.

o V o

THE RISE OF PARLIAMENT

No political contribution that England has ever made to the world is more important than representative government. Yet the idea itself was pan-European. From the thirteenth to the fifteenth century many countries had some form of class representation to act as a check on the power of the hereditary monarch. The Parliament in England has a rough parallel in the French States General, the Diet of the Holy Roman Empire, the Cortes of the kingdoms in the Spanish peninsula, the Polish Sejm, and similar bodies in many other countries. But the English brought representative government, as they did the jury system and Common Law, to an unusual degree of efficiency. Parallel institutions on the continent usually perished with the feudal conditions which gave rise to them, and were supplanted by the professional civil service of an absolute monarch. Even the English Parliament was for a time subordinated to royal power,[1] but it survived and eventually triumphed. The development of Parliament from the old advisory council of tenants-in-chief of the Crown was largely the work of the reigns of Henry III (1216-72) and Edward I (1272-1307).

As Henry III was only nine years old when he succeeded to the throne, he was under the management of other men for many years: of Archbishop Stephen Langton, the hero of the struggle for Magna Carta, who lived until 1228; of William Marshall, a baron who had shared in the same struggle, who lived until 1219; and of Hubert de Burgh, a great Justiciar of the realm, whose power endured until 1232. After Hubert de Burgh's time, Henry III was his own master, though not a very steady or resolute one. He let the finances of the kingdom fall into confusion, first to endow his mother's family, and later his wife's. He filled so many offices with his French 'in laws'

---

[1] During the Tudor period.

43

that he wakened the resentment of the increasingly nationalistic English barons. Strangely enough, the great leader of the opposition was himself a Frenchman.

This leader was Simon de Montfort, born a subject of the king of France and the son of a fiercely orthodox crusader who had warred savagely against the Alibigensian heretics in southern France. He seems to have inherited his father's military skill and valor but to have combined with it a broader statesmanship. He had married a sister of the English king and ruled, ably enough, the province of Gascony as its governor. Coming to England in 1253 he became, with the easy transition characteristic of his class, a 'true born Englishman' and the head of a movement for national self-government.

English politics at this time can only be understood against the background of a general European struggle between Pope Innocent III and the Holy Roman Emperor, Frederick II. Not only were these two men the highest dignitaries in Catholic Christendom, but in their own right as individuals they were among the most remarkable figures of their age. Innocent III was probably the most powerful of all the popes, and Frederick II's brilliant intellect and able, if sometimes cynical, statesmanship won him the popular nickname of *Stupor Mundi*, the 'Amazement of the World.' Nobody could say who was having the better of this struggle—carried on by sword and arrow as well as by excommunication—when the sudden death of Frederick at Parma in 1250 left Pope Innocent with no outstanding rival. The Holy Roman Empire, on the other hand, fell into confusion; it was the end of the great effort begun by Charlemagne in 800 to rule Europe through the double agency of Emperor and Pope.

The death of Frederick II and the collapse of his empire gave opportunity for lesser sovereigns to make something out of his failure. The Pope offered the crown of Sicily to an English prince, and Henry III accepted it for his second son Edmund, then only nine years old. In 1257 Henry's brother Richard, Earl of Cornwall, an abler statesman than the king, was chosen by some German princes, with papal approval, 'King of the Romans.' He tried to make good his authority in Germany, but failed. Both these unsuccessful experiments cost heavily in English treasure.

Meanwhile Simon de Montfort was leading a patriotic reform party among the barons against royal extravagance. In 1264 he won the hard-fought battle of Lewes in Sussex. King Henry himself was taken prisoner. Using the royal authority, now within his control, Simon summoned in 1265 what is regarded as the first English Parliament. It comprised the various 'estates of the realm'—the barons ('peers' or 'lords'), each of whom attended, on royal summons, in his own personal right; the clergy, as represented by the archbishops, bishops and chief abbots; the commons, represented by two burgesses from each borough and two knights from each shire, chosen (if there were any dispute) by election.[2]

Parliament naturally did not spring full-blown from Simon de Montfort's mind, like Athena from the head of Zeus. The English were long familiar with the idea and practice of representative government, especially in local affairs. The old English shire-moots had not ceased to function. The chief citizens of such cities as London, Bristol, Lincoln, Winchester, and Norwich were in the habit of meeting in town council; while the merchants (pretty much the same men) met in the town's merchant guild. William I had given a charter to London; Henry II, Richard, and John had all sold charters to towns, in return for cash, granting them privileges such as electing their own sheriffs or having their own merchant guild regulate all trade within the town. Though neither the Anglo-Saxon Witan nor the Norman Great Council (of barons and prelates) which followed it was elected, both had a representative character. In Magna Carta King John agreed that 'No scutage or aid' should be imposed 'without the common counsel' of the kingdom. Though scutage and aids were special feudal dues, this article was gradually extended by judicial construction to cover other royal levies and taxes. 'Common counsel' was given in the name of the nation by the nobles and clergy in the Great Council, but the king sometimes by special writ would summon knights of the shire to represent the gentry. In 1237 Henry III convened a Great Council at Westminster to which had been added, by summons sent to the sheriff of each county, an unknown number of freemen who voted 'for themselves and their villeins' a tax of one-thirtieth on all movable property.

[2] Very often the citizens or knights were so obviously the leaders in the community that no form of election was necessary, especially since membership in Parliament was not a coveted honor so much as a burdensome duty, like jury service in our time. Sometimes fines were imposed on those who refused to serve.

Earl Simon's addition of citizens ('burgesses') from the towns was a tribute to the growing importance of the merchant class. After all, the 'knights of the shire' were landholding 'gentry'; in most continental countries they would have been called nobles, though English usage narrowed nobility to a relatively few families and passed on the title to a single heir. But burgesses were common freemen of the middle class. In early feudal days they had played a very subordinate part in politics; the great forces of the age were the king, the clergy, the nobility, and the gentry; and land was the only form of wealth which carried with it social standing. But the thirteenth century was, in general, a prosperous age in western Europe. It was a century of cathedrals, universities, gilds, commerce, and great art. Though the largest towns were insignificant by modern standards, and England was even behind other nations in municipal development, the townsman could no longer be ignored. He enjoyed chartered civic rights, his wealth often exceeded that of a nobleman, and the conditions of urban life kept him in closer touch with national problems than were most country gentlemen of the time.

Earl Simon was not without support from the clergy. The Friars Minor or Franciscans had reached England. Though their primary work was charity rather than education, they could boast of some learned men in their order. Thus at the time of the Barons' War, a Franciscan friar wrote in honor of Earl Simon's victory a Latin poem called, after his victory, *The Song of Lewes*. In this there is phrased an amazingly modern theory of constitutional government—a theory which, so far as people speculated on the subject, was that of the Middle Ages, too.

> The king who tries without advice to seek his peoples' weal
> Must often fail, he cannot know the wants and woes they feel . . .
> Law stands high above the king, for Law is that true might
> Without whose will the king would stray and wander from the right.

The Parliament of 1265 did not achieve a permanent settlement. The civil war broke out again that same year. At Evesham, Earl Simon was defeated in battle by the king's warlike son, Prince Edward, then twenty-six. This battle ended the Barons' War and ensured peace for the last seven years of Henry's reign. In 1272 the king died and Edward I, at the time on a crusade in Palestine, succeeded him.

Simon de Montfort's work, instead of being terminated by his death on the field of Evesham, was carried on and greatly developed by the new king, who had crushed him in war.

King Edward I was a wise king and legislator. He has been called the 'English Justinian,' though the term is not too apt, since his greatness lay not in the codifying of ancient laws but in adapting them to meet the needs of a new time. He proceeded experimentally; all his reforms were expedients to end some particular abuse. His development of Parliament was probably the result of a quest for some acceptable method of taxation. 'What touches all should be approved by all'—*Quod omnes tangit ab omnibus approbetur*—was a memorable phrase which he put in the writ of summons to the clergy for his 'model Parliament' of 1295. This Parliament, though not the first of his reign,[3] was the most complete. It adopted Simon de Montfort's precedent of summoning burgesses and knights of the shire to meet with the clergy and the barons, but the relation of these classes was more clearly defined. Moreover, Earl Simon's Parliament had been a partisan body,[4] the product of a rebellion, and it was thus very important that its type of organization should have been approved in quieter times by a king who was under no sort of coercion.

King Edward summoned not all, but a large number, of the tenants-in-chief who held land directly from the Crown. Of these, forty-nine received personal writs of summons, and from that time onwards the issue of a personal writ has been taken to create an inheritable peerage. Thus came into being the 'House of Lords,' the Upper Chamber of the modern Parliament, though the name House of Lords was not applied to it until 1541.

Along with the secular peers were summoned the Archbishops of Canterbury and York and the bishops, who still sit in the House of Lords as 'spiritual peers.' These peers were only part of the Estate of the Clergy, which was represented for about a hundred years after the Model Parliament by archdeacons and elected proctors. In the

[3] That of 1275 contained commoners (knights and burgesses) but not the lower clergy.

[4] The American reader can conceive of Earl Simon's Parliament as being somewhat analogous to a National Party Convention, which represents all states but only one political party.

fifteenth century, however, the clergy, except the spiritual peers, dropped out of Parliament and voted their share of the national taxes in the purely ecclesiastical assemblies of the Convocation of Canterbury and the Convocation of York.

The Estate of Commons comprised two burgesses from every borough and two knights from every shire, burgesses and knights alike being summoned through the sheriff of the county, though the burgesses were elected in their own boroughs and the knights in the county courts, attended by the freeholders of the county and by four villeins from each manor. Knights and burgesses sat together as a single body. When the clergy dropped out, there were only two Estates left in Parliament, the Peers or Lords (including the spiritual peers), and the Commons.

It will be noted that Edward's Model Parliament was not feudal; no one sat in it by right of tenure of land. In the Great Council (*Magnum Concilium*) from which Parliament had grown, membership was wholly based on feudal tenure, as the king summoned to it all who held land directly from him, the 'tenants-in-chief.' But the Peers of the Model Parliament were personally summoned by writ, and their position was hereditary. As the Commons held office by election, tenure was thus eliminated from the structure of Parliament.

King Edward also struck a blow at feudalism from another quarter by his land laws. In 1290 he convened a Parliament—the name was used, but in this case it was merely a meeting of the old Great Council—which enacted a statute called *Quia Emptores*.[5] It was a simple act designed to prevent the complication of feudal tenures by what was called subinfeudation, or the creation of tenancies depending on tenancies. By the new statute if a landholder sold any of his land the buyer would become the vassal or 'man,' so far as feudal services were concerned, not of the man who sold him the land but of his overlord. Now, the biggest landholders were the tenants-in-chief, who held land directly from the king himself. Every time one of these men sold land, he thus created a new tenant-in-chief. Thus a large class of landowners grew up who owed feudal services to nobody except the central government of the Crown.

[5] From the Latin words at the beginning of the statute, 'Because purchasers . . .'

In 1610 Francis Bacon, then Solicitor-General, spoke in Parliament for the abolition of antiquated feudal dues which the king proposed—fruitlessly at that time [6]—to commute for a lump sum of money. Bacon said, 'When the Sheriff calls out the *posse comitatus* [the forces of the shire], no one troubles to ask *"Whose men are you?"* ' Feudalism was practically extinct then. It was not extinct in the days of Edward I, but the king had done much to kill it by separating land tenure from military service and from the position of a Lord of Parliament.

Though personally devout, Edward was not, like his father Henry, a ruler who submitted to every sort of extortion that was made in the name of the Church. He saw with some alarm the tendency of landholders to give their lands to the Church, on condition of enjoying them for their lifetime, and thus securing the exemption from military duties, feudal dues, and ordinary taxes which was usually extended to the properties of the Church. So in 1279 he had enacted the statute of *Mortmain*,[7] forbidding the grant of lands to the Church without royal license.

Edward's legislation touched many other matters. He confirmed old chartered rights and liberties, among them the principle that no taxes could be levied without common consent, which in effect meant Parliamentary grant; worked out a law for entailed estates; made stringent provision for the pursuit of criminals by 'hue and cry' and for keeping watch in walled towns; expelled the Jews from England [8]; and followed the precedents of Henry II in organizing the courts and processes of law. He conquered Wales and undertook in vain the conquest of Scotland. Parliament is his greatest monument, though the king never knew how great was to be the structure whose cornerstone he had laid. Indeed, could he have read the future, he might even have viewed with some alarm his part in building an institution which in time to come would depose his own son, and later

[6] This was later done under Charles II.

[7] *Mortmain*, a picturesque Latin phrase for the 'dead hand' which protected the land from dues and services to the king.

[8] The Jews had formed a class of bankers and money lenders in medieval England. They were very unpopular, alike from the religious bigotry of the times and because a debtor never loves a creditor. Oliver Cromwell was the first ruler after Edward's time to permit them to return.

still displace the Throne as the central power in the national government.

It must be insisted that Edward's Parliaments were very far from having the importance that Parliament attained in the fifteenth century, or, still more, in the present day. They were primarily tax-granting bodies. They could and did tender advice and complain of grievances, but they were little apt to legislate in the modern sense except on the initiative of the king or of his ministers. Over the administration, the power of Parliament was even less. The vigorous protests of the Lords and Commons, backed by a threat to refuse to grant money, might induce a king to drop a particularly unpopular official; but the entire conduct of foreign policy and the appointment of all national officials were in the king's hand. Nor was he obliged, at this period, to summon Parliament at stated intervals. If he could get along without new revenues, he did not have to call Parliament at all.

Why were the English Parliaments so much more successful than the similar institutions of other European countries? There are really many reasons. For one thing, the structure of Parliament was of an unusually effective type. In France, the States General comprised three houses—clergy, lords, and commons; in Sweden the national Diet had four—clergy, lords, citizens, and peasants. A two-chambered legislature, such as gradually developed in England, was obviously more compact and convenient; it is the form which has been imitated most widely in modern Europe and America. Far more important was the fact that the House of Commons included two of the strongest classes in the nation—the country gentry and the city merchants. In most other countries the gentry counted as lesser nobles and held themselves aloof in disdain from the citizens, with the result that the growth of royal power and the consequent decline of the feudal authority of the nobility meant also the decline of representative government. In England, as the Lords weakened, the Commons grew stronger.

Another factor was undoubtedly the comparative security of England, which saved the country from militarism and from the despotic government which militarism almost always involves. England knew less of foreign invasion and of civil war, after the establishment of Norman rule, than almost any other European country. The king had no large standing army with which to enforce his will, and thus he had to conciliate the subjects whom he could not coerce.

Another reason for the dependence of the king on Parliament was simply lack of money. As supreme landlord of England he could collect the customary feudal dues from his tenants-in-chief without summoning Parliament, but these did not suffice for the efficient conduct of government even in normal times, and in war proved utterly inadequate. The English kings were warlike and ambitious, even for the times, and therefore were forced to call Parliament into frequent session for special grants. Parliament often coupled its grants with requests for the redress of grievances, but, taught by experience that kings were apt to evade the detailed fulfilment of promises made 'in principle,' petitions were later phrased as definite bills which the king had to accept or reject as they stood. Thus the parliamentary power to tax became the power to legislate as well.

Parliaments of one sort or another existed in Scotland, France, and most of the little states of Germany, Italy, and Spain, but they declined almost everywhere on the continent during the later Middle Ages. Therefore, it was natural that when England founded colonies overseas in the seventeenth century, they were granted assemblies similar to the English Parliament, whereas the Spanish, Portuguese, and French colonies were denied representation. The Congress and the state legislatures of the United States today are thus derived from the English Parliaments of Simon de Montfort and Edward I.

ENGLISH PENETRATION OF SCOTLAND, WALES
AND IRELAND

THUS far we have made only very incidental mention of the parts of the British Isles outside England. By the reign of King Edward I, however, English influence had extended in many ways to Scotland, Wales, and Ireland, and the 'history of the English-speaking peoples' began to take on a larger meaning than the 'history of England.' It will be necessary to turn aside from the narrative of purely English affairs to introduce these other peoples who have shared so greatly in British achievements but who have also retained national traditions of their own.

Great Britain is only about twice the size of the State of New York, yet it comprised at least three separate sovereignties in the later Middle Ages. After the Norman Conquest the island was made up of the Kingdom of England, the Kingdom of Scotland, and the more or less tribal region of Wales, not always united under a single ruler. The adjacent islands were not originally under English rule. Ireland (about the size of Maine) was mainly Celtic, though it had been much affected by the invasion of the Northmen. The romantic little Isle of Man, with a mixed Celtic-Norse population, was for a time a dependency of Norway until it was ceded in 1266, together with the Hebrides, to King Alexander III of Scotland. The Channel Islands were part of the original Duchy of Normandy, and remained under the English Crown after King John had lost the mainland Duchy. The Channel Islanders continued to speak Norman French, to observe Norman laws and customs, and to retain a feudal system of landed property down to our own time. The Hebrides, Orkneys, and Shetlands became attached to Scotland, but the Faeroe Islands remained Danish.

The Irish play no part in general European history until their conversion by St. Patrick and other missionaries in the fifth century. Then, with all the traditional zeal of the recent convert, they became missionaries in turn and had a share in the conversion of the Anglo-Saxons and even of the distant Germans. The form of Catholic Christianity developed in Ireland was called the Celtic. In fundamentals it was at one with Rome, but it differed in small details, such as the date of Easter or the form of the tonsure (the shaved crown of the priest), and also in laying more stress on the 'regular clergy' (monks and abbots) than on the 'secular clergy' (priests and bishops). Irish culture blossomed most brilliantly in the monasteries. The exquisite illumination of Irish manuscripts (such as the *Book of Kells*) equals the best work of its kind done anywhere in Europe. Early Irish epic verse, so say those who can read Erse, has something of the vigor and vividness of Homer. Learned scholastic philosophers came from the Irish Church. But the lack of political unity in the island exposed it to invasions: first by the pagan Northmen, and again by their civilized descendants, the Normans.

The great Irish King, Brian Boru, defeated the Northmen at Clontarf in 1014 and thus put a temporary stop to these invasions. But in 1154 Adrian IV (Nicholas Breakspear, the only Englishman who was ever elected Pope) granted Ireland to King Henry II. Norman, or Anglo-Norman, knights and younger sons, hungry and adventurous, began to go over to Ireland. Henry himself took little interest in the matter until after the murder of Becket, when he was in hot water with the clergy and glad to escape from his embarrassments by a foreign expedition. In 1171 he led an expeditionary force into Ireland. Henceforth the English kings assumed the title Lord of Ireland, until Henry VIII took the title of King of Ireland. English rule long remained limited to an eastern district called the Pale, seventy to a hundred miles of coast around Dublin. Medieval English kings gave little attention to Irish affairs, which were left to the mismanagement of Celtic chiefs and Norman barons; but Edward I, though he never visited Ireland in person, convened the first Irish Parliament at Dublin in 1295, the year of his famous Model Parliament of Westminster in England.

Between the different parts of Great Britain there were natural barriers which in that age of poor roads were as formidable as the sea which divided Great Britain from Ireland. What made Wales was less the distinction of language than the line of hills extending from the mouth of the Dee, near Chester, to the mouth of the Severn, near Gloucester. Anyone traveling by road or railway from London to Aberystwyth or Harlech begins to see, not far beyond Wolverhampton, the lines of 'alp on alp' which mark off Wales from England. There is an equally prominent geographical barrier between England and Scotland. This barrier is simply the high country—hills and moors—on the east-west line of the Solway Forth and the River Tweed, a belt of rugged countryside for some twenty miles to the north and to the south of this line. In the Middle Ages this border country was almost a no-man's land, with only a scattering of hamlets and battlemented keeps; even some of the parsonages and farm houses were fortified. It was not in any sense a racial frontier, for the people of northern England and of southern Scotland, however frequently they have fought against each other, are very much of the same type: they have the same stalwart, big-boned frames, the same soft voices and pure vowels, the same high-bred manners, the same rosy, high-colored, weatherbeaten complexions, the same traditions of legend and balladry. Both are descended largely from the Angles of old Northumbria.

Wales and Scotland, in the time of King Edward I, were more largely Celtic than was England. But the difference was only one of degree. Not only were many Englishmen of Celtic descent,[1] but Celtic speech still lingered in some western parts of the country, notably in Cornwall. On the other hand, the Welsh 'marches' (border country) had many Anglo-Saxon and Norman settlers. Though the Scottish highlands were Celtic, the lowlands were largely Angle, and numerous English and Norman knights and nobles figured among the Scottish aristocracy. The Norman Conquest of England sent thousands of refugees from northern England across the border into Scotland. 'These refugees spoke English, but an English that differed in many respects from the English of London and the Midlands . . . This Northumbrian English became in time the speech of the whole Scottish lowlands.'[2] The many Scandinavian raids which Scotland had suffered, in common with England and Ireland, also left a very con-

---

[1] For a discussion of this point, see Chapter I.
[2] R. L. Mackie, *A Short History of Scotland* (1930), p. 62.

siderable Norse element in Scottish life, especially in the extreme north; the Shetland Islander, for example, is practically an English-speaking Scandinavian.

Though many English kings had claimed a vague suzerainty over both Wales and Scotland, none of them before Edward I were greatly concerned to enforce their claims. Even Edward, an eminently practical ruler, was probably moved to conquest more by annoyance at the turbulent condition of the Welsh Marches and the Scottish Border than by any abstract conception of British unity. The Welsh Marches comprised the counties of Shrewsbury, Hereford, and Gloucester, and were divided among a number of barons called the Lords Marcher, who held lands from the King of England but within their own fiefs wielded almost sovereign powers. The royal sheriffs did not enter their lands. Their special duty, the defense of England against the Welsh, they performed well enough, but the system was not a good one. It permitted too much private warfare. The Lords Marcher were almost always at strife with someone; if the Welsh were quiet, they fought among themselves.

Celtic Wales west of the Marches was not without a culture of its own. In farmhouses and princely halls alike men sang the ancient bardic poems or composed new ones. Then, as now, the Welsh were the most musical of the peoples of the British Isles. Though the native princes were often at war with each other, and would even league with Norman Lords Marcher against men of their own kindred, they were all proud of their ancient tongue, their military tradition, and their faithfulness to the Christian teachings which had been planted among them by Roman missionaries before the legions had left Britain. Gradually, some degree of unity had been given to the country by Llewellyn the Great, recognized in his own day as Prince of Wales. His power descended to his nephew, Llewellyn ap Gruffyd, who acted as a great English baron as well as Prince of Wales, and supported the cause of Simon de Montfort in the Barons' Wars.

War broke out between Edward I and Prince Llewellyn, who was defeated and killed by English forces in 1282. Edward then by the Statute of Rhuddlan (where he summoned the English Parliament) reorganized the Principality of Wales. He wisely left Welsh law and custom in force, though for judicial purposes he divided the country into four shires with a Justice in each. He named his son Edward (a 'native-born Welsh prince,' as he was born at Carnarvon in 1282) Prince of Wales, a title since then conferred on the eldest sons of English kings.[3] He established centers of military power in the magnificent castles which he built at Carnarvon, Harlech, and other places. The Marcher Lordships, that is Wales outside the Principality, were not shired until 1535.

Wales entered slowly into full partnership with England. For a long time the Welsh regarded the English as alien conquerors, but they often gave a personal loyalty to the king (especially after the Welsh Tudor dynasty ascended the throne in 1485), and their skill with the bow and arrow made them highly valuable in England's foreign wars. They have preserved their native Celtic language, though most of them speak English as well. They still maintain many of their old traditional customs, such as the annual festival of poetry and song, the Eisteddfod. The Wales of today, however, is in some major respects very different from the Wales which King Edward knew. Then it was the most rural part of his dominions, a land of shepherds and small farmers; now, with the advent of the industrial revolution, it is a main center of the British coal industry. Then, it was devoutly Catholic in faith and inclined to conservatism in politics, a home of lost causes and ancient traditions; now, it is evangelical Protestant in creed and generally radical at election time. Yet Prince Llewellyn and David Lloyd George would be at one in their enthusiasm for the rocky land of their forefathers and for the beauties of its native tongue.

Curiously enough, there is a distant corner of southwestern Wales, farthest from the English border, which is the most English part of the country; indeed Pembrokeshire bears the popular nickname of 'Little England beyond Wales.' Much of this 'English' character, however, is due to the immigration of Flemings from the continent in the time of Henry I and Henry II, so that 'Little Flanders' would be almost as appropriate a name.

Succeeding with his conquest of Wales, Edward I made a failure

---

[3] When, as at present, there is no son of a king, no one bears the title of Prince of Wales.

of his plan of union with Scotland. At first things looked promising. King Alexander III of Scotland died in 1286. His heir was a granddaughter, herself a daughter of the King of Norway, and in 1290 a betrothal was arranged between Edward, Prince of Wales, and the seven-year-old princess Margaret. She was sailing to Scotland in that year to take up her crown and wait till marriageable age, but she died in the crossing, and with her perished the English plan for a peaceful union between the two British kingdoms.

Failing with one plan, Edward attempted another. The death of the little Maid of Norway, as the people called the heir to the Scottish throne, left the succession in dispute. No fewer than eight candidates claimed the throne on various theories of hereditary right. Civil war seemed in prospect. Thereupon King Edward offered to arbitrate on the condition—which the candidates concerned did not think unreasonable—that the claimant should do homage for his Crown to the King of England. Doubtless the claimants thought that Edward's suzerainty would be the purely nominal overlordship claimed—but not enforced—by several previous English rulers. The award was delivered in 1292 in favor of John de Balliol against Robert de Brus and other competitors. Both Balliol and Brus (Bruce as the name later came to be written) were descendants of David, Earl of Huntington, a brother of the Scottish King William the Lion. They were both of mixed Norman, English, and Scottish descent, and both had fiefs on the Scottish side of the border. On the basis of strict hereditary right, Balliol had probably the best claim and Edward's award was not unfair.

King John Balliol discovered, however, that he could hold his throne only on condition of being in fact as well as in form a feudal vassal of Edward. He was summoned frequently to England to render service or to hear complaints brought by his own subjects to Edward's court. Irritated by Edward's exactions and mocked by his Scottish subjects as merely a *toom tabard* (empty coat), he at last revolted. This gave Edward the excuse he needed to declare Scotland forfeited to himself as overlord according to the recognized feudal principle that a rebel vassal loses his right to a fief. In 1296 he invaded Scotland, forced John Balliol to abdicate and retire to his Norman estates, garrisoned the Scottish castles with English soldiers, and made himself King of Scotland in his own name and right.[4] Few of the nobles, warlike though they were, seemed disposed to question Edward's claim. Why should they care? Many of them were as much Norman or English as they were Scottish; to expect them to be filled with pure national patriotism and to scold them for lacking it (as in the romantic novels of the nineteenth century) is as much an anachronism as to have expected them to fight their wars with cannon.

Nationalism is born earlier, however, among the masses of the people than among a feudal nobility. A hitherto unknown knight, William Wallace, said to be of prodigious size and strength, led an insurrection, won the adherence of many Scots, and during Edward's absence inflicted a severe defeat on the English army of occupation at Stirling Bridge in 1297. Next year, however, Edward came in person with a strong army and defeated Wallace's forces at Falkirk. This battle advertised to the world the military efficiency of the English infantry armed with the long bow, the chief instrument of English victory in the wars against Scotland and France. William Wallace lived a hunted life for six years until he was captured in 1304, sentenced for treason, and put to death in 1305. 'He was the first,' says the historian Green, 'to sweep aside the technicalities of feudal law and to assert freedom as a national birthright.' He did not die in vain, for the course of war itself created a patriotic feeling among the Scots. Noblemen who had hitherto treated Edward's wars from the standpoint of feudal allegiance, party preference, or family advantage now for the first time began to feel nationally. Among them was a remarkable warrior, Robert Bruce, the grandson of Balliol's unsuccessful rival for the Scottish throne.

Bruce, like most other Scottish nobles, had played politics with the issue of Scottish independence, taking one side or the other as it might seem to suit his interest. One might almost say that he was tricked into consistent patriotism, for it was only after he had slain one of his enemies, the 'Red Comyn,' a partisan of Edward, that he ceased to vacillate. He had burned his bridges with a vengeance, for he knew that Edward would never forgive him now, especially since

---

[4] King Edward caused the Stone of Scone, reputed to be the very pillar on which Jacob slept and had his vision of the angels, to be removed to England and placed in his coronation throne, where it has ever since remained.

the murder had been committed (like that of Becket) in the precincts of a church. He had drawn on himself at once the hostility of Comyn's Scottish friends, the wrath of England, and the outraged dignity of the clergy. Though in 1306 Bruce assumed the crown of Scotland, he had to spend years as a hunted fugitive fleeing from his foes. In adversity he grew from a selfish politician into a statesman and hero. Undaunted by defeat, uncomplaining under hardship, placing the welfare of his followers before his own, and devoting every effort to securing Scottish independence, he became at last a worthy successor to the patriot martyr Wallace.

Fortunately for Bruce and for Scotland's cause, King Edward was a dying man. He summoned his last energies for a final invasion of Scotland, but he died at Burgh-on-Sands near Carlisle. On his tomb in Westminster Abbey are the words: *Edwardus I, Malleus Scotorum, Pactum Serva,* 'Edward the First, the Hammer of the Scots, Keep Faith,' the last phrase being the king's chosen motto. In the main he had been true to it, though sometimes he regarded more the letter than the spirit of an agreement, as when he dealt with the whole Scottish nation by the technicalities of feudal law without regard to the spirit of a free people. Yet Edward I ranks high on the list of English kings, perhaps being second only to Alfred in the affections of the people. As much as any man he was the founder of Parliament; he was a wise statesman, patriotic and public spirited at all points; and even his wars with Scotland and Wales were not mere examples of imperialistic ambition: to at least an equal degree they represented a desire to secure the English borders from rapine and to extend the bounds of civil law and good government.

King Edward II was not the man who could succeed where even his father had failed. Castle after castle fell to the Scottish patriots before Edward, to save at least the strategic fortress of Stirling, led an army personally into Scotland. In 1314 the English and Scottish armies met at Bannock Burn and the Scots were completely victorious. Though the war dragged on for several years, this victory really assured Scottish independence. By the Treaty of Northampton, 1328, this independence was formally recognized by England.

It is impossible to assess completely the gain and loss of the long war for Scottish independence. Scotland had found herself. Norman barons, Angle lowlanders, Celtic highlanders, and Norsemen had been welded into a common nation. The memory of the heroic struggle for national freedom still glows and still inspires alike Scottish literature and Scottish valor. Yet the history of the nation for the next four hundred years is a very chequered one. The long period of peace with England, which had but few interruptions previous to Edward's reign, gave place to an age of border warfare. Scotland, usually an ally of France [5] (because France was an enemy of England), was never indeed conquered but frequently suffered from defeats and from victories almost as costly as defeat. Nor was the country often at peace within itself. Many Scottish rulers died violent deaths at the hands of assassins. The highland clans were forever fighting among themselves or raiding the lowland villages. The turbulent nobility of the lowlands and border country were almost as lawless as the highlanders. The country remained backward in both economic and political development, and many Scotsmen, like the Swiss, made a career of war and went to foreign lands as professional soldiers when there was not enough fighting to do at home.

The most fruitful era of Scottish history, though not the most picturesque and romantic, has been the period since the Union of 1707.[6] Scotland has never been subordinated to England by being united with her. On the contrary, Scotsmen have played a part in common British history far out of proportion to their numbers, especially in science, invention, commerce, and colonization. Though modern Scotland has but an eighth part of the population of England, a fair half of the Prime Ministers of Great Britain in the last half century have been of Scottish birth or descent. Ever since 1603 the rulers of Great Britain have traced their ancestry back to the Scottish house of Stuart (Stewart).

[5] This 'auld alliance' has left deep and abundant marks on Scottish customs and in many words and phrases of Scottish dialect. Thus *tassie* from the French *tasse* for a cup, *douce* from the French word for sweet, and many others. The Edinburgh housewife of the eighteenth century who, before throwing water out of an upstairs window, cried 'gardyloo!' may or may not have realized that she was speaking French, *Gardez, l'eau!*

[6] See Chapter xiv. From 1603 to 1707 the two countries had the same dynasty but differed in their national governments. Even now Scotland retains her own church system and, to some extent, her own legal procedure.

VII

THE HUNDRED YEARS' WAR

WHEN the modern reader is told of a 'hundred years' war' over the French Crown the phrase conveys too much. Medieval warfare was not continuous but sporadic; it consisted of a number of isolated raids and sieges during the warmer months, for armies rarely campaigned in winter time. Usually only a few hundred soldiers were involved, though occasionally a great battle might bring together some twenty or thirty thousand. The fighting men were very badly equipped. We hear of complete suits of armor for men and horses—the art of body armor reached its perfection in the fifteenth century—but forget that only those of high birth had either the right to wear such armor or the money to purchase it. Leather jackets, wooden shields, iron-pointed wooden pikes or spears, crossbows or longbows made up the usual infantry equipment. Even the knights often were reduced to riding scarecrow horses comparable to Don Quixote's Rosinante. The capture of a store of provisions or of firewood filled an army with joy; the capture of a good suit of armor was chronicled in the dispatches as the capture of heavy cannon would be today.

In one sense, the Hundred Years' War was merely the last phase in a struggle of four hundred years. From the time when William of Normandy took the realm of England in 1066 to the last embarkation of English soldiers withdrawn from Guienne in 1453, there was no enduring peace, though hostilities were often suspended for long periods of truce. The last phase of this conflict had, however, some special characteristics of its own. It involved on the part of the English kings a novel claim to the French Crown, never made before the reign of Edward III, and it gradually developed into a national struggle between two peoples instead of remaining a merely feudal conflict between the French Crown and its rebellious Norman or Angevin vassals who happened also to rule England. During the fourteenth and fifteenth centuries the French and English peoples seemed to regard each other as natural enemies, an idea revived by the colonial conflicts of the eighteenth century.[1]

King Edward I devoted his main attention to the conquest of Wales and Scotland and gave only incidental attention to his French fiefs. Edward II (1307-27) was an unlucky king, defeated by the Scots, defied by his Parliaments, detested by his nobles. Using Parliament as an instrument, the barons deposed him and placed on the throne his young son as King Edward III (1327-77). In 1328 Edward III married the Countess Philippa of Hainault and in 1329 did homage to King Philip VI of France for his fief of Guienne. This was the last domain in France still held by the King of England and was growing smaller year by year as the French Crown reclaimed it piecemeal. Little by little, claiming here feudal dues, there the patronage of an abbey, again the right to build a castle or to set up a court, the King of France, as feudal overlord, was eating up the Duchy.

It was largely to stop this process of attrition and save what was left of Guienne that Edward threw down the gauntlet and began organized war with France in 1338. He made an alliance with the townspeople of Flanders (northern Belgium), a French fief containing the great trading cities of Ghent and Bruges. English wool was the raw material for the Flemish weavers. Edward III had some understanding of the economic and political interests of the English in the Netherlands. Later (but not until William III) this interest developed a sort of English 'Monroe Doctrine' for these countries, the policy of keeping them out of the hands of any great military power who could use them against England.

Probably in order to gain the alliance of the Flemish, who were in nominal allegiance to the King of France, Edward III advanced a claim to the French throne. The claim itself was rather dubious. It was based on the contention that the French line of succession, like the English, passed through a female heir when direct male heirs were lacking; hence Edward, as son of a daughter of a French king, claimed a right to the throne in preference to Philip VI, who belonged only to a collateral Valois branch of the French royal fam-

[1] See below, Chapter XVIII.

ily; but the French nobles and high clergy preferred the male line and gave their allegiance to Philip of Valois.

The first English invasions led to no result. 'The war was carried on by a series of forays, sieges and chivalrous but unscientific exploits of arms' [2] in true medieval fashion. In 1340, however, Edward III, as ready to fight by sea as by land, met a large French fleet off Sluys and captured over a hundred ships. After that, in spite of much piracy and irregular warfare in the Narrow Seas, Edward was able to transport troops to France at will. In two great battles, Creçy in 1346 and Poitiers in 1356, the English won striking victories, due largely to their use of the long bow in support of the cavalry. The Genoese crossbowmen, employed by the French, were relatively ineffective, and in general the French at that time understood very little how to employ infantry with advantage, relying almost entirely on massed charges by their heavy cavalry. The English were earlier to realize that the archer and man-at-arms were becoming as important in war as the knight. The victory of Creçy led to the capture of Calais.[3] The French inhabitants were driven out, and Englishmen were settled there. It might be called the first English colony on the continent (for Normandy and Guienne were feudal possessions, not colonized). It was more of a garrison-fortress and trading station than a colony; nevertheless it sent two burgesses to the English Parliament. For two hundred years it was the headquarters of the English woolen export trade. At Poitiers, Edward, the 'Black Prince,' son of King Edward III, captured the French King John II. The Treaty of Bretigny in 1360 ended this first phase of the Hundred Years' War. England obtained all Guienne (including Gascony), free of any feudal vassalage, and full sovereignty also over Calais. King John was set free on condition of paying an enormous ransom; when he found that this could not be paid, he returned to captivity. He passed the rest of his life tranquilly, well treated, in the Savoy Palace, London.

[2] Oman, *The Art of War in the Middle Ages* (1924), II, 126.

[3] To this occasion belongs the pleasant incident of the 'six burghers of Calais' who offered their lives as a ransom for their fellow citizens but were saved by the personal plea of the tender-hearted Queen Philippa to her stern husband King Edward.

There was no question of expansion in these English conquests in France. Save for a few merchants and soldiers, no Englishmen settled in Guienne, and the English occupation was a mere military garrisoning of a completely alien territory. It does not follow that English rule was altogether unpopular. England, which grew no vines, imported the wine of Guienne and caused a flourishing local trade throughout the province. Law and order were better maintained by the alien conquerors than by the French kings in other parts of France, which had been devastated by the English wars and ravaged by bands of freebooting professional soldiers or hordes of hungry peasants. The time was to come when all Frenchmen would feel nationally and resent the presence of foreign rule over any part of their nation; but in Edward's time French patriotic feeling was largely provincial, and men from Flanders, Burgundy, or Gascony were quite willing to enlist under an English banner and serve an English king, especially since these English monarchs were mainly of French descent and still habitually spoke the language of their ancestors.

In 1367 the war was renewed by the ill-advised expedition of Edward, the Black Prince and Governor of Gascony, into Spain, where there was civil war between two claimants to the Crown of Castile, the largest of the Spanish kingdoms. The new French king, Charles V, commonly called 'the Wise,' intervened on the other side of the Spanish quarrel. Bertrand du Guesclin, 'Constable of France,' won great successes over the English by a new type of tactics. Instead of seeking battle with the old, joyous, headlong impetuosity of the French chevaliers, he avoided pitched conflicts, laid waste the land around the English armies so that for want of supplies they had to retreat, and then harried their withdrawal by guerrilla attacks. A combined French-Castilian fleet defeated the English at sea. The heir to the throne, Edward the Black Prince, died in 1376 and his father the following year, leaving the English and French wars as a legacy to the young son of the Black Prince, Richard II (1377-99).

King Richard II is in many ways a very attractive figure. He had to deal with a rebellion of peasants under Wat Tyler against what remained of serfdom and its vexatious legalisms. With great presence of mind, facing an armed mob whose leader had just been murdered, he offered to be himself the leader of the people and promised them emancipation if they would quietly disperse to their homes. Whether or not his promises were sincere, they were ineffective, because the barons would not listen to any concessions. Richard loved peace and trade more than war, and in 1396 he negotiated a thirty years' truce with France and married a daughter of the French King Charles VI. He was a patron of art and letters, and his court poet was Geoffrey Chaucer. But his arbitrary rule led to his deposition by a malcontent faction of nobles headed by Henry, Duke of Lancaster, son of John of Gaunt and grandson of Edward III, who took the throne as Henry IV (1399-1413). Richard died a prisoner, as had Edward II.

Henry IV was the first ruler of that branch of the Plantagenet dynasty which is called the House of Lancaster. Since he owed his throne to revolutionary violence rather than to strict hereditary right, rival claimants arose in later years to challenge the Lancastrian rule. Civil war was latent in Henry's revolution, though it did not actually break out until the reign of his grandson Henry VI. The three Lancastrian rulers (Henry IV, Henry V, and Henry VI) depended much on the support of Parliament, for though Henry IV claimed the throne by descent, he really owed it legally to Parliament's Act of Deposition of Richard II. The Lancastrian dynasty renewed the wars in France, though Henry IV was kept too busy quelling revolts in Wales and in northern England to devote much time to French affairs. The reign of his son Henry V (1413-22) reopened the Hundred Years' War.

Henry V, a brilliant young soldier with Edward III's thirst for martial glory, revived Edward's old claim to the whole land of France. In 1415 he won at Agincourt the most resounding English victory of the age. By the Treaty of Troyes in 1420 he was recognized by King Charles VI as heir to the French throne, and to bind the bargain he married the princess Katherine, the daughter of the French monarch. He had an ambitious dream of uniting France and England permanently under one rule and then hurling this combined realm against the Mohammedans in a new crusade. But he died almost immediately after his triumph in France, leaving the throne of England and the throne-expectant of France to his infant son, scarcely nine months old.

The reign of Henry VI (1422-61) is a double tragedy in English history. The child king grew to manhood and developed many amiable qualities, but no ability to rule. In his time England lost her French possessions and also embarked on a disastrous civil war, the so-called War of the Roses. The loss of France was due in part to the brilliant victories of a French peasant girl, Jeanne Darc (called in England Joan of Arc), and in part to the growing sense of a common nationality among the French provinces. With all France united, England could never have conquered her, for the population of France in those days was much greater than that of England. But the Dukes of Burgundy, great feudal princes intensely jealous of the French Crown, took the side of England until 1435, when they became reconciled to France. Jeanne Darc, in the meantime, had relieved the siege of Orléans, crowned the French prince as King Charles VII at Rheims, and followed these triumphs by a series of swift offensives against the English. Captured by the Burgundians, she was delivered to the English, tried by a packed court on charges of sorcery and blasphemy, and burned at the stake in Rouen in 1431. This sorry vengeance did the English cause no good. 'Joan the witch' became to the French people 'Jeanne the martyr' and her cult has grown until in our own generation she has been officially canonized by the Roman Catholic Church. After 1453 the English held nothing in France except Calais, which they lost in 1558.

The Hundred Years' War contributed greatly to the break up of the old feudal system. So protracted a war could no longer be conducted on the old basis of vassalage. Professional soldiers, hired for fixed terms and definite wages, largely took the place of the feudal levy. The English army was a small volunteer force; unlike the modern army, however, it was paid off at the end of a year or a campaign, and dismissed to civilian life, very much as a ship's crew is paid off at the end of a voyage. Permanent English regiments date only from the time of Oliver Cromwell in the seventeenth century.[4] Sometimes at the end of a campaign a captain and his company, no longer in employment, preferred to keep together and live by their wits, selling their valor in any market that would buy it. It was thus that a famous English captain, Sir John Hawkwood, went to Italy and

---

[4] Except, of course, for palace guards in immediate attendance on the king.

enlisted his 'free company' in the service of the Republic of Florence.[5]

The navy was managed in much the same way as the army. It had never been completely feudal, though the Cinque Ports (the five south-coast cities of Sandwich, Dover, Hythe, Romney, and Hastings) were supposed to supply ships for the Royal Navy and continued to do so until the time of Henry VII. The king had only a few ships of his own; in wartime he chartered private vessels, which thus formed the bulk of the navy. The crews were hired, or pressed into service, from the merchant marine, and paid off, like the soldiers, at the end of each campaign. Piracy and privateering were common in the Narrow Seas around England, and indeed in all European waters.

Probably the loss of France was in the long run a blessing to England. But it did not seem so to the Englishmen of the time of Henry VI. Bitterly ashamed that the laurels of Creçy and Agincourt had been dragged in the mud by the statesmen and generals of Henry VI, they placed much of the blame on the king himself, who was certainly never a man of war. Discontent was rife, and the House of York, claiming a superior right to the throne, waged civil war against the ruling House of Lancaster. Henry VI was deposed, restored, again deposed and imprisoned. He died in prison, possibly murdered, while Edward IV (1461-83) assumed the throne. Edward IV was a handsome, warlike, luxury-loving monarch, who governed with a cynical ruthlessness but considerable ability, and rested his strength not on Parliament and the Church (as the Lancastrians had to some extent done) but on the citizens of London and the good will of the middle classes. His son, Edward V, died in the Tower of London, a prisoner of Edward's brother Richard, who took the crown as Richard III (1483-5). Though he ruled capably, the nation could not forgive him for his usurpation. In 1485 he was killed on Bosworth field, the last king of England to die in battle. The victor was connected on his mother's side with the House of Lancaster, but in his father's line he was descended from the Tudors, a Welsh family. Henry VII is thus usually considered not the last victor in the

[5] Readers of Conan Doyle's *The White Company* will be familiar with these exploits. Some eighteenth-century irregular forces, like Roger's Rangers (see Kenneth Roberts' *Northwest Passage*), were of the Free Company type.

wars of Lancaster and York, but as the founder of a new dynasty. The Tudor rose unites the white rose of York and the red rose of Lancaster.

The Wars of the Roses form probably the ugliest part of English history. The callous murder of several princes who might possibly advance claims to the throne, the wholesale execution of their followers among the nobility, the tangle of treasons which shifted victory to one side or the other, the sordid and selfish motives of most of the contestants make an unsavory picture. Yet the effects on English life were not so profoundly evil as might have been expected. Continental writers noted with wonder, not untouched by envy, that towns and villages were rarely burned, commerce scarcely interrupted, and the peasants seldom molested. The wars were so exclusively a game of baronial politicians who sought the Crown for themselves or their party, that the average Englishman hardly concerned himself with them. The most important result of the contest for the throne was to weaken the feudal nobility and strengthen the monarchy. Many nobles had been killed and the House of Lords was consequently reduced in size, while the Crown itself, through confiscations, acquired lordships and lands. Proscriptions and confiscations filled the royal treasury at the expense of feudal estates. The commercial middle classes, weary of the war, were willing to forego many traditional limitations on royal power to enjoy peace and security.

Tudor power rested on a new basis. There had been kings quite as powerful, quite as arbitrary, as Henry VII, but their strength had been personal. William the Conqueror had been a despot, but Stephen's reign was a mere anarchy. Edward I had been a strong ruler, but his son was deposed and murdered. Richard II had been absolute for a time, but only to be deposed and slain in his turn. Edward IV was an autocrat, but his son died in the Tower of London. No king had been able to hand on his personal power, unimpaired, to a successor. But the power of the Tudors was institutional as well as personal. It belonged to an abstraction—the Crown, the Throne, the State; it belonged also to the man who was king. All Tudor monarchs, even the young, inexperienced Edward VI, were of strong character. They were capable statesmen and chose able ministers—

Fox, Wolsey, Somerset, Burleigh. They strengthened existing institutions—the Council, the Law Courts, the Justices of the Peace. Feudalism was dead at last; barons had sunk to be courtiers; the age of national monarchy had come. Before the new era, however, let us turn for a last glance at the age which had come to an end.

VIII

'MERRIE ENGLAND' AT THE END OF THE
MIDDLE AGES

ENGLAND of the fifteenth century was far indeed from having the world importance of the British Commonwealth of Nations in the twentieth. Several other countries then seemed more important. Setting religion aside, in no essential respect could the Asiatic civilizations of the Arabs, the Hindus, or the Chinese be reckoned below that of Europe. Within Europe, the Byzantine Empire, though fighting a losing battle with Mohammedan invaders, still enjoyed standards of comforts and luxury unknown to the British Isles; the Holy Roman Empire and the Kingdom of France both outranked England in area, population, wealth, culture, and prestige; the city states of Italy, with their superior art and commerce, considered the Englishman as little better than a warlike barbarian.

The population of England has been variously estimated, but at the time of the Hundred Years' War it probably did not much exceed two and a half millions. Modern London is thrice as populous. Except in southern Scotland and in a few parts of Wales and Ireland, English was little spoken outside its native soil. Most Englishmen were peasants. London, the largest city, probably did not then exceed fifty thousand souls. Her closest rivals, such as Bristol, Norwich, and York, scarcely numbered ten thousand apiece. Though the cloth manufacture was steadily increasing, England still shipped much wool to the looms of Flanders. Though 'merchant adventurers' were beginning to widen the bounds of English trade, bankers from Lombardy, merchants from the German Hanseatic League, traders and sailors from Italy, craftsmen from France and Flanders played a leading part in national commerce, and debts were frequently paid in the ducats of Venice or the florins of Florence.

Yet when medieval Englishmen spoke of 'merrie England' (that is to say, 'pleasant England') they were not merely voicing the insular satisfaction of ignorance. We have abundant foreign testimony to the effect that the common people in England were better governed, freer, and in some respects more prosperous than the subjects of greater or wealthier states. It would, of course, be preposterous to present medieval England as a paradise. The average man was a drudging peasant who could read no word in any language, who had never been a dozen miles from home in his life, who shivered all winter in a cold and dirty hut, whose diet, though hearty, was coarse and monotonous, whose clothing was filthy and ragged, whose children more often than not died in infancy from lack of medical knowledge and care. The Black Death, or bubonic plague, which swept across England, and indeed all Europe, in the middle of the fourteenth century, killed off perhaps a third of the people in England. But such evils were common to all countries then. If England of the fourteenth and fifteenth centuries be compared not to modern England but to continental Europe at the same period, the common man had some reason to congratulate himself on a goodly heritage.

For one thing, personal freedom came earlier to England than to most countries. Serfdom lasted in France, though in diminishing degree, down to 1789; in Prussia to 1810; in Russia to 1866. In England serfdom had practically vanished by the fifteenth century. There were peasant risings, the *Jacquerie,* in France during the Hundred Years' War; in Germany in Luther's time; in England under Richard II. The English Peasants' Revolt under Wat Tyler in 1381, however, seems not to have been a mere explosion of discontent at unendurable miseries like the *Jacquerie.* In a small way, it may be compared to the French revolution of 1789, a movement of hope and aspiration among peasants whose lot was slowly improving. The Black Death, by creating a serious labor shortage, had raised wages all over England. Peasants who could not make a good living on the estates of their landlords were wandering the country to look for employment at good terms. Parliament, obsessed with the fixed medieval idea that there was a 'just price' for every commodity and a 'just wage' for every task, tried in vain to keep wages standardized by legislation. So the landlords called on the lawyers to enforce the old, traditional, half-obsolete dues and tasks upon the former villeins.

Naturally, this reactionary policy caused profound indignation. A Kentish priest, John Ball, England's first 'equalitarian,' harangued the peasants, declaring, 'Things cannot go well in England until everything shall be in common; when there shall be neither vassals nor lords and all distinctions levelled. Are we not all descended from the same parents, Adam and Eve? And what reasons can they show why they should be more the masters than ourselves?' Among the peasants the argument of a common descent from Adam and Eve took the form of the familiar jingle:

> When Adam delved and Eve span
> Who was then the gentleman?

The Kentish peasants, joining with some detachments from other shires, marched on London, demanding total abolition of serfdom. We have seen [1] they gained nothing by their movement, since Parliament cancelled the promises of the king. Yet serfdom continued to decline. The new money-economy was fatal to the old manorial system of subsistence agriculture. Some landlords preferred to commute fixed services for money rentals; others turned tilled land into pasture, to engage in the profitable wool trade with the continent. The displaced villeins flocked to town, or sought employment as hired agricultural laborers.

A kind of rural middle class came into existence, the 'yeomen' who were not gentry but who either owned their lands or leased them on easy terms for long periods. These sturdy, independent farmers often served in the army as archers. At home they attended courts and sometimes took part in elections. The sixteenth-century writer Harrison, in his *Description of England,* is full of admiration for the yeoman class:

This sort of people have a certain pre-eminence and more estimation than labourers and the common sort of artificers . . . They are also for the most part farmers to gentlemen . . . and with grazing, frequenting of markets, and keeping of servants, do come to great wealth, insomuch that many of them are able to, and do, buy the lands of unthrifty gentlemen, and often setting their sons to the schools, to the Universities and to the Inns of Court,[2] or otherwise leaving them sufficient lands whereon

[1] See p. 65.
[2] Where the practice of law was studied.

they may live without labour, do make them by those means to become gentlemen . . . And albeit they be not called 'master,' as gentlemen are, or 'sir,' as knights appertaineth, but only 'John' or 'Thomas,' yet they have been found to have done very good service. The kings of England in foughten battles were wont to remain among them (who were their foot-men), as the French kings did amongst their horsemen, the prince thereby showing where his chief strength did consist.[3]

Townsmen in all countries and periods of the Middle Ages tended to be freer than countryfolk. No towns in England had the vast political powers and virtual independence of the city-states in Italy and Germany and the Netherlands, but many towns and cities had charters which gave them much more control over local laws and taxes and commercial regulations than any city enjoys today. Serfs resident for 'a year and a day' in a chartered borough were cus-tomarily set free from all servile obligations. Handicraft and trade in England, as in most parts of Europe, were regulated by gilds. For the gild we have no precise modern equivalent, since its functions are today divided among many agencies. Like a trade union it included workingmen; like a chamber of commerce it included employers; like an insurance company it guaranteed its members against desti-tution due to accident, illness, or unemployment; like a trade school it trained young men in the 'mystery' of their craft; like a Bar Asso-ciation or Medical Association it penalized unprofessional conduct; like a modern Rotary Club it brought businessmen together socially. In many towns the citizens were the gildsmen and the gildsmen were the citizens, so that the political government depended also on these economic organizations.

The town was one of the two social ladders in the Middle Ages (the Church being the other) by which the humblest serf might rise to power, wealth, or fame. Usually a lad was apprenticed for a term of seven years, during which time he lived at his master's shop, learned the trade, and gave his services in return for board and lodg-ing. When 'out of his indentures' at the end of the seventh year, he was a free craftsman or journeyman, able to ply his craft. If he throve well enough to set up a shop of his own and employ apprentices in turn, he was a 'master.' Traces of the old apprenticeship system lin-

[3] Harrison, *Description of England* (1577 edition), Book III, chapter IV.

gered down into the nineteenth century, and there are still gilds in London, though they have become merely social or benevolent societies and have none of their old regulative powers and duties.

The English enjoyed a greater number of legal privileges and freedoms than was common in most parts of Europe. The development of English law from the time of Henry II increasingly tended to make the jury rather than the judge the final authority on the guilt or innocence of an accused person.[4] No arrest or punishment, even by the highest authority, was lawful unless it followed the forms prescribed by common or statute law. Torture was rarely employed to extract evidence, and simple hanging was the ordinary form of capital punishment, though treason, heresy, poisoning, and a few other offenses might be punished by crueler deaths. Minor cruelties, such as branding, flogging, the stocks, and the pillory, were often employed against offenders, but the most common penalty was a fine. Imprisonment was generally used as a means of detention until trial rather than as a punishment for a fixed period of years; prisons were jails rather than penitentiaries. Traitors and prisoners of state were often confined in the Tower of London, and offenders of rank, too patrician to be hanged, were there beheaded. Fortunately for England, royal power was usually strong enough to prevent the abuse of authority by feudal overlords, who could not lawfully inflict any but minor penalties on their villeins.

English government was far from democratic, but equally far from autocracy. Its general principle was that England was a nation of classes (or 'Estates') and that each class had its rights and privileges. During the time of the Lancastrian kings Parliament reached a considerable degree of power, though this must not be exaggerated. It registered some definite gains.

It not only turned its former petitions into 'bills,' but used on occasion the power to impeach the king's ministers and try them for their offenses (for Parliament was a court as well as a legislature), or punish them out of hand by a special 'bill of attainder.' Obviously this legal power was subject to great abuse, and during the Wars of the Roses it became an engine of oppression in the hands of the victorious party to use against its opponents. It is interesting to note that

[4] See above Chapter IV for the beginnings of the jury system.

the Constitution of the United States, though making formal provision for trial or impeachment by Congress, after the model of the British Parliament,[5] specifically forbids bills of attainder. Parliament also became more definite in its structure, dividing with precision into the two Houses, of Lords and Commons, in place of the original vaguely organized grouping into Estates of lords, clergy, knights of the shire, and burgesses of the towns.[6] The town franchise varied according to local custom, in some places being very democratic and in others very exclusive; the county franchise became fixed in the fifteenth century for 'forty shilling freeholders,' landowners whose lands had an annual rental value of at least forty shillings.

On the whole, England had attained a tolerable balance of authority and liberty. At all events, foreign observers were struck by the reign of law, the restrictions on feudal tyranny, the relative infrequency of private war and family feuds. But the disorderly times of the Wars of the Roses permitted some great landowners to abuse their power by having private armies of retainers, to whom they gave livery of clothing and equipment, and maintenance of their lawsuits before the courts. Partly as a reaction against these abuses, the pendulum swung too far in the other direction, and under the Tudors threatened England with the type of royal tyranny that was growing up on the continent. Fortunately, legislation by Parliament and trial by jury had become traditions too deeply rooted to be altogether set aside.

The slow absorption of the conquering Norman aristocracy into the general mass of the population was hastened by the loss of the French fiefs of the Crown, first in the time of John, and again in the time of Henry VI. The French tongue gradually yielded to English among the aristocracy, whose estates were now all on the English side of the Channel. In 1362 English was introduced into the royal courts of law. Many legal documents, however, were still written in Latin down to the eighteenth century, and almost innumerable terms borrowed either from Latin or from Norman French are still used by lawyers. The king still gives his assent to laws by the French formula *Le roi le veult* (the king so wills it).

[5] In both Britain and the United States impeachments are brought by the lower House and tried by the upper.

[6] For the origins of Parliament, see Chapter v.

To make a language something other than a mere collection of local dialects there is needed the cement of a written literature. The development of a true English literature came somewhat slowly. So greatly had the coming of the Normans changed the language, not only by introducing French words into the vocabulary but by wearing away Anglo-Saxon grammatical forms, that the old masterpieces of Anglo-Saxon, such as the epic poem *Beowulf*, were no longer understood by the masses of the people. Scholars wrote exclusively in Latin. Latin was the common speech of the clergy, so that a priest, monk, or friar might wander from Poland to Portugal and be understood at every monastery which gave him a night's shelter. The English kings and the court circle long remained French in speech and manners, though, as we have seen, English was gaining even among the upper ranks of society. A really accomplished Englishman in the fourteenth or fifteenth century had to be trilingual: able to read a learned Latin book, to chat French in polite circles, and to speak English when dealing with shopkeepers and servants.

English enters real world literature only with Geoffrey Chaucer (c. 1340-1400). Chaucer had traveled in France and Italy, he had certainly been influenced by Dante's poetry and probably by Boccaccio's prose. But with all his cultured cosmopolitanism he, like the hero of the Gilbert and Sullivan opera, 'remained an Englishman,' and if this be not 'greatly to his credit,' at least it is greatly to our advantage, for his usage fixed the forms which the new language was to take. He has helped us in another way, by choosing to depict the common types of Englishmen of his day, from the grave and courteous knight and the university scholar with his books of Aristotle, to rough sailors and millers, all bound on a common pilgrimage to St. Thomas Becket of Canterbury.

Another window by which we may look into fourteenth-century England is opened by *Piers the Plowman*, ascribed with some uncertainty to William Langland. It is a bitter attack on the insolence of wealth, the corruption of the clergy, and the oppression suffered by the poor; reading it one can understand the popular sympathies that underlay the Peasants' Revolt. The people enjoyed also the legends of King Arthur and the ballads which told of the deeds of the chivalrous outlaw Robin Hood. More or less under the patronage of the Church there were simple popular dramas, the mystery plays, miracle plays, and morality plays.

This use of everyday English enabled the laity to break the monopoly of learning, almost of thinking, which the clergy had so long enjoyed by their knowledge of Latin. The introduction of printing into England by Caxton about 1476 completed the destruction of the clerical monopoly, for it resulted in books being multiplied and made available in every large town and in every studious home.

All this restless ferment of the fourteenth and fifteenth centuries, the criticism, impulse to change and improvement, challenges to hitherto accepted ways of life, came to a head in the cracking and splitting of the Roman Catholic Church, which we call the Reformation. Some early signs of this appear with John Wycliffe, the chief English heretic, who has been called the 'morning star of the Reformation.' He attacked the power and wealth of the clergy, contended that no priest of impure life could validly administer the sacraments, and even questioned the miracle of transubstantiation (the change of bread and wine in the mass into the body and blood of Christ). Though expelled from Oxford, Wycliffe was not otherwise persecuted, and he died as a parish priest in 1382. His followers, the so-called Lollards, were cruelly punished under the statute of 1401 'On Burning the Heretic' (*de Haeretico comburendo*), but the sect never quite died out till it merged with the later Protestant movement for which it had prepared the way.

Wycliffe handed on a torch to the Hussites of Bohemia, who in turn influenced the later German reformers of Luther's time. Although the claim must not be exaggerated, it may be said that England became, in a sense, what the historian Froude called the 'sea cradle of the Reformation.' Milton, in a well-known passage of his *Areopagitica*, declared that out of England had been 'proclaimed and sounded forth the first tidings and trumpet of Reformation to all Europe. And had it not been the obstinate perverseness of our prelates against the divine and admirable spirit of Wycliffe, to suppress him as a schismatic and innovator, perhaps neither the Bohemian Huss and Jerome, no nor the name of Luther and Calvin, had ever been known: the glory of reforming all our neighbors had been completely ours.' As things were, however, the Lollards sank into obscurity, and, while almost every reign brought out some political controversy between papal claims and royal power, these conflicts seldom involved any question of heresy.

Medieval England was far less differentiated from continental Europe than modern England. The general atmosphere of the Middle Ages was at once too local and too cosmopolitan for nationalism. Man's immediate allegiance went out to a city, a landlord, a province rather than to a whole nation; while general institutions, such as feudalism, the manorial system of agriculture, gild regulation of industry in the towns, the scholarship of the monasteries and universities, the use of Latin by the learned, the powers and duties of the Catholic clergy, were not national but universal. An English clergyman was first of all a Churchman, as when Thomas Becket put the interests of the Pope ahead of those of his king; an English noble felt more in common with a French noble, whose language he spoke and whose code of chivalry was his own, than with an English peasant or shopkeeper.

Yet England came probably closer to nationality in the modern sense than any other state of that time. There was a single common law for the whole nation, not laws that varied from province to province as in most European kingdoms. Allegiance to the English king was demanded of sub-vassals, not merely of tenants-in-chief of the Crown. England came nearer feeling as one and acting as one in international affairs than either France or the Holy Roman Empire; while the Italian and Spanish peninsulas were still divided into small separate states, as the Balkan region is today. Unlike Scotland, Ireland, and Wales, where English contested ground with native Celtic tongues, England knew no linguistic frontiers within her domains. The Normans for a time had constituted a class, but never a section; their fiefs were fairly evenly distributed throughout the country. Though there was more Danish blood in the eastern shires, and more Celtic blood in the west country, both Danes and Britons had become thoroughly assimilated to the common English stock.

An illustration of the extent to which England was at once part of a cosmopolitan civilization and yet able to give it a national twist of her own is afforded by the greatest medieval art, church architecture. The Norman style is practically identical with the Romanesque, round-arched style which prevailed throughout the greater part of

Europe until near the end of the twelfth century. The early Gothic, or pointed-arched, churches in England are very similar to those in France—often, indeed, the work of French architects. But the last phase of English Gothic, the perpendicular style, with its straight vertical lines, tall square towers, and fan-vaulted ceilings was characteristically national. Gothic, perhaps, had passed its best period in both England and the continent. But the point is that English architecture stiffened into rigidity at the very moment when continental Gothic was melting into opulent curves and flamboyant decoration; if they both erred, they did so in opposite directions.

This nationalization of architecture in the later Middle Ages is symbolic of many things. We have already seen how continental Parliaments and French juries acquired new significance when transplanted to English soil. The universities were a part of the common civilization of Catholic Christendom, but Oxford and Cambridge drew slowly farther away from their French, German, and Italian contemporaries. They lost the emphasis on specialized professional training and developed more as general schools of humane culture, first for the clergy, later for the gentry. So different did they finally become, that the Americans copied their undergraduate colleges in the seventeenth century from Oxford and Cambridge, and their graduate universities in the nineteenth century from Heidelberg and Göttingen.

The main legacy of medieval England to modern Britain and the United States was institutional. We have already noted the importance of Parliament, of the common law, of trial by jury. Of scarcely less significance was the tradition of local government. Continental Europe passed from feudal decentralization to bureaucratic despotism; England, however, had never been so loosely organized as feudal France or the Holy Roman Empire, and never became so highly centralized as the France of Louis XIV or the Prussia of Frederick the Great. The old Anglo-Saxon units of tun, hundred, and shire did not wholly disappear under Norman and Angevin rulers. The ecclesiastical unit of the parish retained some vitality in handling local affairs. The judicial system, though providing for higher royal courts, entrusted an almost incredible range of administrative as well as of judicial duties to country gentlemen, unpaid for their services, who held lifelong royal commissions as justices of the peace. This absence of a large professional class of government officials, together with the absence of a large standing army and the growing prestige of Parliament, saved England from the encroachments of royal power which extinguished traditional local liberties in most other parts of Europe.

PART II

BRITAIN IN THE DAYS OF EMPIRE

◦ IX ◦

THE NEW MONARCHY

THERE was nothing mystical about the year 1485 to herald the passing of the Middle Ages or the coming of modern times. Henry VII had replaced Richard III on the throne: one more battle, one more monarch—how could anyone living then know that the Wars of the Roses had ended, and that the crown would rest more firmly on a Tudor brow than ever on that of Yorkist or Lancastrian? No omens in the sky revealed the coming of a modern England—Protestant, commercial, and imperial—to replace the medieval England—Catholic, rustic, and bounded by European horizons.

Continuity in change is, indeed, the outstanding characteristic of British history. The outward forms of government stand today very much as they did in the fifteenth century: King, lords, and commons; jury trial and common law; chartered rights, shires, boroughs, justices of the peace. Inwardly, of course, these institutions have profoundly altered, but so slowly that in the main they keep the old names and forms, as petrified wood follows the grain and pattern of the parent tree, though what once was wood is now stone. The old fortress prison of Paris—the Bastille—is now an open square, symbolizing the clearance of old French institutions by the Great Revolution; the similar fortress prison of London—the Tower—was kept in perfect repair, as a museum. In many respects more of medieval life has been preserved in England than in any other country in the world: old castles still stand, old official records exist in unusual abundance (perhaps because England was so seldom harried by war), old customs are kept up from love of tradition.

With the important exception of the alterations which the Reformation brought to the English ecclesiastical system, the Tudor period (1485-1603) was rather conservative than revolutionary. Although the Tudors were masterful sovereigns and conducted a

83

vigorous administration through the royal Council, Parliament remained the normal channel for granting taxes and enacting laws, and even grew in power from the moment when it enacted Henry VII's right to the Crown. Though the personal power of the ruler also increased, this power rested on popular consent. Every Tudor ruler had to face some local uprising, and face it without a standing army; a strong revolutionary movement might have dethroned any one of them. The fact that no successful revolution against the Crown took place until the reign of the Stuart King Charles I is proof that the monarchy did not altogether lose touch with national sentiment.

King Henry VII met his first Parliament at Westminster on 7 November 1485. The Commons were present in their usual number, but very few Lords attended and a majority of them were Lords Spiritual—archbishops, bishops, and abbots. If Henry VII had summoned no new peers to Parliament, the nobility of England would have become practically extinct in a short time, as only the eldest son of a peer became, on his father's death, a peer by hereditary right, his brothers and sisters being in the eyes of the law simply commoners. So far from letting the nobility die out, however, the Tudors built up a new nobility of their own creation. What would be the splendor of a court which had only commoners to attend it? Every king likes an aristocratic atmosphere about the throne. But every king prefers that his nobles should owe their distinction to himself and shine with a reflected glory.

Although Henry VII officially dated his accession to the throne 21 August 1485, the day before the battle of Bosworth in which he won the crown, his first Parliament asserted its power by a bill enacting that 'the crowns of the realms of England and France [1] rest, remain and abide in the most royal person of our new sovereign lord King Henry VII.' While in France, Spain, and the Holy Roman Empire representative institutions decayed, in England Parliament met not indeed regularly but generally every year or two, even if only for a few weeks. Even when several years elapsed with no summoning of Parliament, the basic principle of representative government was preserved, that no new law and no new tax could take effect without parliamentary consent. Henry VIII, his son and successor,

---

[1] The kings of England long continued a nominal claim of the French throne.

made even more frequent use of Parliament than Henry VII, probably because he needed some agency of public opinion to back his fight against the Catholic Church. In 1543 he declared, 'We at no time stand so highly in our estate royal as in the time of Parliament, wherein we as head and you as members are conjoined and knit together in one body politic, so that whatsoever offence or injury during that time is offered to the meanest member of the House is to be judged as done against our person and the whole Court of Parliament.'

It is often contended that the Tudor sovereigns were conciliatory towards Parliament because they had found in it a passive tool for their own designs. In some measure this was true. New boroughs were enfranchised, especially in Cornwall, to return obedient members. Pressure was sometimes applied at elections. Most legislation that was passed was initiated by the king or his ministers. The general tone of the formal parliamentary resolutions and addresses to the throne was more than respectful, it was almost sycophantic. But we have evidence of contested elections, especially in the shires, and even of refusal to return candidates desired by the government.[2] In Parliament itself debate was, on the whole, free, and government measures were not infrequently amended or rejected outright. The absence of abbots after the Reformation from the House of Lords decreased the influence of the parliamentary peerage, and the entry of substantial owners of former monastic lands in the House of Commons increased that of the Commons. When the struggle between Crown and Parliament began again in the seventeenth century it was the Commons and not (as in the thirteenth and fourteenth centuries) the House of Lords which took the lead.

Francis Bacon, who was a lawyer and a judge as well as a philosopher, said of Henry VII, 'He may justly be celebrated for the best law giver to this nation after King Edward the First.' A very healing measure, after the harsh proscriptions and attainders that had marked the Wars of the Roses, declared that no person who in good faith had obeyed the ruling king *de facto* should afterwards be prose-

---

[2] 'In 1547 the Council ventured to recommend a minister to the freeholders of Kent. The electors objected; the Council reprimanded the sheriff for representing its recommendation as a command . . . and that Government candidate had to find another seat.' A. F. Pollard, *Henry VIII* (1919), p. 252.

cuted for such service. This secured the innocent adherents of the defeated party in a civil war from being punished for being on the losing side. Another statute imposed a limitation of five years on claims for land after due and proper notice had been given. Another limited the enclosure of common lands, which was so persistent a source of complaint in Tudor times and afterwards, because, so Bacon said, Henry did not want England to become like France where 'all is noblesse and peasantry, and no middle people.' Careful of the sea as well as of the land, Henry enacted that certain imports should be brought to England only in English ships.

Perhaps Henry's most important task was the one which confronts all governments in all ages, the establishment of order and the repression of crime. The Wars of the Roses had the usual effect of protracted civil war, the breakdown of law and the increase of private violence. The Venetian ambassador (all the ambassadors of Venice reported carefully and elaborately on the social conditions of the people among whom they were placed) declared that in no other country were there so many 'thieves and robbers' as in England. Few honest citizens dared venture abroad at night. Wealthy landowners brought troops of armed retainers to overawe judge and jury in cases where their interests were involved. By the end of Henry's reign, however, England was as orderly a country as could be found in Europe. This was the more remarkable, since there was no regular police force, no standing army, and a new dynasty on the throne. On several occasions Henry VII had to deal with pretenders to the throne or conspiracies directed against it.

The Yorkist party, though defeated at Bosworth in the person of King Richard III, was not quite extinct. The young Earl of Warwick, son of the Duke of Clarence and nephew to Edward IV and Richard III, and Elizabeth, daughter of Edward IV, both had some claims to the throne. Henry met these claims by marrying Elizabeth and by keeping Warwick in the Tower of London. Plots, however, continued. In 1487 the Yorkist party in Ireland made a descent on England, bringing with them the son of an Oxford tradesman called Lambert Simnel, whom they claimed to be the true Earl of Warwick. The boy, though he had been 'crowned' in Dublin, was treated mercifully by the king and made a turnspit in the royal kitchen, eventually being promoted to be one of the king's falconers. The next pretender, Peter or 'Perkin' Warbeck, son of a boatman, was put forth as the veritable 'Richard, Duke of York' (younger brother of Edward V and, with him, murdered by Richard III in the Tower of London). He found some support in Ireland and Scotland, but he was captured and imprisoned and, after he had escaped and been retaken, executed. The Earl of Warwick was also put to death, thus removing the last dangerous claimant to the throne.

The chief agency of Tudor strong monarchy was the Council, which in some respects overshadowed the Parliament. It was not the old occasional Great Council out of which Parliament itself had evolved, a meeting of the feudal baronage, but a whole-time, working group of expert administrators, a Council of the chief ministers and advisers of the Crown. Unlike a modern cabinet or ministry it had no direct connection with parties or with Parliaments, although most of the Councillors were members of the House of Commons or House of Lords; it was responsible neither to the people nor to the people's representatives but to the sovereign alone. Moreover, this Council was more than an advisory or executive body; it had also certain judicial functions.

To repress the lawlessness of the times King Henry erected a court consisting of certain members of the Council, together with two chief judges, which had the power to deal with cases of treason, sedition, high offenses against the State, and cases in which private persons could not be brought to ordinary criminal justice because they overawed judges and juries. This court was commonly called, from its place of meeting, the Court of Star Chamber. It was not bound by the ordinary rules of the common law, and so it was not required to make use of juries and it could force the giving of evidence, even by the employment of torture. Obviously such a court had within it every possibility of tyranny. Two points, however, should be noted. The Court of Star Chamber usually dealt only with great issues and powerful rebels; the ordinary safeguards of the common law still prevailed in everyday criminal cases. Again, public opinion at first welcomed the innovation, dreading much more the lawless power of wealthy private individuals than the power of the king.

Popular also was Henry's activity in putting down the customs of 'livery and maintenance,' that is the support of private armies of re-

tainers by noblemen. Bacon represents Archbishop Morton as saying
to Parliament,

. . . it is not the blood spilt in the field that will save the blood spilt in the
city; nor the marshal's sword that will set this kingdom in perfect peace;
but that the true way is to stop the seeds of sedition and rebellion at the
beginning, and for that purpose to devise, confirm and quicken good and
wholesome laws against riots and unlawful assemblies of people, and all
combinations and confederations of them by liveries, tokens and other
badges of factious dependence.

During the Tudor period Ireland was for the first time effectively
brought under English control. Hitherto Ireland had been divided
into two unequal parts, the small English 'Pale' around Dublin,
where English law prevailed, and a large area which was nominally
subject to the King of England, by his secondary title of 'Lord of
Ireland,' but in fact governed by a mixture of Celtic tribal custom
and the power of the Norman barons, who represented English
authority in very lawless fashion. Under Henry VII, in 1495, Poyn-
ing's Law subordinated the Irish Parliament to the English Council;
no session could be called unless King and Council were satisfied that
it was necessary, and had arranged for its program of business. Henry
VIII elevated Ireland to the rank of a kingdom and took the title
of King of Ireland. Under the same king Wales obtained regular
representation in the English Parliament. The Tudors were, indeed,
generally partial to Wales, being themselves of Welsh descent.

The aspect of Henry VII's reign which caused the most unfavorable comment at the time was not the increased authority of the
Crown or even the extraordinary power given to Star Chamber and
other courts of royal prerogative—both were in general welcome to
honest and peaceable men—but the methods he used to fill the royal
treasury. Parliament had granted him certain customs duties ('tonnage and poundage') for life, but this and his traditional feudal dues
did not suffice for the needs of an expanding nation. The pernicious
medieval notion that a king was just a greater landed proprietor
who should 'live of his own,' as other wealthy men did, confused the
needs of the ruler as a private person with the needs of the general
government. It drove Plantagenets, Tudors, and Stuarts alike to all
sorts of devious and sometimes dishonest shifts to make a 'balanced

budget.' Henry confiscated the estates of rebels, revived obsolete dead-letter laws for the purpose of exacting fines, and often compelled wealthy men to pay forced loans under the title of 'benevolences.' Those who lived luxuriously were told that they were well able to pay, as their profusion was proof of their wealth, while those who lived sparingly were told that they must have saved a good deal and could well afford to grant money to their king. Two of the king's officials, Empson and Dudley, were made the scapegoats of this policy and were executed, under Henry VIII, technically for treason but really because of their unpopularity.

It is due to Henry VII, however, to say that the masses of the people suffered little from his exactions; the wealthy few paid ransom for the community. This is true of many aspects of Tudor tyranny. Individuals high in rank, fortune, or place were the common victims of arbitrary arrests and imprisonments, unjust confiscations, executions on flimsy evidence under all the Tudors, especially under Henry VIII, and the eminence of these objects of royal wrath and greed gave a dark color to the times. But the grievances of the poor were of a different sort. They suffered little, as a rule, from royal tyranny.[3] The greatest social misery of the age was the transformation of tilled land into sheep pasture, as the growing prosperity of the wool trade tempted landlords to evict their tenants and promote wool growing for the Flemish market. 'Sheep,' said the wise Sir Thomas More, 'are eating men.' But private individuals were to blame for this policy; Henry VII even legislated against it, as did several of his successors, notably the Protector Somerset in the reign of Edward VI.[4]

Hugh Latimer, Bishop of Worcester, in a sermon preached before Edward VI on 8 March 1549, thus describes the decay of the yeomanry, the small farmer-owners or substantial tenant farmers, in some parts of England:

My father was yeoman, and had no lands of his own, only he had a farm of three or four pounds by year at the uttermost, and hereupon he tilled so much as kept half a dozen men. He had a walk for a hundred

---

[3] Except, perhaps, the closing of the monasteries where the poor were wont to receive alms. See below, p. 101.

[4] See below, p. 103.

sheep, and my mother milked thirty kine. He was able and did find the king a harness armor . . . He kept me to school, or else I had not been able to have preached before the king's majesty now. He married my sisters with five pound, or twenty nobles, apiece. He kept hospitality for his poor neighbours, and some alms he gave to the poor. And all this he did of the said farm, where he that now hath it payeth sixteen pound by the year, or more, and is not able to do anything for his prince, for himself, nor for his children, or give a cup of drink to the poor.

This agricultural change must not be thought of, however, as sudden or catastrophic. It was but a phase of the gradual transition from an England almost entirely rural to an England of commerce and industry. Agriculture could no longer be confined to the customs of the manor. Industry could no longer be regulated adequately by the craft gilds. The landed gentry had surplus income to invest, whether in sheep runs, in deer parks, or in mercantile enterprises. Master craftsmen were expanding their business and eager to borrow capital. John Winchcombe, called Jack of Newbury, had about 1550 some sixty or seventy men working under him to make cloth; he is the first known factory owner of the period, but he soon had many successors. The age of capitalism was at hand.

Local government, outside the chartered boroughs, was very largely in the hands of the Justices of the Peace. They were country gentlemen, serving for honor and not for pay, on royal appointment. Their functions were almost as much administrative as judicial. New laws, down through Elizabeth's time, imposed fresh duties on them. They had to oversee poor relief, the regulation of wages, the repression of beggary, the management of roads and prisons. They were aided in their work by locally elected—often self-elected—parish vestries, which looked after church affairs, chose constables to keep the peace, provided for the poor, and in some cases (all too rare!) supported schools. This Tudor system of local government is the background to American as well as English institutional history, for it is the form with which the first English colonists were familiar.

Tudor England must, to be understood, be viewed in its European setting. Italy, though divided politically into many states, was the center of commerce as well as of art and letters. France was making a strong recovery from the injuries of the Hundred Years' War. The crafty and politic Louis XI (1461-83) had made France almost as

united as England [5] and far more subject to royal despotism. Under
his successors Charles VIII, Louis XII, and Francis I, France plunged
into a series of wars against the Austrian House of Habsburg, with
dominant influence over wealthy Italy the chief prize of victory.
Another great power arose in western Europe, when the marriage of
King Ferdinand of Aragon to Queen Isabella of Castile united the
two largest monarchies in the Spanish peninsula. The conquest of
Moorish Grenada ended the last stronghold of Mohammedanism
in western Europe, and practically completed Spanish unification. In
the same year, 1492, that Grenada fell, the Genoese sailor Christopher Columbus, outfitted with a Castillian fleet, sighted land of the
western hemisphere. Thus the newly-made Spanish nation became
heir to a vast overseas empire. Ferdinand died in 1516, the 'maker'
of Spain, so far as one man might be. Three years later Cortez was
on his way to the conquest of Mexico. The sixteenth century was
truly the Spanish century, the great century (*el Siglo* as the Spaniards call it) of the colonization, conversion, and conquest of Spanish
America.

Henry VII and all his Tudor successors wanted to play a great part
in this new Europe. Wisely they decided to abandon that projected
conquest of France which had cost the Hundred Years' War, though
until the reign of Mary Tudor the English still held Calais. By the
Treaty of Etaples (1492), Henry VII terminated the French wars
in return for a subsidy. By the agreement of the Great Intercourse
he obtained favorable commercial terms with Burgundy. In 1499 he
concluded peace with Scotland and in 1502 negotiated a marriage
alliance between King James IV of Scotland and Henry's daughter
the Princess Margaret. This wedding of 'the thistle and the rose,'
emblems of the two nations, led ultimately to a peaceful union of the
two Crowns a century later in 1603.

Henry's greatest diplomatic success, though one which was to have
some very disconcerting consequences,[6] was the marriage alliance
arranged with mighty Spain. His eldest son Arthur married the Princess Katherine, younger daughter of Ferdinand and Isabella. Arthur

---

[5] English law was more uniform than French; it was not until after the revolution of 1789 that France received a truly uniform legal, administrative, and
financial system.

[6] See Chapter x.

died soon after the marriage, and Katherine was then engaged to Henry VII's surviving son, Prince Henry, then eighteen years of age, but the marriage was not completed until he had ascended the throne as King Henry VIII.

Not only was Henry VII one of the makers of modern England; he was also, in one sense, a founder of the British Empire. He had always been interested in seafaring and discovery and he actually entered into negotiations with Bartholomew Columbus, the brother of Christopher, for financing a voyage of exploration. Finding that Spain had already taken the first step, Henry VII was not discouraged, and in 1497 gave his support to an expedition of the Venetian John Cabot, who sailed with his son Sebastian from Bristol across the Atlantic to the 'new found land' which is today Newfoundland. They were the first Europeans since the Norsemen five centuries earlier to reach the North American continent—the coast of Labrador. The new region, however, did not seem inviting to settlers and the English took no step for many years to follow the voyages of the Cabots. Portugal, Spain, France, and Holland were all more active than England in the sixteenth-century race for empire.[7]

[7] See Chapter XVI.

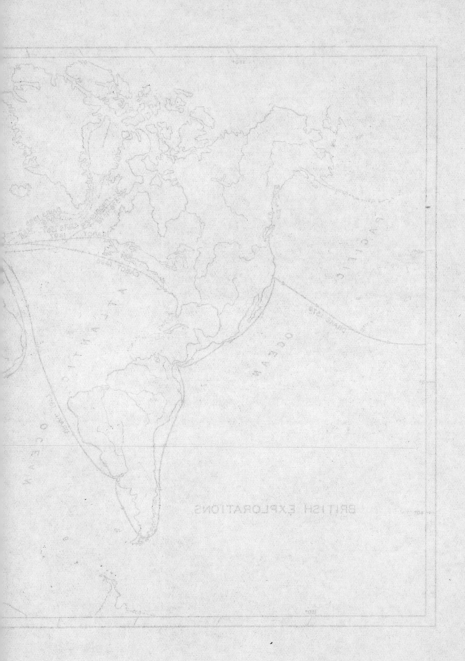

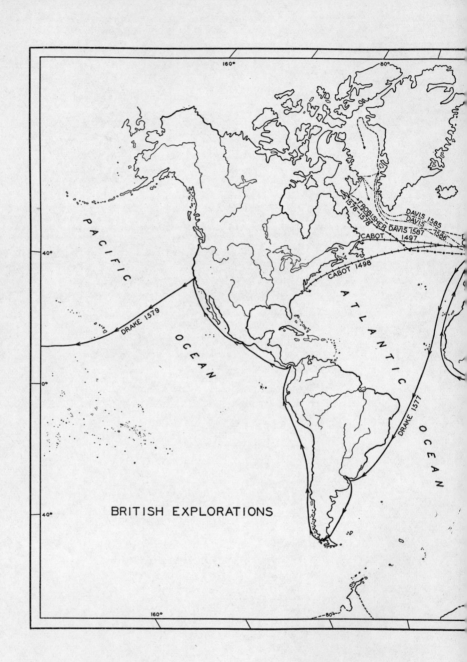

BRITISH EXPLORATIONS

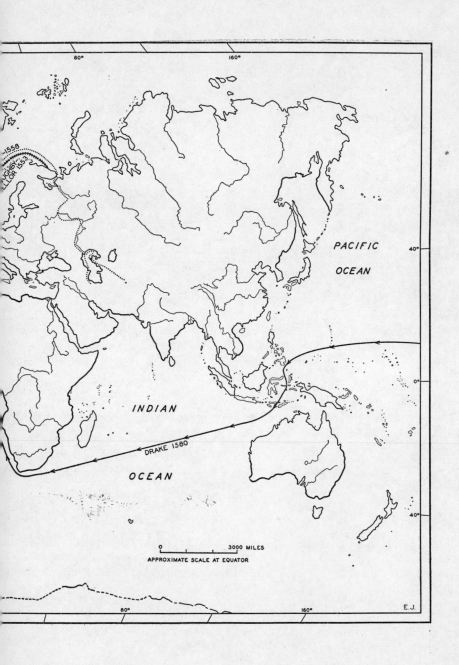

PACIFIC
OCEAN

INDIAN

OCEAN

DRAKE 1580

—1558
UGHEY
ELLOR 1553

40°

0°

40°

0   3000 MILES

APPROXIMATE SCALE AT EQUATOR

80°   160°

80°   160°

E.J.

◦ X ◦

RENAISSANCE AND REFORMATION

THE Tudor period is associated in English history with two great intellectual movements which profoundly altered the destinies of all Catholic Christendom—the Renaissance and the Reformation. Neither movement was directly of British origin, though Wycliffe's teachings had an indirect effect in preparing men's minds to receive Luther's and Calvin's doctrines. The main glory of the Renaissance, especially on the artistic side, certainly belongs to Italy, and the main battlefield of the early Reformation was Germany; England at best was an apt and forward pupil.

In one respect, indeed, England was notably backward. So far as the Renaissance was an expression of craftsmanship and appreciation in painting and sculpture, England could not be compared to Italy, France, Spain, or the Netherlands. Not until late in the seventeenth century did England make any important contribution in either field. In architecture there were, indeed, some very remarkable achievements, such as the chapel of Henry VII at Westminster and that of King's College at Cambridge; and the half-timbered houses of the well-to-do were so attractive that they are widely imitated even today. But there is little in this that suggests the new styles, based on classical models, that came in with the Italian Renaissance and did not generally prevail in England till the Stuarts had succeeded the Tudors; rather it was a final phase, a beautiful sunset, of the medieval Gothic, which lingered later in England than in most continental countries. In some of the lesser arts, such as gold and silver work, fine glass, furniture, and fashionable dress, the English imitated the Italians, and a common phrase of the age spoke of these devotees of continental modes as 'Italianate' Englishmen. But in the greater arts even appreciation was laggard. As late as the early seventeenth century 'diaries and guide books of travel in Italy, written by scholars and men of cultivation, describe the treasures of palaces and churches, and above all the monuments of antiquity; but scarcely a word is wasted on the pictures, even in detailed accounts of Florence . . . On the other hand, good taste in architecture, gardening, carving in wood, engraving in metal, and other arts that minister to the uses of life, was then natural and widely spread.'[1]

The literary influence of the Renaissance produced rich fruit only in Elizabethan times.[2] Many English scholars wrote with grace and wit, and fashionable courtiers could turn out a very passable imitation in English of the Italian lyrics, but, with some exceptions, the whole period between Chaucer and Marlowe is a barren stretch in the fields of English literature. Until the fierce struggles of Catholic and Protestant were healed by the Elizabethan compromise, most of the literary talent of the nation was devoted to theological controversy.

If the Renaissance spirit in letters reached England so late, and in art still later, what, then, was England's share in the movement? Chiefly scholarship. The study of Greek, long neglected in the Middle Ages, was taken up with ardor by English as well as by Italian, French, and German scholars in the later years of the fifteenth century. Under the impulse of the new learning, both Oxford and Cambridge experienced an intellectual revival. For a long time, printing presses for English books were to be found only in London and in these two university towns. Bishop Fox, formerly Chancellor of Henry VII, founded in 1516 Corpus Christi College at Oxford, for the study of classical languages. Cardinal Wolsey, Chancellor under Henry VIII, founded in 1524 the college now known as Christ Church. John Colet, Dean of St. Paul's in London, founded in 1509 St. Paul's School, in which Latin, Greek, Hebrew, and mathematics were all studied. Erasmus of Rotterdam, the greatest scholar of the age, paid long visits to England under Henry VII and Henry VIII, and lectured at Oxford and Cambridge. A hun-

---

[1] G. M. Trevelyan, *England under the Stuarts* (1930), p. 7.

[2] See Chapter xi. Inness says that in Henry VII's reign 'Colet's figure is almost the only one—apart from such representatives of erudition and scholarship as Grocyn and Linacre—which stands forth holding out a promise of intellectual progress. In effect there was no literature; in this respect Scotland was in advance of England with the verse of William Dunbar.' A. D. Inness, *England under the Tudors* (1937), p. 56.

dred years later the sound learning of the Latin Grammar Schools and the Universities of Oxford and Cambridge was transplanted from old England to New England by the Puritans, and newly embodied in the Boston Latin School and in Harvard College in Cambridge, Massachusetts.[3]

One cannot better the generous enthusiasm of Erasmus in paying tribute to the giants of the English Renaissance. 'I have found in Oxford,' he writes, 'so much polish and learning that now I hardly care about going to Italy at all, save for the sake of having been there. When I listen to my friend Colet, it seems like listening to Plato himself. Who does not wonder at the wide range of Grocyn's knowledge? What can be more searching, deep and refined than the judgment of Linacre? When did Nature mould a temper more gentle, endearing and happy than the temper of Thomas More?' Archbishop Warham and many other educated prelates were patrons of the New Learning, though nearly all the scholars were fiercely critical of clerical abuses, and in England, as in Germany and the Netherlands, the Renaissance paved the way for the Reformation.

The greatest of the figures in the English Renaissance, however, died a martyr to his orthodox Catholic faith, and has been by Roman authority recently admitted to the list of saints. Thomas More, though an able statesman in the service of his ungrateful master Henry VIII, is today remembered chiefly for his urbane and graceful fiction *Utopia*, a description of an ideal imaginary commonwealth which has enriched the language with the useful adjective 'Utopian' to hurl at any inconvenient reformer. The book was a triumph of English genius but not, in its original form, a contribution to English literature, since, like most learned men of the time, More wrote his most important work in Latin. To the student of English history the book is less important for the reforms it suggests than for the abuses that it by inference attacks. Thus war is denounced, complete religious toleration advocated, the cause of the poor championed and the privileges that go with wealth condemned. The brutalities of the criminal law are pointed out in a spirit that would have been remarkable in the full tide of the humanitarian movement three centuries later. The historian Green declares, 'It is not too much to say that in the

---

[3] See Chapter xvii for colonial education in America.

great principles More lays down he anticipated every one of the improvements in our criminal system which have distinguished the last hundred years.'

Another direction, perhaps an unfortunate one, in which England became Italianate was politics; not in constitutional form, but in practice and method. The age of More's idealism was also the age of Machiavelli's realism. The merits and vices alike of such kings as Edward IV, Richard III, Henry VII, and Henry VIII were those which might be found among the shrewd, practical, public-spirited and art-loving, but utterly unscrupulous despots in the Italian city-states. 'All the great Tudor statesmen, with the exception of Wolsey and the elder Cecil, were men of Italian training. Thomas Cromwell was completely saturated with Machiavelli's political philosophy; Francis Walsingham, Elizabeth's right-hand man, was denounced by King James of Scotland as "a very Machiavel." ' [4] This should not be taken as meaning that Machiavelli's doctrines were popular in England; on the contrary, the great Italian political scientist was seldom mentioned except to be denounced. Rather, the Tudor statesmen got their theory of political conduct in the very place where Machiavelli himself did—the actual practice of the European world of the Renaissance. It was a world of powerful and irresponsible sovereign states which were competing for political power and commercial wealth. These rulers and their ministers perhaps were less trammeled by traditions of chivalry or scruples of religion than statesmen of the thirteenth century might have been. The chief difference, however, was not that statesmen had become morally worse—for the Middle Ages knew many evil rulers—but that national governments were more clearly defined and more sharply thrown into competition. In the exaltation of the absolute rights of the state, the exemption of politics from the operation of the moral law prevailing in private life, and the acceptance of perfidy as a normal, if regrettable, part of diplomacy, the despots of the sixteenth century bear an uncomfortable likeness to the dictators of the twentieth.

Three figures tower above the rest in the international politics of the early sixteenth century—Emperor Charles V, ruler of Austria, Spain, the Netherlands, Burgundy, half of Italy and most of America,

---

[4] Conyers Read, *The Tudors* (1936), pp. 54-5.

the greatest landlord Europe ever knew between Charlemagne and Napoleon; King Francis I of France, and King Henry VIII of England. Charles V was grave, cautious, steadfast, the ruler of more lands than one man, however well supplied with councillors, could manage. Francis I was a dashing soldier, a generous patron of art, a somewhat irresponsible statesman, monarch of a very powerful kingdom. Charles, Francis, and Henry VIII held the destinies of Europe in their hands. Their appearance together was not entirely fortuitous. They were the product of an age when the old feudal and ecclesiastical controls were being broken and when the monarch was rising in solitary grandeur, the director, the savior of the state. *Le nouveau Messie est le roi,* 'the king is the new Messiah.'

Compared with either the Habsburg Austro-Spanish inheritance or with the Kingdom of France, England was but a minor power. But united and compact, tolerably prosperous and well-administered, little England counted for enough to make her alliance sought, and she was able to augment her importance by playing off Spain against France. This balance-of-power policy, which was to become a set tradition of English diplomacy, is usually dated from the reign of Henry VIII, and especially from the ministry of the able, ambitious, and overbearing Cardinal Thomas Wolsey. Under Wolsey's energetic leadership, London became for a time a center of the new diplomacy. How far he was conscious of making a new departure in British policy is a matter of dispute among historians; some think that he was merely using the new power of Spain as an instrument in the old quarrel with France; others that he desired, perhaps with a hope of himself being Pope some day, to support the Papacy against France with Spanish aid; others that he planned a general European peace with diplomatic negotiation substituted for war. But whatever his personal motive may have been, Wolsey's typically Renaissance conception of diplomacy as a game of skill in which victory goes to the power which can most adroitly balance the rival ambitions of other states had a profound effect on the future.

Henry VIII (1509-47) has been more variously estimated than any other English sovereign, from Froude's picture of him as a champion of national rights against ecclesiastical corruption and tyranny, to Dickens's verdict that he was 'a blot of blood and grease on the history of England.' This difference of opinion is not due entirely to the fact that he was the central figure in the English Reformation, and that so long as there are Catholic and Protestant historians there will be two versions of the reign in which the Church of England seceded from that of Rome. Apart from this, there were contradictions in Henry's own character. When he came to the throne he was greeted with as much enthusiasm as any monarch in British annals. A handsome young man of eighteen, athletic, cultured, a musician, a Latin scholar, a skilful fencer and yachtsman, full of the zest of life, bluff and hearty, and with no foreign mannerisms, he was well fitted to attract the applause of the crowd. He had also some of the abilities which impress statesmen. He was a thorough patriot, an advocate of ship building and sea power, and he labored unceasingly for the greatness of England. Though personally autocratic and imperious in the last degree, he made more use of Parliament than had any monarch since the time of Henry VI, and he treated it with more respect than his own ministers did; where Wolsey bullied the Commons, Henry flattered and cajoled them. His religious convictions seem to have been sincere, and he was an amateur of theology, actually writing a pamphlet in defense of the seven sacraments against Martin Luther, which won him the title (still borne by British kings) of Defender of the Faith.

On the other hand, Henry was essentially selfish; Wolsey summed him up in the famous phrase, 'rather than he will miss part of his appetite he will hazard the loss of one-half of his kingdom.' Those who withstood his will, no matter how great their services, how noble their characters, or how clear their innocence of the particular charges brought against them, were crushed with as little remorse as a tiger would show to a deer. His six marriages, two ending in judicial annulments and two ending in the execution of the unhappy queen, do not show him more licentious than many other monarchs of that age, but they do show a ruthlessness in personal relations which paralleled his ruthlessness in matters of state.

The break with Rome might have come to England, as it did to Scotland, as a popular movement independent of, or even opposed to, the policy of the ruler. There was enough background of Lollardy in England, and enough Protestantism coming in from Holland and Germany and Geneva along the paths of trade, to make this quite possible. On the other hand, England might have remained, like

France, a predominantly Catholic State with a considerable Protestant minority. If Henry VIII had not, almost accidentally, come into collision with the Pope on a purely political question, one or the other of these destinies would probably have been that of England, for Henry VIII was theologically Catholic rather than Protestant, and all his predecessors, since England was converted from heathenism, had been Roman Catholics and many of them very devout. There had been secular quarrels innumerable between State and Church, as in the reigns of Henry II and John, but these were no more acute than the similar quarrels of French, German, and even Spanish monarchs with popes or clergy. Charles V, the pillar of the Church in the Holy Roman Empire, had been involved in a temporal dispute with Pope Clement VII and had sent an army against him. The 'Most Catholic kings' of France had also warred against papal armies.

Queen Katherine had borne to Henry six children, but only the Princess Mary had survived. In default of a son, she would succeed to the throne. But though English law admitted a female heir, there had been no queen actually reigning in her own right unless we count Matilda, King Stephen's rival, whose unsuccessful attempt to take the throne had cost nineteen years of civil war. Henry felt that the English people were entitled to a male heir, that the throne might be stable and the nation secure. He remembered the Wars of the Roses, arising from a disputed succession. He also knew whom he wished to marry and to raise up a prince to succeed him: Anne Boleyn, maid of honor at the court. A pretext for the dissolution of the marriage was not lacking. Henry had married his brother Arthur's widow, which was contrary to canon law; though the Pope had given him a dispensation which had quieted his conscience at the time, he now revived the question as to the legality of his marriage. This so-called divorce, or more accurately a suit for the annulment of an illegal marriage, after being considered by a Papal Commission in England, was in 1529 transferred by Pope Clement VII to Rome. Impatient at Wolsey's procrastination and lack of success in handling the case, Henry deprived him of his post of Chancellor. Wolsey retired to his archdiocese of York, but imprudent letters to foreign ambassadors led to a charge of treason and the cardinal might have been executed had he not died on his way from York to London.

Meanwhile (1529) Henry summoned his Parliament, commonly called the Reformation Parliament. His previous Parliaments had been brief, but this one was to last—of course, not in continuous session—for seven years. Its first measures were designed rather to bring pressure to bear on the Pope by hostile legislation than to make a complete and final break. But the Pope, independent of any personal reluctance he must have felt to overturn a papal dispensation and to annul the marriage of an honorable and faithful queen, was in no position to quarrel with Charles V, who was Katherine's own nephew. It became plain to Henry that nothing was to be hoped for from the Papacy, so he made his own arrangements for disowning Katherine and marrying Anne Boleyn. Wolsey's place was taken by Thomas Cromwell, who had none of Wolsey's scruples in breaking altogether with the Pope. Though Cromwell's ruthless character is most unattractive, his elevation to power was in a sense a triumph of the common man over the two dominant classes in medieval England—the clergy and the gentry. 'He was the first great minister of the crown baseborn and yet not a cleric.' [5] Henry had the first essential of a great ruler, the ability to detect ability in others, though he was as ready to break his tools as he was keen-sighted in finding them.

One by one the knots which bound the Church of England to Rome were elaborately untied. Practically every step was taken with the formal sanction of Parliament. This was chiefly to place the sanction of public opinion on measures so novel and revolutionary, but it was also a method that accorded well with the strange character of the king, who all his life had little regard for justice but much for legality. In 1529 certain clerical fees, such as those for marriage and burials, were limited by statute. In 1530 the English clergy was collectively charged with violating the law of *praemunire* (carrying cases out of the king's jurisdiction to a foreign—in this case the papal—court) and forced to recognize Henry as head of the Church in England, though the convocation of the clergy insisted on adding the qualification 'so far as the law of Christ allows.' In 1533 Henry took control of matters of church law. In 1534 he forbade the payment of 'annates' (the first year's revenues of a church official) to the Pope. Later in the year an Act of Supremacy completed the

---

[5] Conyers Read, *The Tudors*, p. 66.

formal side of the Reformation, ending all connection with Rome. The bishops and abbots accepted this, except the saintly Bishop John Fisher who, together with the great Catholic layman and ex-Chancellor, Sir Thomas More, was executed for treason in refusing to take the prescribed oaths.

Although the king remained Catholic, without being Roman Catholic, and in 1539 had persuaded Parliament to enact of a Bill of Six Articles, affirming the principal doctrines of the Catholic Church which the Protestant sects had abandoned, he undertook a general attack on the monasteries. In 1536 he had the smaller monasteries dissolved on the ground that they were more corrupt than the larger establishments. This provoked the most serious insurrection of his reign, the so-called Pilgrimage of Grace, in Lincolnshire and Yorkshire. In 1539 the larger monasteries were dissolved in turn. The total revenues of the monastic lands at the time of the dissolution were about £135,000, equal to about one-half of the revenue of the Crown; expressed in terms of modern price levels this might amount to about two million pounds stirling ($10,000,000) a year. The estates of the monasteries lapsed to the Crown and about two-thirds of them were given or sold—chiefly the latter—to royal officials or private persons. These splendid estates thus operated as an endowment of newly created nobles and bound them by ties of interest and obligation to the king. A little of the confiscated revenue went to public purposes, such as school endowments, and some of the abbey churches became cathedrals; but most of it was plundered with no advantage to the public. The poor, deprived of the casual charity they had been accustomed to receiving from the monks, were in many cases reduced to destitution.

The last years of Henry's life constituted a reign of terror. Executions were numerous, beginning with that of Thomas Cromwell, who had fallen from the king's favor in 1540. Roman Catholics were beheaded for denying the royal supremacy over the Church, and Protestants were burned for denying the miracle of transubstantiation in the mass. The strong-willed monarch who had defied Pope, Emperor, and King of France still held the nation in his mighty grasp, and great nobles were waiting in the Tower of London to be beheaded when the tyrant, prematurely aged at fifty-five, died in 1547. The condemned men were released at once.

Although the will power of the ruthless king counted for much in the breach with Rome, the Reformation in England did not depend upon royal command. Probably a majority of the people under Henry VIII were still Catholic, but there was at any rate a large Protestant minority and a growing one. There were Oxford and Cambridge scholars, parish clergy, town merchants and craftsmen, and country yeomen who were accepting the new-old doctrines, the freedom of the individual soul and conscience, the direct approach to God, the return, as it was believed to be, to the simple teachings of the Gospel without the accretion of centuries of Romanism. English Protestantism became more clearly defined in the next reign.

Henry VIII, married six times, had only one legitimate son, Edward, by his third wife, Jane Seymour. The frail boy who now inherited the crown at the age of nine had a good share of the Tudor ability and, like all the Tudor rulers, a thorough education. His reign (1547-53) ended before he came of age, and was entirely covered by two regencies or protectorates of older men, first that of his uncle, Edward Seymour, Duke of Somerset, and later that of John Dudley, Duke of Northumberland. Both men were Protestants, and Edward VI inclined the same way himself. Thus his reign, even more than that of Henry VIII—who had never entirely abandoned Roman Catholic theology even when politically most hostile to the Church— gave the Protestant doctrines an opportunity to spread. No one at this late date can say how many Englishmen were Catholics and how many were Protestants, but it is certain that the latter greatly increased in number during Edward's reign. Archbishop Cranmer had the opportunity of introducing many reforms which he had not been permitted to carry out under Henry VIII. The Parliament of 1547 repealed the 'six articles' by which Henry VIII had tried to impose uniformity of belief; abolished old statutes for burning heretics which dated back to Lollard days, and also some new definitions of 'treason' which Henry VIII had introduced; and, in 1549, approved a 'Booke of Common Prayer,' which owes much of its beauty to the literary genius of Cranmer. A second Prayer Book issued in 1552, after Northumberland had succeeded Somerset, went still further in the Protestant direction and is the basis of the liturgy in the Church of England to this day.

Like all Tudor rulers, Edward had to face local rebellions. These came from two sources, religious and social discontents. Thus the conservative peasantry of Devon and Cornwall rebelled against the new English Prayer Book, preferring the old Latin ritual. (It is interesting to note that the sailors and townsmen, perhaps because of their more frequent contact with new ideas from the continent, took to Protestantism much more readily.) The popular indignation against the enclosure of common fields for the benefit of rich landlords flared up at the same time in an insurrection in East Anglia under Robert Ket. To his credit, Somerset did what he could to redress the wrongs of the peasantry, and when in 1522 he was executed by his enemies of Northumberland's faction he was sincerely mourned by the poor.

The death of Edward VI in 1552 opened a quarrel over the succession. Henry VIII by will had left the crown to Edward and his heirs; failing such heirs it would go in succession to his half-sisters Mary and Elizabeth, in spite of the fact that both had been previously declared illegitimate. Northumberland, however, had hit on a device to continue the power of his regency. His fourth son, Lord Guildford Dudley, was married to Lady Jane Grey, the granddaughter of Henry VIII's sister Mary. Edward VI had been induced to declare Lady Jane Grey his heir, and Northumberland proclaimed her Queen of England in London. The country rallied around Mary, however, and Northumberland paid forfeit with his life for his bold bid for dynastic power. Mary was generous enough to be content with imprisoning the 'nine days' queen' and her husband in the Tower of London, but a later rebellion under Sir Thomas Wyatt caused both to be executed. At the time of her death Lady Jane Grey was but a little over sixteen, beautiful, amiable, scholarly, one of the most innocent victims ever sacrificed to the ambition of those about her.

Mary I (1553-8), daughter of Henry VIII and the unhappy Katherine of Aragon, whose broken marriage had broken also the ties between England and Rome, was of course a devout Catholic. To her, Protestantism was thrice detestable, as a soul-destroying heresy, as the movement which had laid waste her mother's life, and as the party which branded her as illegitimate and had tried in vain to bar her from her right to the throne. She restored the mass and the old Latin service and permitted the monasteries to reopen, but she failed to get back the abbey lands which had passed into private ownership; it was only too evident that many of the rich were quite willing to take any religion, whether Catholic or Protestant, from the Crown, but would not permit royalty itself to force them to disgorge their plunder!

Mary risked her first popularity by marrying a Spanish prince, Philip, who was later King Philip II. This provoked Wyatt's rebellion, which cost the leader his life and led to the execution of Lady Jane Grey and the imprisonment of the Princess Elizabeth. Philip stayed only a short time in England and took little interest either in his English queen or in the affairs of her nation. The terrible persecution of the 'heretics,' which won for the well-meaning and conscientious Mary the popular nickname of 'bloody Queen Mary,' was not due to Philip's influence (indeed he advised her against it) or to considerations of state among the queen's advisers, but to her own morbid hatred of the Protestants. The punishment of burning, abolished under Edward VI, was now revived by Parliament, and some three hundred persons went to the stake, among them Archbishop Cranmer, the Bishops Ridley and Latimer. The terrible stories of the time were collected by an exiled Protestant, John Foxe, whose *Acts and Monuments of the Church,* popularly called 'Foxe's Book of Martyrs,' spread throughout England and had a tremendous effect in spreading the Reformation. In many cottages the Bible and the 'Martyrs' were the only two printed books to be found. The 1559 edition, printed in Switzerland, tells the famous story of the burning of Latimer and Ridley at Oxford. Each was bound to a stake in a separate fire but close together in a space in front of Balliol College. 'Be of good cheer, Master Ridley,' Latimer said, 'we shall this day light such a candle, by God's grace, in England, as I trust shall never be put out.'

Mary's reign ended in tragedy. Philip, now King of Spain, involved her in a war with France in which England lost her last French stronghold, Calais. The persecution had not succeeded in stamping out heresy, though it had driven many Protestants to take to the sea; English Protestantism and English seamanship joined themselves together, as they were seen to be in the reign of Elizabeth. Philip himself remained cold and indifferent to Mary. There was no child born of the marriage to inherit the throne. The loveless queen died in November 1558, just after the French captured Calais. The Crown passed, therefore, to Elizabeth, who was a Protestant, though not an extreme one, and with Mary ended the last opportunity to restore England to the Catholic fold.

THE ELIZABETHAN AGE

Though the reign of Mary Tudor had left an unhappy memory, the greatest glories of the English Crown are associated with three queens reigning in their own right: Elizabeth, Anne, and Victoria. The reign of Elizabeth (1558-1603) enjoyed a degree of stability and balance in the structure of both Church and State greater than England had known since the Wars of the Roses began, and greater than England was again to know till after the revolution of 1688. It marked also the first great flowering of English literary genius, if we make an exception of the isolated figure of Chaucer, and in particular the greatest chapter in the world history of the drama. Not least, it marked the first active movement for colonization overseas. No Elizabethan settlement survived the queen's own lifetime; permanent foundations began with her successor James I. Yet not without warrant is the conventional dating of the 'First British Empire' from the reign which saw the growth of English sea power, serious inroads on Spain in the Old World and the New alike, voyages to lands hitherto unknown, and Raleigh's bold, though unsuccessful, ventures in Virginia—the land of the Virgin Queen.

How much of the greatness of the Elizabethan Age may be safely ascribed to the queen herself is a much mooted question. Certainly she came to the throne with unusual talents for government. She was twenty-five years old when the royal messenger found her under an oak in Hatfield park and told her that she was Queen of England. As the daughter of Henry VIII and of Anne Boleyn she was naturally Protestant, since a consistent Roman Catholic would have had to pronounce her illegitimate; but her mind was positive, realistic, and secular and she cared relatively little for either religious visions or religious forms. When she persecuted it was always because she feared a political enemy, not because she hated a theological heretic.

She was national and patriotic to the highest degree; 'mere English' she declared herself. Though she did not travel on the continent, she was an accomplished linguist, able to read Greek, Latin, and Hebrew and to speak in German, French, and Italian. Her training by Protestant governesses and tutors, chief among them the famous educational reformer Roger Ascham, fellow of St. John's College, Cambridge, in English country houses in the 'home counties' accentuated her Englishry. She had learned to be wary, tactful and at times disingenuous during the reign of her half-sister Mary, when a single false step might have brought a charge of treason and the headsman's block, as it did to the simpler and honester Lady Jane Grey.

Though Elizabeth had friends and favorites among the courtiers, she put responsibility for administration in the hands of experienced officials. Her Privy Council, or at least the working part of it, became a very expert body. Her chief officials were not the Lord Chancellor or the Lord Chamberlain, with their old traditions of ecclesiastical, legal, or feudal attachment, but Secretaries of State (for the greater part of the reign Burleigh and Walsingham), who administered home and foreign affairs and, being themselves members of Parliament, introduced and guided bills through the legislature as cabinet ministers do today. There were no paid officials to enforce these acts of Parliament; the justices of the peace saw to their enforcement in the counties and the mayors in the towns. These unpaid agents of government often complained of the 'stacks of statutes' that the Privy Council sent down to them to be read, learned, and enforced; for though there was no trained civil service for national administration the Council took on itself to regulate anything and everything it thought needed attention—the making of soap, the hiring of apprentices, the price of bread, the eating of fish on Friday, the kind of sports permitted on Sunday, and (a perpetual Tudor preoccupation) the minimum amount of land to be kept by every 'house of husbandry.'

All this paternalism took time to be developed. The immediate problems confronting the young queen were the foreign war with France, which had just cost England Calais, and the religious settlement. After protracted negotiations, England made peace with France in 1559, though the promised restoration of Calais to England was never carried into effect. Elizabeth at first temporized with the religious issue, stopping the burnings of heretics and using an English form of service but not definitely declaring for Protestantism. The Pope had at one time hopes of her conversion, and Philip II of Spain, widower of her half-sister Mary, hoped for an alliance—perhaps even a matrimonial one.

When Elizabeth finally made her religious settlement with the co-operation of Parliament, it was a compromise or middle way, which did not satisfy either the Roman Catholics or the Calvinistic Protestants who were later called Puritans, but it did seem to please the great majority of the people. An Act of Supremacy abolished papal jurisdiction and made the monarch the Supreme Governor (not 'Head') of the Church of England. An Act of Uniformity restored the English Prayer Book as used under Edward VI. Subjects were required to attend the church services, under penalty of a small fine, but there was no inquisition into their private faith; 'I will open no windows into any man's soul,' said the prudent queen. Although the ecclesiastical settlement was now definitely Protestant, it preserved the stately outward fabric of the medieval Church, and new bishops were duly consecrated by bishops who had served under Henry VIII, thus maintaining the continuity of the Church of England back to the days of Augustine and the first missionaries.

The social problems of the time attracted the attention of the government. The coinage, greatly debased under Henry VIII, was restored to full value by the government, acting through the London merchant and financier Sir Thomas Gresham. The termination of the French war enabled the government greatly to reduce expenses. Elizabeth was, to be sure, always extravagant in her personal habits, but it takes a great many royal gowns to equal the cost of a single battle! A number of well-meant but futile laws were passed against the transformation of agricultural land to sheep pasture; their local enforcement depended on the justices of the peace, who were themselves the chief enclosers of land. Other laws regulated the conditions of apprenticeship.

The Elizabethan poor law was a constructive effort to deal with the pressing social needs created by the break-up of feudalism, the enclosure of lands, the rise in prices, and other circumstances of the new age. Begging was forbidden. Churchwardens and certain householders in each parish were made Overseers of the Poor. In conjunction with the justices of the peace, they had the power to levy a poor-rate, purchase materials for work, and build 'places of habitation' for poor people, the 'poor house' or 'workhouse' familiar in later British history, and in American history as well. Though the system was greatly changed in the nineteenth century, its fundamental principle was that the State should compel the taxpayer to support those who were in no wise able to support themselves. The State assumed the task of administering charity which had once been the monopoly of the Church.

Much of Elizabeth's early reign was taken up with foreign policy. England enjoyed many years of peace, but it was peace amid perils. The dominant state in Europe was Spain, ruled by Philip II, who, possessing most of the New World, denied to other nations the privilege of trading with it. France, torn by civil wars between Catholic and Huguenot, was at once Spain's ally in repressing Protestantism and her enemy in the struggle for secular power. The Netherlands, fallen to Philip of Spain by dynastic accident rather than by any natural connection, was seething with revolt. Ireland, the half-conquered island, was driven into open rebellion against English rule by dislike for the innovations which Protestant England was making in religion.

Scotland, still an independent kingdom, was rapidly becoming Protestant, but in the Calvinistic rather than the Anglican form. Moreover, the Scottish queen, Mary Stuart, widow of Francis II of France, was not only a devout Roman Catholic but a partisan of the 'auld alliance' of Scotland with France and a claimant to the throne of England. If Elizabeth really were illegitimate, as Rome contended, the lawful ruler of England would be Mary 'Queen of Scots.' It was an age of political assassinations, and the murder of Elizabeth was doubly a temptation to the fanatic, since it would not only destroy a Protestant ruler but place on the throne a Catholic. The Scottish peril was the most immediate, if that of Spain was in the long run the most formidable. The tradition of war between England and Scotland had become a persistent evil legacy handed down from generation to generation. James IV, though he had married the daughter of Henry VII, had died fighting the English at Flodden. James V died after hearing of the defeat at Solway Moss, further saddened by the reflection that his successor was a baby girl and that the Stuart name would die with him; 'It came with a lass and it will go with a lass,' he groaned. During Mary's minority Scotland was governed by the French Regent and Queen Mother, Mary of Guise. Scotland was, in fact, almost a French province until in 1560 French troops were withdrawn from Scotland by agreement with England.

The Reformation came to Scotland more slowly than to England, partly because the government took the Catholic side. James V, Mary of Guise, and Mary Stuart all held sincerely to the old faith. A few Protestants were burned, among them Patrick Hamilton, a disciple of Luther, and George Wishart, a friend of Knox and a disciple of Calvin; but there was no persecution on such a wholesale scale as that under Mary Tudor in England. The Scottish nobles, or at any rate the anti-Guise faction, were attracted not only to Protestantism but to the monastic lands which they could take over from the admittedly corrupt Scottish Church. A majority of the Scottish people were turned to Calvinism by the teachings of John Knox and his zealous fellow Reformers. Their temper was as stern and implacable as that of their foes. Cardinal Beaton, the chief persecutor of the Protestants, was murdered (1546) to avenge the death of Wishart. Images were torn from the churches. Knox himself bitterly assailed the policy of Mary of Guise and Mary Stuart (who returned from France to Scotland in 1561) and of Mary Tudor in England by his tract on the *Monstrous Regiment of Women*, designed to demonstrate that the Salic law which in many continental countries barred women from the throne was in accord with Scripture and the law of nature. This unfortunate pamphlet won Knox little thanks from Elizabeth when she came to rule England, but in most respects the English queen was well pleased to witness the triumph of the Scottish Reformers, which not only buttressed the Protestant cause in England but gave embarrassment to her rival the Queen of Scots. The triumph of the Scottish Reformers was completed by an expeditionary force which Queen Elizabeth sent to Edinburgh in 1560 and which expelled the French garrison supporting Queen Mary.

The tragic struggle between the two queens, the inspiration of so many dramatists and novelists, ended in Elizabeth's favor, mainly because Mary's subjects were hostile to the religion which she professed. It is always hard for a ruler when his faith is different from

that of the nation which he rules. Henry IV, a Protestant king of
Catholic France, changed his religion to secure a firmer hold on the
Crown; Christina, a Catholic queen of Protestant Sweden, abdicated. Mary decided to abide the issue. She made her position even
more untenable by unfortunate ventures in matrimony. After the
death of King Francis, she married her kinsman Lord Henry Stuart
Darnley, thus securing the perpetuation of the Stuart name in the
dynasty. But apart from his Stuart name and handsome appearance,
there was nothing to Darnley. Cold of heart and empty of head,
unfaithful and yet insanely jealous, as his murder of Mary's Italian
secretary Rizzio showed, he so completely alienated Mary that,
when he in turn was murdered, she speedily married one of his
slayers, the Earl of Bothwell. Scotland now rose against her; she
was defeated, deposed, imprisoned, and escaped to England, but
only to change a Scottish prison for an English one. At first her imprisonment was a polite one, with residence in a variety of English
country houses and every luxury except freedom, but fresh conspiracies hardened Elizabeth's heart, and on 25 October 1586, Mary
was condemned for alleged conspiracy to accomplish Elizabeth's
death. Elizabeth put off signing the death warrant until 1 February
1587. Mary was executed at Fotheringay Castle, Northamptonshire,
8 February 1587. Her son, James VI of Scotland, was brought up
a Protestant and the regency during his minority was not unfriendly
to England. Eventually he succeeded to the English throne as King
James I, founder of the Stuart dynasty in England.

After Scotland, Elizabeth had Ireland to deal with. Though nominally subject to the English Crown since the reign of Henry II, and
partly colonized by English and Norman knights, there were few
signs of English rule or of the Anglo-Norman blood in most of the
island. In the English Pale, comprising the counties of Dublin,
Louth, Meath, West Meath, and Kildare, and in a few others outside the Pale, there were traces of English organization. An Irish
Parliament, subordinate to the English Council, represented the 'obedient' districts. Outside these, Irish chieftains ruled and the people
talked Erse, the native Celtic tongue, instead of English. The Pale
was garrisoned by a few hundred English soldiers, and the entire
revenues of the Crown in Ireland barely sufficed to pay for this garrison. The Tudors tried to control the more powerful native and

'Anglo-Norman' chiefs by giving them English honors and titles; such as the Earls of Kildare, Desmond, Ormonde, and Clanrickard.

Under Henry VIII the Irish monasteries had been disendowed. Lingard, the Catholic historian, suggests that if the prayer books of Edward VI had been translated into Erse, the Irish people as a whole might have been won to Protestantism. As things were, the Irish could see in Protestantism only an alien heresy imposed by foreign rulers. Catholic enemies of England on the continent naturally sought to profit by the discontents of the Irish Catholics, and thus Elizabeth's reign meant in Ireland a struggle between Catholicism as represented by Spain and Protestantism as represented by England, and the Irish suffered the hard fate of a small nation which has become a pawn in a game among Great Powers.

Elizabeth and her Council had not given up hope that Ireland could be won to Protestantism. The subservient Irish Parliament was induced to pass the Acts of Supremacy and of Uniformity. Thus the English Prayer Book was enjoined, though a tardy concession permitted the use of Latin and Erse in the church services. The Jesuit missionaries, however, conducted a secret and perilous mission throughout Ireland, reconverted many, and confirmed others in their native faith.

A series of insurrections under Shane O'Neill, Earl of Tyrone, and his successor Hugh O'Neill, kept English armies busy in Ireland. Sir Walter Raleigh and Edmund Spenser were among the English who served in Ireland. Efforts were made to 'plant' the country, wherever land had been forfeited by rebellion, with English settlers, but none of the Elizabethan plantations survived as discernible units beyond the queen's reign. The great migration of English and Scottish settlers was to come under James I (VI), who first united the forces of the two countries; the province of Ulster was still Catholic and natively Irish in Elizabeth's day. Some attempts were made to land Spanish troops in Ireland and thus open a back door to England, but all were defeated.

Elizabeth and her ministers did some constructive work in Ireland. They introduced English land laws and systems of tenure, established sheriffs, justices of the peace, and the use of the jury, and founded a college, Trinity, in Dublin, which became one of the most distinguished schools in Europe. The use of the English language began to spread; it is perhaps no accident that modern 'dialect' English in Ireland retains so much of the accent and flavor of Elizabethan English—some linguists have even said that if we could hear Shakespeare actually talking at the Mermaid tavern or reciting his verses on the stage of the Globe theater he would sound more like a modern Irishman than like a modern Englishman. But the harshness of the wars in Ireland, the famine that followed in the wake of the sword, and the division of Ireland into hostile religious camps began the bitterness which, sharpened by the actions of Oliver Cromwell, down to this very day affect Irish, and Irish-American, politics.

Elizabeth's continental policy was governed by the apprehension of a possible Spanish attack on England. There was no open war between Spain and England until 1558, but there was often severe tension, because of Spain's efforts to crush Protestantism and, even more, England's efforts to break Spain's uncompromising monopoly of trade and colonization in the New World. There was unofficial war of the Elizabethan seadogs upon Spanish sea-borne trade long before there was official war between Elizabeth and Philip. Since anything that would weaken Spain in the Netherlands tended to the greater security of England, Elizabeth permitted the Dutch sailors, the famous 'beggars of the sea,' to use English ports. Elizabeth had personally little sympathy with the Dutch patriots, though many of her subjects had more; to her they were extreme radicals in both religion and government and she desired neither Calvinism nor republicanism to spread. But she could not afford to neglect any weapon against the mighty power of Spain. She lent the Dutch from time to time about two million pounds—an immense sum in those days—and in 1586 sent an expeditionary force under Robert Dudley, Earl of Leicester (elder brother of Guildford Dudley, the husband of Lady Jane Grey). This expedition was only moderately successful and is best remembered for the heroic death at the battle of Zutphen of Sir Philip Sidney, poet, essayist, courtier, soldier, the perfect gentleman of the English Renaissance, who died passing his cup of water to a common soldier who lay wounded by him, saying, 'Thy necessity is greater than mine.' The English also gave hospitality to some thirty thousand fugitive Netherlanders, fleeing from

Spanish tyranny. But the greatest service which England performed for the Dutch was the indirect one of defeating the Spanish navy.

Philip of Spain, exasperated and not unreasonably so, at the many raids by English privateers on Spanish trade in the New World,[1] decided to end matters by sending a huge naval expedition or Armada to England in 1588. The crushing disaster to this expedition concluded the long, irregular struggle for command of the seas with Spain, for two subsequent expeditions sent against England were scattered by storms before they came near enough to be a danger. The English navy, which before the Tudors had been a rather occasional affair, taken on and paid off, had been quite continuous since 1509. 'This great royal fleet, erected by Henry VII, and consisting of some thirty large and twenty smaller vessels, forms the fountain-head from which the navy of Drake and Blake, Rodney and Nelson, directly descends to the superdreadnaughts and submarines of today; from 1509 onwards there is no break in personnel and no cessation in the replacement of ship by newbuilt ship.'[2] The base of the Elizabethan voyages to the New World was the navy commanding the seas at home. The regular fleet was augmented by privateers. A sailor's skill could be turned with equal success to handling a trading vessel in a storm or a warship in battle; it was plain good seamanship (along with the excellent equipment, the powerful guns, provided by John Hawkins at the Admiralty) that defeated the apparently greater naval might of Spain. The Spaniard, in many ways the boldest explorer and adventurer of the sixteenth century, was on the whole more a soldier than a sailor; his treasure fleets were huge transports in convoy, and his warships floating platforms to carry armies. English sailors and fishermen, on the contrary, had learned to think with the twist of the tides and the shifting of the winds, and they often preferred to fight in ugly weather.

English naval superiority was the more important since there was still almost no English army. On land, and in time of peace, England was the weakest of all the European Great Powers, and long so remained. The Tudors were content with a few hundred palace guards and a half-trained popular militia; the regular professional armies

---

[1] See Chapter xvi for Elizabethan ventures overseas and in the New World.
[2] J. D. Upcott, *Three Voyages of Drake* (1936), p. 11.

later raised by Cromwell, James II, and William III were never
very large and were intensely unpopular. It is an interesting fact
that while Scotland and Ireland have furnished more than their due
proportion of famous British generals, most of the great British ad-
mirals were of English birth. The navy is considered the 'senior
service' and the popular heroes of English tradition have been Drake,
Blake, and Nelson rather than Marlborough or Wellington; Trafalgar has inspired more songs than Waterloo!

Just as Elizabeth weakened Spain by giving surreptitious aid to
the Dutch insurgents, she weakened France by similar aid to the
Huguenots. She dallied insincerely with French proposals of royal
alliance by marriage, aided Frenchmen against Spaniards when it
seemed feasible, made one unfortunate venture in active war to regain a French port, and ended her reign in friendship with the able
Henry IV. Elizabeth's reign had marked the culmination and the
defeat of the great reaction against the Protestant Reformation, generally called the Counter-Reformation, a movement for the reconquest of Europe for Roman Catholicism. It had failed to sustain
Mary in Scotland; the Scottish people were now predominantly
Presbyterian. It had failed to free Catholic Ireland from English
control. It had failed to hold the Dutch-speaking provinces of the
Netherlands. It had failed to conquer England by the Great Armada.
Elizabeth's reign ended with the English and Dutch allied against
Spain, no longer in danger of conquest, and on friendly terms with
a tolerant French government.

Like other Tudors, Elizabeth was tactful in dealing with Parliament. Naturally impatient and imperious, not infrequently arbitrary
and despotic, she yet knew how to yield gracefully when yield she
must. When Parliament insisted on the abolition of certain legal
monopolies created by royal grant, she not only conceded the matter
at issue but thanked her good Commons for calling such abuses to
her attention. Had her successors, the Scottish Stuarts, possessed a
tithe of the tact and national feeling which kept Elizabeth popular,
for all her many faults of temper, deceitfulness, and vanity, the
great conflict between Throne and Parliament which filled the seventeenth century might never have arisen.

In many other respects, however, the Elizabethan period was of
a piece with the Jacobean which succeeded it. The founding of the

colonies, begun under Elizabeth, was continued under James. The genius of the English language which blossomed under Elizabeth still awaited its crowning glory, the King James version of the English Bible. Even Shakespeare spans the two reigns, and his genius is as much Jacobean as Elizabethan. Most of what we think of as Elizabethan culture and civilization belongs to the latter part of the great queen's reign, after the immediate peril of Spanish conquest had been removed.

Indeed, it is interesting to think what epitaph historians of the continent might have written of English civilization had the Spaniards succeeded in destroying it in 1588. Doubtless mention would have been made of the great feats of arms of William I, Richard I, Edward III, and Henry V. Profounder students might have pointed out the interrupted possibilities of national development foreshadowed by the Parliament and the jury, the verse of Chaucer, the English cathedrals, the philosophy of Roger Bacon and of Thomas More. Yet the single city of Florence had, up to that time, contributed more than all the Kingdom of England to the general culture of Europe. But the reign which saw *The Faerie Queene* of Edmund Spenser, with its blend of chivalric tradition and Protestant religious idealism, the penetrating essays on scientific method by Francis Bacon, the thunderous 'mighty line' of Marlowe, the comedy of manners as developed by Ben Jonson, scarcely needed a Shakespeare to make it memorable. Shakespeare himself, it is needless to say, achieved the double triumph of being at once the world's profoundest dramatic poet and the world's most popular playwright. Even in his own day he was widely honored, though as much for his lyric verse as for his dramas, and at no time since then have his plays left the stage, except for the short Puritan interval that placed all playhouses under a ban. Carlyle hardly exaggerated the place of Shakespeare in the tradition of the English-speaking peoples when he declared that the British would rather lose their Empire of India than the writings of this one Englishman.

The Elizabethan-Jacobean drama owed its origin to many sources —the old medieval mystery and morality plays which developed out of church festivals, the studies of the learned in the Greek and Latin drama, the spirit and methods of the Italian Renaissance, and the vigorous tragedies of chivalry which had developed on the Spanish stage. It was a drama robust and untamed; so much so that in the eighteenth century, under the influence of French standards of taste, it was usually presented in modified versions with many of its extravagancies pruned away. In every direction the new English drama seemed to widen the boundaries of the imagination. It took its themes from everywhere—Holinshed's chronicles, Plutarch's biographies, Boccaccio's stories, old Roman comedies, or the actualities of apprentice life in London. It wandered over every known land and every age of recorded time in search for settings of these plots. Its characters included literally everyone, from kings to beggars. It paid little attention to unities of time, place, or atmosphere, and placed the jests of clowns alongside the deathbeds of heroes. With no need for elaborate stage setting, gorgeous rhetoric taking the place of accurate scenic backdrops, the action of the drama was unconfined by any practical considerations of cost. The English language for the first time revealed its full possibilities. Unashamed of simple, homely words, unashamed equally of 'purple patches,' the dramatists not only used an exceptionally wide vocabulary but used old words and phrases with new meanings. In other times and places, such, for example, as ancient Greece, seventeenth-century France, and nineteenth-century Norway, plays have been presented with fewer faults, with more economy of effort and greater finish of detail, but none have shown the same catholic range and elemental power.

KING AGAINST PARLIAMENT

So long as two partners in a business are personally friendly they will not need lawyers to weigh every syllable of their agreement, but as soon as they become mutually distrustful the terms of their contract with each other assume great importance. The Tudor period did not solve the problem of fixing a frontier between the king's prerogative and the privileges of Parliament, because the two were seldom in practical conflict and it is not the English way to cross a bridge till the stream is reached. But these disputed issues remained latent, and they flashed into life under the Stuarts. The importance of the Stuart period in English history is that it defined the rights and powers of the various organs of government. The constitution emerged from the mere accumulation of tradition and precedent which it had been in past centuries, and took on the form of positive law.

The sixteenth century had been a kind of bottle-neck for European legislative assemblies; few passed through it undiminished. In England, almost alone, Parliament persisted with no abatement of its theoretical claims, though practically very anxious to stay on good terms with the sovereign. It did not meet every year and seldom sat for more than five or six weeks; its chief business was to pass upon the measures laid before it by the Council, and its most important privilege the right to reject measures it disliked. This privilege was freely allowed by the Tudors. In 1593 Elizabeth informed Parliament through the Lord Keeper: 'To say yea and no to bills, God forbid that any man be restrained or afraid to answer according to his best liking, with some short declaration of his reason therein.' But if Parliament turned to a discussion of foreign affairs or royal marriages or religious establishment the queen sometimes sent messages or broad hints, called 'rumors,' to stop it. 'I would to God,

Mr. Speaker,' said Peter Wentworth, a member from Tregony in Cornwall, in 1575, 'that these two were buried in Hell, I mean rumors and messages.' The horrified House of Commons committed him to the Tower for a month. But when financial questions, such as taxation or the abolition of monopolies, were under discussion, Parliament, touched on the pocket nerve, could be as bold as Wentworth.

King James ruled over Scotland as James VI from 1567 to 1625 (including a long regency), and over England as James I from 1603 to 1625. Had he been never so able he would at first have been less popular than Elizabeth, for he was a Scotsman and to the average Englishman of that day a 'foreigner.' In another way his Scottish origin was a handicap in England. Scotland had failed to develop a powerful and efficient Parliament, and James, who had been accustomed to treat the Scottish Parliament as a mere tool, altogether failed to comprehend the independent spirit and deeply rooted tradition of the English legislature. He had also an inadequate understanding of the English common law and very little sympathy with English customs and prejudices.

Personally the king had some good qualities. He was well-intentioned, he was bookishly learned, and in some respects he was wise. He wanted peace at home and abroad, and he was in advance of his age in desiring a complete union of England and Scotland. But his handicaps were fatally numerous. He was pedantic, clumsy, and slovenly, not in the least royal in appearance or manner; he cherished worthless favorites and raised them to honor and power; he tactlessly harped on his 'divine right' as monarch till he frightened his English subjects into the belief that he aimed to destroy their liberties. Finally, he managed to offend both his Scottish and his English subjects by his ecclesiastical policy.

Queen Elizabeth had hoped to comprehend all her people within the national Church of England. A large number of Roman Catholics, however, stood loyal to the Pope; and within the Protestant communion many found the Established Church too ritualistic and wanted to 'purify' the service from everything that even suggested Romanism. The Catholic minority were called Recusants, the radical Protestants Non-conformists or Dissenters. Both groups were subject to fines for failure to attend church services, and Roman

Catholics were also suspected of political disloyalty, since they would not admit that Elizabeth was rightful Supreme Governor of the Church.

When James became King of England the Puritans, or purifiers of Protestantism, were divided into three main factions. A majority, the Puritan party in the narrower sense of the word, wanted to lessen the power of the bishops and simplify the ritual of the Church of England but to leave the establishment otherwise intact. Others wanted to follow Scotland's example and create a Presbyterian Church, strictly Calvinist in doctrine and governed by representative bodies, such as synods, instead of by bishops. Most radical of all were the Independents or Brownists, followers of the Reverend Robert Browne, who, for a time, favored a policy of making each individual congregation a law unto itself in doctrine and in ritual; they are the Congregationalists of later times.

On James's accession the Puritans presented him with a Millenary Petition of 825 clergymen, objecting to the wearing of the surplice, the use of the sign of the cross, and other ritualistic features of the Anglican service. James convoked a conference at Hampton Court to discuss these matters. He sided altogether with the high-church bishops and accused the Puritan party of aiming at a Scottish Presbyterian system which 'agreeth as well with a monarchy, as God and the Devil.' He regarded the royal appointment of bishops as an essential buttress of royal power—'No bishop, no king!' He warned the Puritans that if they would not conform he would 'harry them out of the land.' He made this threat good to the extent that many hundreds did go to tolerant Holland and some even sought an asylum in the wilderness of America.[1] The one useful result of this disastrous conference was the appointment of a committee of learned divines to make a new translation of the Bible—the famous Authorized or King James version, which became the basis of education in every English home in Great Britain and in the colonies.

The Roman Catholics were intermittently persecuted. The purpose of the penal laws of Elizabeth's time had been political rather than religious; so they were put into force whenever the Catholics seemed dangerous and relaxed when they seemed harmless. 'Cathol-

---

[1] See Chapter xvi for the settlement of New England.

icism meant for one man ruin; for another a certain picturesque distinction. In one district it was the pass to the highest county society; in another it was the butt of intolerable injuries and insults.' [2] Priests were not permitted to carry on their services, but many wealthy Catholic laymen maintained secret rooms and passages where they could be concealed in case some zealous official tried to enforce the dormant law. One result of the persecution was a 'gunpowder plot' to blow up King James and Parliament, ending in the arrest of Guy Fawkes and other conspirators, an incident still celebrated by English children as Guy Fawkes Day.

With a singular talent for making enemies, King James managed to offend his subjects in several directions at once, and to destroy nearly all the reverence for the Crown which had grown up in Tudor times. The Puritans, who were very strong in Parliament, were alienated by his imposition of high-church ritual upon them. The lawyers were alarmed at his disregard of the principles of common law. The adherents of constitutional government could not but be uneasy at a monarch who wrote, 'As to dispute what God may do is blasphemy, so it is sedition in subjects to dispute what a King may do.' Even those who might have acquiesced in absolute monarchy, so long as it meant efficiency, were critical of his vacillating foreign policy, his extravagance, and his favoritism for worthless courtiers. His very merits counted against him. Thus a plan for uniting Scotland with England in an organic union encountered too many national prejudices and had to be dropped. The two kingdoms, with the same ruler, continued to maintain their separate Parliaments, chanceries, courts, defenses, and tariffs. Again, a sensible plan for abolishing the remnant of feudal dues holding over from medieval times broke down on the question how much compensation should be granted to the Crown for abandoning them.

As has so often been the case in English history, the chief bone of contention between Crown and Parliament was the revenue question. That Parliament alone could levy new taxes was generally admitted; but just what was a 'tax'? The Crown, as director of foreign policy, claimed to direct English trade. Elizabeth had given the monopoly of the Mediterranean trade to a London group which

[2] G. M. Trevelyan, *England under the Stuarts* (1930), p. 85.

called itself the Levant Company, and collected an 'imposition' of five shillings and sixpence on each imported hundredweight of currants. After James's accession, the Levant Company surrendered its legal monopoly though it did not go out of business. Though the currant trade was now free, the Crown continued to collect its old imposition. In 1606 a London merchant, John Bate, refused to pay the duty, but the court sustained the Crown. The decision was probably correct, for there were precedents in favor of the legality of impositions. Nevertheless the decision angered the merchant class who feared that it might lead to increased taxation, without consent of Parliament.

James ended the war with Spain in 1604, shortly after coming to the throne, on conditions advantageous to England. In 1607 the colony of Jamestown was planted in Virginia and the first permanent beginning of English settlement made in America. In 1608 a beginning was made at the 'plantation' of Protestant English and Scottish settlers in Ulster. James mediated between Spain and the Dutch Republic. He married his daughter Elizabeth to the Protestant Elector Palatine of the Rhine and thus gained an interest in German affairs. Thus far he had not done badly with the foreign policy of the nation, but the death in 1612 of Robert Cecil, Earl of Salisbury and son of the famous Lord Burghley of Elizabeth's reign, deprived him of his wisest adviser. His management of foreign affairs rapidly deteriorated. To please the Spaniards he had Sir Walter Raleigh put to death on trivial charges [3] in 1618. He meddled ineffectively, neither withholding aid nor giving any that mattered, in the German Thirty Years' War in the interest of his son-in-law the Elector Palatine. He entered into a 'Spanish Marriage Project' and let his son Charles go to the Spanish court to seek a bride in the country which the Englishmen of the time most hated.

When the Commons wished to discuss the foreign policy of the government in 1621, James informed them of his will that 'none shall presume to meddle with anything concerning our government or deep matters of state,' to which the Commons made the spirited reply, 'That the liberties, franchises, jurisdictions of Parliament are

[3] Raleigh had been imprisoned on dubious charges of treason in 1604; he was set free to go on an expedition to find gold in Guiana, South America, but he found only conflict with the Spaniards, who demanded his execution.

the ancient and undoubted birthright and inheritance of the subjects of England.' The issue had been joined, but only in words. There is something to be said on both sides. The House of Commons wanted a maritime (and religious) war but were not eager to vote taxes for it. James was a man of peace and, on the whole, was tolerant (perhaps more tolerant of Catholicism than Presbyterianism) and did not hold that the English had any great cause for war with Spain. James was more concerned to assert his divine right in theory than to enforce it in practice. He had quarreled with all his Parliaments, but he had not ventured to cast Parliament aside and govern alone. This final rashness was reserved for his son and successor King Charles I (1625-49).

Charles was a younger son of James, his older brother Henry dying too soon to inherit the throne. He had at first intended a Spanish marriage, but the plan miscarried and resulted only in fresh ill-feeling between England and Spain. Then he turned to France and married the Princess Henrietta Maria, another Roman Catholic match hardly better liked by the intensely Protestant English than the Spanish project. His own religious policy was that of his father, to impose the Prayer Book and religious forms of the Established Church of England on Scottish Presbyterians and English Puritans whether they consented or not. He also continued his father's feud with the privileges of Parliament and the customs of the common law. His handsome presence, personal courage, and royal dignity contrasted with James's lack of all these qualities, but he added to James's somewhat high-handed attitude towards Parliament a disastrous obstinacy which brought the parliamentary controversy to open war.

One point must be made in justice to King Charles. It was he, rather than his Parliamentary opponents, who represented what is called 'the spirit of the age,' for the seventeenth century was the high tide of absolute monarchy in Europe. In the crystallization of national states out of the feudal chaos of the Middle Ages the nations had usually grouped themselves around the throne and the king had become, like a flag, a symbol of national patriotism and unity. Thus it was in France, Spain, Portugal, Sweden, Denmark, Prussia, Austria, Russia, and most of the smaller German and Italian states.[4] In Tudor times, monarchy had been exalted in England. No doubt Charles sincerely regarded his opponents as antiquated reactionaries clinging to obsolete feudal institutions, obstacles in the path of efficient national government.

The new reign started badly. Charles summoned Parliament in his first year and found it unforthcoming. Contrary to usual practice it voted the customs dues known as 'tonnage and poundage' for one year only, not for the king's life. It violently (and justifiably) complained of the mismanagement of the war with Spain then proceeding. In 1626 Charles summoned Parliament once again, but it proceeded to criticize the management of the Spanish war under the court favorite George Villiers, Duke of Buckingham and Lord High Admiral. To save his minister, Charles again dissolved Parliament. England drifted into another petty war with France on the pretext of affording aid to the distressed Huguenots. This campaign, like practically all those undertaken by England in continental Europe at that period, was mismanaged and ended in complete failure. The blame for the futile wars undertaken under James I and Charles I must be divided between ruler and nation. Neither James nor Charles understood war or chose to office other men who could remedy their deficiencies; the nation, as represented in Parliament, rightly distrusted such men as Buckingham, but clung pathetically to the delusion that wars could be cheaply won without any great increase of taxation. Fortunately, these wars were on so small a scale that they did not menace English security or seriously mar English prosperity.

A far greater danger to the future lay in the attempts made by Charles to find the necessary war revenues by devious means without the sanction of Parliament. Had he succeeded, England would probably have gone the way of France towards absolute monarchy. In 1627 he levied a forced loan and imprisoned five gentlemen who refused to pay. Charles's third Parliament in 1628 enacted a Petition of Right, to which the king had to assent before any revenues would be granted. This recited the precedents on which Parliament relied, such as the Great Charter of John's time, and laws enacted under Edward III against forced loans and 'benevolences.' On the strength of these precedents, the king was petitioned 'that no man

---

[4] The Dutch and Swiss republics were exceptions.

hereafter be compelled to make or yield any gift, loan, benevolence, tax, or such like charge, without common consent by Act of Parliament.' The Petition of Right also declared against arbitrary imprisonments, such as had been inflicted on the five knights who had refused to pay the forced loan. It further objected to the billeting of soldiers on private homes and the grant of commissions of martial law.

In 1629 Charles dissolved Parliament and tried to see whether or not he could carry on government without it. For eleven years he governed alone. This does not mean that England thereby became legally an absolute monarchy, for Charles admitted that he had no authority to levy new taxes without Parliamentary grant, but he hoped to find revenues that could not be called taxation. He curtailed England's commitments abroad and let the Thirty Years' War in Germany continue without him. He tried to build up the navy without a subsidy from Parliament, by using a medieval device called 'ship money,' the right of the king to compel seaport towns to build ships for national emergencies or to furnish money for the purpose. Finding his device successful, he extended the levy to the inland counties.

John Hampden, a Buckinghamshire squire who had frequently sat in Parliament, refused to pay his ship money assessment on the ground that it was illegal taxation. The case was carried to the courts, and although a majority of the judges decided in favor of the king on the ground that he was the sole judge of what constituted an emergency necessitating levies for the equipment of the fleet, the nation at large was convinced by the arguments of the minority. Other devices favored by the king were fines imposed on persons holding estates by military tenure who had neglected to receive knighthood, the reclaiming of lands which had once belonged to royal forests, and the sale of monopolies.[5] The law was thus wrested to the king's advantage so that the letter of the Petition of Right might be kept even if its spirit were violated.

The two most important ministers of the Crown during Charles's

[5] The sale of monopolies had been attacked by Parliament under Elizabeth and James I and made illegal (save for the holders of inventors' patents) under the latter; Charles in 1621 was selling monopolies to corporations instead of to individuals.

personal rule were the Archbishop of Canterbury, William Laud, and the Earl of Strafford, Thomas Wentworth. Both were able, sincere, and zealously devoted to the king's policies in Church and State. Laud, the son of a clothier, became President of St. John's College in Oxford, held high offices in the established Church, and rose by his ability to the highest position, the archbishopric of Canterbury, in 1633. The Pope offered to make him a cardinal if he would join the Church of Rome, thinking that because he was the deadly enemy of the Puritans he might be at heart a Roman Catholic. But the Pope mistook his man. Laud was a married clergyman, a high-church Anglican, who wanted merely to preserve dignified historic customs and traditions against the iconoclasm of the Puritans. With the support of the king he was able to use all the coercive powers of the special royal courts, the ecclesiastical Court of High Commission, and the civil Court of Star Chamber, to punish clergymen who would not use the prescribed ritual or laymen who were 'recusant' about attending the services.

Many Puritans went overseas, disgusted if not rebellious, and in their New England handed on a separatist spirit that was later embodied in the American Revolution. The larger number who stayed in England, like the Cambridgeshire squire Oliver Cromwell (who at one time had contemplated emigration to New England), became increasingly impatient of Laud's tyranny until their exasperation at last burst forth in the Great Rebellion.

But it was not alone Laud's ecclesiastical system which pressed upon the Puritans. They objected to the secular administration of Charles I, which was so largely directed by Wentworth. Sir Thomas Wentworth, a member of the House of Commons for Yorkshire, had been one of the leaders of the opposition to the Court in Parliament down to 1629, and had helped to draft the Petition of Right. His objection was more to the inefficient way in which absolute government was being exercised than to absolutism itself. When Buckingham, symbol of Court corruption, had been removed by assassination, and after Charles had agreed to the Petition of Right, Wentworth thought that the road was open for competent royal government—differing in this from John Eliot, John Pym, and other leaders of the opposition. In 1629 he entered the king's service and became President of the Council of the North, an administrative body wielding special powers for repressing lawlessness in the wilder rural parts of England. Then he was made Viceroy or royal 'Deputy' in Ireland. He gave that distracted country a better government than it had known for a long time. He tolerated the Catholic majority, reformed the administration of the Protestant Church, encouraged the linen industry in Ulster, balanced the budget, and organized a small but well-disciplined army of 5,000 men, the largest military unit in all the British Isles. His motto was 'Thorough,' which might be translated as efficient but dictatorial. For his services he was made Earl of Strafford.

Great as was the popular discontent with Charles's personal rule, England lay quiet until Scotland gave the signal for revolt. In Scotland the issue was religion rather than taxation or constitutional privilege. The attempt to force the English form of church service on the Presbyterian Scots led in 1638 to riots in the churches and to the signing of a National Covenant to uphold the Presbyterian system. Charles unwisely attempted coercion, and there followed two short struggles commonly called the Bishops' Wars. Charles found it impossible to carry on the contest without more money to pay his troops, so he summoned Parliament in 1640.

The Parliament met in angry mood, and Charles was forced to dismiss it before it had voted subsidies; hence it is known in history as the Short Parliament. But the Scottish war continued to go against the king, so he summoned Parliament again later in the year. This new Parliament, the most famous in British history, was the Long Parliament which lasted (according to its own interpretation of the law) from 1640 to 1660, though actually it was not in session during Cromwell's dictatorship.

The Long Parliament was resolved to sweep away all the abuses and arbitrary usurpations of power committed during the eleven years of Charles's personal rule. It began by prosecuting Strafford for an alleged plot to use his Irish army to subvert the English constitution, and Strafford was duly executed in 1641. In the same year a Triennial Act ensured that there should never be an interval longer than three years between two sessions of Parliament. A comprehensive bill vindicated the common law by sweeping away the 'extraordinary' courts which functioned without juries, such as the Court of Star Chamber, the Council of the North, and the Council of Wales, while another act abolished the ecclesiastical Court of High Commission. All forms of customs, ship money, and other sources of royal revenue independent of Parliamentary grant were abolished.

Thus far the reformers in the Long Parliament were fairly well agreed, but when it came, in November 1641, to the enactment of a Grand Remonstrance, violently attacking every phase of Charles's government, it carried by only eleven votes. Parliament was beginning to divide into a radical party, represented by such men as Pym and Cromwell, and a moderate faction, represented by such men as Hyde and Falkland. The attempt made by Charles to arrest the radical leaders on the floor of Parliament, though it was unsuccessful, aroused fierce hostility. The final break came on the militia bill, designed to take the control of the militia (and there was next to no standing army) away from the king. In 1642 Charles rallied his followers at Nottingham. Many of the Lords and not a few of the Commons joined his cause.

The war which followed, the English Civil War or the Great Rebellion, is far more interesting in its political than in its military aspect. Politically it was a struggle which determined the future course of the English-speaking nations: were they to follow the example of continental Europe and become subject to autocratic monarchy—not perhaps wholly without parliament, but with a subordinate parliament—or follow the course based on the principle of representative self-government? It was a war of parties more than of classes or of sections. In general the great towns, including London, and the eastern shires sided with Parliament, while the rural North and West supported the king; in general, also, the nobility of the Court, the established clergy, the Roman Catholics, and the high-church Anglicans were royalists or Cavaliers, as the phrase went, while the Puritan squires and townsmen were parliamentarians or Roundheads. In every county, however, almost in every town, there were some who took one side and some the other; the poorer peasantry, who made up the majority of the whole population, either followed their landlords or remained neutral to the end. Charles I had not been well treated by his parliaments. On the other hand he had not tried to understand them, and he had not acted honestly by them. Fundamentally in his relations with Parliament he relied upon force and upon his 'divine right.' The English were not going to let themselves be ruled by these things.

The fact that the war was a struggle of civilians, partisans in a political quarrel, determined its military character. It was waged in rather desultory fashion, by plucky but untrained men, from castle to castle and town to town over a great part of England and Scotland. Victory was determined by two facts. The parliamentarians controlled the wealthiest towns and the seaports, so that they were better able to hire good soldiers; and they had the good fortune to find in Oliver Cromwell a genius at organization, whose 'New Model' army of stern Puritans of various sects was one of the best-disciplined and reliable forces that had ever taken arms. Cromwell's victories at Marston Moor (1644) and Naseby (1645) determined the issue in England, and the defeat of the gallant Marquis of Montrose determined it in Scotland.

Charles surrendered to the Scots, who delivered him to their allies the English. After prolonged negotiations and hesitations, the radical party in Parliament (now purged of all its conservative members) brought him before a special tribunal under a charge of treason, a crime which hitherto had usually meant disloyalty to the king. They brought in a verdict of guilty and Charles was publicly beheaded in front of Whitehall palace on 30 January 1649. The excuse for an execution which was neither legal nor politic (since most Englishmen viewed the execution of a king with horror) was that experience had shown that Charles could never be bound by pledge or agreement to accept in good faith any real limitation of his power. To Cromwell and his partisans the choice seemed to lie between the king's life and their own; indeed, between the king's life and that of English liberty. But it proved easier to kill a king than to build a commonwealth.

COMMONWEALTH AND RESTORATION

WITH the death of King Charles in 1649 England became in form what she had been in effect since the king's surrender in 1646—a republic. Later in the same year the Long Parliament declared England to be 'a Commonwealth and Free State . . . without any King or House of Lords.' Scotland and Ireland were to be merged with England into this consolidated Commonwealth. An earlier resolution declared in words that later were to echo in the American Declaration of Independence, 'That the people are, under God, the original of all just power.'

No government ever undertook its tasks with a clearer conception of the principles of popular sovereignty than the Commonwealth. But to translate these principles into facts proved difficult, even impossible. The very Parliament which declared itself the spokesmen of the people was not representative; it had been elected nine years earlier, under widely different circumstances, and a majority of its membership had deserted to the king, or fallen in battle, or been excluded by a 'purge' which barred out conservatives. In the phrase of the time, it had become a mere 'Rump Parliament.' The logically democratic course would have been to hold a fresh election on a wide franchise. But republicanism was the creed only of an idealistic minority, mainly Puritans of the middle classes. If all England could have freely voted it is not improbable that the people would have recalled Charles's exiled son and put him on the throne; in which event the regicides would have lost their power and probably their lives. Parliament dared not take the chance.

Another fatal obstacle to a democratic republic was the religious question. Most of the Scots and a majority of the English Parliament wanted an exclusive Presbyterian establishment in the Church. Cromwell's New Model army of veterans, who had once been amateur volunteers but were now almost professional soldiers, wanted complete religious toleration for the Protestant sects, not Presbyterians only but Independents (Congregationalists), Baptists, Quakers, and other denominations. Most of Ireland wanted the one thing which neither Parliament nor the Puritan army would ever allow, a Roman Catholic establishment. To reconcile all these divergent desires was beyond the skill of Cromwell, who already had the power, though not the name, of dictator.

Cromwell is an interesting human type; he may, perhaps, be called the reluctant dictator. In theory he was a moderate man, desiring chiefly religious toleration and constitutional civil government. He had little sympathy with the more extreme Puritans—'Levellers,' 'Diggers,' 'Fifth Monarchy Men,' and the like—who wanted to found a democratic Utopia forthwith, based on universal suffrage and, in some cases at least, equality of property. He had equally little sympathy with the leaders of Parliament who wished to force a Presbyterian establishment on all the Puritan sects alike; he agreed with his Latin Secretary, John Milton, that 'new presbyter was but old priest writ large' and that ecclesiastical tyranny was objectionable in the name of any church. But Cromwell had faults of his own. He was impatient, imperious, and hot-tempered, with a soldier's hasty contempt for politicians. Though he did not seek absolute power, he was ready to grasp it whenever it seemed to him that no other course would secure the safety of England, the gains of the revolution, or the ascendency of his own Puritan party. Such a man, with a triumphant army behind him, would not be apt to put up with much parliamentary opposition. It has to be borne in mind, too, that the period of the Commonwealth in England was one of great economic difficulty. The Civil War and the wars with Holland and Spain were destructive of capital and financially exhausting. The Cromwellian government had to deal with a politically discontented people in a period of economic depression.

His first task, however, was to secure the success of the revolution in Scotland and Ireland. Scotland, shocked at the execution of a Stuart monarch, would willingly have put his son on the throne as Charles II, provided guarantees were given that the Presbyterian Church would be sustained. The Scots had a good army and a good general in David Leslie, a veteran of the Thirty Years' War in Germany. Cromwell was nearly trapped at Dunbar between the hills and the sea, but the Scots, urged on by their clergy, attacked too soon, and Cromwell was victorious on 3 September 1650. On the anniversary of this battle he defeated another Scottish army at Worcester in England. Ireland had already been subjugated, with such violence that for years to come 'the curse of Cromwell' was the most bitter of Irish oaths. In 1653 both Scotland and Ireland were incorporated with England into a single centralized Commonwealth or republic, but the union, in itself wise and statesmanlike, had the fatal defect that it rested on force and was not viewed with favor by the majority of Scotsmen or of Irishmen.

Cromwell became increasingly discontented with the conduct of the Long Parliament, which would not pay the soldiers, submit to new elections, or tolerate any form of worship except the Presbyterian. In 1653 he turned Parliament out of doors as arbitrarily as Charles had ever done. Yet he did not wish to rule without Parliament. He experimented with a nominated Parliament of Puritans, called Barebone's Parliament after the name of one of its leaders (Praise-God Barebone), but this proved no more satisfactory. Later in the same year Cromwell and his advisers accepted a written constitution known as the Instrument of Government, the first written constitution ever made in English-speaking lands [1] and the most complete constitution, perhaps, that had up to that time been made in any country. It provided for a Lord Protector (Cromwell himself), a Council of State, and a single-chambered Parliament elected from England, Scotland, and Ireland. Very wisely, it reformed the distribution of representation so that it corresponded more closely to population; a reform which was unfortunately lost at the downfall of the Commonwealth, and was not again realized until 1832. Religious toleration was granted to all sects except 'Popery and Prelacy' (Roman Catholicism and high-church Anglicanism) and those who 'practise licentiousness.' Adherents of the royal cause were not to be admitted to Parliament.

The new constitution, though it had many theoretical merits, did not work smoothly, and in 1657 a second constitution was tried, the

[1] Of course there had been royal charters, Parliamentary statutes, colonial charters, and the like, which covered certain constitutional questions, but none was so comprehensive as The Instrument.

so-called 'Humble Petition and Advice,' which added an upper house
to Parliament and gave to the Protector the right of nominating his
own successor. This was a close approach to monarchy, and Cromwell, like Julius Caesar, coquetted with the idea of taking the title
of King. Like Caesar again, he decided against it, partly because the
name of King was unpopular with his followers and partly because
he already enjoyed the power without the title. The whole constitutional question remained unsettled at the time of his death in 1658.

Though Cromwell had failed to establish what he called 'government by consent' and had, in fact if not in theory, ruled more auto-
cratically than any Tudor or Stuart, his Protectorate had many
merits. It gave the country tranquillity after years of civil war, extended toleration to a wider variety of Protestant sects than had
ever been given liberty before,[2] established more firmly than ever
English supremacy at sea, made political union and freedom of trade
between England, Scotland, and Ireland, gave aid to oppressed Protestants on the continent, encouraged the growth of the merchant
marine, and forecast the eventual merging of the English and Scottish administrations. Many of his reforms perished with him, but his
emphasis on sea power and empire building was continued after the
monarchy had been restored. For example, the Navigation Act of
1651, which confined British imports to goods carried either in
British vessels or vessels belonging to the country producing the
goods, an act of quasi-monopolistic imperialism and intended as a
blow at the Dutch, who were the middlemen of Europe, was re-
enacted under Charles II.

But Cromwell's commonwealth collapsed speedily after his death.
His son Richard had taken the Protectorate, with many misgivings,
but held it for only a few months. The 'Rump' or remnant of the
old Long Parliament, which had never regarded Cromwell's dissolution of 1653 as legal, came back into power in 1659. There were
royalist risings and demonstrations everywhere. The situation was
being watched by General George Monk, commanding the Commonwealth forces in Scotland. He was a resolute, fair-minded, public-

---

[2] Roman Catholics and Anglicans were penalized on the ground that they were
politically dangerous. Practically all other sects were tolerated. Jews legally were
readmitted to England for the first time since the reign of Edward I, though
there were a fair number of them in England in the Tudor period.

spirited man, not politically minded but interested in the peace and
stability of the country. He would support any government which
was likely to be stable and which would also be reasonably free. He
was a friend of Oliver Cromwell, and was loyal to him, but Richard,
he said, had deserted himself. At last George Monk, fearing anarchy,
moved down from Scotland with a section of the army. In 1660 the
Long Parliament was finally dissolved and a new 'Convention Parliament' elected. It invited Charles to return from exile and reign
as King Charles II. He promised pay for the army, religious toleration subject to such regulations as Parliament might make, and
constitutional rule. For his services in bringing about the restoration,
Monk was made Duke of Albemarle.

Thus ended, apparently in complete failure, the Puritan experiment of a republican Commonwealth, after enduring fourteen or
eleven years, according as it is dated from 1646 or 1649. It might
almost be considered a kind of backflow from New England into old
England. The British Isles had become a Puritan Commonwealth,
with membership in a religious congregation a virtual qualification
for holding office. There was no theater, no mixed dancing, no games
on Sunday, no celebration of Christmas and other feast days. Probably Cromwell's Puritanism was better fitted to New England than
to England, Scotland, or Ireland. It furnished a background and a
precedent for the American Revolution, in which New England Puritans played a large part. Republicanism never appeared again in
Great Britain, save as the creed of a few isolated individuals, but it
was to have a great future in America.

The permanent importance of the republican interlude in English
history was threefold. In the first place, it put a definite end to absolute monarchy. Charles II never repeated the mistake of his father
of trying to govern in open defiance of Parliament. His brother
James did so, and was speedily dethroned. No later ruler ever made
the attempt. The place of Parliament in the constitution had been
established once and for all. In the second place, by way of reaction,
it left in England a profound distaste for dictatorship, military rule,
standing armies, and regimentation of private life. If England never
again had a republic, it is equally true that England never again had
a dictator. What the people wanted was the historic government by
'King, Lords, and Commons,' the safeguards of personal liberty in

the common law, the old traditions of the unwritten constitution, a Protestant but not Puritan Church establishment, a strong navy, a weak army, the subordination of the military to the civil power, and the right of private persons to enjoy themselves in their own way. All these wishes were realized.

The third permanent result of the Commonwealth period was that its incessant, though unsuccessful, constitutional experimentation encouraged political thought and discussion as never before. Milton's *Areopagitica* is the classic statement of the case for 'the freedom of unlicensed printing.' The Levellers, for the first time in England since John Ball and the Peasants' Revolt,[3] carried on a propaganda for abstract democracy. Theorists like Harrington debated the finest shades of constitutional balance. Among the hundreds of reforms enacted, discussed, or proposed at some time or other during the revolutionary period, G. B. Adams enumerates:[4]

> Free public schools; a public post office; public work for the employment of the poor; female suffrage; voting by ballot; the establishment of a national bank; freedom of the press . . . the improvement of local government; a system of recording land transfers; a simplification of marriage laws . . . a simplification of appeals; steps toward the union of equity and common law . . . the payment of judges by fixed salaries, no longer by fees, and tenure during good behavior; more liberal means of defence to persons accused of crime; better facilities for the collection of debts; and prison reform and the relief of prisoners for debt.

In short, about half the entire budget of political, legal, and social reforms actually realized in the eighteenth, nineteenth, and twentieth centuries in Great Britain, the Dominions, and the United States of America!

The reign of Charles II (1660-85) was, however, not adapted to sweeping projects of reform. It was a reaction against the high-strained Puritan idealism, though a reaction which did not go all the way. Old-fashioned Cavaliers who had fought for Church and King under Charles I found themselves only a degree less alien to the spirit of the times than the surviving remnant of the Puritans. The new age was practical and prosaic, given to compromises and expedi-

---

[3] See above, p. 72.
[4] G. B. Adams, *Constitutional History of England* (1921), p. 329.

ents, eager only in the pursuit of pleasure. Charles himself typified its spirit. He was an absolutist at heart, but unlike his father he was too prudent to fly directly in the face of public opinion. By private conviction he was Roman Catholic, but he did not avow himself such until he lay on his deathbed. He was more popular than many better kings, for he was tactful, witty, debonair, and his profound selfishness was hidden by a gracious manner.

Though the reign was not warlike, Charles's foreign policy was in the main unfortunate. He engaged in needless wars with the Dutch, partly because of his secret alliance with France and partly from commercial rivalry. Because the navy had been suffered to fall into disrepair, the English met reverses at sea. New York, however, was conquered from the Dutch. Charles's marriage to a Portuguese princess brought Bombay in India and (temporarily) Tangier in Morocco to England; indirectly it resulted in an alliance with Portugal which is still in effect, and (after the Methuen Treaty, 1703) encouraged the habit of drinking port. A new Navigation Act directed that the products of Asia, Africa, and America should be imported into England only in English ships. Colonial shipping was included in the description 'English,' but foreign ships could not carry English colonial goods, nor could colonial ships trade with foreign colonies—the French, Dutch, and Spanish West Indies, for example—but only with England. These restrictions were often evaded by smuggling, but smuggling invited official repression, and this in turn increased colonial irritation. The seeds of the American Revolution thus were sown.[5]

With the fall of the Puritan Commonwealth, the Church of England was restored to its old dominant position. A whole series of repressive measures aimed to keep the dissenting sects powerless and helpless. The Corporation Act (1661) required all members of a municipal corporation to take the sacrament according to the rites of the Church of England. A new Act of Uniformity (1662) imposed the Prayer Book and the Anglican ritual on the clergy. The Conventicle Act (1664) forbade religious assemblies other than those of the Church. The Five Mile Act (1665) prohibited ministers who had refused to agree to the Act of Uniformity from coming within

[5] See Chapter xix.

five miles of any incorporated town. The Test Act (1673), aimed chiefly at the Catholics though it affected Protestant dissenters too, required all office holders to take the sacrament of the Established Church. The enforcement of these laws was very imperfect, but was severe enough to drive thousands of Puritans into exile in the American colonies. The worst phase of the persecution was in Scotland, where the adherents of the Presbyterian Solemn League and Covenant were hunted down as traitors to the Crown. Very little of the persecution was due to Charles personally, who would have been willing to tolerate Presbyterians and even Quakers if, in return, he could have secured toleration for the Roman Catholics. The temper of the time was so intolerant, however, that all his attempts in this direction proved a failure.

A few useful reforms marked the reign. Old feudal dues were abolished at last, as had been in vain proposed in the time of James I. An act of Habeas Corpus (1679) gave new securities against arbitrary arrest and imprisonment, and proved one of the most valuable privileges for all English-speaking nations. The House of Commons strengthened its control over finance. But the real constitutional importance of the reign is that it marked the first definite attempt at government by party.

Of course party strife did not come into existence with the reign of Charles II. Yorkist and Lancastrian, Cavalier and Roundhead, were partisans. But the party system means more than this. It is a means for avoiding civil war, not for making it. Each party tries to persuade the people to give it confidence, so that party rule will mean majority rule and also criticism by an organized minority, willing to assume for itself the responsibilities of government should the party in power fail.

The origin of the two-party system was the conflict over the exclusion of Charles's brother James from the throne. As Charles had no legitimate children, on his death James would succeed as the nearest heir. But James was openly a Roman Catholic and many feared that were he on the throne the Protestant Church would be in danger. The Court party, or Tories, maintained that, however regrettable it might be to have a Catholic king, Parliament had no right to alter the succession to the throne. The Country party, or Whigs, held that

Parliament did have such a right.[6] The two parties, thus established, still exist, the Whigs being the direct ancestors of the Liberals and the Tories of the Conservatives. In recent years a new Labour party has introduced a complication in the simplicity of the two-party system, but British custom still recognizes a leader of the government party and a leader of the principal opposition group. The British colonies and Dominions have taken over the English party system, and throughout the history of the United States there have usually been only two major parties. In general, experience has shown that the two-party system has worked more smoothly, by assuring the government in office a working majority, than the multi-party system, as in France, which leaves the government dependent on the uncertain support of several independent groups; and it is certainly infinitely more democratic than the single-party system of the totalitarian states, such as Germany, Italy, and Russia, which offers the voter no choice at all.

Charles's first ministry was headed by a sincere and able, but very old-fashioned, Cavalier, Edward Hyde, Earl of Clarendon. He remained for seven years in office, though not always in the king's confidence; but eventually his administration became unpopular. This was due not alone to real faults of his administration, such as the persecution of the Puritans, but to other events which roused a vague popular discontent, such as the outbreak of an epidemic of the plague in London in 1665, a great fire in the city the following year, and the victories of the Dutch fleet. He went into exile, as in those days the fall of an unpopular minister was almost always accompanied by prosecution on charges of misgovernment.

A new coalition ministry, called the Cabal,[7] formed a triple alliance of Britain, Holland, and Sweden, then the three chief Protestant powers in Europe, to check the ambitions of Louis XIV of France. But Charles entered into a secret treaty with the French monarch a little later for an alliance with France, war against Hol-

---

[6] Like so many names of parties and sects, the terms Whig and Tory were coined by enemies. 'Whig' meant a Presbyterian rebel in Scotland; 'Tory' a Catholic rebel in Ireland.

[7] The name meant a conspiracy, but it gained added point from the fact that the initials of five prominent ministers (Clifford, Arlington, Buckingham, Ashley, Lauderdale) made up the word.

land, a secret pension from France (which would render him more independent of Parliament), and a promise to declare himself a Catholic when the time was ripe. Louis failed to conquer Holland, and public opinion forced England to break with France. The Earl of Danby became the most powerful minister and carried on the Tory policy of persecuting dissenters. Anthony Ashley Cooper, Earl of Shaftesbury, led the Whig opposition. To stir up sentiment against the Catholics, he made use of the pretended revelations of an informer named Titus Oates, who claimed to have evidence of a 'Popish plot' to kill the king so that the Catholic James would be on the throne, burn London again,[8] and massacre the Protestants. The mysterious murder of the magistrate before whom the information was laid convinced many that there was truth in Oates's accusation. A number of innocent Catholics were executed before the falsity of the plot was exposed, or, to be more accurate, before the popular rage and excitement died down. It is a hideous episode in the history of intolerance, comparable with the witch-killings in Salem, Massachusetts, in 1688-92.

The Whigs had carried matters too far. There was a strong Tory reaction; Shaftesbury fled to permanent exile in Holland, the Exclusion Bill was dropped, the city charter of London was annulled, and Sidney and Russell, two theoretical republicans, were executed on dubious charges of treason. In 1685 Charles died, proclaiming himself a Roman Catholic on his deathbed, and his brother assumed the throne as James II.

James II was a sincere believer in despotism and, had he not professed an unpopular religion, he might have gone far indeed in making the 'divine right' of James I and Charles I a reality. The future would show which weighed the more with the triumphant Tories, their political creed that no one had the right to resist a king or their religious faith that the Church of England must not give place to the Church of Rome.

Corrupt, cynical, and licentious as was the reign of Charles II, it marked in many respects a great advance in English national development. Party politics, though still often violent, was a good substitute for civil war or the absolute rule of either King or Lord Pro-

---

[8] Popular rumor credited the papists with the great fire of 1666.

tector. Commerce flourished and general prosperity prevailed. There was a new interest in science, and Charles II was himself an amateur in this field. The Royal Society, still the world's premier scientific association, was founded in 1662. Puritanism found its noblest literary expression in the dark hour of defeat in Milton's *Paradise Lost* and Bunyan's *Pilgrim's Progress*. Drama, suppressed during the Commonwealth, flourished during the Restoration. The greatest of the Restoration dramatists was John Dryden (1631-1700), but there were others, such as Congreve, whose plays are still sometimes acted and more frequently read. Coffee was coming into fashion, and the coffee-houses were the clubs of men of letters, politicians, and the gentry, who wanted to talk or hear the latest news. Pamphleteering, letter writing, such diaries as those of Pepys, informal and readable memoirs enrich our understanding of the times. Sir Christopher Wren, who designed St. Paul's cathedral and many other churches after the great fire in London, was an architect of genius who made most effective use of old classical forms. Though England had not yet worked out a native school of painting, foreign artists, such as the Flemish painters Rubens and Van Dyke, did some of their best work in England under royal patronage. The growing enlightenment of the times diminished superstition, and the witchcraft prosecutions which had reached their height under James I were now few and far between.

◦ XIV ◦

THE TRIUMPH OF THE BALANCED CONSTITUTION

KING JAMES II (1685-8), brother of Charles II, had originally been an Anglican and had married Anne Hyde, daughter of Lord Chancellor Clarendon, the most famous minister of King Charles. His two daughters were Protestants and married to Protestant princes: Mary, the elder, to William, Prince of Orange and chief magistrate (Stadholder) of the Dutch Republic; Anne, to Prince George of Denmark. After the death of his first wife, who never lived to become queen, James married an Italian princess, Mary of Modena, who was of course a Roman Catholic. James openly declared himself a Catholic and in consequence, as we have seen, efforts were made to exclude him from succession to the throne.

Meeting the Privy Council immediately after the death of Charles, James said in a happily phrased speech: 'I have often heretofore ventured my life in defence of this nation, and I shall go as far as any man in preserving it in all its just rights and liberties.' He had, as a matter of fact, fought on the continent against the English in Cromwell's time, but he had also fought in the navy in Charles II's Dutch wars, and was considered a competent Lord High Admiral.

On the very threshold of his reign he encountered a rebellion. The Duke of Monmouth, an illegitimate son of Charles II who claimed that a secret marriage had made him legitimate, stirred up the Protestant peasantry of southwestern England against a 'Romanist king.' But Monmouth was easily defeated in the battle of Sedgemoor, in Somerset, on 6 July 1685, the last pitched battle ever fought in England. Monmouth was executed, and with him many of his humble and credulous followers. Some 320 were put to death and 800 transported as convict laborers, practically slaves, to the West Indies. These 'Bloody Assizes' of Judge Jeffreys are still a memory of horror in the West Country. The king gave the pris-

141

oners to courtiers who, after all expenses were paid, made about ten pounds apiece from each one transported into slavery; James's queen, Mary of Modena, made a good deal of money in this manner. Another rebellion, on an even smaller scale, took place in Scotland, where the Duke of Argyle was executed for treason.

Like Charles II, King James desired to emancipate the Roman Catholics from hostile legislation, and to this end issued in 1687, and again in 1688, two Declarations of Indulgence, dispensing all his subjects from the Test Act (requiring office holders to take the sacrament according to the rites of the Church of England) and from the Penal Acts. On the face of the matter, this meant that he was more tolerant and liberal than Parliament, which opposed such emancipation. But while bigoted Anglicans were naturally hostile to any measure which would give power to Dissenters or Roman Catholics, many who were not bigoted at all joined in opposition to the royal policy. Some feared that James really aimed at a restoration of Catholicism, and that he merely included the Dissenters in his proclamation because he could not well do otherwise. This view was strengthened by attempts to force Catholics into office in the army and in the universities, and by the cruel persecution of the Presbyterian 'Covenanters' in Scotland. Others objected on legal grounds. If a king could suspend the operation of any law, or 'dispense' his subjects from obeying it, a precedent would be created which could be turned against good laws as well as bad, and leave to Parliament only the empty shadow of power.

England was alarmed also at the attempt of James to build up a standing army. Charles II had made a small beginning by taking over some half dozen Commonwealth regiments which had followed Monk to restore the monarchy. James, using Monmouth's rebellion as a pretext, greatly increased the number, and tried to overawe London by an encampment of 20,000 men on Hounslow Heath, under a Roman Catholic commander. Hitherto the Tudors and Stuarts had lacked military force to render them absolute; James saw the lack and resolved to remedy it.

Alarmed at the danger to the Church of England, the bishops refused to co-operate with the king's policy. When he ordered the clergy to read his Declaration of Indulgence in church, seven of the leading bishops [1] drafted, signed, and presented to the king a petition protesting that the Declaration, unconfirmed by Parliament, was illegal. When the petition was printed and circulated, the furious king had the bishops committed to the Tower of London and brought to trial on a charge of publishing a seditious libel. The jury brought in a verdict of not guilty and the people cheered this victory for law and freedom. Indeed, no precedent did more to establish the liberty of petition in English-speaking countries than this 'seven bishops' case.'

The country might have endured the tyranny of James a little longer, had it not been for the birth of a son to his Catholic queen, opening up a prospect of a long line of Roman Catholic sovereigns. So alarmed was the nation at this possibility that a report was industriously circulated that the son was really an impostor smuggled into the palace to ensure a Catholic succession. Absurd as this rumor was, many believed it because they wished to do so. Both Whig and Tory leaders, the former alarmed for English liberty and the latter for English religion, now joined against James. Secretly an invitation was extended to William of Orange, husband of James's eldest daughter Mary, to take the throne. In November 1688, William sailed for England with a considerable army, including not only Dutchmen but Scotsmen, Englishmen, Swedes, Germans, and Swiss. They landed safely at Torbay in Devonshire. Whole sections of King James's army deserted him, and he fled the country without offering resistance, thus ending the last attempt in English history to establish either an absolute monarchy or a dominant Roman Catholic Church. The revolution reached Scotland, too, where there was some resistance but only on the part of a small minority. The real test would be Ireland, the only Catholic country under the Crown. Here James resolved to make a stand.

In Ireland there was war for nearly two years, but in 1690 William was victorious at the Battle of the Boyne. Brave Sarsfield, the Irish general, surrendered at Limerick in 1691. Unhappily the Irish Parliament, representing only the Protestant minority, did not permit the promised extension of religious liberty to Ire-

[1] Archbishop Sancroft, Bishops Trelawney of Bristol, White of Peterborough, Turner of Ely, Lake of Chichester, Lloyd of St. Asaph, and Ken of Bath and Wells, the author of the *Morning and Evening Hymn*.

land but continued in force the penal laws against the Catholics.

In the American colonies the victory of King William was welcomed. The government of Charles II had cancelled the Charter of Massachusetts; that of James tried to consolidate New York, New England, and New Jersey into a centralized dominion under autocratic rule.[2] When the news of the revolution of 1688 reached America several months later, colonial self-government was restored.

A majority in Parliament would have liked Mary, the daughter of James, to be queen in her own right, and her husband merely Prince Consort, but William would have none of this. Accordingly Parliament stated 'that the said late King James the Second having abdicated the Government and the Throne being thereby vacant, . . . William and Mary, Prince and Princess of Orange be and be declared King and Queene of England, France and Ireland,[3] and the Dominions thereunto belonging.' The English kings kept until 1815 the quaint title of King of France, dating from the reign of Henry VI, but it was no longer a serious pretension to the French throne. Thus began the joint reign of William III (1689-1702) and Mary (1689-94). Since the usual line of succession had been set aside by placing a daughter instead of a son of the exiled monarch on the throne, William and Mary really ruled by the will of the people, as expressed by Parliament, and not by hereditary right.

This great victory for popular government was celebrated by the historian Macaulay in 1848, a year of violent revolutions on the continent of Europe, in words which are still more applicable today:

Now, if ever, we ought to be able to appreciate the whole importance of the stand which was made by our forefathers against the House of Stuart. All around us the world is convulsed by the agonies of great nations. Governments which lately seemed likely to stand during ages have been on a sudden shaken and overthrown. The proudest capitals of Western Europe have streamed with civil blood. All evil passions, the thirst of gain and the thirst of vengeance, the antipathy of race to race, have broken loose from the control of divine and human laws. Fear and anxiety have clouded the faces and depressed the hearts of millions . . . And, if it be asked what has made us to differ from others, the answer is, that we never lost what others are wildly and blindly seeking to regain. It is because we

---

[2] See Chapter xvi.
[3] Scotland acted separately through her own Parliament.

had a preserving revolution in the seventeenth century that we have not had a destroying revolution in the nineteenth.

The 'glorious revolution of 1688,' as Englishmen long called it, was the last revolution that England has ever known. Henceforth all political changes, no matter how drastic, were made in due legal form by Act of Parliament. There have been no dictators since Cromwell, no armed rebellions since Monmouth's, no political violence on a larger scale than a local riot since William displaced James. Of all major countries on earth, not even excepting the United States (which had one civil war), England[4] has been the most peaceable and 'civilian' in its political life.

To consolidate the gains of the revolution a considerable number of important measures were approved by Parliament. By far the most significant of these was the Bill of Rights, which has proved a model for the bills of rights embodied in the federal and state constitutions of the United States and has been widely imitated in continental Europe and Latin America. Among its chief provisions were:

That the pretended power of suspending of laws . . . by regal authority without consent of Parliament is illegal . . .

That the levying of money for or to the use of the Crown by pretence of prerogative without grant of Parliament for a longer time or in other manner than the same is or shall be granted is illegal.

That it is the right of the subjects to petition the king . . .

That the raising or keeping a standing army within the kingdom in time of peace unless it be with consent of Parliament is against law.

That the subjects which are Protestants may have arms for their defence . . .

That election of members of Parliament ought to be free.

That the freedom of speech and debates or proceedings in Parliament ought not to be impeached or questioned in any court or place out of Parliament.

That excessive bail ought not to be required nor excessive fines imposed nor cruel and unusual punishments inflicted.

That jurors ought to be duly impanelled and returned and jurors which pass upon men in trials for high treason ought to be freeholders.

[4] *England* is used here in the narrower sense; Scotland and Ireland have known subsequent civil strife.

That all grants and promises of fines and forfeitures of particular persons before conviction are illegal and void.

And that for redress of all grievances and for the amending, strengthening and preserving of the laws Parliaments ought to be held frequently.

During the same year, 1689, a Toleration Act ended the long and tragic story of religious persecution in England. Freedom of worship was granted to Protestant dissenters. The law was not a very generous one, for though it swept away a mass of persecuting statutes it did not apply to Roman Catholics, or to those who denied the Trinity, and it did not repeal the Test and Corporation Acts, which barred those not of the Church of England from important public office; it granted religious liberty to dissenters, but not religious equality. Yet this grudging concession was interpreted widely enough in practice so that even Catholics and Unitarians were not molested in Great Britain—Ireland remaining an unhappy exception in this matter, as in so many.

Some liberties came to England almost by chance. Thus the freedom of the press, for which Milton had pleaded, came into effect not by any royal proclamation or parliamentary bill of rights, but merely by the refusal of Parliament in 1695 to renew the licensing act which had just expired at the end of the previous year. Again, the bill creating martial law courts for mutinous troops (Mutiny Act) had to be annually renewed, thus indirectly depriving a sovereign who did not have the approval of Parliament of the ability to maintain a standing army for any great length of time, for an army without discipline is a broken reed.

Other important measures required new elections to Parliament each three years (Triennial Act, 1694); required an alleged case of treason to be proved by the testimony of at least two independent witnesses (Treason Act, 1696); established the Bank of England; funded the national debt on a permanent basis; and reformed the coinage. The Act of Settlement (1701) secured the throne to Princess Anne, James's younger daughter, since William left no direct heirs, and after Anne to the nearest Protestant heir thenceforward; thus forever barring Roman Catholics from succession to the throne. The Act also severely limited royal power in other ways. Every ruler was required to join in communion with the Church of England; no sovereign born outside the realm (as was William) might involve England in a war for his foreign possessions, except by act of Parliament; no sovereign might leave his own dominions without consent of Parliament; no foreigner might hold high public office; persons holding 'an office or place of profit under the king' were not to be members of the House of Commons; [5] judges were to hold office during good behavior and to be removed only 'upon the address of both Houses of Parliament'; no royal pardon could bar an impeachment by Parliament. Some of the many reforms of William's reign were Whig measures designed to limit royal power in general; some Tory measures designed to limit the power of William in particular, since he was considered by the Tories a 'foreigner' interested more in Dutch wars than in English affairs. Some were proposed by William, some readily accepted by him, some strongly but vainly opposed. Thus the interaction of party strife between Whig and Tory, and between King and Parliament, all worked together in the end for the greater liberty of the subject.

Most of William's reign was filled with war. He had taken the throne in the first place less from ambition to reign over England than to secure the English alliance against France for his passionately loved native country, the Dutch Republic. Louis XIV of France made the natural counter-offensive stroke of giving recognition and support to the exiled James II. Thus the war in which England engaged from 1689 to 1697 might not inaptly be termed the War of the English Succession. The navy not only kept Great Britain, in spite of some reverses, from invasion, but enabled William III to take an army over to the main theater of war in the Spanish Netherlands (Belgium). The Treaty of Ryswick (1697) forced France to give up her principal conquests, except Strasbourg, and to acknowledge William III as King of England.

The Peace of Ryswick, however, proved to be only the prelude to a greater war. The direct line of the Spanish royal family was threatened with extinction as Charles II, prematurely old and sickly, had no children. His sisters had married into the royal families of

---

[5] Had this provision not been modified, it would have rendered impossible the later growth of the cabinet system of government by which ministers of the Crown are chosen from Parliament. A later law, however, permitted members of the Commons to take office after standing again for election.

two powerful and ambitious neighbors, the Austrian Habsburgs and the French Bourbons. The Spanish Habsburg dominions were a heterogeneous group of states loosely held together by a weak and inefficient despotism, and, by their weakness and lack of cohesion, inviting partition. Both the English and the Dutch dreaded that the Spanish Netherlands might fall to France; in the hands of Spain it was no menace to either country, because Spain was both weak and distant, but in the hands of France this country would be a pistol pointed at England's heart (as Napoleon called it) and at that of Holland, too. It was also considered important that the French should not gain the Spanish colonies in the New World. Rather than have these Spanish possessions fall to France, both of William's two nations, English and Dutch, were resolved to fight; but William first tried diplomacy, and negotiated partition treaties for the division of the Spanish Empire among rival claimants on the death of King Charles II. But all these plans were upset when in 1700 the Spanish king, to prevent the division of his empire, bequeathed all his domains to Philip, grandson of Louis XIV. Louis accepted, and war became inevitable. When the exiled James II died in 1701, Louis acknowledged his son as 'King James III of England and VIII of Scotland.' William III made ready for war, but died in 1702. The war continued under his successor, Queen Anne, daughter of James II.

William III ranks with Alfred, William the Conqueror, Henry II, Edward I, and Elizabeth as one of the rulers of England whose personal qualities and policies were profoundly important in determining the course of English history. He was never popular in his own right, though most Englishmen preferred him to James II. Cold, aloof, and preoccupied with continental wars, he remained to the end an alien element in English life. Yet it was by means of his reign that England made permanent and solid advances in political liberty and stability, assured the Protestant succession, and broke the ascendancy of the despotic King Louis XIV in Europe. William had both the advantage and the disadvantage of being a European statesman. He did not think in terms of England only; that was his advantage. He involved England in continental wars; that was his disadvantage.

The War of the Spanish Succession (1701-14) was on the grand scale. The Dutch kept some 200,000 men under arms, counting both army and navy and including foreign mercenaries in the Dutch service. The total English force was of similar size. The Holy Roman Empire supplied about 100,000 men, and some of the individual German states, such as Brandenburg, also sent contingents. Louis XIV of France and his grandson and ally, Philip V of Spain, had a slightly smaller force than the allies opposed to them, but had the advantage of a compact command and of fighting on inner lines. All told, there may well have been a million Europeans under arms, not counting the fighters in the Great Northern War between Russia and Sweden, which raged at the same period (1700-1721).

Most of the soldiers were volunteers, enlisted for long terms of service, and forming a distinct class of professional soldiers aloof from the civil population. No one then dreamed, and least of all in civilian England, that it was every patriot's duty to serve his country in battle. Fighting took place mainly in the late spring and summer, the campaigning season, and armies in bad weather entered winter quarters and ceased fighting till the roads were hard once more. Strategists aimed at destroying field armies or capturing fortresses and capital cities rather than at exhausting the entire enemy population and breaking its will to resist. There was, as always, much cruelty in war (for example, when Louis XIV in a previous war had ravaged the German Palatinate of the Rhine), but there was little passion. The old crusading spirit of the sixteenth-century wars of religion had died out, and the nationalist fanaticism of our own times had scarcely developed. War was a cold-blooded game of kings fighting for dynastic interests, or of ministers interested in colonies, commerce, and the balance of power. The ally of one war was as often as not the enemy of the next. War had not yet become 'total war'; it was fought by limited methods and for limited objects.

Fighting in the War of the Spanish Succession began in the Spanish Netherlands in 1702, where French, Dutch, and English armies did most of the work; in northern Italy, where Austrian troops and their allies from Savoy defeated Spanish garrisons; in Spain, where a futile attempt was made to place the Austrian Archduke Charles on the throne against Philip V. In 1704 Gibraltar was taken, giving the British the key to the front door of the Mediterranean. Later in the year the English general John Churchill, Duke of Marlborough, destroyed a combined French and Bavarian army at Blenheim, the greatest English military triumph in continental Europe since Agincourt. Fresh victories brought Marlborough new laurels, but the prolongation of the war, costly in both lives and money by the standards of that time, caused the public to wonder if England had not done enough and whether the war was not being needlessly prolonged in the interests of Holland, Austria, or the Whig party.

Party feeling remained high throughout Anne's reign. It is the period when the party system, which had been growing in definiteness ever since the time of Charles II, became fully conscious of its possibilities. William III had endeavored to maintain a balance between Whigs and Tories, though he leaned more to the former. Queen Anne (1702-14) made the same attempt, though she leaned more to the latter. But Anne discovered that it was impossible to form a coalition ministry for any length of time, as Whig and Tory were so bitterly opposed. So the custom arose that a ministry must be all of one party, and must take or leave office as a unit, according to the wishes of the House of Commons. This rule has not been an unbroken one, for there have been party coalitions since, especially in wartime, but it represents the normal course of British politics.

In general, the Whigs of Anne's time were the war party, favorable to the Dutch alliance, tolerant towards Dissenters, strong in the commercial classes and the big towns; the Tories were the party of country squires and country parsons, the landed interest, hostile towards Dissenters, inclined to a policy of isolation from continental wars, though both parties supported a strong navy. During her reign the two parties alternated in office, and self-seeking politicians like Marlborough shifted from party to party as they thought might best suit their interests.

War-weariness brought the Tories into power in 1710, and they started negotiations with France which ended in the Treaty of Utrecht in 1713. Philip V, King Louis's grandson, was to remain unmolested on the Spanish throne, though France and Spain were never to have the same ruler. The balance of power was satisfied by the transfer of the Spanish Netherlands to Austria, together with Milan, Naples, and Sicily, in Italy. The Dutch were allowed to garrison fortresses in the Austrian Netherlands, as Belgium was now called. The British kept many of their naval conquests: Gibraltar and the Mediterranean island of Minorca from Spain; Newfoundland, the Hudson's Bay fur-hunting grounds, Acadia (renamed Nova Scotia), and the West Indian island of St. Kitts from the French. A commercial agreement, the *Asiento*, permitted one British ship a year to trade with Spanish South America; and another agreement gave to British merchants the right to import slaves into the Spanish colonies. These agreements lapsed in 1740.

Marlborough had been forced from command to clear the way for the Treaty of Utrecht, as the Tories feared that he might insist on prolonging the war. New men were elevated to the peerage in order to overcome the Whig majority in the House of Lords. The victorious Tories, bitterly hostile to the Dissenters, carried an Occasional Conformity Act (1711), which held that an occasional taking of the sacrament according to the custom of the Church of England did not qualify a man for public office unless he were in good faith a member of that Church; and a Schism Act (1714), which forbade Dissenters to teach schools. Both measures were poorly enforced and soon repealed.

The death of Queen Anne threw the victorious Tory party into confusion. One section headed by St. John, Viscount Bolingbroke, was at odds with another headed by Harley, Earl of Oxford. Anne had many children but they all had died before her, so the nearest Protestant heir was George, Elector of Hanover, an unpopular, middle-aged German who could speak little English, but who could trace his descent back to King James I. The Catholic claimant was 'James III,' son of the exiled James II, and commonly called by his opponents the Pretender to the throne. His followers were called Jacobites, from Jacobus, the Latin form of James. Some Tories were Jacobites, desiring to recall the exiled Pretender and keep the House of Stuart still on the throne; others declared for George of Hanover. The Whigs had the advantage of being united for King George and the Protestant Succession, so the new King George I (1714-27) placed his confidence in the Whig party, which dominated politics from 1714 to 1760.

Probably the greatest political event of Anne's reign was not the triumph over France in arms, but the union between England and Scotland. The two countries had been continuously under the same ruler since James I of England and VI of Scotland came to the

English throne in 1603, but—save for a brief period under Cromwell's dictatorship—the two countries had never been organically united. The fear that Scotland might choose a ruler other than George, and thus divide the two countries entirely, induced both England and Scotland to accept an Act of Union in 1707. This merged the English and Scottish Parliaments into a single Parliament of Great Britain, opened up freedom of trade and colonial enterprise to both nations, and left to Scotland her Presbyterian Church establishment and some old customs of Scottish law. Ireland retained her own Parliament, but this was of little advantage to her, since it still represented only the Protestant minority of the people.

By the end of Anne's reign, the main foundations of the British constitution as it is known today had become firmly established, and the controversial issues which had distracted the nation since Elizabeth's time had been settled. It had been decided that neither England nor Scotland should be republics or absolute monarchies but be governed as limited or constitutional monarchies. Except for some backward-looking Jacobites, all agreed that the two nations should have the same monarch, that the monarch must be a Protestant, that Parliament had the right to fix the succession to the throne, and that the monarch must act at all times by the advice of responsible ministers. Custom, not law, demanded further that these responsible ministers be of the party which commanded a majority in the House of Commons. There remained a capstone to the British party system still to fix in place, the recognition of a leader of the ministry, or Prime Minister. In the reign of George I this final step was taken.[6] With respect to the religious establishment, it was agreed that it should be Anglican in England and Presbyterian in Scotland but that other sects should be tolerated.

In literature the reign of Anne is regarded as an 'Augustan Age.' It is the age of Addison and Steele and of their essays in the *Spectator*, polished, wise, tolerant, quietly humorous. It is the age of the satiric verse of Pope, and the slashing journalism of Defoe and Swift, who are best known to the world at large for their ventures in fiction, *Robinson Crusoe* and *Gulliver's Travels*. Such men were a real factor in politics, and Defoe was a tower of strength to the

[6] See Chapter xv.

Whigs as Swift was to the Tories. It was also the age of Newton, one of the greatest scientists of all time, who was also a public official and held for years the office of Master of the Mint, an interesting example of the characteristic English union of the speculative with the practical genius. It was the age of John Locke, equally famous for the philosophy of his *Essay on the Human Understanding* and his defense of constitutional freedom. Voltaire, the intellectual dictator of European thought, had the penetration to see, and to point out to his fellow Frenchmen, that the England of Newton and Locke was really more significant than the England of Marlborough. 'Peace hath her victories, no less renowned than war.'

◦ XV ◦

EIGHTEENTH-CENTURY BRITAIN

WITH the end of the War of the Spanish Succession and the definite establishment of the Hanoverian line on the British throne, there opened a new era, mundane and materialistic in many ways, but bringing a degree of stability, tolerance, and prosperity that the British people, or indeed any people, had rarely known. The English constitution was now the British constitution, and the Scottish and English peoples, no longer rivals in trade, shared in a common effort to develop the resources of a common empire. Though many unjust religious discriminations remained on the statute books, the zeal to enforce them had vanished and, except in unhappy Ireland, the Roman Catholic, the Protestant Dissenter, and even the Deist were almost as free as the Anglican.

The social order, to be sure, contained many injustices. Schools were few, the debtor might be mewed up in prison, profiteers grew rich from the miseries of the African slave trade, appointments to office went by kinship or favor rather than merit, the common thief faced the same doom on the gallows with the murderer, one clergyman did the work for which another got the pay; no great wind of social reform had blown over the land since Commonwealth days, and vested private interests took precedence over public needs. But these abuses were old, the like of them existed almost everywhere, they were the way of the world. Compared with other nations of the time, Great Britain was an eminently free land. If class distinctions were wide, they were not rigid; a merchant's son could become a landed gentleman and his son's son a peer of the realm. There was still a large class of independent yeoman farmers; the factory age had not yet imprisoned mankind indoors. If many were very poor, yet more people could afford their daily beef and wheaten bread than in most European countries. If one offended the laws, there must be open trial and twelve unanimous jurors before one could be punished; the eighteenth-century French Bastille and the twentieth-century German concentration camp were not in the Briton's ken. On the whole, the literature of the time mirrors a happy people; foreign writers were frankly envious, and British authors somewhat complacent.[1]

To this happy state of affairs King George I contributed, but only in a negative sense. He was not a papist and not a tyrant; the religious and political quarrels which had racked Britain for generations could slumber. He was not English, and he was too old to learn new interests; this meant that his ministers could make their own decisions in cabinet meetings from which he nearly always absented himself. Thrown on their own responsibility, the ministers became accustomed to doing without the royal presence, and thus began a tradition which in time to come would bind the hands of stronger kings. England had known the coming of foreign rulers before, but William the Norman, Henry Tudor the Welshman, James Stuart the Scot, William of Orange the Dutchman had mattered because of what they were; George the Hanoverian mainly because of what he was not. He had, and sometimes insisted upon, his views on foreign affairs. Domestic affairs he left to his ministers.

One of the cabinet or ministry became recognized in political practice, though not as yet in constitutional theory, as Prime Minister, the man who bore the burden of decision. There was nothing at all new in the possession of great authority and responsibility by one of the king's subjects; indeed, in almost every reign one or more individual statesmen had stood out head and shoulders above the rest. Robert Walpole, the first Prime Minister, had no greater power than Wolsey under Henry VIII, Cecil under Elizabeth, or Clarendon under Charles II. What was novel was not the power, but the political status of the man who wielded it. In name and form adviser to and servant of the Crown, his position really depended on the support of a majority in the House of Commons. He had not one master, but hundreds, unless by his political skill he could make himself their master.

For twenty-one years, from 1721 to 1742, Walpole directed Brit-

---

[1] Swift was bitter enough, but Swift was Irish!

ish policy. So long a continuous service in supreme ministerial office has few parallels in any country, whether the minister depends on royal, parliamentary, or popular favor; today a five years' British ministry is considered very stable, and in France a single year is above the average. A ministry can be upset by royal hostility, party defeat, or factional intrigue. Walpole could cope with all these dangers. Both George I (1714-27) and George II (1727-60) had moments when they disliked Walpole or his policy, but they recognized that he had the support of the Whig majority in Parliament. To cast him aside would encourage the Tories, and neither king nor nation dared risk a Tory victory. Not all Tories were Jacobites, but so many were that the distant shadow of James III, the 'Old Pretender,' frightened even the reluctant into Whiggery.

There remained the danger of faction. Granting that only Whigs could be trusted with office, it did not necessarily follow that Walpole was the only possible Whig minister. Ambition, jealousy, or honest difference on questions of policy might, and sometimes did, lead to revolts in the party ranks. But Walpole understood practical politics very well—perhaps too well for his own reputation. One man could be held in line by honors, another by office, another by flattery, another by family favor, still another perhaps by direct cash payment. Walpole never said that 'all men have their price,' but he did say, almost without exaggeration, of his talkative opponents, 'all *those* men have their price,' and he had bought them often enough to know! Again, Walpole was always ready to yield his own wishes to keep himself and his party in office. Thus, when he introduced an excise on wine and tobacco in 1733, itself a sensible measure enough, he found that his foes had represented it as a monstrous official tyranny; so the unpopular measure was quietly dropped.

A more important instance of Walpole's readiness to yield to popular demand was the so-called War of Jenkins's Ear.[2] A cardinal feature of Walpole's policy was to maintain peace at any reasonable price, because peace meant commercial prosperity. He had kept Britain out of the War of the Polish Succession, and took credit for the fact that in one year 50,000 soldiers had died and among them 'not one Englishman.' But while the average Briton cared little for the

[2] For this war see Chapter xviii.

niceties of the continental balance of power, he was much concerned over the commercial and colonial rivalry with Spain and France, so in 1739 Walpole gave way to the national sentiment for war. He had, however, no taste for war and little skill in conducting it, so the surrender of his better judgment kept him in office only three years longer.

In the meantime, the War of Jenkins's Ear had broadened into the general European conflict known as the War of the Austrian Succession (1740-48). This was one of the many wars of partition that disgraced the age. At one time or another, plots were hatched for the partition of the Spanish Habsburg territories, the Austrian Habsburg territories, Sweden, Bavaria, Prussia, Poland, and Turkey, though only in the case of Poland were the robber Powers wholly successful. In 1740 it was Austria's turn to be the victim. Maria Theresa, Queen of Hungary, Archduchess of Austria, and ruler by various titles in many other parts of Europe, had no sooner taken the throne which the chief European Powers had all agreed to respect by the so-called Pragmatic Sanction, than several of them broke their promises and entered into a conspiracy to partition her domains. France, Prussia, and Bavaria were the ringleaders in the partition plot; Great Britain took the other side. The struggle was inconclusive: King Frederick of Prussia obtained Silesia, but the other Powers were unsuccessful. Great Britain and France agreed to a mutual restoration of colonial conquests at Aix-la-Chapelle in 1748.

During this foreign war, Great Britain was faced by her last civil war, but a struggle rather Scottish than English. In 1715 there had been an insurrection on behalf of the exiled Stuarts, led by the Earl of Mar. Thirty years later, in 1745, there was a much more serious insurrection headed by Prince Charles Edward, son of the exiled 'James III and VIII,' called by his friends the Young Chevalier, and by his enemies the Young Pretender. He had little support outside the Highlands, for the Presbyterians of lowland Scotland dreaded a Catholic ruler. Had he been a Protestant he might have been welcomed; for Scotland was still barely reconciled to the new union with England, and there were still Scotsmen who felt it a humiliation that Edinburgh was no longer the political capital of an independent nation. Moreover, a Hanoverian seemed a more alien

ruler than a native Scottish Stuart. Even with the handicap of the
Catholic faith of himself and his father, Prince Charles was able to
win some initial successes, enter Edinburgh, and overcome the handful of troops that opposed him in the lowlands.

When the Jacobite army entered England, however, there was another story. Englishmen had no sentimental affection for the name
of Stuart; quite the contrary in fact. England had no wounded national feelings to assuage. If the fires of Protestantism burned a little
less fiercely among the Anglican squires than among Scottish Calvinists, this was balanced by the greater attachment of Englishmen
to their political institutions; 'the constitution in danger' was an
English rallying cry which matched the Scottish cry of 'the kirk in
danger.' Here and there, especially in the far north of England, old-
fashioned Tories might theoretically hold that Parliament could not
set aside a succession which God had ordained, or drink a loyal toast
to the 'King over the water' by passing a wine glass over a water
pitcher; but very few carried their enthusiasm to the fighting point.
Moreover, England was fighting France at the time and, while
France might still mean to some Scotsmen 'the auld ally,' to nearly
all Englishmen France was rather 'the old enemy,' and it seemed
mere treason to join an insurrection that would give aid and comfort to the national foe.

So Prince Charlie was forced to retreat from England without a
battle. At Culloden, in Scotland, the Jacobite army was broken in
1746; the last battle ever fought in Great Britain till the Second
World War.[3] Charles, after romantic adventures and hairbreadth
escapes that have been the fortune of novelists ever since, returned
to France. The Scottish Highlanders were disarmed, their native
dress temporarily forbidden, their traditional rights as chieftains
diminished or expunged, and the country opened up by highroads
and policed by military garrisons. The whole hopeless and romantic
story of the 'Forty-Five' was but an interlude of poetry in an otherwise prosaic patch of history, a knight errant's quest for the Crown
in a setting of commercial wars.

The desire of Maria Theresa to win back her lost province of Silesia from Prussia brought about a diplomatic revolution which allied

---

[3] Sedgemoor, in Monmouth's rebellion, was the last battle in England.

France with her old enemy Austria. Russia, Sweden, Saxony, and several other countries entered the anti-Prussian coalition. But Great Britain, solicitous for Hanover as well as naturally hostile to France, took the side of Prussia.

In the colonies, strife had already broken out between Britain and France.[4] On the European continent Great Britain played but a minor role, and the main burden of the war fell on King Frederick the Great of Prussia. Yet William Pitt, the most important member of the war ministry, though nominally subordinate to the Duke of Newcastle, sustained Frederick with large subsidies, so that France would be kept busy fighting Prussia while the British army and navy thrust the French from America and from India. He had formerly opposed the policy of sending aid to Hanover and Prussia, and he still insisted that the colonial struggle was, for Britain, the most important aspect of the contest with France; but he saw the possibility of linking together the campaign on the Elbe, the campaign on the Ganges, the campaign on the St. Lawrence, and the naval struggle on the high seas, so that each would reinforce the others.

While the war was still raging, though the essential British victories had already taken place, George II died. His grandson and successor, George III (1760-1820), was not content with the limited monarchy of his immediate predecessors; he wished to be the King, a living political force, not merely the Crown, a legal figment. He knew it was too late in the day to defy Parliament, after the manner of Charles I or James II, but he did not see why he could not have some voice in the selection of his own ministers and in the determination of national policies, in the fashion of Charles II or William III. He was thorough patriot, with both feet on British soil, instead of looking forever to Hanover like the first two Georges. His simple life, his domestic tastes, his obvious honesty and good intentions won him at first a certain popularity; he was 'farmer George' as well as King George to many of his subjects. Moreover, the fact that Jacobitism as an effective political force, if not as a sentimental tradition, had died with the failure of the rebellion of 1745 made him free to negotiate with Tories as well as with the numerous Whig factions who shared political power in the seventeen-sixties.

---

[4] For the colonial campaigns, see Chapters xviii and xxxiii.

Whether or not it was too late for a sovereign of tact and talent to take an active hand in British politics is an open question, but certainly it was too late for George III to do so. With all his good qualities, he was a master blunderer. He rushed into politics with all the valor of ignorance, chose his tools unwisely, offended the most influential statesmen, sacrificed his own popularity, sacrificed also a large part of his empire. His aim, that of Bolingbroke's *Patriot King*, was to rule above parties as a personal sovereign able to summon either Whigs or Tories to his counsels, or both together, as national interests might require. His actual achievement was to create a synthetic coalition of Tories, discontented Whigs, and mere political adventurers who were content to bear the label of the 'King's Friends'; a coalition with no man of outstanding ability to head it and no particular principles to represent.

King George's political ineptitude was shown at the very beginning of his reign in the appointment of the Earl of Bute as his personal representative in the ministry and, later, as Prime Minister. Bute was a Scottish nobleman of reactionary opinions, mediocre ability, and great personal unpopularity. Anxious to make peace with France, now that Britain's colonial conquests were secure, Bute opposed Pitt's war measures against France's ally Spain and thus forced Pitt to resign. The Duke of Newcastle also was shaken out of the ministry and Bute stepped into his place as nominal head of the cabinet. The discontinuance of subsidies to Prussia had left Frederick the Great with a bitter hostility towards the British, though Frederick himself had more than once left a trusting ally in the lurch. Bute's blunders in foreign policy, however, came too late to undo the work of Pitt, and the Treaty of Paris, which closed the Seven Years' War in 1763, placed the British nation at a new high level of power and prestige.[5]

Bute soon retired from an office where he had been neither happy nor successful, and King George looked for other agents to help him govern. Sometimes he had to do the best he could with factional Whig leaders; twice, he found leaders for a reorganized Tory party, Lord North and William Pitt, younger son of the famous Whig statesman of the same name who had become Earl of Chatham.

---

[5] For the Treaty of Paris, see Chapter xviii. An almost simultaneous treaty signed at Hubertusburg ended the conflict between Austria and Prussia.

North had skill in parliamentary tactics, but his career was wrecked on the rock of the American Revolution.[6] Pitt, twice as able as North and ten times as able as Bute, would serve the king only on his own terms. Thus King George's every attempt to inject royal influence into politics ended in failure: his first tool, Bute, had broken in his hands; his second, North, he broke himself by his colonial policy; his third, Pitt, developed a will of his own. His later years, clouded by insanity, were inactive. King George's statesmanship left only two legacies to British history, a quarrel with the American colonies, and a refusal to grant to Ireland the concessions which Pitt might otherwise have made.[7]

The royal venture into politics met with fierce opposition from many of the Whig leaders in Parliament. John Wilkes, a demagogue, cynic, and libertine, became by accident a champion of British freedom. He was prosecuted and expelled from the House of Commons for a criticism of the royal government in issue forty-five of his paper *The North Briton*. Several years later he was again elected to the Commons, expelled as unfit by a hostile party majority, and, when again chosen, the Commons declared his opponent elected on the ground that his previous expulsion had disqualified him for office. This was a blow not so much at Wilkes—who was rather enjoying his notoriety—as at the freedom of the electors, and it roused such bitter criticism that it never became a precedent.

The political situation in the latter part of the eighteenth century was paradoxical. It would be easy to represent the times as shameless and cynical. Votes and seats in Parliament were purchased almost as openly as cattle in the market. Both King George and his Whig opponents played the dirtiest kind of politics with weapons which ranged from bribery to slander. An inept colonial policy lost the thirteen American colonies; oppression in Ireland led to rebellion; mismanagement in the navy led to serious mutinies; the army administration was a by-word for inefficiency.

Yet the same period which saw all these scandals and abuses saw also some of the greatest speakers and greatest thinkers in parliamentary history. Out of the crowd of professional politicians rose such figures as the Earl of Chatham; his son William Pitt; the ardent

---

[6] For the political setting of the American Revolution see Chapter xix.
[7] For Ireland, see Chapter xxvii.

reformer Charles James Fox; Sheridan, equally famous as dramatist and as orator; Erskine, the vindicator of the freedom of the press, and Edmund Burke, the profound philosopher in politics. Probably neither before nor since has British political oratory sustained so high a level. Outside the walls of Parliament, too, there was much penetrating political thought. The same year, 1776, which witnessed the American Declaration of Independence saw also Adam Smith's *The Wealth of Nations,* the classic cornerstone of modern economic science; Jeremy Bentham's *Fragment on Government,* which brought all institutions to the test of reason and utility; and Tom Paine's *Common Sense,* a vindication of the American Revolution by a recently transplanted Englishman.

Nor were practical achievements lacking. The American seaboard colonies were lost, but the French Canadians were well treated, being allowed by the Quebec Act of 1776 the free exercise of the Roman Catholic religion and their own civil laws; they were thus secured in the British Empire. If Ireland remained disaffected, Scotland at last became reconciled to the English connection. If India had been disgracefully plundered by officials of the East India Company, the evils had been thoroughly exposed by the parliamentary investigation of Robert Clive and the impeachment of Warren Hastings (two mighty empire builders who were made the scapegoats of other men's faults as well as their own), and to some extent remedied by Pitt's law which strengthened government control over the affairs of the East India Company.[8] The voyages of Captain James Cook opened up the island world of the Pacific to British exploration, conquest, and settlement.[9] In spite of maladministration, the navy still commanded the seas. Political test cases of the time ended in vindicating the freedom of the press and the freedom of elections. Lord Mansfield declared in a famous judicial decision that slavery could not exist under English law; and, though this decision did not affect slavery in the colonies, there was already the beginning of a fierce attack on the African slave trade which in the next generation would end it, and in yet another generation end colonial slavery itself.

Something of the same paradox which we have noted in British political life may be noted also in religious life. On the surface, the

[8] See Chapter xxxiii for Indian affairs.
[9] See Chapter xxxv for Pacific discovery.

Hanoverian period was the Ice Age of English religion. Episcopal appointments were made in exactly the same manner and spirit as any other political jobbery. There was little mysticism in the average clergyman, usually an impoverished younger son of some country gentleman, who took his bottle and his fox hunt along with the squire and hated dissenters with a feeling less theological than political. Quite outside the Church, and even outside the dissenting chapels, there grew up a generation of miners and factory hands who were practically pagan. The situation was worse yet in Ireland, where the established Church was regarded as an alien English importation, disliked by the Roman Catholic majority and by the Scottish Presbyterian minority. Even Scotland, though pleased to have her national Kirk established, was entangled in questions of politics and patronage that made the more devout look back with longing to the heroic days when the Covenanters fought and died for the principles of Calvinism.

But over against this general background of a religious 'call' turned into a mere professional 'calling,' of fanaticism watered down into dull bigotry, of a Church content to be an ecclesiastical department of the State, one may mark two hopeful signs of life and vigor. One was the Wesleyan or Methodist movement, and the larger evangelical movement of which it was a part: the revival of personal piety. The other was a keenness in philosophical controversy which made English theology a matter of moment to all Europe.

John Wesley, the son of a Church of England clergyman, and himself trained for the same profession, had no intention of founding a separate church. The term Methodist, which eventually became a denominational name, was originally given half-derisively to a young group of Oxford students whose 'methodical' lives awoke the wonder of their more worldly fellow classmates. They aimed to bring about a revival in the Established Church, and also to reach the poor and ignorant who had remained untouched by its ministrations. So Wesley and his fellows took the world for their parish, engaged in outdoor field preaching, and led revival meetings that changed the lives of thousands. By permitting the laity to preach, they offended the conventions of the Established Church and were eventually forced to organize as a new denomination—the youngest of the major Protestant churches. George Whitefield fathered a

related movement of Calvinistic Methodists, which was especially
strong in Wales. Charles Wesley, brother of John, contributed more
largely than any other man in history to the Protestant hymnals.
Wesley was much influenced by William Law's *Serious Call to a
Devout and Holy Life* (1728). Law himself was much influenced
by the works of German mystics and pietists. Wesley also had some
inspiration from a Moravian, Peter Böhler, whom he met in London in 1738. Subsequently, Wesley went to Germany and visited
the great Moravian settlement at Herrnhut in Saxony.

Historians have agreed to consider the Wesleyan movement as
a main turning point in British life. Macaulay expressed the hope
that the time would come when no one would attempt to write even
a political history of the reign of George II without considering it.
Lecky considered Wesley's work as the factor which averted an
English social revolution which might have been as terrible as that
of France. O. G. Robertson goes so far as to call Wesley 'probably
the most striking of eighteenth-century figures' and to bracket his
movement with the French Revolution as the 'two most tremendous
phenomena of the century.' [10] Certainly, later evangelical revivals
within the Church of England and also within the older dissenting
sects owe a limitless debt to Wesley's inspiration and example.

The British contribution to the philosophy of the Age of the Enlightenment has been unduly obscured by the greater fame of the
French *philosophes*. It is true that no one Briton either filled the
stage of his own time so fully as Voltaire, or influenced in so revolutionary a fashion the thought of coming generations as Rousseau.
But the French themselves generously admitted their debt to the British. Newton's physics did more than any other one thing to convince thinkers of the existence of a reign of law throughout the universe. The writings of the early British Deists inspired the Deists
of France, just as the analysis of the British constitutional balance by
such theorists as Locke inspired the political science of Montesquieu,
and the Scotsman Joseph Hume's skepticism of old philosophic
dogmas influenced the philosophy of Kant and his German disciples.
It was only in Britain that orthodox Christianity found such vigorous champions as Bishop Butler, whose *Analogy* drew a parallel be-

[10] *England under the Hanoverians*, p. 210.

tween revealed religion and the 'natural religion' of the Deists and the 'reign of law' which atheists themselves accepted; and Bishop Berkeley, who showed that matter itself was only an inference from our sensations, and that these sensations in turn were merely states of mind.

The chief glory of the eighteenth century was not British trade and empire, not new machines and factories, or victories by land and sea; rather that, in politics and philosophy alike, Great Britain provided a vast forum where all the great questions of human interest could be intelligently discussed. Bolingbroke could argue as cogently for a revival of royal power as Fox could oppose it. Dr. Samuel Johnson's Tory batteries carried a weight of metal which matched the radical artillery of Priestley or Paine. Butler and Berkeley asked no odds of the ablest skeptics. Jeremy Bentham constructed political reform on the geometric lines of pure reason, while Burke contended that national institutions were an organic growth, which might be pruned if necessary but could never be safely uprooted. So, while the great debates of statesmen echoed in the halls of Parliament, every coffee house was a little parliament whose debates were often just as full of wit and wisdom. The pious discipleship of Boswell has preserved for us those in which Dr. Johnson took part, but doubtless a thousand equally interesting discussions have been lost to us forever.

The same life and vigor which informed political and philosophical controversy can be traced in the literature and art of the time. The early Hanoverian period was, to be sure, somewhat less brilliant in letters than Queen Anne's time.[11] Swift, Bolingbroke, Defoe were 'holdovers,' much of whose best work had already been done, and no new Popes or Drydens were discovered. But on the foundations of the novel laid by Defoe were added the great constructions of Richardson and of Fielding, as well as the lesser work of Smollett and Sterne. Gay's *Beggars' Opera* was musical comedy worthy of the nineteenth-century work of Gilbert and Sullivan; while Goldsmith's *She Stoops to Conquer* and Sheridan's *School for Scandal* were dramatic comedies which combined the craftsmanship of a Molière, the humanity of a Shakespeare, and the light vivacity of a Congreve.

[11] See Chapter XIV.

The vanishing social order of the English village was given a worthy epitaph in Goldsmith's *Deserted Village* and Gray's *Elegy in a Country Churchyard*.[12] Some songs of Gray and Collins foreshadow the coming day of romantic poetry; as did also the revived interest in the Middle Ages. Two great literary frauds, or semi-frauds, indicate this interest. Chatterton, the 'marvelous boy,' to interest people in his imitations of old English poetry passed them off as genuine, while MacPherson reconstructed old Celtic legends of the Scottish Highlands as veritable fragments of 'Ossian.' Bishop Percy's *Reliques of Ancient English Poetry*, a collection of genuine old verses, attracted attention to the half-forgotten ballad literature.

In painting, the age was Britain's golden age. The grim satiric realism of Hogarth, the mastery of form and creative imagination of Sir Joshua Reynolds, the reality and fine color of Gainsborough's portraits, Constable's landscapes, the powerful work of Romney and Scottish Raeburn placed British painting at once on the highest level, the more remarkable as prior to the eighteenth century Great Britain had contributed very little to the art. Handel's genius, though owing much to his German origin, made a new era in British music. The Wedgwood chinaware, the exquisite furniture, the gay colors of fashionable clothing, the woven tapestries of the formal dance made up a pattern of graceful living which is still our wonder, and perhaps our envy, today.

[12] Actually the village social order never quite vanished; there is yet something of its antique charm in England. Goldsmith's beautiful, if too highly colored, picture was drawn from an Irish, not an English, village where his brother was clergyman.

PART III
THE FIRST BRITISH EMPIRE

○ XVI ○

FROM ISLAND TO EMPIRE

THOUGH sea-cradled England was ideally situated for overseas expansion and eventually developed the widest domain ever gathered under one Crown and one flag, the English awoke to their opportunity with singular tardiness. Save for Cabot's voyage to Newfoundland,[1] which did not result in any immediate settlement, the English had taken no share in the first imperial ventures of Europe in the New World. Pope Alexander VI, by his line of demarcation in 1493, had divided the colonial world between the Portuguese and the Spanish. This monopoly neither Spain nor Portugal proved strong enough to enforce, but not until the time of Elizabeth [2] did the English seriously contest it. Both the French and the Dutch were more active in the early race for empire.

The first Englishmen to venture overseas were not settlers or even conquerors. Some were smugglers, often operating with the connivance of local Spanish authorities, with no worse intention than trade. Some were prospectors for gold and silver mines, hoping to emulate in Guiana or Virginia the Spanish successes in Mexico and Peru. Some were privateers engaged in irregular warfare against those whom they considered enemies of their country and their faith. Some were little better than pirates, justifying themselves to their easily satisfied consciences that gold stolen from the Indians by the Spaniards might well be stolen in turn by honest Britons. Most of them, perhaps, were a mixture of all these: equally ready to trade, to hunt gold, to fight, and to plunder.

Another aspect of English expansion was the search for a Northwest Passage to the Far East. If the English were late and reluctant colonizers they were bold navigators and explorers. The names of

[1] See p. 92.
[2] See Chapter XI.

169

Gilbert, Davis, Frobisher, and Hudson on maps of the Far North testify to their daring. But this effort, though it blazed many a path for later claims and settlements, was fruitless in its own day. No colonies were then founded in the Far North, and the supposed routes to Asia ended either in land or in impassable ice. It was farther south, within the Spanish zone of influence, and in rivalry with the Spaniards, that the first attempts at empire were undertaken.

John Hawkins of Plymouth made in 1562 a successful trading voyage to the west coast of Africa, where he took on a cargo of slaves, and then to the West Indian island of Hispaniola (the modern Haiti), where he sold the slaves for gold, silver, pearls, and sugar. The slave trade was already well established by the Spaniards and Portuguese, but he was the first Englishman to take an independent share in the sinister traffic. Having profited so well by his first voyage, he fitted out a second expedition in 1564, the queen, the Earl of Leicester, and other dignitaries taking shares in it. The third and larger venture of 1567 ended in disaster. When the squadron put in at the Mexican port of St. Juan de Ulúa, it was treacherously attacked and escaped only with heavy losses. As Spain refused compensation, Hawkins, Drake, and other captains resorted to reprisals which, as is usually the case with reprisals, often fell upon the innocent.

The maritime enterprise which excited most admiration was the voyage of Francis Drake around the world in 1577-80. With the permission of his queen and the help of 'divers friends adventurers,' Drake fitted out five ships and left Plymouth on 15 November 1577. The largest ship, the *Pelican* (later called the *Golden Hind*), was listed at a hundred tons, but was probably larger by modern measure. The total crew of the five ships was 164. The ships were fully armed, the *Pelican* carrying fourteen nine-pounder cannon. A storm forced a delay of three weeks; then, 'with happier sails we once more put to sea.' By Christmas the fleet had reached the coast of Morocco, fifteen hundred miles from home. Thence they sailed to the Cape Verde Islands, belonging to Portugal, then across the Atlantic to Brazil, taking delight as they went in 'beholding the most excellent works of the eternal God in the seas, as if we had been in a garden of pleasure.' They sailed leisurely down the coast of Brazil, trading with the natives, and by June had reached Patagonia (modern Argentina), where Drake had to quell a mutiny and execute, after formal jury trial—for the English common law followed the English flag even into unknown lands—one of his officers.

Having sailed through the Straits of Magellan, the ships entered the Pacific on 7 September 1578. Three weeks later the *Marigold* sank with all hands. Turning northwards, the squadron reached the coast of Chile. Entering Valparaiso on 5 December, the English boarded a Spanish vessel, 'easing the ship of its heavy burden' of wines and gold. At Tarapaca they found a pile of thirteen bars of silver and took it quietly while the custodian lay asleep. They also encountered a string of light llamas, each carrying two sacks of silver, eight hundred pounds in all, tended by a Spaniard and an Indian boy; the English drove off the llamas and silver without harming the drivers. Off Avica, in February 1579, they captured two Spanish ships with over fifty bars of silver the size of brick bats. Turning west from the Pacific coast, the expedition reached the islands which were later called the Philippines by October; by May 1580, it was at the Cape of Good Hope; while on

the 26th of September (which was Monday in the just and ordinary reckoning of those that had stayed at home in one place or country, but in our computation was the Lord's Day or Sunday) we safely with joyful minds and thankful hearts to God, arrived at Plymouth, the place of our first setting forth, after we had spent two years, ten months, and some few odd days besides, in seeing the wonders of the Lord in the deep, in discovering so many admirable things, in going through with so many strange adventures, in escaping out of so many dangers, and overcoming so many difficulties in this our encompassing of this nether globe and passing round about the world which we have related.

The English called on each other to resist the temptation to ignoble ease and to follow the example of Francis Drake. After one of his voyages, a follower wrote it up as *Sir Francis Drake Revived: Calling upon this Dull and Effeminate Age to follow his Noble steps for Gold and Silver*. It is difficult to imagine what the Elizabethans would have considered an 'exciting and hardy' age if they regarded their own time as 'dull and effeminate'! Drake's men appreciated the outstanding character of his voyages and some of them kept journals and log books; these were developed into the memorable narratives, the 'prose epic of the English people'—commonly known as *Hakluyt's Voyages*. Richard Hakluyt, from whom we have just freely quoted, was a clergyman and, among other benefices, a canon of Bristol cathedral, and Bristol was in those days second only to London among English ports.

Sir Walter Raleigh, the perfect courtier of the age, was the first to make any real attempt to found a New England overseas. His scheme took the form of a co-operative company to plant in North America a colony to be called Virginia, in honor of the Virgin Queen Elizabeth. The expedition of 1584 and two later ones failed. Another in 1587 made a temporary settlement which existed for some months and then disappeared, leaving behind it no sign except the mysterious word 'Croatan' carved on a tree. Elizabeth died with her dream, and Raleigh's, still unfulfilled. It was reserved for the Scottish Stuarts to bring to fruition what the Welsh Tudors had planted.

The motives which took the English to the New World were not markedly different from those which animated their rivals, the Spanish, the Portuguese, the Dutch, and the French. Commerce was first with them all. America had been discovered in the first place by men looking not for new lands but for new trade routes to the Orient. The Spaniards were the most fortunate in finding gold and silver; other explorers hunted in vain, though some American treasure houses—the gold of California and the Klondike, the silver of Nevada and Colorado—were still undiscovered. Lacking direct access to the precious metals, the next best thing was to find some commodity which could not be produced in Europe and thus monopolize the market. The Portuguese, and later the Dutch, did this with some success in the 'spice islands' of the East Indies. Sugar cane, cultivated by African slave labor, proved a similar source of wealth in the West Indies. At a later date, the cultivation of tobacco on the mainland, the use of timber for naval stores, the fisheries around Newfoundland, and the fur trade with the Indians in the north made the exploitation of the continent the subject of international rivalry. For a long time, however, the continental colonies were grossly undervalued as compared with the sugar islands of the Caribbean.

The English came too late to get the larger islands. Cuba was Spanish; Haiti poised uncertainly between France and Spain. Gradually, however, during Stuart times an English insular empire was pieced together out of Barbados, Jamaica (Cromwell's conquest), the Bermudas, the Bahamas, and the Leeward Islands.[3]

Apart from the purely commercial motives which led European adventurers abroad to seek their fortunes, there was the hope of national power, of military glory, and of service to Christianity in spreading the Gospel among the heathen. All these motives seem to have been weaker with the English than with the Spanish or the French. On the other hand, the English were moved more than most of their rivals by a desire to find an outlet for their surplus population, a topic widely discussed in the pamphlet literature of the seventeenth century. At first glance this seems strange indeed. England was not in those days as densely populated as many continental countries and had, in many respects, a higher standard of living than any of them. But there were in England many men, no longer peasants, who were footloose. Sometimes they found occupations in town and bettered themselves; often, however, they became vagabonds and 'sturdy beggars,' charitably supported by the parish rates or driven from town to town as unwelcome tramps. Would it not be a good plan, men said, to ship them to a new, fertile, and almost uninhabited land?

Many a nation would have undertaken conscious, direct empire building to realize these possibilities. But that was scarcely the English way. The government had small revenues and its military force was insignificant. There was no large class of professional bureaucrats and trained administrators. Kings, ministers, and Parliament assumed great power in controlling all sorts of private affairs, from trade to religion, but they conceived their duty to regulate these matters rather than to initiate them. Individuals started schools; the government laid down rules and conditions. Individuals traded; the government collected tariffs. Individuals settled colonies; the government issued charters to the companies that 'planted' them. Other nations too, notably the French and the Dutch, made much use of the chartered company in the earlier stages of colonization,

---

[3] For the development of the West Indies see especially Chapter xxxvii.

but none employed the device for so long a time or in as many parts of the world as did the English.

Various groups of Merchant Adventurers and companies for trading with 'Muscovy' (Russia) and the 'Levant' (Turkey) had been organized to conduct commerce along European trade routes. In 1600 Elizabeth had chartered a company to traffic in India and the East Indies.[4] The first American colonies were planted in Stuart times by similar companies. The tradition of the chartered company came down to much more recent times, as in the exploitation of Rhodesia by the British South Africa Company. The familiar saying that the British Empire was created in a fit of absence of mind really means no more than that it was created rather by private initiative than by official planning.

Not until the reign of James I can we speak of a transatlantic British Empire. James sacrificed the life of Raleigh to please an offended Spain, but he refused Spanish demands to curb English colonial enterprise. His religious intolerance drove abroad a few persecuted Puritans to settle in the New World, though this was, of course, not the intent of his policy. The union of the English and Scottish crowns, by strengthening England's security in Great Britain, may possibly have had some effect in facilitating ventures abroad, but it is noteworthy that for many years to come the colonial enterprises remained English rather than British, and Scotsmen, save as individual emigrants, were denied any share in them.

The first successful American plantation was made through a commercial venture of the London Company, a chartered corporation authorized to settle lands along the Atlantic between the thirty-fourth and forty-first parallels of latitude. Over a hundred settlers landed in 1607 on the shores and islands of the James River and founded a fort at Jamestown. At first the colony seemed likely to share the fate of Raleigh's Roanoke Island venture, and of many other now half-forgotten experiments of the age, all the way from Panama and Honduras to Nova Scotia and Maine. Probably only the vigorous and somewhat autocratic management of Captain John Smith kept the infant colony alive. Famine slew many of the settlers; Indian tribes, by turns friendly, suspicious, or hostile, killed others.

---

[4] See Chapter xxxiii for the East India Company.

For almost two decades more settlers returned, discouraged, to England, or died of the hardships of the wilderness, than remained to make their homes in Virginia. Very often the light burned low, but it never quite went out. The growing of tobacco maintained the interest of English investors, whereas the growing of maize, or Indian corn, kept alive the hungry settlers.

In 1619 burgesses, chosen by the actual settlers, met with councilors appointed by the London Company in the first American representative assembly. Individual land ownership replaced some early experiments in collective settlement. In 1624 the English government took over directly the responsibilities hitherto borne by the London Company under various charters. Henceforth Virginia was a royal province with an appointed governor, though representation of the settlers was assured by an elected House of Burgesses.

While Virginia was thus evolving from a private commercial speculation into a dignified dominion of the Crown, other plantations were under way. Some were undertaken by chartered companies, and others were grants to individual proprietors. Their territories were defined by the terms of royal grants, sometimes in conflict with the boundaries claimed by earlier settlements.

Among the earliest and most interesting of these new ventures were the settlements of Plymouth and of Massachusetts Bay (both now comprised within the state of Massachusetts). The Plymouth Company was organized to plant a colony in the northern parts of Virginia. A first attempt to establish a colony in the region which is today the state of Maine proved a failure. But a later attempt, after the company had been reorganized as the 'Council of New England,' resulted in permanent settlement. A number of nonconforming 'pilgrims,' harried by persecution in England and afraid of losing their English nationality if they remained permanently in tolerant Holland, saw in the wilderness a chance to keep both their faith and their native tongue.

In 1620 the *Mayflower* sailed from Plymouth in Devonshire to found a colony of New Plymouth in America. The settlers suffered as much from famine and the rigors of an unfamiliar climate as the first colonists in Jamestown had done, but they were fortunate in finding friendly Indians to teach them how to grow the Indian corn. A much larger settlement, mainly of discontented Puritans, was made a few years later around Massachusetts Bay on the site of the present city of Boston.

The government of both colonies was largely in the hands of the actual settlers. By additions to the number of 'freemen' of the company, the franchise was widened to include many later immigrants. The General Court of the Massachusetts Bay Colony developed into a true legislature. An attempt was made, however, to preserve the original Puritan coloring of the community by restricting the vote to members of an approved church congregation. No 'godless' men should share in the rule of the New England Zion!

The other New England colonies were practically offshoots from Massachusetts Bay resulting from the discontent of various dissenters with Bostonian orthodoxy. Two settlements, later united as Connecticut, were founded to the west around Hartford and New Haven. No less than four dissident groups established themselves within the area of Rhode Island, now the smallest state in the Union. The most interesting of these was Providence on Narragansett Bay, founded by Roger Williams, a Baptist who held a number of unusual doctrines, including a belief that civil authorities had no jurisdiction in questions of religious faith and that there should be no union of Church and State.

Another type of colony was the foundation by an individual proprietor. George Calvert, Lord Baltimore, whose name still clings to the great city on the Chesapeake, was given Maryland. His powers were modeled on those of the county palatine of Durham, where the old-time bishops, as bulwarks of England against the Scots, had enjoyed an exceptionally independent position. As a Roman Catholic he desired to make Maryland an asylum for his fellow Catholics, but Maryland was never a Catholic colony, like French Quebec, for the English would not have sanctioned discrimination against all Protestants; it was merely a colony in which Catholics enjoyed protection. Eventually, it had more Protestant than Catholic settlers.

William Penn, the Quaker statesman and philanthropist, satisfied an old claim against the Crown in the time of Charles II by accepting a tract of land in America. He was personally the proprietor, though his powers were somewhat more limited than those of Lord Baltimore in Maryland. The Quakers, or Friends as they called themselves, suffered more than other dissenting sects from persecution because they not only held unorthodox views of God but maintained unconventional customs towards man. However eager people are to vindicate divine dignity, they are seldom less careful of their own, and the Quaker who refused to doff his hat to a magistrate, to take oath in court, or to fight for King and country, was naturally unpopular even among worldlings who cherished no religious zeal. Massachusetts drove Quakers out of the community and hanged them if they returned to it; in old England they were at times as badly treated as in New England. Penn hoped to find a quiet home for these harmless, industrious, but uncomplying people in the new land of Pennsylvania.

But into this Quaker colony poured a horde of other immigrants. The good soil and relatively moderate climate attracted settlers from many nations. Virginia and Massachusetts had been 'mere English,' but Pennsylvania was soon cosmopolitan. The valleys in the hills contained many German settlers, popularly miscalled to this day the 'Pennsylvania Dutch.' There were also real Dutch from Holland, Scotsmen, Irishmen, Welshmen, Swedes, French Huguenots, and Swiss. Though the Quakers found the freedom they sought, and a good livelihood as well, they were not numerous enough to dominate the political life of the colony for as long a period as the Puritans did in Massachusetts. They have, however, left deep traces on American life in social custom and zeal for education. American evangelical piety owes as much to such Pennsylvanians as the Quaker William Penn and the Moravian Count Zinzendorf as to the Winthrops, Brewsters, and Cottons of New England.

Between New England and Pennsylvania the Dutch had thrust a wedge. The Dutch legal claim to their New Netherland was based on the voyages of Henry Hudson, who, though an Englishman, sailed in the Dutch service when he entered the river which bears his name. The Dutch colonial policy was strictly commercial, and their colony was little more than a fur-trading post governed by the autocratic authority of the officials of the Dutch West India Company. The Dutch absorbed an earlier settlement of Swedes and Finns on the Delaware; and New Netherland in the widest sense included not only the Hudson valley from New Amsterdam (New York City) to Rensselaerwyck (Albany), but the present area of New

Jersey, Delaware,[5] and western Connecticut.[6] Pursuing, as a commercial community should, a wise tolerance of alien creeds and races, New Netherland even under Dutch rule was rapidly becoming a cosmopolitan rather than a nationally Dutch community. More than a dozen languages were spoken in the streets of New Amsterdam.

Not so much the conflict of charters and legal claims, or the desire to occupy the rich Hudson valley, as the opportunities which New Amsterdam offered for smuggling and violation of the Navigation laws determined the English government to annex New Netherland. Cromwell had planned such a conquest, as part of his struggle with the Dutch, but in this, as in so many matters of foreign or commercial policy, the restored Stuarts carried to completion the unfinished projects of their arch-foe. Charles II placed his brother the Duke of York (later King James II) in command over a vast tract of land in the New World, including the area settled by the Dutch; and, in 1664, an English naval force arrived before New Amsterdam and forced the Dutch to submit. Thenceforward, except for a short interval of Dutch reconquest in 1673, New Netherland was New York, and New Amsterdam was New York City. The Duke sublet eastern and western New Jersey to Sir George Carteret and Lord Berkeley, respectively, as proprietors. The Quakers were later able to buy an interest in both parts of New Jersey. Eventually New York, New Jersey, and Delaware each became a separate colony.

The government of King James II made a short-lived attempt to consolidate all the northern colonies—New York, New Jersey, and the New England colonies—into a single royal domain. In this enlarged Dominion of New England there was no provision for popular representation; the old colonial charters were cancelled, and popular town meetings were discontinued. The English revolution of 1688, however, deprived James's officials of home support and William III restored the old colonial charters in 1689 with little change. Maine and Plymouth were incorporated with Massachusetts, but New Hampshire was recognized as a separate colony. In 1665 New Haven had merged with Connecticut, and in 1644 Rhode Island

---

[5] Claimed also by Pennsylvania.
[6] Claimed also by the New Englanders.

with Providence; so now there were four New England colonies: Massachusetts, Connecticut, Rhode Island, New Hampshire.

Charles I had granted Sir Robert Heath in 1629 the right to settle a wide tract of land between Virginia and the Spanish colony of Florida; little was done, however, to plant this region of 'Carolana' until the reign of Charles II, when eight proprietors were granted a new patent in 1663. It was hoped that, since tobacco from Virginia and sugar cane from the West Indies were amply supplying the market, the new province would furnish silk, wines, olive oil, and fruits, so that England would no longer have to enrich her French rivals. In 1729 'Carolana' broke into North and South Carolina. Among the early South Carolinians were French Huguenots, Scotsmen, and English immigrants from the West Indies. The expected silk and wine were not forthcoming; and for many years the chief economic value of both Carolinas was the sale of wheat, maize, hogs, cattle, and naval stores to the West Indies plantations. Eventually, however, South Carolina developed her own slave plantation system for the growing of sugar cane, rice, and indigo.

John Locke, the philosopher, as secretary for Lord Ashley, one of the proprietors, worked out a fantastic constitution for Carolina which never went into effect and is of interest only as showing how persistently attempts were made to transplant old social forms to the new country—and how vain they were! This still-born constitution provided for a complex feudal structure; in addition to the proprietors themselves, as overlords, there would be inferior orders of nobility, the Caciques (an American Indian term) and the Landgraves (a German one), and a legislature in which these orders of nobility and the common settlers would alike be represented.

The last of the thirteen colonies to be established along the Atlantic seaboard was Georgia, the philanthropic experiment of James Oglethorpe, who secured a charter in 1732 for a colony where debtors could retrieve their broken fortunes and start life over again. The same humanitarian impulse showed itself in the attempt of the proprietor to discourage slavery and to encourage small holdings. But South Carolina was already beginning to draw profit from rice culture on slave plantations, and the Georgians so insistently wished to follow their lucrative example that the original restrictions could not be maintained.

Although, as we have seen, the thirteen colonies started in many different fashions—some, like Virginia, being founded by chartered companies; some, like Pennsylvania, being grants to individual proprietors; some, like New York, being royal foundations; they all tended towards a common form. In all cases the imperial authority was strengthened and that of the proprietor or the private company diminished. The general pattern of government in the colonies was, in English terms, 'representative' but not 'responsible.' In most cases a royal government represented the Crown, and a legislature, at least in part elective, voiced the wishes of the property-holding inhabitants. The authority of the governor was not a mere legal fiction, nor was he in any way bound to subordinate his views of public policy to those of the colonists. Many of the British Crown Colonies of our own time, such as the West Indies islands, have a very similar type of government.

Although the thirteen colonies formed a natural geographic group and had a common English background, it would be a mistake to think of them as bound to each other. Each had its separate government and its direct dependence on the Crown. Four New England settlements (Plymouth, Massachusetts, Connecticut, and New Haven) had, indeed, once formed a Confederation in 1643 for their common defense, and, as we have seen, James II had projected an even more inclusive Dominion of New England; but neither of these attempts at union had proved enduring, and even had some such plan succeeded it would only have sharpened the contrast between the New Englanders and the Southern colonists.

Moreover, the thirteen colonies did not stand alone; they formed but a part, though a very large part, of an imperial system of colonies, dependencies, and plantations in many parts of the world. The larger English islands in the West Indies, such as Jamaica and Barbados, had a form of government similar to that of the mainland colonies, and were then considered much more important and profitable ventures. The English claimed, although against French opposition, the right to fish off the banks of Newfoundland and to barter with the Indians around Hudson's Bay for furs. They had cast covetous eyes on the French colony of Acadia, which they were later to own as Nova Scotia. Several attempts had been made, from Raleigh's time onward, to colonize Guiana. Some slave-trading stations on the

African coast were at least incipient colonies. The settlement of Englishmen and Scotsmen in Ulster was called a 'plantation' and often
compared with those of Barbados and Virginia.

Few seventeenth-century Englishmen, indeed, saw much difference between a Protestant immigrant in northern Ireland, an East
India Company trader bartering cloth and casting up accounts amid
the ruins of the dying Mogul Empire, a planter superintending
gangs of Negro slaves in the cane fields of Jamaica, or an American
backwoodsman barricading his cabin against an Indian raid. All alike
were Englishmen seeking their fortunes abroad, and alike subject to
English law, and especially to the commercial laws of the mother
country, whose interests must ever be the paramount consideration.

Yet natural environment and the force of circumstances were shaping a new nation on the American continent, almost before the colonists themselves were aware of it. How and why these English
settlements developed a distinct national character of their own must
be our next study.

OLD WINE IN NEW BOTTLES

THE settling of America was much more than the mere political adventure and commercial speculation which most men of the seventeenth century thought it to be. It was also, in the apt phrase of Edward Eggleston, a 'Transit of Civilization.' Most of the settlers were grown men and women, fixed in habit, accustomed to the traditions and institutions of their homelands. They carried with them the whole of their civilization, even to its prejudices. If, as very commonly happened, they brought with them also some grievance against the government, either for banning their peculiar form of worship or for failing to afford them ample opportunity to make good living at home, this fact did not, of itself, make them foreign. A discontented John Bull may be as thoroughgoing an Englishman as anyone; indeed his very grumbling resentment at real or alleged misgovernment has been considered a characteristic British trait.

The distinctly English character of most of the early settlers appears on the very map. Where the place names are not borrowed from the Indian natives they are usually taken from the map of Britain, or named in honor of British rulers. There would be nothing unfamiliar to an Englishman in finding on the map of Massachusetts a Boston, a Cambridge, a Plymouth. The loyalty of the Southern colonies was attested by a Virginia (honoring Elizabeth), a Jamestown, a Williamsburg, a Carolina, a Maryland, an Annapolis, a Georgia, a College of William and Mary. Even the Middle Colonies, less purely English, had a preponderance of English names. New York and New Jersey honored the greatest of the shires (owing to the accident that James was Duke of York at the time of the conquest of New Netherland) and the Channel Islands. It is not fanciful to see a certain homesickness in these first names given to places in the American colonies, especially since later settlements, even during the colonial period, drew far less frequently from English place names and more often commemorated the name of some prominent settler.

As to the actual proportion of English blood in colonial times, we are reduced in large part to conjecture. A study based on family names in the census of 1790, shortly after the close of the colonial period, shows that British [1] names amounted to about 77 per cent of all those borne by white men; German names were about a tenth as numerous; then followed, in order, the Irish, the Dutch, the French, and a scattering few of other European nationalities. It should be remembered that immigrants then, like immigrants today, often changed a foreign-sounding name to an English one, either to assimilate themselves to the dominant English group or simply because they were tired of hearing it mispronounced. This makes the one statistical test which can be applied, the test of name, somewhat uncertain. For later times we are able to check the evidence of family names by official statistics of immigration, but such figures for the colonial period are too imperfect to be of much use. One estimate for 1776 places the English at about two-thirds of the whole white population of the thirteen colonies; the Scotch-Irish at about one-sixth; the German at about one-tenth, with others in smaller proportion.

Besides the white European immigrants, almost a fifth of the colonial population consisted of Negro slaves, and there must be added an indeterminate, though probably not very large, native American Indian element even within the settled colonies. But, with every possible deduction for the uncertain, it is beyond doubt that a considerable majority of the whole population (Indians and Negroes included) were of British descent, and that the English element was much greater than that of other Britons.

Nor is there any question that the influence of the English was far in excess of their actual numerical strength in the population. The fact that the English were preponderant among the earliest immigrants, as in Virginia and New England, meant that the eighteenth-century German or Irishman found a pattern of life already

---

[1] No sharp distinction here can be made of English, Welsh, Scots, and Scotch-Irish, as these peoples have so many family names in common.

laid down for him on English models. English governors enforced English law. The English language prevailed in the schools and courts. Most immigrants learned to speak it in their traffic with the outside world, though among themselves (as among the Dutch in the Mohawk Valley in New York or the 'Pennsylvania Dutch' from Germany) they often fell back on their native tongue. All colonies had some non-British settlers, but they were most numerous in the Middle Atlantic colonies such as New York and Pennsylvania, where pamphlets, periodicals, church services, and private academies not infrequently used Dutch or German.

The Scotch-Irish, so called, have a story of their own, and a very heroic one it was. They were, for the most part, Scottish Presbyterians who had settled in the 'plantations' of Ulster, but had been driven by poverty to seek new homes overseas. More than any other immigrant element they settled in the western backwoods, and perhaps their characteristic merits and faults were due more to environment than to racial origin. They were bold, adventurous, and enduring, the most staunch and stalwart of men, but often reckless, defiant of legal authority, and given to waging war with the savage Indians in a manner hardly less savage. The bond of a common language and of a common Protestantism tied them closely to the English colonists, especially to the English Puritans, and they can hardly be considered a separate national community.

Although physical differences prevented, and still prevent, racial assimilation, in one sense the Negro slave became the most 'English' of them all. If he had a native African culture to lose, it was forgotten on the voyage to America. Only in the West Indies and, to a less degree, on the rice plantations of South Carolina did he retain any African words at all. His religion became whatever type of Christianity his masters might choose to teach him. Old beliefs might linger in the form of superstition and conjuring, but on the Sabbath he was, as his descendants still are, the most devout of evangelical Christians. Under slavery he took whatever first name his master gave him; when free, with a family name now necessary, he usually borrowed his master's. The beautiful music of the spirituals, the greatest Negro contribution yet made to world civilization, was developed after his enforced immigration to America. Just as the Negro in Haiti, even in the act of rebelling against France, boasted of his

'Latin' culture, so did the Negro in Barbados or in Carolina adopt the ideas, along with the cast-off clothing, of his English masters.

This is not to deny that there is a characteristic racial quality in the songs of the plantation Negro, in his folklore and animal stories of the 'Uncle Remus' type as well as in his modern triumphs as poet, musician, and actor. He may well have given an unconscious coloring and twist to English civilization. But English civilization, and that alone, was the material with which he worked. Even the traditional Negro dialect is much more like seventeenth-century English, as spoken by white men of the servant class, than like a blend of English and African.

The Negro 'hit' was court English in Elizabeth's time; the supposed Negro words 'dem,' 'dey,' 'dat,' for them, they, that, appear in verses written in the modern dialect of Surrey. African speech has left hardly a trace even upon dialect in the United States. Slave speech caught its first accents from the bond servants and convicts who worked alongside the Negro and from illiterate overseers.[2]

Although the American colonies were largely English they were not a complete mirror of all phases of English life. Emigrants left from every shire, though among the Puritan settlements the eastern counties seem to have sent the greatest number. Local English differences tended to disappear where Yorkshire, Devonshire, and Kent lived side by side in a new continent. More important than differences of place were differences of class. Very few of the British aristocracy settled overseas themselves, though several noblemen promoted plantations and helped induce other men to emigrate. Life for the rich was too comfortable to make a venture in the wilderness attractive. Peasants also, attached to the soil by long ancestral custom, are usually reluctant emigrants. It is the townsman, the 'burgess,' who moves most readily to a new home. Many writers have called America an extension of the British middle class; this certainly contains some truth, but needs closer analysis.

In general, English emigrants to America in the seventeenth and eighteenth centuries fall into two economic divisions: those who fared overseas at their own cost, and those who had to be assisted. As the transatlantic voyage was costly, those who financed the trip were apt

[2] E. Eggleston, *The Transit of Civilization* (1933 reprint), p. 112.

to demand years of service in return. Indentured servants and contract laborers served for a fixed term, very much as apprentices did in the Middle Ages, and thenceforward were free men. Convict labor was sometimes employed on the plantations, though chiefly in the West Indies. It should never be forgotten that some of these convicts were men of high character who had been condemned for political offenses, such as participation in Monmouth's rebellion. On the mainland, at least, they made but an inconsiderable part of the population. Religious refugees might come from any social class, but most of the English Puritans and French Huguenots were townsfolk, so this element reinforced the predominantly middle-class character of the new settlements. It would probably be a fair guess that about half of the American people, of colonial stock, are descended from moderately well-to-do artisans, yeoman farmers, merchants, or professional men, and most of the rest from town laborers, apprentices, and indentured servants. But these latter, though scarcely middle class in the old country, often rose to a fair degree of prosperity and became independent farmers or merchants in the new.

It was in the sphere of religion that the English colonies differed most greatly from England. Certain of the colonies, to be sure, maintained the established Church of England. Virginia and other Southern colonies were Anglican from the start, and Maryland and New York became for a time preponderantly so. But Puritanism took an Independent or Congregationalist form in New England, breaking altogether the ties with the old establishment. Presbyterians were numerous among the Scotch-Irish of the frontier. There were many Quakers in Pennsylvania and her neighboring colonies. Baptists were common in several colonies, and there was a growing number of Methodists, though neither sect then had anything like the relative numerical importance which both enjoy today. Many of the Dutch clung to their old national Reformed Church. There was a sprinkling of German and Swedish Lutherans and of German Moravians and Mennonites. What England called 'dissent' and 'non-conformity' was far more marked in the new country than in the old.

One reason why all attempts at religious exclusiveness broke down in America was the wide variety of sects and the fact that no one of them towered above the rest in importance. The persecuted Puritan could flee from Virginia to Massachusetts. The persecuted Quaker could flee from Massachusetts to Pennsylvania. The Catholic found refuge in Maryland and the Baptist in Rhode Island. Rhode Island, as we have noted, had no religious establishment at all. Maryland, so long as it remained under Lord Baltimore's influence, tolerated all Trinitarian Christians. Pennsylvania, New York, and the Carolinas were, in the main, highly tolerant. Every shade of religious belief could find refuge somewhere, though not, as yet, everywhere. The English Government, though giving general support to the interests of the Church of England, wisely did not imitate the French policy of barring the colonies to heretics. What persecution there was in English America was local and temporary. The tolerant atmosphere of the eighteenth century dissolved nearly all remaining restrictions on religious freedom.

In a word, one might summarize colonial America as a string of mainly English settlements with a disproportionate representation of the middle-class and dissenting Protestant elements of the English population. Yet by the time of the American Revolution it was evident that there were wide differences between American and English ways. Today the divergence has become still wider, nor can it be wholly accounted for by the coming in of new immigrants from continental Europe, for if America is not altogether like England, Scotland, or Ireland, still less does she resemble Germany, Italy, or Poland. What forces have brought about this difference?

The first, and unquestionably the most important, of these forces was the wilderness. This had a double effect. It daunted at the start not only the faint-hearted and the physically infirm but those as well who valued the quiet life of a scholar or the lively pleasures of court or city more than the chance of a career in a rough new country. Thus it tended to select certain types, such as the restless, the adventurous, the discontented; those who were at odds with Church or State or social custom. Again, it imposed on all who came a simple way of life, close to physical realities, in which luxuries and refinements had to be sacrificed. In many ways, pioneer societies are alike. The first settlers of later British colonies, such as Canada, Australia, and New Zealand, lived over again many experiences of the first Virginians and the Pilgrim Fathers of Plymouth. It is scarcely surprising that even today observers find many common traits in the American, the Canadian, and the Australian.

One effect of pioneer conditions is to level social ranks. No one can be excused from manual labor when the combined efforts of a whole community are scarcely sufficient to win security and comfort for them all. Our twentieth-century problem, even in new communities, is to find work enough to employ everyone. In seventeenth-century America there was the opposite problem of finding hands enough to do the necessary work. Drake, the greatest of the Elizabethan sea captains, said, 'I should like to see the gentleman that will refuse to set his hand to a rope. I must have the gentlemen to hale and draw with the mariners.' Captain John Smith told the idlers in Virginia, 'He who will not work, neither shall he eat.' The European aristocrat, the 'gentleman of leisure,' seemed a traitor to the community. The idea that work was not only the doom but the duty of every son of Adam became an American tradition; a tradition which in our own time keeps even the millionaire of sixty going daily to his office.

American democracy was not deliberately introduced. On the contrary, many purposeful attempts were made to plant aristocracy in the new soil. In the previous chapter mention was made of the quaint feudal constitution prescribed in vain for Carolina. The Dutch of New Netherland gave vast estates to patroons, just as the French in Quebec tried to establish their seignorial system as it existed in the land of the Grand Monarch. Various speculating 'proprietors' often dreamed of leaving to their heirs a lordly principality.

Even the New England Puritans, for all their self-governing churches and their disdain of bishops and kings, did not at first understand the very democracy they were shaping. What they wanted to create was a theocracy, a government by the will of God as revealed in his Holy Word. The magistrates who were to interpret and enforce that will should have much honor and implicit obedience unless they proved unfaithful to their calling. The influential minister John Cotton agreed with his master in theology, John Calvin, that an aristocracy was to be preferred to either absolute monarchy or unrestricted democracy. 'Democracy,' he wrote, 'I do not conceyve that ever God did ordeyne . . . If the people be governors, who shall be governed?'

The aristocracy, under the theocratic label, which the Puritans desired and which existed for some time in Massachusetts in the days of the stern and able Governor John Winthrop, was not, indeed, the traditional rule by the gentry. The gentry might have a large part in it, but only if they were godly men. The Puritan clergy and the holders of legal office were to be the true 'judges in Israel.' Seditious and libelous speeches against authority were punished in New England exactly as in old England, by stocks or pillory for minor offenses, and by flogging, branding, and ear-cropping for serious or repeated defiance. There was an element of popular election in the government, it is true, but this was limited not only by the usual property qualification but by the additional condition of active church membership.

But the Puritan theocracy was not destined to endure for more than a few decades. The people of Plymouth and of Rhode Island were of a milder temper than the stalwarts of Massachusetts Bay, and to Massachusetts itself there came new colonists who sought rather a better living for themselves than the building of a New Zion.[3] Along the western frontier of the colony arose a new breed of men, rough, simple, practical, and democratic; in the words of Vernon Parrington, the 'Puritan' was being transformed into the 'Yankee,' and there seems warrant for his conclusion that cheap land and self-help created an economic democracy that rendered any form of political aristocracy impossible in the long run. The fisher folk of the shore and the foresters and trappers of the Maine woods were also natural democrats.

Although English settlement in colonial times extended only to the Appalachian ranges, in contrast to the bolder ventures of the Spaniards and the French, there was even in the English colonies in the seventeenth and eighteenth centuries a marked sectional difference which often flared out into political hostility. The Westerners complained that colonial governors and legislatures would not protect them from the Indians and would not give them representation

[3] Cotton Mather tells of a minister who spoke of religious truth as being the 'main end of planting this wilderness,' whereupon a settler called out, 'Sir, you are mistaken, you think you are preaching to the people at the Bay [Boston]; our main end was to catch fish.' See T. J. Wertenbaker, *The First Americans* (1927), p. 111.

in proportion to their growing numbers in the colonial legislatures. The Easterners retorted that the frontiersmen brought the Indian wars on themselves by greedy land-grabbing, and that property and culture should be considered, as well as mere population, in any system of representation.

In writings of Colonel William Byrd of Virginia in the early eighteenth century one finds many amusing pictures of frontier democracy, especially among those who had left the stricter rule of Virginia to settle over the line in North Carolina.

Wherever we passed we constantly found the Borderers laid it to Heart if their Land was taken into Virginia; they chose rather to belong to Carolina, where they pay no Tribute, either to God or to Caesar . . . [One magistrate] taking upon [himself] to order a fellow to the Stocks, for being disorderly in his Drink, was, for his intemperate zeal, carry'd thither himself . . . They are rarely guilty of Flattering or making any Court to their governours, but treat them with all the Excesses of Freedom and Familiarity.

This influence of the frontier on American life has been the special study of a whole school of American historians. Possibly some of them may have exaggerated its importance, but without question it is a key to much that is most characteristic of the American. With what faults does the world reproach him? Rudeness, lawlessness, wastefulness, and preoccupation with material gain; the faults of the frontiersman. With what merits does the world credit him? Initiative, energy, self-reliance, and indomitable cheerfulness in misfortune; the virtues of the successful pioneer. What other qualities, of themselves neither good nor evil, but capable of being either, are generally attributed to him? Love of change, appetite for novelty and experiment, impatience with custom and tradition, 'rugged individualism,' a boyish delight in physical sport, and a hero-worshipping admiration for spectacular feats; the qualities one would *a priori* expect of a frontier settlement. The fact that the typical American humor, as in Mark Twain, is the 'tall story,' such as might be told to amuse a lumber camp where each man tries to 'cap' the tale last told, is not without significance. It is national in the same way that the epigram is characteristically French or the bull is natively Irish.

Quite apart from these nebulous and debatable questions of national psychology, however, the influence of pioneer conditions can be traced very concretely on certain specific institutions. Take, for example, the question of the land laws and systems of land tenure. English land law in the seventeenth century was a jungle of technicalities, many of them relics of medieval feudal tenures. New complexities were added during the period of colonization by the privileges of chartered companies and proprietors in the early overseas settlements. Quit rents and other relics of proprietorship long remained to vex the American farmer. Unsuccessful experiments in communal farming were made by the early settlers of both Virginia and Plymouth. The principle of primogeniture prevailed in several of the colonies. Yet eventually land law in America tended towards plain individual ownership, freed of all limitations and technicalities, with complete freedom to sell and bequeath at will. Simple systems of registry made it as easy to transfer land as any other property. Jefferson and other reformers were able, during the eighteenth century, to root out primogeniture and substitute the equal rights of all children.

There was one institution in the colonies which operated in the opposite direction from democracy. That was, of course, chattel slavery. The English slave trade began with the African voyages of Sir John Hawkins, though this was merely an encroachment on an already flourishing Spanish traffic. The Spaniards had at first enslaved the Indians, but had later turned to Africa, partly because the Indian was a poor plantation hand, dying off rapidly in a condition of routine slave labor, and partly because the Spanish Government itself awoke to a belated sense of duty and put forth ordinances to save the Indians from the selfish greed of the conquistadores. The English plantations in the West Indies, like the Spanish, French, Dutch, and Danish, were worked by slaves from the start. For a time political captives and other convicts of British birth worked alongside Negro slaves, but this temporary enslavement of the white convict soon disappeared, leaving the labor in the cane fields entirely to the African.

In 1619 the Dutch sold to the Virginians the first cargo of slaves to labor in an English colony on the mainland. Until the end of the seventeenth century, slavery was the exception rather than the rule in Virginia, Maryland, and other American continental settlements. Planters made much use of the labor of indentured servants from England, who were bondsmen for a fixed term of years and by their own consent.[4] But successive deliveries of slaves made the eighteenth century a golden one for both slave trader and plantation owner. The percentage of Negroes to the whole American population was about twice as great at the end of the colonial period as it is now. Since the natural increase of white man and black in America is not very dissimilar, the higher birth rate of the Negro being offset by a higher mortality rate, this difference is almost wholly due to the cessation of the slave trade early in the nineteenth century.[5] Thereafter the constant stream of European immigration had no offset in corresponding immigration from Africa.

All shipping communities took part in the slave trade: the Spaniard, the Dutchman, the Englishman, the Yankee. A curious triangle of trade was the sale of West Indian molasses to make Yankee rum, which in turn was sold in Africa in exchange for slaves. The British Government deliberately fostered and encouraged both the slave trade and the slave plantation system. Slaves were not always taken directly from Africa; in many cases they were re-imported into the mainland colonies after having been seasoned and acclimated in the West Indies. During the colonial period no colony refused to take slaves; Massachusetts and Georgia, it is true, at their very beginning tried to keep out slavery, but the religious scruples of the early Puritans in the former case, and the humanitarian objections of Oglethorpe in the latter, proved unavailing in the long run. The reason why most of the slaves found their way to the Southern colonies was wholly economic. The small farm system of New England was not well adapted to slave labor; the slave could only be a general farm laborer or a personal servant, and he was not an efficient all-round farmer, while few Yankee pioneers could afford the luxury of household servants. Only on large plantations, where gang labor could be employed under overseers, was slavery a direct source of

[4] At least in theory, always by their own consent, but during the seventeenth century there was frequent complaint that boys and drunken sailors were kidnapped into service abroad.

[5] Even after the legal slave trade ceased in 1808 there was much smuggling, but importation was at nothing like the eighteenth-century rate.

profit. Where the climate permitted the growth of sugar cane, rice, or tobacco, there, and there only, did slavery take firm root.

The plantation system also permitted the concentration of great wealth in a few hands, and thus made possible the luxury slave, who was butler, coachman, or footman in a great household. A great estate in Jamaica or South Carolina came to resemble a feudal manor. Like the manor, the plantation was practically self-sustaining. It not only raised its own food but made provision for making clothing, clouting shoes, building cottages, casting candles, mixing soap, making horseshoes and nails on the estate. The owner or master was 'monarch of all he surveyed' when at home, which gave him a sense of dignity and power that raised noble souls to chivalry and degraded baser ones into tyranny. Like the feudal baron, he was impatient of control from above and a great friend to freedom for himself and his own class; as Burke pointed out, freedom to the slaveowner is doubly dear since it is his personal badge of rank and dignity. There is, or should be, therefore, nothing surprising in the paradoxical appeal of the Jamaica legislature to self-government and the 'rights of Englishmen' when the British Parliament at last developed a conscience and began to restrict colonial slavery in the West Indies; a Polish noble would have protested with the same angry sincerity if a king had interposed his authority to free the serfs.

The West Indies and the seaboard of South Carolina were, however, the extreme exceptions. Most mainland colonists, even in the South, owned no slaves at all. Most slaves were held, as Professor Phillips has pointed out,[6] in small lots of one, two, or three Negro families. The future possibilities of the cotton estate were still unrealized, and the tobacco culture could almost as readily be carried out on small farms as on large estates, while the sugar, rice, and indigo plantations took up relatively little space. The great tobacco estates of Virginia and Maryland ceased where the plain gave way to the broken country of the mountains. Even in the Carolinas and in Georgia, the back country had but a minority of Negroes.

One effect of Negro slavery was to make the term and idea of 'servant' distasteful to the white laborer. 'Help,' 'hired man,' 'hired girl' and similar euphemisms took its place. The term 'master' for

[6] U. B. Phillips, *American Negro Slavery*. See also his *Life and Labor in the Old South*.

employer, till then in general use, began to drop out of the American vocabulary, for it now suggested 'owner.' Less and less, as time went on, was the immigrant willing to become an indentured servant and labor along with the Negro slave. As convict slavery, Indian slavery, and indentured apprenticeship became rare, the idea gradually took possession of the colonial mind that only those of Negro blood could or should be held to unwilling service; what had been to the seventeenth century merely a distinction of legal status now became a clear-cut distinction of race.

The institution of slavery apart, most of the conditions of American settlement tended towards the leveling of class distinctions. Perhaps the real American revolution was not the severing of the merely political tie between Great Britain and thirteen of her American colonies, but the slow and peaceful building up of a new social order, simpler and more democratic than that of any European country at the time, in the century and a half that preceded the separation.

The early Puritan founders of New England, some of them graduates of Cambridge University, had a fairly high average of culture, though it was often narrowed by religious prejudice. They believed in an educated ministry; the clergyman must have such schooling that no layman could convict him of ignorance of the learned tongues. They believed it also essential that even the layman should be able to read the Scriptures. Whatever one may think of Calvinism in its other aspects, it has certainly been the cornerstone of many a school system. The Dutch, Scotch, and Swiss Calvinists had been pioneers in the creation of publicly supported schools, and the Puritan settlers of New England were familiar with all these undertakings. But theirs was a greater urgency. The preamble of the Massachusetts School Law of 1647 confessed that public provision for schools was necessary 'that learning may not be buried in the grave of our fathers.' It added, in a phrase that now brings a smile, that such ignorance would give great opportunity to 'the ould deluder Satan.' To thwart this wily potentate, and balk him of Yankee souls, each township of fifty householders was to have a schoolmaster to teach reading and writing, and each township of a hundred householders to have a Latin grammar school. The latter provision could not always be enforced in the outlying frontier districts where the four R's—reading, writing, 'rithmetic, and religion—seemed a quite sufficient education without any spice of Latin.

Harvard College in Cambridge, Massachusetts, and William and Mary College, in Williamsburg, Virginia, were the first foundations in the sphere of higher education. Harvard was started as a venture in public education in 1636, chiefly with the aim of maintaining a trained ministry. John Harvard's gifts enlarged the resources of the college and gave it a permanent name. Yale, founded in 1701, was in part a conservative protest against the increasing theological liberalism of Harvard. The eighteenth century brought still other foundations, a College of New Jersey in Princeton (now Princeton University), which met the needs of the Presbyterians of the Middle colonies; a King's College in New York City (now Columbia University), mainly under Church of England influence; a Philadelphia academy, which eventually became the University of Pennsylvania, without direct denominational ties. As the century advanced, the preponderantly theological emphasis declined in all the higher schools, and more and more students went to them with no intention of entering the ministry. The colleges became more 'Hellenic' and less 'Hebraic,' less professional and more generally cultural in aim. In this respect American higher education was but following a course parallel to that of the older European universities. Towards the end of the century one finds complaints that most of the college students were 'unconverted' and had never joined in communion with any Christian fellowship.

Every student of American history has heard of Governor William Berkeley's boast that there were no free schools or printing presses in seventeenth-century Virginia and his hope that none would come there. This was, however, only an individual expression of opinion by a peppery old reactionary, and, to do even Berkeley justice, he was not using 'free school' as equivalent to 'school.' There were a number of schools in Virginia in his time, and perhaps only Massachusetts and Connecticut had a higher educational standard than Virginia. What he meant was that the schools of Virginia were, like most of those in England at that time, voluntary schools supported by the fees of the students. Even so, he exaggerated, as at least two endowed free schools then existed in Virginia.

It is true, however, that the Massachusetts principle of public education was long in spreading beyond New England. New York, which had made a timid beginning in public education during the Dutch period, fell back into complete individualism under English rule. With trivial exceptions, the Middle and Southern colonies depended on the private school, the charity school, and the private tutor. The Society for the Propagation of the Gospel did something to promote learning as well as piety in the interest of the Church of England, and some of the clergy took pains to give instruction to the poor of their parish. Many of the wealthier planters, in Virginia and in South Carolina especially, sent their children to the 'public schools' and universities of England. Others kept private tutors, the more penurious ones getting cheap instruction from qualified indentured servants. Girls rarely went to any of the larger schools; if they were not taught entirely at home they attended 'dame schools' which taught the rudiments of reading and writing together with knitting and the catechism to very small classes of little girls. The American institution of coeducation had not yet become part of the national tradition.

On the whole, the educational effort of the colonies was creditable. In spite of the material handicaps of a pioneer environment, the proportion of children taught to read and write was at least as great as in most of the countries of western Europe, and the tax-supported public education of Massachusetts and Connecticut was distinctly an advance over the completely *laissez-faire* education of England. The colleges, it is true, were small and poorly endowed: half Latin academy, half theological seminary. They had neither the prestige nor the resources of Oxford or Cambridge; yet there seems some ground for the belief that the Harvard boys had to work much harder at their books than did most of the English university students. College was not yet in America what it was already beginning to be in England (and often became in twentieth-century America), a pleasant and leisurely way for a gentleman to spend a few youthful years before tackling the serious business of life. Overwork and overseriousness marked these early colleges and Latin schools, where holidays were rare and living conditions of a Spartan severity. Discipline seems to have been of about equal rigor in English and American schools; the use of the rod was an English tradition that crossed the Atlantic with undiminished vigor. In the seventeenth century, students at Harvard, unless they were of age, were still subject to corporal punishment.

The mere matter of schooling is not, of course, the whole of culture. The student of American colonial history will want to inquire also into the level of arts, the struggle of science against superstition, the facility of self-expression of the common man and also of his intellectual leaders. A verdict is not easy. The evidence is abundant, but conflicting and even confusing, as in the instance of one of the most important of the Puritan leaders, Cotton Mather. He was to some extent responsible for the disgraceful witchcraft panic in the town of Salem, where nineteen men and women were hanged for alleged dealings with the devil. He was also one of the first to use preventive inoculation for smallpox, which he boldly introduced into his own family against the current opinion of conservative physicians. Now, how shall we rate such a man? Was he in advance of his age or behind it?

Three colonial Americans, at least, ranked with the great thinkers of Europe. One of them, Benjamin Thompson (later Count Rumford), must be credited mainly to the Old World, since his scientific achievements are associated with his prolonged residence in Europe. But Benjamin Franklin was so thoroughly and characteristically American that some writers have even considered him the most typically American figure in history. Jonathan Edwards, for all the grim extravagance of his theology, is acknowledged to be a past master of logic and metaphysics. It is an interesting fact that the same environment which produced the sage and mundane Franklin, who never rose above and never fell below the level of common sense, should have produced also the agonized visions of the mystical prophet Edwards. There is much vigorous prose in the writing of the founders of the new colonies, such as Bradford, Winthrop, and John Smith, who contributed vigorous descriptions of the American scene as well as indispensable materials to the historian.

It is true that the colonists had little opportunity to hear the best music, and that they were dependent on Europe for painting and sculpture. But they had not lost touch with beauty. There were few buildings in America between 1820 and 1900 that can compare in grace and simple dignity with the homes and little churches of the seventeenth and eighteenth centuries. The recent reconstruction of colonial Williamsburg, some of whose buildings were designed by Sir Christopher Wren, is a revelation of good taste and gracious living. The furniture, china, glass, and metalwares of colonial times are valued today at extravagant prices, not only from an antiquarian love of rare things but also from an artistic appreciation of beautiful things. Most of the architectural forms used in America, however, and most of the styles of furniture were borrowed from Europe. The chief American innovation was that of building houses in wood, furnished in abundance by the native forests, in place of the stone or brick cottages of the English countryside. Public buildings, however, were usually built of durable materials.

The fate of the English language on American soil has been the subject of many studies, and need not long detain us here. Some writers, such as H. L. Mencken, have even spoken of an 'American language' as distinct from English. The differences between the two in accent, pronunciation, vocabulary, and idiom are indeed considerable; but, if they amount to a difference in language, one must speak also of the 'languages' of Lancashire, Somerset, lowland Scotland, and several other parts of Great Britain, and perhaps even of the 'Yankee,' 'Southern,' and 'Western' languages in the United States, since the sectional differences within the two countries are as great as any differences between them.

One point might be noted. Not all the differences are novel Americanisms introduced in the restless atmosphere of the New World; some, on the contrary, are evidences of American conservatism. In the Southern mountains, especially in the western parts of Virginia, one can still hear words and phrases that were in current English use in the seventeenth century but have dropped out of modern British speech. Too often it is forgotten that, while America does indeed branch off from England, it is from the England of the seventeenth century and not of the nineteenth or twentieth, and that England also has been altering her language in the meantime, not perhaps so rapidly but quite as constantly.

∘ XVIII ∘

AMERICA—FRENCH OR BRITISH?

TWICE in history have France and England been persistent enemies. The first occasion was the great medieval dynastic struggle which we call the Hundred Years' War.[1] The second was the commercial, colonial, and naval rivalry which began with the coming of William III to the British throne and did not end until Napoleon went into exile after Waterloo. To be sure, there were many years of peace between 1688 and 1815, but likewise there were long periods of peace during the fourteenth century; the significant fact is that when there was war in either period France and England were always to be found on opposite sides. In a word, they were at all times opponents, if not on the battlefield then in the councils of diplomacy, very much as France and Germany have been in recent years.

The European aspects of this national contest are elsewhere discussed;[2] here we are concerned only with the colonial aspect, and especially the American. By the beginning of the eighteenth century it was plain enough that the northern parts of America would be either British or French. Spain, Portugal, and Holland, the only other colonizers, had practically attained the limits of their colonizing activity and their chief sphere of interest lay in the tropics; but everywhere in eastern North America France was a formidable opponent to Britain.

Superficially, the odds might seem to have been with France. The France of Louis XIV was unquestionably the greatest power in Europe. To hold the ambition of that monarch in check, the British had to find allies in the Dutch, the Austrians, and many other continental peoples. France was a larger country than Great Britain, much more populous, perhaps wealthier, beyond question more mili-

[1] See Chapter VII.
[2] See Chapters XIV, XV and XXVII.

199

tary. The centralized government of France, a drawback in time of peace, was an advantage in war; the king combined diplomacy and strategy in one person and he was not troubled by parliamentary opposition or the consequent rise and fall of ministries.

In the colonies, too, France had certain advantages. She had started her colonizing work in America long before the English were active there. The territory opened up by French enterprise was incomparably vaster in extent than the little string of seaboard settlements which England had planted. A tremendous empire of the waterways, including the whole region of the Mississippi, the Ohio, the Great Lakes, and the St. Lawrence, was, at least on diplomatic paper, French.[3] Within that area the power of the French Government was unhampered by local rights and privileges. While English governors were bargaining and bickering with their American subjects, French governors were merely issuing commands to theirs.

Another advantage which the French had was their generally amicable relationship with the Indian tribes. More than any other colonizers, the French have succeeded in getting along in friendly fashion with native peoples, not only in the eighteenth century but since. But the success of the French in America had another cause. The Indians noticed that the Spaniards came hunting gold and enslaving natives to work in the mines; that the English drove them away from their hunting fields (sometimes with a legal pretext and sometimes without) and settled in compact farming communities; whereas the French, for the most part, were content merely to trade in furs and for the rest to leave the natives alone.

But to offset these French advantages, the British had two that were decisive: sea power and colonial population. That the French were stronger than the British by land mattered little in the colonial struggle, for the colonies could be reached only by sea. Louis XIV and his successors were much more interested in the European struggle than in the colonial; they considered colonies as valuable economic ventures and strategically convenient to hold in check their English enemies, but they regarded a new French province on the Rhine or even a dynastic claim in Spain or Italy as incomparably

[3] Note the great number of French place names on the map of this region today.

more important than all America. The greatest energies of France were exhausted by the military struggle for European ascendancy, first against Austria and Spain and later against Prussia. Her geographic position, with exposed frontiers, as well as the ambitions of her kings, prevented her from regarding colonial empire as more than a secondary issue, a desirable but incidental prize of victory.

With the British it was otherwise. Taught by the experience of the Hundred Years' War, they wisely relinquished all ambition for conquest on the European continent. Except for certain naval bases, incident to sea power, they stood entirely aloof from the costly territorial scramble which engaged (and still engages) the attention of the continental powers. When they intervened, as they frequently did, in continental wars, it was either to secure the balance of power by preventing the rise of any single empire to the domination of the continent or to strike a blow at a rival in colonial expansion.

Colonial expansion which is associated with sea power, mercantile marine, and commerce is much more soundly based than colonial expansion which is a side issue to European military ambition. The economic roots of the British colonies ran deeper. Much of the wealth of France was tied up in uneconomic fashion, by gild regulations in manufacturing and by feudal usages in agriculture; British wealth was much more fluid, much more easily available for new enterprises. The British monarch and Court cost less than the French, the British army cost less, there was less peril of foreign invasion, less wasteful extravagance among the aristocracy, a cheaper religious establishment, a better system of taxation, a more powerful middle class. A practical, perhaps prosaic, commercial spirit was evident in the policies of the government; eighteenth-century Britain looked at the world and its problems largely through the same businessman's spectacles that the Dutch used.

Besides the advantage which the British had in being able, and inclined, to concentrate their main efforts on sea power and overseas expansion, they had the advantage of actual settlement. Though French America was so much more extensive than British America, most of it was wilderness inhabited only by the Indian tribes. There was a large compact settlement in what is today the province of Quebec, a small one at the mouth of the Mississippi, and a still smaller one in Acadia. The upper course of the Mississippi, the Ohio

Valley, and the Great Lakes region saw the Frenchman only as soldier, missionary, trapper, trader, or explorer, all of them migrants who were few in number and formed almost no permanent settlements. Away from the waterways there were vast areas, as large as modern American states, which had no French inhabitants at all. Canada, the most populous part of French America, had a population of about 20,000 at the time of the Treaty of Utrecht in 1713; the British American colonies on the mainland had a population in the neighborhood of 300,000. New England alone had almost five times as many white inhabitants as Canada.

There were good reasons why French America grew so slowly. The Frenchman has always been a reluctant emigrant from his own country, as he is today. Many, moreover, who might have been willing to break the strong ties of affection which bound them to the ancestral home, were little attracted by what New France had to offer. The English colonies offered religious freedom (at least locally), cheap land, local self-government, a lax and easy social system; whereas the French colonies would admit no heretics, they had a land system as feudal as any in western Europe, they granted no measure of home rule. The French Huguenots, an extremely capable group of men, enriched with their labor England, Prussia, Holland, South Africa, New York, South Carolina, and many other lands, since both France and the French colonies refused to tolerate them.

To the British colonists the European wars of the age were known by the names of their rulers. Thus they thought of the War of the League of Augsburg as 'The war we fought when King William ruled'—hence King William's War. Similarly, the War of the Spanish Succession became Queen Anne's War, and the War of the Austrian Succession, King George's War. The last great struggle with France, which coincided with the Seven Years' War in Europe, had a name of its own that marked its unusual importance and its burning memory—the French and Indian War, a war in which the Indian scalping knife and tomahawk were allied with the French bayonet.

The American conflict was, of course, for the control of the West Indies as well as the mainland; as we have already noted, the island colonies were considered by far the more valuable. The French developed flourishing plantations, based on Negro slavery, in Guadeloupe, Martinique, and the western part of the Spanish island of Hispaniola, which the French termed St. Domingo (the modern Haiti). The English island of Jamaica, captured from the Spanish in Cromwell's time, was set about with French and Spanish colonies. Spain, still something of a power in the Caribbean, was frequently an ally of France, and Spain still held Florida, neighbor to Georgia and the Carolinas.

The colonial wars in the days of King William (1689-97) and of Queen Anne (1701-13) were inconclusive, but on the whole the advantage lay with the British. By the Treaty of Utrecht in 1713 the British rights to Newfoundland and to the fur-trading posts around Hudson's Bay were conceded by France, and the colony of Acadia (Nova Scotia) was transferred from the French to the British. The British also got control of the island of St. Kitts in the West Indies, which the French had hitherto contested. They obtained from Spain a favorable commercial treaty, giving them the right to ship slaves from Africa to Spanish America and to send one ship a year of general merchandise.

In the meantime the Act of Union between England and Scotland in 1707 had transformed the English colonies into British colonies. Though Scotland had but little share in the original building up of the American colonies, and her independent colonial venture at Panama had been a complete failure, she now blended her efforts with those of England with such success that very few in the later eighteenth century and still fewer in the nineteenth thought of England as a predominant partner in empire building. The influence worked both ways. Not only did Scottish influence play a great and growing part in imperial administration, but colonial trade stimulated the growth of Scottish commerce.

The interlude of peace which followed the exhausting War of the Spanish Succession, a peace broken on the continent by minor wars but preserved for Britain by Walpole's policy of keeping out of avoidable conflicts, ended in 1739. War was forced on the reluctant ministry by popular clamor, an interesting evidence that, contrary to a very common belief, it is not always governments which make wars and nations which desire peace! Spain again was the center of difficulty; the British had abused their commercial privileges in Spanish America by much lawless smuggling, while the Spanish officials, at once feeble and violent, had punished some of the smugglers cruelly, without, however, being able to check the traffic. The severe treatment of a certain Captain Jenkins, whose ear had been cut off as a vigorous warning to those who engaged in it, stirred so much popular sympathy in England that the war which followed a few years later bore commonly the name of 'The War of Jenkins's Ear,' which has the same partial degree of appropriateness as if the American war with Germany in 1917 had been called 'The War of the *Lusitania.*' This petty colonial war with Spain was soon caught up into the much greater conflict over the Austrian Succession, or King George's War.

Colonial opinion took war for granted. Peace had never been considered as more than an armistice, though many hoped that it was an armistice which would long endure. There were frontier disputes for almost every mile of the boundary of French America. The French were blamed for encouraging Indian attacks on British settlements in time of peace. Commercial and national rivalry were intensified by religious bigotry on both sides. Though religious passions did not run as high in the eighteenth century as formerly, New France still refused to tolerate 'heretics' and New England still considered Catholics 'papistical idolators.' An expedition of New Englanders, under the governor of Massachusetts, seized the French fortress of Louisbourg on Cape Breton Island. But in the general peace which was made at Aix-la-Chapelle in 1748 there was a mutual restoration of colonial conquests. France relinquished Madras in India; the British returned Louisbourg in America.

The expected renewal of conflict really began in the colonies before war broke out in Europe. As early as 1755 there were several pitched battles in America. General Braddock, with a mixed force of Virginians [4] and British regulars, was trapped by French and Indians in the backwoods and his army cut to pieces. The British expelled the French settlers from Nova Scotia, the old Acadia, for disloyalty to their new rulers.

As the war spread, British disasters piled up. The Mediterranean base of Minorca fell to the French in 1756. French and Indian raids, directed by the alert and vigorous Montcalm, kept the whole fron-

---

[4] George Washington was the most notable of the colonial officers.

tier of British America in terror. Not until William Pitt became the real (though not the nominal) head of a war administration late in 1756 was there much hope of retrieving the situation. Within a few months all was changed. Pitt used the conflict between Frederick the Great of Prussia and his enemies to keep French attention engaged on the European chessboard, while he gave support to the ablest men he could find, in both India and America, pressing upon them the need for a vigorous aggressive policy. The fleet was kept up to a high degree of efficiency. In 1758 the great French forts of Frontenac, Louisbourg, and Duquesne were captured, and Duquesne was appropriately renamed Pittsburgh.

So long as Quebec held out, however, there was still some hope for New France. In the following year, 1759, young General Wolfe achieved its capture. His own life paid the forfeit, for both Wolfe and the French commander Montcalm were mortally wounded in the battle on the Heights of Abraham. Although on the scale of modern warfare the taking of Quebec was scarcely more than a skirmish, it has been called by some historians the most important battle ever fought on American soil. The French at Montreal held out for several months longer, it is true, but in 1760 all Canada surrendered.

The British fleet in the meantime had been seizing French islands in the West Indies and, after Spain entered the war, Spanish islands as well. Pitt was anxious to have as many colonies as possible under the British flag before peace negotiations began. But his own downfall from power followed very soon after King George III came to the throne. King George and his favorite minister, Lord Bute, both wanted an early peace; they did not share the boundless imperialistic ambition of Pitt. Negotiations for peace began in 1761 and were completed by the Treaty of Paris in 1763.

It is an interesting commentary on the myopic views of the mercantilist statesman of the age that for a long time they hesitated whether to demand from France the little sugar island of Guadeloupe or the vast empire of Canada. Pitt was for keeping both, but those who wanted an end to the war saw the necessity of some compensation to France for her great losses. Guadeloupe and Martinique were turning out immediate profits; Canada was a speculative investment. What tipped the balance in favor of Canada was not so much any vision of the imperial future, as the argument that Canada would prove to be an ampler market for British manufactures.

All mainland North America east of the Mississippi went to Great Britain, even Florida passing into British hands, though Spain was compensated by being given the land which France had claimed west of the Mississippi. France retained Haiti, St. Lucia, Guadeloupe, and Martinique in the West Indies, and two small fishing stations in the Gulf of Saint Lawrence. Great Britain gained, or had confirmed to her, Senegal, and the West Indian islands of Grenada, St. Vincent, Dominica, and Tobago. She returned to Spain the conquests of Cuba and of Manila.

Far more important in the eyes of the men of that time was the British victory over France in India. This epic struggle belongs, however, to a separate phase of the story of Empire.[5]

[5] See below, Chapter XXXIII.

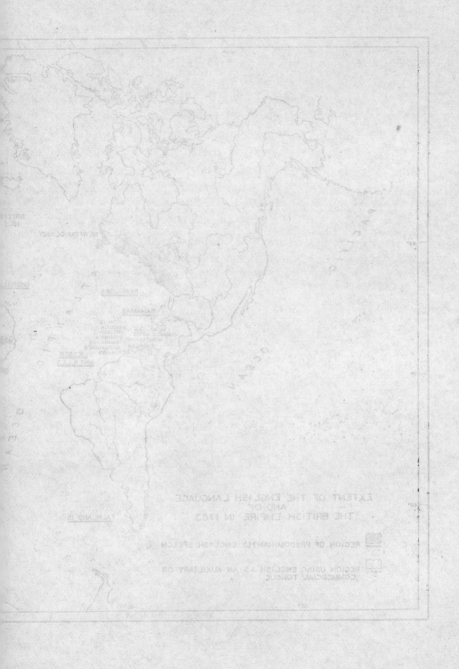

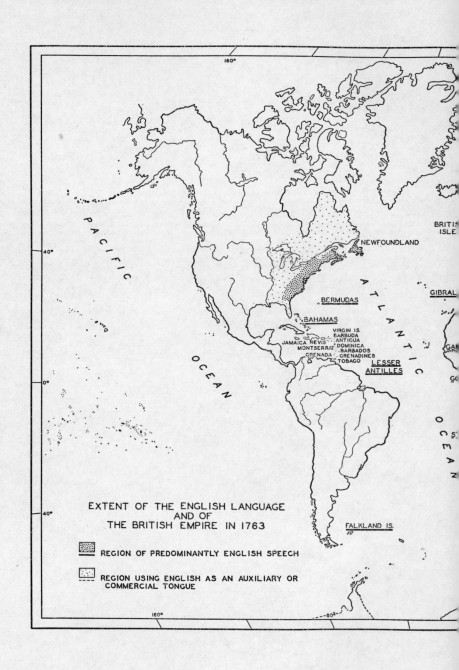

EXTENT OF THE ENGLISH LANGUAGE
AND OF
THE BRITISH EMPIRE IN 1763

REGION OF PREDOMINANTLY ENGLISH SPEECH

REGION USING ENGLISH AS AN AUXILIARY OR
COMMERCIAL TONGUE

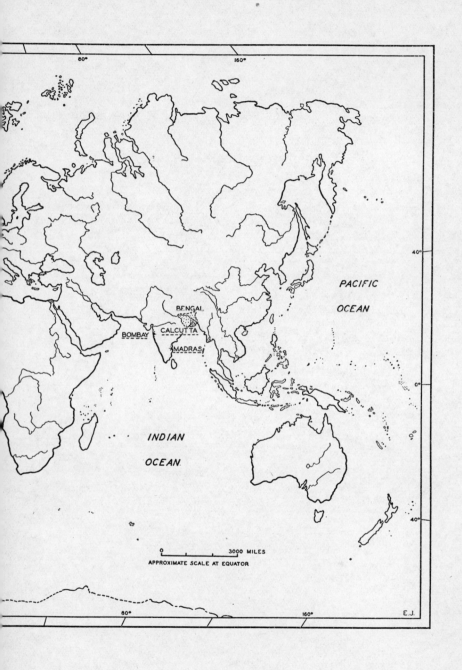

PACIFIC
OCEAN

BENGAL
BOMBAY CALCUTTA
MADRAS

INDIAN

OCEAN

0   3000 MILES
APPROXIMATE SCALE AT EQUATOR

E.J.

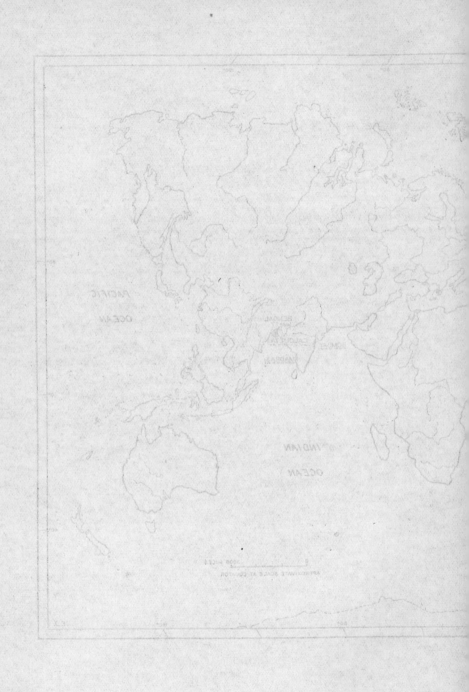

AMERICA—DEPENDENCY OR REPUBLIC?

In human history every question that is settled opens a new one. So long as France remained a dangerous power in the New World there was no question of independence for the English-speaking colonies; whatever grievances the colonists might have, they did not wish to leap from the frying pan of British rule into the fire of an alien French government. But once the French menace was removed, the issues between the motherland and her American colonies became acute. Unfortunately, at this very time, when tactful handling was most required, the British Government began a series of irritating interferences with colonial affairs. The ties of imperial control that had been too lax were now abruptly tightened. From the British point of view this was merely a long overdue attention to imperial duty; from the standpoint of the colonies it looked like deliberate and intentional tyranny.

What were the colonial grievances that first frayed and then snapped the ties of sentiment between Great Britain and her thirteen American mainland colonies? The chief ones may be summed up under the three headings of trade, taxes, and the western lands. Let us look at each of these in turn.

As we have seen, the very essence of colonial policy in the early modern period was the regulation of commerce in the interest of the colonizing power. In this respect British policy differed not at all from that of her rivals, France, Spain, Portugal, the Dutch Republic. In Cromwell's time an ordinance, summing up much previous legislation, was enacted in 1651 with the aim of taking the English carrying trade out of the hands of the Dutch. It provided that colonial goods could be imported into England, Ireland, or other colonies only in English (or English colonial) vessels; that goods from other European countries could be imported only in English ships, or ships owned by the nation whose goods they carried, and that aliens could not engage in the English coastwise trade. In those days the Dutch were the middlemen of Europe, carrying goods from England to France and from France to England and reaping freighters' profits from both. The English wanted the carrier's profit for their own ships.

Cromwell's navigation ordinance was, with a few modifications, made law after the restoration of the monarchy, for his interest in naval and mercantile development was the only part of his policy which the Stuarts approved. The Navigation Act of 1660 permitted a few exceptions to the English monopoly of her overseas trade, if high duties were paid, but certain enumerated commodities, such as sugar, tobacco, and cotton, were to be shipped from English colonies only to England or to other English colonies. Other laws restricted the importation of foreign goods, even in English vessels, to the colonies unless they were first landed in England and then re-exported, and forced colonial exporters to give guarantees that they were not selling enumerated commodities to foreign markets.

This navigation code was not as unjust to the colonies as has sometimes been represented. While it greatly restricted freedom of trade and cut off (had it been always enforced!) a profitable commerce with the Spanish, Dutch, and French colonies, especially in the West Indies, in compensation it gave the English colonists preference against foreigners in the English home market. Colonial shipping also, it should be noted, shared most of the privileges of English shipping. In many ways both the Irish and the Scotch (until the Act of Union) were subject to more discrimination than the Virginians or the New Englanders.

Moreover, the colonists profited by the lax enforcement of the law. So long as New York remained New Netherland it was practically impossible to control the irregular shipment of goods between New England and the Dutch port of New Amsterdam. Even in later times Yankee shippers, evading the law, would buy up surplus quantities of sugar or tobacco and reship them to ports in continental Europe. It is hard to realize the extent to which smuggling took place in the seventeenth and eighteenth centuries. Smuggling was a profitable industry in European waters as well as in the colonies. Sailing vessels of small size carried the world's commerce; they could find port in waters far too shallow to harbor a modern steamer. Contrary winds might prevent the government ships whose business it was to enforce the law from reaching a suspected landing place in time to stop the smugglers, even if the officers had received a 'tip' where to look. The moral support given to the government by public opinion was weak. Men, honorable in every other relation of life, saw no harm in buying goods cheaply because they had not passed the customs; they often regarded the smugglers, or 'free traders' as they were euphemistically called, as social benefactors who helped keep down prices. The hangman himself was scarcely less popular than a revenue officer. Even in time of war, smuggling continued with but few patriotic inhibitions. If this were true of England, one can imagine how much more true it must have been of colonies which had taken no share in the making of the laws which restricted their trade.

The eighteenth century brought new legal restrictions on colonial trade. Since the colonies were designed to be markets for British manufactures, not competitors, every attempt was made to discourage colonial manufacture for export, such as woolens, ironware, and beaver hats. The Molasses Act of 1733 was designed to break up trade between New England and the French sugar islands in the West Indies. The new laws were, however, no better enforced than the older ones. Not until 1764, when a new Sugar Act replaced the old Molasses Act with lower duties but better methods of enforcement, did these laws become a major practical grievance—though they had always been the source of some irritation.

Far more indignation was felt and expressed at the Stamp Act introduced by the ministry of George Grenville in 1765. Its main purpose was to provide funds which would at least partly support a standing army in America. For such an army, now that the French menace had been removed, the colonists had little need and no wish. The Spaniards were distant and the Americans flattered themselves that they better understood Indian warfare than did any European regular troops. Moreover, the Stamp Act seemed a dangerous precedent. Tariffs and customs dues and navigation acts had the excuse that their main purpose was to regulate British trade and promote British shipping; what revenue they yielded was only incidental to this main purpose. But an internal revenue duty was a definite tax, and taxation had hitherto been regarded as the duty of the colonial legislatures. If such 'taxation without representation' were possible, could not an unfriendly Parliament take over the whole field of revenue and leave to the legislatures merely the idle forms of legislative power? Mobs rose against the revenue collectors in almost every mainland colony, and the new Rockingham ministry in the following year repealed the tax, while at the same time asserting not only that such a tax was within the rights of Parliament, but that Parliament had absolute authority in all cases to bind the colonies.

In the Stamp Act debates, no less than three important questions of principle had been raised. The first of these was that of the competence of Parliament to tax colonies or legislate directly for them. The prevalent eighteenth-century British theory might be termed 'the omnipotence of Parliament.' Parliament, on this theory, might for reasons of expediency waive its right to tax and legislate for some particular colony, but the existence of that right was beyond question. The British ministry was also the Imperial ministry; the British Parliament was an Imperial Parliament. Colonial legislatures were minor and subordinate legislatures, like the provincial legislatures of modern Canada.

The American theory was that while the king was King everywhere in his far-flung Empire, Parliament was a local institution of Great Britain. The king's British ministers were his advisers on British and foreign affairs. But there were other legislatures in the Empire besides the British Parliament: not only those of the thirteen American mainland colonies, but also the Irish Parliament and the colonial legislatures of the West Indies. By international law even the smallest independent nation is equally sovereign with the mightiest Power on earth; similarly by the American theory a colonial legislature was equal in status, though not in power and importance, with the Parliament of Great Britain. On any other theory, the Americans would be ruled by men whom they had not chosen and representative government would be at an end.

To combat this argument, the British brought forward the theory of 'virtual representation.' Admittedly, the Americans did not directly choose members to the House of Commons. But what of that? Most Englishmen were without any vote; indeed, whole great cities had no special representation. The House of Lords represented the class of 'Lords, Spiritual and Temporal'; the House of Commons represented the class of commoners. It had at no time been a part of British law or custom that each place should be represented. On this point, at least, the American position was more realistic than the British, though either could be supported by lawyer's arguments. Of what practical use was virtual representation across thousands of miles of salt water, especially on issues on which the economic interests of the mother country and those of her colonies were, or seemed to be, in conflict? When it was urged that Manchester, Birmingham, and Sheffield were not represented in the House of Commons, James Otis gave the common-sense answer, 'If these now so considerable places are not represented, they ought to be!'

The third question at issue between the contending parties was the reserved sphere of personal liberty and individual rights. Both the British and the American colonists agreed that these rights and liberties were very dear, that they should be protected by governments and, if need be, asserted by revolution. But the British contended that the duty to respect these rights was only a moral obligation; the Americans that it was a legal limitation on the powers of Parliament. They claimed that certain constitutional documents and charters, such as Magna Charta and the Bill of Rights, had a sanctity over and above ordinary legislation, which would be invalid if it conflicted with them. Hence, in resisting 'tyrannical' laws of Parliament the colonists were doing nothing contrary to law; they were merely defending the British constitution and the rights of Englishmen against illegal legislation. Some spoke even more generally of 'natural rights,' antecedent to all government. The weakness of the American position lay in the lack of any general agreement on exactly what were the 'indefeasible rights' to which they appealed; the Americans may have thought that they were defending the past, but what they were really doing was to invoke the unborn future. The eventual American Constitution was to embody in its clauses those restrictions on governmental power which the colonists vainly sought to find in the unwritten British constitution.

The Stamp Act is a landmark in American history not only because it provoked a far-reaching controversy on the power of Parliament to lay direct taxes on the colonists but also because it brought about some of the first steps towards colonial union. No common organ of government connected the thirteen colonies; legally they were united only by the authority of the British Crown, which applied just as clearly to the West Indies and to the newly acquired lands in Canada. But under the pressure of the new tax grievance, a 'Stamp Act Congress' of delegates from nine colonies assembled in New York to discuss grievances and petition for redress. It was not a legal body, merely a political convention, but it furnished a precedent for intercolonial federation in the future.

Though the Stamp Act had been repealed, the issue of taxation was raised in another form by Charles Townshend, who, as Chancellor of the Exchequer, introduced a measure for import duties on paint, lead, paper, and tea imported into the colonies, even from British ports. The enforcement of customs duties was made more rigorous, and, what roused the greatest alarm, part of the money thus raised was to be employed in paying the salaries of colonial judges and governors so that they would no longer be dependent on their legislatures. Many of the governors at that time were intensely unpopular. The faults were not wholly on either side. The legislatures were undoubtedly penny-pinchers, with little knowledge of the cost of administering an efficient government, and it must have been exasperating to the best-intentioned governors to find the public services starved for funds. On the other hand, the governors were often appointed not for their knowledge of American affairs but merely to pay off a political debt; they did not identify themselves with American life and interests but kept themselves aloof as if they were ruling over aliens and subjects. This was certainly not true of all, but a single arrogant official in a sensitive community can do harm enough to offset all the efforts of a dozen more tactful men. The colonists felt that if the judges and governors were made independent financially they would henceforth pay no attention to the legislatures. They drew the moral from British history that only control over the purse strings had enabled Parliament to keep the royal power from becoming absolute.

The Townshend Acts, unlike the Stamp Act, were in form customs duties and, as such, less objectionable than an internal revenue tax. But it was so evident that their purpose was revenue rather than regulation of trade that most Americans considered them still taxation.[1] Though most of the duties were later repealed, the tea duty was retained 'to keep up the right' to tax. In 1773 a new Tea Act, passed largely in the interests of the East India Company, which granted that powerful corporation the right to sell tea directly in the American market, roused the fears and resentments of the colonial merchants. Several ports refused to accept cargoes of tea, and at Boston a group of violent young men, disguised as Indians, dumped the tea chests overboard into the harbor. This 'Boston Tea Party,' a trivial affair in itself, was the real starting point of revolution, since it led to acts of coercion that provoked the first armed resistance.

The Coercion Acts of 1774 closed the port of Boston to commerce until reparation was made for the destruction of the tea, reorganized local government in Massachusetts so as to increase the authority of British officials, and provided for the trial of royal officials, accused of offenses, outside the colony where public sentiment was hostile to them. During the same year the new Quebec Act, quite independent in its origin and purpose but unpopular on its own account, was bracketed in the public mind with these other 'intolerable acts.'

To understand why the Quebec Act, intended chiefly to placate the French Canadians, was taken by the English colonists in America as a punitive measure directed against themselves, it is necessary to review briefly the third great grievance of the colonists, the question of the western lands. Under the original seventeenth-century charters certain colonies, notably Virginia, Massachusetts, and Connecticut, were granted a definite extent of seaboard and an indefinite extent of territory to the westward—in the case of Virginia to the northwestward, overlapping the claims of the New Englanders. When the French territories had been conquered, the English colonists took for granted that there now existed no obstacle to their settling beyond the mountains on the wide and fertile forested plains around the Great Lakes, the Ohio, and the Mississippi. To them, the original colonial charters were contracts, morally, if not also legally, binding on the British Government.

[1] Compare the ambiguity of 'tonnage and poundage' in the time of Charles I; Parliament holding such dues to be taxes, while the king denied it. In the later history of the United States similar questions have arisen; for example, were protective tariffs 'revenue measures' or the regulation of trade in the interest of certain groups of producers?

The British, on their part, considered the colonial charters merely as grants which could be modified or cancelled altogether by authority of Parliament. They had no particular desire to have settlers, greedy for land, pouring through the Appalachian passes in the search for new farms. Such pioneers were apt to make trouble with the Indian tribes and thus cause expensive frontier wars and interfere with the fur trade.

Hence in 1763 a royal proclamation set aside the West as an Indian reservation and even required settlers who had already trespassed in that region to withdraw. This restriction was intended to be only temporary, and the wise Earl of Shelburne, who seems to have understood the Americans better than any other British statesman of the time, with the possible exception of Edmund Burke, planned to promote a slow and gradual settlement on lands voluntarily ceded by Indian tribes. But some later ministers treated the passionate land hunger of the frontiersmen with complete indifference and contempt.

The proclamation of 1763 was later supplemented by the Quebec Act of 1774. The boundaries of Quebec were extended over the whole Great Lakes basin and as far south as the Ohio River. Since most of the white settlers within this area were French, the French language, the Roman Catholic Church, and French Civil law were recognized, though the English criminal law was to be used. No representative assembly was introduced, but the French colonists did not at first particularly mind this since they had not been accustomed to one under their own flag. From the French standpoint the British had conceded what mattered most to them—their old laws, language, and religion. If the Quebec Act went far towards alienating the thirteen colonies, it should also be admitted that it probably prevented Canada from becoming a fourteenth state in the American Union; the Canadians were never sure that their conservative, French and Catholic native culture would be as secure within a Protestant, English-speaking independent republic as it was under the protection of the British Crown. English Canadians were, as yet, too few to be a factor in the situation.

But it is easy to see how the whole arrangement must have looked to the New Englanders and Virginians. Our charters cancelled and our western lands confiscated! A despotic government at our very doors! A foreign language and a foreign law to prevail where our frontiersmen go! Worst of all, the 'Papist' Church to enjoy special privileges! Was it for this we crossed the ocean and tamed the wilderness? Was it for this we waged war with French and Indians? We want land where we can settle under English law and with our own representative assemblies and our own Protestant churches. The Indians? They are only savages, and few in number at that; let them go farther west. The French? Let them remain where they are, along the St. Lawrence valley, but not spread over our own northwestern territories, which Providence has destined for Anglo-Saxon settlement.

Other grievances played a part, differing in importance with the local situation of particular districts. Land speculators as well as backwoodsmen were interested in the development of the western lands. Debtors wished for currency inflation and a lavish issue of paper money to that end. Manufacturers wanted to develop the home market without danger that their 'infant industries' would be crushed either by hostile legislation—which had destroyed some once flourishing Irish industries—or by force of underselling. Somewhat blindly, a new nation was reaching out for such economic autonomy as is today enjoyed by the British Dominions.

In the hush before the firing of the guns it may be well to consider also how far a new American nationality had come into existence, as distinguished from mere 'English colonists with grievances.' A secession does not always imply a new nationality, nor does a difference of nationality always imply a secession. Yet, while there are exceptions both ways, it is the rule in modern times for a political separation either to arise from or to result in a separate national consciousness. Were the American colonists of 1774 'Englishmen' or were they not?

No categorical answer can be given. In ancestry they were mixed; as Thomas Paine truly said, America was the child of Europe as well as the child of England, but the English were still a majority by blood [2] and overwhelmingly preponderant in influence. Moreover, the parts of America most active in the American Revolution, Virginia and New England, were also the most English of the colonies;

[2] See above, Chapter xvii, for a discussion of this point.

the Dutch and German settlements of the Middle colonies were much slower to take fire. The Scotch-Irish were in general a revolutionary element, more perhaps because they settled along the frontier than because of their national origin. If the test of nationality be sentiment rather than ancestry, the majority of colonists professed, with every apparent sincerity, a desire to remain within the British Empire if certain particular issues could be settled to their satisfaction. If the test of nationality be language, the slight differences in the mother tongue which arose in the new country were, after all, no greater than the differences in popular speech between one English shire and another.

Yet frontier life, as we have seen, had placed an impress on the English colonists in America.[3] They had developed a laxer, looser, more flexible social system. There was no native nobility; no one overshadowing Established Church (though some of the colonies had church establishments); no landlord class of ruling 'gentry.' An embryonic aristocracy existed, indeed, in the plantations of the South, and, on a much smaller scale, among the wealthy Dutch patroons of the Hudson valley; in eastern Pennsylvania and on the Narragansett Bay, but its influence was more than counterbalanced by the number of small freehold farmers along the western frontier. The independent, undisciplined spirit of the frontiersmen was hard to reconcile even with the staid respectability of the Atlantic cities, and still farther removed from the customs and conventions of European society. New words—'Americans,' 'Continentals'—were coming into use to describe a social awareness that was no longer merely English and colonial, or merely local, such as 'Virginian' or 'Pennsylvanian.' Alongside the movement for autonomy, and growing with it, was a parallel movement for a more democratic life within the colonies themselves.

On the British side there was much good will towards the colonies, but very little understanding. Certainly no one had any intention to tyrannize over or oppress them. Even acts which seemed definitely designed to overthrow American liberty were the temporizing expedients of busy politicians whose minds were much more on the party situation in England than on the imperial situation in

[3] See above, Chapter XVII.

the colonies. Their sin was merely short-sightedness: the commonest of all political sins. If Chatham, Burke, and Shelburne had been able to work out a new imperial constitution, somewhat along the lines of modern dominion home rule, as it is now understood, even then an eventual separation might have taken place, but it could have been postponed for at least two generations.[4] Nor can it be contended that such ideas were unknown to the eighteenth century. As early as 1754 Benjamin Franklin, at the Albany Congress called to meet the Indian menace, proposed a federal council to be chosen by the colonial assemblies under a single president-general to be appointed by the British king. Two decades later Joseph Galloway of Pennsylvania elaborated a plan for joint control of imperial affairs by the British Parliament and by a colonial Parliament, each to have a veto on the measures of the other on questions of common imperial interest.

That all such opportunities were missed was due in part to the pressure of commercial interests on Parliament, and in part to party politics. Arthur Young, the enlightened agricultural reformer of England, put his finger on the former difficulty when he declared that the Revolution was due to 'that baleful spirit of commerce that wished to govern great nations on the maxims of the counter.' Colonies were still considered merely as profitable plantations. The sugar interests, the slave-trading interests, the East India tea interests, the iron industry, and many others had well-organized lobbies to influence Parliament. To have granted complete home rule to the American colonies might have opened the door to legislation that ran counter to the special interests of one or another of these powerful groups; it might even have compelled the entire abandonment of the mercantile system of the times and nullified the navigation laws, throwing open colonial trade to French, Dutch, and Spanish rivals. Men's minds were not ready for so bold a step.

The confusion of party politics added to the difficulty. The Americans saw British politics in terms too clear and simple: on the one side the angels of light, the Whigs,[5] who sympathized with colonial

[4] If this statement seems rash and dogmatic, remember that it was not until the census of 1830 that the United States had a greater population than Canada has today.

[5] The term Whig was so popular in America that a great political party revived and used it more than half a century after the United States had been

grievances; on the other, the angels of darkness, the Tories, with the tyrant George III at their head. When war broke out, the term Tory was applied to anyone in the colonies who wished to remain a British subject, even if he were in fact a Whig. Actually, party lines were in a state of chaos from the time when George III came to the throne in 1760 till the younger Pitt consolidated a new Tory party in the days of the French Revolution.[6] King George III, playing politics for his own hand, built up a party of 'King's Friends' that was sometimes vaguely called Tory but had little party organization and contained many former Whigs. His favorite Prime Ministers, Bute and North, were of this group. The Whigs were split into numerous personal factions. There were conservative Old Whigs, led by the Marquis of Rockingham; imperialistic Pittites, who followed the great William Pitt, Earl of Chatham; Grenville Whigs, who followed George Grenville; Bedford Whigs, who followed the Duke of Bedford; and several smaller groups. By accident of personal leadership, the Old Whigs and the Pittites were friendlier to the colonies than the other groups were, but no faction or party stood for any consistent body of principles or even of prejudices.

Of the four English statesmen who best understood America Chatham was already crippled by ill health, Shelburne was seldom in office, Burke was a mere private member without much influence, and young Charles James Fox was only a fiery critic of the government who had never as yet been entrusted with the responsibilities of power. Grenville and Townshend, the taxers of the colonists, were well-meaning but narrow and dogmatic. Lord North was too closely tied to the king to have an independent policy. The king himself was at first considered a friend by the colonies; impartial observers such as Franklin had praised his honesty and good will. But opposition always roused in him a sulky and stubborn temper; he considered it mere sedition, whether in England, Ireland, or America. The more his Whig opponents in Parliament criticized his American policy the more obstinately he clung to it. The lesser politicians of all factions regarded American affairs as merely an issue to be exploited, in one way or another, for party advantage.

independent. The African republic of Liberia, founded by freed American slaves, used the term Whig as a party name even in the twentieth century.

[6] For British politics during this period see Chapter xv.

The division of opinion was quite evident on the other side of the Atlantic. The proportion of Tory or loyalist sentiment in America during the Revolution has been estimated at anywhere from a tenth to more than a half of the population; probably the former figure is a fair estimate of those openly and at all risks siding with Great Britain, while the latter would include a considerable body of farmers little interested in politics whose motto was Mercutio's 'A plague on both your houses!' The actively 'rebel' or 'patriot' group was certainly a minority, though probably larger than the actively Tory faction; in all civil wars there are more who are swept along with the current than of those who deliberately take a stand on either side. These neutrals were numerous among the foreigners, especially the Dutch and the Germans.

The American Revolution was rather a political than a social revolution; it was more akin to the nationalistic and democratic revolutions of 1848 than to the French Revolution of 1789 or the Russian Revolution of 1917. Yet class lines played a part. Church of England clergymen, government officials (even those of native American birth), many lawyers and judges, some of the merchants and planters were to be found in the loyalist ranks; while the less prosperous members of society, especially the frontier farmers, were usually revolutionists. The Massachusetts merchants, however, whose trade had first been injured by the British commercial laws and later ruined by the closing of the port of Boston, were in the vanguard of revolution, and the heavily indebted Virginia planters were quite as radical.

The British West Indies colonies, perhaps because they so obviously stood at the mercy of the British fleet, took no part in the Revolution, and there was very little revolutionary sentiment among either the French Canadians of Quebec or the handful of British settlers in Nova Scotia. Religion entered into the question also; the dissenting churches, Presbyterian or Congregational, were usually centers of political radicalism, and the doctrine of 'natural rights' resounded from their pulpits. On the other hand, the Church of England was mainly loyalist, and the Quakers, true to their pacifist convictions, with but few exceptions, stood neutral.

The American Revolution was truly a civil war; in fact, a civil war in two senses, firstly as being fought within the framework of the British Empire, and secondly as being a partisan struggle within the colonies themselves. The conflict began in Massachusetts, in April 1775. General Gage, established in Boston, attempted to seize some arms stored at Concord; this led to the battles—or, rather, skirmishes —of Lexington and Concord, followed shortly by a sharp engagement at Bunker Hill. In the meantime the Continental Congress, originally assembled merely to discuss grievances, had resolved to resist the measures of the British ministry by force of arms and had appointed a competent Virginian, George Washington, as commander of the American forces. Very few Americans, even in 1775, dreamed of complete independence, and while the war continued Congress continued to draft resolutions and petitions for 'redress of grievances.' Thomas Paine, himself an Englishman by birth, was one of the first to advocate a complete break with England and his pamphlet *Common Sense* (published in 1776) enjoyed an immense circulation.

In July 1776 congress at last decided to 'cross the Rubicon.' A Declaration of Independence was approved in principle on 2 July and formally adopted two days later. The chief author of the Declaration was Thomas Jefferson and its wording reflects his clear and forcible mind. The statement of grievances against the British Government, though cleverly and cogently worded, was ephemeral matter. It lumped together complaints which had existed from the beginnings of colonization with events so recent that they arose from the war itself. But the fundamental principle of self-determination which Jefferson formulated has become the timeless creed of liberalism ever since:

We hold these truths to be self-evident, that all men are created equal, that they are endowed by their Creator with certain unalienable rights, that among these are life, liberty and the pursuit of happiness. That to secure these rights, governments are instituted among men, deriving their just powers from the consent of the governed. That whenever any form of government becomes destructive of these ends, it is the right of the people to alter or abolish it, and to institute new government, laying its foundations on such principles and organizing its powers in such form, as to them shall seem most likely to effect their safety and happiness.

The Revolutionary War, considered as military history, was the defeat of a professional European army by the wilderness and the frontiersmen who understood it. It has been called, with some exaggeration, a war in which the British won all the battles but lost all the campaigns. The conduct of the war on the part of the British Government was, it must be admitted, a perfect study of 'how not to do it.' The war office was directed by Lord George Germain, a politician who had been dismissed from the army for misconduct during the Seven Years' War; the navy was directed by the grossly incompetent Lord Sandwich. The generals in the field were better, but Howe, Clinton, Gage, Burgoyne, Cornwallis, and the rest were at best men of mediocre qualities, and some of them, notably Howe, were more than half in sympathy with the Americans. Too much reliance was placed on German mercenaries, Loyalist sympathizers, and Indian tribesmen; all three proved to be broken reeds. Too much importance was attached to the occupation of the large cities of the coast—Boston, New York, Philadelphia, Charleston—while the back country remained unconquered.

Of course, the war on the side of the colonists was no miracle of efficiency either. While Washington's troops were starving at Valley Forge, farmers were selling corn and chickens to the British, preferring ready cash to dubious paper money. No American officer had commanded large armies, and only a few had had any military experience worth mentioning. There were intrigues, cabals, and jealousies among the higher officers, and one of the ablest of them, Benedict Arnold, went over to the enemy. The American soldiers were in many ways excellent military material, and in other ways very poor. They had a frontiersman's skill with the rifle and a knowledge of woodcraft which stood them in good stead in a war which consisted mainly of skirmishes and guerrilla fighting. The conquest of the vast Northwest by a small force of Virginia and Kentucky frontiersmen under George Rogers Clark in 1778 and 1779 showed a combination of initiative and endurance in the common soldier of which any army might be proud. But they were citizen militiamen rather than professional soldiers, after all. They did not take kindly to drill, discipline, and obedience, and were apt to enlist for short terms of service and then go back to the farm and get in the crops. It proved very difficult to maintain any considerable force in camp when an immediate emergency was past or when the war moved away from the soldiers' own neighborhood into some distant state. There was more excuse for the American mismanagement of the war than for the British, however, since the whole machinery of national and state government, financial and military organization, had to be built up from the very ground and in the midst of war. In Professor Evarts Greene's apt phrase, 'The American leaders were like manufacturers trying to turn out finished products while the factory was still being built.'

Fortunately for the Americans they were able to secure the services of some very able men: Robert Morris as financial manager, Benjamin Franklin as a diplomat in France, and John Adams as a diplomat in the Dutch Republic. They had chosen the right man as commander of their small army, for George Washington was a true patriot who put the interest of the whole nation above either his personal ambition or the special claims of any section of the country. Intrigues, ingratitude, incompetence, delay, defeat, and frustration dogged his heels for the whole course of the war; he raised armies to see them melt away again; he kept up the morale of his soldiers when they were unpaid and almost unfed and unclothed; but he never swerved from the course of duty which he had marked out for himself. Several competent foreign volunteers helped him organize his raw militiamen into regular armies, among them LaFayette of France, Steuben of Germany, and Kosciusko of Poland.

The victory of the Americans at Saratoga, in 1777, when General Burgoyne and his army were forced to surrender to General Gates, decided France, already straining at the leash, to come to the help of the Americans. Individual Frenchmen of the LaFayette type were genuinely inspired by love of American liberty; but it is impossible to suppose that the French Royal Government was moved by any abstract preference for republican institutions. The king and his ministers were concerned solely with the balance of power. Britain had seized most of the French colonies in 1763; now if France could aid thirteen British colonies to win independence, France would have reconquered her lost prestige and influence as a Great Power. But, before taking so drastic a step as open war, the French wanted to be sure that the American Revolution would not be a mere flash in the pan; so at first French aid was confined to money and munitions and a few volunteers. In 1778 France signed a definite treaty of alliance with the United States. A little later Spain, and still later the Dutch Republic, joined France.

The international situation towards the end of the Revolutionary War was the worst, perhaps, that Great Britain ever faced before 1940. Though her fleet was still supreme on the seas, all three of the other chief naval powers—the French, Spanish, and Dutch—were allied against her; Russia, Prussia, Sweden, Denmark, and several other states had established an armed neutrality to resist British interference with their neutral trade; Ireland was on the verge of rebellion; discontent was rife among all classes at home. Under these circumstances, after a last attempt to reconquer America by way of the south had failed in the Yorktown campaign of 1781, when Cornwallis was compelled to surrender a British army to a combined French and American force under Washington, the British Government decided to liquidate its losing war with the thirteen colonies. Thus the West Indies and Canada might at all events be saved. Lord North resigned and negotiations with the United States were begun by Shelburne. A naval victory of Admiral Rodney in the West Indies saved the British from having to face the loss of colonies in that quarter; victorious France, without supremacy of the seas, was still unable to colonize against British opposition.

The issue at the peace conference was no longer American independence, already an accomplished fact, but certain questions of detail which arose from it. Would the lands between the Appalachians and the Mississippi be wholly part of the United States, or partly British, Spanish, or Indian? Could the Americans retain their old share in the Newfoundland fisheries? What compensation could be guaranteed to loyalists who had lost their property or been driven from their homes because of their desire to remain under the old flag?

The western lands were granted to the United States, with the Great Lakes as a boundary between them and Canada. Certain fishing rights were conceded to the French as well as to the Americans. Spain regained her lost colonies of East and West Florida, including a westward strip of territory through what is today southern Alabama and Mississippi. Congress 'recommended' to the state legislatures compensation for the loyalists, but nothing effective was done; the British themselves had to take the matter in hand by granting land and compensation in Canada and Nova Scotia to loyalist settlers —the 'United Empire Loyalists' of later fame.

This settlement of 1783 ended the war and enabled the United States, in the words of the Declaration of Independence issued seven years earlier, at last 'to assume among the powers of the earth, separate and equal station.' Henceforth there would be in the world two independent political units using the English language and inheriting English institutions. One of them was still, with all its recent losses, the greatest imperial state on earth; the other was a young republic with almost unlimited opportunities for expansion in wealth and power.

PART IV

THE UNITED STATES OF AMERICA

∘ XX ∘

AMERICA PUTS HER HOUSE IN ORDER

INDEPENDENCE is merely another name for responsibility. Just as coming of age means for the individual earning a living and paying taxes, it means for a nation balancing budgets and making its own mistakes of legislation and administration. Painters and sculptors have usually represented Liberty as a Greek goddess enjoying a perpetual picnic on Olympus; a far better symbol would be a Dutch housewife scrubbing pots and pans in the kitchen.

Fortunately for the Americans they had long been trained to shoulder responsibility as individuals and as communities. They had, probably, a better preparation for complete freedom than any other people who ever won independence by war. In their colonial charters they had instruments of government that with very little alteration served as state constitutions and even provided a mine of suggestions for a federal Union. The franchise in most of the colonies, though far from democratic by modern standards, was more liberal than was then enjoyed by the British or by any important nation on the European continent. The prevailing occupation of the people was freehold farming, and many were farmers under pioneer conditions; a narrow way of life, perhaps, but one which throws much responsibility on the individual. Whatever liabilities the new republic was burdened with, it had priceless assets in the political training of its citizens and in their self-confident assurance that they would meet no difficulties which they could not surmount.

All this training and all this self-confidence were needed, for the problems which came with peace and independence were scarcely less urgent than those which had come in wartime. Historians have called the first years of independence the 'critical period' of American history. A great experiment had been undertaken, but one which might easily have failed. Many witnesses, even sympathizers, had little hope that it could succeed. For one thing, the experiment of a large republican state had never been long successful.[1] Europe had known many republics, but almost always on a small scale—such as the Dutch, Flemish, German, Italian, and Swiss 'city states.' Rousseau, the apostle of modern democracy, held it axiomatic that democracies must be small enough so that the citizens personally know one another, and in this verdict he followed the opinion of the ancient Greeks who knew various types of government so well. France had not yet made the experiment of her First Republic; monarchy prevailed in all the larger states of the world.

The greatest immediate peril was lest a federal republic of unprecedented size, thinly peopled, and with most inadequate means of communication, would break up into smaller units. The time-distance from New Hampshire to Georgia was so great that to administer thirteen commonwealths from any single American center was almost as difficult as it had proved to be to rule them all from Britain. There was no single metropolis, no obvious capital city, to bring together the forces of American life; no London, no Paris. In spite of common efforts in the cause of independence, most Americans still felt a far keener love for Virginia, South Carolina, or Massachusetts than for the United States as a whole. Community of language counted for something, but it had not sufficed to keep York and New York in one Empire and it might easily fail to hold New York and Charleston in one Republic.

The Articles of Confederation under which the nation was governed created a 'perpetual union,' but it was a union of the loosest sort; in the terminology of political science rather a confederation or league of sovereign states than a true federation. A common Congress enjoyed fairly extensive legislative power, but taxation, tariffs, and the executive power to enforce decisions were reserved to the individual states. Each state, great or small, had an equal vote, and the opposition of a single one of the thirteen could block any constitutional amendment.

Two illustrations will serve to show the difficulty of carrying on

[1] The failure of the Roman Republic in ancient times, the downfall of the Polish commonwealth and the political inefficiency even of the Dutch federation are instances that every eighteenth-century critic would have in mind. Cromwell's dictatorship had not endeared the republican idea to Englishmen.

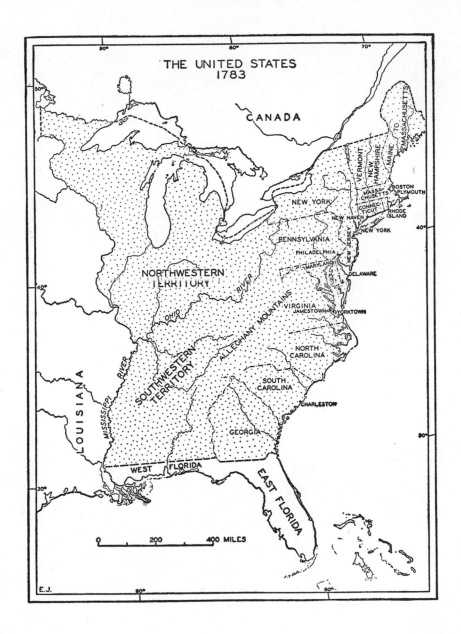

THE UNITED STATES
1783

CANADA

MASSACHUSETTS

VERMONT

NEW
HAMPSHIRE

MAINE
TO
MASSACHUSETTS

BOSTON
PLYMOUTH

NEW YORK

MASSA-
CHUSETTS

CONNEC-
TICUT

RHODE
ISLAND

NEW HAVEN

NEW YORK

NEW JERSEY

PENNSYLVANIA

PHILADELPHIA

MARYLAND

DELAWARE

NORTHWESTERN
TERRITORY

OHIO RIVER

VIRGINIA

JAMESTOWN

YORKTOWN

SOUTHWESTERN
TERRITORY

ALLEGHANY MOUNTAINS

NORTH
CAROLINA

LOUISIANA

MISSISSIPPI RIVER

SOUTH
CAROLINA

CHARLESTON

GEORGIA

WEST   FLORIDA

EAST
FLORIDA

0   200   400 MILES

E.J.

the national government. The states engaged in competitive tariff struggles with each other and refused to grant revenues from this source to the national Union. They also, in most cases, refused to carry into effect the recommendations of Congress on compensating loyalists for property losses in wartime, and thus gave the British a pretext for continuing to hold frontier posts in the Northwest, one violation of the treaty of peace balancing another.

A potent cause of ill-feeling among the American states was the question of the western lands, the same issue, in another form, that had done so much to alienate the colonies from British rule. Each state that possessed claims under the old colonial charters declared them revived by independence, since British decrees annulling those claims were now in turn null and void. Difficulty arose from three sources. First of all, the western claims overlapped; Virginia's, stretching north and west over nearly the whole of the region between the Ohio River and the Great Lakes, intersected the narrower bands of territory claimed by Massachusetts and Connecticut, extending directly west beyond New York. Again, states such as Maryland that had no western claims opposed the whole theory that an eastern seaboard state might hold vast unsettled lands in distant parts of the country in a kind of colonial dependence. Finally, the western settlers themselves wished local home rule; wished it so strongly that in some cases they threatened secession unless it were granted.

The upshot of this dangerous controversy was most fortunate. The states of New York, Massachusetts, Connecticut, and Virginia ceded their northwestern lands as, at a later time, North Carolina, South Carolina, and Georgia ceded claims in the southwest. The Union as a whole profited by this sacrifice by some of the states; there were to be no rival imperial or colonial systems within the common confederation. Thomas Jefferson wished to exclude slavery from all new territories, a step which would probably have averted the eventual Civil War,[2] but this proposal was too advanced for its age, and slavery was tacitly admitted to the southern territories though expressly excluded from the northern. The land ordinance of 1785 set aside a section in every township for the support of common schools. The more general ordinance of 1787 organized the

[2] See Chapters xxiii and xxiv.

Northwest Territory as a district which would have a legislature of its own, a governor and judges chosen by Congress, and the right to be organized eventually as a series of not less than three or more than five states 'on an equal footing with the original States in all respects whatever.' This Northwest Territory became the parent of five states, Ohio, Indiana, Illinois, Michigan, and Wisconsin, whose combined present population is about equal to that of all Spain.

In this way was created a distinctively American 'colonial system.' In nearly every case, each new state has had a probationary or tad-pole period when it enjoyed only about as much home rule as a British colony in America prior to the Revolution, with power divided between an elected legislature and an appointed executive. But on attaining a considerable population each territory has been encouraged to petition Congress for statehood and to prepare a state constitution in a specially elected popular convention. The statehood thus requested has sometimes been delayed by a feeling in Congress that the population was still too small, or that the new constitution was objectionable, or that the admission of the state might upset the delicate balance of sectional or party interests. Thus the admission of Kansas was delayed by controversies over slavery, and the admission of Utah by controversies over Mormonism. Usually, however, the desire to obtain political support from a grateful new state has induced all political parties to vie with each other in advancing territories as rapidly as possible to statehood, and the only ones which remain today are far distant from any of the states—Alaska, Hawaii, Puerto Rico. Some few states have had a very brief territorial period or none at all: Maine was organized directly from Massachusetts, Kentucky and West Virginia from Virginia, Vermont from contested territory claimed by New York and New Hampshire, Texas was admitted immediately as a state, and California almost immediately, the slavery controversy causing a delay of a few months.

Almost as serious as the danger to national unity arising from the rivalry of the different states was the danger to national stability arising from the rivalry of different classes. The danger did not arise from any deep-seated or permanent class antagonism, such as complicated the work of reform in eighteenth-century France or twentieth-century Russia and Spain, but from temporary class friction, due in part to the long war and in part to the financial problems natural to any frontier community. The war had practically compelled Congress to issue unsupported paper money in such quantities that 'not worth a continental' became a national proverb. After the peace many states issued paper money on their own account and passed laws making it legal tender for all debts. Even with this relief many farmers could not pay their debts and found their homes taken for taxation or on mortgage foreclosures. In 1786 distressed farmers of western Massachusetts rose in rebellion under a Revolutionary soldier, Daniel Shays, to demand an end to these court judgments. This pathetic little insurrection was easily crushed, but it seriously alarmed conservatives. In Rhode Island the debtors had their way in the legislature and issued so much paper money that the courts defied the legislature and refused to enforce the laws requiring creditors to accept it. All this social discontent convinced the creditor classes that a stronger central control was necessary to prevent some state legislatures from running amok. Next to radical currency inflation they feared 'laws impairing the obligation of contracts,' such as legislation cancelling farm mortgages or postponing the time of interest payment. Democracy needed a brake, and a new constitution might supply it.

Besides the perils of disunion and of radical legislation there was the more distant but equally formidable danger of interference from foreign powers. Great Britain, it was feared, might seek to undo the work of the Revolution by wooing back disaffected states through commercial concessions while bludgeoning obstinate states by closing her doors to American trade. British forces still garrisoned some western outposts and formed rallying points for Indian resistance to American expansion northwest of the Ohio. The Spaniards strove to win over the farmers of the Ohio and Mississippi valleys to form an independent republic and thus create a buffer between their own colonies and the Atlantic seaboard states. A weak central government could not hold the country together against such forces from without, and in the event of a general European war—such as actually took place a few years later—the United States would be unable to maintain neutrality with dignity and effectiveness.

Such considerations moved men of light and leading in all the colonies to seek something more than the mere amendment to the Articles of Confederation that everyone conceded to be necessary.

The Congress of the Confederation called into session a convention at Philadelphia to revise the Articles. How far would this Constitutional Convention venture to go? It had the right to recommend the most drastic amendments, but its recommendations would have to be approved by each of the states and many states were indisposed to curtail their sovereignty.

The United States has had only one national constitutional convention, but there have been numerous state constitutional conventions either to make or to revise constitutions for the individual states. As a rule such conventions are far superior in personnel to the average legislature concerned only with current legislation and not with changes in the constitution; abler men seek office when the fundamental law itself is in question. So it was in Philadelphia in 1787. Most of the members of the Convention had a sound education, either academic or legal or both. A large majority of the members had served in public office and many of them had been for years members of Congress. With the exception of a few, such as John Adams and Thomas Jefferson, who were away on foreign missions, most of the leaders in national politics were present. Finance, commerce, plantation agriculture, and the law all had able spokesmen in the Convention. The point of view of the small farmers, the distressed debtors, the frontiersmen, however, had little representation; the Convention was a body of liberals but scarcely a body of democrats. It gave far more time to the national question, the strengthening of the federal government, than to economic questions, but it did not forget that the two were bound up together and that a strong central government would give stability to the rights of property.

Rhode Island sent no representatives, and some of the delegates chosen by other states failed to attend or dropped out during the proceedings. At no time did the Convention have more than fifty-five members present, and only thirty-nine signed the constitution when the work was completed. George Washington, representing Virginia, presided. The oldest member was Benjamin Franklin of Pennsylvania, a veteran of eighty-one. Neither took much part in the debates, but without the endorsement of these two, the most loved and honored men in the country, the new constitution would probably have been rejected by the states. James Madison of Virginia contributed more than any other one man to formulating the details of the new constitution. The extreme nationalists were represented by Alexander Hamilton, born in the West Indies and therefore without any overweening attachment to a particular state, though his residence was in New York. He advocated a government in which the states would be mere provinces or departments under appointed governors and in which the President would be a kind of elective king, holding office for life or good behavior.

Hamilton's plan had no chance of acceptance at any time, as he probably knew. It represented to him merely an ideal which might be partly approached by the winding path of compromise. The two plans seriously considered by the Convention were the so-called 'Virginia plan,' which provided for a Congress based on population and a strong national government, and the 'New Jersey plan' according to which the states had equal representation and the government remained much as it had been under the Articles of Confederation except for an increase in the powers of Congress. The two plans divided the delegates into large-state and small-state groups, and the resulting deadlock threatened the whole work of the Convention. Finally, a compromise was proposed and accepted, basing representation in the House of Representatives on population (except that slaves counted for only three-fifths as much as freemen) while in the Senate each state had two votes without regard to size.

Compromise was the watchword of the Convention throughout. It is safe to say that the Constitution was such as no one of the delegates would have made it if the task had been entrusted to him alone. No state and no section, no class and no party had everything its own way. Thus there was a compromise on the important question of national control of commerce. Congress was given general power to lay tariffs and regulate interstate and foreign trade, but export duties were forbidden and the slave trade, in deference to the lower South, was not to be prohibited before the year 1808. The method of election was another compromise: the House of Representatives was to be chosen by those who were voters under state law, the Senate by the state legislatures, the President and Vice-President by a specially chosen Electoral College which had no other duties.

No constitution was ever made in a more businesslike fashion. The whole Convention was so small as to permit intimate and confidential discussion in place of declamatory debate, and much of its work was done in even smaller committees. Press and public were excluded, so that no one yielded to the temptation of directing spreadeagle oratory to the galleries. Abstract political theory played but a small part, classical precedents from Greece and Rome (dear to the eighteenth century) even smaller. Even the Bill of Rights guaranteeing personal liberty was tacked on as a concession in a series of amendments after the Convention had dissolved and the Constitution had already been completed. Almost no legislative or statutory material, such as still clutters up most American state constitutions, found a place; the Constitution briefly defined the organs of government and their powers—that was all. For nearly every clause of the Constitution some precedent may be found in British law, or colonial charters, or the new state constitutions, or other institutions under which Americans had been governed.

Though many of the provisions of the Constitution had English precedents, it is none the less a fact that the American Constitution created a new type and model of government which was far removed from the parliamentary system of the motherland. The mere fact of having a written and rigid constitution at all was un-English, for the British constitution is made up of precedents, charters, and statute laws which can be changed at the will of Parliament. The United States is governed under two kinds of national law (to make no mention of state law): constitutional and statutory. To amend the latter a bare majority of the House of Representatives and of the Senate and the approval of the President suffices, but to amend the former a two-thirds vote of both houses of Congress must also have the concordance of three-fourths of the states, acting by legislatures or by special conventions.

The American Constitution also introduced a much sharper separation of the branches of government than had been for a century the actual practice of the British system. British theorists, it is true, had talked much about an executive power, vested in a king and his ministers, a legislative power divided between the House of Commons and the House of Lords, each representing a separate class of the king's subjects, and a judicial power exercised by independent judges appointed for life. This check and balance system, however, existed rather in theory than in fact. If it were even approximately true under William III, it had become a legal fiction by the time of George III.

With respect to the relation of the executive authority to the legislative, the American Constitution harked back in many respects to seventeenth-century England, though it had no place for the hereditary principle which gave England a King and a House of Lords. The President was an executive of limited but independent powers, whose cabinet (not specifically mentioned in the Constitution, but implied in the power to appoint heads of departments of government) was of his own choice. He was in no way obliged to follow the advice of this cabinet. No possible vote of Congress could force him to dismiss an official, once the appointment had been confirmed by the Senate. Nor could Congress hasten by a single day the coming of a new election which might change the administration. On the other hand the President could not dissolve either branch of Congress or order any election before the calendar demanded it. Neither he nor any of his cabinet could be members of Congress, or join in its debates, or directly introduce bills in either house. The President had the old royal power (already lapsed from disuse in England) of vetoing measures, though they could be passed over his veto by a two-thirds vote of both houses of Congress. His recommendations to Congress were his own opinions, not a 'speech from the throne' written by someone else.

The Senate proved to be a far more powerful body than the British House of Lords. The formal distribution of powers between the two houses of Congress was, indeed, closely modeled after the usages of the two houses of Parliament. In both Great Britain and in the United States money bills had to originate in the lower house; in both, impeachments were brought by the lower house and tried before the upper. But the House of Lords represented a class which no longer had the same relative importance that it had enjoyed in previous centuries, while the Senate represented the equal rights of the states and their still powerful feeling of sovereignty. The Senate had the power, by a two-thirds vote, to confirm appointments and ratify treaties; a British king, advised by his ministers, did not require parliamentary sanction for either appointments or treaties unless some fresh expenditure of money was involved. The House of Lords could be 'packed' by royal (or, rather, ministerial) creation of new

peerages; the Senate could be controlled only through the state legislatures. In the course of time the Senate rose to still greater heights
of prestige because it was a small body, where individuality stood
out, and because its longer term of office, six years, made it more
attractive than the House of Representatives, which was renewed
every two years. Since the Senate, moreover, was renewed by only
one-third each two years, it never changed suddenly with any political landslide, but reflected equally the public opinion of today, of
yesterday, and of the day before.

Another divergence of American constitutional practice from the
British lay in the federal system. The British Parliament of the time
claimed unlimited legislative authority, but the American Congress
could legislate only on certain specified matters; all else was reserved to the states. Congress had power to collect taxes, duties,
imposts, and excises 'for the common defense and general welfare,'
to borrow money, to regulate commerce, to naturalize citizens, to coin
money and fix its value, to grant patents and copyrights, to establish
a postal service, to create federal courts, to wage war and maintain
armies and navies, to legislate for the federal district containing
the capital, and—a conveniently elastic clause—to make all laws
'necessary and proper for carrying into execution the foregoing
powers.' The states were forbidden to make foreign alliances, wage
war on their own account, coin money, 'make anything but gold and
silver coin a tender in payment of debts,' impair the obligation of
contracts, levy tariffs, grant titles of nobility, pass laws of attainder
or *ex post facto* laws (the federal government also was forbidden to
grant titles or pass attainder and *ex post facto* laws), and they were
required to maintain 'a republican form of government.'

Subject to these limitations, and a few similar ones, each state could
adopt any form of constitution it chose. It is strange how little variety, in face of this vast implicit permission, there actually has been
in the state constitutions. They differ in little points of detail, such
as the salaries of officials or the length of the terms of office, but in
important matters they are almost invariably of the same type. Each
has the same separation of powers into independent executive, legislative, and judicial branches that one finds in the federal government, and, with the rarest exceptions,[3] each has two chambers of

[3] Nebraska today has a single-chambered legislature.

the legislature chosen directly by the same voters, though for election districts of different extent. At first the state franchise laws differed considerably, but the growth of democratic sentiment eventually made the suffrage almost universal for free men everywhere.

There was a check on the powers of Congress which did not exist on the powers of the British Parliament, the judicial review of legislation. The Constitution states in explicit terms that 'This constitution, and the laws of the United States which shall be made in pursuance thereof; and all treaties . . . shall be the supreme law of the land; and the judges in every state shall be bound thereby.' This would seem to impose on the courts, in any particular case that might come before them, the duty of deciding whether the statute or executive order in question did or did not conform to the 'supreme law of the land.'

It will be noted how completely the Americans had realized in their own Constitution the special theory of the British constitution for which they had contended in colonial days. They had held that certain fundamental 'rights of British subjects' could not be erased by any statute of Parliament; now they had a fixed constitution supreme over Congress. They had held that the British Empire was in a sense federal, with several legislatures, instead of a single supreme Parliament; now they had a Congress representing all the states and thirteen state legislatures besides. They had emphasized the separation of executive, legislative, and judicial authority, admitting that they were under the King's Crown but denying that they were subject to his British ministry or to the British Parliament; now they had a constitution in which the different spheres of executive, legislator, and judge were as carefully balanced and adjusted as the wheels of a watch.

Americans have been called a restless, innovating people, but they have shown a pious reverence for their Constitution surpassing that of any other nation on earth. The twenty-one amendments to the Constitution enacted up to the present time have left its main outlines quite untouched. The first ten were guarantees of personal liberty added almost at once to ease the doubts of liberals; the eleventh a guarantee of states rights; the twelfth a minor change in the manner of election in the Electoral College; the thirteenth, fourteenth, and fifteenth were designed to secure the full freedom of the Negro;

the sixteenth authorized a federal income tax; the seventeenth provided for direct popular election of the Senate in place of election by the state legislatures; the eighteenth imposed prohibition on the land, and the twenty-first took it away again; the nineteenth granted woman suffrage, and the twentieth abolished the post-election or 'lame duck' session of an expiring Congress. Somewhat greater changes have been brought about by custom and precedent, in the British manner; thus, to take the most familiar example, the Electoral College has lost its freedom to select Presidents and Vice-Presidents at will and now acts only as an agent of the voters. Other changes brought about by custom and precedent are the system of partisan appointments to federal office, the development of the cabinet, the extension of federal responsibility to a wide range of economic activities never contemplated by the makers of the Constitution.

But put all these changes together and they amount to much less than the changes in the government of any other country on earth during the same period. Of all European states Great Britain has changed her constitution the least, and with the least friction, and yet the franchise reform bills, the limitation of the power of the House of Lords, and the grant of complete home rule to Ireland and to the overseas Dominions are structural alterations much greater than any change yet made in the American Constitution. One hardly knows whether to wonder more at the wisdom of a small group of eighteenth-century politicians who could frame a government so well for four million people in a very simple rural community that it would still serve in the twentieth century for a hundred and thirty million inhabitants of the most complex industrial society ever known in history, or at the meek filial piety which keeps those hundred and thirty millions almost unanimously content with their eighteenth-century institutions!

Making the Constitution was only half the battle. The next task, perhaps the harder of the two, was to get it accepted. Against it were arrayed the jealousy of sovereign states, fearing a centralized empire; the suspicion of extreme liberals, dreading lest the President become a dictator; the vague sense of grievance of poor men and debtors who distrusted a constitution made by property-minded men. Knowing the difficulty of getting all thirteen states together, the

Constitutional Convention had taken the revolutionary step of providing that the new frame of government should go into effect as soon as nine states accepted it. But would there be even so many? It seemed very doubtful.

If the new constitution had been submitted to a general plebiscite or referendum of the whole American people it is more than doubtful if it would have carried at all, and practically certain that it would have failed in at least some of the states. That it won the approval of each of the thirteen states was partly explained by the fact that the ratifying state conventions, though chosen usually by a broad franchise, contained a disproportionate number of representatives of the prosperous classes, and partly because of the well-directed campaign of education carried on by the Federalists, as advocates of the new constitution called themselves. Alexander Hamilton, generously forgetting that his own plan of union had been ignored, and stifling his secret doubts of the less centralized plan which had prevailed, joined with James Madison of Virginia and John Jay of New York in preparing a series of papers explaining the new constitution. These *Federalist* papers, moderate and temperate in tone as well as closely reasoned, are often called the greatest American contribution to political theory, just as the Constitution itself is usually considered the greatest American contribution to political fact.

The populous state of Pennsylvania and most of the lesser states approved the Constitution with little dissent, but there were battles royal in Massachusetts, Virginia, and New York, and an American union from which any one of those three was absent was hardly conceivable. Among the opponents of the new frame of government were some dissatisfied members of the convention itself, such as George Mason in Virginia and Luther Martin of Maryland, and some popular heroes of the Revolution, such as the orator Patrick Henry of Virginia. In Massachusetts John Hancock and Samuel Adams were with great difficulty persuaded to accept the Constitution. In New York Hamilton had to face a powerful league of politicians hostile to any closer union of the states. After New York had, by a very narrow margin, come into the new Union, only North Carolina and Rhode Island still remained outside. Their position was insecure and somewhat ridiculous, so they pocketed their mis-

givings and agreed to accept the Constitution, which had already
come into operation.

An important concession was made to the honest misgivings of
those who feared lest a strong central government might be too
strong for the people's liberties. Congress adopted and laid before the
states a series of constitutional amendments, ten of which were almost
immediately enacted into law. They followed closely the form of
certain bills of rights already adopted into the state constitutions,
and these in turn had borrowed liberally from famous English charters and statutes of personal liberty; thus the eighth amendment,
'Excessive bail shall not be required, nor excessive fines imposed,
nor cruel and unusual punishments inflicted,' followed practically
word for word the English Bill of Rights that resulted from the
Whig revolution of 1688. The first article, and the most important,
guaranteed religious freedom, freedom of speech and of the press,
the right of assembly, and the right of petition. Other articles provided for the right to bear arms, to be exempt from billeting of soldiers on private homes in time of peace, to be secure against unreasonable searches and seizures, to a trial by jury, and various other legal
privileges. It is worth noting, however, that many of these restrictions
applied only to acts of the Federal Government; thus, if a state
should enact a law restricting the freedom of the press the first
amendment would offer no redress. Each state in the Union, however, has a similar, and often even more elaborate, bill of rights in
its own constitution.

Nowhere in the Constitution is there mention, even by hint or
implication, of the existence of political parties. Party government
was already an old story in Great Britain; in fact party majorities
were the very muscles which made parliamentary government able
to move. But there was a credulous Utopian hope in the young
American republic that under the new constitution there need be
no place for 'faction.' No one seems to have foreseen that the chief
resemblance between American and British government in future
years would be the two-party system with its alternation of one
faction forming an administration and another an official opposition;
still less, that the American parties would eventually become more
definite and rigid in their organization than the British.

The very fight over the Constitution itself drew party lines between federalists, or pro-constitution men, and anti-federalists. If anyone had been nominated for President except George Washington, a division would have appeared in the Electoral College without delay. But Washington was twice unanimously elected, the only man to whom that compliment has ever been paid, and the only President who did not admit that he was a member of a party.[4] He tried to include in his first cabinet men of very diverse opinions; thus his Secretary of State, in charge of foreign affairs, was Thomas Jefferson, and his Secretary of the Treasury Alexander Hamilton. A few years later, however, Jefferson and Hamilton were the leaders of rival factions that might be called definite political parties.

Since party strife was soon to break out in all its fury, it is very fortunate that the first beginnings of national constitutional life were under the administration of a man who tried to think and work for the whole nation instead of any particular section, sect, class, or faction. Washington's civil triumphs, like his military ones, were much more the result of character than of brilliant intellect. He reasoned slowly, though clearly, and took many of his ideas and policies from others. He was not a philosopher, like Jefferson or Franklin, not a political scientist like John Adams or James Madison, not a profound lawyer like John Marshall, or a dexterous financier like Hamilton. A worried, over-conscientious man, he took his duties very seriously, enjoyed his presidency as little as any man who has ever held it, and suffered more from the libels of a few gutter journalists than he gained pleasure from the applause of millions. When, after two terms of service, he returned to his beloved estate of Mount Vernon as a simple country gentleman once more, he was like a schoolboy come home for his holidays or a soldier on leave from the trenches.

Washington's two administrations created a number of important precedents. He supported Hamilton's financial reforms which filled a bankrupt treasury and maintained the national credit by the assumption of state debts and the payment of both national and state

---

[4] James Monroe was re-elected in 1820 with only one electoral vote against him, but he was an avowed partisan whose party had virtually destroyed the opposition. Washington himself, though he strove to stand above party, was increasingly surrounded by Federalists in the later years of his administration, and that party claimed him, though he did not claim them.

debts at par. He used military force to subdue an outbreak of frontiersmen in western Pennsylvania, who thought an excise tax on whiskey a violation of their natural rights. He refused to be drawn into the conflict between the first French Republic and its foes, and risked great unpopularity by supporting the Jay treaty, negotiated on unfavorable terms with Great Britain. He warned his fellow-countrymen against involvement in Old World alliances and wars. He refused a third term for the presidency, thus establishing a precedent never broken until the election of 1940.

◦ XXI ◦

FRESH WINDS FROM WESTERN FORESTS

In 1790 Congress fixed the seat of national government in the District of Columbia on the Potomac River, on a site ceded by land grants from the states of Maryland and Virginia.[1] Many people, Americans and foreigners, ridiculed the idea of locating the capital city of a great nation in a western wilderness, and several years elapsed before Congress and the President actually moved from comfortable Philadelphia to this frontier outpost. By 1810 the center of American population was close to the city of Washington. Today that center is in southern Indiana, more than five hundred miles farther west, and many complaints are heard that Washington is an eastern city, inconveniently located for the great mass of American citizens! National political conventions and the like rarely meet at Washington, as they find such cities as Chicago and Saint Louis more central, and, were the location of a national capital still an open question, undoubtedly it would now be placed somewhere near the Mississippi.

In this progressive westward movement most of the story of America is told. America is the product of several successive distillations of the pioneer spirit. No sooner did the Tidewater region become densely peopled, orderly, and socially stratified, than the more restless individualists moved into the foothills, the Piedmont, of the Appalachian range. When the hills in turn became too tame, new pioneers sought the mountains, the mountain valleys, and the great plains beyond them. This process continued till the end of the nineteenth century, when there was no longer a frontier zone left to develop. As America was to Europe, so the West has been to the East. But the 'western frontier' is a most flexible term. In 1650 it meant western Massachusetts and central Virginia; in 1750 it meant

[1] Virginia's grant was later retroceded.

243

the valleys of Pennsylvania and western Virginia; in 1800, Ohio and Kentucky; in 1850, Texas, Kansas, and Minnesota; in 1900 the cattle ranches of Montana and Wyoming.

Nine-tenths of the United States would have looked 'western' to European eyes when Washington was President. New York was divided, as it is still, between the city and 'upstate,' but in those days the upstate area was almost entirely a farming region, where it was settled at all. Pennsylvania, similarly, contained populous Philadelphia and a few neighboring counties, which had Eastern, that is to say commercial and conservative, tendencies; while all the rest of the state counted as the land of the pioneer. The 'cohees' of the Shenandoah valley in Virginia were politically more democratic than the 'tuckahoes' of the Tidewater. Even South Carolina and Georgia had their eastern and western divisions.

East of the Missouri River nearly all parts of the United States were once densely forested. Even as early as the eighteenth century much of this had been cleared along the Atlantic seaboard, but there was no state without its forests and but few where the clearings were more than occasional patches of cultivation in the wilderness. European travelers, such as Chateaubriand, grew lyric over the majestic silence of the woods. The pioneers themselves were usually more matter-of-fact about them, regarding the trees as enemies to be laid low with the ax so that the land might be tilled. Wood being in such abundance, practically all houses except a very few public buildings were built of it. This was truer in the West than along the coast. One can find many more old stone barns in Virginia or New Jersey than in Ohio or Kentucky. The crudest homes were log cabins, with the bark still on the round timbers. A grade higher came the house built of logs which had been squared off and stripped of bark, 'lumber' rather than 'timber.' The well-to-do lived in painted frame houses with wooden floors and shingled roofs. Few of the first generation of settlers could afford the time, the labor, or the outside help to build such homes; but they were not at all uncommon in the second generation. Much of the furniture was homemade. Many slept on beds piled with oak leaves, rocked their babies in sugar troughs or pack saddles, wore deerskin clothing, and packed deer's hair into their shoes or moccasins in place of socks. Wild game was the staple food, together with hominy or parched corn. So long as

a man was a good shot he rarely faced starvation, for in few parts
of the world was game more abundant than in the American forests.
Apparently the difficulty of obtaining salt was irksome, for we read
of long and dangerous trips through the woods in search of salt
springs or 'salt licks.' Oxen, cows, and horses were imported from
the East, for the native buffalo was regarded only as a convenient
source of meat and skins.

One of the greatest contrasts between Europe and America was
the much wider spacing of the farms in the latter. Even in the Middle Ages, few Europeans lived in absolute isolation; the custom
everywhere, from England to Russia, was for the peasantry, whether
free or servile, to congregate in country villages and go out from
them to the farmlands for the day's labor. Such villages were by no
means unknown in America, especially in New England. But the
growing tendency was for the farmer to set his home in the midst
of his own acres. He might live half a mile from his nearest neighbor, and his entire social circle comprise a dozen farms. Where the
Indian menace was great, there was a check on this tendency to scat-
ter. Sometimes, as in the first Kentucky settlements, it was necessary
to keep together in a fortified stockade, or at least to live near enough
to one to retreat behind its wooden walls when rumors of an Indian
raid spread panic. But no sooner were the Indians killed, tamed, or
driven away, than the stockade settlements were abandoned and each
squatter took his family away to his independent farm. The way
in which the western land was allotted, a whole solid and square
section being sold to an individual, encouraged this widely spaced
settlement. Then, too, there was always a fringe of restless souls
who took up trapping or surveying because even squatter farming
was too tame and static a way of life; also a group of land-speculat-
ing pioneers who were forever looking for cheaper lands beyond the
frontier of settlement.

The conditions of life along this wide western margin of the
growing nation inevitably developed a certain social outlook, which
in turn affected the political life and institutions of the whole country; for even Eastern politicians could not afford to ignore Western
votes. Though the Western pioneer was of all men the most individualistic, apt to squat on land to which he had no strictly legal
title and resent taxation of any sort as tyranny, he was also nation-

alistic. By the very act of moving west he had broken the ties of state and county which were so strong in the older states. He would brag of his new home, but it was not an abiding city, for perhaps he already had his mind on another farm farther west. The new states were mere arbitrary divisions of land squared off on lines of latitude and longitude out of the federal domain, and states rights never meant as much in Michigan or Tennessee as they did in Massachusetts or South Carolina.

The pioneer was a democrat because he lived in an environment that forced every man to fend for himself. In the West it was almost impossible to get a servant because few people found much attraction in working for others when by the same amount of labor they could have a farm for themselves. The lower South solved the problem by taking Negro slaves westward along the trails of settlement; the Northwest simply did without. There was no proletariat because there were so few towns and cities; no peasantry because the Western farmer had no attachment to ancestral lands or old customs; no capitalists, except a few lucky land gamblers, because there was little capital to invest; few landlords, because so many were freeholders; no aristocracy of social privilege, because men of the leisure class did not want to live in a wilderness. There was not even the old Puritan reverence for the elected or appointed official, the 'magistrate'; on the contrary, all Westerners were loud in the opinion that officials, kept on low pay and chosen for short terms, were merely the hired servants of the public. The clergy were often greatly honored, but the type of religion which flourished in the frontier settlements was not the staid and decorous Anglicanism or Puritanism of the early colonial days; rather it was warmly emotional evangelical religion, with its revivals, camp meetings, and lay preaching. The typical frontier minister dressed like his fellows, lived as simply, made his Bible his library and a pine cabin his church, and differed from his congregation in little except that he drank less and worked even harder.

Another basis of democracy in the newly settled communities arose from psychological rather than economic causes. The very fact that most men and women spent whole weeks in the roughest farm drudgery without seeing a neighbor's face made them all the more desirous of sociability when they got a chance to meet. The Westerner was famous for his hospitality, but this was only in part because of his natural good nature; in part it was caused by the welcome break it gave in a lonely and often monotonous life. A Yankee peddler, with 'notions' from Connecticut in his bag, a schoolteacher 'boarding around' among the parents of his pupils, a circuit rider moving on from pulpit to pulpit might give a cordial host a happy evening of gossip and political discussion. Getting together took many forms, which were often merely excuses for sociability: 'barn raising,' when neighbors joined forces to erect a new roof; corn-husking; spelling matches for adults in a crossroads rural school; a political 'barbecue' when oxen were roasted and stump speeches made; a muster of militiamen; a meeting of the county court for routine legal business; even a religious camp meeting. A man who was a 'good mixer,' cordial, friendly, unaffected, was forgiven many sins; while a man who was haughty, aloof, reserved, was hardly forgiven even his virtues! Practically all English travelers in those days commented on the inquisitiveness of Americans; the manner in which a total stranger in a coach or inn would unhesitatingly proceed, without invitation, to probe your views and air his own on every subject under heaven. Some visitors liked this and called it the natural friendliness of the American; others disliked it and called it intrusiveness.

The position of women in the United States was much enhanced by pioneer conditions, paradoxically enough by the very fact that those conditions bore most hardly on the housewife herself. Hard work faced everyone on the frontier; even boys and girls had to labor long hours; but if anyone had the advantage it was the man. He met his neighbors more often than his wife did, and the keen edge of life was not so often dulled and broken by loneliness. It required exceptional courage for a mother of small children to go into a new land where doctors were few and savage Indians were many. So, if the pioneer was a selected type, brave and enduring beyond most men, his wife was doubly selected. Very few unmarried women ventured to go West at all. Those that did could often take their choice among a dozen suitors. Even in the seaboard states the men outnumbered the women, as far more bachelors than maids came over on the immigrant ships. Women had what economists call 'scarcity value.' Almost any girlish face seemed beautiful to a backwoodsman who had seen nothing for months but the bearded faces of men.

The education of children was a passion with the frontiersmen. In 1824 one writer humorously complained, 'It was democratically believed and loudly insisted that "Larnin'," even the most power-fullest, highest larnin', should at once be bestowed on everybody and without a farthing's expense.' In the conservative East, boys and girls were taught separately and, above the common schools, in academies, endowed colleges, and other private institutions; but in the West the tax-supported public school, imported from New England, became the almost universal form of education, leading up to the public high school and university. Partly from reasons of economy, and partly from the pioneer sentiment of woman's equal rights, these western schools tended increasingly to become coedu-cational. As life grew easier and families smaller, less work was exacted from children and more time granted for their recreation. An anonymous Briton writing of his *Excursion through the United States and Canada* in 1824 declared that 'In America I never saw even the schoolboys playing at any game whatsoever,' and noted American indifference to recreation as one of the outstanding con-trasts with England. Stuart Chase, on the other hand, writing a century later, declared that 'Not far from one quarter of the entire national income of America is expended for play and recreation broadly interpreted.' [2] Thus greatly has the American attitude to-wards leisure changed.

Pioneer life made for versatility. The frontiersman had to learn to do a little of everything for himself and his family. This carried with it a general handiness, an inventiveness and adaptability that have enabled the United States to lead the world in mechanical in-vention and in many branches of applied science; but it had the draw-back of unduly discounting the training of the expert. When the first frontiersman President, Andrew Jackson, was inaugurated, he declared that since the duties of public office were 'plain and simple' he could not but think that 'more is lost by the long continuance of men in office than is generally to be gained by their experience.' The half-trained militiaman was regarded as the equal, or more

[2] C. A. Beard, *Whither Mankind* (1928), p. 338.

than the equal, of the professional soldier. There was some opposition to the first normal schools for teachers on the ground that
'anyone could teach.' Not infrequently 'anyone' did! It is amazing
how many captains of industry and distinguished political leaders
taught school at some time in their youth.

Law and medicine were usually learned by apprenticeship in an
office. The English distinctions between barristers and solicitors disappeared, and there was no sharp line drawn between civil and criminal practice; for many, indeed, the law was only a springboard to
a career in business or politics. Many an American had half a dozen
'careers' in a lifetime: he would attend the common schools in the
intervals of working on his father's farm, earn his way through an
academy or half way through a little denominational college, then
drop out to make money by teaching 'district school' for two or three
years, open a land survey and sales office, study law at night, practice at the bar for a few years, be elected a district attorney or a
county judge, run for Congress, make a fortune in promoting a
railroad or canal enterprise, lose one in a mining venture, move West
to take up timber lands, and finally die, either a rich man, still
ambitious and discontented, or a poor man, still eager and hopeful!
Such was the spirit of America as a whole, but especially of the West.

Until the question of slavery became acute, the West and the
South were more often than not politically allied. Both were agricultural sections whose economic interests often diverged from the
interests of the merchants of Boston, New York, and Philadelphia.
Both were debtor regions, having to borrow capital, and thus interested in 'cheap money' and inflation so that prices might be good and
interest on mortgages easily paid. Local government in the West
was a hybrid between the town system of New England and the
county system of Virginia, drawing certain features from both. Even
territories north of the Ohio had many Southern settlers, and south
of that river the West was simply an extension of Southern settlement. The political genius of Thomas Jefferson saw the possibility
of welding together into a single democratic party the sectional
South, the sectional West, and a large number of discontented minority groups in the East.

Jefferson is one of the most interesting figures in American history.
One cannot call him a typical American, for he was a philosopher,

and a philosopher is in no country the typical man. But his philosophy was intensely American; he believed by reason in the policies which the frontiersman favored by interest or instinct.[3] Though himself a Virginia planter and slaveowner, his sympathies were less with his own class than with the yeoman farmers who did all their own work. He had a vision rather than a creed: a vision of an America stretching from the Atlantic to the Rocky Mountains or beyond, peopled by hardy, self-respecting farmers, with scattered towns and cities that would be hardly more than market centers for the surrounding countryside. In this vision the National Government, like the wise parent of adolescent children, would keep itself tactfully in the background, letting affairs of common interest be handled by town meetings or, at the most, by state legislatures chosen by a very wide suffrage. There would be public schools for every child, but each church would have to seek the support of its own congregation. When Jefferson chose his epitaph he made no mention of the fact that he had been twice President of the United States but modestly boasted of three things: authorship of the Declaration of Independence, authorship of the Virginian statute for religious freedom, and the founding of the University of Virginia. Political liberty, religious equality, and popular enlightenment through education, symbolized by those three achievements, were the great passions of his life.

Even during Washington's presidency Jefferson was uneasy. He feared what he called the 'monarchical tendencies' of the Federalists, the party of the Constitution-makers. He had not been one of the opponents of the Constitution, but he sympathized with their suspicion of strong and centralized government. But it was only after Washington had refused a third term that party strife broke into the open. Washington's successor was a partisan, definitely a Federalist. John Adams of Massachusetts had been Vice-President under Washington. He was the founder of a long line of able and conscientious public servants [4] who combined a keen sense of honor and

---

[3] Of course, the ideas of liberalism and democracy were common to thinkers of western Europe and America, and Jefferson owed much to French influence. For all that, he was emotionally moved less by his abstract theories than by his passionate love of a simple, agrarian way of life.

[4] See J. T. Adams, *The Adams Family*.

public duty with a prickly self-esteem and a lack of tact that rendered almost impossible effective co-operation with other men. Elected President, Adams never became the leader even of his own party. At every stage he found himself hampered and checked either by Jefferson in front of him or by Alexander Hamilton, scornful and overbearing, behind him.

Hamilton, rather than Adams, was Jefferson's real antithesis. Washington admired him and entrusted him with the secretaryship of the treasury, where he justified the confidence of his chief by placing the public credit on the soundest foundation. But Hamilton had in mind much more than a balanced budget and bonds selling at par. He wanted definitely to foster industry by a protective tariff and thus create a large mercantile and industrial class in the United States to balance the agricultural interest. Though he had been active in the Revolution, he admired British institutions, looked with disdain at the crude pioneering environment of America, and wished to build up in the new country a social and economic structure as complex as that of Great Britain. He loved neither tyranny nor democracy, believing that the 'people' were merely the 'mob.' Like Jefferson he had a vision, but a vision which required much less optimism and faith in human nature: a United States firmly united by a strong government and a competent ruling class of merchants, bankers, lawyers, and trained public officials; self-sustaining behind a wall of tariffs and the protection of a strong fleet and army, with busy factories to match the prosperous farms. He was the soul and genius, as well as the active party leader, of Federalism. Unfortunately for his cause, he was almost as tactless as President Adams and even more unpopular.

The French Revolution and the ensuing European conflict sharpened party lines. The Federalists, for the most part, sympathized with the British, either from horror at the radicalism and terrorism of the French Revolution or because even the secession of the United States from the British Empire had not wiped out all affection for the motherland. The anti-Federalists, or Republicans as they called themselves, were usually pro-French, either from enthusiasm for the principles of the French Revolution or because they still considered the British as enemies and the French as allies.

Interests as well as sympathies were involved, however. The

United States was in the decade of the 1790s the chief neutral nation.[5] As a neutral, the nation suffered wrongs from both belligerents. Washington had been compelled to expel the French minister, Citizen Genêt, for trying to stir up a discontent that would force the United States into war on the French side. The Jay treaty with Great Britain, though renewing commercial relations, did not prevent the British from intercepting American trade with France and her allies and, worse yet, impressing American sailors into the British service on the ground that if they were of British birth they could not plead American citizenship. In 1798 there was an acute crisis with France, diplomatic relations were severed, and many of the Federalist party, including Hamilton, expected war and made ready for the conquest of Florida and of the Spanish territory west of the Mississippi, since Spain had sunk to being a mere tool of French diplomacy. To repress American sympathizers with France, Congress passed Alien and Sedition laws, giving the President the right to expel undesirable aliens from the country and making it a penal offence to write, print, or publish 'any false, scandalous, and malicious writing' against the National Government.

The Republican opposition was alert. The legislatures of Virginia and Kentucky denounced the new legislation as unconstitutional and called on the states to agitate for repeal. As Madison, the chief architect of the Constitution, fathered the Virginia resolutions, and Jefferson, the leader of the Republican party, the Kentucky ones, they became classic assertions of state rights. The Kentucky resolutions held that 'whensoever the general government assumes undelegated powers, its acts are . . . void' and that the states had the right to judge for themselves whether the Government had violated the Constitution; the Virginia resolutions, somewhat less drastic in tone, declared that the powers of the Federal Government resulted from 'a compact to which the states are parties' and that the states might 'interpose' their authority if the Constitution were violated. Both appealed to the first amendment of the Constitution as proof that the freedom of the press was guaranteed against the Sedition law. An issue had been raised between 'sovereign nation' and 'sovereign states' that was to be debated afresh in each decade, sometimes by one

---

[5] As in 1914-17 and 1939-41.

aggrieved party or section and sometimes by another, until in 1861 it plunged the country into civil war.

President Adams, unlike many of his party, still hoped and worked for peace with France. Napoleon, who had recently come into power, did not want to face an American war when the British fleet was still on his hands, so he smoothed over the quarrel and no war came. But the Federalist party was rent by schism. Adams was the official candidate for re-election, but Hamilton worked behind his back to induce the Electoral College, which still had some discretion of its own in choosing Presidents, to select Pinckney of South Carolina instead. The Republican party was united behind Jefferson of Virginia and Aaron Burr of New York. It had the support of most of the West and South, a powerful and not too scrupulous party machine in New York, and many discontented small farmers in Pennsylvania and New England. In 1800 it swept the polls. In the Electoral College there arose an unexpected difficulty. Not anticipating the rise of political parties, the fathers of the Constitution had armed each elector with two votes and provided that the candidate with the highest number be chosen President, the one with the second highest Vice-President. But strict party discipline in 1801 caused every Republican elector to vote for both Jefferson and Burr; as a result the election was deadlocked and, in accordance with the Constitution, thrown into the House of Representatives.

The House was deadlocked in turn. Some Federalists wanted to throw the election to Burr out of hatred of Jefferson, their arch-foe, or from the belief that Burr in gratitude would make terms with the Federalist party. But Hamilton, regarding Burr as an unscrupulous intriguer, persuaded his sullen and reluctant party to permit Jefferson to become President as the lesser of two evils. Burr never forgave Hamilton, and later shot him in a duel. The Constitution was amended in such a way that each elector marked his ballot for both President and Vice-President as separate offices. Only twice since then have there been disputed electoral results: in 1824 when John Quincy Adams was chosen by the House of Representatives, since no one had a majority in the Electoral College; and in 1876 when a special electoral commission was created to examine alleged election frauds and miscounts in a close national election. The Electoral College itself became a mere rubber stamp to ratify the victory of a party at the polls.

Jefferson's party, the so-called Republican party, has no organic connection with the Republican party of today; on the contrary it is the direct ancestor of its rival, the present Democratic party. It is the only political party which has maintained its organization and identity throughout the lifetime of the republic. From 1801 to 1861 it was almost continuously in office, with the rarest intermissions; since then, though with widely varying fortunes, it has on the average been about equal in voting strength with the new Republican party founded in the 1850s. The Federalists continued for twenty years after Jefferson's victory a losing battle with the 'democratic Republicans' but they never again held either Congress or the presidency; the allied West and South had defeated the Northeast. The only consolation—or additional exasperation!—for the defeated Federalists was that the triumphant Republicans adopted many Federalist policies when they came to office. They spoke less of state rights, since the federal machinery was now in their own hands.

President Jefferson allayed many fears when he delivered his first inaugural address. Those who had considered him a 'Jacobin' fanatic were surprised to hear him declare: 'Every difference of opinion is not a difference of principle . . . We are all Republicans, we are all Federalists.' He announced that the essential principles of his administration would be:

Peace, commerce and honest friendship with all nations, entangling alliances with none; the support of the State governments in all their rights . . . the preservation of the General Government in its whole constitutional vigor . . . a well-disciplined militia, our best reliance in peace and for the first moments of war, till regulars may relieve them; the supremacy of the civil over the military authority; economy in the public expense . . . the honest payment of our debts and sacred preservation of the public faith; encouragement of agriculture and of commerce as its handmaid.

There was little in this to alarm even Hamiltonians, though some may have feared that the great war raging in Europe would interfere sooner or later with Jefferson's dream of rustic peace and plenty.

One department of the government was still Federalist, the appointed judiciary. President Adams had packed the bench with Federalists and placed at the head of the Supreme Court the famous jurist John Marshall, a Virginian but a political opponent of Jefferson. Marshall held office for thirty-four years and had a greater effect on the interpretation of the Constitution than any other one man. Thus in his opinion in *Marbury* versus *Madison* (1803) he laid down the doctrine that the courts had the right and duty to disallow any law of Congress or act of the government which did not conform to the Constitution; in *McCulloch* versus *Maryland* (1819) he declared that the Federal Government might lawfully establish a national bank, since it could use all means necessary and proper in carrying out the duties assigned to it by the Constitution, even if those means were not themselves mentioned by the Constitution; in the Dartmouth College case (1819) he asserted that a corporation charter was a contract with the state government, which the latter could not cancel by law; in *Gibbons* versus *Ogden* (1824) he insisted that 'the sovereignty of Congress . . . over commerce with foreign nations and among the several states' was as absolute as in a consolidated government.

The greatest triumph of Jefferson's administration was the purchase of the Louisiana Territory. This was a vast region starting with the mouth of the Mississippi River and extending north and west until it reached the Rocky Mountains: it covered almost as great an area as the entire United States when Jefferson took office. Spain had claimed it since 1763, but there were few Spaniards within its bounds; with the exception of a small French colony around New Orleans it was inhabited only by wandering Indian tribes. Napoleon obtained it for France in 1800, but could not hold it in the face of the British fleet. Rather than have it pass by conquest to his foes he was willing to sell the whole. In 1803 Jefferson secured the entire Louisiana Territory for sixty million francs, plus interest and the settlement of certain private claims.

Adams the Federalist had narrowly escaped war with France; Jefferson the Republican was nearly forced into war with Britain. Both men deserve the greatest possible credit for maintaining peace, since in each case the chief pressure towards war came from their own fellow partisans. British Orders in Council, virtually forbidding neutrals to trade with the greater part of continental Europe, now under Napoleon's control, and the continued impressment of American seamen of British birth led to a long series of irritating incidents, culminating in the attack on an American vessel, the *Chesapeake*, by a British warship. In 1807 Jefferson, still trying to find a substitute for war, resorted to a weapon much discussed in these days, the economic boycott. By an Embargo Act Congress forbade American ships to leave port for European waters and all exports to belligerent nations were prohibited. It was hoped that this shutting off of American trade would speedily bring Great Britain, and Napoleon as well, to recognition of the 'freedom of the seas.' But Jefferson miscalculated. His measure hit American commerce a deadlier blow than all the British and French interference with American ships put together. Far better, thought mercantile New England, a trade with some risks than no trade at all. Just before leaving office Jefferson had to rescind the embargo and admit that his peaceful equivalent for war had failed to do anything to vindicate American rights at sea.

James Madison of Virginia was Jefferson's successor. Though a great constitutional statesman he was a weak President; he was unable to maintain peace, as Washington, Adams, and Jefferson had done, or adequately to prepare the country for war. In the nick of time Napoleon promised not to interfere with American trade while Great Britain refused to abandon her Orders in Council restricting commerce with Napoleon and his allied and conquered territories. A little more patience at that point and war might even yet have been avoided; for, unknown to the Americans, the British Government was already considering a suspension of its Orders. But behind the clamor for 'freedom of the seas' and 'sailors' rights' was another cry, the cry of the frontier West, for the conquest of Canada. Irritated by Indian wars in the Northwest, which many Americans believed to have been supported by British officers in Canada, and ever greedy for more land, the backwoodsmen were a war party, expecting an easy conquest of thinly peopled Canada, perhaps even a rising of the Canadians against their British rulers. In 1812 Congress declared war, but the maritime states of the East voted in the minority against it.

Jefferson's optimistic reliance on the militia 'for the first moments of war' received little support from the events of the War of 1812.

Several attempts to invade Canada failed from the inadequacy of
the regular army, small almost to invisibility, and the indiscipline
of the militia. Later in the war the British raided the Atlantic coast
and burned the Capitol and the White House in Washington. But
a long series of naval victories in single engagements between British
and American frigates did something to restore national self-esteem,
and the naval battle on Lake Erie assured American command of
the Great Lakes. The greatest American victory on land, Andrew
Jackson's triumph at New Orleans, was fought in January 1815,
after the treaty of peace had been signed, though before the news
of it reached the United States.

New England's opposition to the war did not cease after it had
been declared. The Federalists disliked it on three grounds: it was
ruinous to trade, it helped 'Napoleon the tyrant' in his struggle to
conquer Europe, and it was 'Mr. Madison's War' started by the
Republican party. They found some economic compensation, however, in the fact that first Jefferson's hated embargo and later Madison's war, by cutting off British trade, had stimulated American
manufacture. The beginning of large-scale cloth manufacture in
Massachusetts, Rhode Island, and New Jersey dates from this period.
In 1814 the New England states sent delegates to a convention at
Hartford, Connecticut, to formulate a policy for their section. Extremists wished to secede and make a separate peace with Great Britain, but the moderate Federalists prevailed and watered down the
Hartford program to proposals for a few constitutional amendments.
But the Federalist party never recovered from the reproach of taking
a disloyal attitude in the midst of war, and it slowly declined towards
extinction even in New England.

Though two or three generations of Americans were taught to
look on the War of 1812 as an American victory, and Canadians on
the other side of the frontier to consider it a local triumph for themselves, the truth seems to be that it was as close to being a draw as
any war in modern history. The Treaty of Ghent which closed it at
the end of 1814 neither affirmed nor denied the British contentions
about the right of search and seizure of neutral ships and impressment of British seamen found on them. Impressment was, in fact,
abandoned by the British themselves in later years, and the seizure
of neutral cargoes is still a bitterly debated question of international

law unsettled in the twentieth century. No changes at all were made in the international boundary between the United States and Canada, though boundary commissions were established to settle parts of the frontier that were uncertain.

There was a happy sequel to the inconclusive War of 1812 in the Rush-Bagot agreement of 1818, which limited naval armament on the Great Lakes to a mere police patrol. The precedent thus established has been continued, so that for more than a century the United States and Canada have enjoyed the longest unfortified frontier in the world. In the same year it was agreed to leave the Oregon country west of the Rockies open to either British or American occupation with no immediate attempt to fix a frontier, and in 1819 the American purchase of Florida ended a long-standing source of friction with Spain.

○ XXII ○

DEMOCRACY, ISOLATION, AND EXPANSION

THREE main trends marked American public life between the close of the War of 1812 and the close of the Mexican War of 1846-8: democracy, isolation, and expansion. So far as the free white population was concerned, at any rate, the new spirit of equality leveled the last barriers of legal class privilege. Americans turned away from European affairs and concentrated on their own immediate interests, especially the rapid development of their western lands. They took, however, a keener interest than ever in the international politics of the New World, and pushed their frontiers from the Rocky Mountains to the Pacific Ocean.

All three tendencies were, in very large part, merely by-products of that westward trend of settlement which we have noted in the previous chapter. Left to themselves, the Atlantic seaboard states would have been less democratic, more closely tied to Europe, and less concerned about expansion. But they were not left to themselves. Each new state beyond the Appalachians increased the weight of the West in both houses of Congress and in the Electoral College; when the Constitution was made there were thirteen stars in the flag, in 1850 there were thirty-one. Of the eighteen new states all were predominantly rural, and all but three (Vermont, Maine, and Florida) lay west of the mountains.

The War of 1812, though in sober fact a stalemate, begat a curious self-confidence in the young republic. For the second time it had stood up to the mightiest Empire in the world. Defeats on land were forgotten and victories at sea embalmed in patriotic legend, and Jackson's final victory at New Orleans left a pleasant taste in the mouth. Indian tribes were easily bribed or coerced into giving up their native woodlands to the white pioneers. The Spanish Empire was beginning to break up in revolution; parts of it might fall

259

to the more enterprising Anglo-Saxon; other parts form a series of friendly fellow republics. The tone of British diplomacy had changed; the United States was no longer either bullied or patronized but treated as France might be treated, a possible ally or a possible rival, but in either case as an independent equal. There were many excuses for the new national self-assurance that 'made the eagle scream' in the patriotic oratory of the day.

Political independence might be secure, but what about economic independence? The United States was only beginning to manufacture. Sydney Smith asked in 1820 the rhetorical question, 'Who drinks out of American glasses? Or eats from American plates? Or wears American coats? Or sleeps in American blankets?' Today the answer might be 'Half the world!' In those days it would have been, 'Half America; the rest, who can afford better goods, buy from Britain.' This dependence on British manufactures seemed galling. So the Republicans adopted the old Federalist doctrine of Hamilton, that agriculture should be balanced by manufactures. National banking, protective tariffs, and expenditures from the public treasury for canals, roads, bridges, rivers, and harbors, in later years for railroad subsidies, became features of the new nationalism. It is curious to see among the advocates of this policy not only Henry Clay of Kentucky but even John C. Calhoun of South Carolina, later to be the archpriest of state rights.

Now that the Republicans had become nationalists, there seemed no longer any excuse for the Federalist party. James Monroe was elected in succession to James Madison, and re-elected with practically no opposition on the Republican ticket. An era of good feeling replaced the old strife of the parties; it lasted only for Monroe's time, but the bitter new quarrels which ended it were due to party splits among the dominant Republicans.

Even in those halcyon days, there was one political storm, but it involved a sectional rather than a strictly party conflict. Missouri Territory demanded admission as a state. Since most of the Missourians were from the South, and some of them were slaveholders, slavery was recognized in the new state constitution. Anti-slavery men wished to keep Missouri in her territorial status until she was willing to come in as a free state. This aroused two sorts of men, those who wished slavery extended, and those who viewed with apprehension the attempt to impose conditions on a new state against the will of a majority of its voters. The quarrel alarmed the aged Jefferson 'like a fire bell in the night.' His own sympathies were divided; he hated the extension of slavery, but he was sensitive, as were most Virginians, to any attempt to coerce either the states, as states, or the South, as a section. Henry Clay and others postponed a sectional clash on the slavery issue by a ready compromise. Missouri could have slavery if she wished, but other territories north of the latitude of 36° 30′ were to prohibit it.

Monroe's administration is now remembered chiefly for the Monroe Doctrine, which formulated the Latin American policy of the United States for more than a century to come. The revolt of Spanish America had extended so widely that Spain, from her own meager resources, was wholly unable to repress it. The Great Powers of the European continent—Russia, Prussia, Austria, and France—had, however, committed themselves to a policy of repressing revolution wherever it might arise. With France as their active agent they had crushed a rebellion in Spain. Would they extend the same policy to Spain's American colonies?

The British ministry hoped not. It was a Tory ministry and certainly had no love of revolutions and no passion for republican principles, but it could see no danger to British institutions in revolutions so far away as Mexico and Argentina. On the other hand, it had a very lively fear lest Spain and her colonies might fall under French influence and be closed to British trade. In 1822 the United States at last extended recognition to several of the Spanish American republics. Great Britain was not yet ready to do this, but in 1823 Foreign Minister Canning proposed to the United States a joint protest against intervention by other powers in the struggle between Spain and her former colonies. Richard Rush, the American minister, laid Canning's proposal before his own government. Monroe was favorably impressed, as were his two immediate predecessors, Madison and Jefferson. John Quincy Adams, son of President Adams, was Monroe's Secretary of State. He was inclined to be suspicious of British diplomacy but he saw in Canning's overtures the possibility of a general declaration of American policy, aimed not only at France's alleged designs in Spanish America but also at Russia's presumed ambitions, for Russia was busily engaged in extending her Alaskan claims to the southward along the Pacific coast.

So Monroe and Adams put their heads together. The lofty idealism and keen, impatient mind of Adams contributed most to the formulation of the Monroe Doctrine, but Monroe's diplomatic tact and skill in phrasing counted for not a little. In December 1823 the President issued his message to Congress. He declared that

the occasion has been judged proper for asserting . . . that the American continents . . . are henceforth not to be considered as subjects for future colonization by any European powers . . . In the wars of the European powers in matters relating to themselves we have never taken any part, nor does it comport with our policy so to do . . . With the movements in this hemisphere we are of necessity more immediately connected . . . We owe it, therefore, to candor and to the amicable relations existing between the United States and those powers to declare that we should consider any attempt on their part to extend their system to any portion of this hemisphere as dangerous to our peace and safety. With the existing colonies or dependencies of any European power we have not interfered and shall not interfere. But with the governments who have declared their independence and maintained it, and whose independence we have . . . acknowledged, we could not view any interposition for the purpose of oppressing them, or controlling in any other manner their destiny, by any European power in any other light than as the manifestation of an unfriendly disposition toward the United States.

The doctrine thus expressed became the cornerstone of American foreign policy, acquiring, like the Declaration of Independence and the Constitution, added prestige with each generation. So many new glosses have been added to the original simple message that it may be worth a moment to point out what the Monroe Doctrine is *not*. It is not a part of international law,[1] and no foreign government is obliged to respect it if willing to risk the displeasure of the United States. It does not in any way extend the influence of the United States over the Latin American countries nor, on the other hand, does it contain any self-denying clause limiting the acquisition of

---

[1] Curiously enough, its first formal recognition by treaty, with the assent of European powers, was in the Covenant of the League of Nations, which, as part of the Treaty of Versailles, the American Senate refused to ratify—thus throwing away an important victory of American diplomacy.

additional American territory by the United States. It has, in itself, no application to existing European colonies, such as Canada.[2] It is not a statute binding even the United States; any of Monroe's successors in the presidency was free to modify or even to repudiate the policy which he outlined. It was and is merely a declaration of policy to the effect that the United States would oppose European attempts at conquering or colonizing independent American territory.

Party strife burst out anew when Monroe left the White House, but at first there was no formally organized opposition party, merely a warfare of personal factions of Republicans. Four candidates appeared in the field in 1824: John Quincy Adams, the Secretary of State, from Massachusetts; William H. Crawford, Secretary of the Treasury, from Georgia; Henry Clay of Kentucky; and General Andrew Jackson of Tennessee. All four had strong support and no one was able to command a majority in the Electoral College, so the election was thrown into the House of Representatives. The Clay men threw their support to Adams and elected him. This was strictly in accordance with law and constitution, but it awakened an immense, if illogical, opposition. Jackson had the widest popular support of any of the candidates, and a new theory had arisen that the Electoral College and the House of Representatives were alike merely 'delegates of the people,' morally bound to carry out any evident popular desire. The fact that Clay was made Secretary of State was denounced as evidence of a 'corrupt bargain,' though, since Clay was well qualified for his post, it looks to the modern eye more like a perfectly frank and reasonable political coalition.

Thus Adams's administration started under a cloud, from which it never emerged. John Quincy Adams has been variously estimated. He has been ranked among the greatest of the Presidents, and also among the weakest. Both estimates are not without warrant; he was, like his father, a man of the highest integrity and ability, and his statesmanlike outlook was even broader; but he disdained the arts of politics and was completely out-generaled by his opponents. In 1828 he was defeated by Andrew Jackson, whose election to the presidency opened a new era in American politics, even more evidently than Jefferson's famous victory in 1800.

[2] Yet, as President Franklin Roosevelt pointed out, the United States would feel menaced if Canada were attacked by an alien power.

Andrew Jackson was the first Western President, the first in fact to be chosen outside the charmed circle of the political leaders of the proud old states of Virginia and Massachusetts. Previous Presidents had been chosen from the cabinet, like British Prime Ministers; Jackson was an army officer with some experience in Congress, but he had never formed part of an administration. He was not, indeed, the illiterate backwoodsman that his enemies made him out to be; he was a chivalrous gentleman with much natural dignity; but he had lived a roving, adventurous life, he had fought deadly duels, and had perplexed American diplomacy by carrying fights against the Indians across the border of Spanish Florida. It was in Jackson's time that the Republican party of Jefferson began to assume on its own behalf the title, hitherto given it by opponents, of the Democratic party. The term 'democratic,' though still viewed with some dislike by British politicians, was now eagerly embraced by Americans, even by those who held slaves.

Jackson was a remarkable man, but, after all, he was much more a product of the new democratic spirit than a cause of it. If he had never lived, some other Western President would have soon been chosen—that 'hardy perennial' candidate Henry Clay of Kentucky, perhaps. The chief changes in law were carried out in the states rather than in the Federal Government. For example, one tendency of the time was towards universal manhood suffrage, no other qualification for the vote being required than that a man should be 'free, white, and twenty-one.' But the franchise was entirely a matter of state law, even for national elections. Again, there was a tendency to multiply elective offices so that the people would choose directly those who were to serve them. In states, counties, and cities scores of offices—sheriffs, district attorneys, coroners, local judges, superintendents of education, and the like—were made elective and for short terms. But no similar change was made at Washington. Federal judges still held office for life; the President still appointed his own cabinet.

Changes there were, however, in national politics; but they were changes of custom rather than of law. One change, a singularly disastrous one, was the growing development of the spoils system.[3]

---

[3] From the phrase used by William Marcy, a New York politician, 'To the victors belong the spoils.'

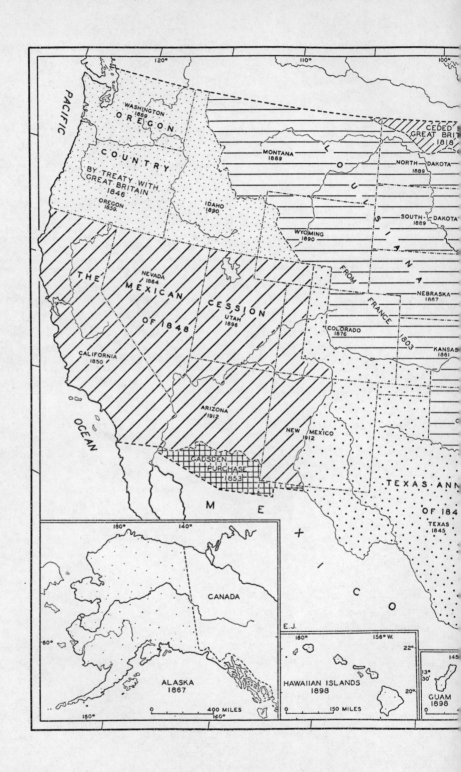

PACIFIC

WASHINGTON
1889

OREGON

COUNTRY

BY TREATY WITH
GREAT BRITAIN
1846

OREGON
1859

IDAHO
1890

MONTANA
1889

LOUIS

NORTH DAKOTA
1889

SOUTH DAKOTA
1889

WYOMING
1890

CEDED BY
GREAT BRIT.
1818

THE

NEVADA
1864

MEXICAN CESSION

OF 1848

UTAH
1896

CALIFORNIA
1850

NEBRASKA
1867

COLORADO
1876

KANSAS
1861

OCEAN

ARIZONA
1912

NEW MEXICO
1912

FROM FRANCE 1803

GADSDEN
PURCHASE
1853

M E

+

I

C

TEXAS ANN.

OF 184

TEXAS
1845

O

E.J.

150°

140°

CANADA

60°

ALASKA
1867

150°

160°

400 MILES

160°

156° W.

22°

HAWAIIAN ISLANDS
1898

20°

150 MILES

145°

13°
30°

GUAM
1898

TERRITORIAL EXPANSION OF THE UNITED STATES

Hitherto the coming in of a new administration, even of a new party, had meant the removal of only a few officials; and the two Adamses had even retained men in high office who were actively working against them. But Jackson, copying the growing practice of local politics, removed federal office holders by the hundreds on purely political grounds. Jackson, of course, was quite unconscious of the harm he was doing. He believed public duties could be performed by any reasonably intelligent and honest American as well as by any other, and he was too intense a partisan to see more intelligence or honesty in a political foe than in a political supporter.

Another change was in the manner of nominating the President. Hitherto nominations had been as a rule the work of a party caucus in Congress, though sometimes state legislatures and other bodies proposed nominees for President and Vice-President. After Jackson's time it became customary for a special party convention to be called to draw up a platform of principles and policies and nominate candidates for President and Vice-President. One important effect of the new method of nomination was to break the old tradition of promotion from Congress or cabinet office to the White House. Nominating conventions cast a wider net, and often swept clear out of national politics and caught a state governor or successful general who had never held cabinet office or served in Congress. Anyone familiar with American politics in Washington's administration, if asked to guess who the next four Presidents would be, would have put Adams, Jefferson, Madison, and Monroe high on his list. But since nomination by convention came into fashion it has seldom been possible to predict a nomination (unless it were the renomination of the man in office) for more than a year or two ahead, and on several occasions a party convention has ended by nominating a man who was not even considered when it first met.

Jackson blended in a curious fashion the nationalist and the state-rights advocate. He believed in reducing the functions of the Federal Government to a minimum, but in maintaining its authority against all opposition. During his administration he vetoed a bill to recharter the national bank, partly from a belief that such a monopolistic institution was unconstitutional and partly from a frontiersman's suspicion of the 'money power.' The frontiersman appeared also in his tacit permission to Georgia to force Indian tribes from the state, in defiance alike of national treaties and of a decision of the Supreme Court. But when South Carolina proclaimed the right to nullify a national tariff law by state action, and backed her stand by threats to secede from the Union, Jackson stood implacably for national sovereignty.

The nullification quarrel was personal as well as constitutional. John C. Calhoun, Vice-President of the United States, was at one time much of a nationalist himself. But as he saw his beloved South falling behind the North in population and industrial wealth, when he discovered that the new industries fostered by protective tariffs kept away from the slave states, he fell back on state rights and a strict construction of the terms of the federal Constitution, as doubtless most Northen politicians would have done had the cases been reversed. He had already quarreled with Jackson on personal grounds [4] and lost the support of the administration as Jackson's successor in the White House, which was transferred to Martin Van Buren, Secretary of State, an adroit New York politician. In 1828 Calhoun prepared an 'exposition and protest,' which was approved by the South Carolina legislature. It declared that a protective tariff was 'unconstitutional, unequal and oppressive . . . The General Government is one of specific powers, and it rightfully exercises only the powers expressly granted, and those that may be necessary and proper to carry them into effect.' It argued that the power of an unchecked majority was tyranny over the minority, and that this tyranny was at its worst when it was of one section of the country over another. To prevent this tyranny, the founding fathers of the Constitution had placed sovereign power in the hands of the states. 'The constitution had formed the states into a community only to the extent of their common interests.' To protect the rights of individual states, appeal might be made to the Supreme Court or to the reserved power of the states themselves. 'To the states respectively—each in its sovereign capacity—is reserved the power, by its veto, or right of interposition, to arrest the encroachment' of the central government.[5] In

[4] Mrs. Calhoun had snubbed Mrs. Eaton, wife of the Secretary of War. The petticoat has played a smaller part in the political life of America than of most nations, but it appears here and there.

[5] Calhoun was quite aware of the obvious objection to nullification, that if each state were made judge of the constitutionality of any federal act no contro-

1830 Jackson openly challenged Calhoun at a public meeting by offering the toast 'Our Federal Union—it *must* be preserved.' In 1832 the South Carolina legislature declared the tariff null and void, as beyond the powers granted to Congress by the Constitution, and forbade the collection of customs duties within the confines of South Carolina. Jackson declared nullification illegal and obtained from Congress a bill authorizing him to use the army and navy to enforce the laws. But a conflict was averted. Congress, frightened at the prospect of civil war, modified the tariff, and South Carolina, on her part, agreed not to interfere with the federal revenue officers. Twenty-eight years later South Carolina was again to raise the issue of state sovereignty and thus plunge the whole nation into war.

Jackson had roused against himself a very composite opposition: friends of Clay and friends of Adams, advocates of the national bank, advocates of state rights, conservatives who were afraid of Jackson's radicalism, and liberals who considered him too arbitrary and dictatorial—'King Andy' in short. But opposition to Jackson was almost the only thing they had in common. They called themselves first National Republicans and later Whigs. The short-lived Whig party, the official opposition to the Democratic party, played a curious part in American history. It refused to identify itself with any class or section of the country and contained wealthy Southern planters and Eastern bankers, as well as the frontiersmen of Kentucky who idolized Clay. It made a point of ignoring the slavery issue and, in truth, most issues. In general, it tended to favor a protective tariff, a program of federal internal improvements, and a national bank, but it contained many individuals who differed from it on all those points. It had a special weakness for nominating popular military heroes—Harrison, Taylor, Scott—with no ascertainable political opinions, and twice this policy led it to success. The real giants of the party, Daniel Webster of Massachusetts and Henry Clay of Kentucky, sought eagerly for the presidency but always failed either of nomination or election.

Jackson was able to defeat Clay and secure re-election, and later to

verted policy could ever be adopted. His answer was that the Constitution itself could be amended by action of three-fourths of the states; they would thus be the ultimate judge and jury in any case arising between the federal government and any single state government.

place his friend Martin Van Buren in the White House as his successor. But Van Buren's single term was clouded by the panic of 1837, brought about in part by Jackson's anti-bank policy, and in 1840 the Whigs were jubilant. They nominated General William H. Harrison, a doughty old Indian fighter somewhat of the Jackson type. Jackson had been born in South Carolina and had moved west to Tennessee; Harrison had been born in Virginia and had moved west to Ohio. Van Buren's champions, unwisely forgetting Jackson's own career, sneered at Harrison as a simple backwoodsman who would be content with a log cabin and a jug of hard cider. Instead of rebutting this charge, which could easily have been done since Harrison was actually a cultured and fairly prosperous gentleman, Harrison's cynical campaign managers boasted of it. They carried log cabin models, jugs of cider, and coonskins in parade and attacked Van Buren as a wealthy aristocrat who lacked the common touch. Jackson's enemies had adopted Jacksonism; the Western spirit of equality had conquered both parties. It was now good tactics in American politics to be of humble origin, to have little money and very plain tastes, and not in any way to set one's self up as better than one's neighbors.

Harrison was triumphantly elected to the cry of 'Tippecanoe [6] and Tyler too!' in a whirlwind campaign of songs and slogans. But the old victor of Tippecanoe died within a few weeks of taking office, and for the first time in American history a Vice-President succeeded in office a deceased President. John Tyler was not really a Whig but rather an anti-Jackson Democrat who devoutly believed in state rights; he had been put on the ticket to attract the followers of Calhoun. The Whig political managers had been too clever; death had made President a man who had little sympathy with them. Tyler refused to charter a national bank, the cabinet resigned,[7] and for the rest of the term the administration was rather Calhoun Democracy than Whiggery. Shortly before leaving office, Tyler signed a bill for the annexation of Texas as a state of the Union, and thereby started

[6] A battle in which Harrison was victorious over the Indians. John Tyler of Virginia was the nominee for Vice-President.

[7] Daniel Webster, Harrison's Secretary of State, held on for a few months to complete negotiations with Britain over the Maine boundary.

a train of events that led to war with Mexico and the annexation of the whole Southwest.

The Mexican province of Texas had a small settlement of Americans on its vast and almost empty plains. Finding Mexican government, or rather misgovernment, a handicap, they proclaimed an independent republic and elected Sam Houston, former governor of Tennessee, President of Texas. The Texans regarded independence as merely a stage between Mexican rule and union with the United States, but, largely because of the slavery question, Texas was kept waiting on the threshold from 1836 to 1845, since it would enter the Union as a slave state.

In 1844, while the Texan issue was still pending, the Democrats nominated James K. Polk of Tennessee on a platform of national expansion. Oregon was to be occupied clear up to the boundary of Russian Alaska, 'fifty-four forty,' and Texas annexed. The Whigs nominated Henry Clay, who refused to commit himself definitely on the Texas issue and was defeated by the bolder course of his rival. On taking office Polk sent an army to protect the new American state of Texas from Mexican reprisals. He tried to obtain recognition of the frontier, and perhaps the annexation of California and New Mexico, by purchase; but the Mexican Government refused to negotiate on these matters. When news reached Washington of a Mexican attack on a small American force near the Rio Grande River, Polk advised Congress to declare war on the ground that Mexico had 'shed American blood upon the American soil.'

A brisk and romantic little war followed, highly popular with all except anti-slavery advocates, who feared the extension of slavery in the new territories which might be acquired, and a very few conservatives of the Southeast, like Calhoun, who feared the reopening of the slavery question. Much to the disgust of the Democratic administration, however, the best generals it could find were Zachary Taylor of Louisiana and Winfield Scott of Virginia, two Southern Whigs. These competent officers defeated dictator Santa Anna's armies and enabled the United States to impose a treaty on defeated Mexico. In the meantime Captain John C. Frémont aided an insurrection of American settlers in California. Among the lesser officers who received praise for their services in the war were Robert E. Lee, Jefferson Davis, George B. McClellan, and Ulysses S. Grant.

The treaty which closed the war early in 1848 acknowledged the frontier claimed by Texas, the Rio Grande River, and transferred to the United States California (except for the peninsula of Lower California) and the territory then called New Mexico, much larger than the present state of that name, lying between Texas and California. From some feeling of compunction or compassion for defeated Mexico, the United States agreed to pay $15,000,000 for the new territory and to assume the claims of private citizens against the Mexican Government. In 1853 a small additional strip of land was purchased from Mexico along the southern border of the United States (the Gadsden purchase).

Polk had been elected not only as an advocate of expansion at Mexico's expense but also on the cry of 'Fifty-four forty or fight,' the annexation of the entire Oregon country. The lion in the path here was Great Britain. The agreement of 1818 had left open the ownership of the whole Pacific coast between California and Alaska; either Britons or Americans might settle there in the meantime. Spain and Russia had withdrawn their claims shortly afterwards. The Hudson's Bay Company desired to hold the valley of the Oregon (or Columbia) River as a fur-trading area; but there were rival fur traders from the United States. In the 1830s they were joined by American missionaries to the Indians, and in the 1840s by farmers from the Mississippi valley.

These farmers did not want to stop on the great plains of Kansas and Nebraska or among the Rocky Mountains; they aimed to cross both plains and mountains in a single trek and reach the wooded and fertile Willamette valley near the Pacific. Conestoga wagons, whose bottoms were shaped like boats and hence could be floated across any not too turbulent river and whose tops were covered with rainproof canvas, were used to carry these immigrants. Oxen were employed more often than horses, since endurance was more necessary than speed. When the first prairie grass appeared in the spring these wagons would leave the Missouri River for the 'Oregon trail.' By the first week in July they would be at Independence Rock in Wyoming, the landmark where prairies began to give way to hilly country. They had to be across the mountains before snow fell or run the frightful risk of being caught on the road by impassable drifts. The swift and treacherous waters of the Snake River and the

Columbia into which it flowed took many lives; the hostile Indians took more. By 1845 there were several thousand American settlers south of the Columbia and the boundary settlement with Great Britain could no longer be postponed.

With Mexico on his hands, Polk did not really wish war or risk of war with Great Britain. In 1846 he agreed to a compromise, extending the boundary along the line of 49°, giving the Americans the long-contested Columbia River valley and awarding to the British Vancouver Island and what is now the province of British Columbia. As the Maine-New Brunswick frontier had been fixed by the Webster-Ashburton treaty of 1842 the Canadian boundary was no longer a source of dispute. Some Northerners complained that Polk had been willing to compromise concerning Oregon in the Northwest, while he stood firm for annexations from Mexico in the Southwest; but on a candid examination this seems to be less a question of sectional favoritism than a very well-justified estimate of the respective risks of challenging Great Britain and challenging Mexico! Historians are still discussing Polk's responsibility for the Mexican War but none now blame him for accepting the Oregon peace.

The most extraordinary of all the Western settlements was that of the Mormons in Utah. The Mormons, whose own name for themselves is the Latter Day Saints, accepted a special revelation from their prophet Joseph Smith, embodied in the Book of Mormon. The Mormon settlements in Missouri and Illinois were viewed with dislike by their neighbors, and when Joseph Smith proclaimed polygamy as a practice of the new church, his congregation was broken up by mobs and he himself was murdered. The new leader, Brigham Young, decided to move to a promised land far to the sunset where 'Gentile' neighbors would no longer disturb them. On the shores of Salt Lake he founded a State of Deseret under the dictatorial control of himself and the clergy. Polygamy apart, the new government was remarkably efficient and under its iron control a prosperous agricultural community developed.

While farmers were seeking a new Zion in Utah or new farms in Oregon, word came of the discovery of gold in California. This started another rush for the Far West, of a different character. Amateur miners in thousands made for California in 1848 and 1849, and statehood was granted in 1850. Never before in American history, perhaps in any history, had a new community developed with such sudden impetus. In 1846 California had been a sleepy Mexican community, very sparsely settled by ranch owners and mission priests, with a small sprinkling of restless American immigrants who were scheming to join it to the Union. By 1850 it was a teeming cosmopolitan mining center [8] with fresh immigration constantly pouring in from overland wagon trails, coastwise ships from the isthmus of Panama, and the great clipper ships sailing around South America. Mining camps are often more lawless than farming communities, and federal authority was weakened by distance. Special vigilance committees, organized without warrant of law but with the intention of repressing crime, were constituted to act as a temporary substitute until the law could be efficiently administered by its own officers. When silver mines were discovered a few years later in Nevada and Colorado there were fresh rushes of immigration, new epochs of lawlessness, and new popular tribunals to repress it. Though mining gave to California her early rapid growth, many who came to find fortunes in the golden sands of her rivers were disappointed in their hopes and turned instead to ranching, farming, and store keeping. Before long California, like Oregon and Utah, was primarily an agricultural region.

The prairies and the mountains developed more slowly than the Pacific coast beyond them. East of the Mississippi, except in part of Illinois, the whole United States was well wooded, but between the Mississippi and the Missouri woodlands became scarcer, while west of the Missouri the prairie was almost unbroken. Over these plains roamed the Indian and the buffalo. Even when the Indians had been driven away, difficulties confronted the pioneer. He did not have to chop down trees and grub out roots, it is true, and the land stretched level before him, waiting for the plow. But if the forest had been the enemy of the earlier pioneers it had also been their friend. On the plains of Kansas and Nebraska, opened for settlement in the 1850s, the settlers found neither wood nor stone to build their homes; the more prosperous imported lumber from a distance, the rest built huts out of the prairie sod. Fencing was another problem; neither the stone fences of New Hampshire nor the zigzag rail fences of Vir-

---

[8] California by the census of 1850 had almost a hundred thousand inhabitants.

ginia were possible; the introduction of barbed wire in the 1870s later solved this difficulty. Clouds of grasshoppers, dry seasons, dust storms, and occasional tornadoes created new obstacles unknown to the backwoodsmen of Pennsylvania, Maine, and Wisconsin. A new agricultural technique, involving irrigation, dry farming, and re-forestation, had to be learned. In many ways the man who moved from Massachusetts to Kansas entered a newer environment than his great-grandfather who had moved from Essex to Massachusetts. British settlers in arid Australia, however, have faced similar problems.[9]

Anyone might have thought that the acquisition of the Louisiana Territory, Florida, Texas, Oregon, California, and New Mexico would have exhausted all expansionist dreams of the American frontiersmen for at least another century. The War of 1812, to be sure, had put an end to all dreams of conquering Canada, though hopes were sometimes felt—especially at the time of the rebellion of 1837 [10]—that Canada might voluntarily join the Union. For the most part visionaries of empire looked southward. Cuba was constantly talked about, and many suggestions made of purchasing it from Spain. Some reproached Polk for not annexing all Mexico when he had his chance. An adventurer named William Walker tried to seize the Central American republic of Nicaragua. Fear of conflict with Great Britain in Central America led to the compromise of the Clayton-Bulwer treaty (1850), by which both countries agreed not to seek exclusive control over a projected canal route across Nicaragua. In 1854 Commodore Perry persuaded Japan to abandon her isolation and sign a treaty of friendship and commerce. American traders were active in Chinese ports and among Pacific islands.

Nor did American diplomatic isolation mean that the people of the United States felt obliged to refrain from expressing opinions on events in the Old World. When Greece rose against Turkey, and later when Hungary rose against Austria, hundreds of public meetings in every state passed resolutions of sympathy and extended every encouragement that oratory could give. Only when it came to action did a prudent people hesitate. The Hungarian patriot Kossuth

[9] See Chapter xxxv.
[10] See Chapter xxxiv.

was welcomed on his visit to America with as much enthusiasm as was ever shown to LaFayette, but the hot-heads who wanted to fight Austria were always overruled. Similar platonic, though sincere, sympathy was expressed for republican France in 1848, for the advocates of German and of Italian unity, and for the Irish Home Rulers. Irritated Europeans might complain that Russian oppressions in Poland were no worse than chattel slavery, or that it came with poor grace for the victors in the Mexican War to accuse the British of imperialism in India, but the American sentiment for world liberty was perfectly genuine, even if sometimes inconsistent.[11]

[11] Domestic critics also pointed out this inconsistency, as witness Lowell's *Biglow Papers:*

> I du believe in freedom's cause
> Ez fur away ez Paris is . . .
> It's wal enough agin' a king
> To dror resolves and triggers
> But liberty's a kind of thing
> That don't agree with niggers!

⚬ XXIII ⚬

SOUTH AND NORTH ON THE EVE OF CONFLICT

THUS far we have traced the history of the United States mainly in terms of western expansion and the sectional rivalry of East with West; it is now time to emphasize another such conflict, that of North and South. The 'West' was a dissolving view, constantly altering both its geographical limits and its characteristic institutions. Such a state as Ohio, for example, was considered Western in Jackson's time, Central in Lincoln's, and Eastern in McKinley's. The South, on the contrary, had relatively fixed boundaries. Lines of westward settlement usually followed the lines of latitude: New Englanders went to Iowa, Virginians to Kentucky, Georgians to Mississippi. Even within the confines of a single state these trends were evident; thus northern Ohio, Connecticut's old 'western reserve' lands, seemed as Yankee as New England, while southern Ohio, the Virginia military grant lands, resembled rather Kentucky.

The boundaries of the South were originally fixed by the institution of slavery, which was profitable only where staple crops could be raised on plantations, and this in turn depended ultimately on climate. The United States, except for the Pacific coast, has everywhere rather an intemperate than a temperate climate; even Florida orchards are sometimes endangered by winter frosts, and North Dakota wheat farmers are sometimes victims of sunstroke in summer. But though the annual range of temperature is wide, there is a great regional difference in the duration and severity of the cold season. The staple crops of tobacco, cotton, sugar cane, rice, and indigo could be profitably cultivated only in regions of comparatively short and mild winters. This resulted, even in colonial times, in a concentration of the Negro slave population in the South.[1] At first this was a difference of economic interest rather than of sentiment; except in

---

[1] For a discussion of colonial slavery see Chapter XVII.

the Quaker communities there was no great hostility to slavery in the North. But the fact that very few Northerners owned slaves made it easy for the state legislatures, acting one by one, to abolish the institution itself; the growing sentiment of the majority was face to face with the economic interest of only a small and diminishing minority.

In the South the trend was all the other way. Thomas Jefferson and many other Virginians of his generation disliked slavery and looked forward to its eventual abolition. But there were fewer Southerners of his opinion in 1830 than in 1776, and fewer in 1860 than in 1830. The invention of the cotton gin by Eli Whitney near the end of the eighteenth century made cotton a cheap commodity in the market, while the rapid expansion of the British textile manufacture in the nineteenth century increased the demand. As the cotton culture pushed westward into Alabama, Mississippi, Louisiana, and Texas, the plantation system went with it. The vested interest in slavery was now so great that it would have required a political earthquake to shake it.

Even in the cotton belt, however, and still more in the upper South, where tobacco and maize were more important than cotton, the majority of white men were not slaveholders. Why, then, did they not outvote the landed gentry who owned the plantations? Why was there next to no echo among the slaveless whites when Helper's *The Impending Crisis*, a Southerner's plea on their behalf, was so widely applauded in the North? One reason, of course, was that men think and feel in groups as well as individually, and no one wants his state or section impoverished by legislative action even if he loses no property of his own. But there were other reasons which had little to do with economics. The mind of the whole South was hag-ridden by fear that the free African would be uncontrollable. The writings of the time are full of references to Haiti, where Negro slaves had overthrown not only their masters but the French colonial civilization which had been established there. Slavery was defended as essentially a police measure to assure white domination. So long as this view was accepted, by slaveless as well as by slaveholding whites, the necessary impetus to overturn the institution would never come from the South, no matter how many economists might demonstrate that slave labor was in the long run unprofitable.

Would this impetus come from outside? That was the fear of the pro-slavery leaders. The abolition of colonial British slavery, against the wish of the majority of the planters in the West Indies,[2] seemed an ominous precedent. A growing anti-slavery propaganda, from old England, New England, the Northwest, and even continental Europe, made the South feel isolated, thrust into the position of defending what was euphemistically called her 'peculiar institution' against the rest of the civilized world. From talking merely of state rights, Southerners progressed to Southern rights, although in so doing they passed from constitutional arguments to a new regional conception which had no formal legal basis. In his last days, Calhoun, the most eminent champion of the lower South, began to dream of what a Briton of today would call Dominion status for the South; even to consider the election of two Presidents, like the two consuls of ancient Rome, one chosen from the free states and one from the slave states.

Let us suppose that Calhoun's imaginary Dominion of the South had been established in 1850, when he was considering it, what would it have comprised? Maryland, Delaware, Virginia, North Carolina, South Carolina, and Georgia of the original states, and Kentucky, Tennessee, Alabama, Mississippi, Florida, Louisiana, Texas, Arkansas, and Missouri of the newer states—fifteen slave states in all. The national capital of Washington in the District of Columbia would be included also and, under the terms of the Missouri Compromise of 1820, the greater part of the territory taken from Mexico in the war which had just been completed. It would have then contained over six million whites, over three million slaves, and about a quarter of a million free Negroes. Its northern frontier would have followed the so-called Mason and Dixon's line between Pennsylvania and Maryland, the Ohio River, and the Missouri Compromise line of 36° 30' north latitude west from the southwestern corner of Missouri.

So vast an area was, of course, far from homogeneous. The part most distinctively differentiated from the rest of the United States was 'the land of cotton,' a strip of fertile soil and warm climate stretching from South Carolina to southeastern Texas and including about half the area of the Gulf States. This was also the 'black belt'

[2] See Chapter XXXVII.

with the largest Negro population; in a few counties Negroes were actually more numerous than whites, especially in the lowlands of South Carolina and along the lower reaches of the Mississippi. The sugar and rice plantations were much more limited in extent than the region of cotton culture, but they were also part of the black belt.

But even in the Deep South there were breaks in the continuity of cottonland—hilly or barren regions where plantations were small and Negroes few. In the upper tier of Southern states there was a diversified agriculture. Tobacco was still important in Virginia and Maryland; Kentucky was famous for racehorses and Missouri for sturdy mules. Texas was a huge transition zone from cotton plantations to cattle ranches, half Southern and half Western in character. Florida, which had to await the twentieth century for its fame as a tourist center, was a sparsely settled region divided between a northern zone of cotton and fruit culture and a swampy south which had been scarcely developed at all.

Southern tradition, which has always tended towards romanticism, has given the world a literary impression of an Old South which was one great cottonland of large plantations, inhabited by three classes: planters, slaves, and the 'poor whites' who owned no slaves and lived a hand-to-mouth existence. The planters were cavalier aristocrats who lived like English country gentlemen; their recreations riding and hunting; their duties the supervision of large estates and care for the welfare of their dependents; their training the ancient classics, etiquette, genealogy, and the gentleman's 'code of honor,' which did not forget the duel; their homes large, white-pillared mansions with hospitable verandas. The slaves were not only cotton and tobacco pickers but also carpenters, coachmen, blacksmiths, horse tamers, butlers, footmen, cooks, laundresses, lady's maids, midwives, and children's nurses; so that the plantation was a whole community in itself and, in Professor U. B. Phillips's excellent phrase, the South was 'rural without being rustic.'

Every part of this picture is true to life and can be verified by authentic records; the error lay in regarding it as the whole truth. It omitted the largest class of all, the host of small farmers and planters who did not have the wealth and culture of the planter aristocracy and yet were not victims of hook-worm, pellagra, or subtropical laziness like the true 'poor whites.' Some owned a few slaves, a family or two of Negroes merely, and others, outside the black belt, did their own work and lived very much like Northern farmers in Illinois or Indiana. Because this class was closest to the American norm it gained less attention from travelers and fiction writers than the classes which could not be found in other parts of the country.

Even the aristocracy was not, for the most part, of ancient lineage. Most of the great planters had grandfathers who were poor but thrifty working farmers. Nor was there much substance in the common contrast drawn between 'cavalier' South and 'Puritan' North. Doubtless in the seventeenth century Virginia presented a laxer, gayer pattern of life than Massachusetts, but by the 1850s the evangelical revival had made the South the most devoutly Protestant part of the nation, with much emphasis on church attendance, Sabbath observance, and orthodox belief, while the old Puritanism of New England was beginning to dissolve into Unitarianism, transcendentalist pantheism, and other 'heresies.' Jonathan Edwards, had he risen from the dead, would have taken much more satisfaction in a Virginia soldier like 'Stonewall' Jackson than in the creedless humanism of Emerson or the frank paganism of Thoreau.

It is not easy to estimate accurately the effect of slavery on either the black man or the white, because in the highly individualistic South each estate was a little kingdom in itself, benevolent or tyrannical according to the character of the owner rather than the text of the law, just as in feudal times the personality of the landlord mattered more to the serf than the policies of some distant king. Usually actual conditions were much better than the laws. The law permitted, under a few restrictions, the breaking up of families by sale of some of the members, but many a planter boasted that a 'servant' (the common euphemism for slave) was never sold from his estate. The law in several states forbade teaching slaves to read or write, lest abolitionist literature fall into their hands, but many planters taught them notwithstanding. The worst abuses took place where the master was an absentee and turned over the details of plantation management to overseers. That such abuses did sometimes occur is proved by newspapers of the time which not infrequently advertised for runaway slaves by the identification mark of brands, stripes, or scars on their bodies. Though the law did little to protect them,[3] the Negroes had two other safeguards, the usual easy-going good nature of their masters, and the fact that they were highly valuable and expensive property, a good field hand often costing as much as a racehorse. Though the importation of slaves from Africa was illegal after 1808, there was a good deal of smuggling. The law in some states placed difficulties in the way of those who wished to free their slaves, and it was easy for a Negro freedman to fall into slavery again, as a legal punishment for even minor offenses.

The effect of slavery on the white South is also hard to generalize. Its champions claimed that it alone made possible the free, gracious, and cultured life of the gentry; its adversaries that it was responsible for the poverty, ignorance, and backwardness of some other classes of the people. Probably both exaggerated, and certainly both confused the slavery question with the associated, but distinct, race question. Slavery was not essential to Southern prosperity, for the twentieth-century South without it has greater aggregate wealth than had the early nineteenth-century South with it. On the other hand, rural poverty in the South was due to many causes, of which slavery was only one. Of at least equal importance was the fact that most of the South had naturally poor soil, and that much of the good soil was being spoiled by unscientific agricultural methods. No doubt the existence of slavery kept European immigration away from the South and discouraged manufacturing, but competition with cheap Negro labor, even if free, would have handicapped the white immigrant in any event.

Down to 1850 the South had in every decade played a greater part in national government than her proportionate population and wealth would have warranted. Presidents Washington, Jefferson, Madison, Monroe, Jackson, Harrison, Tyler, Polk, and Taylor were all of Southern birth, and all except Harrison Southern by residence as well. There were also several Southern Vice-Presidents, but since it was good politics to award the two offices on the national ticket to different sections, the vice-presidency usually went to the North as a consolation prize. Cabinet memberships and federal justiceships were so distributed that the slave states held at least half of the

---

[3] There were anti-cruelty laws on every statute book, but there were few prosecutions because of lack of evidence, since a slave's testimony against his master was not usually received in court.

prominent offices in both Whig and Democratic administrations. From 1801 to 1835 the Chief Justice of the Supreme Court was the Virginian John Marshall, and from 1835 to 1864 the Marylander Roger Taney.

The North had far less regional self-consciousness than the South; many people called themselves Southerners; very few spoke of themselves as Northerners. Politically, as we have seen, the Northwest had been more often allied to the South than to the Northeast: it was Jeffersonian and Jacksonian, and if, by 1850, Westerners had begun to hesitate, it was from fear that Jefferson's liberalism and Jackson's pioneer democracy were no longer embodied in the Democratic party. A Yankee farmer in stony Vermont, an Irish immigrant in the crowded streets of New York City, a German immigrant in the frontier state of Wisconsin had nothing in common except that all were Americans and none were Southerners. But, negative as was the concept 'North,' it may serve for a discussion of certain tendencies in American life which had freer play outside the social system created by slavery. Among these were capitalism (or, more accurately, commercialism), nationalism, and the idealistic movement which found expression in literature and in social reform.

Slavery, of course, is capitalistic in the extreme, since it means the ownership of the laborer by the private employer. But it is a static form of capitalism, as it locks up wealth in land and slaves instead of letting it flow freely as money and credit; it is associated with agriculture rather than with trade and manufacture, and it rests on 'status' rather than 'contract.' Not that the Northern trader and manufacturer had, as such, a quarrel with the slave plantation system. The recent attempt of some historians to make the anti-slavery struggle a simple conflict between capitalism and agrarianism overlooks the fact that the wealthy and conservative men of the North were, with a few individual exceptions, the very last to be affected by the anti-slavery movement. But it is true that the establishment of iron and textile industries in the Northeast created a demand for protective tariffs which ran counter to the need of the Southern planters for free trade, and thus created another sectional issue which more or less coincided geographically with the division on the slavery question.

Nationalism was no more Northern than Southern in the early

days of the republic. The Constitution had been largely framed by one Virginian, Madison, and developed by the judicial interpretations of another, Marshall. Jackson, the Tennessean, had threatened South Carolina with military coercion. Even South Carolina had been nationalist on most points in the days of Pinckney, the Federalist leader, who was Hamilton's preferred choice for President. State rights had been a minority weapon, wielded by any party or section that found itself out of power, the Jeffersonians in 1798, the Federalists in 1814. But a number of causes had gradually increased nationalism in the North. One of these causes was negative: the North did not have a distinctive and endangered sectional institution, such as slavery. Another was economic: a commercial community moves about more freely and has weaker local attachments than a predominantly agricultural community. Again, the North had most of the new European immigrants, who naturally thought in terms of America in general rather than of Pennsylvania or Michigan in particular. An immigrant often becomes a patriot, but rarely a local patriot. Finally, the North had been much impressed by the nationalist views of such leaders as Daniel Webster, who preached that 'It is to the Union we owe our safety at home and our consideration abroad . . . It has been to us all a copious fountain of national, social, and personal happiness.'

The middle years of the nineteenth century saw the first flowering of American literature. Colonial thought had been but a local variety of European philosophy, theology, and social science. The New England Puritans wrote in the same style as the Puritans of old England. The theorists of the Revolution, such as Jefferson and Paine, owed much to the politics of Locke and Montesquieu and to the legal studies of Coke and Blackstone. Franklin, thoroughly American in spirit though he was, shared in the scientific studies and political controversies of France and Britain. Very little had been written in America before the 1820s that might not equally well have appeared in London. American periodicals throve greatly on reprints of English books in serial form, often with little or no compensation to the author because of defects in the copyright laws, a grievance which lay behind Charles Dickens's strictures against the young republic in *Martin Chuzzlewit* and *American Notes*. British textbooks long dominated the teaching in American schools, though the success of

Noah Webster's *Spelling Book* and *Dictionary*, which simplified certain traditional English spellings, amounted almost to a declaration of independence for the American schoolboy.

Washington Irving of New York, whose *Sketch Book* containing the tales of 'Rip Van Winkle' and 'Sleepy Hollow' appeared in 1820, may be taken as typical of the transition from literary colonialism to literary nationalism. He was a warm admirer of British life, a personal friend of Sir Walter Scott, and a student of Spanish as well as of English history and literature. But he turned to good effect the traditions of the Dutch settlers of New Netherland and wrote accounts of explorers of the Far West of his own generation. Of less literary value, but even more important as a reflection of national life, were the novels of Indians and frontiersmen by J. Fenimore Cooper and William Gilmore Simms.

Poetry found its golden day in New England with James Russell Lowell and Henry Wadsworth Longfellow, who, like Irving, were devoted students of both English and continental European literatures but turned frequently to American themes; with John Greenleaf Whittier, Quaker and abolitionist, closer to popular Yankee life and sentiment; and Ralph Waldo Emerson, who expounded in prose and verse alike an idealistic philosophy which was often called 'transcendentalism.' A little outside the New England orbit were the New Yorkers, William Cullen Bryant, poet of nature, and Walt Whitman, robust champion of democracy and the first great American master of free verse. The South produced several good poets and at least one great one, Edgar Allan Poe.[4] Poe, however, reflects neither the life of a section nor that of the nation; he is 'out of space, out of time,' living wholly in the world of the imagination.

Poe and the New Englander Nathaniel Hawthorne were masters of the short story, the field in which American literary genius has usually done its best work. Hawthorne's *The Scarlet Letter*, a brief novel of Puritan days, is considered his masterpiece, and is perhaps still the best American work of fiction. Poe greatly influenced both England and France in developing the technique of the detective story, the story of supernatural horror, and various other types of short-length narrative. Possibly the most important of the longer

---

[4] Born in Boston, but resident in Virginia and Maryland for most of his life.

novels of the epoch was Herman Melville's *Moby Dick*, an adventure story of a whale hunt which gradually transforms itself into a symbol of human striving for the unattainable.

When a people become nationally self-conscious they are apt to take an ardent interest in history; the Amercians were no exception. George Bancroft celebrated the American struggle for independence; Francis Parkman told the story of the French in Canada and in the old American West; William Prescott wrote of the deeds of the Spanish conquistadores. Outside the field of American history, John Motley won the greatest fame by his account of the Dutch Republic. Like the great nineteenth-century literary historians of Britain, France, and Germany, these Americans combined vast erudition, painstaking labor, and literary charm with fierce partisanship, writing as much to praise a nation, an age, or a political ideal as to narrate the events of the past.

The decades from 1830 to 1860 were yeasty, fermenting with new ideas and projects for reform on both sides of the Atlantic. Socialism in various forms attracted disciples, competing with phrenology and spiritualism for the favor of the drawing rooms. Many communistic colonies were founded in the American backwoods by disciples of Fourier, Cabet, and Robert Owen.[5] Thoreau advocated, more sincerely than Rousseau, a life close to Nature. His *Walden*, an account of a personal experiment in simplifying life and of the individualistic philosophy he derived from it, ranks as a classic of American prose. There was a strong temperance movement in both Britain and America; and writers on both sides of the Atlantic discussed the complete prohibition law adopted by the state of Maine. A woman's suffrage movement appeared in New York State as early as 1848. Horace Mann studied the Swiss and Prussian schools to find improvements which might be introduced in the schools of Massachusetts. The New England system of public education spread gradually into New York, Pennsylvania, and the new states of the West.

Abolitionism was only one of a host of movements to make the world better by the idealistic Utopians who saw the millennium just around the corner, but it awoke fiercer opposition than all the other

[5] See Charles Gide, *Communist and Coöperative Colonies* (trans., 1930).

reform movements combined. In the South all constitutional free-doms—speech, press, assembly, and petition—were suspended on this one question. In the North abolitionists spoke, but at their own peril; not infrequently they were mobbed. Yet they were not revolutionists. With very few exceptions they deprecated violent measures and some of them, such as the Quakers, were extreme pacifists. Their utmost defiance of law was usually to offer houses of refuge to escaping slaves along the road to Canada (the 'underground railroad'). Most politicians of all parties deprecated their agitation as hurtful to national unity.

Yet, while the South was certainly in error in believing that the abolitionists were either numerous or popular in the North, it is true that they were the spearhead of a much greater, though less radical, anti-slavery sentiment. The small Free Soil party advocated the exclusion of slavery from the territories. The recapture of fugitive slaves in the free states was a constant irritant to Northern senti-ment, which might have tolerated slavery at least a generation longer had its police power been confined to the slave states themselves. John Quincy Adams, former President, led a fight in the House of Representatives against the 'gag rule,' which banned the presen-tation of petitions on the slavery question to Congress. Workingmen and farmers wanted to take up western lands without coming into competition with slave labor. Could all these forces be brought to-gether, slavery indeed was in danger; not of sudden abolition, but of slow constriction by unfriendly legislation.

President Polk, the Democrat, had successfully carried through the Mexican War, but the presidency in 1848 went to a Southern Whig, General Zachary Taylor of Louisiana, who defeated Lewis Cass of Michigan. Taylor was willing to compromise the slavery issue in the new territories and admit California as a free state, and Henry Clay was ready with his accustomed role as conciliator of the sections. He proposed a series of measures to settle the slavery question 'perma-nently.' The admission of California as a free state was balanced by dropping the proposed 'Wilmot proviso' [6] for the exclusion of slavery from the other territories taken from Mexico; and the abolition of

[6] So named from Representative David Wilmot of Pennsylvania who pro-posed it.

the slave trade (not of slavery itself) in the national capital was balanced by a more drastic fugitive slave law,[7] which made federal officers agents to catch runaway slaves, since Northern local authorities could no longer be trusted with this distasteful task. Calhoun, on behalf of the Cotton States, declared these concessions insufficient, but Daniel Webster, speaking for the North, accepted all the terms of the compromise, even the fugitive slave law, and went out of his way to denounce the abolitionists. President Taylor had died, but his successor, Vice-President Millard Fillmore, accepted the compromise. Talk of secession died down. Within two years the three great senators of that generation, Calhoun with all his misgivings, and Clay and Webster with all their confidence, had died before new events reopened the slavery question.

The election of 1852 seemed to ratify the compromise of 1850, as the Democratic candidate, Franklin Pierce of New Hampshire, was chosen by a large majority over the Mexican War hero on the Whig ticket, Winfield Scott. Pierce was strongly pro-slavery, and as a 'Northern man with Southern principles' was expected to be a conciliator of the sections. But another Northern Democrat unwittingly put a match to the powder magazine, and Pierce's administration was the scene of the fiercest battle yet waged over the extension of slavery.

Senator Stephen A. Douglas of Illinois wanted rapid development of the prairie region beyond the Mississippi and, to this end, favored a transcontinental railroad which would follow in general the old covered-wagon trail to the Pacific. As there was a rival plan for a southern route, he bid for Southern support by dividing the prairie country into two parts, Kansas and Nebraska, each to determine for itself whether it would have slavery or not. This, in effect, abolished the Missouri Compromise, for both proposed territories lay north of the boundary which was to limit slavery according to the law of 1820. The general expectation was that Nebraska, lying west of Iowa, would become a free territory, while Kansas, west of Missouri, would vote for slavery, but Douglas professed personal indifference to the outcome. The question, he said, was for the white settlers themselves to decide and Congress need not be concerned about it. This he called 'popular sovereignty,' his enemies 'squatter sovereignty.'

[7] The occasion of Harriet Beecher Stowe's famous attack on slavery, *Uncle Tom's Cabin*.

This Kansas-Nebraska bill of 1854 created the Republican party; not Jefferson's old party of that name, which had later become known as Democratic, but a novel fusion of Northern Whigs, anti-slavery Democrats, and Free Soilers. It was the most definitely sectional party that had yet appeared, as it had virtually no votes from the South; indeed, at first it was practically confined to the Northwest, though the gradual break-up of the Whig party brought it fresh recruits from the East.

Another effect of the measure was the outbreak of a small civil war in Kansas that smouldered on for several years. To win the territory for slavery, a large number of Missourians crossed the border, some of them intending to stay and settle, but most of them merely to cast their votes and then return home. The territorial government thus created was denounced as illegal by the free-state settlers who set up a rival government of their own. Both groups sought admission as a state, but President Pierce sided with the pro-slavery territorial government. Murders took place on both sides: John Brown killed in cold blood a number of Southern settlers, and Missouri 'border ruffians' sacked and burned the town of Lawrence. Douglas, who cared nothing for the Negroes, cared much for the rights of white settlers, and denounced the administration for imposing slavery on Kansas against the will of a majority of the bona fide settlers. In 1856 Senator Sumner of Massachusetts, who had just made a bitter speech on the 'crime against Kansas,' was pounded into insensibility by the cane of Representative Preston Brooks of South Carolina.

The election of 1856 was fought directly on the issue of excluding slavery from the territories. The new Republican party nominated John Frémont, a Western explorer and adventurer; the Democrats James Buchanan of Pennsylvania; the Whigs were divided among the Democrats and Republicans and an anti-foreign 'American' party, which nominated ex-President Fillmore and made a vain attempt to distract attention from the perilous slavery issue. Buchanan carried the whole South (except Maryland, which supported Fillmore) and enough Northern states to ensure his election.

Representative Wilmot had created one crisis over the western-lands question by his proviso excluding slavery from lands acquired from Mexico; Senator Douglas a second crisis by his Kansas-Nebraska Act, opening up Northern territories to possible slavery; in 1857

Chief Justice Taney created a third, the most serious of all, by rendering a judicial decision which imposed slavery on all territories, whether they wished it or not. Dred Scott was a Negro who sued for his freedom on the ground that he had been a temporary resident both of the free state of Illinois and of the territory free under the Missouri Compromise of 1820, though he had later returned to Missouri. Judge Taney, knowing this to be a test case, went beyond the matters immediately in question and determined, supported by a sectional majority on the court, to clear up a number of cloudy issues. He declared that a Negro was not a citizen of the United States and could not bring suit in a federal court, and that property rights (including slavery) could not be set aside by territorial legislation; only a sovereign state could abolish slavery within its boundaries. If this decision held, the Missouri Compromise, which had been accepted law from 1820 to the Kansas-Nebraska Act of 1854, had always been unconstitutional; the Republican proposal to bar slavery from the territories by congressional action was also unconstitutional; and Douglas's proposal to let the settlers decide the question was unconstitutional too! Seldom, if ever, has so much political dynamite been packed into one judicial decision.

Each year now brought forth a new crisis. In 1859 John Brown, fresh from the little civil war in Kansas, seized the federal arsenal at Harper's Ferry in Virginia, with some vague idea of making it an armed camp for fugitive slaves. His enterprise had not the faintest chance of success. The Negroes themselves held aloof from it, and it was speedily crushed by joint action of the state militia and of federal troops under Colonel Robert E. Lee. John Brown was hanged, and the only abolitionist insurrection was at an end. But a shudder of horror went through the South; it recalled grim memories of the Nat Turner slave rebellion of 1831, when more than fifty white people had been killed.

The election of 1860, like that of 1856, was fought along sectional lines on the issue of slavery extension, but the Republican chances were now much brighter. The business depression of 1857 had swung the commercial community away from the Buchanan administration. The Democrats were split between Taney's decision that all territories were necessarily open to slavery, and Douglas's doctrine that settlers by unfriendly legislation could bar slavery from territories if they wished. The Republicans were united on a platform of no slavery in any territory, and they had two other attractive baits—the offer of free homesteads to settlers of the new West, and higher tariffs for manufacturers. Moreover, they had now a stronger candidate than Frémont.

Abraham Lincoln was a Kentuckian, born in circumstances of great poverty.[8] His restless pioneer father migrated with his family from Kentucky across the Ohio River, and most of Lincoln's youth was spent in Indiana and Illinois. He practiced law in Illinois with some success, and served a term in Congress as a Whig. He first achieved a national reputation by his joint debates with Senator Douglas on the slavery issue, and though Douglas gained the senatorship from a Democratic state legislature, Lincoln won the respect of the young Republican party, not yet too well provided with leaders. Like so many American presidential candidates, he was chosen as an 'available' compromise. Governor Seward of New York, the favorite for the nomination, had many bitter political enemies in his own state; Salmon P. Chase of Ohio was considered too radical; and lesser contenders were eliminated on one ground or another. Against Lincoln no particular objection could be raised. He was a Westerner, who might carry the doubtful state of Illinois; a man of the people, whose youth as a rail splitter would be as good an election asset as was Harrison's 'log cabin and hard cider' in 1840; he was personally honest, moderate in opinion, well liked by the few who knew him, and an excellent public speaker. For these reasons he was chosen over several better-known national figures and a flock of local 'favorite sons.'

The Democratic convention, meeting at Charleston in South Carolina, where pro-slavery feeling ran higher than in any other city in the United States, split after a prolonged deadlock. Two rival tickets were eventually nominated, one nominating for President Vice-President John C. Breckenridge of Kentucky on a platform extending slavery, as of constitutional right, to all territories; the

[8] This is at least as much the rule as the exception for American Presidents. When the pictorial magazine *Life* (Feb. 20, 1939) published pictures of the birthplaces of all the Presidents, it was evident that at least half a dozen could fairly be classed as 'log cabins,' and that nearly all the others were small and cheap wooden frame houses.

other favoring Senator Douglas and squatter sovereignty. A fourth party, essentially the last movement of the Southern Whigs, nominated Senator Bell of Tennessee on a 'Constitutional Union' ticket, with no platform except an appeal to maintain the Union.

There followed what was, by all odds, the most interesting and important election in American history. All four candidates were Western by residence, and all except Douglas were Western by birth. All were men of proved ability, though Lincoln had the least experience of the four in national politics. But personalities were, for once, submerged by issues. In the only other four-cornered fight in American history, the election of 1824, the voters had lined up as 'Adams men,' 'Jackson men,' or supporters of Clay or Crawford; but in 1860 they voted for Lincoln if they wished to keep slavery out of the territories, for Douglas if they wanted to leave the decision to the settlers themselves, for Breckenridge if they held that slavery could not lawfully be excluded from any territory, for Bell if they deemed it safest to ignore the whole issue.

Bell divided the popular vote of the South very closely with Breckenridge, though he carried only Virginia, Kentucky, and Tennessee. Douglas carried only Missouri and part of the electoral vote of New Jersey, though he ran well in many Northern states. Breckenridge carried most of the South but no free state. Lincoln swept the North. The combined popular vote for Douglas and Breckenridge, the two rival Democratic candidates, was greater than that for Lincoln, but it was geographically so distributed that, even if they had joined forces, Lincoln would still have had a majority in the Electoral College.

The Cotton States now resolved on secession. The election of a President and Vice-President (Hamlin of Maine) from the North [9] by a sectional party on an anti-slavery platform convinced them that political power had passed to unfriendly hands. Perhaps their decision was premature, since the Democratic party was still strong enough to block radical legislation in Congress and there was a pro-slavery majority on the Supreme Court. Many Southerners urged delay; perhaps this little-known Lincoln will prove less unfriendly than we feared, they said; why not await the event?

---

[9] Lincoln, though of Southern birth, was considered a Northerner because of his residence in Illinois.

South Carolina, however, knew no hesitation. Of all states in the Union, Calhoun's state held most firmly to the excellence of slavery and to the right and expediency of secession. In December 1860 a special convention voted South Carolina an independent state. A tier of states in the Deep South followed within a few weeks—Georgia, Alabama, Florida, Mississippi, Louisiana, Texas. In February 1861 the Confederate States of America were proclaimed, with a new capital at Montgomery, Alabama, and with Jefferson Davis of Mississippi as President and Alexander Stephens of Georgia as Vice-President. Davis had been a reluctant secessionist, and Stephens an active opponent of secession, but both believed in the right of a state to withdraw at will and both gave support to the new government now formed.

President Buchanan, not knowing what to do, did nothing. By rigid constitutional law he remained in office four months after election, but the defeat of his party had deprived him of all political authority and prestige. Though by no standard was he a successful President, it should be remembered in his behalf that he occupied an almost impossible position. If he coerced the South, he presented the incoming administration with a civil war; if he did not, he presented it with an already divided nation.

Schemes of compromise were mooted in Unionist slave states such as Virginia and Kentucky. One of these, fathered by Senator Crittenden of Kentucky, proposed to legalize the Missouri Compromise line by constitutional amendment, and to insert in the Constitution an explicit guarantee against federal interference with slavery in the states. The seceding states were not satisfied, and gave no indication that they would rejoin the Union on any terms; the victorious Republicans were unwilling to compromise on the issue which had placed them in office, the total exclusion of slavery from all territories, north or south, present or future. They remembered that many projects had been brought forward for acquiring Cuba and other countries around the Gulf of Mexico as future slave territory.

Such was the situation which confronted President Lincoln when, on the fourth of March 1861, he assumed the burdens of office. His inaugural address was a plea for peace. He reiterated that he had neither the power nor the inclination to interfere with slavery where it already existed, that he would take no aggressive step, but that the Constitution and his oath of office constrained him to uphold the Union and enforce its laws. A perplexed and inexperienced pilot had taken the helm, with a mutinous crew, a dangerous sea ahead, and no chart or compass of precedent to guide his course.

o XXIV o

THE WAR FOR SOUTHERN INDEPENDENCE

Any European looking at the crisis of 1861 will be inclined to ask with a natural impatience, 'Since Lincoln did not believe in the right of a state to secede, why did he wait more than a month before taking any action; why not send in the army at once and nip rebellion in the bud?' There were three reasons. One was Lincoln's hope that his 'olive branch' inaugural address might meet some response, that there would be a tide of Unionist sentiment which would bring some seceding states back to the Union and confirm wavering border states in their allegiance. Another was that the regular army was very small and many of its best officers had already resigned and gone South; to crush the Confederacy would require the addition of large forces of half-trained militia or wholly untrained volunteers taken from civilian life, who would be confronted by similar Southern forces, and the contest would be long and doubtful. The third reason was that unless the Confederacy took some military step which would arouse unionist patriotic feeling, the government would be widely blamed, even in the North, for initiating a fratricidal war, and the border slave states would all secede.

The right of secession, like other aspects of state rights, had champions in all parts of the country. From the first adoption of the federal Constitution until the guns spoke in 1861, lawyers and politicians had argued endlessly whether sovereignty inhered in the state or in the nation. As in the quarrels between King Charles I and his Parliaments, or between George III's ministers and the American colonies, a good legal case could be presented by both sides. The Constitution did not say in so many words whether or not a state could secede, nor had the Supreme Court yet made an interpretation which clearly covered the case. Commentaries on the Constitution by lawyers, however learned, resolutions of state legislatures and political conventions, speeches by eminent statesmen on either side were conclusive only to those who already agreed with them.

The real issue for the historian is not the technical legality of secession,[1] but the state of public opinion on the question at this period. There is every evidence that in normal times all parts of the country were strongly attached to the Union. Secessionist sentiment was sporadic and occasional, appearing only when sectional interests seemed exceptionally endangered. The really significant fact about the Hartford Convention of 1814,[2] South Carolina's defiance of President Jackson,[3] the 'Southern rights' movement in the crisis of 1850,[4] and the more radical abolitionists is not that in each case there was a secessionist agitation, but that in each case it failed to win popular favor.

But towards the Union which, with almost negligible exceptions, all parties and sections had supported, there were three distinct attitudes. The lower South generally, and many individuals in other sections, considered the Union a mere compact of sovereign states. They viewed it as a modern Englishman might the League of Nations; he might greatly deplore and strongly oppose any attempt on the part of Great Britain to withdraw from it, but he would not let such a withdrawal alter his primary allegiance to the British Crown. The belief in the Cotton States that, since the states were unquestionably sovereign, no war would follow secession can alone explain the light-hearted and precipitate manner in which they broke the ties that bound them to their sister states.

Another group considered the national authority paramount, but insisted on the autonomy of the individual state as an equally important political principle; their position was not unlike that of an average Canadian to his Dominion and to the British Commonwealth as a whole. This was the usual Northern view and had some support in the Southern border states. Finally, there were the few whose allegiance was entirely nationalist: to whom the state was merely a unit of local government, like an English shire. Only immigrants fresh

---

[1] The legal theory of the government was that no state could secede; so that the war was merely the coercion of individual rebels, not of states as such.

[2] See p. 257.   [4] See pp. 285-6.

[3] See p. 267.

from Europe, or Westerners whose states had been recently carved from federal territory, were apt to take this view.[5]

So Lincoln had to deal with a doubtful and undecided North as well as with a seceding South. Many said with the journalist Horace Greeley, 'Let the wayward sisters depart in peace.' While the President temporized and played for time, Secretary of State Seward proposed a hare-brained plan for averting civil war by a foreign war scare. France and Spain had dubious designs on Mexico and Santo Domingo; let them be sharply rebuked. A wave of patriotic sentiment would then overwhelm the sectional issue. Fortunately, Seward made this suggestion only in a private memorandum to Lincoln, and the latter wisely kept it secret, so no mischief was done. In another direction Seward's self-assertion was more harmful. President Buchanan had surrendered much government property in the South, but the United States still held Fort Sumter in Charleston harbor, South Carolina, and another fort in Florida. After long hesitation, Lincoln resolved to hold Sumter; but Seward had led the Confederate commissioners to believe that the administration would probably evacuate it. When provision ships appeared, the Confederates felt they had been tricked; they fired on the fort and, after two days' siege, it surrendered.

The fall of Sumter on 14 April 1861 was the opening action of the war. This war has borne many names in history, none of them quite satisfactory. In the official documents at Washington it was at first 'The War of the Rebellion,' a name later discarded for 'The Civil War.' Both terms denied by implication that the Confederacy had become really independent, so the South called it 'The War between the States,' though the actual conflict was between two rival federations, the Union and the Confederacy, rather than between states as such. The most accurate title among the many that have been proposed is 'The War for Southern Independence.' To the world at large, however, it is simply 'The American Civil War.'

On learning of the capture of Fort Sumter, Lincoln issued a call for 75,000 volunteers. This forced the hesitating states to choose one

---

[5] There was a further complication. Many who talked of states' rights were really thinking of sectional interests. A citizen of Richmond might regard himself as primarily a 'Virginian,' a 'Southerner,' or an 'American'; a Bostonian might think in terms of Massachusetts, New England, or the United States.

side or the other. Virginia, North Carolina, Tennessee, and Arkansas now joined the Confederacy, and its capital was removed to Richmond, in compliment to Virginia. Kentucky tried for a brief time to remain neutral, Missouri was divided into rival camps, Maryland had many Confederate sympathizers and inspired the greatest of Confederate war songs, 'Maryland, my Maryland'; but none of these states eventually withdrew from the Union. The western counties of Virginia, a mountainous district where slaves were few, remained unionist, and this region was later erected into the new state of West Virginia. Since five slave states remained within the Union (Delaware, Maryland, West Virginia, Kentucky, and Missouri), the Confederacy was less extensive than the 'South'; it drew indeed volunteers from every Union slave state, but within its own borders there were small unionist enclaves, such as eastern Tennessee, which sent soldiers to the other camp.

The Confederate States of America adopted a constitution which was in its main lines identical with that of the United States. There were a few minor technical improvements, some of which might with advantage be adopted today, such as permitting cabinet members to take part in congressional debates, and giving the President authority to veto individual items in appropriation bills. There was also an explicit assertion of state rights, including a prohibition of protective tariffs. There was a positive affirmation of slavery, and a prohibition of any interference with it in the territories. The foreign slave trade, however, was forbidden, except with the slave states remaining in the United States.

After all secessions had taken place, the United States had still more than twice the total population of the Confederacy, and more than thrice its white population. The disparity of the two governments in wealth and industrial power was even greater. Naval power was with the United States, and the Confederacy was blockaded throughout the war, though the long extent of coastline permitted a great amount of smuggling and blockade running. The theory of state rights, whether beneficial or not in time of peace, was unquestionably a handicap in time of war; the whole political history of the Confederacy was one prolonged and bitter controversy between the administration of President Davis and the many doctrinaire critics who accused him of disregard of the rights and privileges of the separate states. 'Southern rights' had come into conflict with 'state rights.'

The Confederacy was not without advantages, however. Since it merely wished to achieve independence it could win the war by holding its own, whereas the Union must conquer the whole of a vast territory, much of it without railroads or good roads, or fail in its professed war aim. The Confederacy included the entire cotton belt, and could make out an effective case for foreign intervention by the necessity which British mills had for American cotton. President Davis had served in the Mexican War and had been Secretary of War in Pierce's cabinet; if his military experience led him—as it did—to frequent interference with strategy in the field, it also enabled him to select from personal knowledge very able generals at the opening of the war. He had, in any event, better officer material at hand than President Lincoln possessed, for the tradition and genius of the South was military while the North was essentially civilian in outlook and habits. Several of the most distinguished Union officers were of Southern birth; for example, General Winfield Scott, General George Thomas, and Admiral Farragut.

Lincoln, on his part, knew much more about politics than war. He had selected his cabinet from every faction of the Republican party, including recently converted Democrats, and several of the members, notably Secretary of State Seward and Chase of the Treasury, had been his rivals for the nomination. A coalition cabinet of this sort may have great political prestige, but is hard to dominate and keep together. Cameron, the Secretary of War, had been chosen to pay a political debt, and he spent his brief time in office paying his political debts in turn. His successor Stanton was more efficient, but so overbearing, dictatorial, and crabbed that scarcely anyone but the patient Lincoln would have endured him as a subordinate. Too many of the Union generals had been hastily chosen because they were popular, politically influential, or prominent in the public eye. The war was half over before Lincoln discovered where to look for the ablest military specialists, or how to give them the free hand they needed when he found them. It is to his credit that he did learn, and the last two years of his administration are models of what a civilian ruler's attitude should be to the army in time of war.

The first major battle of the war was a Confederate victory. In July 1861 a Union force, consisting largely of half-trained and ill-disciplined volunteers under General McDowell, met a similar Confederate force under General Beauregard near Manassas Junction in northern Virginia, so close to Washington that some congressmen came out to witness the fight. After a confused battle, with rumors of defeat brought to both sides by frightened stragglers, the Union lines broke. A blow at the capital at this moment might have been decisive, but victors as well as vanquished had been thrown into disorder by the battle. Even as things were, this battle of Bull Run (the Northern name) or Manassas (the Southern) practically ended the summer's campaign. It also found a military hero for the Confederacy. A certain stern martinet, Thomas J. Jackson, formerly professor at a military school in Virginia, kept his soldiers in such discipline that they stood in the midst of the hottest fire like a stone wall. Henceforth, to all posterity, he was 'Stonewall' Jackson, and his soldiers the 'Stonewall Brigade.'

Lincoln now turned to George B. McClellan, a self-confident young man with an excellent Mexican War record and some minor successes to his credit in West Virginia. In some ways it was a very good choice. General Lee, who should know as well as anyone, later named McClellan the ablest general he had faced. 'Little Mac,' as he came to be known, was a born organizer with a high standard of administrative efficiency and a determination not to be forced into premature action by pressure from amateur strategists in Washington. He was an inspiring commander, much loved by his soldiers. But these merits were offset by serious defects. He was insubordinate, treating the President with cool insolence and the War Department with open contempt. He was also over-cautious, reluctant to begin an offensive until his army had reached an impossible perfection, and inclined to overestimate the numbers against him. For the moment, these defects did not greatly matter. Lincoln patiently endured McClellan's lectures, reproaches, and even refusals to grant him audience, while a long spell of comparative inaction was just what the Army of the Potomac needed for drill and discipline.

Eighteen hundred and sixty-two was the epic year of Confederate triumph. McClellan had created a powerful and well-equipped army, and with it intended to take Richmond, the Confederate capital, in a single campaign, using the peninsula between the York and James Rivers as an approach. The plan had reasonable prospects of success.

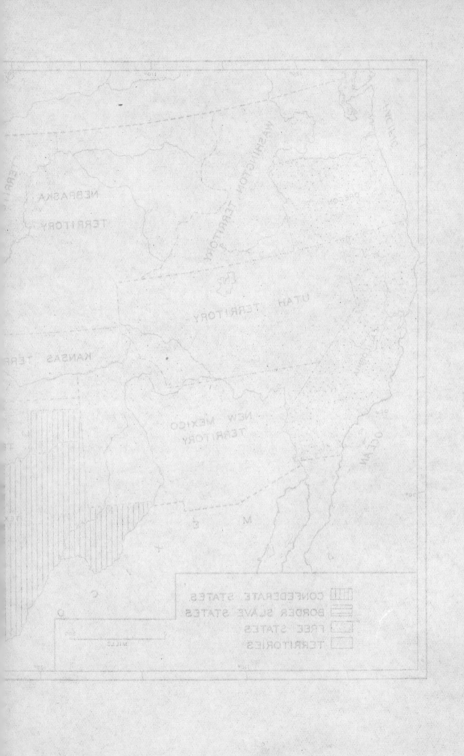

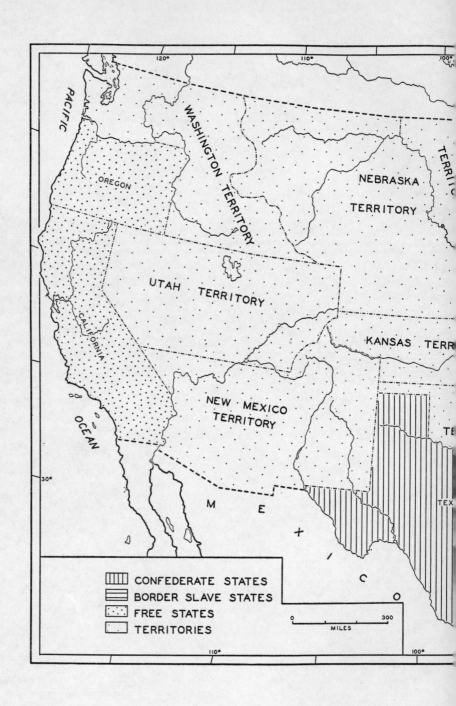

CONFEDERATE STATES
BORDER SLAVE STATES
FREE STATES
TERRITORIES

THE WAR FOR SOUTHERN INDEPENDENCE 1861

1 WASHINGTON
2 MANASSAS (BULL RUN)
3 APPOMATTOX
4 GETTYSBURG
5 RICHMOND
6 HARPERS FERRY
7 FORT SUMTER
8 CHANCELLORSVILLE

9 HAMPTON ROADS
10 ANTIETAM (SHARPSBURG)
11 FREDERICKSBURG
12 ATLANTA
13 VICKSBURG
14 NEW ORLEANS
15 CHATTANOOGA

E.J.

But Stonewall Jackson was so active in the Shenandoah Valley that he frightened the capital. It was feared that while McClellan was taking Richmond, Jackson would be riding into Washington. The military effect of the loss of Washington might, indeed, be retrieved, but hardly its political effect. France, Britain, and other nations would probably have taken the fall of the national capital as an occasion for recognizing Confederate independence, or even for demanding an end to the naval blockade of Confederate ports. So troops on whom McClellan had counted were removed to protect Washington. Lee now summoned Jackson from the valley and struck back with all his forces. McClellan was forced to abandon his peninsular campaign, though he conducted his retreat with masterly skill. Later in the summer Pope, a Union general transferred from the West, was defeated by Lee and Jackson at the second battle of Manassas.

Lincoln placed McClellan again in command to repel an advance of Lee's army into Maryland. At the battle of Antietam (or Sharpsburg) in September McClellan succeeded in compelling a Confederate retreat. Though the battle, the bloodiest single day's action in the war, was inconclusive owing to McClellan's failure to follow it up, it could be represented as a Union victory since it ended the invasion of Maryland. It determined Lincoln to risk the most momentous decision ever made by an American President—a proclamation abolishing slavery in all parts of the Union which would still be in rebellion at the end of the year.

The war had been caused by slavery, but it had not hitherto been fought on the issue of slavery. Without the prolonged and bitter controversy over the extension of slavery into new western territory there would have been no secession, and hence no war, but the secession itself was the ground taken by the government at Washington for military action. President Lincoln had discouraged every premature attempt at emancipation which might alienate the doubtful slave states of the border and drive them into the Confederacy. He declared the restoration of the Union the sole war aim, though he vainly urged on the Union slave states that they anticipate the day when emancipation would come, by voluntarily adopting plans of gradual and compensated abolition within their own borders.

Europe therefore looked on the war as merely a contest of state rights *versus* nationalism. Why should European foreign offices care which constitutional theory triumphed? Nay, should they not rather welcome a break-up of the presumptuous young republic, whose strident and raucous voice had so often been an unwelcome note in world politics? Other causes also tended to swing European governments to the side of the Confederacy. The Union blockade kept Southern cotton, the world's chief source of supply, away from European mills. An end to the war on any terms would restore the normal course of trade. Again, the Union was protectionist, while the Confederacy favored free trade; so export as well as import interests viewed the latter with favor. Napoleon III had designs on Mexico; a divided and impotent United States would facilitate these plans. Nor was self-interest the only factor: many Englishmen felt for the Confederacy a romantic sympathy for a gallant, outnumbered people.

There were also specific instances of diplomatic conflict. The speedy recognition of the belligerency of the Confederacy, though perfectly correct in the circumstances,[6] caused some resentment in the North. Late in 1861, Captain Wilkes of the American navy seized two Confederate agents, Mason and Slidell, from the British steamer *Trent*. The British Government demanded apologies and reparation for this violation of British neutral rights. Both nations now occupied an anomalous position. In the Napoleonic struggle, when Britain was at war and the United States neutral, this right of 'search and seizure' was maintained by the British and denied by the Americans. That no new 'War of 1812' took place in 1861 was because of a few wise heads on either side. Prince Albert successfully urged on the British ministry a courteous tone in the dispatch of protest, knowing that in diplomatic affairs what is said is often less important than how it is said. Secretary Seward, no longer the jingo he had been, and Senator Sumner, spokesman of the abolitionists, successfully urged on President Lincoln the release of the Confederates. That danger had passed. But who could tell how soon some new incident

[6] The United States had virtually recognized Confederate belligerency (though not, of course, independence) by according to its armies all the usages of war, and by proclaiming formal legal blockade of its ports. The Confederates were called 'traitors' and 'rebels,' but were nearly always treated as lawfully armed belligerent opponents. Not a single person was executed on charges of treason or rebellion at the end of the war.

might cause hesitating France or Britain to grant complete recognition to Confederate independence?

There were, of course, reasons for the hesitation of foreign governments. If the South meant cotton to European traders, the North was equally important as a supplier of wheat and of iron ore. Again, prevailing opinion in all European countries was hostile to slavery. Even those who had no love for republics had, as a rule, no love for slaveholders either, and their favorite taunt flung at American democracy had been, 'Yes, a "democracy" where one man in every six is a chattel who can be bought and sold like a horse!' It was the decade in which even a Russian Tsar was freeing his serfs and thus ending the last relic of personal servitude in Europe. If the slavery issue should clearly emerge in the American war, any intervention which might have the effect of perpetuating slavery would be widely unpopular.

Lincoln weighed all these considerations. The Union slave states were no longer doubtful; the heat of conflict had welded them firmly to the free states. The cry for abolition was rising in the North. European intervention might be averted by shifting the issue from union *versus* secession to freedom *versus* slavery. Though Lincoln, while hating slavery, had always contended that the Federal Government had no constitutional power to put an end to it in the states (as distinguished from the territories) in time of peace, he believed also that the power to wage war given by the Constitution to the President, as Commander-in-Chief of the army and navy, included the use of any means necessary to wage it successfully, such as the conscription of soldiers or the emancipation of slaves of the enemy. Others before him, including President John Quincy Adams, had foretold that slavery might come to an end under the war powers of the Federal Government, even if immune to every other attack. So Lincoln prepared his emancipation proclamation and submitted it to the cabinet. Secretary Seward raised a canny objection: if the proclamation were issued in the midst of disasters it would seem merely a desperate expedient of a defeated government to rouse a slave rebellion behind the enemy's lines. So Lincoln agreed to wait for a victory. It was long in coming, and doubtful when it came, but Antietam was the first turn in the tide.

On 22 September 1862 Lincoln told his cabinet that the time had come to issue the proclamation. From the first day of January 1863, all slaves would be free in the parts of the United States still in rebellion. The proclamation involved a curious paradox. In literal, immediate fact it freed not a single slave, for the only states to which it applied would not recognize the President's authority. Yet it doomed slavery, granted the success of Union arms, for it made abolition for the first time the policy of the government and prevented any more concessions or compromises on the question. It found ultimate fruition in the constitutional amendment, urged by Lincoln but not finally carried till 1865, abolishing slavery everywhere, in the Union as well as in the late Confederate states. The border slave states lost their chance for compensation by not accepting Lincoln's suggestions; the Confederate states by continuing the war beyond the time limit he had set.

McClellan's failure to follow up his success at Antietam cost him his place, but his successor Burnside was defeated at Fredericksburg in the winter of 1862. The year ended with the Confederacy in possession of nearly all its territory in the East, many victories to its credit, and superb morale. Lincoln was still unsuccessfully experimenting with generals. The November elections strengthened the Democratic opposition in Congress and reflected popular discontent with the conduct of the war. In the West, however, the balance of generalship was more nearly equal than in the East. The Confederacy had, indeed, two generals of the first water in that region, Albert Sidney Johnston and the dashing cavalry commander, Nathan Forrest. But Johnston was killed early in the war. Forrest's abilities were never given full scope till too late. On the Union side, the course of the western campaigns gradually revealed some highly competent officers, such as Ulysses S. Grant, W. T. Sherman, and George Thomas.

In 1863 the United States followed the example given by the Confederacy the previous year and resorted to conscription. Both armies were filled mainly by volunteers, and the draft was intended to fill the gaps. Exemptions and substitutions were so freely permitted, on both sides, that the working of the draft law led to widespread evasion and resistance.

In the spring of the year a fresh disaster fell on the Union arms. Lee and Jackson caught Hooker, Burnside's successor, at Chancellorsville and broke his army. The cost was high, however, for Stonewall Jackson was accidentally shot by his own men, and Lee never found again the perfect subordinate that Jackson had been. The victory was so important that Lee resolved to follow it up by another blow at the North. In the Antietam campaign of the previous year he had invaded the border state of Maryland; now he would advance farther, into Pennsylvania. As Lee entered the state, Hooker resigned and was succeeded by General Meade.

At Gettysburg, in southern Pennsylvania, the two armies came into collision, in a three days' battle, the greatest of the war. The two armies were ranged on opposite hilly ridges. A series of attacks failed to dislodge the Union forces and Lee was forced to retreat. The same Fourth of July that brought to Lincoln the news of Gettysburg saw also the final surrender of Vicksburg, the last great Confederate stronghold on the Mississippi, to General Grant. This was followed by a campaign in Tennessee. The victories of Sherman and Thomas laid Georgia open to invasion, and in 1864 Sherman marched south. Joseph Johnston, with much skill, fought a defensive campaign against him, but when Atlanta, the capital of Georgia, was in danger, President Davis yielded to public clamor for a more aggressive campaign and put General Hood in his place. Thomas, however, defeated Hood's army, and Sherman was able to continue his march.

Theoretically, the war should have ended with Gettysburg and Vicksburg in 1863, for there was little hope afterwards either of a Confederate triumph or of European intervention. But President Davis was resolved to continue the struggle to the last ditch, and the generalship of Robert E. Lee enabled him to protract resistance to an incredible length. The Confederacy almost repeated in 1864 the brilliant triumphs of 1862, though with dwindling resources and fading prospects of ultimate success. Grant was placed in command of the Union forces and given a greater moral and material support than any previous Union general, and he had strong qualities of his own, a dogged stubbornness, which fitted him well for a war of attrition, and a greater aggressiveness than McClellan or Meade. Yet in the Wilderness in May, at Cold Harbor in June, and for many months before the entrenchments of Petersburg, the Confederates held their own.

The drag of the war began in 1864 to undermine morale on both sides. President Davis was faced with almost open defiance from the governors of Georgia and of North Carolina. Sherman's march through Georgia and Sheridan's down the Shenandoah Valley in Virginia, the 'granary of the Confederacy,' reduced whole counties to waste. The armies at the front lacked food and clothing, and the Confederate currency was sinking towards worthlessness. The last hope of foreign intervention faded when in 1863 the British Government, after American protests, decided to stop the building of warships ultimately intended for the Confederacy. Pro-American demonstrations by workingmen and liberals had convinced the government that no step which even indirectly aided slavery would be supported by the mass of the nation.

But gloom was almost as deep in the North. Lee's obstinate resistance to Grant had convinced many that the Confederacy was unconquerable. The defeatists controlled most of the political machinery of the remnant of the Democratic party, now that the 'war Democrats' were supporting Lincoln. In 1864 they nominated McClellan for President and hoped for victory from the quaint combination of a war hero on a peace platform. The more radical Republicans were impatient with Lincoln's conduct of the war and threatened to run Frémont, the party candidate of 1856, in his place. The news of Sherman's victories in Georgia, however, restored confidence in the administration, and Lincoln was elected by a safe margin over McClellan.

In April 1865 Lee at last surrendered. Grant offered generous terms: the officers to keep their swords, and both men and officers to keep their horses 'to work their farms.' Lee passed his last years as President of Washington College in Virginia, which was eventually renamed 'Washington and Lee University' in his honor. The surrender of the few remaining Confederate forces followed within a few weeks after Lee's famous 'Army of Northern Virginia' had laid down its arms.

Even before the war had entered its final phase, Lincoln was busy with plans for the 'reconstruction' of the Union. His idea was to restore normal civil government as soon as one-tenth of the citizens in any state would take the oath of allegiance. There would be no prosecutions for rebellion or treason. Slavery would, of course, be abolished, and educated Negroes and those who had fought for the Union, but apparently not the others, would be admitted to the franchise.

On 14 April 1865, a fanatical actor named Booth shot President Lincoln at a theater, while an accomplice tried to murder Secretary Seward. No President, and that is saying much, had to face so much bitter abuse in his lifetime, but none has been so honored after his death. Perhaps the fairest summary of Lincoln's personality and achievement was that of the English pacifist, Bertrand Russell: 'To conduct a great war, through years of difficulty and ill success, resolutely, to a victorious conclusion, and to remain throughout conciliatory and calm and large-minded, is a feat which was accomplished by Lincoln, but, so far as I know, by no other historical character.' [7]

But Lincoln was not the only war figure to leave a legend. No other civilian figure on either side became the object of popular devotion, but the generals who had done well were the idols of the next generation. The states of the former Confederacy paid to the memory of such heroes as Lee, Jackson, Stuart, and their compeers a reverence which grew with the passing years. For political success in the next generation a war record was almost essential. The Republican party elected to the presidency Grant in 1868 and 1872, Hayes in 1876, Garfield in 1880, Harrison in 1888, McKinley in 1896 and 1900, all of them war veterans with good military records; the Democrats twice nominated Union generals, McClellan in 1864 and Hancock in 1880. The issues of slavery, from 1848 to 1860, of secession from 1861 to 1865, of reconstruction from 1865 to 1876, dominated American politics, as was natural enough, but to the present hour many Americans still are voting on the old sectional lines of 1848-76 rather than facing new issues as they arise.

If the war left too deep an imprint on the national mind, no one can wonder. It was probably the most extensive and important war fought anywhere in the world between 1815 and 1914. It cost more than 600,000 lives. It introduced into warfare such modern methods as the strategic use of railways, field entrenchments protected by earthworks and wire entanglements, and ironclad warships. Important in itself, it was still more important in its consequences. It lib-

[7] Bertrand Russell, *Freedom and Organization* (1934), p. 335.

erated about four million slaves, exalted national authority above state rights, transferred political power for a generation from the South to the North and from the Democratic to the Republican party, stimulated in a dozen ways the development of industry and manufacture,[8] and marked the transition between the old America, mainly rural and agricultural, and the new America, mainly industrial and commercial. In short, the war was the 'great divide' across American history.

[8] American shipping, however, declined, partly because of wartime Confederate raids, but even more because of the competition of the new British steamships.

THE REUNITED STATES IN THE MACHINE AGE

WHILE the politicians were fighting over again the old battles of the war on party platforms, a profound revolution was under way in the industrial life of America, a change greater than any war could bring, though war certainly hastened it. Ante-bellum America was predominantly rural and, except for a few great plantations in the South, rural at the level of the working farmer rather than that of the country gentleman. Towns and cities were market centers rather than industrial areas. By the end of the nineteenth century, however, the United States ranked with Great Britain and Germany as one of the three chief industrial nations and had greater resources for future development than either.

After Seward had made his purchase of Alaska from Russia in 1867, the United States had reached present territorial limits, except for island dependencies overseas. This area was only a little smaller than the whole continent of Europe, and scarcely inferior in resources of every sort. But, whereas Europe was cut up by mountain ranges, tariff barriers, armed frontiers, and diverse languages, the United States enjoyed a high degree of unity. Two great mountain highlands, the Rockies and the Appalachians, ran from north to south, but there were no important east-to-west ranges, such as the Alps; the whole Mississippi Valley formed a single plain. One language prevailed everywhere; no political or commercial barriers existed. Vast resources of coal, iron, copper, petroleum, and waterpower still lay completely untouched. Reckless waste had locally depleted some good farm and timber land, but not as yet to the point of impoverishing the nation as a whole. The new Union Pacific Railroad, pushed across the West from 1862 to 1869, bound the Pacific coast to the Mississippi Valley. The great distances between farm and market stimulated the development of railroads and, later, of automobiles.

The high cost of domestic service and of rural wages made the use of machinery profitable in the home and on the farm.

Nor were the people less fitted than the land for industrialism. Americans, from colonial days, had been an alert, restless, innovating sort of men, little attached to ancestral soil or to ancestral customs. Among the early American contributions to world industry were such inventions as Eli Whitney's cotton gin of 1793, Robert Fulton's steamship (1807), Cyrus McCormick's grain reaper (1834), Samuel Morse's electric telegraph (1835), and Elias Howe's sewing machine (1846). Eli Whitney had applied the method of interchangeable parts to the manufacture of firearms, and thus made possible the ordering of replacements for any broken bit of machinery by number from the factory.

The outstanding industrial development during the generation immediately following the war was the rapid expansion of the railroads. The older highways had been chiefly the waterways. Mark Twain's *Life on the Mississippi* recounts the great days of river navigation. The Erie Canal, opening up a barge route from the Hudson Valley to the Great Lakes, was largely responsible for developing New York City into the American metropolis. But good waterways were not to be found everywhere. The rivers of the western prairies are shallow in dry seasons, while the Rocky Mountain area has almost no navigable rivers at all. Without the phenomenal railroad building after 1860, the development of the West would have been retarded by at least two generations. Though nearly all railroads were privately owned, some had received substantial endowments from public lands to make them possible. Their owners entered politics to protect their vested interests or to work against unfriendly legislation. The 30,000 miles of American railway in 1860 became 90,000 in 1880 and 240,000 in 1910. Since then, there has not been much extension. Just as the railroad thrust into the background river steamboat, canal barge, and stage coach, so in turn the motor bus and the truck took business from the railroads.

Parallel with the growth of railroading was the development of telegraph and telephone. By 1880 there were already over 100,000 miles of telegraph line in the United States. In 1876 the Bell telephone was introduced; within four years over 50,000 telephones were in operation. In 1866, after repeated failures, a submarine cable was at last successfully in use under the Atlantic.

The iron and steel industry is fundamental in the American industrial system, since it underlies so many forms of specialized manufacture. The iron ore deposits of greatest extent are located near Lake Superior, far from the chief coal areas, and this at first handicapped the United States in competition with Great Britain, where distances are so short from iron mine to coal pit. Shipping on the Great Lakes, however, partly solved this difficulty. The million tons of pig iron produced in 1860 had more than trebled in the next two decades. Improved methods of manufacture revolutionized the steel industry.

The United States possessed reserves of soft (bituminous) and hard (anthracite) coal greater, according to our present knowledge, than any other coal deposits on earth. The story of the second most important fuel, petroleum, is a romantic one, with a slightly buccaneering aspect. At first sold as an 'Indian remedy' for various ills, it later replaced whale oil in lamps. The old-fashioned kerosene lamp, still common in many country districts, was for a time almost universal. The German invention of the internal combustion engine made possible the gasoline automobile, the motor bicycle, the oil-burning ship, the airplane. Tremendous fortunes were made or lost in the oil booms, and John D. Rockefeller, the organizer of Standard Oil, became the wealthiest man of his generation. Secret rebate agreements with the railroads, giving the company favored rates, played a part in the growth of this powerful corporation, but much of its success was attributable to the scientific grading of the different kinds of oil.

Many parts of the United States are rich in waterpower. This has made possible cheap electric light and power for hundreds of cities. Many ingenious applications of electricity were made by Thomas A. Edison, whose electric lamp of 1880 began the modern transformation of night into day. Edison's inventions also did much to develop the phonograph and the motion picture.

It is, perhaps, scarcely necessary to point out that the industrial expansion of the United States after the 1860s was but part of a world-wide development. British inventions, like the steam locomotive, were introduced almost at once in the United States; Ameri-

can inventions, like the telegraph, needed few years to become matters of course in Europe. The great organizer of the American steel
industry was a Scottish immigrant, Andrew Carnegie. German chem-
istry and British engineering underlay many American industrial
processes. But geography and social conditions fostered a greater
utilization of machinery in the United States than in any other country.

When manufacturing was on a small scale, ownership was usually
vested in a single person or in a partnership, but the trend of 'big
business' in the new industrial era was to the corporation. By 1910
nearly four-fifths of all manufactured goods were produced by corporate companies. Some of these were veritable leviathans; in 1901
the United States Steel Company was organized with a capital of
well over $1,000,000,000. Sometimes a trust company would take
over the management of several different concerns which were supposed to be competing with each other. The Sherman Anti-Trust
Act of 1890 forbade every 'combination in the form of trust or otherwise . . . in restraint of trade or commerce among the several states.'
The vagueness of the law, however, made it open to many diverse
interpretations, though a few prosecutions were instituted under it,
the trusts multiplied more than ever.

The rapid industrial growth of the United States attracted ever
increasing numbers of immigrants. Since 1820 more than 40,000,000
immigrants have entered the United States, the greatest mass movement of peoples which history records. The heaviest immigration
took place in the relatively brief period from 1880 to 1914. Down
to the 1840s British immigration prevailed, but in that decade political unrest in Germany and hard times in Ireland stimulated immigration from those countries especially. After 1890, however, German and Irish immigration tended to decrease and the number of
south and east Europeans—principally Italians, Slavs, and Jews—to
augment rapidly.

Estimates made in 1920 placed the descendants of immigrants
from Great Britain and northern Ireland at a little over 41 per cent
of the white population, as compared with 77 per cent in 1790.[1]
Next in number were the Americans of German descent, about 16

[1] See above, p. 183.

per cent, and the southern Irish, 11 per cent. Canada and Poland each contributed over 4 per cent; Italy and Scandinavia about 3½ per cent apiece; Russia and the Netherlands each about 2 per cent, and many other countries smaller numbers. Many Scandinavians and Finns took up Minnesota or Dakota wheat farms or entered the Michigan and Wisconsin lumber camps; Germans, Dutch, and Bohemians (Czechs) were numerous in the cities of the Middle West; Slavs and Hungarians (Magyars) were employed by the thousands in the mill towns and coal mines of the industrial states, such as Pennsylvania; the Irish and the Italians found new homes in New York and New England; Jews, especially from Russian Poland, concentrated in large numbers in New York City; French Canadians often went to New England factories; the Pacific coast had a thin sprinkling of Orientals, and across the southwestern border there was a considerable immigration of Mexicans. But none of these peoples remained fixed in one place. Like other Americans, they moved from city to city and gradually became diffused throughout the nation, though of course in widely different numbers and proportions.

Indeed it is curious how rapidly each generation of immigrants in turn became assimilated to the old colonial stock. During the generation before the War for Southern Independence, a nativist movement popularly called the 'know-nothing' [2] tried to establish a long probationary period for citizenship and to exclude the foreign born from high public office. It was aimed largely at the Irish Roman Catholics, and religious bigotry was at least one of its elements. But a generation later Irish-American politicians and trade unionists were urging legislation to decrease immigration from southeastern Europe and to shut off altogether the cheap Chinese coolie labor which had begun to appear on the Pacific coast. Only in local patches, or under exceptional conditions, did children of any immigrant nationality keep up the language and customs of their parents. There were, and are, vernacular newspapers for each immigrant group, but the sons and grandsons of the immigrants read by preference the more widely circulated newspapers printed in English. Though sectarian schools were numerous, the free public schools were far more widely at-

[2] So called because its adherents professed ignorance of their organization when talking with outsiders.

tended. In the factories and in the trade unions, workmen of a score of nationalities were forced to meet daily.

Because of the rapid fusion of these diverse ores in the common American melting pot, it is not easy to estimate the exact contribution of each national or racial element to national culture. Certainly the United States did not turn into another polyglot Austria-Hungary. In no European country was there a more general loyalty to the flag or a greater standardization of customs and manners. Foreign critics of American life did not complain that the United States was a patchwork of disunity but rather that the country was a monochrome of uniformity. This, of course, can be exaggerated. There is a wide difference between wintry, conservative, self-contained Vermont, and California with her pioneer exuberance, her Riviera climate, and her Spanish architecture. The South, even after losing her war for independence, remained a self-conscious cultural unit and became known politically as the Solid South from the habit of always supporting the Democratic ticket. There are districts in every large city that have a distinctly foreign flavor and where less than half the shop signs are in English. There are queer little unassimilated groups, the Amish Mennonites of Pennsylvania for example, which have kept the same ancestral customs alive for many generations. But these exceptions do not invalidate the generalization that the United States after 1865 was essentially one nation.

Where continental European influence entered the United States it was not always by the gates of Ellis Island, where the immigrants landed in New York harbor. After all, most immigrants came as workingmen with little capital except their stout arms and ambitious hopes. The influx of ideas often followed other channels. Thus the American universities, especially in the field of graduate study and organized research, borrowed heavily from German models, but the chief agents in this movement were not the German immigrants themselves, rather the handful of American scholars, often of colonial ancestry, who visited Heidelberg, Berlin, or Göttingen. French and Russian realistic fiction had considerable influence on American literature. Famous musicians, singers, and actors from abroad made symphony concerts and grand opera possible. The growing American habit of traveling abroad for pleasure broke up many old provincialisms and introduced European conceptions of art and culture.

During this period of rapid industrial development between the War for Southern Independence and the Spanish-American War, political life was much less absorbing than it had been in former generations. Men who in 1840 would have sought a senatorship were better pleased in 1880 to build a railroad—and give orders to senators! No doubt this shift of interest from the affairs of state to the affairs of business contributed to the low standard of party politics during much of this generation; but one must also bear in mind the demoralizing effect of a great war, the difficult problems of reconstruction in the South, and the presence of a rapidly growing host of inexperienced immigrant laborers in the industrial centers.

President Andrew Johnson, who succeeded Lincoln, resembled him in being a self-made man of Southern origin and an advocate of conciliation towards the South. To Lincoln's political tact and skill he never attained, however, and he was soon at open strife with the Republican leaders in Congress. The Radical Republicans, as they were called, insisted that equal civil rights and the political franchise be granted to Negro freedmen before the seceding states were restored to their old position in the Union. This program was embodied in the fourteenth amendment, which stated that no state might 'deprive any person of life, liberty, or property without due process of law nor deny to any person within its jurisdiction the equal protection of the laws'; and in the fifteenth, which declared that the right to vote could not be restricted on grounds of 'race, color, or previous condition of servitude.' These amendments have had a rather curious subsequent history. The fourteenth has been sometimes judicially construed to protect not merely human beings but corporations, as legal 'persons,' from confiscatory legislation and thus has become a bulwark of property rights. The fifteenth, though never repealed, has been successfully evaded by most of the Southern states by tax or educational requirements and other methods, so administered as to exclude Negro voters from the polls.

Finding President Johnson an obstacle to the radical program, the leaders of that faction tried to remove him by impeachment, mainly on the pretext that he had violated the new Tenure of Office Act, which took from the President the right to remove federal officials, even in his own cabinet, without consent of the Senate. Johnson, considering the law unconstitutional, had disregarded it. His acquittal by the Senate established a useful tradition against the employment of impeachment for political purposes, and no subsequent President has ever been impeached.

In 1868 the Republicans made the almost inevitable nomination of General Ulysses S. Grant, hailed as 'the man who won the war,' in spite of his previous lack of experience in politics. He was elected over Governor Seymour of New York, the Democratic candidate, but his administration proved such a disappointment that when he ran again in 1872 he faced a coalition of Democrats and Liberal Republicans with the Republican journalist, Horace Greeley, as their joint nominee. Grant's ineptitude made him the victim of designing politicians, and his second term was even more deeply involved in scandal than his first. His Secretary of War Belknap and his private secretary Babcock were accused of making private fortunes out of public frauds.

The record of the legislative branch of the government was worse than that of the executive. A financial concern, the *Crédit Mobilier*, acting as a construction company for the Union Pacific railroad, placed stock at a cheap rate among the congressmen to win political friendships. This was but one of many scandals. Still lower depths were plumbed by some local governments, such as the 'Tweed ring' in New York City, and the reconstruction governments in many Southern states, where inexperienced Negro voters were herded in droves by Northern 'carpetbaggers' [3] to vote for officials who fattened their purses at the expense of the taxpayers. In retaliation, a secret, shrouded, and hooded order, the Ku Klux Klan,[4] intimidated Negro voters and avenged acts of license and disorder.

In 1876 the Republicans nominated Rutherford B. Hayes, an honest old soldier who had been thrice governor of Ohio; the Democrats Samuel Tilden, a New York lawyer who had successfully prosecuted 'Boss' Tweed, the leader of Tammany Hall in the worst days of municipal corruption. The election that followed was so close that the result hung by the margin of a single vote in the Electoral College, and many votes were in dispute owing to wholesale

[3] So called, as if all their worldly possessions were in a carpetbag!

[4] Not to be confused with the new Ku Klux Klan after the First World War. There were other organizations of similar purpose, though less fame, such as the Knights of the White Camelia.

frauds by both parties in the 'reconstructed' states of the South. A special electoral commission, made up of certain representatives, senators, and judges of the Supreme Court, decided by a strictly party vote not to 'go behind the returns,' and declared Hayes elected on the face of the results as presented by local boards. President Hayes withdrew federal soldiers from the South and thus permitted the local white population to organize state governments as they chose. 'Reconstruction' was at an end.

President Hayes made efforts to establish merit standards in the federal civil service and fight the spoils system. The necessity of this reform was shown by the assassination of his successor, President James A. Garfield, a former Union general, by a disappointed office seeker. Vice-President Chester A. Arthur, who had himself been a spoilsman in lesser offices, now he was in the White House proved a pleasant disappointment, as he took up the Hayes tradition of civil-service reform. Congress passed a measure establishing competitive examinations for many offices, and later administrations have widely extended the scope of the system. Even today, however, more officials are changed when a new administration takes office than is customary in Great Britain or in the British Dominions.

Grover Cleveland in 1884 broke the long string of Republican victories. He was elected, after a stirring campaign, over the popular Republican orator and congressional leader, James G. Blaine. The campaign was decided by Cleveland's victory by a narrow margin in his own state of New York, and this in turn was decided by the unfortunate phrase used by a Blaine supporter—not by Blaine himself, the most tactful of politicians—that the Democratic party was the party of 'Rum, Romanism, and Rebellion'! Cleveland introduced the issue of tariff reform, implying in this case a reduction of the existing high protective rates; he was defeated on this platform in 1888 by General Benjamin Harrison, a grandson of President William H. Harrison. In 1892 he was victorious, winning the only non-consecutive second presidential term in American history.

Cleveland had accomplished much. He had restored the Democratic party to office, had ended many scandals in war pensions and land grants, had made a partially successful effort to extend the merit system in the civil service, and given the first important challenge to the protective tariff system since 1861, though he could not get as much reduction of rates from Congress as he wished. But he had little sympathy with the radical discontent of workingmen and farmers outside the ranks of party politics.

Radicals found, indeed, little comfort from either Republicans or Democrats. In the early days of its existence the Republican party had been considered the radical party, and was called by that name in some sections of the country. Karl Marx had written articles for the European press in support of the Union during the War for Southern Independence. But after the emancipation of the slaves had been accomplished, the 'party of moral ideas' (as it modestly termed itself) became the party of Big Business. Except on the tariff issue, the Democrats were equally conservative. Both parties, however they might 'view with alarm' each other's misdeeds in their platforms, always 'pointed with pride' to the industrial and commercial progress of the nation. There had been occasional setbacks to that progress, as in the panics of 1837, 1857, 1873, and 1893, but no one expected the government (as after the panic of 1929) to rush forward with plans for relief. So the forces of discontent organized small third parties or concentrated on local fights in the state legislatures. A Prohibitionist party fought each election on the single issue of national prohibition of intoxicants. 'Greenbackers' demanded an ample paper currency; 'Free Silverites' an unlimited coinage of silver; disciples of Henry George urged a 'single tax' to absorb all increments in land values. There were some disciples of Karl Marx, and Utopian Socialism was well represented by Bellamy's famous romance of the future, *Looking Backward*. Trade unions agitated for a maximum eight-hour day, government ownership of railroads, and the total prohibition of Chinese immigration. All schools united in denouncing the trusts and the great corporations of other types, but their remedies varied all the way from 'trust busting' to restore the good old Jeffersonian days of small business and unlimited competition, to the Socialist slogan 'Let the Nation own the Trusts.'

Though there were small radical groups in the mill towns, discontent with the existing economic order was most widespread in the prairie country which had been settled between 1850 and 1890. The Indian and the buffalo had been swept aside with incredible swiftness into small reservations. Then followed the day of the cowboy. The cattle ranges of the open plains made possible the driving

of vast herds from western Texas to the stockyards and railway ter-
minals in western Kansas. Later the range extended north to Dakota,
Wyoming, and Montana. The cowboy dressed in Mexican fashion,
with a broad sombrero, fur-protected leggings, jingling spurs, and
fine leather trappings for his horse. He became a hero of American
fiction and folklore and is more alive than ever in the motion-picture
films. But almost from the start he was challenged by two enemies:
the sheep herders (whom no American called 'shepherds') whose
flocks cropped the thin prairie grass so closely that cattle could not
feed where they had passed; and the farmers, whose barbed-wire
fences cut the old open range into patches.

The farmers, locating their homesteads on government land,
pushed their settlement too far into arid territory. A few dry years
on these high plains would suffice to turn rich farmland back into
desert, the 'dust bowl.' Though the nation gave land to settlers for
merely occupying and developing it, the farmers had to buy their
own domestic animals and agricultural machinery, and often had to
mortgage the land, or the crops, to equip their farms. Then would
come the lean years, and they would lose their profits, their labor,
often their homes. It is not by chance that the wheat belt has been
a focus of discontent on many occasions in the past sixty years.[5]

With hard times a new party appeared, the People's party, commonly dubbed the Populists. It drew members from the farmers'
social associations, or granges, and the more political Farmers' Alliance, and its leaders from the small third parties. It advocated free
silver, more paper money, an income tax, government ownership of
railroads, telegraphs, and telephones, direct election of senators (at
that time still chosen by the state legislatures), restriction of immigration, and many other reforms. In 1892 the Populists carried several western prairie and mountain states, the only occasion between
1860 and 1912 that electoral votes went to any third party. They
opposed President Cleveland on the currency question, but they
hoped for an alliance with the radical wing of the Democrats, and
in 1896 a fiery young Democratic congressman from Nebraska,
William Jennings Bryan, received the joint Populist and Demo-

[5] The prairie states supported the Populists in the 1890s, the Roosevelt Progressives of 1910-12, and such local movements as the Farmers' Non-Partisan
League in the 1920s. See Chapters xxvi and xli.

cratic nominations on a platform calling for the 'free and unlimited coinage of silver at a ratio of sixteen to one' to that of gold.

The Republicans chose William McKinley of Ohio, who wished to make the fight on the tariff issue but who was constrained by Bryan's challenge to come out for the gold standard. The battle of 1896 was thus the old fight, renewed in one form or another at least once a generation, between 'sound money' and 'cheap money,' between deflation and inflation, between creditors and debtors. Free silver was favored by the mining states, such as Colorado and Nevada, and also by the Western farmers, who wanted better prices for their crops. Other issues were pushed into the background, and the nation had a refreshing change from the monotonous harping on war memories and the tariff question which had served national politics since 1865. McKinley carried the entire Northeast and Middle West and several of the Southern border states; Bryan won the old Confederate states and most of the states west of the Mississippi and Missouri Rivers. The Republican party, committed now to the gold standard as well as to the protective tariff, the party of Big Business and prosperity, was entrusted with the destinies of the nation for many years to come.

But the election of 1896 was not quite so important as it seemed. Though the gold standard was maintained till 1933, new discoveries of gold in South Africa, Alaska, and the Klondike soon made money cheap, prices high, and farmers prosperous. Though a conservative had been chosen President, within five years a liberal would occupy the White House, and Theodore Roosevelt the Republican would frighten the 'money changers of Wall Street' quite as badly as Bryan the Democrat. Though the election had turned on purely domestic issues, McKinley's administration was made memorable by a war with Spain. Even in a democracy, the decisions of the sovereign People are subject to the whimsical veto power of Fate!

AMERICA BECOMES A WORLD POWER

PRIOR to 1898 the United States had in the main held aloof from world politics. American diplomacy, though occasionally concerned with issues beyond the limits of the Monroe Doctrine, had devoted most of its attention to such matters as the demarcation of the Canadian boundary, fishing rights in Alaskan and Newfoundland waters, the misbehavior of Caribbean dictators, and similar American affairs. Within the New World, American statesmen had been zealously expansionist, acquiring land from Indian tribes, from France (Louisiana), from Spain (Florida), from Mexico (Texas, California, New Mexico), from Russia (Alaska), and by boundary adjustment with Great Britain (Oregon). But in the partition of Africa, the great concern of European diplomacy during the 1880s and '90s, the United States had taken no share. Though Americans had played a part in opening up China and Japan to world trade, the nation sought no treaty ports or spheres of influence in Asia.

The War for Southern Independence had created some acute international problems. Grant's able Secretary of State, Hamilton Fish, together with Charles Francis Adams, Minister to Great Britain, successfully arranged the arbitration of the so-called *Alabama* claims, by which the United States was compensated for the damage done by Confederate raiders outfitted in British ports. This was a great victory for the principle of arbitration, and was useful also in clearing up uncertain legal points regarding the duties of neutrals in wartime. Napoleon III took advantage of the war to place the Austrian prince Maximilian on the throne of a Mexican Empire, but American opposition later forced him to withdraw French aid and permit the restoration of the republic.

In 1895 a new crisis arose. The republic of Venezuela was engaged in a boundary dispute with the colony of British Guiana. President

Cleveland advocated arbitration, and took advantage of the frontier controversy to declare, through the pen of Secretary of State Richard Olney, that 'the United States is practically sovereign on this continent, and its fiat is law upon the subjects to which it confines its interposition.' This ambitious 'Olney Doctrine' was not accepted by Great Britain as a pendant to the Monroe Doctrine, and for a few days a war panic clouded the skies, but British acceptance of arbitration on the specific issue in question ended the incident, and with it the last crisis which has ever threatened war between the English-speaking Powers.

President McKinley had no great personal interest in expansion, but among the leaders of his party such men as Senator Lodge of Massachusetts and young Theodore Roosevelt, Assistant Secretary of the Navy, were ardently in favor of a vigorous foreign policy and a great increase in naval strength. The situation in Cuba gave them a strong argument. The island was a relic of Spanish rule, which had been driven from the American mainland seven or eight decades earlier. Within a short distance of Florida, Cuba afforded a continuous nightmare of insurrections, repressions, and misgovernment. In President Pierce's time, and again in Grant's, Spanish executions of American volunteers in the Cuban cause had aroused patriotic indignation that almost led to war.

Various more or less accidental incidents helped stir the war spirit. General Weyler's policy of forcing Cuban peasants into concentration camps led to terrible suffering. Taking this as a theme, two rival New York publishers, Joseph Pulitzer and William Randolph Hearst, carried on an active anti-Spanish propaganda in their papers. The Spanish Minister at Washington wrote a letter attacking President McKinley, which was stolen and printed. The American battleship *Maine* was blown up in Havana harbor in February 1898. To this day no one knows the exact cause of the explosion, but a commission of inquiry believed that it had an external cause, probably one of the mines in the harbor. American diplomacy took a stiffer tone, and Spain, alarmed at last, offered concessions which might have averted war had they been made earlier. Congress, however, declared war in April.

The war itself was trivial. Most of the American regulars and volunteers who made up its small death roll perished from bad food, bad water, or disease-laden mosquitoes rather than from Spanish bullets. Cuba and Puerto Rico were easily occupied, and Commodore George Dewey seized the Philippines in a single naval engagement. Within four months the fighting was over and an armistice established.

But small wars have often had great consequences. The Spanish-American War marked an emergence of the United States as a World Power. Cuba became an independent republic, the United States retaining the right to intervene when necessary to establish order (the Platt amendment), a right relinquished in 1934. Puerto Rico, the Philippine Islands, and the island of Guam became American colonies. Spain was paid $20,000,000 for the Philippines, a consolation gift to the vanquished which recalls the payment made to Mexico after the annexation of California and the Southwest. Some other acquisitions, independent of the war, were made at about the same period. Thus in 1898 the Hawaiian Islands, which President Cleveland had refused to annex, were admitted by their own request and given territorial status. Small island outposts such as Wake, Midway, and part of Samoa, rounded out a minor Pacific empire.

Some Americans in both parties denounced the acquisition of the Philippines as rank imperialism, and Bryan, again the Democratic nominee, fought the election of 1900 unsuccessfully on that issue. A small insurrection in the Philippines was put down and American rule established. William Howard Taft became civil governor. Yellow fever and malaria in Cuba, and cholera and small-pox in the Philippines were successfully combatted. An admirable system of roads and schools revolutionized Filipino life, and the population doubled under American rule. Yet both parties agreed that the Philippines must have their independence 'some day,' though the Republicans favored a longer period of probation than the Democrats. Though American rule did more for the Filipinos than even optimists had hoped, it did less for American business than even pessimists had feared. Trade with China languished. Planters hesitated about investing in islands whose future was so uncertain. In 1916 Congress voted in principle for Philippine independence 'as soon as a stable government can be established,' and in 1934 the Tydings-McDuffie Act made independence automatic by 1945, unless there should be a change of policy in the meantime, or unless the Japanese gain permanent footing there.

The Chinese crisis of 1899-1900 marked another step towards active American participation in world politics. John Hay, as Secretary of State, enunciated an 'open door' policy, directed against the threatened partition of the Chinese Empire. The United States also took part in the international expedition against the Boxers. When China paid her indemnity to the aggrieved foreign Powers, the United States remitted a share of its own indemnity as a fund to be used for sending Chinese students to American universities: a wise arrangement which did much to cement friendship between China and America.

Relations between Britain and the United States became more cordial than at any previous period. The generally friendly attitude of the British during the Spanish-American War was the more appreciated because of the hostile tone of the press of continental Europe. In Chinese affairs the two nations co-operated. In 1901 the Hay-Pauncefote treaty, replacing the old Clayton-Bulwer treaty, gave the United States a free hand to construct a canal between the Atlantic and the Pacific under strictly American auspices, provided that all ships using it paid equal tolls.

In September 1901, shortly after the commencement of his second term, President McKinley was shot by an anarchist, and Vice-President Theodore Roosevelt assumed the presidency. Roosevelt was of old New York Dutch stock, but his experiences on a Dakota cattle ranch gave him a touch of Westernism, and few people thought of him as a New Yorker. He had a varied and eventful career: a New York police commissioner, an author of popular histories, an Assistant Secretary of the Navy, a volunteer leader of 'Rough Riders' in the Spanish-American War, a governor of New York, and, much against his wish, a Vice-President of the United States. Like many American politicians he had dreaded the vice-presidency as a sort of respectable political burial, but chance had made it a short cut to the presidency. He promised, sincerely enough, to continue McKinley's policies, but his own personality made that impossible.

Roosevelt was never, at least prior to his whirlwind campaign of 1912, really a radical. His concrete innovations in government were moderate and constructive, he viewed doctrinaires with scorn and boasted of being a realistic practical politician. But he was by temperament ardent, impatient, and strenuous, very much the Andrew Jackson type, though with a wider range of intellectual interests. Conservatives were alarmed not so much by what he did as by the manner in which he did it and the uncertainty of what he might do next.

Roosevelt's domestic policies may be grouped under a few heads: regulation of large-scale business by the Federal Government; the conservation of natural resources; and the assumption by the President of responsibility for the initiative in legislation. He avoided the dangerous tariff issue, which has wrecked so many American administrations, and concentrated on the more popular task of taming the trusts. He favored laws giving the Interstate Commerce Commission the right to fix railroad rates, and pure-food laws establishing penalties for misbranded foods and drugs carried in interstate commerce. He established a new Department of Commerce and Labor (later divided into two departments) in the cabinet. He withdrew millions of acres of timberland from private entry to form giant forest reserves, and placed their care under the Forest Bureau of the Department of Agriculture, headed by the zealous conservationist Gifford Pinchot. Many new national parks were established for public recreation and for the preservation of wild animals. When an anthracite coal strike threatened the nation with a fuel shortage and the mine owners refused arbitration, Roosevelt forced them to yield by threatening to open the mines by government authority and run them under military rule.

In the sphere of foreign policy Roosevelt showed the same initiative and energy. He built up the navy and tested its efficiency by a world cruise. He interested himself in army reforms. He participated by representative in the Algeçiras Conference on Morocco. He intervened in Cuba and Santo Domingo to restore order. He persuaded Germany to agree to a peaceful settlement of claims against Venezuela. He received the Nobel Peace Prize for his mediation which terminated the Russo-Japanese War.

The strength and weakness of the Roosevelt method—for an excessive and needless display of strength is often a weakness in diplomacy—is well illustrated by the building of the Panama Canal. Two routes had been suggested for an interoceanic canal, one through the isthmus of Panama, then belonging to the Republic of Colombia, the other through Nicaragua. A private French company had undertaken the construction of a canal at Panama; its engineering was good, but its finances unsound and its sanitation execrable. Unable to complete its contract, it sold its rights to the United States for $40,000,000, while $10,000,000 and an annual rental were to be paid Colombia for the right of way. But the Colombian Congress played a waiting game in the hope that the lease of the French company would expire before the United States assumed its rights, and thus fresh sums be obtained for renewal of the lease. Roosevelt, furious at what seemed to him a mere case of 'racketeering,' took advantage of a rebellion in the province of Panama in 1903 to force Colombia's hand. He recognized the rebel province as an independent republic and landed troops 'for the protection of commerce across the isthmus,' thus effectually preventing Colombia from reconquering her lost canal zone! Then, ignoring Colombia, he bought the canal rights from the newly created Republic of Panama. The canal was constructed under government control with the aid of such able men as Chief Engineer Goethals and Chief Sanitary Officer Gorgas. It was open to traffic in 1914. But there was a sequel, less happy. So much ill will towards the United States had been aroused in Latin America by the cavalier way in which Colombia had been treated, that in 1921 the United States paid Colombia $25,000,000 in consolation money.

In 1904 President Roosevelt was re-elected against a conservative Democrat, Judge Alton B. Parker, also of New York. In 1908, refusing another term for himself, he secured the nomination of William Howard Taft of Ohio, his Secretary of War, who defeated Bryan, for the third time an unsuccessful Democratic candidate. As governor of the Philippines and as Secretary of War, Taft had proved himself an able administrator, and in later life he was a successful Chief Justice of the Supreme Court. But his single presidential term was an unhappy one. Roosevelt had caused the nation to expect aggressive leadership; even apart from Roosevelt the nation was beginning to demand progressive policies. Taft, with all his ability, could meet neither demand.

American liberalism has its high and low tides. One wave had made Jefferson President, another Jackson, another Lincoln. Dur-

ing the Roosevelt and Taft administrations there was a new flowing
of liberal sentiment, which took the rather vague name of 'progres-
sivism.' No one issue predominated, as the slavery question had done
in the 1850s or the currency question in the 1890s; rather a score of
independent, though sometimes overlapping, reform movements
were simultaneously active. Woman suffrage, long confined to the
Rocky Mountain states, was now winning converts in the East. Constitutional amendments for a federal income tax and for direct
popular election of senators were debated in Congress. Direct primaries,[1] the initiative and referendum on state legislation,[2] and the
recall of elected officers by popular petition, were popular measures
in the Western states. Many cities adopted simplified charters, con-
centrating power in the hands of a commission or a city manager,
instead of dispersing it in the traditional American manner among
mayor, council, aldermen, and a long list of separately elected officials. Each state elaborated its code of factory laws, and legislated to
minimize the evils of child labor, though constitutional limitations
prevented the Federal Government from dealing effectively with
such problems.

A new tendency towards national self-criticism appeared in what
had hitherto been seemingly the most self-satisfied of the nations.
In part this was doubtless merely a phase of the world-wide restless-
ness of the years immediately before the First World War. The
social legislation of Germany and of Great Britain [3] had been studied
by many American reformers. The French syndicalist movement had
an approximate American parallel in the new radical union of the
I.W.W. (Industrial Workers of the World). But in the main, the
progressive movement grew from native roots; it was a more searching analysis of the weaknesses of American capitalism than that of
the Populists, but it answered to similar discontents. The popular
periodicals ran articles exposing 'Frenzied Finance,' 'The Shame of
the Cities,' 'The Treason of the Senate,' and other real or alleged
evils. The articles were sometimes too sensational—even Roosevelt

[1] The nomination of candidates by the direct vote of party members.

[2] A referendum on changes in the state constitution, as distinguished from
ordinary legislation, had long been the rule in most states.

[3] For British reforms during this period see Chapter xxxi.

compared them to 'muckrakers' [4]—but at least they put an end to the old complacent belief that everything was for the best in 'God's country.'

In 1910 popular discontent with Taft's conservatism, and especially with the new Payne-Aldrich tariff law, which had failed to keep the party promises of tariff reform, gave the control of Congress to the Democratic party for the first time since 1894. The Republican progressives urged Roosevelt to run for the presidency. In 1912 the party split, the Republican convention renominating Taft, while the insurgents organized as the National Progressive Party, with Roosevelt as their candidate, and adopted a platform which embraced numerous reforms ranging from woman suffrage to federal regulation of corporations. Democratic prospects were so bright that there was an unusually keen contest for the nomination. Champ Clark of Missouri, Speaker of the House of Representatives, was the favored candidate for the nomination, and at first took the lead in the convention, but eventually the choice went to Governor Woodrow Wilson of New Jersey, supported by the liberal wing of the party.

The campaign itself was almost an anti-climax after the fierce struggle in the Republican and Democratic primaries and conventions, though feeling ran so high that a fanatic shot and wounded Roosevelt. Wilson easily swept the Electoral College, though he failed to obtain a popular majority.[5] Taft carried only two small states; Roosevelt several states of the North and West. Apparently the Progressives were no longer a 'third party,' since their candidate ran second, but as a matter of fact many who voted the new ticket were really rather 'Roosevelt Republicans' than Progressives on principle, and they returned to their old party allegiance a few years later.

Wilson was the scholar in politics—a rare figure in American life. Other Presidents had taught school or written books, but only as incidents in a life filled with other activities; Wilson stepped directly from the presidency of Princeton University to the governership of New Jersey, and thence to the White House. He was a Virginian by birth, the first Southerner since Andrew Johnson to become Presi-

[4] A reference to the 'man with a muckrake' in Bunyan's *Pilgrim's Progress*.
[5] Like Lincoln in 1860, he had a popular plurality, though not a majority.

dent. He gave his first attention to the tariff and to the banking question. He succeeded, where both Cleveland and Taft had failed, in making Congress carry out party pledges to lower the tariff. He succeeded in organizing a national banking system. It differed from Hamilton's plan, which Jackson had destroyed, by substituting twelve federal reserve districts in different parts of the country for a single, centralized institution. He created a Federal Trade Commission to prevent unfair methods of competition among corporations engaged in interstate trade, and exempted trade unions from being prosecuted as 'combinations in restraint of trade.' No administration before Franklin Roosevelt's was more fertile in legislative reform.

President Wilson had been elected on purely domestic issues, as most American Presidents have been, and his Secretary of State, Bryan, had very little knowledge of Old World affairs. Mexico seemed the outstanding diplomatic problem of the United States. In 1911 the long dictatorship of Porfirio Diaz had ended—as dictatorships almost invariably do—in civil war. The liberal President Madero, who succeeded him, was murdered, and the reactionary Huerta took his place. Most foreign nations recognized Huerta at once, but President Wilson refused, desiring by his refusal to discourage usurpations and lawless violence among Latin American countries. When in 1914 Huerta arrested some American marines at Vera Cruz, Wilson took active steps to aid the "constitutionalists' who were bent on overthrowing the new dictator. But he did not wish to have a second Mexican War on his hands,[6] so he accepted the joint mediation of Argentina, Brazil, and Chile. Though the mediation failed of any result, Huerta's government finally collapsed and the constitutionalist leader Carranza became for a brief period President of Mexico, pending fresh revolutions.

But serious as was the Mexican crisis, it was soon overshadowed by the coming of the First World War. This burst on the American people with a shock of surprise as well as of horror; the cry of war had been raised so often in recent years that nearly everyone expected an outcome like that of other crises: an alarm, a frantic exchange of notes, a diplomatic conference, and a compromise. When war did

[6] 'Probably no other nation but the United States, and no other President but Wilson would so long and patiently have tolerated such conditions,' S. E. Morison and H. S. Commager, *The Growth of the American Republic*, Vol. II, p. 443.

break out, the presidential proclamation of neutrality was taken as a matter of course by nearly everyone; in spite of the precedent of 1812, hardly any American in 1914 expected the United States to become directly involved in a European conflict. The progressive disillusionment of the American people must be the subject of a later discussion.[7]

The cultural life of the American people between the War for Southern Independence and the First World War tends to be obscured by the rapid material growth of the nation. It is true that no group of poets, historians, and philosophers stands out so prominently as did the New England writers of the immediately preceding period.[8] It is true also that the general rush for wealth gave the impression of a 'gilded age' or 'chromo civilization,' rather Corinthian than Athenian. Many famous American authors, such as Henry James or Henry Adams, and artists, such as the impressionist James McNeill Whistler, spent by preference a large part of their lives in Europe and confessed that they no longer felt at home in the materialistic hurly-burly of the United States. The intellectual leaders who stayed by the ship had their misgivings too. Sidney Lanier, the Southern master of melodious verse, echoed Tennyson's indictment of the prevalent commercial greed; trade 'is only war grown miserly.' William James, the philosopher of pragmatism, denounced the popular worship of the 'bitch goddess Success.'[9] Many professors, so says Henry Canby, had to wrestle even in the classrooms with 'the second generation of industrial pioneers, who . . . believed with that implicit faith which is so much more powerful than doctrine, that the rest of their lives would be spent in a great struggle for wealth and privilege, where the best grabbers would win, and where only freaks and dreamers would take time to speculate on what it was all about and whether the result was happiness.'[10]

Yet there is another side. The first blooming of American culture had been fine in quality but subject to many quantitative limitations. For one thing, it was regional rather than national; it centered in

[7] See Chapter XXXVIII.

[8] See Chapter XXIII.

[9] William James, the brother of Henry James, the novelist, was a pioneer in scientific psychology and an author of outstanding power and originality.

[10] *Alma Mater* (1936), p. 135.

eastern Massachusetts, thinned out through the other Atlantic states, and reached the West scarcely at all. Again, this culture owed much to England but very little to continental Europe,[11] and had few points of contact with the new immigration or with the rougher phases of native American life. It was served by an inadequate newspaper and periodical press and depended on a few small, poorly endowed colleges for sustenance. The task of the years from 1865 to 1914 was rather to broaden the base of American civilization than to heighten its achievements.

There was a great improvement in the press. Editorial writing did not become more significant, rather less so, as the individual journalist was swallowed up in the huge impersonal machinery of a modern metropolitan daily, but the news services placed far more timely and accurate information before the nation's readers than had been possible in earlier years. Literary weeklies and monthlies, supported by a growing volume of commercial advertisement, increased in number, size, and attractiveness. By 1914 the public of the United States probably had better access to current fact than any other public in the world.

The colleges—for even those which had ambitiously assumed the title of 'university' had been scarcely more than colleges—now added courses in natural science, modern languages, and history to the traditional classical curriculum. Professional schools so greatly improved that the ordinary method of becoming a doctor or a lawyer in the twentieth century was no longer as hitherto apprenticeship in an office, but a college career capped by three or four years of hard postgraduate study in the principles of the profession. American scholars imported the graduate school from Germany, with its seminars for training students in research. True universities, in the European sense of the word, began to appear, captained by such educational leaders as Presidents Eliot of Harvard, White of Cornell, Gilman of Johns Hopkins, and Harper of Chicago. The universities were lavishly endowed by wealthy alumni or other philanthropists.

American genius, long recognized in the application of science to

---

[11] There were, of course, exceptions. Longfellow derived much inspiration from the old Scandinavian literature, and German idealism played a part in the Transcendentalist cult.

industry, now made conquests in the field of pure science, notably in biology, psychology, and medicine. If the new generation of literary historians were less distinguished than their predecessors, a much larger number of young men were studying the detailed facts of history and making original contributions to knowledge. The social sciences, such as economics, politics, and sociology, found able expounders. Eminent lawyers, less bound by purely technical precedents, tried to work out a flexible system of jurisprudence which would fit the needs of a rapidly expanding industrial society; some of them, like Dean Pound of Harvard, within academic walls, others, like Associate Justice Holmes, on the highest federal courts.

Perhaps the most notable characteristic of the fiction of the age was its emphasis on local color. All parts of the nation now had their spokesmen. Best known and loved was Samuel Clemens—'Mark Twain' to his readers—who wandered everywhere and wrote of all he saw, but whose sincerest work centers round his boyhood home on the banks of the Mississippi. William Dean Howells, Hamlin Garland, and many others also wrote of the Middle West; Bret Harte, Joaquin Miller, Frank Norris, and Jack London of the Far West; George W. Cable, Ellen Glasgow, Thomas Nelson Page, and Mary Johnston of the Old South; [12] Sidney Porter ('O. Henry') of New York City's 'Four Million'; Mary E. Wilkins Freeman and Sarah Orne Jewett of the New England village. Europe began to read American books; in the 1850s British authors had justly complained that lack of a copyright law had robbed them of the profit of their American sales, but a couple of decades later Mark Twain estimated that he lost many thousand dollars every year because his books were not protected in the British market.

In the fine arts, too, there was progress. Winslow Homer, Thomas Eakins, George Inness, J. S. Sargent, Edwin Abbey enriched American painting, and though they owed much of their technique to Europe, and especially France, they taught almost as much as they learned. Whistler stands apart, perhaps; American by birth, but almost wholly European in his artistic career. Saint-Gaudens ranks as the leading American sculptor, and his Adams memorial has been

[12] Mention should also be made of Joel Chandler Harris, whose 'Uncle Remus' stories, based on Negro folklore, have delighted British as well as American children for many years.

called the greatest American work of art; but many others, such as Barnard, Taft, Borglum, and French, have obtained world recognition.

It was in architecture, however, that a really native school of art developed. The skyscraper, though not unknown in Europe, was for economic reasons especially suitable to America. At first it was a mere utilitarian convenience, a huge box set on end to save ground rentals in the great cities. But its possibilities as an art form were discovered by Louis Sullivan in the late nineteenth century; and the effect of zoning laws, which required a 'step back' structure for the upper stories, has transformed the mere mathematical prism into a dignified and often graceful *ziggurat* worthy of ancient Babylon. Among Sullivan's disciples was Frank Lloyd Wright, who in our own day has applied functional architectural forms to private houses as well as to public buildings. In the more traditional styles, H. H. Richardson and the partnership of McKim, Mead, and White successfully revived the Romanesque, and Ralph Adams Cram the Gothic. City planning became more common, and private homes, after reaching their ugliest in the third quarter of the nineteenth century, thereafter showed the beneficial effects of a better trained architectural profession.

Surely an age is not altogether to be condemned as merely materialist which saw the beginning of social reform and humanitarian restraint on cut-throat competition, founded good schools and universities even in the impoverished South and the crude pioneer West, and had room for such delicate literary talents as those of Edith Wharton, Emily Dickinson, and Stephen Crane. In the words of Professor Schlesinger,

A larger proportion of Americans consecrated themselves to the cause of science and learning than ever before . . . and a greater number of them attained an eminence that compelled the attention of the world . . . A Gibbs, a Newcomb, a Ward, a James, a Mark Twain, a Whistler, a MacDowell, a Saint-Gaudens, stand out not as unexpected flowers along a scrubby roadside, but as among the most perfect blossoms in a well-tended field.[18]

[18] A. M. Schlesinger, *The Rise of the City* (1933), p. 435.

PART V

THE DEVELOPMENT OF MODERN BRITAIN

BRITAIN BECOMES THE ARBITER OF EUROPE

SELDOM has any nation been faced with more difficulties than those which accumulated around Great Britain in the last years of the American Revolution. America, France, Spain, Holland were open enemies. Russia, Prussia, Sweden, Denmark, and the Holy Roman Empire were still formally neutral but they were leagued together to prevent British interference with their trade. India was in a state of civil war which roused French hopes of recovering her lost influence there. Ireland was on the very verge of rebellion. King George III, at the height of his unpopularity,[1] had been forced to let his favorite minister Lord North resign and to accept the Whig Rockingham as Prime Minister. Fox, the new Foreign Minister, was the public man he most hated. Ominous murmurs of popular discontent came from almost every shire.

Within a very few years, however, most of these clouds had blown away. India had been held in leash by the strong hand of Warren Hastings.[2] The United States won independence and Spain won Florida, but France gained little more than the satisfaction of having diminished the empire of Britain. The armed neutrality of the northern Powers lost importance as the war with France came to an end. Ireland was pacified, though only temporarily, by the grant of greater freedom of trade and of more power to her local Parliament.

With the death of Rockingham, Shelburne succeeded as head of the ministry. Fox, who did not like him, resigned and headed a hostile faction of discontented Whigs against him. Shelburne remained in office barely long enough to see the peace negotiations to an end when he was ousted by a coalition of North and Fox under

---

[1] In 1780 the House of Commons had voted that 'the influence of the Crown has increased, is increasing, and ought to be diminished.'

[2] For India see Chapter XXXIII.

the Duke of Portland. In all the factional shifts of the chaotic politics of the time nothing stranger had happened than the alliance of Lord North, Tory and King's Friend, the agent of the royal policy for the coercion of the colonists, and Charles James Fox, radical Whig, people's man and champion of American rights! King George himself was, of course, furious, the nation at large was thunderstruck, the politicians were cynically amused. When the House of Lords rejected a bill for the government of India which Fox had brought forward, King George seized his chance, dismissed the ministry, and appointed the youthful William Pitt, only twenty-four years of age, as the head of a new administration. From December 1783 till his death in January 1806 the history of British policy is mainly the history of Pitt. Indeed, that is to put the matter too narrowly, for Pitt's two greatest monuments were the victory over Napoleon, which he never lived to see, and the rejuvenated (really new) and triumphant Tory party, which continued to rule Great Britain for a full quarter of a century after his death.

Pitt himself, like his father the famous Chatham, had been a Whig. At all times he held many liberal ideas and his connection with the Tory party seems almost as much a political accident as Disraeli's. Yet the new Toryism which broke the long ascendancy of the Whigs and replaced it by an equally long ascendancy of the Tories was more his work than any other man's. It was greatly influenced by the French Revolution, which the new Toryism hated. This Toryism was anti-democratic. Its early gospel was the clever little magazine, *The Anti-Jacobin,* in which George Canning wrote brilliant, satirical verses. It was, in the time of Pitt, Castlereagh, and Canning, well led. Pitt insisted on party discipline and solidarity; he did not wish to be, like North, the head of a mere coalition of King's Friends, half Tories and half Whig place-seekers. He often yielded a cherished plan in face of opposition from the Crown or from the Commons, but he must be the one to decide which measures would be insisted on and which would be postponed. He built up a large and permanent Tory majority in the House of Lords by raising new men to the peerage, and it is hard now to realize that until his time the Lords had been about as Whiggish as the Commons, often indeed more so than the Commons.

Pitt's appointment was a royal challenge to the ministerial system as it had been understood since Walpole's time, for Fox and North between them had a majority of the House of Commons with them to oppose the new ministry. Pitt could not have held on indefinitely against such a majority, but he had no need to do so. He merely awaited a favorable moment for an election and then appealed, successfully, to the voters. Apparently the nation had vindicated King George in his quarrel with the Whig politicians. But the fruits of victory went to Pitt rather than to the monarch.

In many ways Pitt was too far in advance of his party, if not of his times, to effect the reforms which he desired. Left to himself he would have granted full civic rights to the Roman Catholics, even in Ireland, transferred the parliamentary seats held by small decayed villages to the counties and to prosperous towns, and abolished the slave trade. But every move he made to effect these changes was blocked either by the bigotry of King George or by the reluctance of the Tories themselves, and Pitt was not the man to give up supreme office because he could not carry some pet reform.[3] He was more successful in rationalizing the national finances, a task in which he was aided by the growing industrial wealth of the country. His peace budgets presented an increasingly prosperous picture of national well-being. Though not a pacifist in the strict sense, and ready to fight when he thought the national interests demanded it, Pitt, like Walpole, preferred peace because it meant prosperity. He used a diplomatic alliance with Prussia and with the Dutch Republic to maintain peace and the balance of power on the continent. He foreshadowed the later policy of Palmerston and Disraeli in supporting the Ottoman Empire against Russia, though when the Empress Catherine showed that she was sufficiently in earnest, Pitt called off the dogs of war in rather undignified haste. Still, in the main, his foreign policy was successful down to the French Revolution. He had not only maintained the peace but he had broken up the old diplomatic isolation of the American Revolution period and convinced continental nations that Britain was an ally worth having.

Needless to say, the French Revolution awoke the most intense

---

[3] From 1801 to 1804 Pitt relinquished office because of the King's hostility to Catholic emancipation; but in this instance the question was not one of abstract justice; it was bound up with Pitt's union of Great Britain and Ireland and was a central point in the policy of the ministry.

interest in the British Isles. No possible internal event in any other foreign country could have aroused such general attention. France had been for over a century the leading Power on the continent, the chief colonial rival of Britain, and her most frequent enemy in war. British diplomacy revolved around the central problem of holding French ambition in check. British military and naval budgets were constructed from the single standpoint of matching French armaments. Nor were all the relations between the two Powers hostile in character. British and French writers formed a single republic of letters and exchanged ideas almost as though there were no frontier. No English gentleman of fashion thought his education complete unless he had traveled in France, knew the French styles, and could smatter some French phrases.

In general, the first phases of the Revolution were greeted with eager sympathy. Apart from the traditional British good nature, which likes in the abstract to see any foreign country better governed, there was also the subtle flattery that France was abandoning her old institution of absolute monarchy for the British system of a limited and constitutional monarchy in which an elected legislature would have the chief authority. Clubs and corresponding societies of sympathizers sprang up all over Britain, sending resolutions of sympathy and encouragement to the French reformers. The fall of the Bastille in Paris echoed in applause in London; Fox, leader of the Whig opposition, declared it at once the greatest and the best event in history.

One of the first warning notes came not from a crusted Tory but from a famous Whig statesman who had championed the American Revolution, sympathized with the grievances of Ireland and of India, and stood for the supremacy of Parliament over the Crown. Edmund Burke's *Reflections on the French Revolution* appeared before the Reign of Terror had disgusted most of the friends of the Revolution. To some of his friends his misgivings seemed incomprehensible. Had the great orator of liberalism become a renegade, a turncoat? The clue to the mystery lay in Burke's political philosophy, a subtle one not easily understood by matter-of-fact radicals or reactionaries. Burke believed in the kind of self-government that was born and grew to maturity like a living being; he disbelieved in the kind which was made to order on an arbitrary plan. It was not only the violence of the French radicals that alarmed Burke (though that was certainly repellent to him); he found their pedantry, their hostility to history and tradition, their abstract political geometry, their 'natural rights' which came from somewhere in the void and had no legal roots, equally dangerous and offensive.

The third great political leader of the time, Prime Minister Pitt, represented a point of view almost equally removed from the enthusiasm of Fox and from the burning hostility of Burke. To Pitt it was a minor matter whether or not the Revolution was a good thing for France: the important question in his eyes was its effect on England. He was no crusader for the abstract principle of either republicanism or royalism. France would be still France under any government, and a possible menace under any government—Bourbon, Jacobin, or Bonapartist. The Revolution made only this difference, that France could now menace Britain with a double weapon, by her propaganda as well as by her armaments. Very well, then, he would crush sedition in Great Britain by forbidding radicals to hold meetings, expelling undesirable aliens, confiscating subversive papers and pamphlets, prosecuting disaffected persons in state trials. A Tory reign of terror, less bloody than the French one but equally arbitrary, came into being after 1792. The mob was as intolerant as the government. As early as 1791 the laboratory of the great chemist Priestley was wrecked in Birmingham because its owner was suspected of French sympathies.

The execution of King Louis XVI roused a storm of anger in an England that had forgotten—or perhaps too uneasily remembered!— the execution of King Charles I. But Pitt might not have made events in France, however abhorrent, an excuse for war if he had not been alarmed for the safety of Britain. Prussia and Austria had engaged in war in 1792 while the British Government still stood neutral. But in 1793, with French republican armies menacing the Netherlands, the Austrian provinces (Belgium), and the Dutch Republic, Pitt decided that war had become a necessity. Great Britain plunged into a struggle with France which, with two brief intervals, lasted continuously till Napoleon's final overthrow. It was the most stupendous conflict which had engaged British arms for centuries and, until it was eclipsed by a greater in 1914, it often bore the title in British histories of 'The Great War.'

Pitt was as resolute in opposing France as his father had been in the Seven Years' War; he had the same patriotism, the same devoted courage and tenacity, the same personal ascendancy over the mind of Parliament and of the nation. But he failed to realize that he was facing a more formidable foe than Louis XV had been. He clung with a pathetic optimism to the belief that France, whose regular army and navy had been disorganized by revolution, whose rulers were inexperienced, and whose treasury was almost empty, would collapse within a few months. He saw nothing of what even the prejudiced Burke had seen, that the strong wine of the new democratic doctrine was giving the French a zeal which they had never shown when fighting for the mere dynastic interests of the Bourbon family. He realized too late the military genius of Carnot and of Napoleon. In a word, Pitt's statesmanship, in many respects of high quality, failed at two important points: he at once overestimated the danger of French propaganda in Britain and underestimated the danger of French military power on the continent. Had the energy which was put into suppressing 'sedition' at home all been poured into the war with France, England would have been stronger.

The greatest of English blunders was Ireland, but that has been true in each successive century from the twelfth to the twentieth, and Pitt's failure here was due more to the bigotry of King George and of Irish officialdom than to any errors of his own. Eighteenth-century Ireland was a classical instance of misgovernment. Ireland was under the Crown but had her own Parliament and thus in a technical sense enjoyed home rule, but the Irish Parliament was little more than a mockery. It represented neither the Roman Catholics nor the Protestant dissenters, it did not control the executive, it was neither honest nor efficient. The old monopolistic commercial system denied to many Irish products access to British markets. The established Irish Church was really the Church of England erected among a prevailingly hostile people. Cruel and disgraceful penal laws placed the Catholic majority in the position of helots in their own native land. The system of holding the land in great estates was in no way peculiar to Ireland; indeed, it was quite as common in England and in Scotland. But English and Scottish landlords lived by preference on their own land and took a personal interest in their tenants and in the improvement of agriculture; Irish landlords commonly lived in Great Britain and had no interest in their estates except the rent.

Henry Grattan took advantage of the difficulties of Britain in the American revolutionary war to insist on Irish reforms. Restrictions on Irish trade and manufacture were decreased, many disabilities of the Catholics were removed, and the powers of the Irish Parliament increased. But Grattan's Parliament, as people called it, still had the defect of not being open to Roman Catholics and it was still unrepresentative of the masses of the Irish nation. The alien Irish Church and alien landownership still remained as standing grievances. The example of the French Revolution stirred up hopes of complete national independence among the more radical Irish, and France saw in the situation a chance to strike a blow at England's back. From 1796 to 1798 there was a ferocious civil war in Ireland during which rebels committed many atrocities, but the forces of 'law and order' were more atrocious still.

Pitt, who had long advocated Irish reforms, though with insufficient zeal, decided that the only solution for the Irish question was to merge Ireland with Great Britain in a common United Kingdom, just as Scotland had been merged with England by the Act of Union in Queen Anne's time. He wished also to make this loss of a separate legislature palatable to Irish opinion by accompanying it with complete equality for the Roman Catholics, including the right to be members of the common Parliament of the United Kingdom of Great Britain and Ireland. He succeeded, mainly by bribery, in persuading the Irish Parliament to consent to its own extinction, but his plan for Catholic emancipation encountered a granite obstacle in the refusal of King George to consent to anything of the sort. The Union of 1800, though the work of combined force and fraud, did give Ireland a better government than the old system of a local but unrepresentative Parliament, but it was deprived of all merit in Irish eyes by the refusal of Catholic emancipation. The Irish question was not ended, it merely entered a new phase.

One of the by-products of King George's refusal of equal rights to Catholics was the resignation of Pitt. He felt that he had been put in a position of breaking his implicit promise to the Irish nation and would not condone this by continuing to head the ministry. In 1801 Henry Addington succeeded as Prime Minister, almost as great an anti-climax as when Bute had taken over the reins of power from

Pitt's father. King George was not disconcerted; though he admired Pitt he was more at home with mediocrities like Bute, North, and Addington. Besides, peace with France was expected. Negotiations had already been opened and the Treaty of Amiens in 1802 confirmed the popular hope of a truce to the long conflict. Since all Britain's continental allies had failed her, the peace was not expected to be a very favorable one. Great Britain gave up all her overseas conquests made during the war except the islands of Ceylon and Trinidad. Wits called it the 'peace that everyone is glad of and no one is proud of.'

The peace proved to be merely an armistice. British diplomacy, by holding on to the naval base of Malta instead of turning it over, as had been stipulated, to the Knights of St. John, gave Napoleon an excuse to break it. But Napoleon himself was guilty in far more important matters; his fresh invasions of Italy and Switzerland showed that he regarded peace with Britain merely as an opportunity to widen his empire on the continent. War was resumed in 1803, to continue without a respite till 1814. The shadow of invasion hung over England, and the country was conscious of a more acute peril than at any time since the Spanish Armada had sailed the Channel. How far Napoleon's threat of invasion was seriously intended and how far it was a feint to cover plans of conquest on the continent is still a matter of dispute among military historians. Probably Napoleon intended an invasion if a real opportunity should present itself, but the British fleet took good care that such an opportunity should never come. The military record of Great Britain, down to Wellington's campaign in Spain and Portugal, had been a poor one, a mere series of disconnected raids, sometimes on French, Spanish, or Dutch colonies, sometimes on outlying shorelands of continental Europe. But efficiency at sea increased as the war proceeded, and the genius of Nelson, as remarkable in its own way as the genius of Napoleon, brought to the British navy the greenest laurels in its annals.

Horatio Nelson earned a peerage by destroying the French fleet sent to Egypt in 1798. He defeated the Danish fleet near Copenhagen in 1801. In 1805 he destroyed a combined French and Spanish fleet off Cape Trafalgar and thus ended the last serious menace of a French invasion of England. His last great action cost him his life, a price which he was always willing to pay but one which England could ill afford. At least, like Wolfe before Quebec, he had the high satisfaction of seeing the face of victory before he died. Nelson was not a flawless hero; but he belongs in the company of a strange but very remarkable group of men, the romanticists of war, men of strong individuality, sometimes a little off balance and 'queer,' but capable of such great strokes of imaginative daring as rarely come to conventional minds. It has been the peculiar good fortune of England to find more than her share of such eccentric heroes at critical moments in her destiny.[4]

Another hero, no romanticist this time but a grim realist, restored the reputation of the British army. Arthur Wellesley, later Duke of Wellington, belonged to the Irish aristocracy or, as one might more significantly phrase it, the British aristocracy in Ireland. He undertook to provide a stiffening of British aid for the resistance of Spain and Portugal to the French army of invasion which threatened to carry Napoleon's power to the westernmost extremities of Europe. The legal position of the two countries was not quite the same. Portugal was still independent, though her independence was threatened; Spain had been bullied and tricked into accepting Napoleon's brother Joseph as king and had become virtually a French dependency. But the Spanish people rose in revolt against their new French masters on behalf of their legitimate (though unworthy) monarch Ferdinand. From 1808 to 1814 the peninsular war continued. Napoleon himself did not appear on the scene, and his marshals were not the equal of the stern British martinet who confronted them. In the words of Sir Robert Rait, 'The peninsular war was the great military contribution of Great Britain to the destruction of Napoleon's power.' It kept a large French army tied up at a time when it was urgently needed on the more decisive battlefields of central and eastern Europe.

Such a successful campaign was a godsend in the dark days which followed Pitt's death in 1806. He had been recalled to office in 1804 because Addington was not believed strong enough for the critical

---

[4] Wolfe's enemies accused him of being mad, which provoked George II's famous retort that he wished Wolfe would bite some of his other generals! Clive made several attempts at suicide and finally succeeded. The eccentricities of 'Chinese' Gordon, of Lawrence of Arabia, of many Elizabethan sea captains and of several heroes of the Indian mutiny are well remembered.

hour, but his health had already failed him. He lived long enough to rejoice in Nelson's victory of Trafalgar and to sorrow at Napoleon's triumph of Austerlitz; he could say that 'England has saved herself by her exertions' and might yet save Europe 'by her example,' but half a dozen years of dazzling success still awaited Napoleon before England's example was taken to heart by most of his continental opponents.

The British fleet, indeed, protected the nation from any imminent danger of invasion, and Napoleon's 'continental system' for starving out Britain by a continent-wide boycott on British trade proved to be a boomerang. While the British suffered from the loss of their normal trade with the continent, Napoleon's protectorates and vassal kingdoms suffered more from their loss of British trade. Napoleon could hardly clothe his own troops without winking at smugglers' enterprise. Moreover, he was led from one disastrous step to another by the necessity of closing doors to British trade. Had it not been for the continental system, which Russia had disregarded, Napoleon might never have undertaken the futile Moscow campaign, which marked the beginning of the end. The logic of his struggle with the sea power of Great Britain practically compelled the Emperor of the French to make himself Emperor of Europe or perish in the attempt. But the expansion of the national empire of France into a pan-European imperialism meant also the stirring up of latent national feeling among the peoples whom Napoleon subjected to his rule. The war against the dynasties had become a war against the peoples, alike in Spain, Russia, and the Germanies.

It is easy now from the vantage point of a later time to see that economic forces and national sentiments were together undermining the power of Napoleon, and that unless he could have limited his ambitions and compromised with the world he was doomed to ultimate failure. It was not so easy to see this between 1806 and 1812. Napoleon broke every coalition directed against him; incorporated directly into his Empire the Netherlands (in every age the very key to British security), western Germany, and much of Italy; held in vassalage Spain, Switzerland, central Germany, Poland, and the rest of Italy; forced his unwelcome alliance on defeated Austria, Prussia, and Russia. Except in Spain and Portugal, and there were many reverses even there, British military activities on the continent had achieved nothing; as late as 1809 a military expedition to the Netherlands (the Walcheren expedition) ended in utter failure. Britain's attempt to interfere with neutral trade in the many parts of Europe under Napoleon's control brought her into war with the United States from 1812 to 1814, after years of diplomatic bickering, and, though the war was only a minor campaign from the British standpoint, it brought heavy losses to the fleet.[5] Economic distress, rather than political discontent, caused widespread riots among the poor both in town and country. 'Frame breakers' wrecked machinery, and Parliament, with the cruelty of panic, made their offense liable to capital punishment.

After Pitt's death there was a brief interlude of a coalition ministry of 'all the talents,' which included even Whigs. Lord Grenville was Prime Minister, but the most conspicuous figure in the cabinet was Fox as Foreign Minister. Fox had been a pacifist in the earlier stages of the conflict with France, but his dealings with Napoleon convinced him that the French Emperor did not sincerely desire a peace unless peace meant merely conquest without resistance of all the unsubjugated parts of Europe. Fox died only a few months after the passing of his great rival Pitt, and the political stage was left to comparative mediocrities. The Grenville coalition ministry soon fell and the Tory party again held exclusive power under the successive leadership of Duke of Portland (1807-9), Spencer Perceval (1809-12), and the Marquess of Liverpool (1812-27), none of them outstanding statesmen. The ablest of the Tory ministers were Viscount Castlereagh and George Canning, but they were long estranged from each other by personal quarrels, and Canning was doomed to prolonged periods of exile from office. Yet it is due to the Tory governments of the last years of the war to say that they showed all the tenacity of Pitt and had a far more adequate conception of the military effort required to defeat Napoleon. The last years of the struggle were those most creditable to the British nation, and perhaps the national glory stands out all the more clearly from the fact that no single man of genius could claim the laurels that belonged to all. Napoleon overshadowed France as Hannibal did Carthage,

[5] See Chapter XXI.

but as it was Rome and no one Roman which defeated Hannibal, so it was Britain and no one Briton which defeated Napoleon.

The hour was at hand when the long years of patient effort were to meet their reward. Napoleon retreated from Russia to find all Germany in arms against him. In a series of epic battles he was beaten back to France and then forced to accept banishment to Elba. While the peace conference was in session at Vienna, Napoleon made his dramatic return to Paris. Though the British fleet had policed the world's seas, though British money and credit had upheld every coalition against Napoleon, though Great Britain alone of all his enemies had not been forced to periods of national humiliation and subservience by his diplomacy, the British (except in Spain and Portugal) had taken a decidedly minor share in the actual military operations of the war. Their role, however useful, had rarely been dramatic or striking. It was, therefore, a matter of profound national gratification that a large British army under Wellington's direct command played so considerable a part in the final defeat of Napoleon at Waterloo in 1815. A most appropriate curtain had ended the great drama, and applause was not stinted.

The final triumph over Napoleon brought British prestige abroad to the highest point it had ever reached. Napoleon was a captive and spent his last years as a state prisoner on the British island of St. Helena. Isolated France was no longer a menace, and Britain was grouped with the other Great Powers of Europe in a Quadruple Alliance. But Russia, Austria, and Prussia, though they had played an honorable part in the last campaigns and had much influence on the final peace settlement, could not vie with Britain in general prestige accruing from the war. They had all within recent years bowed the knee to Napoleon, while Britain had alone stood erect. Nor had any of the three naval power, industrial wealth, political freedom, or overseas empire. In this combination of advantages Great Britain stood alone in the world.

If a man of the type of Napoleon had stood in such a position it is easy to see what a vast expansion the British Empire might have undertaken. Nothing would have been easier, for instance, than to find some excuse for retaining the valuable colonies of Java and the other Dutch East Indies, which the fortunes of war had already placed in British hands. But the British Toryism of 1814 and 1815 lacked alike the Napoleonic imagination and the Napoleonic greed. It could not rise to the idea of a permanent league of peace, even as far as it was vaguely previsioned in the dreamy mind of Tsar Alexander I; on the other hand it did not sink to the petty thievery of provinces, which engrossed the lesser German princes, or the concept of a league of autocracies against constitutional liberty, which occupied the thoughts of the Austrian Metternich. In the main, British diplomacy at Vienna showed only three preoccupations: the balance of power on the continent, the obtaining of a few convenient naval bases, and the abolition of the slave trade. A word on each may be appropriate.

The general principle of the Congress of Vienna was that of 'legitimacy' or the restoration of each sovereign to his former sovereignty. But in some instances it was impossible to restore former conditions. Austria did not want her old netherlandish provinces which experience had shown were almost impossible to defend against France; both Russia and Sweden could put in a claim for Finland; scores of petty German states had been swept away forever by Napoleon's consolidations. In such cases a secondary principle came into play, that of compensation to the victor Powers, either for their labors and sacrifices during the war or for the relinquishment of territory in other directions. Thus Austria, giving up Belgium to form part of the new enlarged Kingdom of the Netherlands, took her compensation in Italy, obtaining Venice and Milan (the Lombardo-Venetian Kingdom); Sweden, permitting Russia to retain Finland, was granted Norway; Prussia, giving up part of her Polish provinces to the Tsar's Kingdom of Poland, was granted part of Saxony and new provinces on the Rhine. The British representatives, Wellington and Castlereagh, did not question this general principle but they aimed at maintaining a balance of power by opposing dangerously large additions of territory.

Great Britain sought her own 'compensation,' as she had done after the eighteenth-century wars with France, in the form of naval bases and coaling stations or distant colonies. It was not a question of asking for new lands, for the British fleet had been busy during the war picking up stray islands in European and other waters; it was merely a question which British conquests should be restored to their former owners (as Java was restored to the Dutch) and which should be retained. Britain kept Helgoland, off the German coast, a useful guard to Hanover; Malta, strategically located in the central Mediterranean; the Ionian islands, off the coast of Greece; Ceylon, off the coast of India; Mauritius, in the Indian Ocean; Tobago, St. Lucia, and Trinidad, in the West Indies; part of Guiana, in South America; the Cape of Good Hope, in Africa. Most of these acquisitions had little but strategic significance; they were valued only as bulwarks of naval power. True, the Cape of Good Hope was eventually to become the base of a great British Empire in southern Africa, but that was not foreseen by the men of 1814-15, who considered it as little more than a port of call on the way to India.

The changing attitude of the British people to the slave trade is a curious chapter in rapid moral evolution. At the conclusion of the War of the Spanish Succession British diplomats asked for and obtained the right to ship slaves from Africa to Spanish America, and regarded this privilege as one of the most valuable fruits of victory. During the greater part of the eighteenth century the African slave trade was taken for granted as being quite as legitimate as any other branch of commerce. But towards the end of the century there was active agitation against a traffic which Wesley considered 'the sum of all villanies,' which offended even the Toryism of Dr. Johnson, and which the great orators of the age—Pitt, Burke, and Fox—agreed to condemn. Even so, the financial interests at stake were so great that Parliament did not abolish the traffic until 1807. At Vienna the British statesmen tried to make the ban on the slave trade international, and succeeded in having it condemned in principle though not as much was done as the British wished to take active steps to put it down. The main credit for this revolution in public opinion must be given to a handful of zealous reformers, such as Wilberforce, Clarkson, and Sharp, who opposed abstract moral considerations to the tremendous bulk of commercial interest on the other side. Most reforms have been carried by a mixture of humanitarianism and self-interest; this one had no aid from the latter, as many Britons had grown rich from the trade and none stood to grow rich by its abolition. Slavery itself, limited of course to the colonies, lasted a generation longer.

The main merit of the peace was that the victor Powers treated defeated France with comparative leniency. France was shorn of all her conquests and, as a punishment for permitting Napoleon's return, compelled to pay a moderate war indemnity. But the provinces which were French before the Revolution remained French; even the Prussian plan for annexing Alsace was vetoed, and there was no such general removal of landmarks as Napoleon himself had inflicted on the German states. France, which had devastated Europe from Russia to Portugal for more than a score of years, was more liberally treated than Poland, which had offended her neighbors only by her weakness. British statesmanship deserves a share of the credit for this magnanimity.

But the Vienna settlement had the faults of its virtues. If it showed less national passion and vindictiveness than the Treaty of Versailles in 1919, this was partly due to the fact that the aristocratic mapmakers had more class feeling than national sentiment. Their great object with respect to France had been to replace the Bourbons on the throne. Not France as a nation but revolutionary democracy as a principle was the enemy. The liberal nationalists of Germany and Spain who had labored so valiantly to combat Napoleon's upstart despotism found that their efforts had only restored the absolute despots of the old regime. Even the most moderate and conservative steps towards constitutional self-government or national self-determination were frowned on as 'Jacobinical.' The national sentiments in Europe which were in the future to cause so many wars and revolutions were either flouted or ignored.

A few years, however, revealed the abyss, temporarily bridged at Vienna, between British aristocracy and continental autocracy. Great Britain participated for a time in the annual conferences of the Great Powers which aimed to preserve the peace settlement and put down incipient wars and revolutions. But when Metternich turned the machinery for securing peace into a mechanism for assuring absolute despotism and asserted the right to intervene in a foreign country disturbed by revolution, Great Britain opposed him, secretly under Castlereagh, openly under Canning, his successor at the Foreign Office. Canning, indeed, broke altogether with the Quadruple Alliance, opposed French intervention in Spain, and countered it by giving diplomatic support to the Spanish-American colonies which had proclaimed their independence. This step brought together Great Britain and the United States, if not in a common policy, at any rate in parallel action, and assured the independence of the Latin American republics.[6] The British also took a share, though at first a somewhat ambiguous one, in securing the liberty of Greece when the Greek people rose against their Turkish tyrants. Though the Tory statesmen had no crusading passion for either liberalism or nationalism, they did not relish the dangerous principle of invading independent foreign countries on the pretext of quelling revolution which aimed at parliamentary government. British ministers believed the British interests on the continent of Europe were best served by independent countries with parliamentary government. On the whole, British influence on general European politics, where exerted at all, helped more than it hindered the cause of freedom. Even those who were counted reactionary in home politics showed their most liberal side when dealing with the affairs of Italy, Greece, or Spain.

[6] For the Monroe Doctrine and its place in American history, see Chapter XXII.

BRITAIN BECOMES THE WORKSHOP OF THE WORLD

EVEN the important political events that marked the sixty years of King George III's reign (1760-1820) were probably less significant than the economic developments of the time. But for their new industrial wealth, it would have been difficult for the British to have sustained the long struggle against Napoleon and his allies. Behind the diplomacy of Pitt and Castlereagh, the armies of Wellington, the fleets of Nelson, the lavish subsidies to continental allies, lay the force of what is commonly called the Industrial Revolution.[1]

It cannot have been chance which brought to Britain industrial and commercial leadership. Nor can it be attributed to individual or national inventive genius alone, since other European peoples, such as the French, showed quite as much scientific zeal, inventive ingenuity, and skill in the applied arts. The credit belongs in part to certain natural advantages of Great Britain and in part to favorable political and economic conditions. The British natural advantages are too obvious to need elaboration: excellent harbors, close to the world's chief maritime trade routes; an abundance of coal and iron; a mild, yet stimulating, climate which both permits and encourages work the year around; an ocean moat against foreign invasion.

The social environment was equally favorable. Serfdom had vanished; gild regulations and petty governmental restrictions on industrial methods, though they had not quite disappeared, were far less onerous than in most continental countries. The British were not as badly 'overgoverned' as the French or the Prussians. They suffered less than other Europeans from the menace of foreign inva-

---

[1] Some historians have objected to this term, on the ground that the industrial changes in Britain during these years were but a part of a world-wide movement which is still continuing. But, if the term be restricted to the first phase of modern industrial development, it is a convenient phrase.

sion or domestic strife. They had an abundance of free capital for investment; and British commerce stood first in the world, outrivaling even France and the Netherlands. There was also a large supply of free and mobile labor. Among the thousands of workingmen employed in the old-style handicrafts were skilled artisans from France, Flanders, and Germany, many of them religious refugees, who rewarded British tolerance by their industry.

There were also some minor adventitious circumstances which aided in the development of particular industries. The mild, damp climate of Lancashire was almost ideal for textile manufacture, especially for the spinning of cotton thread. Great Britain was one of the greatest sheep-raising countries in the world, so the raw material for the woolen manufacture was abundantly on hand. Coal was not only abundant, but had long been mined for fuel, since Britain had less forest wealth than many other European countries. A familiar figure in eighteenth-century literature was the British householder warming himself by his 'sea-coal fire.' Sheffield had been making cutlery in Chaucer's time. Birmingham had been famous for pikes, swords, locks, nails, toys, and—unhappily—for counterfeit coin, in the early eighteenth century. Potteries existed in Staffordshire long before Josiah Wedgwood made them world famous. Now, textiles, iron, coal, earthenware, and machinery were the specialties of British industry in the nineteenth century; the methods were new, but the industries themselves were long established.

Nor did Great Britain have to await the new industrial inventions to become capitalistic. Whichever aspect of capitalism we may choose to stress, placing emphasis on the rights of private property, on freedom of contract, or on the division of the manufacturing population between laborers and the owners of capital, we find it almost as much in evidence in Walpole's time as today. The weaver worked in his own home instead of in a large factory, but he usually had to buy his thread from and sell his cloth to a richer man, and not seldom he had to rent his very tools. We hear of strikes and labor riots, the beginnings of trade unionism and even of the closed shop.[2] The worst

[2] 'As early as 1700 the wool-combers of Tiverton had formed a friendly society . . . Shortly afterwards . . . this "unchartered corporation" of the wool-combers spread all over England and felt itself strong enough to attempt to regulate the industry, to the effect that no man should comb wool under

evils of the age arose indeed from an excessive tenderness for property rights, as for example in the legal sanction for the slave trade and the ferocious penalties imposed on thieves and poachers. There still existed some restrictions on perfect freedom for private business, such as the tariff laws and navigation acts, the power of magistrates to fix wages and regulate the conditions of apprenticeship, the privileges of a few chartered monopolies, such as the East India Company. But Adam Smith and other economists were subjecting such relics of past paternalism to trenchant criticism. The spirit of the age was against them, and one by one they were weakened or removed. Thus in 1795 Parliament stopped the practice, dating back to an act of 1662, of forcing a workingman to return to his original 'place of settlement' if the parish to which he went considered that he was likely to become a charge on the poor rates. Long before the act was actually repealed it had been disregarded so frequently that it was virtually obsolete.

Preceding and accompanying the industrial revolution was an agricultural revolution. Its permanent effects were of less importance, since Great Britain has in recent decades cultivated industry at the expense of agriculture. Perhaps no other nation on earth employs today so small a proportion of its whole population in the raising of food or is so dependent on foreign imports for daily bread. But even today the failure of British agriculture is rather quantitative than qualitative. Some of the best of the world's livestock—horses, cattle, sheep, swine—are still raised in the British Isles. Certainly in the eighteenth century the great and rapid improvement in the food industry attracted as much general attention as the developments in the textile or the iron and steel industries. It involved scientific stockbreeding, the rotation of crops, the use of artificial manures, the draining of swampland, and the enclosure of open fields. Unfortunately it involved also a decline in the number of independent landowners and the virtual disappearance of the old yeoman class. Agriculture advanced as a science at the very time that it was declining as a pattern of social living.

The process of 'enclosure' has several meanings. In Tudor times

2 shillings per dozen; that no master should employ any comber that was not of their club.' P. Mantoux, *The Industrial Revolution of the Eighteenth Century* (trans., 1929), p. 79.

it usually meant the turning of farmland into sheep pasture, and caused great social misery and much ineffective protest and restrictive legislation.[3] In the eighteenth and early nineteenth centuries it meant in part the consolidation of the old open fields into compact individual holdings, and in part the division of the commons, or village waste and pasture land, among the landowners of the district in proportion to their holdings. This greatly increased the productivity of the land, but it deprived many poor cottagers of their old free pasturage and access to firewood. Special acts of Parliament were required for these enclosures, but in a legislature consisting mainly of landlords, such acts were easily passed with little scrutiny of details.

The English and Scottish landlord was often a progressive land reformer even when he was most conservative in affairs of state. He had both capital and knowledge. He was able to buy pedigreed stock, to apply expensive fertilizers to poor soil, and to clear standing water from soggy lowlands. In expectation of higher rents, he often aided his tenants to make similar improvements. Against such competition the independent yeoman, without much capital or education and often too set in the old ways to make even the improvements which lay within his power, struggled in vain. The coming of machine industry brought other handicaps. Many small farmers had eked out their income by spinning or weaving during the hours when the farm did not require their attention, but they were unable to compete with the cheap thread and cloth turned out by the factories.

Closely connected with the improvements in agriculture was the building of good new roads for travel and transportation. The eighteenth century was the greatest epoch of road building in Britain since the Romans had left the island. The opening of the Scottish Highlands to general trade, as well as to military policing, after the rebellion of 1745 did as much as anything to transform that region from a picturesque and romantic barbarism to a full share in the civilization of the rest of Scotland. Hundreds of new turnpike roads, charging toll to their users to meet the cost of their upkeep, were authorized by Parliament for nearly every part of Great Britain. At

---

[3] This process still continued in the eighteenth century in the north of Scotland, where many Highland 'crofters' were driven from their homes by landlords greedy to profit from the wool trade.

the end of the century Telford and MacAdam (whose name survives in the 'macadamized' roads of today) introduced practical engineering principles into roadmaking. As the roads improved, mail and passenger coach service became possible even between distant cities. Inns for the accommodation of travelers multiplied. In the latter part of the eighteenth century, England, which hitherto had depended entirely on natural rivers and inlets, developed a series of artificial canals which opened up much of the interior of the country to barge transport. Of course the nineteenth century saw a much greater extension both of roadbuilding and of inland waterways, but without the pioneer work of the previous century the development of machine industry must have been greatly retarded.

Thus far, however, we have considered only the setting of the industrial revolution and the factors that favored its progress. Without any new inventions at all the Britain of 1800 would have differed greatly from the Britain of 1760, owing to the enclosed fields, the improved farming, the new roads and canals. But it required the steam engine, the new textile machinery, and the factory system to make Britain the workshop of the world.

Probably the most important single invention since printing was the improved steam engine which the Scotsman James Watt experimented with in 1764 and patented in 1769. Not that the principle of the steam engine was in any sense new. The ancient Greeks of Alexandria ran toys by steam power. Frenchmen, Dutchmen, and Englishmen of the seventeenth century had all experimented with different types of steam pumps. Two British engineers before Watt's time, Savery and Newcomen, constructed steam-driven pumps which were used on a quite extensive scale in the early eighteenth century. But these steam pumps, or 'fire engines' as they were often called, were unsatisfactory. Much power was wasted owing to the necessity of condensing the steam by cooling the boiler. The direct pressure of steam, moreover, was little used; the real purpose of the engine was to use atmospheric pressure after creating a vacuum through the use of the steam—it was an air pressure engine rather than a steam engine in the full modern sense. The chief practical application of the steam engine, though it was employed also in other ways, was the pumping of water from coal mines. It required the genius of Watt to transform a dubious experiment into an industrial necessity.

Watt's essential step was to provide a separate condenser for the steam so that energy would not be lost by the alternate process of heating and cooling, as in Newcomen's engine, the type then most generally in use. But his contribution to the steam engine did not stop with this single invention. He also made use of the 'expansive force of steam to press on the piston . . . in the same manner as the pressure of the atmosphere is now employed' and thus made steam a direct as well as an indirect motive power. He applied the steam engine, hitherto a mere pump, to the turning of wheels. He invented the governor, which assured regularity of action. When all his improvements were completed, and the process took many years, the steam engine had become the main motive power of manufacture.

But an inventor, even one as practical and level-headed as Watt, cannot by himself transform industry. He requires the aid of other men to finance his undertaking and assure its application. Fortunately Watt found such men. John Roebuck and Matthew Boulton, businessmen, and William Murdoch, technician, helped Watt mightily to transform his laboratory plans into commercial facts. The firm of Boulton and Watt for a long time dominated the steam-engine market, though it had to engage in many suits for violations of patent rights against other inventors or claimants to invention. The rapid expansion of coal mining and the development of the machine-tool industry were also essential to the success of the steam engine, for of what avail would it have been if there had lacked cheap fuel to heat the boilers or accurate cylinders to contain the steam?

Indeed, steam, coal, and iron formed an inseparable trinity. Coal was the fuel which was chiefly used for heating water into steam; steam pumps cleared the coal mines of water; coal (in the form of coke) came into general use, in place of charcoal, for the smelting of iron ore; improvements in the puddling and rolling of iron made possible the cheap and reliable engines essential to the use of steam power. With abundant supplies of coal and of iron ore conveniently at hand, Britain was peculiarly situated to take full advantage of Watt's invention.

Second in importance to the development of the steam engine, and the closely associated industries of coal and iron, was the revolution of the textile trade through the invention of new machinery. The making of textiles consisted of two main processes, usually handled by different persons. One was the spinning of fibers of wool or flax or silk, and in later times of cotton, into thread. In the early eighteenth century this was done usually by the spinning wheel, itself a machine but a very simple one which any housewife might own and use for herself. Then came the weaving of the thread into cloth. This was done on hand looms set up in cottages and worked either by full-time weavers or by farmers and farm laborers who devoted part time to this employment. The marketing of the cloth was a businessman's enterprise, with which the worker had almost as little direct connection as he has today. Since spinning wheels and hand looms were cheap and simple they could be set up almost anywhere, and the textile industry was therefore much more widely dispersed over the whole country than it is now.

During the eighteenth century a large number of inventions transformed the entire textile industry. In 1733 John Kay's 'flying shuttle' doubled the speed of weaving on the hand loom. In 1767 James Hargreaves invented a spinning jenny, which turned eight spindles with a single wheel. About the same time Richard Arkwright used rollers driven by water power to spin and wind thread. Samuel Crompton's 'mule' was a hybrid machine, combining the principles of the jenny with those of Arkwright's water frame. These successive inventions reversed the situation created by Kay; thread was now cheap and weavers in demand. Edmund Cartwright came to the rescue in 1787 with his power loom, though it was not until the nineteenth century that the machine came into general use. At first, hand power or water power was used to run the new machinery, but before long the steam engine had become the heart of the textile factory.

The factory system of organizing labor existed in some industries, such as the silk manufacture, before the era of steam engines. But it was the rare exception, the domestic or 'putting out' system, by which the work was done in the laborer's own home, being the general rule. The new machines, however, were costly and the steam engines costlier still. It was out of the question to set them up in every cottage. Down to the middle of the nineteenth century there were still many hand-loom weavers, but they were fighting a losing battle in their competition with the machines and factories. Almost every inventor had some unhappy experience with rioters and 'frame breakers' who complained that he had 'taken the bread from the mouths of poor folk,' but the new machines had on their side the teachings of the economists, the interests of the manufacturers, and the support of the government. A riot which might ruin the inventor never stopped the effects of his invention.

Even those who found employment in the new factories, and at fairly good wages (as wages went in those days), experienced in some respects a change for the worse. Since the factories concentrated labor in one place, their growth meant a movement from the country or the small village to the town. With but few exceptions these first industrial towns were mere slums. The old medieval towns and cities had been crowded and insanitary, but they had also been centers of art and culture and amusement, and they had been small enough so that a short ramble placed the townsman among open fields and under smokeless skies. William Cobbett, who hated great cities anyhow, called London 'the Wen,' and in truth there was something tumor-like in this rapid growth of new social tissue. Factory and mining towns had little park space or recreation ground, rarely any public library or museum, and next to nothing in the way of good schools. The chapel and the inn were almost the only variations to break the dull monotony of dwelling houses, shops, and factories. Not one of the inhabitants of such a town lived there because he liked it; the need of being near the factory was the only cause for its location. The air was heavy with soft-coal smoke and the waters poisoned by factory chemicals.

Factory labor was utterly devoid of interest. The old-fashioned apprentice was learning a useful trade; he was also creating the whole of something which might be a real work of art and was in any event a challenge to good craftsmanship and pride of skill. The new-style apprentice was merely a machine tender. His hours were usually long, the twelve-hour day being the prevailing rule, and one often much exceeded in practice. After many years of labor he had little more skill than a new man could acquire in a fortnight. Since the machines made little demand on physical strength, especially in the textile trade, children could be employed as readily as strong men, and much more cheaply. Child labor in itself was an old story. Long before the age of factories small children had labored on farms, or helped their parents in cottage industries, or even gone from home as apprentices to some neighbor's shop; and, so far from seeing anything wrong in the custom, humane men like Daniel Defoe rejoiced that the children of the poor could at so early an age be 'useful' to their parents and to society. But child labor wore a different aspect when it meant a mere routine of dull toil in a blind alley occupation. The 'master' in many cases no longer knew his 'apprentices' by name or face. They had become merely industrial units, 'replaceable parts' in a huge profit-making machine.

Even in those industrial Dark Ages Parliament recognized that something must be done to prevent the unlimited exploitation of childhood. In 1802 Sir Robert Peel, father of the famous statesman and himself a wealthy manufacturer, introduced a bill limiting the labor of apprenticed children in the textile factories to twelve hours, providing for their schooling in reading, writing, arithmetic, and religion, and establishing certain rules for safeguarding health and morals. As a precedent for future reform this law was highly valuable; in itself it accomplished little. The inspectors appointed under the act showed little zeal in enforcing it, and manufacturers were able to evade its provisions by hiring children who were not technically 'apprentices' to the trade. Real betterment of conditions had to await a humaner generation.

The industrialization of Great Britain had a threefold effect on the people. It created conditions favorable to the increase of population; to a still more rapid growth of the great cities; and to a general development of the new industrial area of the north relatively to the more stable population of the southeast. We have no accurate statistics of British population before the census of 1801, though from parish registers of births and deaths, and from the tax returns on house property we can frame plausible estimates. All the evidence points to a slow, but fairly steady, growth in the population from Queen Elizabeth's time to the middle of the eighteenth century, a general reflection of growing commerce and prosperity, and then a suddenly accelerated leap forward. In England and Wales in 1750 there were about 6,500,000 inhabitants as compared with perhaps 4,250,000 in 1600. In 1801, by actual count, England and Wales had over 8,800,000. By 1851 this figure had doubled, and by 1911 it had doubled again. Scotland grew at a similar pace. The case of Ireland is peculiar. In the early nineteenth century Ireland was one of the most rapidly growing countries in the world, three times as populous as Scotland; then, with the famine years of the 1840s, there began an actual decrease, owing largely to heavy emigration, which eventually brought Ireland's population below that of Scotland. The temporary increase of Irish population was mostly rural, due in great degree to the introduction of the cheaply cultivated potato; the permanent increase in England, Scotland, and Wales was urban, a rapid expansion of commercial cities, mining towns, and milltowns.

The chief industrial towns were not new; such places as Manchester, Birmingham, Sheffield, and Newcastle were centuries old. But they had for the most part been small market towns or villages and very few of them had been important enough to send members to Parliament. Manchester, the center of the cotton handicraft, had about 20,000 inhabitants in the middle of the eighteenth century. The establishment of the new machine manufacture meant a rapid growth, and the census of 1801 showed 95,000. Liverpool, Lancashire's shipping port, displaced Bristol as the leading Atlantic port. The whole county of Lancashire trebled in population during the eighteenth century, while rural Wiltshire scarcely increased at all. The Scottish Highlands, in many districts, actually showed a decrease. In 1700 Great Britain had a remarkably evenly distributed population, save for the difference between the arable lowlands and the hilly parts of Wales, northern England, and Scotland, which were good only for sheep pasture. So far as there was any concentration—and it was not very pronounced—it followed the Thames valley and the Bristol Channel. A century later there had already developed a huge industrial area in the midlands and the northwest, stretching from Birmingham to Preston, with smaller regions of concentration around London, the Newcastle coal mines, the South Wales mines, and the wasp waist of Scotland between the Clyde and the Firth of Forth. The fourteen decades since 1800 have merely emphasized this concentration, without in any important respect changing its direction.

The redistribution of population had political consequences hardly less great than those arising from the hardships of the poor under the new industrial conditions. An ill-paid factory hand has an obvious grievance against the powers that be. But even a well-paid factory hand is accustomed to change and novelty and more apt to welcome innovations than a peasant whose ancestors have farmed the same acres for centuries. Moreover, it was the restless sort of farmer or farm laborer who gave up country life to move to town. The John Bull of eighteenth-century caricature was a true national type, perhaps even a national ideal. He is always represented as a heavy, stalwart, hearty fellow (a little coarse under Gillray's pencil); stolid, rubicund, and rural. Whether Whig or Tory, he was essentially conservative in the sense of loving old ways because they were old. The new town-bred type of the nineteenth century was a different sort of man—thinner, paler, quicker in movement, more restless and alert in mind, less attached to the customs and traditions of his forefathers. Politically he was apt to be radical; religiously either a dissenter or a complete skeptic.

The rapid growth of northern England also emphasized the injustice of the existing representation in the House of Commons, and united the millowner and the millhand in a common political grievance. It had been anomalous in the early eighteenth century that parliamentary representation was scattered almost at random, according to the accidents of history, but it was not a serious regional injustice. Cornwall and some other parts of the south were even then overrepresented and some important northern towns undervalued, but for England as a whole the House of Commons roughly corresponded to the distribution of landed and mercantile wealth which it was intended to represent. By the early nineteenth century, however, a whole new England of industrial towns and cities, mainly in the north, had come into existence without any increase of political weight at all. A representative system which had once been a picturesque anomaly (which, however, did not work badly) had now been transformed by the shifting of population into a grievance that grew with each succeeding year.

Class friction rather increased than diminished with the return of peace. Though there had been years of great distress during the long struggle with France, the very fact of war tended to keep up farm prices and stimulate the growth of certain branches of manufacture; the full costs of war include the depression that follows the artificial war-prosperity period, as we of the twentieth century know but too well. Moreover, the psychology of reconstruction differs from that of wartime. During a great war many patriots cheerfully put up with hardships and even injustices lest any attack on the government give aid and comfort to a foreign foe, but when the foe at the gates is no longer a present menace they give more attention to evils within the gates. Great wars are commonly followed by revolutionary disturbances; Britain, indeed, escaped a revolution, but by no wide margin.

King George III had long been insane. The Regent, who later became King George IV (1820-30), had betrayed his former Whig friends and adopted the high Toryism of his father, with equal bigotry and a great deal more cynicism. His debts, his frivolities, his notorious quarrels with his wife, Queen Caroline, his cold-blooded repudiation of his previous wife, unrecognized by law,[4] Mrs. Fitzherbert, were hardly offset by certain minor merits, such as an easy good nature and a taste for art and social amenities which won from his few admirers the title of 'the first gentleman of Europe.' Though Queen Caroline was eccentric, empty-headed, and at least doubtful in her conduct, she was made almost popular by the king's persecution of her, and the attempt to divorce her by act of Parliament failed under the pressure of hostile public opinion. The new king's brothers were all disliked in varying degrees, from the mild contempt felt for the amiable Duke of Clarence, who afterwards succeeded as King William IV (1830-37), to positive hatred for the Duke of Cumberland, a reactionary who fought against parliaments and constitutions in Hanover and would certainly have done the same in Great Britain if the Hanoverian law of succession had prevailed there.[5] If the Princess Victoria, daughter of the Duke of Kent, had not stood between him and the succession, Britain might very easily have become a republic.

Aristocracy as well as royalty stood in danger. The Tory party had been in power too long for its own health, and the arrears of reform legislation demanded by the nation had become formidably great. Roman Catholics, Jews, and (in theory) dissenters were still barred from Parliament and from other important public offices. Nearly half of the House of Commons was chosen by nobles and country squires, through their influence in small decayed villages. There was still no provision for public education. The government of towns and cities was conducted with a minimum of efficiency by

---

[4] As a Roman Catholic she could not have been Queen in any case.
[5] In Hanover the throne passed only to the male line.

sleepy oligarchies. The criminal law, though somewhat ameliorated by the efforts of reformers, was savage in its long list of capital punishments, while the civil law was a jungle of tangled precedents, and the influence of John Scott, Earl of Eldon, as Lord Chancellor kept legal reform at bay for a generation. The poor law was rapidly pauperizing a whole generation of laborers by the adoption of the vicious principle of supplementing low wages by grants from the taxpayer (the Speenhamland system, named from the Berkshire district where—with the best of intentions—it was first employed), while rapid industrial changes were throwing thousands into temporary unemployment.

For discontent the Tory Government had no answer except repression. A series of riots and public demonstrations in 1819, much more the result of economic distress than of political agitation, caused a panic in official circles and induced the ministry to introduce six new acts for repressing sedition, by restrictions on public meetings and on the sale of cheap periodicals and pamphlets. In the popular mind, the Tories had become merely the party of high rents, protective tariffs, costly bread, sinecures, pensions, and privileges.

Nor were the Whigs in any position to offer an effective alternative. Their leaders were as aristocratic as the Tories themselves, and their liberalism seemed limited to criticism of the government in power, suggestions for improving the position of Catholics and dissenters, and a platonic sympathy with revolutionary movements in conveniently distant continental nations. They took little interest in the grievances and demands of the working class. Moreover, they were a minority in both houses of Parliament, and a weak and divided minority at that.

Popular sentiment more and more passed to a group—it was scarcely a party—called the Radicals. By imperceptible gradations the more advanced Whigs merged with the more moderate Radicals, and a later generation recognized Whigs and Radicals as simply the right and left wings, respectively, of British Liberalism. But in the 1820s many Whigs were but one degree less frightened by the Radicals than were Tories themselves. Who were these dangerous firebrands; these British Jacobins?

One can hardly speak of the Radicals as a type, though they all agreed in denouncing certain abuses and in demanding certain reforms. There never lived in England two men more unlike in all that makes up personality than the dry, precise, scholarly doctrinaire Jeremy Bentham, high priest of the Utilitarians, and the rugged, witty, swashbuckling peasant William Cobbett, the most popular pamphleteer of his whole generation. Even if one might find common to both a certain prosaic matter-of-factness, an emphasis on the practical, which made them immune to the romantic appeal which the traditions of the past held for such men as Edmund Burke and Walter Scott, one would be confounded by the presence in the Radical ranks of such men as the romantic poets Byron and Shelley, who in certain moods outdid both Bentham and Cobbett in revolutionary emphasis. Surely, only the presence of grievances great enough to irk all sorts of intelligent men could bring together such allies!

Some reformers were specialists, indeed were Radical at all only on certain issues. Thus William Wilberforce, who did so much to abolish the slave trade, was a high Tory on most other matters. Cobbett was, in the most literal sense of the word, a reactionary, though a democrat, for he wished merely to bring back the customs of older and, in his opinion, better times, when England was the home of independent and prosperous yeomen farmers. Major John Cartwright also appealed to the past, believing that medieval England had been a true democracy. Sir Samuel Romilly and Sir James Mackintosh devoted themselves to reform of the criminal law. Others specialized in campaigns against colonial slavery, factory slavery, prison and asylum mismanagement, cruelty to children or to animals, imprisonment for debt, or any of a hundred other abuses.

A very good example of the specialist in reform was Francis Place. Though he was interested in many things, he is remembered today mainly for his work in achieving the emancipation of the trade unions. Laws against 'combinations' had made it a penal offence for workingmen to join in a concerted strike or organize in any manner to force employers to raise their wages. In theory, employers also were forbidden to enter combinations to keep wages down or to restrict output, but it was notorious that the laws against combinations of employers were not enforced while those against workingmen were often put into effect. A successful tailor, Francis Place devoted himself to securing the repeal of the anti-combination laws. Place was not himself in Parliament, but he was a close friend of men who were and who profited by his knowledge of the subject and his political tact and skill. In 1824 Parliament at last legalized the trade unions, though half repenting of its liberality it placed some restrictions on their activities the following year.

Setting aside a few theorists, like William Godwin, Shelley's father-in-law, who advocated an idealistic type of anarchism, most of the Radicals aimed at reforms which could be realized without any real revolution. Some would have been content with a political victory of the middle classes, including free trade, equal rights for all religions, curtailment of aristocratic privileges, and a broader franchise for the House of Commons. Others wanted universal manhood suffrage, abolition of the Church establishment, and other drastic reforms. Very few actively agitated for abolition of the Crown or of the House of Lords, though many held both institutions in contempt. Still fewer dreamed of any general assault on the rights of private property. The typical Radical leader was as often a prosperous manufacturer as an underpaid mechanic. The philanthropic millowner Robert Owen did indeed advocate a kind of Utopian Socialism, but it was to be realized through voluntary association rather than by means of state action. In one sense the Radicalism of the early nineteenth century was the exact opposite of the Radicalism of the twentieth century; it considered government at best merely a necessary evil and favored a restriction rather than an extension of the powers of the State.

XXIX

THE TRIUMPH OF LIBERAL REFORM

In 1827 the long ministry of Lord Liverpool came to an end, and
with it the period of mere immobility and resistance in politics. For
the next twenty years or so, until the ship of state reached the relatively placid waters of the mid-Victorian 1850s, the social order was
under constant challenge. Equal rights were secured to all forms of
religious belief. Trade was unshackled from the restrictions of tariff
and monopoly. The criminal law was civilized and the civil law
rationalized. Colonial slavery was abolished, and colonies of English
speech granted greater home rule. The House of Commons and the
municipal governments became more representative; and privileges,
pensions, pluralities, and sinecures were lopped off from sundry
branches of Church and State. Many of these reforms were the work
of Conservative ministers, who, indeed, differed from their Liberal opponents rather in the speed than in the direction of change.

Toryism, to be sure, was never all of a piece. Among the Tories
who ruled Britain almost continuously from 1783 to 1830 there
were many who had been Whigs, and some who were to become
Whigs as soon as being one was not equivalent to a sentence of exile
from office. Pitt had once been a reformer. Some Tories favored
religious equality, some agreed with Adam Smith on free trade, a
few even admitted the necessity an eventual reform of Parliament.
Lord Eldon's obstinate resistance to any and every proposed change
was exceptional rather than typical. Though the Duke of Wellington was sometimes bracketed with him as leader of the ultra-Tories,
he was personally a man of another type. He held most of Eldon's
opinions, but he was ever ready to subordinate mere political doctrine to prevent a national crisis; thus on several occasions he presided—a grim and disapproving midwife!—over the birth of a new
reform.

Over against the high Toryism of Eldon and Wellington stood the more liberal Toryism of such men as George Canning, Robert Peel, and William Huskisson. Canning was one of the most picturesque personalities of his time as well as one of the ablest men of his party, but his restless ambition, his indiscreet wit, and his occasional petulance made him enemies among both Whigs and Tories. Though he favored equal rights for the Roman Catholics, he expended most of his liberalism on foreign soil, and his greatest claim to fame is his open challenge to Metternich's system of alliances and the support he gave to the Latin American republics.[1] Peel, the son of a manufacturer, was a skilled parliamentarian with a businessman's point of view. He did not dislike change; but he did dislike hurry, and his conservatism consisted in never moving till he thought public opinion was ripe. Thus in the course of his long career he first opposed, then later accepted, Catholic emancipation, parliamentary reform, and free trade. Though he and Huskisson both represented a party committed to protective tariffs (as, indeed, both Tory and Whig parties were, in differing degree), they believed in gradual reductions and adjustments of tariff duties. Peel was responsible for some useful administrative reforms, such as the organization of the London police force, whose members were long called 'peelers' and are still called 'bobbies' in his honor.

Canning's appointment as Prime Minister was popular 'out of doors' but it almost split the Tory party in Parliament; Wellington and even Peel refused to serve under him, and, while he had a certain amount of Whig support, Earl Grey, leader of the Whig party, would not co-operate with him. He died a few months after taking office and was briefly succeeded by that 'transient and embarrassed phantom' Viscount Goderich. Then in 1828 the Duke of Wellington took office with Peel's support. A strongly Tory ministry was faced with a threefold popular demand: equal rights for dissenters, equal rights for Roman Catholics, and parliamentary reform. Wellington was stubborn on the last demand but he yielded on the others.

The case of the Protestant dissenters was a curious one. Since the Toleration Act of 1689 their worship had been authorized, except in the case of Unitarians, and since the Hanoverian succession they

[1] See Chapters XXII and XXVII.

had been permitted to hold office, the last serious attempt to bar them from such privilege being the Tory act against 'occasional conformists' in Queen Anne's time. But they held office only by a subterfuge, a connivance by the government at the violation of its own laws. It had become the custom to evade the Test and Corporation Acts, directed against any who held certain public offices without taking the sacrament according to the rites of the Church of England, by annual acts of indemnity excusing those who had inadvertently failed to 'qualify' for office. Lord John Russell, on behalf of the Whigs, moved for the repeal for the Test and Corporation Acts. The Tory ministers at first opposed the motion, but rather halfheartedly, as men do who know that they are striving against the inevitable; only Lord Eldon in the House of Lords made a tenacious fight against the reform. It was carried without overmuch difficulty and thus cleared the stage for a more dramatic struggle over the rights of Roman Catholics, which was the inevitable next issue.

The Roman Catholic question was nine parts national to one sectarian. Very few objected seriously to granting political rights to the handful of Catholics in Great Britain, and they were irreclaimable fanatics of the type who had been responsible for the Gordon riots of 1780,[2] a type which had become much rarer during the past fifty years. The real question which perturbed the ministry was Ireland, a nation with so many causes for discontent that it seemed equally dangerous to grant equal rights to its Catholic majority or to deny them. To grant Catholics the right to sit in Parliament might mean—eventually it did mean—the entrance into the House of Commons of a large body of Irish Catholics hostile to British rule and ready to throw their votes in opposition to any British ministry. To refuse this right might mean revolution.

The Tory ministry had already been shaken by the resignation of Huskisson and other Canningites, whom the ultra-Tories nicknamed 'liberals' (of course, not in the later party meaning of the term), over the proposal to grant to unrepresented great towns two seats taken from disfranchised corrupt boroughs. The ministry by reject-

[2] Lord George Gordon, a half-crazed zealot, raised a riot in London protesting the repeal of certain penal laws against the Catholics, and for several days the city, which then had no effective police system, was at the mercy of a drunken mob.

ing this very moderate measure of parliamentary reform had lost
its progressive wing. One of the new members of the ministry was
defeated for an Irish seat by Daniel O'Connell, an Irish Catholic
orator of great power. By law, O'Connell could not enter Parliament, but the overwhelming vote cast for him was proof of an
aroused Ireland. Wellington and Peel, hitherto foes of Catholic
emancipation, now in 1829 removed the remaining Catholic disabilities rather than face the risk of an Irish civil war. But this step in
turn displeased the more bigoted Tories. Not content with the compromise by which Catholic emancipation was forced to go hand in
hand with a higher property qualification for the Irish franchise—so
that, if Catholics were to enter Parliament, they should at all events
represent the interests of the well-to-do—they agitated against Wellington and Peel as traitors to the Protestant constitution. Wellington's ministry, having already lost its left wing, now lost its right
also, and was thus in a doubly crippled condition.

The unlamented death of King George IV in 1830 necessitated
the election of a new Parliament. The election almost coincided with
a revolution in France, and, though Great Britain less than any other
nation has taken its political fashions from foreign countries, the
example of the fall of the reactionary monarchy of Charles X and
its replacement by a moderate parliamentary monarchy resting on
the middle classes, a Whiggish sort of regime, could not fail to awake
much British interest and sympathy. More influential probably than
the French Revolution was the existence of hard times in the manufacturing districts, economic distress, as usual, finding an outlet in
political agitation.

Earl Grey, the new Whig Prime Minister, though conservative
by temperament and an aristocrat to his finger tips,[3] had become
convinced of the necessity of a reform bill which would remodel the
House of Commons and make it a real reflection, if not of the nation
at least of all the propertied classes of the nation. Parliament as it
existed in 1830 was certainly far from that. Both houses, and that
to an almost equal degree, represented landlordism. Aside from a
few university members, the House of Commons consisted of county
members and borough members. Each county, irrespective of popu-

---

[3] 'His cabinet was the most aristocratic of the century,' E. L. Woodward, *The
Age of Reform* (1938), p. 76.

lation, returned two members, elected by the 'forty shilling free-holders.' Though this placed a monopoly of political power in hands of landowners it did ensure (except in Scotland) that each knight of the shire had a substantial body of voters behind him. In Scotland only the holders of certain feudal 'superiorities' could vote, and this made the franchise even narrower than in England. The greatest injustice lay in the boroughs. Not only were large towns often un-represented and small decayed villages—in two or three cases with no living inhabitants—represented, but the system of voting was absolutely chaotic. Sometimes the franchise was based on residence, sometimes on payment of local rates and taxes, sometimes on the holding of property of a certain value or of a certain type, some-times on membership in a close corporation of hereditary freemen of the town, or even vested in certain holders of public office. There were towns, such as Preston, where nearly everyone voted; others where not one man in a hundred had the vote. The situation was made worse by the fact that elections were open; no secret ballot protected the tenant who feared to offend his landlord or the shop-keeper who feared to offend his best customers. In the smaller vil-lages the preponderant influence of a single rich man was usually so great that a mere nomination of a candidate insured his election and made the polling an empty formality.

Everyone expected some sort of reform bill, but when the Whigs introduced it the Tories were divided between derision and horror at its provisions. The extension of the franchise was moderate enough: householders whose premises were worth ten pounds a year to have the vote in the boroughs, and the addition of certain well-to-do tenants in the counties to the existing freeholders. But the rotten boroughs were dealt with in a drastic way: all boroughs of less than 2,000 inhabitants to lose their separate representation; [4] all boroughs of less than 4,000 to lose one member; the seats thus saved to go to large towns and cities and to populous counties. No more convenient little pocket boroughs whence the village squire could send his son, or his brilliant young friend from Oxford, or the man who paid him for his 'influence,' to the House of Commons;

[4] Of course a disfranchised borough could share in county elections; it was merely merged with a larger constituency as a raindrop loses its identity in a pool.

a system from which Whig landlords as well as Tory had long profited—what on earth could such aristocrats as Earl Grey and Lord John Russell mean by proposing anything of the sort? The second reading of the bill passed in the Commons by the margin of only a single vote and shortly afterwards the Whig ministry decided to appeal to the country in a general election. King William won a brief popularity by agreeing to dissolve Parliament.

The election of 1831 was possibly the most exciting one which Great Britain has ever known since the revolution of 1688 had established the supremacy of the House of Commons in the constitution. The pressure of public opinion was so great that even the narrow and unrepresentative body of electors was affected by it and returned a majority of reformers. A new reform bill, substantially like the old one, was carried after long and bitter debates through the Commons, but it was rejected in the House of Lords. Riots followed in Bristol and elsewhere. The ministry brought forward a third bill, slightly reducing the number of disfranchised boroughs. Grey asked the king to promise the creation of enough new peers favorable to reform to carry the bill through the House of Lords. At first the king demurred and asked Wellington to form a Tory ministry which might carry a milder compromise measure. But the country still loudly demanded 'the bill, the whole bill, and nothing but the bill.' Francis Place, the emancipator of the trade unions, proposed a run on the banks to bring pressure on the government. The Duke of Wellington found it impossible to form any ministry that the House of Commons would support, and the king agreed to create new peerages if necessary. Earl Grey resumed office and the House of Lords sullenly gave way to the inevitable and permitted the measure to pass.

Looking back on the English Reform Act of 1832, and the similar measures passed for Scotland and Ireland, it is hard to understand the passionate excitement of the times. The small electorate had been increased by only 50 per cent. Later reform bills, passed with relatively little opposition in 1867, 1884, 1918, and 1928, enfranchised much greater numbers. To describe the bill, as is often done, as marking the advent of middle-class or bourgeois rule in Britain is an exaggeration. Many, though not all, of this class now had the vote, but for generations to come they continued to send chiefly members of the landed aristocracy to Parliament, and that class is still well represented in every ministry, by no means excluding Labour ministries. Even as a party triumph the effect of the Reform Act was shortlived. It ended, indeed, the period of uninterrupted Tory ministries, but the Tories were back in office (though only for some four months) two years later under Peel; and, under the successive designations of Tories, Conservatives, and Unionists, they have since held power as frequently as their Whig, Liberal, and Labour opponents.

Wherein, then, lay the importance of this particular measure; why have historians generally selected it as a watershed between the days of aristocracy and those of democracy? Four reasons suggest themselves. The most important, perhaps, was the manner in which the bill was carried, proving that a sustained popular demand, reflected in the House of Commons, can always in the long run override the most tenacious opposition of the Lords. Again, though the shift in the balance of power was slight, it was all in the direction of the merchants and manufacturers and those parts of England where industry predominated over agriculture; it meant that the landed aristocracy, though still the most powerful class, had to share power with the businessmen. Moreover, it abolished the old aristocratic privilege of virtually appointing men to Parliament; every man in the House of Commons was now sent there by a real constituency. Finally, the settlement of the question of parliamentary reform removed the key log from a jam of proposed legislation; it thus made possible a large number of other reforms which the old unreformed Parliament might not have approved.

Four measures in particular occupied the attention of the new reformed Parliament: the abolition of colonial slavery, the restriction of child labor, the reform of the poor law, and the reconstruction of municipal government. With these achievements to their credit, the Whigs were practically content, though their Radical allies continued to agitate for free trade, a wider franchise, the secret ballot, and many other reforms. Indeed, the tempest over the Reform Bill was succeeded by a relative political calm. Whigs were not disposed to press their victory unduly, and Tories found that reform was not revolution and that most of the ancient landmarks still stood intact. Sir Robert Peel, the Tory leader, gracefully adapted himself to the new situation, accepted parliamentary reform as an accomplished fact though he had opposed it so long as the issue was in the balance, and popularized the new name 'Conservative' for the Tory party. Somewhat more slowly, the term 'Liberal' came into general use for the Whigs and Radicals. The old names still lingered, however, though they took on new meanings: Tory came to mean a very backward-looking Conservative, and Whig a similarly tradition-bound Liberal.

In British as in American history, the abolition of the slave trade long preceded the abolition of slavery itself. British warships watched the west African coast to seize slavers while plantation owners in Jamaica still used slave labor brought in at an earlier time to cultivate sugar cane. But the one step brought the other nearer. Emancipation was a simpler task than in the United States (a fact often forgotten by British critics of American slavery) because there were no slaves in the mother country; the issue was entirely colonial. It is most improbable that the British West Indies would have voluntarily set their slaves free for many a long year after the British Parliament itself was ready to act. In 1833 Parliament extinguished colonial slavery, paying compensation to slave owners and providing for a transition period of apprenticeship between slavery and complete freedom.

The restriction of child labor in the factories was not precisely in line with either Whig or Radical ideas, as both Liberal factions in those days deprecated governmental interference with private business, but it was a humanitarian act supported by kindly men of all parties who had been aroused by reports of great abuse and hardship, amounting almost to conditions of slavery. In fact Lord Ashley, later Earl of Shaftesbury, who led the parliamentary movement for factory reform, was himself a Tory. There were precedents for government regulation of child labor in the factories dating back as far as 1802, but the law of 1833 was the first which dealt at all effectively with the problem. It excluded all children under nine from textile factories, limited the hours of labor for persons under thirteen to nine hours a day and those of persons under eighteen to twelve hours, and provided for inspectors (only four at first) to enforce the law.

The reform of the poor law in 1834 was a courageous, though not very sympathetic, attempt to deal with one of the most serious problems of the time. Elizabethan legislation had established the excellent principle that society at large (represented in this case by the parish) was responsible for seeing that no one actually died of want. Under conditions which developed in the eighteenth and nineteenth centuries, the responsibility of the parish worked badly in practice, especially after the Speenhamland system of supplementing inadequate wages by grants from parish rates came into vogue. Economists of the new hard type, such as T. R. Malthus, the student of population growth, held that a continuation of poor relief on the old basis would make England a nation of paupers. The new Poor Law of 1834 had a double aim. It improved the efficiency of administration of poor relief by combining parishes together into 'unions' whose resources were adequate for the work, and it saved money by discontinuing payment to paupers who lived at home or were partly self-supporting. As a means test, the pauper must be willing to seek relief in a union work house where, as the harsh phrase of the times went, his situation would be less 'eligible' than 'the situation of the independent labourer of the lowest class.'

No other Whig measure so completely alienated the working class or revealed so clearly that the alliance between the factory owner and the factory hand which carried the Reform Bill was but a temporary one. To the ratepayer the reform was welcome. It prevented, or aimed to prevent, complete destitution, but it limited relief to the genuinely destitute. To the workingman, who might himself be forced to seek poor relief, it was 'robbery,' and one excited orator declared that he would undertake to prove that the poor man had a better title to relief under the time-honored Elizabethan law than the goldsmiths of London to their plate 'or the grinding shopocrat to his fraud-begotten profits!' The union work houses were dubbed 'Bastilles' and compared unfavorably with prisons. One can read in various of the novels of Dickens how bitterly one writer, after he himself was out of the reach of want, condemned the administration of the law. But in the course of time the harsher regulations were modified, and the removal of the depressing effect of the old poor law on wages probably more than balanced the loss to the workingman by the new restrictions on relief.

The reform of Parliament almost of necessity involved the reform of the boroughs which had elected the greater part of the Commons. Local government in Britain had both the strength and the weakness that comes from a system which has grown rather than been artificially made to order. In rural districts not only judicial duties but manifold administrative tasks of the most varied sort fell on unpaid amateurs such as the justices of the peace. In the boroughs chaos prevailed; sometimes the municipal officials were elected by a broad franchise, sometimes by a narrow one, sometimes they formed a close corporation and elected their own successors. Yet for all this illogical confusion, with the resulting waste, inefficiency, and jobbery, Englishmen were not unjustly proud that they had preserved more of local initiative than most continental nations. The justice of the peace, the vestryman, the alderman, the town councillor, the mayor were usually local men, proud of their town or village or city and counting it honor to serve it. The problem before Britain was to combine professional expertness and efficiency, bureaucracy at its best, with a local self-reliance which would avoid the faults of bureaucratic rule, 'apoplexy at the center and paralysis at the extremities.'

On the whole, Great Britain may congratulate herself on the extent to which this difficult problem of local government has been solved. The Municipal Reform Act of 1835 created councils elected by town ratepayers, thus introducing a uniform representative system. In many towns they took over duties hitherto entrusted to special bodies, such as the improvement commissioners. Not until 1888 was an adequate system of county government adopted, when a system of county councils was created. In 1894, for smaller rural units, a system of parish councils was set up. Along with the democratization of local government went a parallel, and equally valuable, development of public utilities and services on professional lines, alike for police, fire protection, streets, parks, and often public tramways and gas and electric plants.

In 1834 William Lamb, Viscount Melbourne, succeeded Earl Grey as Prime Minister and as leader of the Whig party. He had been one of the Canningite liberal Tories and he still remained almost the most conservative of the Whigs. Even less than Grey did he understand or sympathize with the Radicals and their program; his advice to reformers, 'Why can't you let it alone?' matched Walpole's 'Let sleeping dogs lie.' Peel briefly took office towards the end of the year, but the consequent election failed to give him a majority and Melbourne returned to power. His greatest service to the nation was probably the manner in which he guided by wise and friendly counsel the first steps in statesmanship of the inexperienced young queen who succeeded her uncle William IV in 1837. He planted the Whig theory of government in her mind.

Queen Victoria's uniquely long reign (1837-1901) has given its name to a whole historical epoch. Probably it saved the monarchy, for, looking back on a long succession of blundering, unpopular, or, at best, negative and colorless rulers, many Englishmen said in 1837 that there might never be another coronation. It is true that British rulers no longer had much scope for action, since their powers were now all held in commission by a cabinet responsible solely to the House of Commons; Victoria could never have given England the personal rule of Elizabeth or even have played party politics in the manner of Queen Anne. But the Whig theory that the ruler was merely the Crown, a symbol like the flag, forgets the subtle influence of one personality on another. A British ruler can at least advise his own 'advisers,' his last shred of constitutional power; and this advice is not seldom taken. A mere symbol of Britannia on the open stage, the ruler is sometimes the prompter's whisper behind the curtains. Moreover, the ruler has another power, unknown to the constitution, the influence of prestige with the Court and the crowd, which can make certain customs fashionable or unfashionable. Thus George IV loved a gay life, and the young bloods who surrounded him imitated his loose morals and extravagance; Victoria liked dignity and decorum and thereby won a strange immortality by transforming her name into an adjective, the term 'Victorian,' which is still applied, in admiration or in derision, to a certain tradition of moral earnestness combined with conventional respectability in social life, art, and letters. Doubtless there were other and stronger causes for this trend of the age, the chief being the growing social influence of the Puritan-minded middle class; but it is at least an interesting fact that the queen so completely shared the middle-class ideals.

In 1840 Victoria married a husband of her own choice, Prince Albert of Saxe-Coburg-Gotha, whose brief career, ending in 1861, left a permanent impress on her political outlook as well as on her personal life. At first he was less popular than the queen: he was formal and precise in his manner, and a shade more liberal on domestic questions and a shade more conservative on foreign policy than most of the British ministries in his time. In recent years more justice has been done to his sense of public duty and his interest in science and invention. There were many children, and thus the direct succession was placed beyond a doubt. Fortunately for everybody, the accession of Victoria broke the old connection with Hanover, where a female could not inherit the throne, and thus saved both Britain and Germany from dangerous complications when Bismarck absorbed Hanover in his aggrandizement of Prussia.

By the time Victoria had come to the throne a new industrial revolution, or a new phase of the old, was under way. This was the revolution in communications brought about by the railroad. Like the steam engine and the new textile machinery this invention was largely of British origin. Steam power was applied to boats by several inventors, among whom the most successful was the American Fulton, early in the nineteenth century. Steam had also been applied, but less successfully, to land transport. Had the roads been better the automobile might have preceded the locomotive, but as things were the only successful engines ran on rails, such as Richard Trevethick's railroads in the coal mines. The essential step was George Stephenson's improved locomotive of the 1820s, which proved such a success as to drive from the field alike the horse-drawn railcar, the stationary engine which pulled cars uphill with a rope, and the steam engine on the roads. Within a generation from the time when Stephenson first ran his *Rocket*, a network of railways covered Great Britain and the more commercially advanced parts of the European and American continents.[5]

Until about 1850 the rapid increase of British industrial and commercial wealth did little to raise the general standard of living among the poorest classes. The 1830s and '40s were in general hard times. This doubtless was a main cause of the political discontent which marked the period. After the Reform Bill of 1832 had become law, agitation did not cease. Since both Whigs and Tories seemed content with the new franchise law, an agitation began outside Parliament for manhood suffrage and other radical reforms. The most

[5] The statesman Huskisson, a leading light among the liberal Tories, was killed in 1830 by one of the first locomotives.

important of these movements was called Chartism, because it supported a People's Charter with six demands: (1) manhood suffrage, (2) equal election districts, (3) the secret ballot, (4) annual elections for the House of Commons, (5) no property qualification for members of Parliament, and (6) payment for members of Parliament. The first demand was the essential one; the others aimed to make it more effective. The Charter is interesting for its omissions; it made no mention of monarchy or House of Lords, apparently taking for granted that whoever controlled the Commons would rule the nation. Neither did it mention the economic issues that were really foremost in the mind of nearly every Chartist. This was partly because the Chartists were not in agreement on their economic program: some, like Feargus O'Connor, wanted a 'back to the farm' movement; some, like J. Bronterre O'Brien, the nationalization of the land; some, like Ernest Jones, a complete program of Socialism. They all wanted the vote as a key to power, though they had different ideas about what to do with power when they had it.

Many middle-class Radicals agreed with the working-class Chartists in favoring universal suffrage, but the movement which most interested them was the Anti-Corn-Law League for free trade, especially in grain. This was an early example of what is now called a pressure group, operating by propaganda outside the regular political parties but influencing them by the promise of support or threat of opposition. These tactics, now so familiar, were comparatively new in the 1830s, and some politicians even thought they might be illegal. The League's slogan of 'cheap bread' had the almost unanimous support of the town workingmen, but from the organization itself many held aloof, fearing that it might distract attention from the more important issue of the vote. As one Chartist put it, when the workers had the ballot they would repeal the Corn laws 'and all the other bad laws.' The Chartists had a definitely class-conscious distrust of political movements, even reform movements, coming from the factory owners.

Some turned their attention from politics to economic activity. Trade unions multiplied. Though they had been legalized by Place's efforts in the laws of 1824 and 1825, they still sometimes encountered trouble with the law on one ground or another. Thus in 1834 certain laborers in Tolpuddle village, Dorsetshire, were sentenced to transportation as convicts because their farm laborers' 'friendly society' had taken secret oaths and the court held that this constituted a conspiracy. Though Robert Owen's ideal of organizing all industry on a co-operative basis ended in paper projects and Utopian speculations, a real co-operative movement was started at Rochdale in 1844, applying Owen's ideas on a limited and practical scale to retail trade.

Another subject of agitation was factory reform. Though the law of 1833 had curbed some of the worst abuses, it did not content the workers. Their goal was the ten-hour day even for adults, and they scouted the argument of economists that 'all profits are made in the eleventh hour,' and that of the doctrinaire Radicals that a grown man or woman should be free from any legal limitation on the 'right to work.' Ashley, who had the reform in hand in Parliament, secured by laws passed in 1847 and 1850 a ten-and-a-half hour day for women and young persons, and indirectly (since so many women and young people were employed in the textile industry) limited the actual operation of the factories to this period, thus securing a shorter working day for men as well. A Mines Act of 1842 ended the horrible abuse of the underground labor of women and children. Similar restrictive laws were adopted for many other trades.

The question of the Corn laws agitated the 1840s more than any other issue. Three policies were advocated: the Tory plan of a sliding scale, by which the duty on grain imports varied inversely as the price, so that when wheat was a drug on the market farmers would have ample protection against foreign competition, while if prices stood at famine level the duty would be merely nominal; the Whig plan of a small fixed charge; the Radical plan of total abolition of all duties. John Bright and Richard Cobden, Radical orators, presented the case for free trade so strongly that Sir Robert Peel, who succeeded Melbourne in 1841, was already more than half convinced before the Irish potato famine completed his conversion. He had already in 1842 cut down tariffs drastically on raw materials and manufactured products, balancing the loss by an income tax which has never since been discontinued. In 1846 Peel carried a measure which virtually, though not quite formally, established free trade in grain. The protectionists of his own party, led by Lord George

Bentinck, an aristocratic sportsman, and Benjamin Disraeli, a brilliant Jewish novelist, almost immediately thereafter turned him out of office and Lord John Russell came in with the Whigs as Prime Minister. Peel never again formed a ministry, but if, like Samson, he had sacrificed himself, he had brought down with him the whole temple of protectionism. Till after the First World War, Great Britain remained the greatest exponent of free trade.

One small reform of the time is an interesting evidence of how minor events can be more important in their consequences than the clamorous issues that fill the minds of contemporary journalists and politicians. England at various times was much excited over such ephemeral questions as the divorce of George IV, the dismissal of Queen Victoria's Whig attendants of the bedchamber by Peel, or the use by the Roman Catholic Church of territorial titles already used by Anglican bishops. These issues are now merely historic curiosities, but Rowland Hill's device of the prepaid postage stamp and the low and uniform penny rate for sending letters, sanctioned after much bureaucratic opposition in 1840, not only changed the postal systems of every country in the world (and created the hobby of philately) but brought the habit of correspondence for the first time within reach of the poor.

The early nineteenth century poured as much of its vast creative energy into books as into political battles or steam engines. Probably it was the most brilliant period of English lyric poetry. In the last days of the eighteenth century a number of romantic poets, notably William Wordsworth, Samuel T. Coleridge, Robert Burns, and William Blake, had carried English verse to Himalayan heights. Their work was continued in the new century by Walter Scott's spirited revival of the old ballad literature, Byron's equal facility in romantic sentiment and in cynical epigram, Keats's gospel of pure beauty, Shelley's exquisite artistry. Pegasus not seldom descended to earthly pastures. The reaction into Toryism of such young radicals, once admirers of the French Revolution, as Wordsworth, Coleridge, and Southey, is as historically significant as the similar movement to the right of statesmen like Pitt, while the new poetic radicalism of Byron, Shelley, and Moore is as interesting as the more prosaic radicalism of Cobbett, Bentham, or Brougham.

Prose literature did not lag behind poetry. Sir Walter Scott followed his early popular successes as a poet with more enduring achievements as the greatest of historical novelists; the publication of *Waverley* in 1814 opened a new era in romantic fiction. Scott himself recognized in Jane Austen a subtler realistic talent than his own. In *Pride and Prejudice* (1813) contemporary domestic society is depicted with inimitable charm and wit. The essay, as handled by De Quincey, Lamb, Hazlitt, and Macaulay, never has enjoyed a greater vogue. The rapid increase in the reading public and the development of such critical periodicals as the *Edinburgh* and the *Quarterly* emancipated the author from his old dependence on a personal patron; a pleased public was a sufficient guarantee of a livelihood. Most of Macaulay's brilliant essays appeared in the *Edinburgh Review*. His later large scale *History of England*, a majestic pageant of the reigns of James II and William III, obtained a wide circulation from the start.

Nineteenth-century British art scarcely rivaled the achievements of literature. Though Blake, Turner, and Constable carried on something of the fine tradition of the earlier age of Gainsborough and Reynolds in painting, public buildings and monuments were usually uninspired, and there had been a change for the worse in the minor arts of furniture, decoration, and costume from eighteenth-century standards. Nevertheless, large-scale production of clothing, furniture, chinaware, and substantial building materials, though temporarily playing havoc with the canons of fine living for a favored class, enabled an increasing number of plain people to enjoy substantial comforts. In the latter part of the nineteenth century, popular taste gradually improved, after reaching a climax of ugliness shortly after the mid-century.[6] The influence of such prophets of aesthetic reform as Ruskin and Morris in late Victorian times wrought substantial progress.

[6] 'The ugliest zone of building will be found to lie between 1860 and 1880.' R. C. K. Ensor, *England, 1870-1914* (1936), p. 155. Much the same could have been said for the United States in the same period.

XXX

THE SPACIOUS DAYS OF QUEEN VICTORIA

THE reign of Queen Victoria appears almost a golden age when contrasted either with the social and political discontents that immediately preceded it, or the tense and menacing aspect of foreign affairs which immediately followed it. Writers of the 1920s used Victorian as a synonym for complacent self-satisfaction. To be sure, there were clouds enough even in that sunny day if one were to look for them. The one European war in which Britain engaged, the Crimean War against Russia, was a tissue of blunders, and some of the minor colonial wars were badly handled. An Indian mutiny threatened the very base of British rule. The problem of urban poverty gave increasing concern to a more sensitive national conscience. New scientific theories seemed to many perplexed souls to undermine the grounds of religious faith. Indeed, practically all the writers of the time, no matter how widely divergent might be their remedies, were at one in regarding England as needing a drastic treatment to recover full spiritual and material health. Newman thought Catholic faith was the need of the hour; Carlyle, stronger and more veracious rulers; Ruskin and Morris, a blend of art and socialism; Dickens and Kingsley, more interest in the poor; Arnold and Meredith, a broader cosmopolitan culture. Victoria's poet laureate Alfred Tennyson was always worrying about something: the weakness of the fleet, the condition of the slums, or the waning of religious faith. Indeed, the more one looks for evidences of Victorian complacency, the more it seems to dissolve into a mist of doubts and dissatisfactions.

All this and much more is true enough; indeed the old robust serenity which simply took the world for granted vanished, possibly forever, with the coming of industrialism, democracy, and nationalism. In their various ways, Rousseau, Watt, Napoleon, Darwin, and

Karl Marx have spoiled beyond redemption the contented social order and intellectual outlook of the powdered-wig epoch. But there is another side to the picture. If the Britain of Gladstone's day was more worried and perplexed than the Britain of Walpole's time, this was, in part at least, because of the fact that responsibilities increase with greatness. In wealth and power and prestige Great Britain stood higher than ever before. A new empire was built up in Africa and the Pacific to compensate for the loss of the eighteenth-century empire in America.[1] From Waterloo till the Germans began to create a large navy at the very end of the nineteenth century, Great Britain was never menaced by any direct foreign peril; some distant colony, such as India, might at the worst be endangered, but never the motherland. War was a matter for professional soldiers in distant countries; it never came home to the average citizen in the way in which it did then on the continent, or does in Britain today.

The peril of revolution, with the single exception of Ireland, seemed as remote as that of war. After the Chartist movement[2] had faded with the business revival of the '50s, no significant political movement of the poor appeared for half a century. Nearly all discontented persons adhered to the Radical wing of the Liberal party, a group which looked to Parliament for reforms and viewed revolutionary violence with horror. As late as the '70s there were still a few republican clubs, but they were without real popular support. The trade unions sometimes employed violence in their strikes, but never on any very menacing scale. Marxian Socialism won a recruit here and there, but not in such numbers as to play any real part in the politics of the time.

British security and prosperity appeared the brighter from contrast with other lands. If there be any truth in the charge of Victorian complacency, it is doubtless in the common Victorian habit of comparing Britain favorably with other countries. France, the nearest and most familiar of them, underwent the revolution of 1848, Louis Napoleon's drastic dictatorship, defeat at the hands of Prussia, and the terrible episode of the Paris Commune. Tennyson was not the only one who blessed 'the narrow seas that keep asun-

[1] See Chapter XXXII.
[2] See Chapter XXIX.

der' and wished they were 'a whole Atlantic broad'—a phrase which curiously brings to mind the attitude of American isolationists in the twentieth century. Italy and Germany won national unity, to the general applause of British opinion, but at the cost of several wars. Spain and Spanish America seemed a prey of endless revolutions. Even the United States underwent the shock of one great civil war. Everywhere in continental Europe revolutionary Socialism, religious disbelief, and relaxation of moral standards seemed more in evidence, or at all events more outspoken, than in Great Britain. A typical *Punch* cartoon shows a foreign fanatic trying in vain to rouse a British workingman to 'pour incense on the altar of equality,' while John Bull answers that he would rather 'smoke his 'baccy on the hearth of liberty!' The true Victorian attitude was not that all was well with England, rather that much was ill in England, but that Englishmen could better it, and in any case had no reason to swap their own troubles for the greater ones endured by other lands.

For the first time since Waterloo the British people were more interested in foreign than in domestic affairs. The period from 1848 to 1871, relatively quiet in Great Britain, contained revolutions in France, Germany, Italy, Austria, Hungary, Switzerland, and many other countries; the American Civil War; the Crimean War; the Franco-Austrian War in Italy; the three wars of Bismarck's Prussia with Denmark, Austria, and France respectively; the unification of Italy and of Germany; the establishment of the Second Republic, the Second Empire and the Third Republic in France. In none of these events, except the Crimean War, was Britain directly involved, but in all of them she was keenly interested and concerned. The importance of foreign events brought to the front Viscount Palmerston as the most conspicuous figure in British politics. Domestic reforms rarely interested Palmerston; he had the distaste of many conservative Whigs, such as Walpole and Melbourne, for the restless, incessant current of reforms which the Radicals desired, and he resembled Canning and the Liberal Tories in being readier to advocate reform abroad than at home.

The really interesting thing about Palmerston's foreign policy is the way in which it combined two qualities usually opposed to each other, liberalism and jingoism. He was as keen to assert British predominance and to protect British interests as any militarist or imperialist, while being at the same time as concerned over the rights of oppressed nations as any sentimental liberal or pacifist. Probably he conceived Britain, with her uniquely strong fleet, as a sort of schoolmistress of Europe who would keep all the children in order and protect the little boys from being bullied by the big ones. In the crises of 1848 and 1849, to the horror of Queen Victoria and Prince Consort Albert, he was constantly lecturing the despots and giving verbal encouragement to the liberal revolutionists. When by some high-handed act Palmerston had put himself in the wrong, he appealed to public opinion to support him, and public opinion rarely failed. Thus when he blockaded the Greek coast to secure payment of damages due to a certain Don Pacifico, a money lender of Portuguese birth but of British citizenship, his action was absurdly disproportioned to the actual grievance, but a resounding speech declaring that every British subject, like a Roman citizen of old, must feel the whole might of the empire behind him to protect him against wrong or injury won a victory from an enthusiastic Parliament. Both Queen Victoria and Prime Minister Russell complained that Palmerston sent off vitally important dispatches without consulting them, and, when he incautiously gave approval to Louis Napoleon's seizure of the dictatorial power in France, Russell forced Palmerston to resign.

On an issue of military preparedness shortly afterwards, Palmerston in turn forced out Russell (his 'tit-for-tat with John Russell' as he lightly termed it), the Conservatives under the Earl of Derby took office but failed to secure a majority in Parliament, and a coalition of Liberals and 'Peelite,' or free-trade, Conservatives assumed office under the Earl of Aberdeen. Aberdeen's brief and unhappy ministry (1852-5) was a tragedy of good intentions. The Prime Minister was a lover of peace who was horrified at the thought of war with Russia, but as he had not the personal authority to impose his will on the cabinet, Parliament, and the country at large, the only effect of his pacifism was to convince Russia that Britain would not fight. General British sentiment was for resistance to Russian aggression in co-operation with France and Turkey. Conservatives feared for the safety of India, and even Radicals considered that Russia was the most dangerous enemy to human freedom in Europe.[3] Only a few pacifists, such as John Bright and Richard Cobden, opposed the Crimean War (1854-6). Perhaps the fact that Britain had been at peace for forty years had made war seem not the sordid calamity it is, but the bright, romantic adventure it appears through the mists of distance; there is certainly a touch of this feeling in Tennyson's *Maud*.

The Crimean War was fought by the regular army with the aid of some volunteers. The army, unused since Waterloo except in India and other colonial fields, had become a somewhat rusty instrument. The services of supply were quite unprepared for the fearful responsibility of maintaining a large expeditionary force on hostile soil in a remote Russian province. The higher officers of the army were elderly veterans who had been trained in the methods of a bygone generation. Little attention was paid to the physical well-being of the common soldier. There was much friction between British and French commanders about plans of campaign. Had the inefficiency of the British and French not been far surpassed by that of the Russians, the war might have ended in disaster, but the Russia of Nicholas I was the very embodiment of political corruption and administrative incompetence. The fall of Sebastopol ended the real resistance of Russia, and in 1856 peace was signed at Paris. The mouth of the Danube, in southern Bessarabia, passed from Russian control; the Black Sea was neutralized; Turkey was admitted as a European power; a general declaration laid down rules for naval warfare.[4] The settlement thus made did not prove lasting; in 1870 Russia launched a new fleet on the Black Sea and in 1877 reopened the whole territorial settlement of the Near East.

The only real gain which Great Britain made from the Crimean War was the improvement in army administration brought about by its very blunders. A corps of volunteer nurses under Florence Night-

---

[3] Tsar Nicholas I only a few years earlier had sent in a Russian army to aid Austria against the Hungarian patriots, a deed which roused immense indignation in England.

[4] These included: (1) abolition of privateering, (2) neutral flags to protect enemy goods, unless contraband of war, (3) neutral goods, even on enemy ships, not to be taken unless contraband, (4) blockades to be recognized only if actually effective. At the Paris conference the British insisted on the public discussion of the Italian question, in spite of the fervent objections of Austria.

ingale, aided by articles from special correspondents in the press, revealed the sufferings of the soldiers in the hospitals and opened the way for modern scientific nursing.

The Aberdeen ministry had proved a failure in its conduct of the war as well as in its attempts to avert war. The resolute and energetic Palmerston as Prime Minister saw the war through its last stages. By the irony of fate Palmerston, who had been the benevolent bully of Europe and the most constant asserter of British ascendancy, fell in 1858 on the ground that in introducing a bill to repress conspiracies against the lives of foreign rulers, a most reasonable measure, he had been guilty of truckling to the arrogant demands of the French Emperor! Derby again formed a Conservative ministry, but it was short-lived, and in 1859 Palmerston was back in office. He continued to devote his main attention to foreign affairs, supporting the movement for national unification in Italy, while viewing with suspicion the parallel activities of Napoleon III. Lord John Russell, as his Foreign Secretary, shared to the full his enthusiasm for Italian unity. With respect to the War for Southern Independence in America, the ministry steered a tortuous course,[5] divided by hatred of slavery, desire to obtain Southern cotton, desire to maintain British neutral rights, and a wish to keep out of trouble. Palmerston punished a Chinese seizure of a ship flying the British flag by an armed invasion and the burning of the Emperor's palace. He showed less resolution when Prussia attacked Denmark in 1864 on the Schleswig-Holstein issue. After declaring in Parliament that Prussia and Austria might expect that if they attacked Denmark 'it would not be Denmark alone with which they would have to contend,' Palmerston found that Napoleon III was not ready to fight and decided that prudence was the better part of valor since Britain alone could scarcely be expected to take on two Great Powers over an issue only remotely involving British interests.

Palmerston's absorption in foreign affairs had delayed parliamentary reform for over a decade. Russell and Gladstone, his Liberal colleagues, wanted a slight extension of the franchise, but not until Palmerston's death in 1865 was it possible to take up the issue with any hope of success, since the question held hardly the slightest

---

[5] See Chapter xxiv.

interest for their chief. Russell, now for the second time Prime Minister, brought forward a very moderate bill admitting to the franchise the more prosperous section of the working class. Gladstone warmly supported the measure but, though Palmerston was no longer there to interpose his veto, other conservative Liberals remained. One of them, Robert Lowe, denounced the workingmen as unfit to vote and warned England that democracy was but a flat and dreary plain, where every molehill seemed to be a mountain and every bush a forest tree!

Lowe's gloomy eloquence frightened a sufficient number of Whiggish Liberals [6] to defeat Russell's ministry and bring in the Conservatives under Lord Derby. Disraeli, Derby's shrewd parliamentary manager, decided not to await a new election but to go ahead with a reform bill in Parliament as it stood. To be sure, there was a nominal Liberal majority in the Commons, but the recent vote had shown that it was divided on the franchise issue. A ministry which could dexterously devise a reform bill which would not frighten the Conservative rank and file and yet would please the enfranchised workingman might then face the voters with confidence. Disraeli's method was virtually to let the House of Commons write whatever bill it pleased and then himself assume the responsibility—and the credit—for it. His original measure was even more conservative than Russell's, but he accepted amendments till the suffrage in the boroughs included all rate-paying householders, an addition of almost a million votes, practically doubling the existing electorate. For the first time in British history a very large number of the working classes had the franchise. There was also a redistribution of seats to conform to the movements of population.

Disraeli's new franchise law and Derby's approval of it sincerely shocked many at the time. What did Conservative mean, if a ministry of that name was willing to father, for temporary party advantage, so revolutionary a change What was to become of parliamentary responsibility if a House of Commons which had just rejected a small increase in the vote from Liberal hands should immediately turn around and accept a greater change from Conservatives? Such critics forgot that Disraeli, a Jewish man of letters with strong

[6] Nicknamed 'Adullamites' from the cave of Adullam to which in Old Testament times the rebels and malcontents resorted.

sympathies for the poor, had always been rather a Tory Democrat than a Conservative in the literal sense of the word; he had never feared innovation or reform and he believed that the old English institutions which he sincerely loved—the Throne, the Lords, the Church—would be safer in the hands of the British workingman than in the hands of the middle classes. Perhaps he was right, for although he lost the election of 1868 to Gladstone and the Liberals, taking the whole period since 1867 the Conservative party has been stronger than it was between the reform bills of 1832 and 1867.

The reform bill of 1867 began a new era in party politics. The veterans of the past generation—Peel, Russell, Palmerston, Derby— had vanished. The Peelites, Gladstone among them, had completed their transition from Conservatism to Liberalism, and party lines were once again strictly drawn. Two leaders of transcendant political genius so dominated the scene that elections were really plebiscites for William Ewart Gladstone or Benjamin Disraeli. The fate of ministries was less frequently settled by debates and votes in the House of Commons and determined more often by popular elections and speeches made directly to the voters.

The first round in this duel of the giants was Gladstone's. Disraeli had counted on the gratitude of the newly enfranchised voters to put him back in office; Gladstone, realizing that in politics gratitude is given chiefly for favors yet to come, was ready with a positive program including the disestablishment of the Irish Church. The ground was well chosen, since the Irish Church represented only a small minority of the Irish people and its establishment seemed merely a symbol of alien English supremacy. Even Disraeli, in his heart of hearts, had no belief in the Irish establishment, but he could not, with the Conservative party behind him already dubious over the reform bill of 1867, openly accept Gladstone's drastic proposal. Gladstone coupled Irish disestablishment with a measure of land reform. Irish tenants turned out of their holdings were to be compensated for all the improvements they had made, a custom existing in Ulster and now extended to other parts of the country. Both measures passed easily in the new Liberal Parliament, though Gladstone was soon to discover that he had merely touched the fringe of the difficult Irish question instead of having found, as he had hoped, a final solution.

Gladstone's first and greatest ministry (1868-74) was characterized by administrative reforms of the highest importance. Thus Edward Cardwell as Secretary for War reorganized the army, abolishing flogging in peace time and the purchase of officers' commissions, introducing short terms of service, and making important changes in administration. Lord Selborne consolidated the courts of appeal by a comprehensive Act of Judicature. William E. Forster introduced a system of tax-supported schools to supplement the existing voluntary schools; they were to be free to the very poor (but charging fees to others), open to all religious faiths, and administered by locally elected school boards. Later, in 1891, all fees for these board schools were abolished. The school boards had the power to compel the attendance of children who did not go to some other school.

In 1872 the secret ballot was introduced. This had been an old Radical and Chartist demand for many decades; its advocates contended that the system of open voting was an invitation to bribery and coercion, its opponents that the secret vote was unmanly and 'unEnglish.' The actual effect of the law was not very great, except perhaps in Ireland, where it encouraged tenants to vote against the wishes of their landlords more freely than before.

By 1874 the great Liberal ministry had done its work. Gladstone himself had little more at the moment to advocate save the abolition of the income tax, while Disraeli from the opposition bench gibed at the ministry as a row of 'exhausted volcanoes.' In the election of that year Disraeli and the Conservatives were successful. The Liberals had made many enemies by their many reforms, for each encroached on some vested interest. The nonconformists did not like Forster's Education Act, for, instead of making the schools altogether secular, like the American or French schools, the new law left intact the control of the Church of England over its great system of voluntary schools and even aided them by grants from the public purse. Others were displeased at what they considered the weakness of the Liberal foreign policy. During the Franco-Prussian War Russia had launched a fleet on the Black Sea, in violation of the Treaty of 1856, which ended the Crimean War, and British protests were in vain. The payment of reparations to the United States for damages done by Confederate privateers, such as the *Alabama,* outfitted from British ports, was a wise stroke of statesmanship as well as a victory for arbitration, but many voters could see only the immediate humiliation of paying damages and not the remoter good of improving Anglo-American relations.

Disraeli was in his own way as much a reformer as Gladstone, but he had to be more cautious in order not to lose touch with the Conservatives behind him. During his administration (1874-80) he sponsored a number of important reforms such as a Trade Union Act, enlarging the freedom of the labor unions; an Artisans' Dwelling Act; a Food and Drugs Act; and a general Public Health Act. Aside from these humanitarian laws he did not venture on much domestic legislation. Like Palmerston, his real concern was with foreign affairs. He knew, however, that he lived in a changed world; no longer was it possible for an England, secure and aloof, to lay down rules for 'lesser breeds without the law.' The consolidation of Germany and of Italy had brought new Great Powers on the European scene; imperialist expansion was in the air, and a new race for colonies begun in Africa and in the Pacific island region. Palmerston had ridiculed the Suez Canal venture; Disraeli on his own responsibility arranged the purchase of the shares in this enterprise belonging to the Khedive of Egypt. He added 'Empress of India' to the titles of Queen Victoria. He annexed the Fiji Islands in the Pacific, a step twice rejected by previous ministries.

By these and similar measures Disraeli made himself the exponent and his party the champion of the new, or rather newly revived, doctrine of imperialism. No longer were colonies to be considered fruit ripe to drop from the tree but rather as branches permanently attached to the parent trunk. In 1876, Disraeli moved from the House of Commons to the Lords, and took the title of Earl of Beaconsfield. In his new environment he turned his attention more than ever to foreign affairs. Russia was again on the move, and Disraeli shared Palmerston's tradition of supporting Turkey at all costs against Russia for the sake of the safety of India. Gladstone, on the other hand, saw more in the Balkan troubles than a distant strategic menace to India; his thoughts turned to the millions of Serbs, Bulgars, Greeks, and Armenians who were struggling to be free from Turkish misrule, and, even if Russia should bring armies to their help, he thought Britain should stand aside and give no aid to save the Turk from the doom which his own misdeeds had brought upon him.

Whether the Ottoman Empire was or was not worth supporting against Russia is a question on which statesmen were divided in Crimean War days and again in Disraeli's time, and historians are still debating it. On the answer to that question Disraeli's diplomacy must ultimately be judged. But what is beyond any challenge is the skill with which he carried out his policy, mistaken or not; he wished to avoid war with Russia on the one part and to diminish the results of Russia's victory over Turkey on the other. He achieved both objects. By a firm stand he induced Russia to submit her claims to an international peace congress at Berlin in 1878. At that conference, where his dexterity aroused Bismarck's admiration, he whittled down the Greater Bulgaria which Russia had envisaged, obtained a leasehold over Cyprus for Great Britain, and contented Austria-Hungary by permitting her to occupy and administer the provinces of Bosnia and Herzegovina. Never did his personal prestige stand higher than when amidst cheering crowds he boasted that he had brought back 'peace with honor.' To be sure, there was an ironic postscript to that diplomatic victory. Within the next few years Bulgaria was to annex eastern Rumelia, thus wiping out the strategic frontier which Disraeli had won for Turkey; while Austrian rule in Bosnia, affronting Serb nationalism, was the immediate occasion of the World War of 1914.

Some of the later ventures of the Beaconsfield ministry in imperialism proved unfortunate. One military expedition was defeated by the Zulus in south Africa; another by Afghans just beyond the Indian frontier. An attempt to annex the Boer republic of the Transvaal encountered opposition from some of the Dutch ranchers.[7] Gladstone used these incidents with telling effect in his electioneering campaign in Midlothian, almost the first instance of a British party leader 'stumping the country' in a direct oratorical appeal to the voters. In 1880 the Liberals were triumphantly returned and Gladstone for a second time became Prime Minister.

Gladstone's second administration was far less fruitful and successful than his first had been. His increasing radicalism had cost him the confidence of Queen Victoria, who daily sighed for a return of Lord Beaconsfield, whose wit and tact had made the routine of pub-

[7] For South African affairs see Chapter xxxvi.

lic business a positive pleasure to her. Foreign affairs pressed for attention, and untoward events broke out in remote parts of the empire. Thus Gladstone incurred odium from imperialists by withdrawing from the Transvaal, and from 'little Englanders' and pacifists by intervening in Egypt. His failure to rescue General Gordon in the Egyptian Sudan lost him many friends. But far exceeding all other troubles was the question of Ireland, which dominated the politics of the time.

If Britain has often sinned against Ireland, at all events she has been adequately punished, for in each successive generation the Irish question has perplexed British politics. Ireland was an aid to Spain against Elizabeth's England; a war zone for Cromwell; the last hope for the exiled James II; a military pawn for Louis XIV and for Napoleon; the stumbling block which wrecked the Tory party (over Catholic emancipation) in the 1820s; and the immediate occasion, through the Irish potato famine, of the repeal of protection in Peel's time. Conservative and Liberal ministries alike had to pass coercion bills to restore law and order when Irish tenants refused rent to their landlords and boycotted [8] or shot the landlord's agent or the incoming tenant, and no jury could be found to convict. Gladstone had removed one major Irish grievance by disestablishing the Church. There still remained two unsolved problems, the land question and the issue of national home rule. To many Englishmen, knowing only the surface facts, Ireland had no grievance at all. If most of the Irish were tenants who had to pay rent, why, so were most Englishmen and Scotsmen. If Ireland had no Parliament of her own, neither had Wales or Scotland; and Ireland had more members than her share by population in the common Parliament of the United Kingdom. They did not sufficiently realize that memories of past wrongs and acute present poverty made the average Irishman view his landlord as an alien exploiter and the common government of the United Kingdom as an alien tyranny.

The Irish had found a leader, Charles Stewart Parnell, a Protestant landlord, cold and aloof in manner, the last man whom one would expect to be the leader of the Catholic peasantry. Parnell

---

[8] The very word 'boycott,' now of world-wide application, arose from the refusal of the Irish peasantry to have any dealings with a certain unpopular Captain Boycott.

aimed to steer a middle course between the legal and parliamentary methods of his predecessors in the home-rule movement, Daniel O'Connell and Isaac Butt, and the open rebellion advocated by the Fenians and other radical societies. He would fight the battle in Parliament by building up a strong Irish Nationalist party, pledged to vote against every government and obstruct every debate until Irish claims were granted; outside Parliament he advocated a general refusal to pay rents until they were fairly adjusted. In the meantime serious disorders, amounting to positive anarchy in some districts, were taking place throughout Ireland. In 1882 Lord Frederick Cavendish, the Viceroy of Ireland, and Under-Secretary Burke were assassinated. An attempt was made years later to implicate Parnell as approving the assassination but the evidence was shown to be a forgery.

Gladstone tried to combine conciliation and coercion. He carried a new Irish Land Act, by which rents were judicially fixed at a 'fair' figure—a long departure indeed from individualism and *laissez-faire!* Even this device proved no solution, and the problem of alien landlordism had to be finally solved, under Conservative auspices, by George Wyndham's Land Act of 1903, which provided for the extension of government loans to enable tenants to buy independent holdings.

Aside from the Irish question, the most important measure of Gladstone's second ministry was the extension of the franchise to a large group of voters who had not been included even by Disraeli's generous measure of 1867. Many of these were farm laborers. The franchise reform of 1884 was followed by a fresh redistribution of seats in 1885. Most men now had the vote, but it was not until 1918 that women were granted the suffrage, and then only over the age of thirty; the last step taken, in 1928, gave women the vote on the same terms as men. The Act of 1918 also abolished the privilege of voting in more than one constituency,[9] thus realizing at last the old Radical demand 'one man, one vote,' though 'man' now included 'woman.'

The election of 1885 left Parnell's Nationalists holding the bal-

[9] A minor exception to this rule is the right of certain university graduates to vote for a member of Parliament for their university as well as for their home constituency.

ance of power between Gladstone and the new Conservative leader, the Marquess of Salisbury. Salisbury formed a ministry but proved unable to work with the Irish, so in 1886 Gladstone for the third time took office. The price of power was willingness to introduce a home-rule bill, providing for an Irish Parliament and ministry, which Parnell could endorse. Gladstone's conversion to home rule was somewhat sudden but there is no reason to suppose it merely a pretext to win the Irish vote; after all, Gladstone had a lifelong passion for the rights of small nations, he had already made many concessions to Irish opinion, and there was nothing out of character in his becoming a champion of Irish nationalism. But he could not carry his party with him. Old-fashioned Whigs deserted him at the outset, and even Radicals like John Bright and Joseph Chamberlain opposed his plan. The Liberal party split as disastrously over home rule as the Conservatives had split in Peel's time over free trade; and the analogy holds for yet another step, for just as Gladstone and other Peelite Conservatives eventually joined the Whigs to create the Liberal Parties, so now the Liberal Unionists like Chamberlain became permanent allies of the Conservatives, in a Unionist Party.[10]

The Liberal split over home rule brought in the Conservatives for a long lease of power. From 1886 to 1905 they were continuously in office, save for an interlude of three years (1892-5). Lord Salisbury, like Palmerston and Disraeli, was primarily interested in foreign affairs. On domestic issues he was almost of the old Tory pattern—it is significant that he had opposed Disraeli's Reform Bill of 1867—though he permitted his colleagues to carry through reforms which lay within their special departments. The partition of Africa, in which Great Britain took an ample share, occurred mainly under his administration, and he ended his career by carrying to final, though long delayed, victory the Boer War.[11] In European affairs he aimed to keep the peace and preserve the balance of power. He was less concerned than Disraeli had been about the preservation of the Ottoman Empire, and kept a freer hand in dealing with Near Eastern

[10] This name almost supplanted Conservative for the period 1886 to 1922 while the issue of Irish home rule remained undecided, though Conservative has been since revived.

[11] See Chapters xxxvi, xxxvii.

affairs. On the whole, he preferred Germany to France, since France was a more active rival in Africa, but he was wary of entering into any close alliance with Bismarck. By keeping his temper with President Cleveland in the Venezuela dispute [12] he averted the last possibility of an Anglo-American war.

There was a moment in the 1890s when Irish home rule seemed to have another chance. Parnell and Gladstone were in alliance, the swing of the pendulum seemed likely to bring Gladstone back to power, and, as the Liberal Unionists were already in the Conservative camp, their opposition could no longer cause division within the Liberal ranks. But a personal scandal undid Parnell. He was accused of an illicit love affair with Mrs. O'Shea; the Irish Catholic clergy were shocked, and so were the Puritan nonconformists and evangelicals who formed so large a section of British Liberalism. The Nationalist party split into Parnellite and anti-Parnellite factions, a division which long outlasted the death of the great Irish leader. The election of 1892 brought Gladstone back to office, but hardly to power. His majority depended on the support of the Irish and most of his attention was given to the preparation of a new home-rule bill. This time he put it through the House of Commons but it was rejected by the Lords. Shortly afterwards he resigned, and in 1894 the queen chose the Earl of Rosebery as his successor. Rosebery shelved the issue of Irish home rule until such time as England, 'the predominant member of the partnership of the Three Kingdoms,' became converted to it, a phrase which, like Salisbury's reference to 'the Celtic fringe,' won as little favor in Scotland and Wales as in Ireland. In 1895 Rosebery took advantage of a defeat on a minor issue to resign. The voters returned Lord Salisbury to office with an ample Conservative majority.

The third and last Salisbury ministry was occupied mainly with problems of foreign policy, a dispute with France over the Sudan, the quarrel with the Transvaal and the Orange Free State which culminated in the Boer War, and the Boxer rebellion in China. In 1901, in the midst of war, Queen Victoria died, the great century and the great reign ending almost together. The twentieth century has departed from the old Victorian landmarks in many ways, bring-

[12] See pp. 319-20.

ing in a type of state socialism equally alien to the conservative Tory and the individualistic Radical of the queen's day, and a policy of foreign alliances and understandings alien to the Victorian tradition of national isolation and independence. Something of the Victorian tradition of decorum and respectability also passed with the queen who embodied it; the week-end holiday replaced the Puritan Sabbath, and social customs generally became easier, laxer, and freer from convention.

So many and so great were the changes in British life while Victoria was on the throne that one is at a loss where to begin for even the briefest summary. It was a great age of scientific advance, the new concept of evolution expounded by Charles Darwin, popularized by Thomas Huxley, and developed into a philosophy by Herbert Spencer, revolutionized both biological and theological thought. Scarcely less important was the development of physical science by such British men of genius as Faraday, Kelvin, and Clerk Maxwell. Scientific nursing is associated with the name of Florence Nightingale, as scientific surgery is with that of Lord Lister. The combined effect of many inventions, annihilating time and space, such as the railroad, the telegraph, the cable, the telephone (not all of them, to be sure, wholly British or wholly confined to this period), brought the entire British Empire closer together for purposes of effective administration than were the shires of England a hundred years earlier.

Or one may be more interested in social betterment than in scientific progress; to such a one the Victorian age is that of Livingstone and foreign missions, of Lord Shaftesbury and factory reform, of Edwin Chadwick and municipal provision for public health, of Forster and the beginnings of universal popular education, of Kingsley and the Christian Socialists, of John Stuart Mill and the agitation for women's rights. Never before had humanitarianism made such rapid progress, though much remained to be done in the new century.

Politically the age is interesting in many ways: as a transition from exclusive aristocratic rule to a mixture of upper, middle, and working class influence; as the period of the most perfect balance of the two-party system and of the highest prestige for parliamentary institutions; or as an age of relative diplomatic isolation and of growing interest in overseas colonization, the Empire taking the place of the European Concert in the minds of British statesmen.

The historian remembers that the Victorian age was the heroic age of literary history. It had a Freeman to tell the story of the Norman conquest, a Stubbs to analyze medieval institutions, a Froude to defend Tudor imperialism, a Gardiner to describe the Commonwealth of Cromwell, a Macaulay to vindicate the Whig revolution of 1688, a Seeley to glorify the expansion of empire in the eighteenth century, a Green to popularize the whole story of English national life, and a Carlyle to introduce to the British public the French Revolution and the Prussian monarchy. None of these men were wholly without bias, but they all combined vast learning, literary skill, and a burning sincerity in what they had to say.

It was the great age of prose fiction. The inventive energy of Dickens, the meditative satire of Thackeray, the mundane realism of Trollope, the humane philosophy of George Eliot, the dramatic violence of Charlotte and Emily Brontë, the reflection of social problems in the pages of Kingsley, Disraeli, and Mrs. Gaskell, the intricate psychology of Meredith, the poignant pessimism of Hardy, the optimist call to adventure in Stevenson; even, on a slightly lower level, the reform propaganda of Charles Reade and the historical melodrama of Bulwer-Lytton—take all these from English literature and what a gap is left! The Victorian novelists have been accused of two faults, a tendency to point the moral needlessly in the interest of edification, and a neglect of artistic form. Both charges are largely true, but over against them one must in justice set their four great virtues: fertility, vitality, humanity, and humor.

The Victorian essay was somewhat heavily weighted by its 'message.' None the less Ruskin, Carlyle, and Matthew Arnold could find effective phrases for what they had to say. And the light touch which the essayists lacked was present to perfection in the satiric operas of Gilbert and Sullivan, who almost alone redeem the period from the charge of barrenness in dramatic art.

Victorian poetry, like Victorian prose, always had something definite to say. It may not have reached the intensity of the great romantic poets of the immediately preceding epoch, but it had a wider range of interest. Of the two greatest Victorian poets it may be said that Alfred Tennyson was interested in all subjects and Robert Browning in all men. The religious perplexities of the Age of Darwin are mirrored variously in the reverent skepticism of Tennyson, Clough, and Matthew Arnold, the open paganism of Swinburne and Fitzgerald,[13] the Catholic faith of Francis Thompson, and the courageous, adventurous challenge to the unknown of Browning and Stevenson. Political controversy also played its part. Elizabeth Barrett Browning, the wife of Robert Browning, was concerned for Italy's freedom, Swinburne wanted a world-wide republican revolution, William Morris advocated socialism, and, towards the end of the period, Henley and Rudyard Kipling preached the gospel of imperialism.

[13] Edward Fitzgerald's best-known work, his translation of the *Rubaiyat* of Omar Khayyam, contains more of the translator than of the original poet.

XXXI

BRITAIN AND THE ARMED PEACE

In 1901 King Edward VII (1901-10) succeeded his mother, Queen Victoria, on the throne. In 1902 Arthur Balfour succeeded his uncle, Lord Salisbury, as Prime Minister. During the same year Great Britain broke a long tradition of diplomatic isolation [1] and made a definite military alliance with Japan. With the new century there came new men, new measures, and new problems.

The turning point in British diplomatic history was Germany's decision to build up a formidable fleet. So long as it was a question of 'the elephant *versus* the whale' there was little chance that Britain would become alarmed about Germany, no matter how powerful the German army might be. Nor were Anglo-German relations in general unfriendly. The most widely read historians of the Victorian time, such as Green and Freeman, emphasized the Germanic origin of the English people even to the point of exaggeration. Carlyle had praised Germany's victory over France as the 'hopefullest public fact' of his time. Queen Victoria was always sympathetic with Germany, though she objected to Bismarck's policy in 1864 and 1866 and was even ready to intervene if her ministers had advised this. Gladstone had welcomed German participation in African colonization. With the nation at large, the fact that the Germans and the British were the only two European Great Powers which adhered to the Protestant faith counted for something. Across the North Sea the German liberals were strongly Anglophil, regarding Great Britain as a sort of golden mean between Prussian autocracy and French radical republicanism.

Isolated incidents, it is true, can be cited of Anglo-German fric-

[1] During the Crimean War there was a temporary alliance with France. At all times Britain had an alliance with Portugal, but that was an ancient legacy, not a new departure.

tion even in Bismarck's time. Though British statesmen welcomed in principle German colonial activity, many concrete cases of overlapping and conflicting claims caused difficulty—notably in Samoa, New Guinea, and Southwest Africa. Bismarck had a habit, vexing to British ministries only too well aware of their anomalous position in Egypt, of making difficulties over Egyptian affairs whenever Britain raised objections to German colonization. To some extent he played off Russia against Britain in Balkan politics; thus at the very time when he was blessing the Mediterranean agreements for the *status quo* in the Mediterranean and in the Near East, he was supporting Russian policy in Bulgaria, which threatened that *status quo*. Yet Bismarck's dismissal brought a change for the worse; Wilhelm II, virtually his own Chancellor, played Bismarck's truculent game with a cruder hand, with bluster and without *finesse*. An openly anti-British party, no longer content, as Bismarck had been, with what Germany had already gained, now demanded a remapping of the colonial world to Germany's advantage.

All this is true enough, yet it is impossible to read the periodicals of the '80s and even most of the '90s without being impressed by the fact that for every wakeful hour which Germany caused John Bull, France and Russia caused ten. Far more than Germany, France was the colonial rival of Britain in Africa, and as late as 1898 there was real danger of war between the two countries. Though Britain was not so definitely anti-Russian under Salisbury as under Palmerston and Disraeli, yet there still lingered in the public mind a feeling that if the British Empire had a heel of Achilles it was India, and that Russia, which could reach India by the overland route, was the only real menace in that direction.

At the very end of the nineteenth century a series of events changed the whole perspective of British policy. The German Kaiser's telegram to President Kruger of the Transvaal [2] threatened by implication a German intervention in South Africa. Germany also refused to support British proposals to aid the oppressed Armenians in Turkey. During the Boer War, German press opinion was even more hostile to Britain than that of most European countries, though almost universally throughout the continent sympathy was with the

[2] See Chapter XXXVI.

Boers. In Far Eastern affairs Britain befriended Japan; Russia, France, and Germany were anti-Japanese. In the Spanish-American War, British opinion in general supported the United States; continental European opinion favored Spain. The Russian Government strove to merge the Dual Alliance of Russia and France with the Triple Alliance of Germany, Austria-Hungary, and Italy in a common front against the 'Anglo-Saxons' and Japan during the Boer War, and the German Kaiser renewed the attempt later in the secret treaty of Björkö (1905).

Behind all such particular incidents stood the general problem of naval security. As the only nation at once insular and industrial, Britain was the only one which could be starved out by a naval blockade. Naval supremacy was far more vital in the twentieth century than it had been in the days of Drake, Blake, and Nelson. Then a strong fleet meant merely freedom from invasion; now it meant also security against famine. Germany's decision in 1898 to build a great fleet was certain, therefore, not only to start a dangerous naval race but to cause the British to look abroad for allies.

Yet so recent were the memories of African quarrels with France and of Asiatic and Balkan quarrels with Russia, that the first steps of the British ministry away from isolation were towards association with Germany. Colonial Secretary Chamberlain spoke with enthusiasm of Britain, Germany, and the United States as natural allies. Actually, it is uncertain whether the British or the German governments initiated the negotiations which went on intermittently from 1899 to 1902. They failed partly at least because the German foreign-office expert Holstein thought that better terms could be obtained from Britain at a later date.

On the failure of these negotiations the British Government, in which Lansdowne was Foreign Secretary, looked elsewhere. The Anglo-Japanese alliance of 1902 was restricted to Far Eastern affairs and involved Britain in military obligations only if two Powers joined together against Japan. In the Russo-Japanese War of 1904-5 Britain took no part, though the sinking of some British fishing boats by Russian warships in the North Sea—the 'Dogger Bank incident' of 1904—nearly involved Britain in the war, and might easily have precipitated a general world conflict if British desire for peace had not brought about a peaceful settlement.

The next step was a cordial understanding with France, reached in 1904 by a mutual adjustment of outstanding colonial disputes. France obtained a free hand in Morocco, and accorded Britain similar freedom of action in Egypt. The status of Siam, Madagascar, the New Hebrides Islands in the Pacific, and of sundry colonies in West Africa was better defined, and French fishing rights in Newfoundland waters were definitely settled. There was also a general arbitration treaty, but no formal alliance or military obligation.

Almost immediately after the formation of this *Entente Cordiale* Germany resolved to test its strength. Under the treaty of Madrid, 1880, Germany had certain legal rights in Morocco which the French and British, in their negotiations, had ignored. France had also offended Germany by independent negotiations with Italy, Germany's ally. Germany won a diplomatic victory in getting the whole Moroccan question submitted to an international conference held at Algeçiras in 1906, but while the Algeçiras Conference recognized Germany's interests and confirmed Morocco's independence, it also gave France and Spain joint powers to police the country in the interests of law and order. Even more ominous from the German point of view was the close co-operation between British and French diplomacy; the *Entente Cordiale* had proved its strength and, though no alliance, proved more enduring than many formal alliances.

The substitution of a Liberal for a Conservative ministry at the end of 1905 made little difference to the continuity of British foreign policy. Premiers Campbell-Bannerman and Asquith and Foreign Secretary Grey believed as strongly in the entente with France as its authors, Premier Balfour and Foreign Secretary Lansdowne. Indeed, Grey carried it a step farther by negotiating an agreement with Russia in 1907, recognizing the respective interests of both countries in Tibet, Afghanistan, and Persia. The Triple Entente of France, Russia, and Britain was now complete.

From 1904 to 1914, as again during the 1930s, the peace-loving British public had the unpleasant sensation of sliding irresistibly towards a precipice of war which they could see but might be unable to avoid. Military circles agitated for conscription and for an immense enlargement of the fleet; pacifists urged a general limitation of armaments; alarmists wrote books, plays, and magazine articles dealing with imaginary German invasions of Britain.

In a last attempt to break through thickening clouds of mistrust, Lord Haldane, the Liberal War Minister and an admirer of German culture, went on a personal mission to Germany in February 1912. He discovered that the two governments no longer spoke the same diplomatic language, for while the British Government was willing to pledge itself to non-aggression, the German demanded unconditional British neutrality, in other words a complete abandonment of France and Russia. In the same year Winston Churchill, First Lord of the Admiralty, proposed in vain a naval holiday which would enable both nations to delay expensive warship construction without affecting their relative naval strength. Germany did, however, accept (in fact, if not in form) a ratio of 10 to 16 in battleship construction, and the danger of a superior German fleet was less acute in 1914 than it had been five or six years earlier.

In spite of the growing tension in international affairs, domestic politics overshadowed questions of foreign policy in the popular mind. Prime Minister Balfour had the misfortune to hold office at a time when the long reign of Conservatism was about to come to an end. Difficulties and perplexities thickened around the government. Half of England was angry that the Boer War had taken place at all; all England that it took so long to win it. The importation of indentured coolies into the South African mines at the end of the war gave to the opponents of the ministry a chance to raise the cry of 'Chinese slavery.' An Education Act of 1902, though containing many useful provisions, angered the nonconformists by providing grants out of taxation to Church of England and to Roman Catholic schools. As a climax, the ministry split on the issue of a protective tariff. After half a century of free trade, Joseph Chamberlain had become convinced that protection, or 'tariff reform' as he euphemistically called it,[3] had become necessary both as a weapon against foreign tariffs and as a means towards imperial unity by enabling the British Government to grant preference to colonial products. But Balfour was unconvinced, many Conservatives were frankly for free trade, and the average workingman saw nothing in protection except 'dear bread.'

There were also special causes for the dissatisfaction of the work-

---

[3] In American politics, on the contrary, 'tariff reform' is almost exclusively used in the sense of decreasing rates.

ing class. Social reforms, such as old-age pensions, were long overdue. The Taff Vale railway sued a trade union for civil damages and won its suit, thus endangering the funds of any trade union whose activities in a strike might be judged to have injured the property rights of any private business. The newly launched Labour party, which had elected only 2 members to the House of Commons before the decision of 1900, elected 29 [4] at the next election, in 1906. Trade unionists had become convinced that only by political action could their economic rights be preserved.

In 1905 Balfour resigned, and King Edward appointed the Liberal leader, Sir Henry Campbell-Bannerman, as Prime Minister. An election took place almost immediately, in January 1906, which returned a Liberal majority so overwhelming that it was not dependent on either of the two minor parties, Labour or the Irish Nationalists, though on most issues it could count on the support of both. Never before or since has the Liberal party enjoyed so powerful a mandate from the voters to carry out its program. During the Boer War, indeed, the party had seemed peculiarly weak and ineffective. It had lost its great captain Gladstone, and his would-be successors were at odds on the question of the war and foreign policy generally. Lord Rosebery, Henry H. Asquith, Lord Haldane, and Sir Edward Grey were liberal imperialists who favored a strong navy and army, a traditional 'balance of power' foreign policy, and a vigorous prosecution of the Boer War. Campbell-Bannerman, John Morley, and young David Lloyd George from Wales formed a pro-Boer group who, at the risk of being called unpatriotic, denounced the war as a national sin. The end of the war, however, lessened the Liberal breach on foreign policy, while the Conservative schism on the tariff question grew daily wider.

The Liberal ministry found itself very soon in acute conflict with the House of Lords. The Lords indeed permitted the passage of a Trade Disputes bill, which freed trade unions from the liabilities to civil damage suits asserted in the Taff Vale decision, but they rejected an Education bill and a bill abolishing plural voting. In 1908, with Asquith now as Prime Minister, Parliament passed an old-age pension law and much minor social legislation, but the Lords rejected

---

[4] Not including many trade unionists affiliated with the Liberal party.

a liquor-licensing bill. These repeated rebuffs were very irritating to the Liberal ministers, who commented bitterly on the fact that the House of Lords would pass any Conservative measure but seemed free to reject any Liberal one, no matter how great a majority it might have in the House of Commons. The crisis came in 1909 when the new Chancellor of the Exchequer, David Lloyd George, introduced a budget to cover the new cost of old-age pensions and the increase of the navy. There were increases in the income tax, a higher rate on large incomes (supertax), an increase in the inheritance tax (death duties), new charges on liquor and tobacco, and finally, the most contested point of all, a tax on the increase of land values (unearned increment). Though by long tradition and constitutional custom, not by positive law, the House of Commons was supposed to have sole control over finance bills, the House of Lords rejected the Finance Bill in which the whole budget is incorporated. The Liberals at once appealed to the country, with the election cry, 'The Peers against the People!'

The Liberals won the election of January 1910, but their majority was so greatly diminished that they were now dependent on Labour and Irish votes. The death of Edward VII and the succession of George V (1910-36) in the same year brought about a temporary party truce and prolonged, though futile, negotiations between party leaders in the hope of a solution of the constitutional issue. A second election in December brought no change in relative party strength. The Liberals now insisted on a definite curtailment of the power of the House of Lords, with the threat of the creation of new peers in the background (as in 1832) if the Lords would not agree. Under this threat the Lords gave way, and permitted the Parliament Act of 1911 to become law.

The Parliament Act is one of the most important structural, or constitutional, statutes in British history; indeed of all laws since the revolution of 1688 it has made the greatest change in the form [5] of the British constitution. By its provisions the House of Lords lost all power to reject revenue measures. Other laws could be delayed by the Lords, but if passed in unaltered form by the House of Com-

---

[5] Of course, some other measures, such as the franchise laws of 1832, 1867, and 1884, may have been more important in changing the substance of political power.

mons for three successive sessions and over a period of not less than two years they would then become law. The maximum duration of Parliament between elections to the House of Commons was reduced from seven years to five. Both parties promised a reform of the House of Lords so that it would no longer be so predominantly representative of one class—the landlords—and of one party—the Conservative—but nothing was done about the matter.

That the power still retained by the House of Lords of delaying bills for two years is important is shown by the fate of two major measures of the Liberal ministry. In 1912 the Commons passed a measure disestablishing the Church of England in Wales, on the ground that Wales was mostly nonconformist. The Lords promptly rejected the bill; it was twice repassed, and finally placed on the statute books in 1914; but in the meantime the coming of the First World War postponed its application and it was not finally carried into effect until 1920, and then with some modifications of financial detail. The momentous issue of Irish home rule was even more profoundly affected by opposition from the Lords. The advent of the war not only postponed the coming into effect of the bill in 1914, but, owing to the outbreak of a rebellion in Ireland during the war, resulted in its complete abandonment. A wholly new measure, excluding Protestant Ulster from the jurisdiction of the Irish Parliament, replaced it.[6]

After the titanic struggles over the Lloyd George budget and the Parliament Act, the energies of the Liberal ministry were somewhat exhausted. Their most important positive achievement (after the Parliament Act) in the last years of their power was the National Insurance Act of 1911, modeled somewhat after Bismarck's legislation in Germany, which created a fund paid jointly by the worker, his employer, and the taxpayer for the emergencies of illness (old-age pensions, already established under a statute of 1909, were entirely at taxpayers' cost). The system has been since greatly developed and extended. National Health Insurance has proved to be the greatest benefit in the whole scheme of social reform of 1906-14.

Always in the background of this stirring drama of party politics and social reform there was the growing menace of international war.

[6] See Chapter xxxix for Ireland since the war.

The causes and events leading to the world conflict of 1914-18 cannot be fully told in a book which aspires to trace the history of the English-speaking peoples only, for most of its roots were deep in the soil of continental European politics. Had a tidal wave completely submerged the British Isles in Victoria's time, there is no less likelihood that there would have been a conflict between the continental Powers—though the outcome might well have been different! Franco-German hostility had been chronic ever since the days of Richelieu, and acute since the Franco-Prussian War of 1870; an Austro-Russian war had been conceivable in any year since the Congress of Berlin in 1878, but, as we have noted,[7] Anglo-German rivalry really dates from the last five years of the nineteenth century, and Great Britain was not definitely committed to the cause of France until 1904, or to that of Russia till 1907. Even then the British avoided the forms of an alliance. There was no treaty obligation on the British to go to war for the defense of France.

But it may be argued that there are moral as well as legal obligations. Once Britain and France had entered into military and naval 'conversations,' and the English Channel had been left for the British fleet to guard while France policed the Mediterranean, Britain could not well free herself of the duty to protect the French coast, at least in a defensive war, and France was bound by an alliance to unpredictable Russia. From 1904 onwards it is impossible to discuss British foreign policy without frequent reference to continental rivalries which had nothing directly to do with British interests.

In 1908 a reform party of 'Union and Progress,' commonly nicknamed the 'young Turks,' overthrew the despotism of Sultan Abdul Hamid II and established a constitutional government over the Ottoman Empire. Men of good will all over Europe applauded, but it placed Austria-Hungary in a position of some embarrassment. For thirty years, under the authority of the Congress of Berlin, the Dual Monarchy had administered the affairs of the dual provinces of Turkish Bosnia and Herzegovina. Might not a reformed Turkish Government try to reclaim them? To prevent this, Austria-Hungary annexed the provinces in question. Turkey's anger was brief and easily appeased, as she had long since given up the provinces

---

[7] For Anglo-German rivalry, see pp. 400-404.

for lost; but Russia and Serbia, who had no legal rights there at all, were both deeply angered. Russia wanted 'compensation' for Austrian gains, such, for example, as opening the Straits at Constantinople to Russian trade in wartime as well as in peace; Serbia hoped that when the decrepit Ottoman Empire fell to pieces, Bosnia and Herzegovina, mainly Serb in speech, would fall to her share. Russia retired grumbling in the face of what was virtually a German ultimatum in 1909, while an Austro-Hungarian army mobilization forced Serbia to acquiescence. A Great Power like Russia, jealous of its prestige, rarely gives way twice (in public, anyhow!) on the same issue; the events of 1908-9 made it improbable that in any future conflict of Austrian and Serbian interests Russia would yield.

Morocco, already once a storm center of European diplomacy,[8] became so twice again: in 1908 when a German consul at Casablanca aided German fugitives from the harsh discipline of the French Foreign Legion to escape, and in 1911 when Germany countered a French military occupation of Morocco by sending the German cruiser *Panther* to Agadir. On this occasion David Lloyd George, as Chancellor of the Exchequer and spokesman for the government, declared that 'If a situation were to be forced on us in which peace could only be preserved by the surrender of the great and beneficent position which Britain has won . . . then I say that peace at that price would be a humiliation intolerable for a great country like ours to endure.' This was practically an announcement that Britain would fight on the side of France if war arose. Germany, however, accepted a compromise, giving France a virtually free hand in Moroccan affairs in return for a large slice of the tropical Congo region.

Italy's attack in 1911 on the Turkish dependency of Tripoli (Libya) was the starting point for a new series of Balkan troubles. It encouraged Serbia, Montenegro, Greece, and Bulgaria to launch an attack on the Ottoman Empire to liberate their fellow nationals still under Turkish rule. The First Balkan War of 1912 was a series of defeats for Turkey and ended with the Treaty of London (May 1913) by which the Turks relinquished to the Balkan League all European Turkey except the immediate region of Constantinople and the Straits. Disappointed at her small share of the gains, Bul-

---

[8] For the Algeçiras conference, see above, p. 403.

garia attacked her former allies before the summer was over, and was speedily crushed in the Second Balkan War by a coalition of Serbs, Greeks, and Rumanians, and the Balkan lands were reallotted, much to the advantage of Serbia and Greece, by the Treaty of Bucharest (August 1913).

Though Serbia had won a large amount of land in Macedonia, she remained land-locked, for Albania had been erected into an independent kingdom between Serbia and the Adriatic, thus depriving Serbia of an anticipated seacoast. For this, the Serbs blamed Austrian diplomacy. The Austro-Hungarians, on their part, were alarmed at the growing Yugoslav (southern Slav) agitation, which would tear from the Empire not only Bosnia and Herzegovina but Dalmatia, Croatia-Slavonia, and other provinces. In 1913 the Austro-Hungarian Government had gone so far as to sound out Germany and Italy regarding the expediency of an attack on Serbia, but they advised against it.

On 28 June 1914, a Bosnian fanatic assassinated the heir to the joint thrones of Austria and Hungary, Archduke Franz Ferdinand, nephew of the reigning Emperor, at Sarajevo. The Austro-Hungarian authorities believed that this murderous blow was but a manifestation of a widespread conspiracy on both sides of the border, involving high officials of the Serbian Government. Securing the assent of Germany to vigorous measures on 5 July, the Austro-Hungarian authorities prepared an ultimatum to present to Serbia, which was presented on 23 August. The next twelve days were perhaps the most crowded and chaotic period in European diplomatic history. Probably no European civil government (as distinguished from some military chiefs) wanted a general European war, and all foreign offices except that of Austria-Hungary sought, with greater or less sincerity and persistence, some solution that would avoid even a Balkan conflict; and yet war came.

Crises almost as serious had been more than once peacefully bridged over in past years. The peculiar menace of the Sarajevo crisis was that it occurred at a time when European international relations were electric with tension. Austria-Hungary felt it a life-and-death matter to stamp out the Yugoslav propaganda, and rejected a

Serbian reply which seemed satisfactory even to the German Kaiser:
declaring war as soon as the time limit of the ultimatum expired.
Russia felt that a second diplomatic defeat in the Balkan region, following upon that of 1908-9, would end all her influence over the
small states of southeastern Europe and surrender that whole region
to German and Austrian domination. Germany, with no sure ally
in the world but Austria-Hungary (for Italy was already inclining
to the other camp), felt it necessary to support any demand of her
ally in public, whatever misgivings German statesmen might feel
in private. In vain the German Ambassador to Britain, Count Lich-
nowsky, warned his government that the enmity of Russia and
Britain was more to be feared than that of a divided and decadent
Power like Austria-Hungary. France saw no alternative but loyalty
to her defensive alliance with Russia. Italy alone of the continental
Great Powers found a loophole of escape from the net of treaty obligations, and, declaring that the war against Serbia was not a defensive one, remained neutral, though for half a year longer still
nominally a member of the Triple Alliance.

Great Britain exercised her influence to moderate and reconcile
the opposed governments. No one now questions that Sir Edward
Grey wished for peace in 1914, though many still criticize his methods of securing it. Some say that the British Foreign Secretary should
either have made definite promises of aid to France, which might
have stopped Austria and Germany in time, or else have proclaimed
complete neutrality, which would have forced Russia and France to
make their peace with Germany; such critics forget, perhaps, that
Grey had to reckon with a shifting public opinion, even within the
cabinet itself, and that a premature stand for either peace or war
might have had to be retracted a few days later as conditions and
popular sentiment changed. A juster criticism of Grey's policy is that
he hardly realized the extent to which his own past diplomacy had
involved Britain in continental affairs. He reiterated that Britain
had no formal treaties of alliance with France or Russia (though in
1912 the British and French governments had agreed to consult
together in future crises), but the total diplomatic situation by 1914
had reached such a phase that every Frenchman felt that he had a
right to count on British assistance.

Using Russian mobilization as a ground for action, Germany declared war on Russia and France and proceeded to invade France by way of neutral Belgium and Luxemburg, in accord with long-prepared military plans. This put an end to British hesitation. Britain, Germany (through the transferred obligations of the Kingdom of Prussia), and most of the other European Powers had in 1839 guaranteed Belgian neutrality. But safety as well as honor was at stake. Great Britain has always regarded the low countries (Holland, Belgium, Luxemburg) as a first line of defense, which must not be permitted to fall into the hands of any powerful and aggressive foreign state. Thus, equally to honor an ancient pledge and to secure herself against an obvious danger, Britain went to war.

It was tragic indeed that the German Empire and the British Commonwealth, both of them exceptionally tenacious and resolute peoples, should for the first (though not the last) time in history have confronted each other in a general war. It is not the least of this tragedy that no direct quarrel at the time would probably have led them to fight each other. The naval race was less acute in 1914 than it had been several years earlier. The colonial problem had been eased by a compromise over the Berlin-Bagdad Railway project and by British assurances that if Portugal's African colonies should come on the market Germany would be able to purchase a large share without British opposition.

Nor should too much be made of trade rivalries. Germany was a keen competitor of Britain in various world markets, but also a good customer for British wares; in fact, within a few years after the war the British favored lenient treatment of the vanquished in the hope that the restoration of German prosperity might help in restoring British trade. The United States was also a growing rival to British commerce and yet Anglo-American relations improved steadily throughout the whole period of Anglo-German tension.

No traditional feud, no ancestral quarrel, underlay British policy in 1914, or any hope for territorial gain or commercial advantage. The British had simply felt themselves, rightly or wrongly, menaced by the German fleet and by the aggressive turn of German policy under Wilhelm II. To meet this supposed peril they had aligned themselves with Germany's foes on the continent, and thus assumed moral obligations which in 1914 involved them in war. The spark kindled at Sarajevo, in a remote corner of the Balkans, became a world conflagration involving the British Empire, and eventually even isolated America, but the British were not to be numbered among those who struck the spark or those who fanned it into a flame.

PART VI

THE SECOND BRITISH EMPIRE

THE BRITISH EMPIRE AFTER THE AMERICAN
REVOLUTION

By the American Revolution, 1775-83, Great Britain lost the bulk
of her first Empire, though Great Britain still held many possessions overseas: French-speaking Canada, Nova Scotia, Newfoundland, sundry islands in the West Indies, a few trading posts in
Africa and central America, a few naval bases such as Gibraltar and
St. Helena. The East India Company directed the affairs of Bengal,
Madras, and Bombay in India and had great influence among the
native princes.[1] Captain Cook had laid a basis for later English colonization of Australia by his discoveries, though actual settlement
had not begun. In western Canada, a region then almost unexplored,
Great Britain had extensive claims, though practically the only white
settlers were the trappers and officials of the Hudson Bay Fur Company. 'In all the oversea possessions of Great Britain at the end of
the American Revolution, the white population was not more than
170,000, more than half of whom were French Canadians.'[2] This
was less than a tenth of the white, English-speaking population in
the lost thirteen colonies.

The year 1783 terminated the First British Empire in another
sense. Not only had Great Britain lost her best colonies, but the
principles of the old colonial system were now widely challenged.
Economists and statesmen increasingly denied that colonies were, or
ever could be, a source of profit; and up to that time colonization had
been advocated chiefly on the argument of profit. Adam Smith and
others denied that monopolies imposed by the parent country on its
dependencies could force trade into profitable channels. Josiah
Tucker, Dean of Gloucester, was typical of the new attitude. He

[1] For India, see Chapter XXXIII.
[2] E. Porritt, *Evolution of the Dominion of Canada* (1920), p. 60.

urged that colonial empire and commercial prosperity were independent of each other, and that 'if this defeat should terminate in a total separation from America, it would be one of the happiest events that has ever happened to Great Britain.' His view seemed to be proved sound by the undeniable fact that British commerce with the United States flourished more than had commerce with the colonies before the Revolution. As one American pamphlet of 1786 put the matter:

England, unable to conquer America with an army of soldiers, was now able to conquer her with an army of traders. So great a number of clerks had poured in from Great Britain and had found employment in the stores of the large towns, that the sons of citizens had no chance to be brought up to trade.

Probably this new commercial approach would have been carried even farther had it not been for some lingering relics of the old protectionist and mercantilist ideas. Thus when Lord Shelburne, who had negotiated the peace treaties between Great Britain and her former colonies, contemplated a free-trade treaty with the United States, a certain misguided Lord Sheffield agitated against the proposal and defeated it. Shipping of the United States was excluded from the British West Indies and placed, in British ports, under the same restrictions as the ships of any other foreign nation. The states of the United States had not yet made their Federal Constitution, but the restrictive commercial policy of the British Government drove them closer to union. 'The futile efforts of the states to retaliate separately showed them that a stronger Federal union was necessary. It is time that Lord Sheffield should be accorded his due as a prime mover of the Federal Constitution.'[3] Not until 1938 was a wide trade agreement negotiated between Great Britain and the United States, on the proposal of Secretary of State Cordell Hull, and it was not nearly as comprehensive an agreement as might have been possible in 1783.

Although the government and the people took a pessimistic view of the still existing colonies, they did not abandon them. Canada was convenient as a place of settlement for United Empire Loyalist

[3] S. E. Morison, *History of the United States* (1927), I, 52.

refugees from the United States,[4] and Australia for the dumping of convicts from British jails.[5] The West Indies still produced sugar. India was still a good market for British merchandise. The lesser colonies were convenient naval bases and ports of call. There were questions of prestige to be considered; every government that has ever existed has felt some sentimental regret at hauling down the national flag from any territory where it has once been raised. Finally, official positions in the colonies had become a vested interest for members of the aristocracy who were considered eligible to such posts.

None of these factors weighed at all with the 'philosophical radicals' who were in the vanguard of the anti-imperialist movement. Jeremy Bentham urged the French, during their Revolution, to abandon their few remaining colonies entirely, and expressed the hope that Britain would then follow so excellent an example. *The Edinburgh Review,* then a Whig opposition periodical, asked in 1803 what the British intended to do when their Australian colony of New South Wales grew up. 'Are we to spend another hundred of millions of money in discovering its strength and to humble ourselves again before a fresh set of Washingtons and Franklins?'[6] From the time of the American Revolution till the middle of the nineteenth century an active agitation against colonial expansion was one of the common characteristics of liberal and radical British politics, and even the Tories, who had succeeded to the Whigs of Marlborough's and Chatham's generations as the party of militarism and imperialism, defended colonial empire, if at all, rather on political and military than on economic grounds.

The naval successes of the wars against Napoleon, however, brought into British hands a large number of French, Dutch, and Spanish colonies. Some of the most valuable of these, such as Java, were returned to their former owners. But numerous additions were made, none the less, to the British possessions overseas: Cape Colony in southern Africa, Ceylon off the coast of India, and part of Guiana in South America from the Dutch; Tobago and St. Lucia in the

[4] See Chapter xxxiv.
[5] See Chapter xxxv.
[6] See Manning, *British Colonial Policy after the American Revolution* (1933), p. 6.

West Indies and Mauritius in the Indian Ocean from France; Helgoland, Malta, and the Ionian Islands as European naval bases. Of these acquisitions, only Cape Colony was to prove of outstanding importance, and that importance was little understood in 1815 when the Cape of Good Hope was considered merely a port of call on the trade routes to India and the Far East. But the British hold on India had become firmer, and the development of Australia greatly extended during the period of European conflict. The ascendancy at sea, which Nelson's victories had assured, had laid all the world open to British maritime enterprise, and also enabled the British to prevent, if they so wished, any colonization overseas by any other country.

Still, the colonial impulse was not strong. Napoleon himself expressed wonder that the British had not taken more territory after the war, as they very easily might have done. Some new events weakened yet further the desire for expansion. Spain's mainland American colonies revolted and set up as separate republics with constitutions modeled after that of the United States. Brazil drifted away from Portugal, as a separate Empire. These occurrences seemed to confirm the lesson of the American Revolution that when colonies mature they cannot be retained. A certain tendency to find consolation for the assumed inevitable political loss of overseas colonies in continuing cultural ties found expression among many early Victorian writers. Thus Bulwer-Lytton: 'And when the day shall come (as to all healthful colonies it must come sooner or later) in which the settlement has grown an independent state, we may thereby have laid the seeds of a constitution and a civilization similar to our own.'[7]

This view of colonial enterprise is similar to that of the early Greeks, who would send out to some distant land, such as Sicily, emigrants from a Hellenic city to found a new and completely independent settlement; it is in contrast with Roman colonial policy, which made the new settlement a political extension of Rome.

The abolition of colonial slavery in 1833 aroused fierce discontent among the Dutch farmers in Cape Colony and the British planters in the West Indies,[8] a discontent that would probably have resulted in wars of secession had the disaffected colonists possessed

---

[7] *The Caxtons*, Part xii, Chapter 7.
[8] See Chapters xxxvi and xxxvii.

the numbers and strength of the slave states of the United States of America. It also further reduced the profitableness of the not very prosperous sugar plantations. Compensation had been paid to slave owners, but the amount so paid was inadequate in the opinion of the planters, and in any case did not solve the labor problem. An even heavier blow to the West Indies was the adoption of a free-trade policy by the British Government; the loss of preference in the British market subjected the planters to competition from foreign sugar growers. Thus two enlightened and liberal policies, emancipation and freedom of trade, both proved injurious to the peculiar economic system of the West Indies which had grown up under slavery and monopoly. 'What of it?' said the typical British liberal. 'If these colonies cannot stand free competition and free labor, why should we sacrifice the British consumer's interests to those of the colonial planter?'

It cannot be said that there was much immediate effect of the American Revolution on the methods of colonial government. Down to the Canadian rebellion of 1837,[9] the various parts of British North America were governed in very much the same way that the thirteen colonies had been. Governors, appointed on grounds of party spoilsmanship—though sometimes an able man was accidentally chosen by this system—enjoyed independent authority; while the Colonial Office (itself for a long period attached to some other office, such as the Secretary of State for War) exercised a distant and negligent paternalism. It should be remembered, however, that the British population of the entire colonial empire long remained extremely small as compared with that of Great Britain. Canada was still largely French, though there was a growing British element; Cape Colony mostly Dutch or native African; the West Indies chiefly Negro or mulatto.

One of the first signs of a reviving interest in colonial affairs was the propaganda of Edward Gibbon Wakefield, a man eccentric even among empire builders, who first became interested in colonial administration when serving a term in prison. He favored a deliberate and systematic policy of settling new lands, instead of relying on chance and accident. Land was to be sold at a good price, to bring capital into the colonies; high-class laborers were to be induced to

[9] For the evolution of responsible government in Canada, see Chapter xxxiv.

emigrate, in place of paupers, criminals, and human driftwood; government was to be left to local settlers instead of being managed by distant British officials. These ideas found many eminent Britons to support them, even in the ranks of the philosophical radicals who had so long opposed any colonial acquisitions at all. Wakefield's *Art of Colonization*, published in 1849, had perhaps a greater influence than any other book in this field until Sir John Seeley published his *Expansion of England* in 1883. His National Colonization Society of 1830 encouraged emigration, especially in Australia and, later, in New Zealand (1840).

During the later years of Queen Victoria's long reign the sentiment for imperial expansion rose rapidly. Before the nineteenth century was ended an enlarged British Empire had been created, vaster in extent than any empire hitherto known. It included practically the whole of the great sub-continent of India, for the British Crown had taken over the responsibilities of the East India Company; about a third of Africa, about half of North America, the whole of Australia and New Zealand, and, for the use of the navy and the merchant marine, naval bases, harbors, ports of call, and coaling stations in every continent, every ocean, and every important island group the world around. One man in four was a British subject; one acre in four British territory.

The 'new imperialism' was not exclusively British. Before 1763 Great Britain had to meet keen competition from the French and the Spanish and, in lesser degree, from the Dutch and Portuguese. From 1763 to about 1880 the British had very little competition from any quarter in active colonization, which may have been one reason for the relative relaxation of their effort in this direction. But during the last two decades of the nineteenth century and the first fourteen years of the twentieth, there was again the stimulus of competition. France was building up a new empire in Africa, Indo-China, and the South Seas to compensate not only for the one she lost in the eighteenth century but for the recent humiliation of the Franco-Prussian War. King Leopold II of the Belgians seized the opportunity of the Congo Free State and transformed central Africa into his private rubber plantation. Bismarck, no enthusiast for colonial enterprise personally, was reluctantly persuaded that Germany needed a place in the tropical sun and in consequence seized four parts of Africa and sundry islands in the Pacific; his successors regretted that he had taken so little. Italy gained Eritrea, Somaliland, and Tripoli (Libya), besides making an unsuccessful attempt to conquer Abyssinia (Ethiopia). Portugal pushed her coastal settlements in Africa farther into the interior. Russia was ambitious in the Balkans, in Persia, in central Asia, in Manchuria and Korea; Japan was her rival in the Far East and inflicted military defeats on both China and Russia. The United States acquired the Philippines, Hawaii, and other islands in the Pacific; Puerto Rico, the Panama Canal Zone, and, later, the Virgin Islands in the Caribbean.

There were many causes for this new colonial race. Expanding commerce demanded new markets; expanding industry, new sources of raw materials. Steamships, railroads, cables, telegraphs, and telephones made it possible to administer central Africa or the Fiji Islands more easily than George II and his ministers could administer the Scottish Highlands. The advance in scientific hygiene made it possible for white men to live in the tropics for years at a time. Many of the worst tropical scourges, such as malaria and yellow fever, could now be kept within bounds. Europe enjoyed a period of internal peace from 1871 to 1914 unprecedented in history; it could turn attention outwards to imperial expansion in other parts of the world. The wars of the period were either colonial wars (such as those in Manchuria, Cuba, and South Africa) or struggles in the half-civilized Balkans, almost a colonial area in itself.

In some respects the new imperialism was more humane and enlightened than the old. It did not rest on slavery. Forced labor existed under disguised forms (for example, in the Congo) and 'free contract' often was but a polite mask for economic oppression; but the actual buying and selling of human flesh had disappeared from the market.[10] There was much missionary activity, and whatever the blunders of ill-informed missionaries may have been, they were at least in intention always the friends of the native. David Livingstone, the Scottish explorer-missionary, did much to put down native slavery in Africa; later missionaries exposed abuses in the Congo Free State. Some provision, however inadequate, was made in most colonies for the education and social welfare of native peoples. Abso-

[10] Slavery still exists in out-of-the-way corners of Africa and Asia, but it is nowhere openly countenanced by colonizing Powers.

lute commercial monopolies were no longer considered expedient; though, with the exception of the British, most colonizing nations tried to maintain a protective policy to favor their own merchants against foreigners, none went so far in their restrictions as all the colonial powers had done in the seventeenth century.

Another difference between the old imperialism and the new was the closer tie between imperial enterprise and national patriotic sentiment. With some exceptions, the colonizing powers of the sixteenth to the eighteenth century had considered colonies primarily as commercial investments. A tiny island that returned dividends was valued more highly than half a continent that showed no immediate profit. That was why when colonies ceased to 'pay' so many favored abandoning them altogether. But now there was an ardent expectation that colonization meant a new Britain or a new Germany or a new Italy beyond the seas, where under the old flag countless generations would trade and labor and fight, if need be, in common with the motherland. Alfred Tennyson's ironic rebuke to those who said that Canada was not worth keeping is typical of the new spirit:

> So loyal is too costly,
> Friends, your love is but a burthen,
> Loose the bonds and go!

Some poets, such as William E. Henley and Rudyard Kipling, made the glories of the British Empire their main theme.[11]

The great service of Benjamin Disraeli, the Earl of Beaconsfield, to British imperialism was to dramatize it. Sudden, brilliant strokes of policy, such as the purchase of the Suez Canal shares of the Khedive of Egypt, the addition of 'Empress of India' to the titles of Queen Victoria, the annexation of the Fiji Islands and of Cyprus,[12] made many Britons for the first time conscious of their imperial responsibilities. Some of his ventures were, to be sure, less happy, such as his unsuccessful attempts to add Afghanistan and the Trans-

---

[11] There were anti-imperialist poets, too, such as Wilfrid Scawen Blunt, who replied to Kipling's *The White Man's Burden:*

> . . . 'Trash!
> The white man's burden, Lord, is the burden of his cash!'

[12] Technically, Cyprus was merely leased to Great Britain by Turkey; practically it was under British administration.

vaal to the British Empire, and caused the nation to turn temporarily to the anti-imperialist Gladstone. But Gladstone himself felt
constrained to protect British interests in Egypt by armed intervention; and more complained of his abandoning the Sudan than of his
occupying Egypt.[13] The Conservatives under Lord Salisbury annexed a large part of Africa, including the former Boer Republics
of the Transvaal and the Orange Free State.[14] Joseph Chamberlain,
as Colonial Secretary, staked his political career on an unsuccessful
effort to persuade Great Britain to agree to a policy of protective
tariffs against the outside world and free trade within the Empire.
Queen Victoria became a keen imperialist and expansionist, and two
great Imperial Jubilees held to honor her fiftieth and sixtieth years
on the throne (1887, 1897) gathered together representatives of
every part of her far-flung empire.

Indeed, out of these Jubilees grew the custom of holding periodic
colonial conferences, in 1887, 1894, 1897, 1902, 1907, and 1911,
to discuss matters of common interest, such as tariffs, navies, defense
generally, and the possibilities of imperial federation. Very little of
a concrete character was accomplished. The colonial conferences were
renamed Imperial Conferences and provision made for their meeting at short intervals. Many specific problems were discussed, and
some adjusted. But no general plan of imperial government, defense,
or tariffs was approved. Most of the Dominions[15] seemed to prefer
local autonomy to a share in any super-government of the Empire.
They made generous contributions to the navy, but refused to assume
any binding obligations in the matter. They granted, in several cases,
preference to British over foreign goods, but insisted on their right
to protect local industries from all competition. The British public
was unwilling to abandon the free-trade policy followed ever since
the 1840s in order to give preference in turn to colonial imports.

In spite of the efforts of many enthusiasts, no logical pattern of
government had been worked out for the British Empire by 1914.
The visible ties of unity were so few and tenuous that foreign critics
commonly expected the fabric to fall asunder under the shock of

[13] See Chapter XXXVII.
[14] See Chapter XXXVI.
[15] New Zealand, on occasion, urged Imperial Federation, but the larger Dominions hesitated.

war. Broadly speaking, the Empire [16] fell into four main divisions: the United Kingdom of Great Britain and Ireland; the Indian Empire; the Dominions; and the Crown Colonies. They all alike had a common ruler, though he went by the title of King in most parts of his realm and that of Emperor in India. Usually the King-Emperor was represented by a Viceroy, Governor-General, or Governor in each unit of the Empire. Judicial appeals, on matters of imperial interest and importance, could be carried to the Judicial Committee of the Privy Council, which was thus a sort of Supreme Court for such affairs. Theoretically, the British Parliament was also an Imperial Parliament able to legislate for the whole Empire or any portion of it, but in practice this power had been tacitly relinquished for the Dominions.[17] There was no common currency, tariff, legal system, or right of citizenship to bind the Empire together. The real links of union were invisible: sentiment, common interests, and need for the protection of the British fleet. The First World War showed that these ties sufficed.

The difference between a Dominion and a Crown Colony lay in the degree of self-government enjoyed. Canada, Newfoundland, Australia, New Zealand, and South Africa shared with the United Kingdom the institution of responsible government, which meant that the voters controlled executive as well as legislative policy. Each Dominion made its own laws, levied its own taxes (including tariffs), determined whom it would admit as an immigrant and what active share (if any) it would take in British wars. Its governor had as much power, and no more, as the king in Great Britain and Ireland: the right to appoint a ministry, but always subject to the proviso that it be a ministry acceptable to the parliamentary majority; the right 'to be consulted, to advise and to warn'; the right to be the formal and ceremonial agency through which the ministry acts, and whose name and authority give it the legal right to act. But questions of policy are the responsibility of the ministry.

[16] Even the phrase 'British Empire' was not strictly official, though it was common in popular usage. Since the First World War the new term 'British Commonwealth' is more favored.

[17] Some nominal powers which the home government still possessed in 1914 have since been abandoned. See Chapter xxxix.

Every overseas Dominion [18] was once a Crown Colony, or a group of such colonies. It would be incorrect to say that these colonies are not in general self-governing, though none of them have the plenitude of power enjoyed by the Dominions. In most Crown Colonies there are legislative bodies, elected either in whole or in part by the people; but the governor is more than a symbol of rule, he is expected to wield actual executive authority. In a very few cases only, such as the rock fortress of Gibraltar, there is no popular representation. The vast Indian Empire, though administered entirely apart from the Colonial Office, resembles the average Crown Colony in being partly self-governing and partly administered by appointed British officials.[19]

There were also a number of curious and interesting fragments of the British Empire which could not accurately be grouped under any of these four main heads of United Kingdom, India, Dominions, and Crown Colonies. Within the British Isles themselves the Isle of Man and the Channel Islands had local legislatures with centuries of history behind them. There were sundry Protectorates, such as the native States in India and in the Malay Peninsula. There were districts, such as Rhodesia in South Africa and North Borneo in the East Indies, administered by Chartered Companies. There were 'leaseholds,' such as Cyprus in the Mediterranean and Wei-hai-wei in China. There were areas held by joint tenure, such as the Sudan, administered by both Egypt and Great Britain,[20] and the New Hebrides Islands, administered by both France and Great Britain. Samoa, for a time, was protected by three Powers: Germany, Britain, and the United States. There was the strange case of Egypt, nominally a dependency of Turkey, practically a dependency of Great Britain. There was the still stranger instance of Sarawak, a part of Borneo ruled by a hereditary line of sovereigns of the Brooke family, a local British 'dynasty.' There were spheres of influence, as in Afghanistan and southern Persia, which, strictly speaking, were not within the British Empire at all, however great British influence there might be. Since the First World War still another type of tenure has come

[18] Ireland was not yet a Dominion in 1914, but an integral part of the United Kingdom.

[19] For India see Chapter xxxiii.

[20] For Egypt and the Sudan see Chapter xxxvii.

into existence, the mandated territory responsible to the League of Nations.[21]

Probably never in human history, even in the Holy Roman Empire of the Middle Ages, has any political system existed so intricate and complex as the British Empire. At the margins it faded away into a twilight zone which might be called either British or non-British as one chose to define the terms. Just as it would be hard for the political scientist of six centuries ago to say with absolute certainty whether at a given moment Poland, Burgundy, and Milan were inside or outside the Holy Roman Empire, so in 1914 one might be similarly puzzled to place Cyprus, Egypt, the Sudan, and the New Hebrides in their relation to the British Empire. This ambiguity was not without dangers. The shadowy suzerainty claimed, but not exercised, in the nineteenth century over the Transvaal led eventually to the Boer War; the paramount British authority exercised, but not claimed, in Egypt led to bitter controversies with France; the triple protectorate over Samoa almost brought on a conflict with Germany. A little more logic might have done the Second British Empire no harm.

But it is only fair to point out that the unique flexibility of the British system had its advantages as well. It gave the Dominions what they wanted—autonomy—without imposing on them imperial responsibilities. It enabled each Crown Colony to have whatever degree of home rule the local situation demanded, without following any such uniform pattern as the territorial system of the United States. It saved the face of proud Hindu and Malayan rulers, who had to follow the 'advice' of British officials, but kept their crowns and thrones. It permitted an almost infinite variety of political experiment and adjustment, so that when a blunder was made it could the more easily be unmade. Indeed, the failures of British rule, as in Ireland, had occurred at those few points where the imperial system had failed to show its wonted adaptability to local conditions.

[21] See Chapters xxxviii and xxxix.

INDIA: CHARTERED COMPANY AND EMPIRE

INDIA is not a nation. It is the general name for a vast sub-continent, almost three times as populous as the United States and eight times as populous as Great Britain, containing scores of races, languages, religions, and nationalities. India is not a colony. It is in part a special dependency of the British Crown, known as British India, and in part a series of native states, more than five hundred in number, under British protection. At no time has India been reckoned a colony or been subject to the jurisdiction of the Colonial Office; and the Indian Civil Service is a distinct body apart from the colonial service generally. If the Indian Empire be considered as a unit, it is the largest dependent state in the world; the greatest extant example of all the problems, advantages, and drawbacks of imperialism. If Japan, let us say, were to undertake the management of the whole of Europe, the task would be scarcely more difficult and intricate than British rule in India. The fact that in recent years partial home rule has been extended to British India has made the problem more complex, rather than simpler, for the hardest task which can confront any government is to rule a heterogeneous group of alien people, whose conflicting aspirations must in great degree be somehow satisfied by the ruler. Sheer autocracy, which does not have to give an account of itself to the governed; and democracy, which turns over all responsibility to them, are both easier tasks.

Yet this tremendous political fact of the Indian Empire came into existence merely as the by-product of a private trading venture. The East India Company, incorporated by royal charter of Queen Elizabeth in 1600, began as a 'regulated' company, which merely conferred on its members the right to participate in the monopoly of trade granted by charter to the Company. Within a few years it was converted into a joint stock company; the traders thenceforth were its paid officials, and its profits were annually divided among its shareholders. The history of British India is a romance as remarkable as that of Spanish America, but it is of a different character. It was, in its initial stages, less military; or, rather, for the first 140 years not military at all. Englishmen went to India only for trade. Thus a 'factory,' which meant not a place of manufacture but a trading post for the Company's 'factors' or agents, was acquired by the year 1608 at Surat on the west coast near Bombay. Bombay itself came into British hands as part of the dowry of Catherine of Braganza, the Portuguese princess who married King Charles II. Other factories were maintained at Madras and Calcutta, with a few armed guards.

Thus matters might have stayed indefinitely had India possessed a strong central government. But for India these were years of political disintegration. The strong Mogul Empire had begun to break down into a kind of feudal anarchy, not unlike the collapse of Charlemagne's Empire in Europe of the early Middle Ages. Local viceroys—nawabs, nizams, rajahs, maharajahs, and the rest—became practically independent sovereigns, with consequent disputed successions and civil wars. There was a French East India Company operating like the English Company from depots on the coast of India. Gradually the two companies were drawn into, or began to take part in, Indian politics. When in 1740 the War of the Austrian Succession [1] drew France and Britain into a struggle in Europe and on the high seas and in America it was inevitable that India, too, would become involved.

The French had been the first to see the advantage of native political support for the commercial penetration of India. Joseph Dupleix made alliances with various princes in return for support against the English traders. The French under Admiral La Bourdonnais captured Madras, though they returned it to the English by the Treaty of Aix-la-Chapelle in 1748. Fortunately for the British, at this critical juncture the East India Company had in its employ a poor young 'writer' or clerk named Robert Clive, whose loneliness and melancholy were driving him desperate. He had already fought a duel and tried to commit suicide. Now he transferred to the mili-

[1] See Chapters xv and xviii for other aspects of these wars.

tary side of the Company's forces, and proved to be one of the boy geniuses, such as Alexander, who sometimes appear in military history. He captured the city of Arcot and held it against a prolonged siege, at once bringing him into prominence as the ablest among many able officers in the Company's service.

The Seven Years' War was the foundation for British political power, as distinct from trade, in India. Until then the East India Company had been merely a commercial corporation, though it had been forced to engage in politics and war to defend its interests against French rivals and native rajahs. But in 1756 the ill will between Surajah Dowlah and the English traders at Fort William near Calcutta had led to the capture of the English factory and the tragedy of the Black Hole of Calcutta, a military jail 18 feet square where of 146 British prisoners only 23 survived, the rest having been stifled to death by the heat of an Indian June night. The answer to this atrocity was an expedition by Clive from Madras to Bengal. In 1757 at Plassey, not far from Calcutta, Clive defeated a huge native force equipped with some French artillery.

This victory made the British masters of all the populous province of Bengal. Though Mir Jafar, who had deserted Surajah Dowlah at Plassey, succeeded him as Nawab of Bengal, Clive was the real power behind the throne. Eventually the East India Company assumed the *diwani*, or right to collect and administer the Bengalese revenues. Other victories in southern India made the Company secure against the French, who remained after the Treaty of Paris in 1763 only as traders.

Clive's life ended in tragedy. He had conquered an empire and had striven manfully to curb abuses in the Company's administration, but he had built up an enormous private fortune from the gifts and bribes of native princes and a parliamentary inquiry into his conduct brought on a return of his old suicidal melancholy. Though the House of Commons coupled a mild rebuke with a generous resolution that 'Robert Clive rendered great and meritorious services to his country,' he committed suicide in 1774.

Step by step the Company's power grew. The conditions which led to the taking over of the administration of Bengal—rivalry among native princes, confusion between the Company's authority and that of the princes, famines, lapses of government into anarchy—were paralleled in the presidencies of Madras and Bombay, and with the same result, the assumption of political responsibilities. The process was hastened by wars between the Company and certain powerful Indian rulers, such as the Mahratta confederacy which threatened the existence of British power in Bombay, and Haidar Ali of Mysore who all but conquered Madras. After two wars against the British in which Haidar Ali gained signal success, he died in 1782, saying according to report, 'I can conquer the land, but I cannot dry up the sea.' This saying, whether authentic or not, was certainly the moral of Britain's eighteenth-century wars. By the possession of sea power, the British could always reinforce their garrisons, whether in Asia or in America, while the French and their native allies could be cut off from European support by British cruisers.

Governor-General Warren Hastings, whose services to British dominion in India were scarcely less than Clive's, like Clive became an object of parliamentary censure and on more serious charges. He was impeached and brought to trial in 1788 and was not finally acquitted till 1795. The greatest orators of the age, Burke, Sheridan, and Fox, were among his accusers, and so moving was their eloquence that millions of people believed Hastings the greatest villain in British history. He had, indeed, been guilty of acts of extortion and of the very dubious practice of lending out British soldiers to fight in native wars for financial gain, but modern historians believe that he prevented more acts of dishonesty than he committed. The real villain in the piece was no single man, but a vicious system of administration which turned over the rule of millions of subjects to a profit-making private Company.[2]

Fortunately these abuses led to reforms. In 1783 Fox, the Whig leader, brought forward an India Bill to take political power and patronage away from the East India Company. It failed, but William Pitt the younger, leader of the Tories, carried a compromise measure in 1784, which reduced the East India Company to something like the status of a nationally regulated public-service corpora-

---

[2] During this period many wealthy agents of the Company came back to spend their money in Great Britain. They were nicknamed 'nabobs,' from the native title of *nawab*. A fault of the system which had momentous consequences was the tea duty levied to aid the Company, which led to the first conflicts of the American Revolution. See Chapter XIX.

tion. An official Board of Control was to look after civil and military administration from London, while in India the Governor-General and Council held the power and responsibility. In 1813 Parliament ended the trade monopoly enjoyed by the East India Company, except in China, where the monopoly continued for twenty years longer.

During the French Revolutionary and Napoleonic Wars France made unsuccessful endeavors to recover her lost position in India by stirring up native princes against the British. In 1784 Lord Cornwallis succeeded Warren Hastings as Governor-General of the East India Company's territories. It was he whose capture by Washington and Lafayette at Yorktown in 1781 had practically ended the American Revolutionary War. His failure in America is unfortunately better known than his subsequent success in India. He was an honest and conscientious administrator who put an end to many of the worst abuses of Company rule. By increasing the salaries of Company officers and preventing them from trading privately, or accepting 'presents' on their own account, he established the tradition of what became the incorruptible Indian Civil Service in later years. He made the so-called Permanent Settlement of the land revenue of Bengal, on terms perhaps too favorable to the *zemindars* or tax-farming class, and defeated Tipu, the heir of his father Haidar Ali as ruler of Mysore. A later Governor-General, Lord Wellesley (brother of Arthur Wellesley, who later became the Duke of Wellington), had to renew the fight with the warlike Tipu, who was now allied with France. Tipu died in battle, and the old royal line, which his father had deposed, was restored in Mysore. Then followed a prolonged struggle with the Mahratta confederacy, in which Arthur Wellesley's victory at Assaye secured British supremacy in the heart of India. It was not until yet another campaign had been fought, however, that these stubborn and valiant Mahrattas finally accepted British rule. The fall of Napoleon and the peace treaties of 1814-15, which stabilized the map of Europe, stabilized the map of India as well. British influence was paramount in all parts of the peninsula, and while the French kept trading posts in Pondicherry and Chandernagore, they pretended to no political influence.

At what proved to be the last renewal of its Charter, in 1833, the East India Company became practically a corporation for administering British India. In 1828-35 the Governor-General was Lord

George Bentinck, and his legal adviser the eminent historian Thomas Babington Macaulay. Together they planned and established a system of education for Indians, modeled after the British and using the English tongue. With the collaboration of missionary bodies, university colleges have been developed in the chief cities of British India. Bentinck was also able to put an end to the ancient, firmly held, custom of *suttee*, the sacrifice (supposed to be voluntary) of Hindu widows on their husband's funeral pyre. After him came the great reforming, 'Westernizing' Governor-General, Lord Dalhousie, 1848-56, who introduced railways, telegraphs, and irrigation projects. He had to undertake a war with the powerful Sikh confederacy of the Punjab in northern India, and he also advanced into Burma in the northeast. He carried out, on feudal principles familiar in medieval England, the 'doctrine of lapse,' that where no natural heir existed for a throne in one of the numerous native kingdoms it would escheat to the East India Company as the paramount suzerain of all India.

In 1857 the Indian Mutiny, or Sepoy Rebellion, shook British control over India and led to the termination of the East India Company. The Sepoys (or *sepahis*) were the native soldiers in the British army, and they outnumbered the British troops six to one, though nearly all the higher officers were British. Many parts of India did not join the rebellion at all, and many regiments remained loyal to the British connection at all times. There were a number of causes for the outbreak. The ruling princes were alarmed at Dalhousie's policy of rapid expansion of British India at the expense of native states. Conservative Hindus objected to the Westernizing policy in general, and in particular to the abolition of *suttee*, the activity of Christian missionaries, the sending of native regiments out of India to Afghanistan, Burma, and other foreign countries, and to the use of greased cartridges [3] in the army. An attempt was made to revive the old Mogul Empire, centering at Delhi, and to drive all British civilians out of India. At Cawnpore practically all the British were murdered after surrender; at Lucknow a small British garrison held out against a prolonged siege until relief arrived. The fighting

---

[3] To the Hindus the cow was sacred; to the Mohammedans the pig was unclean. Thus the use of cartridges greased with animal fat was sure to insult both religions.

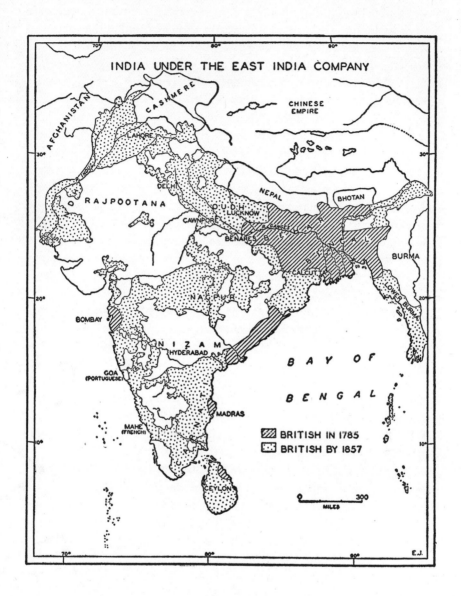

INDIA UNDER THE EAST INDIA COMPANY

AFGHANISTAN

CASHMERE

CHINESE
EMPIRE

LAHORE

R. INDUS

DELHI

RAJPOOTANA

NEPAL

BHOTAN

OUDH
LUCKNOW

CAWNPORE

R. GANGES

BENARES B

B E N G A L

BURMA

CALCUTTA

LOWER BURMA

NAGPUR

BOMBAY

20°

N I Z A M

B A Y   O F

HYDERABAD

GOA
(PORTUGUESE)

B E N G A L

MADRAS

MAHE
(FRENCH)

10°

BRITISH IN 1785

BRITISH BY 1857

CEYLON

300

MILES

E.J.

INDIA UNDER THE EAST INDIA COMPANY

continued for several months before all the embers of insurrection had been trodden out.

The Indian Mutiny persuaded the British Government to place British India directly under the authority of the Crown. A Secretary of State for India in the British ministry took the place of the old Board of Control, and the Governor-General took the title of Viceroy. The actual administration was very little altered at first by this change. The civil service of the East India Company became the Indian Civil Service of about 1,500 officials recruited by open competitive examination. These men spent their active career in India and filled most of the legal and administrative posts except that of Viceroy, which went always to some British nobleman of political experience. John Stuart Mill feared that the transfer of authority from the Company to Parliament might lead to ignorant meddling with Indian affairs by British politicians, and he pointed out that nothing is more dangerous than for a well-meaning but uninformed democracy to undertake the detailed regulation of the affairs of a distant and alien people. But those fears have not been realized. The good and the evil of British rule in India was that of bureaucracy: the rule by a highly trained, honest, and benevolent alien official class, who were well acquainted with the people whom they governed but who refused in any way to assimilate with them. Parliament, except on questions of very broad policy, has rarely interfered with the administration of the country.

Disraeli, as a stroke of policy which would at once please the queen and stimulate the interest of the British people in imperial affairs, had Victoria crowned Empress of India in 1876. It is interesting to note that no British 'Empire' was thus created (the term is merely a popular phrase for all the lands under the British Crown); Victoria was Empress only in India; elsewhere she remained simply Queen.

The British possession of India has profoundly, and sometimes unfavorably, influenced British foreign policy. It made the British Government pro-Turkish in the days when Russia was considered the greatest menace to India, and thus led to the Crimean War, and, a score of years later, to Disraeli's opposition, at the Congress of Berlin, to Russia's reaping the fruits of her military victory over Turkey. It led to several small wars with Afghanistan, a mountainous buffer state to the northwest of India; to the annexation of Burma, east of India; to the temporary occupation of Tibet in 1904, and, in great degree, to the Anglo-Japanese alliance of 1902.

The advantages and disadvantages of British rule in India make up a very important and interesting, though perhaps insoluble, problem. On the credit side, peace has been maintained, the *Pax Britannica*, over a country which had once been the scene of hundreds of wars. Justice in the courts, orderly administration, a degree of self-government which is at least greater than existed before the British came (for ancient India had known practically no form of government except absolute monarchy), a rapidly growing population, scientific methods of fighting famines and epidemics, excellent railways and roadways and irrigation works, generous provision for higher education, suppression of such ancient evils as *suttee, thugee* (human sacrifice by fanatical sects), *dacoity* (banditry), and infanticide—such are some of the claims which the British offer to the world in vindication of their rule.

On the debit side, Indian malcontents point out that after generations of British rule the great majority of the common people are illiterate and so near destitution that famines are still of frequent occurrence; that, while Indian revenues are spent in India, they are often spent for objects of more interest to the British than to the native population, such as the upkeep of a large army and the carrying on of costly border wars; that British colonies are permitted to exclude Hindu immigrants; that alien ways and customs have been introduced against the wishes of the people, and machine-made goods dumped on the market to the detriment of artistic handicrafts of the old time; and that, in any event, 'good government is no substitute for free government.' They urge further, that many of the good things brought in by British rule would have come in anyhow by commercial and cultural contact, as they have to some extent in independent Asiatic states such as Turkey, Persia, China, Japan, and Siam (Thailand).

There was enough force in these contentions to induce the British in the twentieth century to modify their policy of paternalistic bureaucracy by inviting the peoples of India to an ever greater share in the management of their own affairs. The Morley-Minto reforms of 1909 very cautiously began this process by admitting more natives to various legislative and executive councils; they were still, however, outnumbered by appointed official members. In 1919, after the First World War, a much bolder step was taken. A system of 'dyarchy' or double rule was created in the provinces. The provincial Legislative Councils, with a large elective majority, had certain subjects transferred to their management; other questions, such as national defense, were reserved to the British authorities. In 1935 British India and the Native States were united in a federal union, and a central legislature of two houses created with an elected majority in each. At the same time Burma was separated from India and given a constitution of her own.

Even with all these concessions, India is not self-governing in the sense in which that word can be applied to Great Britain or to the Dominions, such as Canada. The franchise, though widened with each successive reform, is still very narrow; it would be more correct to say that the 'educated classes' of India have a share of self-government than that 'the people' do. Moreover, the Governor-General (Viceroy) has still great emergency powers; he is not a mere formal or ceremonial executive like the governors of the Dominions. Agitation continues. Some Hindus desire complete independence; others formulate their demands as Dominion Home Rule —a status like that of Canada, Australia, or Ireland. One of the most interesting native leaders is Mohandas Gandhi, commonly known by the religious title of Mahatma Gandhi, who used the method of boycott and passive resistance—refusals to pay taxes, to attend court, to buy foreign goods—to force concessions. Others have advocated, and sometimes employed, violence. On the other hand, some native princes seem averse to a complete withdrawal of British influence, and the Mohammedans oppose universal suffrage on the ground that they would be swamped by a hostile Hindu majority.

The real difficulty is not to make out a case either for or against British rule, but to find a substitute. India, it must be repeated, is not yet a nation, though she may be on the road to becoming one. Suppose the British element entirely eliminated, the problem is hardly simplified. There are over two hundred languages and dialects in use in different parts of India. The most widely spoken languages are two forms of Hindustani: Hindi, written in a Sanskrit script and used by Hindus; and Urdu, written in Arabic and used by Mohammedans; but only a minority of the people know either. Religion counts for more than language in drawing national lines in all parts of Asia, and the religious situation is singularly complex. There are about 240,000,000 Hindus, over 70,000,000 Mohammedans, and millions of Buddhists,[4] Sikhs, Christians, Parsis, pagans, and other sects. The Hindus are divided into hereditary social classes or castes, who are kept so rigidly apart by social custom that the mere close presence of an outcaste Pariah is contamination to a high-caste Brahmin.

Then there are dangers from without. An independent India would not only be subject to raids from warlike neighbors, such as the Afghans, but would face the serious peril of being permanently conquered by Germany, or Japan. This prospect inclines many of the sincerest Indian patriots to prefer the evils which they endure rather than 'fly to others that they know not of.' In a more peaceful world, with a strong League of Nations or other international organization, an independent India might be free from all but internal perils; until that should be, it is difficult to see any more hopeful future for India than the evolution of self-government within the framework of the British Empire.

In 1942, with Japan already in possession of Burma and at the very gates of India, Great Britain offered Dominion status to India after the war. Though most native leaders rejected the offer as inadequate, it will probably be a basis for Anglo-Indian relations in the future.

---

[4] Gautama Buddha was a Hindu, but his religion has spread more rapidly towards the Far East than in India itself. Such neighboring countries as Ceylon and Burma, within the British Empire, and China and Japan, outside it, are far more largely Buddhist than India.

XXXIV

CANADA: DEPENDENCY AND DOMINION

THE case of Canada is of special interest to the student of the civilization of the English-speaking nations. Geographically, Canada is part
of the American continent and has for her only neighbor the United
States. Commercial and cultural ties innumerable bind the Dominion
to the Republic, and many Canadian customs are American rather
than British.[1] Moreover, there is a close parallel in the way in which
the two countries have developed by the progressive settlement of
the 'Wild West' and by constant immigration from Europe. Both
have been molded by frontier conditions and have developed a pioneer psychology. But politically Canada is part of the British Commonwealth of Nations, and a particularly loyal and devoted part,
as has been revealed on the battlefields of the First and Second World
Wars. Canadian political forms reproduce those of Great Britain
with great closeness. Canada, again, contains a large province—Quebec—which is French in language, in customs, in Catholic faith, and
in historical traditions. Yet, with all this, Canada has an individuality
which is alike distinguishable from that of France, Great Britain,
and the United States.

When Canada became British in 1763, the Canadian boundaries
included on the southern side the territory which now makes up the
states of Michigan, Illinois, Indiana, Ohio, and Wisconsin. The
British Government thought to keep this region, provisionally at
least, as an Indian reserve.[2] This plan came to nothing, as in 1783
the area in question became part of the United States. Without this

---

[1] Canada uses a decimal currency based on the dollar. Canadians drive to the
right of the road instead of to the left. Canadian villages are mainly made up of
wooden houses. Railroads, hotels, newspapers, and periodicals show a great deal
of influence from the United States.

[2] Thus conflicting with certain claims of American seaboard colonies, such as
Virginia, to western lands. See Chapter XIX.

439

rectification of the frontier, the United States would have had no share in Lakes Superior, Michigan, or Huron, though New York would have had the south shore of Lake Ontario and touched the east end of Lake Erie. Over 25,000,000 people now live in this formerly Canadian territory; in 1763 no one lived in it except wandering Indian tribes and a handful of French trappers and missionaries.

Indeed, the settled area of Canada was little more than the Saint Lawrence valley from Quebec to Montreal. Here there were about 65,000 French *habitants;* the Quebec Act of 1774, legally securing them in their language, religion, civil law and customs, satisfied them under British rule. American invasion of Canada in the Revolutionary War and again in the War of 1812 met with no sympathy from the French Canadians. Nor has Quebec ever made the slightest attempt to rejoin France; indeed, the anti-clerical policies of the French Revolution cut off France from the sympathy of the very devout Catholic peasantry of the Saint Lawrence region, and each subsequent generation has increased the difference between the French in Europe and their lost kinsfolk in America. There have been many quarrels, indeed, between the British and French in Canada, and some extreme French Canadian nationalists have even talked of an independent Quebec, but very few have looked abroad either to France or to the United States.

By 1791 there had been a considerable influx of British settlers into Canada. Some of them were United Empire Loyalists who had left the United States after the Revolution to live again under the old flag. Besides these political refugees, there was a growing number of British immigrants who sought a livelihood in a new land. William Pitt, then Prime Minister of Great Britain, judged the time ripe for a new colony. So he divided Canada into Lower and Upper —Lower Canada, the French-speaking part, with headquarters at Quebec; Upper Canada, the new English-speaking region, which ultimately had its center at Toronto. There was a Governor over all, and in each of the two provinces a Lieutenant-Governor and a two-chambered Legislature. The upper chamber, called the Legislative Council, was appointed by the government for life; the lower chamber was an elected assembly. This was almost precisely the form of government which had been employed in most of the thirteen colonies before the American Revolution; constitutional and representative, but not parliamentary or responsible.

Under this Canada Act of 1791 both provinces developed steadily, although their political life was troubled. The War of 1812 interrupted this development, but not for long. For the second and last time white men fought white man (and drew red Indians into the game) in the beautiful region which centers around Niagara Falls. Looking along the vista of the Niagara River, lined with power stations and other industrial plants, it is difficult indeed to imagine the battles of Chippewa or Lundy's Lane; still more difficult is it to visualize the horizons of Lake Erie broken by the smoke of cannon from the rival fleets of Commodore Perry and Captain Barclay.

The War of 1812 settled none of the issues which had caused it, but it led to a permanent peace. Thereafter mixed commissions set up by the British and American governments settled one by one over the next hundred years the frontier disputes and other questions arising between Canada and the United States. The most fruitful agreement of all bears the names of Richard Rush, American minister to Great Britain, and Charles Bagot, British minister to the United States, in 1817. This agreement provided that neither the British nor the Americans would increase their armament on the Great Lakes. In effect, it created an undefended frontier, first in the inland lakes, and then, tacitly, along the whole Canadian boundary.

Her international difficulties solved, Canada could turn to domestic problems. By 1837 both Upper and Lower Canada were almost as ripe for revolution as the thirteen colonies had been in 1775. The causes, however, were somewhat different. There was little question of the relation of the home government and the colonies, and no attempt to tax Canada from London; the Canadian grievances were local and domestic. Both provinces complained that the governors had too much power and the assemblies too little. Each province also had special grievances of its own. The French in Lower Canada, under the vigorous leadership of Louis Papineau, had a national grievance against a regime which reserved its best posts for the British minority. The British in Upper Canada, led by the fiery agitator William Lyon Mackenzie, resented the monopoly of such posts by a small group of reactionary United Empire Loyalists nicknamed the 'Family Compact'; they also objected to the reservation of vast tracts of land for the support of the clergy—the 'clergy reserves.' Curiously enough, the two rebellions, French and English, though running concurrently, were practically independent of each other. They were both suppressed with very little bloodshed, and a British High Commissioner was sent out to investigate the grievances which had caused the rebellion, for the British Government realized that there was no smoke without fire.

This High Commissioner was Lord Durham, one of the Whigs who made the English Reform Bill of 1832. He spent about eight months in Canada, returned to England, and, after consultation with the colonial specialists Gibbon Wakefield [3] and Charles Buller, prepared a Report which has been called the most important document in the history of colonial government. He recommended the undoing of the Canadian Act of 1791 by a union of Upper and Lower Canada into a single province, in the hope that British immigration—for hardly any immigration now came from France—would in the long run assure a British character to the colony. With respect to Lower Canada he said, 'I expected to find a contest between a government and a people: I found two nations warring in the bosom of a single state; I found a struggle not of principles but of races.' This merger was effected by the British Parliament in 1840, and in 1841 the first Parliament of united Canada met at Kingston, Ontario.

Another of his recommendations was even more important, though it was not so soon adopted. Durham urged that the ministry of Canada should, after the British fashion, be responsible to the elected branch of the national legislature. Hitherto, British governors had appointed such ministers and other officials as they pleased, paying little attention to the wishes of elected legislators. If the principle of parliamentary responsibility were now conceded, the consequences would be far-reaching. The Governor would be reduced to the status of a constitutional monarch, such as the sovereigns of Great Britain had been since the House of Hanover came to the throne, who could do nothing save by the advice of his ministers. The Prime Minister, responsible to a local Parliament, would be the real ruler of Canada. After several experiments, by a number

[3] See p. 421.

of governors who were appointed in rapid succession, Lord Elgin resolved to let responsible government be carried out to its logical conclusion. He let the Prime Minister pick his own cabinet, and in 1849 accepted a 'rebellion losses bill,' which indemnified people who had suffered from the rebellion of 1837 without regard to which side they had taken. Some Canadian Tories were so angry at this 'subsidy to rebels' that they stoned the Governor and burned the Parliament buildings—a rather strange manifestation of 'loyalty'! Responsible government was not established by an Act of Parliament, either British or Canadian; it simply became, from Lord Elgin's time onward, a custom or convention of the constitution, as in Great Britain.

After the adoption of the Durham Report and the new policy of responsible government, great progress was made in Canada. The old French feudal system, called seigneurial tenure, which only survived in inconvenient payments and legal forms, was abolished in 1854. The 'clergy reserves' were abandoned, and Church and State virtually separated. The British Government conceded the right of Canada to make her own tariff schedules—a very important matter, for Canada gave protection to her own industries, even against British imports, and refused to follow the mother country along the path of free trade. In Lower Canada (Quebec) population increased from about 65,000 in 1763 to 600,000 in 1837 and 1,111,000 in 1861; mainly by natural increase, since most European immigrants went to Upper Canada (Ontario). In Upper Canada the population reached 1,396,091 by 1861. The arrangements of 1840 had provided for an equal number of representatives from Lower and Upper Canada; at first that provision had favored the British element, but now that Upper Canada had the greater population it favored the French minority. Unless the two divisions of Canada were organized as separate provinces, but bound together in a federal union, there was danger of conflict on this issue of representation.

There were other reasons why a new federal constitution seemed necessary. Outside Canada, in the narrow sense in which the term was then used, there were other possessions of Great Britain in North America. There were three so-called Maritime Provinces (Nova Scotia, New Brunswick and Prince Edward Island) with a considerable British population; [4] the oldest of British colonies, New-foundland; the unsettled plains and mountains of the West under the authority of the Hudson's Bay Company. Some or all of these colonies might be willing to join with Quebec and Ontario into a larger federal union.

Then there was the question of the United States. For a long time there was a fatalistic opinion in Great Britain that Canada, sooner or later, would be attracted into the orbit of the Republic. The same opinion was widely held in the United States; indeed, the conquest of Canada had been one of the objects of the War of 1812, and Charles Sumner had hinted in the Senate that the trans-fer of Canada to the United States after the American Civil War would promote better relations between the English-speaking peoples. Most Canadians viewed the idea with disfavor: the French because their peculiar and specialized local culture might dissolve if Quebec were merely one state in a vast English-speaking republic; the British because they still felt strong affection for the land of their fathers. But how resist the tremendous pull of Canada's gigantic neighbor? Only, it was urged, by a national policy, making British North America a federal nation, instead of a string of small colonies.

A number of able and determined statesmen worked out plans of federation, including such men as Sir John Macdonald, the Conservative leader, George Brown, the Liberal chief, Charles Tupper from Nova Scotia, and Sir George Cartier of Quebec. In 1867 the British Parliament passed the British North America Act, based almost without amendment on the Canadian proposals. This created the Dominion of Canada, and the term Dominion has since been used, in a general sense, for all colonies possessing complete self-government. It repealed the union of 1840, Lower and Upper Canada reappearing as separate provinces under the names of Quebec and Ontario. With these were included New Brunswick and Nova Scotia, and all four provinces together formed the federal Dominion of Canada. Prince Edward Island joined in 1873, but the old colony of Newfoundland remained outside the gates. On one occasion, in 1895, Newfoundland sought admission, but was so heavily burdened

[4] These developed from the old French colony of Acadia, lost to the British in 1713. See Chapter xviii.

with debt that the Dominion refused to assume Newfoundland's financial obligations. Newfoundland remained a separate dominion until, in 1933, financial troubles again forced the colony to seek aid; on this occasion, however, she turned not to Canada but to Great Britain and temporarily gave up her legislative independence in return for British assistance.

Canada's expansion has been mainly towards the west. A belated survivor of the seventeenth-century chartered companies, which had planted British rule in India, in Virginia, and in New England, the Hudson's Bay Company held sovereignty over most of the west under a charter of 1672. A trading company, interested chiefly in furs, it had used its power well and had in the main pursued an enlightened policy towards the Indians. But it was not suited to administer settled agricultural areas and, in fact, did not want to have such responsibilities. In 1869 the Hudson's Bay Company surrendered its sovereign powers to the Crown, retaining its functions as a trading and land company. Its territory east of the Rocky Mountains was formed into the province of Manitoba and included in the Dominion of Canada in 1870. Before the transfer was completed there was an armed rising of the half-breeds (French-Indians) of the Red River district, who wished to be left under the administration of the Hudson's Bay Company. A small military expedition under Colonel (later Field Marshal) Garnet Wolseley went from Thunder Bay on Lake Superior to the Red River by boat and portage; the rebels dispersed without further fighting.

There have been a number of boundary adjustments between British North America and the United States since the War of 1812. In 1842 the Webster-Ashburton agreement fixed the extreme eastern frontier between Maine and the maritime province of New Brunswick. About the same time a far more important dispute arose in the west, over the mountainous region known as Oregon.[5] The Hudson's Bay Company had trading posts in the northern part of this region; in the southern portion various American traders and trappers, notably the German-born John Jacob Astor, who had founded the fur-trading post of Astoria at the mouth of the Columbia River in 1811. For a long time both nations agreed on a joint occupation, without

[5] For the importance of the Oregon issue in American politics see Chapter XXII.

prejudice to their ultimate legal claims, but by 1845 American expansionists were demanding the whole region north to Alaska, which would have shut Canada completely away from the Pacific, while the British insisted on the Columbia River boundary. A compromise agreement in 1846 extended the existing line of division between the Great Lakes and the Rocky Mountains clear to the Pacific at 49° north latitude. This left the Columbia River to the United States, but the line of division bent southward to give all Vancouver Island to the British.[6] In 1871 the mountain area on the British side of the line, known as the colony of British Columbia, joined the Dominion of Canada. From the prairie territories lying between Ontario and British Columbia the new provinces of Saskatchewan and Alberta were organized in 1905. In 1903 a joint commission fixed the disputed boundary between Canada and Alaska.

The Dominion of Canada, when thus completed, contained nine provinces. These fall naturally into four groups, from east to west: the Maritime Provinces of Nova Scotia, New Brunswick, and Prince Edward Island; Quebec, with its French traditions and characteristics; Ontario, and the western provinces of Manitoba, Saskatchewan, Alberta, and British Columbia, extending from the Great Lakes to the Pacific Ocean. In the Far North are territories belonging to the whole Dominion. One of them, the Yukon, is the seat of the Klondike gold fields. Each province sends representatives to a House of Commons, elected directly by the people according to the population of the province (Quebec has always 65 members; all other provinces in proportion). There is a Senate appointed for life by the Governor-General on the advice of his ministry. The Dominion Government has all powers other than those delegated to the provinces; this is the reverse of the principle of the United States Constitution, by which the states have all the powers other than those delegated to the Federal Government.

The most important difference between the government of the Dominion of Canada and that of the United States is that the Dominion follows strictly the British system of responsible government. The ministry must be of the same party as the majority in the House of Commons. The Governor-General must at all times act on the

[6] Some details of the channel boundary were settled by arbitration in 1871.

advice of his ministers, just as does the king in Great Britain. Parliament may be dissolved, and new elections held, before the maximum term has expired if the ministry so wishes. Though there is an appointed, instead of a hereditary, upper chamber, British usage is followed in giving the lower house, elected by the people, sole control over the executive, chief control over finance, and the initiative in legislation; the Canadian Senate, like the British House of Lords, is merely a slight brake on legislation.

In political usages each province imitates the Dominion, as the Dominion imitates Great Britain. Over each province is a Lieutenant-Governor, appointed by the Governor-General on the advice of his ministers. The real power is in the hands of the provincial ministry, which is responsible to the legislative assembly, usually of only one chamber,[7] elected by the people. The powers of the provinces are enumerated in the British North America Act and include direct taxation, local government, local courts, public lands, and (under certain restrictions in the interest of religious minorities) education.

Political life in Canada down to the First World War followed British traditions very closely. There were two great parties, the Conservative and the Liberal. Third parties sometimes came into existence, especially on economic issues, among the farmers and ranchers of the wheat-growing provinces of the western prairies, but they seldom rose to more than local importance. In general, French Canadians supported the Liberals, and the old British Loyalist element of Ontario the Conservatives. The Conservatives were usually advocates of a high protective tariff and opponents of reciprocity with the United States, though neither party had an absolutely consistent record on the question. The Conservatives stressed the imperial ties which bound Canada to the mother country and the other British Dominions; the Liberals laid more emphasis on Dominion and provincial home rule. The question of church schools was, next to the tariff, the most frequent source of party dissension. Political ties were very strong and ministries stable and enduring. Two men, indeed, very largely dominated the political history of the Dominion for half a century after confederation had been established in 1867,

---

[7] Quebec has retained an upper chamber.

Sir John A. Macdonald, the Conservative, and Sir Wilfrid Laurier, a French Canadian who was leader of the Liberals. In 1911, in an election turning on the issue of reciprocity with the United States, the Laurier Government was turned out of office and the Conservatives came into power under Sir Robert Borden.

One of the most urgent tasks of the Dominion was to complete a transcontinental railroad. This was even more vital than the building of the Union Pacific to bind California to the East in the United States, for the Canadian provinces were strung together like beads in a single line; without national railroad communications they would have no real unity, and some of the western provinces might even have felt constrained to find markets by joining the United States. The building of the Canadian Pacific Railway is one of the greatest romances in the history of railroading. The line was begun in 1880. As far westward as Lake Superior there was a fair amount of settlement to support and encourage the company, but between Lake Superior and Winnipeg in Manitoba was a thousand miles of prairie and rocky wilderness without a single permanent settlement. Then the terrible Kicking Horse Pass in the Canadian Rockies had to be overcome before the way was clear into the smiling valleys of British Columbia. On 7 November 1885, the last spike was driven home and Canada had been completely spanned. It is a curious fact that the United States has never had a single continuous transcontinental railway; Canada has now three lines from the Atlantic to the Pacific.

Early railway building in Canada, as in the United States, was occasionally linked with political scandal. In both the Dominion of Canada and Newfoundland there have been many instances of the jobbery, spoilsmanship, and 'pork barrel' distribution of public improvements to influence elections, which are the dark shadows of politics in the United States. Perhaps such confusions of public development with private opportunities are almost inevitable in a new, rapidly developing country.[8] On the other hand, Canada has been relatively free of frontier lawlessness. Instead of the vigilance com-

---

[8] This cannot be attributed to 'democracy,' for many scandals occurred before Canada had attained self-government; and at no time have elections either in the United States or in Canada been as venal as they were commonly in Great Britain before the reform of 1832.

mittee and the lynching bee there has been the stern efficiency of the Mounted Police. The Canadian record of fair dealing with the native Indian population is also somewhat better than that of the United States. One of the best British traditions which Canada has preserved is that of justice and efficiency in the criminal courts.[9]

[9] For Canada since 1914 see Chapters xxxviii and xxxix.

XXXV

AUSTRALIA AND NEW ZEALAND

Viscount James Bryce, familiar to all Americans for his monumental study of *The American Commonwealth,* made shortly after the First World War an equally significant comparative analysis of *Modern Democracies,* devoting particular attention to the British Dominions. He selected Australia as being, in many respects, the most clear-cut example of democracy in all the world:

If any country and its government were to be selected as showing the course which a self-governing people pursues free from all external influences and little trammeled by intellectual influences descending from the past, Australia would be that country. It is the newest of all the democracies. It is that which has travelled farthest and fastest along the road which leads to the unlimited rule of the multitude. In it, better than anywhere else, may be studied the tendencies that rule displays as it works itself out in practice.[1]

Australia is the sole example of a whole continent ruled by one people and speaking one language. The country is only a shade smaller than the continental portion of the United States, but so much of its area is desert that the total population is about that of New York City and less than that of Greater London. Yet, though sparsely peopled, Australia has so much productive energy and so high a standard of living as to be a real power in the world. Its development in a century and a half from a neglected convict settlement to a powerful and prosperous federal Dominion is as stirring a story as the growth of the United States or of Canada.

In 1781 a French observer made the interesting remark that the English had compensated themselves for the loss of one empire— the American—by gaining another, Australia. The vast island conti-

[1] J. Bryce, *Modern Democracies* (1921), ii, p. 166.

nent had for some time been known to the Dutch. Skippers of the Dutch East India Company had explored its coasts, and one of them, Abel Tasman, discovered the neighboring islands of Tasmania and New Zealand in 1642. The English also had their curiosity attracted to this great lone land. Captain William Dampier of Somersetshire, a great sailor though inclined to piracy in his unguarded moments, had sighted Australia in 1688 and was later sent out by William III on an official expedition in 1699, when he sailed along the coast of western Australia.

Australia was not quite empty of human life but very nearly so. In the whole continent there were only some 150,000 inhabitants, a dark, primitive, stone-age race who had no writing, no knowledge of metals, but who did produce fire by rubbing sticks together and who hunted with a curved throwing-stick or boomerang. They were neither Mongols nor Malays, and in no way akin to the brown Polynesian Maoris of New Zealand; no one knows when or how they came to Australia. They did not present so serious a problem to white settlers as the American Indians in Canada and the United States.

The claims of the British to Australia were laid by the remarkable voyages of Captain James Cook, a Yorkshireman who had started life as a haberdasher's apprentice, or dry-goods clerk, and had sailed before the mast as a seaman. In 1768 he was forty years of age, a lieutenant in command of the *Endeavour*. Though this was a ship of the Royal Navy, it was sailing on a scientific expedition largely financed by Joseph Banks, a rich young man with a keen interest in natural history. Cook made scientific observations on the transit of Venus at Tahiti, then he sailed to New Zealand, sighting it on 6 October 1769. He explored the coast of both large islands of the New Zealand group and then went to Australia. On 28 April 1770 the *Endeavour* dropped anchor in a fine harbor which the botanist Banks called Botany Bay—a name of ill omen in later years when it became a convict settlement! Then Cook sailed home by way of New Guinea, Java, and the Cape of Good Hope. He lost his life a few years later, killed by natives on a Hawaiian beach. In the history of the British Empire, Cook's voyages were as significant as those of Cabot, Drake, Raleigh, and Hudson.

The American Revolution had stopped up one outlet for the transportation of prisoners. In 1779 a parliamentary committee inquired into possible new penal settlements and in 1786 an Order in Council appointed the east coast of Australia. 'If we compare the high hopes with which Virginia was started, with this crude avowal of a convict colony, we can recognise the measure of England's disappointment and disillusion.' [2] On the other hand, it is only fair to recognize that so long as free immigrants could go to Canada and the United States there was no reason for them to take the longer, costlier voyage to Australia, whose natural wealth in gold and other resources was then not even suspected. Had there not been convict settlement, for a long time there would have been practically no settlement at all.

In May 1787, Captain Phillip of the Royal Navy was sent out in the *Prince of Wales*, carrying 212 marines, their 28 wives, 600 male convicts, 185 female convicts—and 3 voluntary settlers! William Pitt, then Prime Minister, and Sydney, his Secretary of State, in undertaking this very costly method of transporting convicts to the opposite end of the earth,[3] doubtless had the humane thought that they could make life over in an absolutely new environment. Captain Phillip was made Governor of all eastern Australia. Taking on board from Capetown some cattle, sheep, pigs, and poultry, as provisions for his little company, he sailed onward to Botany Bay in 1788. Unfortunately he also had on board some rabbits, which so multiplied in the new land as to become a serious pest. He first settled Port Jackson, then, a few miles north of Botany Bay, Sydney, named after the Secretary of State.

At first the colony of Port Jackson existed on the verge of starvation, as had the first English settlements in Jamestown and Plymouth, and it was kept alive only by the arrival of a second expedition from England in 1790. The Cape of Good Hope in South Africa, then still in Dutch hands, was the nearest place whence stores could be obtained and it was 6,200 miles from Sydney, a voyage of 38 days. The early governors were naval or military officers. Their main problem was to keep the colony from starvation; to do this every free colonist as well as every convict had to have set tasks. It was complete State Socialism in this pioneer-military colony period, gradually yielding

[2] Egerton, *A Short History of British Colonial Policy* (1932), p. 227.

[3] One officer remarked, 'It will be cheaper to feed them on turtle and venison at the London Tavern!'

to private enterprise. About 1824 a nominated council was established and the period of unmitigated military rule came to an end.

This colony, which took the name of New South Wales, was not self-supporting for several years after its foundation. About 1801, however, the investments of Captain MacArthur in sheep farming began to bring in large returns. Within a generation the wool-growing industry was the main basis for Australian economic life. Captain Bligh, Governor from 1806 to 1808, made trouble in the colony by his arbitrary methods and was deposed by his own officers, as he had previously (1789) been deposed by his crew in the *Bounty*. Colonel Macquarie, who came out in 1809, was the greatest of the early governors of New South Wales. He judiciously helped ex-convicts, even making some of them magistrates. He had the country surveyed and a road made to the rivers and pastures west of the Blue Mountains.

Other colonies were settled soon after the establishment of New South Wales in 1788: Tasmania (once called Van Diemen's land and used as an additional convict settlement) in 1803; Moreton Bay, later Queensland, in 1825; Western Australia, in 1829; Victoria from about 1835 (though tied to New South Wales politically till 1851); South Australia, where many of Wakefield's theories of colonization were tried, in 1836. The British settlement of New Zealand did not begin until 1840. By 1851 representative government was established for all the Australian colonies except Western Australia, which had a very small population, but each remained an independent colony for half a century longer. Australia was not a political entity but merely a geographical expression.

Exploration was the romance of early Australian history. Distance, hunger, and thirst—the enemies of all explorers—were more formidable than in North America, for Australia has few rivers and fewer lakes. The early Australian explorers had little opportunity of using boats, drinking water on the march, catching fish, or shooting waterfowl. They had to ride all the way or, if their horses failed them, walk. The great explorations began with the journey of Bloxland, a settler from England; Wentworth, a colonial; Lieutenant Lawson of the army; and Evans, a surveyor. They crossed the Blue Mountains, which hemmed in the settlers of New South Wales as the Appalachians had hemmed in the first Americans, and in 1813 surveyed a route for Macquarie's road to Bathurst. In 1817-18 John

Oxley, a surveyor, found the Murrumbidgee River, which flows into the Murray. Hamilton Hume, a grazier, in 1824 followed the course of the Murray, and in 1829 he and Captain Sturt solved the mystery of the rivers beyond the Blue Mountains—the Lachlan, the Macquarie, the Murrumbidgee, the Murray—which all flowed into the Darling. Settlers followed, and within a score of years squatters covered, thinly but almost continuously, the vast arable region of the Darling; New South Wales, Victoria, and South Australia were in touch with each other.

South Australia was being settled in the reign of William IV (1830-37), and the capital was named for his queen, Adelaide. Victoria was named for Queen Victoria, and the capital, Melbourne, for her Prime Minister. In 1840 Captain Eyre rode from Adelaide two thousand miles along the coast to Perth in Western Australia. In 1841 Leichardt opened up by exploration the semi-tropical regions of Queensland, also named in Victoria's honor. This ended the epic period of Australian exploration, the 'Elizabethan stage' of Australian history as it might be called, though much exploring was done later in the vast desert interior. In 1859 South Australia offered a prize to the man who should cross the continent from south to north, and in 1860 Robert Burke, William Wills, and six other men started from Victoria with camels and other supplies provided by the Victorian government. They traveled from Cooper's Creek to the Flinders River in the north, then to the Gulf of Carpentaria; thence back overland, with vanishing supplies, to a death from starvation near Cooper's Creek. Yet within ten years Cooper's Creek was the home of prosperous squatters.[4] In 1862 J. McDouall Stuart successfully made the journey and surveyed a route for the telegraph line across the continent. Railway lines followed closer to the coast; there was not enough inland settlement to warrant such transcontinental railroads as were built in Canada.

By the middle of the nineteenth century, say by 1851 when gold was first discovered and home rule granted to most of the Australian settlements, the success of British colonization had been already established. The convict element in New South Wales, which had been

---

[4] The Australian squatter was often a great capitalist with a sheep ranch covering many miles; he should not be confused with the American squatter, who was usually a small farmer, too poor to buy land.

50 per cent of the population as late as 1819, was now less than 1 per cent, and transportation of criminals had been discontinued since 1840. Tasmania received no more convicts after 1852, or Western Australia after 1867; the other Australian colonies, and New Zealand, had no convict settlements. Unoccupied land, on the Wakefield system, was put up for auction at a substantial price, and the money thus raised was used to bring out settlers from the British Isles. Much of the land was in very large properties, especially in sheep runs. Into this slowly, though surely, developing continent of Australia, with about 400,000 white inhabitants in 1850, there was thrust the sudden excitement of a gold rush. As in California in 1849, and later in the Klondike and South Africa in the last years of the nineteenth century, thousands of gold seekers from every country on earth poured in to make their fortunes. Victoria and New South Wales, especially the former, became huge mining camps. Within a decade the population of Australia had nearly trebled.

Development of the resources of Australia differed in certain respects from that of the United States and Canada. From the very beginning, and continuously thereafter, the government played a large part in matters which other English-speaking communities had left mainly to private initiative. The early New South Wales Government had engaged in sheep farming and in marketing. There, and in the other Australasian colonies, people grew up familiar with direct government employment of labor and management of industry. They had few individualistic scruples about the proper sphere of government or the economic doctrines of *laissez-faire*. A dry-farming region (such as the wheat belt in Canada and the United States) is often inclined to invoke the aid of the state because of the large provision that must be made for irrigation, and for relief in lean years. Arid Australia was pre-eminently such a region. Hence a kind of opportunist State Socialism—a 'Socialism without dogmas' it has been called—became characteristic of the Australian colonies.

Other causes made for radical democracy. The gold miners were a restless, hardy, self-assertive sort of men, as they had been in California. The small farmers had grievances against the great estates of the squatters. There was friction in some of the colonies between democratic lower chambers and more aristocratic upper chambers. The concentration of the population in the large seaport capitals of

Sydney, Melbourne, Adelaide, Brisbane, Perth, Hobart—half of all the people of Australia live in them—has encouraged a rapid development of trade unionism. Indeed, in no other part of the world, except perhaps New Zealand, have these unions been so politically powerful. In recent years Australian politics has been in general a duel between a powerful Labor party and a composite opposition under either a Liberal or a National label. With the exception of some of the Rocky Mountain states in America, the colonies of Australia and New Zealand were the first communities in the world to grant complete equal suffrage to women.

The radical democracy in Australia, unlike that of similar parties in Europe, has been strongly nationalist. It has stood for a 'white Australia' with the complete exclusion of colored labor, whether from China, India, or the Pacific Islands. It has, in recent years, given little encouragement even to European immigration. It has been protectionist, with tariffs against even British imports. It has favored compulsory military training in time of peace. These differences from British Radicalism were not doctrinal but due to local conditions. The white Australian policy was adopted partly to prevent such racial problems as have arisen in the United States and in South Africa, and partly to shut out the competition of cheap labor. Protectionism is a policy almost invariably followed by newly settled countries that wish to develop their infant industries. Australian armament has been caused largely by fear of Japan.

Many attempts to federate the Australian colonies failed in the nineteenth century. Even more than was the case with the provinces of British North America, the movement for federation had to overcome the jealousies of the separate colonies.[5] Not until 1900 was a common constitution adopted for the whole Commonwealth of Australia. New Zealand, because of distance, did not come into the Commonwealth at all; but the five continental colonies of New South Wales, Victoria, Queensland, South Australia, Western Australia, and the island of Tasmania entered the union, and there were two federal territories, Northern Australia, formerly belonging to South Australia, and Papua, a part of the island of New Guinea, formerly belonging to Queensland.

[5] Some of the railways, erected by individual colonies, had different gauges, to the serious impediment of traffic.

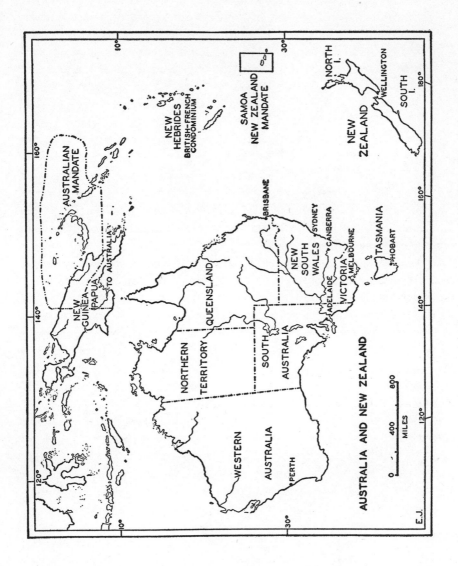

AUSTRALIA AND NEW ZEALAND

In very many ways the Australian Constitution resembles that of the United States more than that of the Dominion of Canada. Both Australia and Canada, it is true, adopted the British system of responsible government alike for the federal and for the local ministries and legislatures. But the local units in Australia are called States, not Provinces; the upper house is a Senate, and the lower house a House of Representatives; the Senate is elected by the people, on a basis of equal representation (six members) from each state, not appointed by the ministry as is the Canadian Senate; there is a Supreme Court to protect and interpret the Constitution; and, finally, the powers of government which are not enumerated belong to the states and not to the Commonwealth, whereas in Canada the Dominion Government absorbs the powers not specifically granted to the provinces. Each state has a Governor, but instead of being elected by the people, as in the United States, or appointed by the Federal Government, as in Canada, he is appointed by the British Government, in the same manner as the Governor-General for the whole Commonwealth. This difference matters little, however, as alike in the Commonwealth and in the individual states the real executive power is in hands of ministries responsible to a party majority of the legislature. Unlike most of the Canadian provinces, the state legislatures are usually divided into two chambers. The Commonwealth has a new made-to-order capital in a federal district at Canberra.

New Zealand is in many respects very much like Australia, and in others unlike. Both Dominions are of almost purely British stock, and both have radically democratic governments with a strong tendency towards political experiment and a paternalistic State Socialism. But the physical setting of the two countries is very different. Australia is a huge island-continent; for the most part with a warm, dry, sunny climate not unlike the southern shore of the Mediterranean, the Union of South Africa, or the southwestern part of the United States. New Zealand, 1,200 miles to the southeast, is only about the size of the British Isles and enjoys a similar oceanic climate; mild, temperate, and moderately rainy. Both North and South Islands, the largest islands of the New Zealand group, have magnificent mountain ranges and fjords worthy of Norway or Alaska.

Like so many of the early American colonies, New Zealand began with a land-owning corporation, the New Zealand Land Company, backed by Gibbon Wakefield, who had already done much to promote settlement in Australia. In 1840 the British Government somewhat reluctantly (for these were the days when expansionist sentiment was weakest) extended its protection to New Zealand. Governor Hobson negotiated with the natives in the same year the Treaty of Waitangi, which guaranteed to them the possession of their land. The New Zealand natives were not in the least like the primitive savages of Australia. They were Maoris, of Polynesian race, a vigorous, warlike people, skilled in many arts and crafts. The too eager zeal of the British settlers for land awakened their suspicion and, as in the case of the American Indians, much trouble arose from genuine misunderstandings about the nature of land purchase on both sides; the white man often believing that he had bought exclusive possession of a tract of land, while the native thought he had sold only hunting or grazing rights, or an individual share in land that belonged collectively to the whole tribe. Wars followed, as fiercely contested as South African struggles with the Zulus, or American contests with Iroquois or Sioux.

The ablest of the statesmen of New Zealand was Sir George Grey, who was Governor from 1846 to 1854 and again, after a period of service in Cape Colony, from 1861 to 1867. By even-handed justice he put an end to the Maori wars and secured the confidence of the native chiefs. He also fostered carefully the development of self-government among the British immigrants, and made New Zealand almost a model colony. After completing his governorship, he made his home in the country and engaged actively in public life, serving in 1877-9 as Prime Minister. The historian Froude, an ardent imperialist, paid a visit to South Africa, Australia, and New Zealand in 1885, and described his visit to Sir George Grey in his *Oceana*. Grey had built a spacious country house, made gardens, collected a library and many works of art. Life, it was evident, could be lived as comfortably and graciously in this remotest fragment of the British Empire as in Great Britain.

From 1852 to 1876 New Zealand was a federation of six small provinces. After 1876 the colony had a unitary government, and in 1907 was formally declared to be a Dominion. In spite of Sir George Grey's advocacy, New Zealand refused to federate with Australia. Responsible government, with a ministry nominally appointed by the Governor-General but actually dependent on an elected Parliament, exists here as in all other British Dominions. The House of Representatives is elected by universal suffrage, which, since 1893, has meant woman suffrage also. The Legislative Council, a rather weak upper chamber, was at first appointed for life, like the Canadian Senate, but the term of office was later limited to seven years.

Since about 1890 New Zealand, even more than Australia, has been one of the most interesting laboratories of social experiment in the world. Under John Ballance, Richard Seddon, and their successors, the Liberal-Labor group put through programs of reform that anticipated, and in some cases exceeded, all that has been done in the United States under the New Deal of the 1930s. Graduated land taxes are levied to break up large estates and promote closer settlement. Conciliation Boards and Arbitration Courts have jurisdiction over labor disputes. There are old-age pensions and various types of public insurance. The government owns the entire railway system and many coal mines, and municipalities conduct all kinds of public utilities.

The verdict to be passed on Australasian social democracy will depend on the point of view of the critic. Opponents of the policies recently pursued in Australia and New Zealand urge that government is very costly, with reckless borrowing; that trade unionists have been given unfair privileges over other workers; that there has been a good deal of jobbery and pork-barrel legislation; [6] and that the selfishness of the politically dominant labor element has kept population from growing through normal immigration, Australia having only 7,000,000 inhabitants and New Zealand about 1,600,000.

On the other hand, it is generally admitted that there has been little of the cruder kinds of corruption, such as bribery; that law and order have been well maintained, and (at least in recent decades) an enlightened and humane policy pursued towards native races; that the highest standards of popular education and welfare have been upheld; and that, if Bentham was right in making 'the greatest happiness of the greatest number' the test of government, Australia and

[6] Seddon frankly, not to say naïvely, avowed that 'It is unreasonable and unnatural to expect the Government to look with the same kindly eye on districts returning members opposed to the Government as on those which returned Government supporters'!

New Zealand are very nearly at the head of the nations. And, however socialistic may be their governmental policies, their hardy outdoor life and pioneer heritage have made the Australian and the New Zealander as personally self-reliant as anyone; if not precisely 'rugged individualists' they are at any rate rugged individuals!

◦ XXXVI ◦

SOUTH AFRICA

WITHIN the British Empire are three great continental federations: the Dominion of Canada, the Commonwealth of Australia, the Union of South Africa. Canada, in spite of a French origin, and Australia from the start were predominantly British, as were also the unitary Dominions of New Zealand and Newfoundland. South Africa, alone of the fully self-governing parts of the Empire, lacked a British majority. About half the white population was Dutch, and both Dutch and British elements were outnumbered by a native Negro population. This mixture of peoples created difficulties which were not resolved without war: wars of white men with black and of white men with each other.

The history of South Africa is a blank until Portuguese explorers and Dutch merchants visited there. The aboriginal Bushmen had not progressed beyond the stone age. The more highly developed Hottentots and Zulus, who drove the Bushmen into the deserts, knew something of the use of iron, herded cattle, formed elaborate military tribal organizations, but had no writing and no records of their own past. America, after Columbus, was never a 'dark continent' in the sense in which that phrase has been used of Africa. The splendid waterways permitted easy penetration of the North American wilderness, and the temperate climate was adapted to European settlement. But Africa, well known along the coast, remained 'darkest Africa' in the interior until the middle of the nineteenth century. In the seventeenth and eighteenth centuries the Cape Colony was but a resting place for the ships of the Dutch East India Company, half-way between Holland and India.

The settlement at Cape Town contained a vegetable garden, a few stores, and residences for company officials. Sailors were refreshed with grapes, plums, and lemons, and thus protected against scurvy.

461

A few of the Dutch took up farms a little way inland. After the revocation of the Edict of Nantes by Louis XIV in 1685, a considerable number of French Huguenots came out to make a new life for themselves in the Dutch colony at the Cape, just as others went to the Carolinas to live under tolerant British rule. In Africa, as in America, they blended admirably with the people about them, and their names, their influence, even their physical type can still be traced in South Africa today.

The French Revolution cost the Dutch their Cape Colony. Since the French had occupied the Dutch Republic in 1795, the British, at war with France, sent a naval expedition to the Dutch colony which was so vital on the route from Europe to India. The Dutch governor and garrison did not welcome their 'liberators' and made a stout resistance, but in vain. In 1802, however, when the Peace of Amiens made a temporary truce in the war between Britain and Bonaparte, Cape Colony was restored to the Dutch, which practically meant to their new French masters. The Peace of Amiens did not last long, however; the French remained in possession of Holland, so a new British naval expedition took over the colony in 1806. When Napoleon's empire fell in 1814, and Dutch independence was restored (though the Dutch Republic was now the Kingdom of the Netherlands), all the Dutch colonies were given back by the British except Cape Colony in Africa and British Guiana in South America. Doubtless the Cape was retained because of the importance of the route around Africa to British India; there was no Suez Canal in those days, and the only all-water route to the East had to pass the Cape of Good Hope.

As the western movement towards the Rockies was the great American romance, both in Canada and the United States, so the trekking of the Dutch Boers (farmers) from the Cape northwards is the romance of South African history. The Boers liked space, and where settlement was too close or public authority too interfering, they packed up their goods in wagons and moved on to fresh pastures. The huge South African ox-drawn wagon, roofed with an arching canvas tilt, is a familiar feature of Boer life. As they moved into the high, dry plateaus away from the coast they became ranchers rather than farmers, and, like Abraham, counted their wealth in flocks and herds. The people were devoutly Protestant, like their

Dutch and Huguenot forefathers, they spoke a local Dutch dialect (the Taal or Afrikaans), they believed in 'white supremacy' and had little patience with what they considered the sentimental British views on dealing with native peoples; in manners and customs generally they were highly conservative, as civilized men are apt to be when isolated among native barbarian tribes, lest they lose their precious heritage from the past. As Olive Schreiner, the greatest literary genius South Africa has produced, once phrased her defense of Boer conservatism, if they had abandoned their stiff, old-fashioned, straight-backed chairs, it would have been to sit on the ground as the natives did!

As in the case of the first American colonies, settlement in South Africa was long restricted to the seaboard. About 14,000 Europeans, mainly Dutch, found themselves under the rule of a British Governor. The Dutch system of local magistrates, chosen from the citizen farmers (burghers) in each district was, however, continued. Thus when a small rebellion broke out among some Dutch settlers in 1815, it was suppressed by the Landrost (magistrate) of Uitenhage at Slagter's Nek. Five rebels were hanged, and the incident was later used to stir up feeling against the British rule under which it took place; but, as one British writer pointed out, 'Dutchmen were in command of the forces that attacked them; a Dutch official prosecuted them; a Dutch judge sentenced them; a Dutch magistrate hanged them; and all that the English Governor did was to pardon one of them!'

After 1820, with some financial assistance from Parliament, the British undertook to settle their own countrymen at the Cape. Men of means, such as pensioned officers from the Napoleonic wars, were encouraged to come out and to bring with them servants or laborers. Some four or five thousand Englishmen came out, founded Port Elizabeth, and took up land put at their disposal by the government. Four years after these 'settlers of 1820,' a British syndicate secured a tract to the north and east of Cape Colony in a region called Natal. This, and the rest of the land northward to the Limpopo River, was under the 'Black Napoleon' Zulu chief, Chaka, from whom the syndicate obtained assent to take up land. Natal gradually became a populous frontier colony, mainly British in stock but with a considerable Dutch minority. The settlers governed Natal independently until 1842 when the Governor of the Cape, Sir Benjamin d'Urban, took it under his jurisdiction. Durban, the fine port of Natal, bears his name. In 1856 Natal was organized as a separate colony.

The Dutch of Cape Colony felt that they had many grievances. The British authorities had made English the official language, though they did not alter the so-called Roman-Dutch system of law [1] which they found in the country. The missionaries, especially those of the great London Missionary Society, which had been founded in 1794, were extremely influential with the British authorities. Partly through their influence the celebrated Ordinance Number 50 was issued by the Governor, securing full civil rights to free colored persons lawfully residing within the colony. Though this ordinance did not apply to slaves, the emancipation of all British colonial slaves by Act of Parliament in 1833 brought the entire native population within its scope. Financial compensation was allowed to owners, but there were legal delays, and the sums obtained were considered inadequate by the Boer slave owners. The government, too, had a fluctuating frontier policy, sometimes displaying vigor against marauding tribes, but shrinking from the cost and responsibility of extending the area of British rule. This grievance was much like that of the colonial farmers in the western parts of Virginia and Pennsylvania before the American Revolution, who complained that their governors, living safely and comfortably along the seaboard, did not adequately protect them against the Indians.

By reason of all these accumulated discontents, a large number of Boers started their Great Trek towards the north in 1836. They were not looking for the vast treasures of gold that lay, unsuspected, under their feet. Their object was merely, as they declared in the Resolutions of Winberg, to 'enjoy a quieter life than we have hitherto had.' Such quiet was not, however, to be obtained by the mere process of moving away from British officials. There were warlike native tribes with whom to contend. Five hundred settlers—men, women and children—were wiped out by the Zulus at Weenen, 'the place of weeping,' on 17 February 1838. The Dutch pioneers or *Voortrekkers* saved their settlement by defeating the forces of Chaka's brother and

[1] 'Roman-Dutch,' because of the influence of Roman law on Dutch law.

successor Dingaan later in the same year. They also challenged the British possession of the colony of Natal.

By the year 1854 there were two British colonies—Cape Colony and Natal—and two independent, Dutch-speaking republics, founded by Boer Voortrekkers—the South African Republic beyond the Vaal River, commonly called the Transvaal, and the Orange Free State, named in honor of the famous dynasty of Orange. There were, as yet, no railways, little trade, and a predominance of pastoral life. The Boers had little desire for closer union; they liked open spaces and disliked British ways and official interference with their own customs. Only the native danger exerted any influence towards the union of South Africa. Altogether nine Kaffir wars are reckoned by South African historians (Kaffir, from the Arabic word for unbeliever, being the general name applied by white settlers to the Negroes of Bantu stock who inhabited South Africa).

Sir George Grey, who had already been Governor of South Australia and of New Zealand,[2] was Governor of the Cape Colony from 1854 to 1861. He was a great exponent of the policy of directly governing the natives by extending the frontier to the northeast. He believed that the government could civilize the natives 'by employing them on public works which will open up the country; by establishing institutions for the education of their children and the relief of their sick; by introducing among them institutions of a civil character suited to their present conditions.' The Grey policy was put into effect only in certain frontier areas. The home government, while assuming sovereign rights, maintained native administration in the huge provinces of Basutoland, Bechuanaland, and Swaziland, each under the guidance of a British commissioner who was directly responsible to the British Government in London.

In 1867 something happened in South Africa analogous to the California gold rush of 1849 or the Australian gold rush of 1851. This was the discovery that the land between the Orange River and the Vaal was diamond-bearing. A quiet, sleepy land of widely spaced ranches, such as the region around the de Beers farm, now became the scene of diamond-washing and surface mining, of camps, traders, and company promoters. The Orange Free State claimed the terri-

[2] See Chapter xxxv.

tory, but so did the native tribe of the Griquas, whose chief asked for British protection. This was granted, and in 1871 Griqualand West was proclaimed at the new mining town of Kimberley to be British territory. In 1886 gold was discovered on the great reef in the Transvaal called Witwatersrand, and soon the town of Johannesburg rivalled Kimberley. Nobody contested that the Rand was Transvaal territory, so in the heart of the pastoral Republic there grew up a crowded, clamorous, cosmopolitan mining community which made the old policy of isolation no longer possible. Industrialism, growing cities, urgent problems of tariffs and transportation made some form of union an urgent necessity. But could two peoples so different as the Boers and the British agree to any common frame of government?

The resourceful and sagacious Governor Grey had proposed federation but could not interest the British Government of the time in it, although the Transvaal Volksraad (Assembly) had in 1858 voted for federation with Cape Colony. Twenty years later, Lord Carnarvon, Secretary of State for the Colonies in Lord Beaconsfield's imperialistic administration, again took up the matter. In 1874 and 1876 he sent his friend the historian J. A. Froude to South Africa to survey the situation. But the Boers were becoming less favorable to the idea, and the First Boer War made it hopeless for a generation to come.

The First Boer War came at the end of a period of troubles. In 1877 the South African Republic (Transvaal) was financially bankrupt, and was threatened with invasion by the Zulus, the most warlike race in South Africa. Lord Carnarvon, still Colonial Secretary, sent Sir Theophilus Shepstone, a South African-born official, to annex the Transvaal, and this annexation was at first received without opposition, though equally without enthusiasm, by the Boers. In 1879 the British had to fight a Zulu war, in which they lost 800 soldiers in the battle of Isandhlwana, though they avenged this defeat shortly afterwards in the battle of Ulundi. It was in this little war that the son of the former French Emperor Napoleon III lost his life while serving with the British forces. When the war was over, and Zululand was pacified and annexed, the Boers rose in arms to regain their independence.

In 1881 on Majuba Hill, in the extreme north of Natal, the Boers defeated about 1,300 British soldiers, who suffered heavy losses, including General Colley. Before news of the battle reached England, British Prime Minister Gladstone had made up his mind to concede independence (with reservation as to foreign relations) to the Transvaal, and when the news arrived he persisted in his opinion, though his political opponents insisted that the prestige of British arms demanded that Majuba be avenged. Accordingly he made the Convention of Pretoria, 3 August 1881, replaced by a still more generous Convention of London three years later, 27 February 1884. The Transvaal was recognized as independent, but was not to make treaties with any foreign state, except the kindred Orange Free State, or with any native tribe, unless with British approval.

At this time an empire builder, at once dreamer and man of action, was beginning to become a power in South Africa. This was Cecil Rhodes, who had gone to South Africa in 1870 to preserve his health in a warmer, dryer climate. Being energetic and ambitious he had not lived the life of a professional invalid, but had entered business. He made an enormous fortune in the diamond fields and in 1881 carried out a great amalgamation of mining interests, the De Beers Company. In 1884 he induced the British Government to take over as a Protectorate the native region called Bechuanaland, where the missionaries Robert Moffat and David Livingstone had labored so fruitfully. In 1889 he formed a Chartered Company which took over, under the British flag, a vast area north of the Transvaal called by his own name, Rhodesia.[3]

Meanwhile Johannesburg and the Rand were filling up with miners and mine promoters. Just as the Dutch in Cape Colony had been discontented with British rule half a century earlier, so now these British Uitlanders (outlanders; aliens) complained of Boer rule in the South African Republic of the Transvaal. But they could not trek, because they wanted to stay by the mines. They complained of misrule, excessive taxation, and denial of citizen's rights. No immigrant was granted the vote till after fourteen years' residence, which to Englishmen seemed excessive. To remedy their situation the Uitlanders agitated, and then, finding the Boer authorities obdurate, conspired. Before a revolution could be engineered, however,

[3] For Rhodesia see Chapter XXXVII.

Leander Starr Jameson, a physician and friend of Rhodes, led a premature raid into the Transvaal from Bechuanaland. His small force of some 600 men was rounded up and forced to surrender by President Paul Kruger at Doornkop. No rising took place at Johannesburg.

The Jameson Raid of 1896 was disastrous in many ways. It deepened President Kruger's stubbornness into obstinacy; he was now convinced that the British were in a conspiracy to subvert the independence of the Transvaal, and he refused to make adequate concession to the Uitlanders. The British had been discredited by a major blunder. Cecil Rhodes, who had favored revolution though he disapproved of the premature action of Jameson, had to resign his premiership of Cape Colony. Worst of all, the incident almost brought on hostilities with Germany, for Kaiser Wilhelm II took on himself the responsibility of telegraphing to President Kruger 'sincere congratulations that without appealing to the help of friendly Powers you and your people have succeeded in repelling with your own forces the armed bands which had broken into your country, and in maintaining the independence of your country against foreign aggression.' The dynamite in the Kruger telegram lay in the phrase 'without appealing to the help of friendly Powers,' which seemed to the British to imply that Germany claimed a right to intervene by force in South African affairs if she saw fit. Nothing, except the building of the large German fleet, had so unfavorable an influence on British public opinion in regard to Germany.[4]

The defeat of the Raid did not stop the Uitlander agitation. Sir Alfred Milner, the new High Commissioner for South Africa, insisted that the British Government give support to the demands of British residents of the Transvaal. He was backed by the Colonial Secretary Joseph Chamberlain and by the British goldmining interests. Both sides were obstinate, each apparently convinced that the other would give way before a mere show of force. Doubtless, also, the Boers had in mind the Kruger telegram and expected eventual foreign aid if matters came to war. The Second Boer War (1899-1902) proved to be a major colonial conflict. The vastly superior resources of the British Empire made eventual victory inevitable, but the Boers, who knew the country thoroughly, who were trained

[4] For the European diplomatic background of the times see Chapter XXXI.

almost from the cradle to ride and shoot, gave so good an account of themselves that they won the admiration of their British conquerors. The Orange Free State joined the Transvaal, so both Boer Republics were drawn into the contest. Though the size of the armies involved was smaller, the struggle in South Africa lasted nearly as long as the American Civil War, and the swift audacious Boer, mounted on his own steed, proved almost as difficult to surround and cut off as the armies of Jackson and Lee.

The war ended at last with the Treaty of Vereeniging. British rule was established over the entire territory of the Transvaal and the Orange Free State, but many concessions were made to the vanquished. The Boers were to have representative government, their own language, and an appropriation of three million pounds (about $15,000,000) to restock their devastated farms. Many British Liberal politicians (including Mr. Lloyd George) had strongly criticized the government for carrying on the war at all. They were resolved that, as soon as possible after peace had been restored, the former Boer Republics should have full responsible government in the British Empire (and such government was actually established in 1909). A minority of the Boers have remained unreconciled, and in 1914 there was a small rebellion of the disaffected,[5] but the great majority were completely won over by the new British policy and it may be said of the Second Boer War that, to a degree almost without parallel among the thousand wars of history, it left the combatants better friends than it found them.

'Reconstruction' was certainly more harmonious in South Africa than it was in the United States after 1865. The chief difficulty arose in the Rand gold mines. European labor was expensive; native labor not reliable, so the unhappy experiment was made of importing the cheap, docile Chinese on long-term labor contracts. This proved unpopular in both South Africa and Great Britain, and in 1905 was used effectively as an election cry by British Liberals to turn out the Conservative Government, already weighted down by the responsibility for a costly and perhaps avoidable war. The Liberals took the risk of conceding full responsible government, of the Dominion type, to both the Transvaal and the Orange River Colony.[6] The question

[5] See Chapter xxxviii.
[6] The old name of Orange Free State was eventually restored.

of union was left for the South Africans themselves to settle. After protracted negotiations, a scheme of union was at last drawn up, and approved by the British Parliament, in 1909. In 1910 the new Union of South Africa started work in its three capitals: Pretoria, the executive center, Capetown, the legislative seat, and Bloemfontein, seat of the highest court.

The Union is a federation, but a more centralized one than the Dominion of Canada, and still more so than the Commonwealth of Australia or the United States of America. There are four provinces: Cape Province, Transvaal, Orange Free State, and Natal. All four have a mixed Dutch and British population, though in varying proportion. The two languages [7] stand on a footing of complete equality. Since the First World War, German Southwest Africa has been held by the Union as a mandated territory from the League of Nations. Of the ten million inhabitants of the Union, only about one-fifth are of the white race, either British or Boer.

There is a Governor-General and his ministry, which is responsible to the House of Assembly elected by the people. The Senate, mainly indirectly elected, though with a few appointed members (chosen, in part, to represent 'the reasonable wants and wishes of the colored races'), is the less important chamber of the two. Each province has a local Provincial Council. Except in the Cape, where a limited franchise was accorded to natives, the Negro population is not directly represented in the Union.

The first Prime Minister of the Union was General Louis Botha, who had fought against the British in the Second Boer War. He was supported, and later succeeded, as Prime Minister, by General J. C. Smuts. General Hertzog (who later held the Prime Ministership) led a Nationalist opposition, and there is a small Labour party. Most of the British voters eventually entered into coalition with the moderate Dutch element who followed Botha and Smuts. Nothing in the history of the British Empire is more striking than the acceptance of Boer leadership by the British in South Africa, unless it be the readiness of the Boer leaders to co-operate whole-heartedly with the Empire which had conquered and absorbed them!

[7] Since 1929 the local South African form of Dutch (Afrikaans) has been preferred to Dutch as known in Holland.

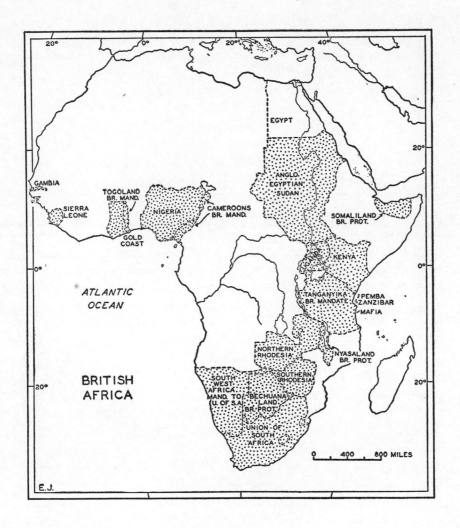

20°　　　　　0°　　　　　20°　　　　　40°

EGYPT

20°

GAMBIA

ANGLO-
EGYPTIAN
SUDAN

TOGOLAND
BR. MAND.

SIERRA
LEONE

NIGERIA

CAMEROONS
BR. MAND.

SOMALILAND
BR. PROT.

GOLD
COAST

0°

KENYA

ATLANTIC
OCEAN

TANGANYIKA
BR. MANDATE

PEMBA
ZANZIBAR
MAFIA

NORTHERN
RHODESIA

NYASALAND
BR. PROT.

BRITISH
AFRICA

20°

SOUTH
WEST
AFRICA
MAND. TO
U. OF S.A.

SOUTHERN
RHODESIA

BECHUANA-
LAND
BR. PROT.

UNION OF
SOUTH
AFRICA

20°

0　　400　　800 MILES

E.J.

CROWN COLONIES AND OTHER DEPENDENCIES

THUS far in our survey of the Second British Empire we have devoted our attention, save for the special case of India, to the completely self-governing portions. But there remain to be considered, however briefly, a number of dependencies whose degree of self-government, though often very considerable, is in no case absolute. This dependent empire is the responsibility of the British Government. A large part of it, administered through the Colonial Office, consists of Crown Colonies; other parts, such as Egypt, are in special treaty relationship with Great Britain but are not technically within the Empire.[1] The reasons for dependence vary greatly. Thus the Fiji Islands are a Crown Colony because their population is native (i.e. non-European) and only semi-civilized. The Falkland Islands, off the coast of South America, have a British population, but too few in number to sustain their own government. Jamaica has a large population, but the white settlers are far outnumbered by the descendants of Negro slaves. Cyprus, Malta, and Gibraltar in the Mediterranean are chiefly important as naval bases. Generally speaking, the dependent portions of the Empire are in tropical or sub-tropical regions, unfit for wholesale European settlement, or are already densely settled by non-European peoples; their importance is strategic or commercial rather than as homes for emigrants.

The common tie of the British Empire is the highway of the Seven Seas. Many of the Crown Colonies are islands, or groups of islands. The oldest group is the British West Indies, the first valuable overseas possessions of the Crown. Another such group is the far-flung oceanic empire of Polynesian and Melanesian islands in the Pacific. Another consists of Malay States, insular or peninsular, between the

[1] For the organization of the British Empire and the relation of its parts to each other see Chapters XXXII and XXXIX.

471

Pacific Ocean and the Indian Ocean. There are also scattered or isolated islands, such as Ceylon, off the coast of India but no part of the
Indian Empire, or St. Helena, Napoleon's last residence, in the
South Atlantic. But territorially the largest group of dependent possessions is continental, the various British colonies and protectorates
in tropical Africa.

'West Indies' is a geographical expression. There is no central government for the entire group and many of the individual islands have
separate governments of their own. The oldest colony is Bermuda,
where a ship's company was wrecked in 1607 while on its way from
England to the new plantation of Virginia. The indomitable leader,
Sir George Somers, had the crew make a couple of pinnaces out of
the trunks of trees, and they completed their voyage. Connection,
chiefly economic, between the West Indies and the thirteen mainland
colonies remained close throughout the old colonial period. The chief
islands of the British West Indies were Jamaica, the Bahamas, Barbados, Bermuda, Grenada, Trinidad, and the Leeward and Wind-
ward Islands. Many other Powers had colonies in the Caribbean, and
the colonial wars of Britain, France, Spain, and Holland largely centered around this region. Today, these empires are much reduced.
France holds Martinique and Guadeloupe; the United States Puerto
Rico and the formerly Danish Virgin Islands; the Netherlands
Curaçao. But Cuba and the old island of Hispaniola (now two republics, Haiti and Santo Domingo) are independent states. Spain
has lost her entire Caribbean empire.

Moreover, few of the West Indies have the political and economic
importance which belonged to them in the old days of the slave plantation system. Then the West Indies had a social life somewhat like
that of the 'black belt' of the Old South; an aristocracy of planters
supported by estates cultivated by gangs of slaves. The proportion of
Negroes to whites was, however, on most islands very much greater
than in any part of the mainland, and the elements of virile democracy which developed in the Southern states were almost lacking in
these tropical island colonies. Emancipation was imposed on the
planters against their will by the British Parliament. Troubles between whites and blacks in Jamaica led on more than one occasion to
intervention by the British Government. In 1839 the British ministry
of Lord Melbourne was almost overthrown by a constitutional con-

flict with the Jamaican planters which echoed in the halls of Parliament; and in 1865 a Negro rebellion, savagely repressed, set half England debating whether Governor Eyre was a tyrant or a savior of society. As a result of these conflicts, Jamaica lost some part of the constitutional powers which she enjoyed under the old colonial system. In other of the West Indies islands there was less racial strife, but almost everywhere there was some economic decline, caused by the competition of foreign-grown sugar or by the failure of the islands to develop manufactures in an age in which industry overshadows agriculture. The islanders remain farmers and planters, producing excellent sugar, coffee, and fruits. They live a fairly tranquil, if not very dynamic, existence, and recent years have opened up to them a new and important source of income, the tourist industry.

There are several other British dependencies in America: the timber-cutting district of British Honduras in Central America; the large but very thinly peopled colony of British Guiana, with its sugar plantations on the coast, worked mainly by coolies from India, and its jungles and magnificent waterfalls in the interior; the sheep-raising Falkland Islands; and the whaling station of South Georgia. The British have also somewhat vague claims, based on exploration, to the ice-bound mountains of the Antarctic, at present of no commercial importance.

The Pacific island group is very much more extensive than the West Indian, though its economic importance is hardly greater. There is a marked contrast between the two in population. Whereas the native Indian Caribs had practically disappeared during the seventeenth century, so that the population of the West Indies was mainly immigrant, either from Europe or Africa, there is a large, though perhaps decreasing, native Polynesian and Melanesian population in Oceania. The Polynesians are among the most attractive of the dark-skinned races, tall, stalwart and athletic, fluent in oratory and song, friendly and genial in manners. Typical of the race are the Samoans, the Hawaiians, and the Maoris of New Zealand. But they were not without their faults. Their early proneness to cannibalism was cured by Christian missionaries, but their easy-going indifference to the economic values left them a prey to the greed of European traders. The attempt to maintain native kingdoms resulted only in the exploitation of their subjects by white traders and planters; imperialism became necessary to restrain the trader by the official.

On one occasion this anomalous situation almost led to war between Great Britain and the United States, on the one hand, and Germany on the other. The Kingdom of Samoa would hardly be remembered today, save by professional students of diplomacy, had not Robert Louis Stevenson's search for health brought him to the islands. In his *Footnote to History* one can read the story of how foreign consuls, British, American, and German, put up chiefs and pulled them down at will to suit the commercial interests of planters of their own nationality. Eventually, after the experiment of a 'condominium' or joint government by all three interested Great Powers had failed, the island group was divided, most of it going to Germany, part to the United States, Great Britain receiving compensation elsewhere. Since the First World War, German Samoa has been a dependency of New Zealand under the mandate system. Australia has a similar mandate for German New Guinea and neighboring islands. The New Hebrides group has been long governed by a French and British condominium.

Fiji, acquired in 1874 at the beginning of the great modern wave of expansionist imperialism, is typical of Melanesia. The Melanesians are a darker race than the Polynesians, almost Negroid in appearance. There are also in Fiji Hindu laborers on the plantations, much more diligent workers than the light-hearted Pacific islanders. Other British Pacific island groups include the Tonga Islands, the Solomon Islands, the Gilbert and Ellice Islands. Perhaps the most romantic story of Pacific colonization is that of Pitcairn Island, founded by mutineers from the *Bounty* who had revolted against the harshness of Captain Bligh in 1790. The Pitcairn Islanders are descendants of these sailors and of the native wives whom they brought over from Tahiti. They govern themselves under the supervision of a resident British officer.

The Straits Settlements are a group of colonies and protectorates connecting the Nearer with the Farther East. The Dutch were the first to engage actively in trade in this region, but their main settlements were in the Spice Islands beyond the Straits. During the Napoleonic wars, since Holland was annexed to the French Empire, the Dutch colonies fell a prize to the British navy. In 1811 Lord Minto,

Governor-General of India, took a naval and military force to Java and occupied it, together with Sumatra. He was accompanied by an East Indian Company official, Stamford Raffles, son of a sea captain, who was born in the West Indies. Raffles was made Governor of the occupied settlements. At the Peace of 1815, the British handed back Java and Sumatra to the Dutch, but the far-seeing Raffles had meanwhile seen the potentialities of a neglected little island called Singapore, near the tip of the Malay peninsula.

Now, all the shipping between Europe, India, and the Far East goes by Singapore, the greatest emporium of the Orient. The picturesque little island, a scene delightfully combined of hill, wood, and sea, has a temperate, equable climate, and has attracted a large population of Malays, Chinese, Hindus, and Europeans. Apart from Singapore, most of the Straits Settlements are on the mainland and are governed by native Sultans with the advice and assistance of British officials. Tin and rubber are the chief exports of this region. The Straits Settlements also include the Keeling (or Kokos) Islands, and tiny Christmas Island, 250 miles southwest of Java, famous for its nitrates. The British also control, under various titles of sovereignty, North Borneo, Brunei, and the strange dependency of Sarawak, governed by a line of British 'rajahs' of the Brooke family—all of them on the great island of Borneo, most of which is Dutch. Some of the islands in the Indian Ocean, such as the Andaman Islands, are attached to the Indian Empire; others, such as Ceylon and Mauritius, are Crown Colonies. In 1941 and 1942 all the Malayan and insular East Indian dependencies of the British Crown were seized by Japan.

Six hundred miles beyond the Straits Settlements is Hong Kong, an island off the coast of China which was ceded to Great Britain by the Treaty of Nanking in 1842. This island, like Singapore, is a meeting place of ships from every land; it is the regular depot for trade between Australia and the Far East. The high wooded granite ridge of the little island offers cool situations for the clustering houses. Europeans find the climate favorable, but the bulk of the population consists of Chinese. Great Britain also leases Wei-hai-wei in northern China and holds concessions in various treaty ports, such as Shanghai. The International Settlement at Shanghai, originally in 1843 assigned by the Chinese authorities to the British, has been thrown open to all peoples. It is a model municipality, administered by an international council elected by the local rate-payers, including Chinese residents. Chinese law does not obtain in Concessions and Settlements, for by treaty they are 'extra-territorial' and have their own magistrates. For a long time British and other foreign merchants claimed similar rights of extra-territoriality and exemption from laws other than their own in Japan, but with the beginning of the twentieth century these privileges were surrendered. Japan seized Hong-Kong in the Second World War and drove out British subjects from all Chinese ports.

The last great group of Crown Colonies is in Africa. Until the nineteenth century, Africa south of the Sahara was known only as a shoreline which European traders visited for barter or slave catching. In 1795 an English scientific society, called the Africa Association, sent a young Scottish surgeon, Mungo Park, to explore the interior from the mouth of the Gambia River in northwestern Africa. Park spent five months in the interior and discovered the upper waters of the Niger. In 1805 he was sent out again, this time by the British Government. He penetrated to the region of the upper Niger and then went downstream in a canoe; he was killed by natives at Boussa, but twenty-five years later the Cornish explorer Richard Lander found Park's copies of the Book of Psalms and Isaac Watts's hymns, preserved as magic charms by the tribe which had slain him.

The desire to give the Central African natives the Gospel and to put an end to the horrors of the native slave trade was the motive of the great explorer David Livingstone. The London Missionary Society, founded in 1795, maintained a station at Kuruman in Bechuanaland, which Livingstone joined in 1840. In 1852, with four native servants, he started from Quilimane in Mozambique and walked, through the regions of the Zambezi and the Congo, across Africa to St. Paul de Loanda, and back again to Quilimane, spending four years in this work, preaching and healing (for he was a qualified physician) as he went. He had discovered the Victoria Falls of the Zambezi. His last journey, 1866-73, took him to the sources of the Nile. He explored the country about Lake Tanganyika, and was believed to be lost there. *The New York Herald* sent an expedition in 1871 under Henry Moreton Stanley to search for him.

Stanley found Livingstone, who accepted medical and other supplies but refused to give up his work and come home. In 1873 Livingstone died. No man since the apostle Paul had spread the gospel more widely, no previous African explorer had adventured more extensively, and no man had done more to heal what he had stigmatized as 'the open sore of the world,' the African slave trade.

Stanley, who was no missionary but a journalist, made many journeys in Africa, some for Gordon Bennett, publisher of *The New York Herald*, some for King Leopold II of Belgium. He was a Welsh boy who had emigrated to New Orleans, clerked in a store there, served briefly in the Confederate army, and then sought a new career as a reporter. His last great expedition was made from Zanzibar through central Africa in 1889 to find one of the white officials of the Egyptian Sudan, then being swept by ferocious bands of Mohammedan fanatics. This man who went by the name of Emin Pasha, though he was really a German named Eduard Schnitzer, Stanley found, safe and contented, botanizing on the shores of Lake Albert Nyanza.

The opening up of central Africa by the explorations of Livingstone, Stanley, and many others led to a more speedy partition of this region among the European Powers. International conferences at Brussels (1876) and Berlin (1884-5) laid down rules for the taking up of native African territory, so that there would be no conflict over jurisdictions. Leopold II of Belgium obtained the vast central basin of the Congo River as the Congo Free State; originally intended to establish peace, promote commerce, and abolish slavery in this region, it became more and more a privately exploited rubber plantation, whose abuses became so notorious that pressure from Great Britain and other Powers eventually forced King Leopold to sell out his rights to the Belgian nation, and the Congo Free State became the Belgian Congo. The rights and claims of Germany, France, Portugal, and Great Britain in tropical Africa were also adjusted by treaty.[2] There was a great deal of friction among the interested Powers but, rather surprisingly, no war. Within the Congo area, which included considerably more than the Free State, the terms of the Berlin Act forbade slavery, the sale of arms and intoxi-

[2] See Hertslet, *Map of Africa by Treaty.*

cants to natives, religious discrimination, and interference with the freedom of trade and navigation. Some of these provisions have been violated by colonizing Powers (as by Leopold II), but their very existence is a proof that the professed ideals of the new imperialism of the nineteenth century at least surpassed those of the old imperialism of the sixteenth, seventeenth, and eighteenth centuries. The British record, particularly with regard to freedom of trade in the Crown Colonies and protectorates, is better than most.

The British colonies in tropical Africa are mainly unsuited for British settlement, though perhaps an exception may be made in favor of the mountain highlands in Kenya and parts of Rhodesia. Rhodesia was administered by the Chartered Company of British South Africa from 1890 to 1923, when it was divided. Southern Rhodesia, suited for white settlement and with a population of more than 50,000 whites (amidst over 1,000,000 Negroes), obtained responsible government, like the Dominions; but Northern Rhodesia, with a very scanty white population, became a Crown Colony. The Zambezi River is the boundary between the two. Both colonies are monuments to the genius and energy of Cecil Rhodes.[3] Great Britain also extends her protection over large regions in South Africa where there is little or no white settlement—Basutoland, Bechuanaland, and Swaziland.

Some of the colonies in western Africa have already a respectable antiquity, such as Gambia (1783) and Sierra Leone (1787). The latter was used as a home for freed slaves, just as was the near-by Republic of Liberia, which was founded under American patronage. Nigeria, partly a product of the private commercial enterprise of the Royal Niger Company, developed into one of the largest, most populous, and most valuable colonies in western Africa; it has over 20,000,000 native inhabitants. Great Britain controls also, in western Africa, the Gold Coast and the parts of Togoland and Kamerun acquired as mandates from Germany in the First World War.[4]

In East Africa also chartered companies did much of the pioneer work. Thus the British East African Company for a time adminis-

---

[3] For the career of this remarkable man see Chapter xxxvi. His well-known will, bequeathing a fortune to found scholarships at Oxford for British colonials, Americans (and Germans!), is an interesting expression of his political dreams.

[4] For the mandates see Chapters xxxviii and xxxix.

tered great tracts of land granted by the Sultan of Zanzibar. Eventually the British Crown took over its rights and claims. Uganda, Kenya, Nyassaland, Zanzibar, and British Somaliland are all virtually under British rule, though, with the exception of part of Kenya, rather as protectorates than as colonies. Since the First World War, German East Africa has been added, under the name of Tanganyika. Native sovereigns and chiefs remain in office, under the direction and overruling authority of British officials, very much as in the native states of India.

Northern Africa is very different from the rest of the continent. Instead of being the newest land to be explored by white men, it is perhaps the oldest; instead of being inhabited by Negroid peoples of various types, it is inhabited by white (though deeply sunburned!) races; instead of being a mixture of primitive paganism, Mohammedanism, and Christianity, it is almost solidly Mohammedan. Like other parts of Africa it was partitioned among European colonizing Powers during the nineteenth and twentieth centuries. France obtained Algeria, Tunis, and Morocco (except a small fragment of the last, which went to Spain); Italy obtained Tripoli and renamed it Libya; Great Britain obtained, in name and form, no colonies here at all, but for practical purposes gained the best prize north of the Sahara, Egypt, the land of the Nile, the most ancient of civilized lands.

Egypt was a dependency of the Sultan of Turkey, ruled by viceroys or Khedives who governed the country as though they were independent sovereigns. France, more than any other European country, had taken an active interest in Egyptian affairs. Napoleon tried to make the land a base of operations in the Orient generally, and a generation later France backed the ambitions of Khedive Mehemet Ali against the Sultan, who had the general support of Great Britain. The extravagance of Ismail, his grandson, bankrupted Egypt and had a great effect on British policy, for it enabled Disraeli to purchase his interest in the Suez Canal enterprise on behalf of the British Government, and it also led to a joint French and British control of Egyptian finance.

Against this 'government by foreign bondholders,' a patriotic Egyptian party under Arabi Pasha raised the standard of revolt with the war cry of 'Egypt for the Egyptians.' The British retaliated by bombarding and seizing Alexandria in 1882. The French took no part; so Great Britain assumed entire responsibility for establishing law and order throughout Egypt. The status of Egypt from 1882 to 1914 is exceptionally hard to define. Theoretically Egypt was a tributary of the Ottoman Empire, governed by its own Khedive. Practically the Khedive took orders not from the Sultan but from the British Consul-General Sir Evelyn Baring (later Lord Cromer). Not until 1904 did France recognize the British position in Egypt, in return for a similar recognition of the French position in Morocco. British rule was never popular, and there were occasional outbreaks against it, but the rapid increase of population, the erection of great engineering works to control the flow of the Nile, the protection of the peasantry from plunder and rapine were the pleas advanced by British imperialists for their right to remain in virtual control of Egypt, however legally anomalous their position might be.

A still more complex question was that of the Sudan, a huge tropical dependency of Egypt on the upper Nile. Gladstone, who had been reluctant to intervene in Egypt, was still more reluctant to hold this distant land by a British army of occupation. He sent Charles Gordon, commonly known as 'Chinese Gordon' because of his services as volunteer in the Chinese army, to withdraw outlying garrisons. But Gordon had ideas of his own; once on the spot he felt it a crime to leave the country to marauding bands who followed a Mohammedan fanatic called the Mahdi. Gladstone, hoping to force this intractable agent into obedience, delayed sending relief. At last it was decided to send succor, but when the relief expedition reached Khartum, in January 1885, the city had been taken and Gordon killed. Though the Mahdi himself died soon afterwards, his followers plundered at will for thirteen years longer. Then an expeditionary force under Herbert Kitchener broke the power of the desert dervishes at Omdurman in 1898.

Almost immediately a fresh crisis arose. Major Marchand, a brave French explorer, had raised the French flag on the Nile at the town of Fashoda after a long expedition through the heart of Africa. The French claim was that the Sudan had become a no-man's land from long abandonment, and that one Power had as good a claim as another to colonize there. The British held that the Sudan had never ceased *de jure* to be a dependency of Egypt and that the French were therefore intruders. A good legal case might be made out for either side (or, an anti-imperialist might say, for neither), but the decisive factors in the situation were that France could not wage a colonial war against the superior naval power of Britain, or risk any war indeed so long as Germany remained a potential enemy. So the entire course of the upper Nile was placed under the joint rule (or condominium) of Egypt and Great Britain, while France had to content herself with territorial gains farther to the west.

PART VII

THE ENGLISH-SPEAKING PEOPLES BETWEEN TWO WARS

◦ XXXVIII ◦

THE FIRST WORLD WAR

IT is not the purpose of this chapter to give an account of the World War of 1914-18, nor of the peace negotiations which closed it. That belongs to world history. Our purpose is merely to indicate the special role played by the British Commonwealth and by the United States of America in this almost cosmic conflict.

Most British wars, thanks to the advantages of a strong navy, had been wars of limited liability. In general, the British had subsidized continental allies, preyed on hostile shipping, and sent abroad small forces of professional soldiers augmented by volunteers. Even in the life and death struggle with Napoleon no general system of conscription was introduced, though the navy had the power to 'press' sailors into its service; and no one in authority so much as dreamed of conscription for the Crimean War or the Boer War. Civilian life flowed placidly in a current of its own.

The First World War ended this separation of the civilian from the soldier; for the first time in centuries the British nation was as much at war as the British army. Though no enemy set foot on British shores, British towns along the North Sea were bombarded by German cruisers within the first few days of the war, and London was later a frequent target for Zeppelin raids from the air. Conscription was adopted in 1916, even though the call for volunteers had raised an army of unprecedented size. The government was forced to undertake, piecemeal to be sure, and reluctantly, a system of wartime socialism, involving the regulation of prices, wages, and conditions of labor, priority of production and transportation, and of every other phase of national economy. Before the end of the war, food and fuel were rationed as though the British Isles were a single beleaguered city. News also was 'rationed,' and war correspondents lost the irresponsible freedom which had marked their reports on the Crimean War, the Boer War, and the Spanish-American conflict. But in one respect Britain remained freer than most belligerent nations; the press was in general permitted to comment freely, even adversely to the government, on its editorial pages.

In a military sense Great Britain was more completely involved than in any previous modern war. British soldiers fought mainly on the western front, from the Flemish coast to the junction with the French armies in the Somme valley; but smaller forces were active at one time or another in Italy, northern Russia, Macedonia, Gallipoli, Palestine, Mesopotamia, German Africa, and the Pacific islands. Before the war was over the Empire had placed about 9,000,000 men under arms and about 1,000,000 of them had given their lives for their country. Though some other belligerents suffered and sacrificed even more greatly, no other touched the war at so many points, engaged in battle on so many fronts, or contributed in such diverse ways to the final result as the British.

Every colony and dependency in the Empire contributed to the British war effort, and some fought independent campaigns, such as the conquest of German Southwest Africa by the South African Union. Canada enrolled nearly 650,000 men, chiefly for service on the western front; Australia about 500,000, and New Zealand over 200,000, largely for the campaigns against Turkey; South Africa 136,000, employed chiefly in Africa. Canada and New Zealand adopted measures for compulsory overseas service; Australia, though having compulsory military training even in time of peace, left overseas service to volunteers. The effort of the Dominions was wholly spontaneous, since not one of them was legally obliged to send a ship, a soldier, or a penny to aid Britain except by the vote of its own elected Parliament.

The status of India and of the dependent portions of the Empire was not the same; but it is worth noting that many Indian princes offered assistance beyond their legal obligations, and it is significant that, although there was much unrest in India during the war, the country as a whole was less disturbed than either just before or immediately after it. Indeed, there was open rebellion in only two parts of the British Empire. In 1914 a few irreconcilable Boers, under Generals Beyers, De Wet, and Maritz, rose in protest against the war with Germany's neighboring colony of Southwest Africa. This revolt, however, was put down by South African forces commanded by former Boer generals, such as Botha and Smuts. In 1916 there was the brief 'Easter week rebellion' of the Irish extremists, which left a legacy of ill-feeling in Ireland but was in itself of little military importance.[1]

The British, owing to the mobility of their forces assured by the mastery of the sea, were the most active of all belligerents in the colonial campaigns. As soon as Turkey made war, the British Government severed all ties between the Sultan and his nominal subjects in Cyprus and Egypt. Egypt, from 1914 to 1922, became a British Protectorate, and Cyprus, no longer a mere leasehold, became a Crown Colony. The German islands in the Pacific, south of the equator, were taken over mainly by Australia and New Zealand. The German colonies in tropical Africa were captured in co-operation with French and Belgian forces; in only one case, German East Africa, was there serious resistance.

The Ottoman Empire proved a hard nut to crack. An attempt to force the Dardanelles by a combined land and sea expedition had to be abandoned, and a British force was captured by Turks in Mesopotamia. In the later years of the war, however, these losses were retrieved. Colonel Lawrence and other British agents roused the Arabs against their Turkish rulers; General Allenby took Jerusalem and occupied Palestine and Syria; General Maude captured Bagdad and thus avenged General Townshend's defeat in Mesopotamia.

The professional army which was sent to France and Belgium at the opening of the war was so small by comparison with the vast conscript armies of the continent that for weeks it could do nothing but carry out an orderly retreat. At the Marne, however, it was able to co-operate with the French in the counterattack which ended the German offensive. Then the war settled down to a four years' deadlock of the trenches. The British army was expanded by constant recruiting, taking over larger and larger sections of the front, until it shared equal responsibilities with the French. The deep mud and incessant rains of Flanders gave the British the worst physical conditions faced by any soldiers in the war.[2] That under these conditions

---

[1] For Irish affairs see Chapter xxxix.
[2] 'The author has visited the fighting fronts from the sand-dunes of the Belgian coast to the entrenched camp of Saloniki and observed the conditions under

newly levied armies, often of briefly trained civilians, maintained their spirit undiminished for four years is amazing. No army in the world showed better spirit, though the French and Germans both had undergone years of military training in time of peace.

The British war effort was seriously handicapped by lack of munitions and uncertainty of strategic objective. There was a shortage of shells for field cannon in the early days of the war, until Lloyd George, as Minister of Munitions, reorganized production. There was also a division of opinion between 'westerners,' such as War Minister Kitchener and Field Marshals French and Haig, who wanted to concentrate on the western front where a single smashing success might decide the whole war; and 'easterners,' such as Munitions Minister Lloyd George and First Lord of the Admiralty Winston Churchill, who wanted to save manpower by defensive tactics in the west until effective blows had been struck in Turkey and the Balkans. This uncertainty of policy had an unfortunate effect. British forces in the Near East were inadequate for their tasks; battles in France and Flanders were too costly for the results achieved. The Somme campaign, however, brought into war the most novel British contribution to warfare, the armored automobile or tank, moving on caterpillar treads like American farm tractors, which could move over rough ground and break down barbed wire defenses and earthwork entrenchments. It helped bring about the defeat of Germany in 1918, and in German hands prepared the defeat of France in 1940.

Of course, the greatest British contribution to the war was sea power. France and her allies might, conceivably, have won the war without the aid of the British army; they must have lost it without the aid of the British navy. Yet there was no decisive victory by sea comparable to the defeat of the Spanish Armada or Nelson's triumph at Trafalgar. Indeed, the war was singularly devoid of overt naval battles. Several German cruisers engaged in commerce raiding until they were hunted down. Minor battles occurred off the coast of South America, and one major conflict, the Battle of Jutland, near Den-

which men fought from the polders below sea-level to the glacier-clad heights of the Alps. He has no hesitation in saying that, of all the combatants, those who fought on the plains of Flanders endured the most terrible physical conditions' (Major Douglas Johnson, *Battlefields of the World War*, p. 25).

mark, in 1916. Not even Jutland, however, was decisive. The real war at sea was the invisible pressure of the British blockade and the German attempt to strike back by using the submarine.

Neither Great Britain nor Germany remained long bound by the precedents and usages of international law. The British found it necessary to shut Germany off almost altogether from overseas commerce by widening the list of contraband of war, and even to ration the trade of such small neutral states as Holland, which might reship imported goods to Germany. Against the British blockade the Germans could use only one weapon, the submarine, and were forced to use it illegally in order to use it efficiently. To give fair warning to the merchant vessel and to permit its passengers and crew to seek safety, as required by international law, would expose the submarine to dangers from some watchful cruiser lurking in the neighborhood. So ships—neutral ships often—were struck unawares by torpedo, and there was great loss of civilian lives. In 1915 the sinking of the great liner *Lusitania*, a British merchant ship, cost the lives of over a thousand civilians, more than a hundred of them being American citizens.

The United States in 1914 had no thought of the possibility of entering the war. Force of circumstances, rather than any definite plan, made the country a munitions base for one side only; had Germany commanded the seas she could have shared in the American trade. Yet the indirect effect of the British blockade was to bring the United States into economic partnership with the Entente Allies against the Central Powers. There were also ties of sentiment. American opinion in the mass condemned Austria-Hungary's hasty ultimatum to Serbia while peace negotiations were still proceeding, the German declarations of war on Russia and France, the German invasion of Belgium, the ruthlessness of German military administration in occupied countries, and the sinister, though unsuccessful, appeal to German-Americans to place their loyalty in their native rather than their adopted country. The mere fact of possessing a common language simplified the task of British propagandists. All Americans could read any British book, periodical, or newspaper without the need of a translator. German propaganda, though considerable in quantity, had to be specially written to order, as relatively few Americans had a reading knowledge of German or indeed of any continental European language.

Against the forces pulling the United States towards war there were certain resistances: German-Americans who still retained a sentimental affection for the 'old country'; Irish-Americans, carrying on a hereditary feud against Britain; Russian Jews with enduring resentments against Tsarist Russia; even some Americans of British stock who mistrusted British policy, hated despotic Russia, feared Japan, or admired the scientific and industrial triumphs of Germany. There were also pacifists and isolationists, who loved German militarism as little as anyone, but who desired to keep the United States out of war and, knowing that intervention was possible only on the side of the Entente Allies, threw their influence against Entente propaganda.

We have no exact measure of the relative strength of these opposing forces, but a survey conducted by the *Literary Digest* a few weeks after the war began (14 November 1914) showed that of 367 newspapers from all parts of the nation '105 report that they favor the Allies, 20 the Germans and 242 are neutral . . . The feeling of the cities and towns represented is reported as favoring the Allies in 189 cases, for the Germans in 38, and neutral or divided in 140.' In other words, of those who had active opinions, there were in 1914 about five Americans who would have preferred a British victory to one who would have preferred a German triumph. The great mass of the neutral, indifferent, or hesitant decreased as the war proceeded, especially after American lives had been taken by German submarines.

The Administration tried to follow a neutral course at first. Both President Wilson and his Secretary of War Bryan were ardent pacifists; both had also concentrated on a program of domestic reform,[3] which war would confuse or interrupt. Even the submarine sinkings brought only reiterated warnings from the White House. Early in 1916, it is true, President Wilson sounded out European Powers on the possibility of a conference to end the war, with the hint that if Germany made unreasonable demands the United States would 'probably' join the Entente Allies. But this was not a definite enough assurance for the European statesmen, at that time confident of winning the war without American aid; so nothing came of his pro-

[3] For the American political background see Chapter XXVI.

posal. The attack on the *Sussex* a few weeks later caused Wilson to threaten an end to diplomatic relations with Germany. Secretary Bryan, feeling that this might be a step towards war, resigned, and Robert Lansing was appointed in his stead. President Wilson was, however, really his own foreign minister at all times; he relied little on either Bryan or Lansing and generally wrote important diplomatic dispatches himself. If he were swayed by anyone, it was probably his confidential adviser, the adroit and politic Colonel E. M. House, who visited the chief European capitals on special missions.

Germany, however, suspended submarine operations for a season and the elections of 1916 passed off with little direct reference to the war peril. The Republicans nominated Associate Justice Charles Evans Hughes of the Supreme Court, who had taken neither side in the Taft-Roosevelt feud of 1912 which had split the party.[4] They accused the Democratic Administration in general terms of leaving the country unprepared, but would not frankly declare for war. Ex-President Theodore Roosevelt, indeed, openly opposed neutrality and abandoned his newly hatched Progressive party to campaign against Wilson, but he could not swing the Republicans to his own aggressive position. The Democrats used with telling effect the slogan, 'He kept us out of war!', but since neither party had advocated war the issue was anything except clear cut. Wilson was victorious in the closest election in more than a generation; indeed, until the vote of California was counted the result hung in doubt. His popular majority, however, was relatively much greater than the majority in the Electoral College, and he considered the result a vindication of his policies, both foreign and domestic.

Fresh from his triumph at the polls, President Wilson appealed to the belligerents to state their war aims. The Entente Allies did so; the Central Powers offered a secret conference instead. Rejecting the terms offered by the Entente, Germany resumed unrestricted submarine warfare. President Wilson proposed 'armed neutrality' to Congress, with the active defense of American merchant ships. A group of pacifist senators talked to death the measure in the last hours of Congress; and when the new Congress assembled in April 1917, it was to debate a declaration of war.

[4] See Chapter XXVI.

Various factors had increased the tension between the American and German governments. Several attempts had been made to sabotage American munitions factories by agents in the pay of the German and Austrian embassies. The German Foreign Minister Zimmermann had naïvely offered Texas, New Mexico, and Arizona to Mexico in the event of war with the United States. The munitions trade and the even vaster traffic in foodstuffs had greatly increased the economic ties between the Americans and the British; victory for the German submarine would have meant ruin to millions of American farmers as well as to thousands of manufacturers. But the decisive factor was certainly that the British blockade, however dubious legally, had violated only American property rights; the German submarine counter-blockade had taken American lives.

Congress not only voted for war by large majorities in both Houses, but made it a war of unlimited liability. It would have been easy to have limited American participation to hunting down submarines, loaning money, and furnishing munitions; easy also to have satisfied 'national honor' by sending a small expeditionary force of volunteers to the front. Instead, conscription, though hateful to a nation of individualists, was adopted almost at once. The blunder made by both sides in the War for Southern Independence of favoring the wealthy by permitted exemptions from the draft was not repeated; on the contrary, the idle rich boy could not claim the deferred status granted to the mechanic in the shipyard or the munitions factory.

The immediate economic effect of the war was a tremendous stimulus to production in every field, industrial and agricultural. Grain prices rose so high, even after a legal maximum had been fixed, that the western plains were overplanted and the farmers' war boom was followed by a post-war depression from which the grain belt did not soon recover. Because other belligerents suffered more than did the United States, a false idea has prevailed in many European circles, at least prior to the depression of 1929, that participation in the First World War had been, on the whole, profitable to the United States. This was far from the fact. The national debt was increased twenty-fold from 1916 to 1919, and most of it was spent unproductively. The war loans (which should really have been called 'war and reconstruction loans,' since they included vast sums loaned after the armistice) amounted to over $10,000,000,000 (£2,000,000,000) and are still unpaid; indeed, even the interest on them was defaulted by the debtor nations after the coming of the depression of the 1930s.[5] Though there was a tremendous increase in the nominal national income, much of this represented mere wartime inflation of costs and prices; a dollar in 1920 bought less than half a dollar in 1915. Translated from statistical tables into terms of human experience this meant acute hardship for the fixed-income classes, such as bond and annuity holders, civil servants, and salaried men. As neutrals, most Americans would probably have been materially better off.

The efficiency of the American war effort has been variously estimated. It took nearly a year to place an effective army in the field, and it was only in the final Meuse-Argonne campaign that the American military contribution can be compared with the French or the British. There was some disappointment at the slow pace of manufacture of aircraft, motors, ships, and artillery. But 'efficiency' is a relative term. The American nation, essentially unmilitary and civilian, required time to transfer its whole economy and psychology from a peace to a war basis, but, at all events, in no previous American war had there been so little friction between civil and military authority, so little amateur meddling with strategy, so little dishonesty in the services of supply. Though President Wilson knew very little about war, at least, in the language of the Oriental proverb, he 'knew that he knew not,' and left military details to the specialists while he busied himself with the problems of statescraft. American aid alone made possible an early and decisive victory.

By 1917 the war had passed into a more active phase. There was a double revolution in Russia, the first establishing a constitutional republic still in alliance with Britain and France; the second, a Communist dictatorship bent on withdrawing Russia wholly from the war. Germany retreated to new entrenchments in the west, but broke Russia and invaded Italy. The submarine campaign had reached the climax which brought the United States into the war. The British won their first major successes in the Near East. The divergent effects of these events almost balanced each other, and so

[5] The only exception was a small, post-armistice loan to Finland.

when Germany launched her last great offensive in the spring of 1918 the outcome of the war seemed as uncertain as when she launched her first in the late summer of 1914. Once again guns thundered along the Marne and German armies pushed close to Paris and to the Channel ports. Most of the ground reconquered by the British and the French in 1916 and 1917 was lost in a few days. Russia and Rumania made separate peace with Germany, and the eastern front no longer existed.

The strain was great, but Germany's effort was her last. Marshal Foch was given supreme power and a free hand; the Allies were no longer a mere coalition but a single army. The 'defeatism' of 1917 disappeared, and the nations of the West rallied for a final struggle. In July and August the tide turned, and from then to the final armistice of 11 November 1918 there was not a moment's slackening in the ceaseless, remorseless hammering of the exhausted German front.

The terms of the armistice owed much to the diplomacy of President Wilson. On 8 January 1918, he had summed up the objects of the war in a series of fourteen propositions, vague at some points but far more definite than any statement of war aims hitherto offered by any belligerent on either side. The first four points (open diplomacy; freedom of the seas; removal of economic barriers; limitation of armaments) and the last ('a general association of nations') were designed to insure a pacific atmosphere in the post-war world; the others dealt with the specific problems of territorial readjustment (equitable colonial adjustments; self-determination for Russia; the evacuation and restoration of Belgium; rectification of the 'wrong done to France' in the matter of Alsace-Lorraine; Italy's new frontiers to follow national lines; the peoples of Austria-Hungary to enjoy 'autonomous development'; Rumania, Serbia, and Montenegro to be restored and Serbia given access to the sea; the peoples of the Ottoman Empire to have autonomy and the Dardanelles to be open to shipping at all times; Poland to be united, freed, and given access to the sea). In subsequent addresses, he spoke less of these details and more of the importance of a League of Nations and his other general international objectives.

When Germany surrendered, it was on the basis of President Wilson's 'points,' but with two explicit modifications. Great Britain and her allies insisted that the restoration of occupied territory must include also reparation for damages done to civilian life or property, and reserved for future discussion the question of the freedom of the seas. There were also other implicit modifications of the Wilsonian terms; thus the actual collapse of Turkey and Austria-Hungary made it no longer practical to talk merely of autonomy for their subject races; they had already attained independence and the task before the peace conference was merely to decide where the new frontiers should be drawn.

Twice during the war Great Britain made major changes in the cabinet. In 1916 David Lloyd George displaced Premier Asquith as head of the coalition government. He discontinued general cabinet meetings and placed the direction of the war in the hands of a war directory of five: himself; the Conservative leader, Bonar Law; two famous colonial administrators, Lords Curzon and Milner; and Arthur Henderson (later G. N. Barnes) to represent Labour. He also held occasional meetings of an Imperial War Cabinet, containing representatives of the Dominions and of India, to co-ordinate imperial policy.

Before the conference met, both the British and the American governments faced the people at an election. There had been no British general election for eight years (though five was the maximum term), owing to the political truce which the war necessitated. No doubt Lloyd George was right in thinking that he needed a mandate before going to the peace conference, especially since the electorate had just been widened to include women and propertyless men. But the result was curious and somewhat disconcerting. The coalition government obtained a very large majority, but one made up mainly of Conservatives; and the Labour party, now stronger than the Liberals, became for the first time the official Opposition. The Liberals, divided into factions, never fully recovered, and have held third place ever since.

The American election was the regular biennial election for Congress. President Wilson unwisely made a partisan appeal to the voters, who disregarded or resented it and returned a Republican majority in both Houses. He also roused resentment by his decision to attend the Peace Conference in person—though the fact that all other belligerents were represented by the responsible heads of their governments might seem a sufficient justification for this step—and by selecting a peace commission which included no prominent political leader from the Republican party.

So divergent were the views of the Allied and Associated [6] Powers that most of the Paris Peace Conference consisted of negotiations among the victors on what should be demanded from Germany and her allies, before the latter were even admitted. Italy, Japan, and the lesser states cared little about the general terms of the treaty and were chiefly interested in territorial problems within very limited areas. The French, British, and American delegations were the only ones which ranged over the whole problem of post-war reconstruction.

Before the Peace Conference had been long in session, the British and American delegations discovered so great a similarity of point of view that French and Italian critics resentfully spoke of an 'Anglo-Saxon bloc.' The Covenant of the League of Nations and the International Labor Organization were mainly of combined British and American authorship. Both governments supported the claims of neutral Geneva as capital of the League instead of belligerent Brussels, the French choice. Both opposed a permanent garrison on the Rhine or the separation of the Rhineland from the rest of Germany. French pressure forced them to agree to a fifteen years' occupation of the Rhineland, to a temporary separation of the Saar district from Germany, pending an eventual plebiscite, and to a separate guarantee treaty to France (an agreement which, opposed by the American Senate, never came into effect).

During the 1918 election, British ministers had spoken rashly of intentions to 'punish the Kaiser' and 'collect the costs of the war,' but once at Paris the British delegation showed no interest in the fate of the Kaiser, now peacefully interned in neutral Holland, and only W. M. Hughes, representing Australia, said anything about recovering the whole cost of the war. The British did, however, insist, against the wishes of the Americans and against the advice of some experts on their own staff, on including soldiers' pensions and separation allowances as 'damages to civilians'; for otherwise the countries which had been actually invaded, such as France, would have got nearly the whole amount of reparations, and British public

[6] Faithful to traditions of diplomatic isolation and independence, the United States had made no treaty of alliance.

opinion demanded some compensation for the heavy material losses of the war.

Apart from this one issue of reparations, the British stood for moderation. They insisted, even against President Wilson's objections, that a plebiscite precede the transfer of any part of Upper Silesia from Germany to Poland. On the Adriatic issue they took a stand midway between the American, favoring the claims of the Yugoslavs, and the Italian. They admitted the obligation of the secret Treaty of London with Italy in 1915 as binding on both Britain and France—though not, of course, on the United States, which had never adhered to any of the secret wartime treaties and had given them no official recognition—but they pointed out that Fiume, which Italy desired, was not covered by the terms of the treaty. In this Fiume controversy, indeed, were planted the first seeds of Italian distrust of British and French diplomacy which eventually led Italy to follow a hostile course towards her wartime allies.

As at the end of so many wars, the British took their own compensation outside Europe. German New Guinea and the neighboring Bismarck Archipelago were to be held in mandate by Australia; German Samoa by New Zealand; German Southwest Africa by the South African Union; the greater part of German East Africa and smaller parts of Togoland and Kamerun by Britain. Asiatic Turkey was so divided that Great Britain obtained mandates for Mesopotamia (Iraq) and Palestine; France for Syria. Cyprus and Egypt were freed from any dependence on Turkey. President Wilson, on behalf of America, refused all territorial gains and all share in the general reparations account.

The mandate system itself was a compromise between Wilson's ideal of trusteeship for the newly acquired territories and the interests of the Powers which held the mandates. Three classes of mandates were recognized to meet differing conditions. Iraq and Palestine, for example, fell into Class A as nations to be prepared for eventual independence. East Africa (Tanganyika) was an example of Class B, a dependency which must maintain equal commercial rights for all members of the League of Nations. Southwest Africa, New Guinea, and Samoa were of Class C, for which the protecting Power was responsible to the League but under no obligation to maintain a commercial 'open door.'

Though the British territorial gains bulked large, they were actually of secondary value. Egypt and Cyprus had been so long under actual British control that their change in legal status was little more than a change of name. Palestine was merely the annexation of a problem: the holding of an even balance between Jewish Zionist immigrants and resentful Arab tribesmen. Iraq had some valuable oil wells, but the hopes at first cherished of considerable agricultural development proved illusory. The former German colonies had very little commercial value under either German or British rule.

In other respects, too, the peace settlement brought a chill of disappointment. Security, the great gain hoped for through four years of war, was not attained; Germany in the 1930s developed as menacing a power as in the early years of the century, and an even more aggressive spirit. Italy and Japan, hitherto good friends of Britain, drifted into hostility, and even France often pursued a divergent policy. Soviet Russia threatened British interests in China, Persia, and India by inflammatory propaganda. Ireland was openly in rebellion. British markets on the continent were wrecked by the poverty resulting from the war, and unemployment became a chronic problem. Over the British Empire, commemorating its million dead, rose a marble forest of war memorials. For the most part they bespeak only sorrow for the dead, pride in their courage, and a faint hope that their sacrifice was not in vain.

A similar disillusionment appeared in the United States. The Senate rejected the League of Nations Covenant and the Treaty of Versailles of which it formed a part. This was due in part, no doubt, to partisan political hostility towards President Wilson, and in part to the jealousy which the Senate has always shown to executives of any party who have been too active in the sphere of foreign affairs. There was also the old American tradition of diplomatic isolation, the fear of 'entangling alliances' and 'Old World diplomacy.' Finally, a force none the less potent because its vagueness almost escapes definition, there was a reaction against the war itself. This was not a definite conviction that the nation had been wrong to enter the war; rather it was part of the same blind, unformulated sense of disappointment with its results which denied to Clemenceau the presidency of France, deposed Orlando from the premiership of Italy, and was a few years later to reduce Lloyd George from the headship of an all-powerful coalition government to the leadership of the smallest faction of the divided Liberal party. Not only the unpopularity of the Treaty of Versailles, but other discontents arising from the war and post-war economic conditions swung the pendulum back to the Republican party in 1920 and sent President Wilson into private life, broken in health, in influence, and in everything but courage.

○ XXXIX ○

FROM BRITISH EMPIRE TO BRITISH
COMMONWEALTH

HISTORIANS have frequently spoken of the 'First British Empire' as a convenient name for the random collection of colonies, dependencies, and chartered-company holdings administered under the old mercantilist colonial system from the time of James I to the American Revolution, and of the 'Second British Empire' as the label for the even larger assemblage of lands under the British Crown built up from the Revolution to the First World War. We have followed that customary usage in this book. But recently there has been a tendency to distinguish still a 'Third British Empire' or, as many writers prefer to speak of it, a 'British Commonwealth of Nations' in the years since that war. The distinction need not be too closely pressed. No sudden shift of policy transformed the first Empire into the second or the second into the third. In true British fashion the change was gradual, halting, uneven, and incomplete: an evolution rather than a revolution. But in the long view the differences in the imperial organization of the three periods are greater than is commonly realized.

Perhaps the change has been one of motive and purpose more than of outward constitutional form. In the first period, as we have seen, colonies were considered as economic experiments, 'plantations,' existing in theory solely for the benefit of the mother country though often permitted a great deal of home rule in point of fact. In the second period, colonies of British origin were given almost complete self-government, and other dependencies, such as India, were administered by British officials rather as a political trust than as an economic venture. Free trade prevailed and attempts at monopoly were generally abandoned. In the third period, the self-governing dominions were accorded not only liberty but equality, being recognized as identical in status with the British Isles themselves. Ireland, too, acquired Dominion rank, and India was accorded partial self-government. Free trade with the world at large was relinquished, but within the British Commonwealth an economic alliance, based on reciprocity treaties and agreements, was established.

In view of the magnificent and spontaneous effort of the Dominions during the First World War,[1] and the terrific sacrifices entailed by it, there was every reason to expect a change in their constitutional relations to Great Britain. They had, as nations, 'come of age.' They naturally assumed, and were without question accorded, the position of independent nations in perpetual alliance with Great Britain. At the Paris Peace Conference the Dominion Premiers and other accredited diplomatic delegates acted simply as colleagues of the British Prime Minister and the other British members of the Conference. India was represented by two native delegates as well as by the Secretary of State for India. The Dominions and India were, in their own right, Member States of the League of Nations. Of course, the diplomatic independence of India has not the same significance as that of the Dominions, for the Government of India is partly British and partly native,[2] whereas that of the Dominions is altogether autonomous. But so far as international law is concerned, India, like the Dominions, has an independent legal personality.

Many people expected a federal union, roughly parallel to that of the United States of America, to arise from the war within the British Empire. Dominion Premiers had, from time to time, sat in the British cabinet during the war. Had these meetings regularly continued thereafter they might have become customs or conventions of the British constitution. But no such development occurred. There is, in fact, no one institution common to all the peoples under the British Crown except the Crown itself, and the king rules by a separate title in the different parts of his realms—Emperor in India, King in Great Britain and in the Dominions, but not Emperor of the whole Empire as such by any legal form. The forty-eight states of the American Union have pooled a certain amount of their sovereignty and entrusted that portion of it to the President, Congress,

[1] See Chapter XXXVIII.
[2] For India see Chapter XXXIII.

and the other federal authorities. The United Kingdom and the Dominions have not pooled their separate sovereignty at all. If they ever take common action or adopt a common policy, they do so only after consultation and agreement, as though they were independent allies.

The system—or lack of system—of the British Commonwealth of Nations is both weak and strong. Being neither a single state nor a federal union, the Commonwealth could be dissolved by agreement at any moment. The only reason its parts stay together is that they want to stay together. This may be what Burke meant when he spoke of ties of empire 'light as air, but strong as links of iron.' The full equal sovereignty of the self-governing portions of the Commonwealth received formal recognition by the Imperial Conference of 1926 and by the Statute of Westminster of 1931.

Since 1887, when Joseph Chamberlain was Secretary of State for the Colonies, there had been about every three years a colonial or imperial conference attended by the premiers and other ministers of the Dominions as well as by the British Prime Minister, the Secretary of State for the Colonies (or Dominions), and sometimes by the Foreign Minister and other ministers.[3] This conference is merely a consultation. It has no binding authority even on the governments represented. Resolutions unanimously adopted by the conferences, however, are apt to be accepted by every part of the Commonwealth, each by its separate legislative or executive act.

At the Imperial Conference of 1926 a report on constitutional matters drafted by Lord Balfour declared 'That nothing would be gained by attempting to lay down a constitution for the British Empire,' because it had so many widely sundered parts, distant from each other in development as well as in location. But, continued the report, one part of the Empire had reached full development—'we refer to the group of self-governing communities composed of Great Britain and the Dominions':

They are autonomous Communities within the British Empire, equal in status, in no way subordinate to one another in any aspect of their external affairs, though united by a common allegiance to the Crown, and freely associated as members of the British Commonwealth of Nations.

[3] See Chapter XXXII.

The conclusions of the Imperial Conference were later embodied in the Statute of Westminster, which translated agreement into positive law. One of the clauses of the Statute provided, in somewhat cryptic language, that 'it would be in accord with the established position of all members of the Commonwealth in relation to one another that any alteration in the law touching the Succession to the Throne of the Royal Style and Titles shall hereafter require the assent as well of the Parliaments of the Dominions as of the Parliament of the United Kingdom.'

An opportunity for testing this provision unexpectedly occurred in December 1936. The British Crown had really become stronger during the twentieth century, in spite of the fall of so many thrones on the continent. King George V (1910-36) had reigned in troubled times. From 1909 to 1914 there were the constitutional crises of the Parliament Act and of the Irish Home Rule controversy; from 1914 to 1918 the First World War; from 1919 onwards the problems of post-war reconstruction. His tact, kindliness, and devotion to duty had, however, enabled him to win a popular affection that resembled that which gathered about Queen Victoria's last years. His eldest son and heir was a young man of attractive personality who had made many 'good will tours' about the Empire when Prince of Wales. In 1936 he took the throne as King Edward VIII. A difficulty arose about his marriage. He wished to marry an American lady, twice divorced, whom his ministers did not regard as an acceptable wife for a reigning sovereign. Rather than give her up he abdicated, the only really voluntary abdication in English history.[4] He was succeeded by his brother, the Duke of York, who took the title of King George VI.

The abdication crisis of December 1936 involved some peculiar problems of imperial law. If the people of any Dominion had desired to separate from the British Commonwealth of Nations, they could have used the opportunity given them under the Statute of Westminster by refusing to agree to the change in the succession to the throne. Instead, each Dominion introduced and passed a bill

---

[4] The removal from the throne of Edward II, Richard II, Henry VI, Charles I, and James II was, in each case, really a deposition rather than an abdication, no matter what forms may have been used.

through its own legislature recognizing the abdication of Edward VIII and the succession of George VI.

The Dominions from the time that they became self-governing have made their own tariffs. This involved the negotiation of commercial treaties with other countries. Those treaties were negotiated by the Dominion concerned through the medium of the British ambassador to the country with which the treaty was being made. In 1923, however, the Government of Canada signed a fisheries treaty with the United States through its own ministry of Marine and Fisheries. Since 1920 Canada has created a diplomatic service of her own, with legations at Washington and Tokio; Ireland also set up a diplomatic service. The diplomatic representatives of the Dominions, like those of the United Kingdom, are nominally appointees of the king, in whose name they act, but the king must act on the advice of the particular government concerned. Thus it is theoretically possible for the king, as representing Great Britain, on the advice of his British ministers, to sign a treaty, while he rejects it in Canada, on the advice of his Canadian ministers! In such a case, Canada would not be bound by the provisions of the treaty. Fortunately, continuous consultation reduces to a minimum the possibilities of actual friction arising from this unbounded freedom. The Dominions are completely sovereign states, in foreign as much as in home affairs. The United Kingdom, however, because of tradition, experience, wealth, and because the cabinet and Foreign Office have the most effective machinery for the conduct of foreign affairs, does retain to a considerable extent the direction of imperial policy.

In other ways, also, the Dominions have acquired new symbols of sovereignty. It has now become customary for even the Governors-General, representing the Crown, to be appointed by the advice of the Dominion ministries. Some Dominions have discontinued the practice of carrying legal cases on appeal to the Judicial Committee of the Privy Council. Ireland (Eire) has exercised her right to declare neutrality in the Second World War, while still remaining within the British Commonwealth of Nations.

While the political ties of Empire have thus become more nebulous, the economic ties have been strengthened. In a world of ever-increasing protective tariffs, Great Britain, for over eighty years the Rock of Free Trade, at last adopted a protectionist policy, combined, however, with reciprocity both within and without the Commonwealth. The agreements reached at the Imperial Conference in Ottawa in 1932 simultaneously decreased tariffs within the Commonwealth and increased them to the outside world, and adopting in principle a quota system providing for the purchase of a certain minimum proportion of various commodities from Dominion sources. Yet this did not preclude similar trade agreements with states outside the British Empire, as is evident from the far-reaching reciprocal trade agreements negotiated with Great Britain and the Dominions by Secretary of State Hull on behalf of the United States of America.

Ireland has changed her status more greatly than any other part of the Commonwealth. In the First British Empire Ireland had been really a colonial dependency, though, like many other colonies, with a legislature of her own. In the Second British Empire, from the time of the Napoleonic wars to the First World War, Ireland had been an integral, and nominally equal (though reluctant), part of the United Kingdom of Great Britain and Ireland. In recent years Ireland has been divided into two altogether separate parts, Northern Ireland (Ulster), which is still a part of the United Kingdom, though having a local legislature as well, and the Irish Free State (later renamed by its Celtic title of Eire), which ranks as a Dominion of the British Commonwealth.

During the First World War Ireland was profoundly disaffected; so greatly, indeed, that Germany may have reckoned on the Irish crisis as likely to cause Great Britain to remain neutral until she had crushed France and Russia. Northern Ireland—Protestant, industrial, partly Scotch-Irish in origin, strongly unionist in sentiment—threatened rebellion if 'home rule' were imposed on Ireland; southern Ireland—Catholic, agricultural, natively 'Celtic,' and nationalist—threatened rebellion if it were denied. In 1916 the Sinn Fein, a radical group much farther to the Left than the official Nationalist party of John Redmond, broke into open rebellion, seizing public buildings in Dublin and requiring military action to suppress it. Several leaders were executed. The attempt, under the shrewd statesman Sir Horace Plunkett, to bring Northern and southern Ireland into an agreement on a compromise Home Rule bill, in place of the one which had been approved by Parliament but suspended on account of the out-

break of war in 1914,[5] ended in failure. Premier Lloyd George at
the end of the war projected a new plan, with separate legislatures
for Northern and Southern Ireland. Northern Ireland accepted, and
has thus a local Parliament while still enjoying representation in
the common British Parliament. Southern Ireland demanded an
independent republic for the whole of Ireland. A minor guerrilla
war was waged from farmstead to farmstead in parts of Ireland
between the Irish Republican Army and a special British constabu-
lary force, the 'black and tans' (so called because they wore a black
police cap with their khaki uniform). In 1922, however, the Sinn
Fein leaders, weary of fruitless strife, agreed to a new plan offered
by the British Government, called the Articles of Agreement, giving
Southern Ireland the name of the Irish Free State and the legal
status of a British Dominion, with complete control of its own Parliament, ministry, and revenues, including tariffs. A minority of
Sinn Feiners refused to acquiesce in the Treaty and have remained
since then in permanent opposition.

The moderate Free Staters, under Premier Cosgrave, eventually
were defeated by a more extreme party under Eamon de Valera,
whose principles were frankly republican. He proposed and carried
through the Irish Parliament measures abolishing the oath of allegiance to the Crown, suppressing the office of Governor-General,
suspending payments on the old land-purchase debts due from
Ireland to the British treasury for loans made to Irish tenants, and
establishing a President. The Irish Free State was renamed Eire,
and a new constitution adopted. Douglas Hyde, an elderly, amiable
Celtic scholar, was elected President with the support of all Irish
parties. Ireland, however, still remained 'in association with' the
British Commonwealth, probably because De Valera had come to see
that a complete break with Great Britain would end the last faint
chance of inducing Northern Ireland voluntarily to merge her lot
with the rest of the country. Though Eire was formally neutral in
the Second World War, there was far less Irish hostility to Great
Britain manifest than during the First World War when Ireland
was still an integral part of the United Kingdom. The exact legal
status of Eire is almost past definition. A 'republic' and yet 'asso-

[5] See p. 407.

ciated with' the British Crown; a neutral within a belligerent Commonwealth; a sovereign Dominion occupying part of one small island —a supreme example at once of the British genius for compromise and of the Irish fondness for paradox!

In speaking of the British Commonwealth of Nations, it must not be forgotten that the equality of status which characterizes it applies only to Great Britain, Ireland, and the Dominions of Canada, Australia, New Zealand, and South Africa.[6] India, as we have seen, is a 'dyarchy' or joint-rule, with certain matters reserved to British control and others transferred to local legislatures.[7] The Crown Colonies and other dependencies are grouped under Great Britain rather than under the Empire, or Commonwealth, as a whole, and yet most of them enjoy a considerable measure of local self-government.[8]

There are also dependencies whose relation to Great Britain is essentially external or diplomatic, and yet very important. Such a case is Egypt: a protectorate till 1922; since 1922 an independent kingdom. By the Anglo-Egyptian Treaty of 1936 the British and Egyptian Governments are in permanent alliance. Great Britain undertakes the defense of Egypt. The Treaty authorizes a British garrison to remain for the protection of the Suez Canal. Such a case is that of the mandated territories, held in trusteeship from the League of Nations, either by Great Britain or by her Dominions. The colonies in Africa and in the Pacific which had formerly been German were administered with little difficulty, if not with much profit, but the formerly Turkish countries of Palestine and Iraq (Mesopotamia) gave many a headache to British statesmen. The boundaries of Iraq, and the oil claims of the Mosul area, had to be adjusted with Turkey and with French Syria. Arabs demanded a union of both Palestine and Iraq with other Arabian States in a common federation. Jewish Zionist colonists in Palestine complained that, in deference to Arab susceptibilities, Britain was unduly restricting immigration; while, on the other hand, agents of Hitler and Mussolini stirred up anti-British feeling among the Mohammedan Arabs by representing Britain as the champion of the Jews.

[6] Newfoundland, formerly a Dominion, voluntarily reverted to Crown Colony status because of financial difficulties in 1933.

[7] See Chapter XXXIII.

[8] See Chapter XXXVII.

Iraq was given in the 1930s a status similar to that of Egypt. The British mandate was formally relinquished, but the independent Arabic-speaking kingdom which was established is closely allied to Great Britain and much under British influence. During the Second World War the British army was compelled to reoccupy Iraq because of the activity of German agents in the Near East.

The Second World War found all parts of the British Empire-Commonwealth in a state of transition. Some units of it may pass, as did thirteen American colonies in the eighteenth century, to complete independence; others to such nominal independence as is today enjoyed by Egypt and Iraq. Some colonies are already verging on full Dominion status, such as Rhodesia. India may eventually attain the status of a Dominion. There is even the possibility of a general federation for the entire Commonwealth such as many predicted, though vainly, would result from the First World War. Closer relation with the United States may well be expected of an era which opens, in 1940, with the location of American naval bases on British colonies in the Atlantic and the Caribbean. Portions of the Empire-Commonwealth may even pass to foreign conquerors in our epoch of frequent and terrible wars. All that is certain is that the imponderable ties of sentiment and interest which bind together the lands of the British Crown have thus far proved stronger than the 'links of iron' forged by other empire-building states.

○ XL ○

GREAT BRITAIN IN OUR OWN TIME

THE First World War did not have such obviously revolutionary effects on British life as on that of most continental belligerents. Neither communism nor fascism won the allegiance of a hundredth part of the nation. The Throne stood unshaken amidst a welter of wrecked European monarchies. Labor, though immensely more powerful than before in politics, remained moderate and evolutionary. In Great Britain itself—as distinguished from Ireland, Egypt, and India—there was no prospect of revolution.

There were, indeed, political changes, though they kept within the bounds of parliamentary tradition. A new franchise law of 1918 established adult suffrage.[1] The Labour party displaced the Liberal as the great rival to the Conservatives. All three parties broke into personal factions, which tended to blur beyond recognition the outlines of the old party system, and for many years [2] there were coalition, or so-called 'national,' governments supported by the adherents of more than one party.

Such a government was in office at the end of the war. Prime Minister David Lloyd George headed a coalition government which had the support of the Conservative party, of many Liberals, and of some Labour members; on a show of votes it seemed almost invulnerable. But there is an old saying of Lord Beaconsfield that 'England does not love coalitions.' They are tolerated in wartime and other periods of acute crisis, but the tendency in normal times is for them to break up into party rivalry. Lloyd George was a Liberal, at one time even

[1] At first woman suffrage was limited to voters over thirty, but in 1928 the age limit was made the same for women as for men.

[2] From 1915 to 1923, and again from 1931 onwards. After 1918, however, all coalition ministries depended on a Conservative plurality in the House of Commons, and their policy was colored by that fact.

counted a Radical, and the Conservatives who had submitted to his dynamic leadership during the war now became restive. On 19 October 1922, a meeting at the Carlton Club, a Conservative political association, decided that the Conservatives could no longer support the ministry, not only for personal and partisan reasons but because it was carrying on a more vigorous policy in the Near East than they cared to endorse. Since most of the supporters of the coalition ministry were Conservatives, Lloyd George had no choice but resign, which he did the next day. Andrew Bonar Law, a Canadian-born Conservative, succeeded him as Prime Minister.

The Liberal party was shattered beyond repair. So long as former Premier Asquith lived he had followers who could not forgive Lloyd George for replacing him during the war. But there were deeper causes for the decline of the party than this passing schism. Fear of socialism caused many property-minded Liberals to seek the securer shelter of Conservatism, while impatience for social reform caused Liberals of a more radical stripe to join the ranks of Labour.

Premier Bonar Law retired in 1923 because of ill health and was succeeded by Stanley Baldwin, who had hitherto been a loyal wheel-horse of the Conservative party rather than a conspicuous leader. He looked the very type of John Bull, was fond of country life, had a certain taste for classical literature and a gift for writing, but was essentially unoriginal and unimaginative. He 'went to the people' on the issue of a protective tariff, but did not obtain a majority for the Conservative party, and so James Ramsay MacDonald, the Labour leader, became head of the first Labour Ministry in British history. Premier MacDonald could not have held office without Liberal support, but his was not a coalition government, for the Liberals did not share the responsibilities of office. King George V may have had strange thoughts as he entrusted the seals of office to an avowed Socialist who had been an outspoken opponent of British participation in the First World War, but he was doubtless pleased to note that if a revolution in politics had indeed arrived, it had done so in a comfortable and reassuring British manner.

Premier MacDonald was, in truth, no firebrand. An earnest, handsome, self-made Scot, a sincere advocate of peace and of parliamentary government, he seemed rather an old-fashioned Radical than a class-conscious Marxian. He combined with his premiership the charge of foreign affairs, and took an interest in the new plans for collective security then interesting Europe. His formal recognition of Soviet Russia, however, caused some misgivings, and rumors of Communist intrigues in the British army caused many Liberals to withdraw their votes from support of his ministry. In 1924 the Conservatives took office once more under Stanley Baldwin.

The second Baldwin ministry (1924-9) roughly paralleled in time and temper the Coolidge administration in the United States.[3] Except for the general strike of 1926 it was the quietest and most prosperous period between the two World Wars. The economic situation of the world at large, still sufficiently serious to awaken misgiving, seemed to be improving. Britain, France, and even Germany temporarily stabilized their finances, and the British Government made regular payments on its external debt to the United States. The Locarno Peace Pact brought the nearest approach to Franco-German reconciliation in the entire span of the years since 1871. No great projects of reform seemed necessary, though the problem of unemployment even in those days gave great concern to the nation.

Strikes also were a plague of reconstruction days. In 1920 railwaymen struck all over the country. A series of partial coal strikes led up to one in 1926 which affected all the mines. Railwaymen, transport workers, and many other unions struck in sympathy, but the general sympathetic strike lasted only eight days and was accompanied by relatively little disorder; the trade unionists themselves feared the possible consequences of a prolonged tie-up of industry and were as eager as the other classes of the community to find a way out. The mine strike outlasted the general strike by several weeks, but it ended without improvement of the conditions either of the mining industry or of the miners.

Another serious economic problem was that of housing. During the war there had been, of course, little building. With the advent of peace the government subsidized municipal enterprise in slum clearance and the erection of model flats and workmen's cottages. In 1939 the four millionth house built under the official housing plan was completed in the United Kingdom. The cost of new government undertakings, unemployment allowances, old-age pensions, and

[3] See Chapter XLI.

other services added to interest on the huge war debt, both internal and external, kept taxation at levels unprecedented for Great Britain in time of peace, and higher than in most foreign countries. German reparations came in only by driblets and eventually ceased altogether. Yet if general prosperity had continued, some sort of economic balance of these difficulties might have been reached in time.

The world depression, which shriveled into nothingness the partial recovery of the post-war decade, brought an ominous increase in unemployment and a falling of revenue. In September 1931, over 2,800,000 workers were unemployed. A 'flight from the pound' set in and the dwindling gold reserve of the Bank of England forced the government to abandon the gold standard and free trade; also to cut the salaries of public officials and curtail unemployment allowances.

Premier Ramsay MacDonald, who had succeeded Baldwin's Conservative Government with a second Labour ministry in 1929, had now to face an ugly dilemma. The Premier and his Chancellor of the Exchequer, Philip Snowden, were convinced that only a serious reduction of expenditure could save Britain from financial ruin. Most of the Labour ministers and members of Parliament, however, opposed retrenchment because of the hardship it would work on the unemployed. By ordinary British political procedure, Premier Mac-Donald would have resigned, and King George would either have summoned the opposition leader, Stanley Baldwin, in his place, or have dissolved Parliament and ordered a new election. The times were so critical, however, that Premier MacDonald was persuaded to hold office at the head of a coalition ministry and seek support from Conservatives and Liberals as well as from the remnant of Labour still loyal to his leadership. A National Government ministry was formed, as if the economic crisis were as serious as a great war—which was doubtless the case. In 1931 the coalition faced a general election; it won an almost ten to one majority in the House of Commons over the portion of the Labour party in opposition and still smaller dissident fragments of the Liberals.

The formation of the National Government did not save the gold standard, though it permitted the eventual balancing of the budget. The pound sterling sunk by about one-third in terms of the dollar, which had not yet been devalued. The depreciation of the pound stimulated export trade by enabling the British to meet the competition of those continental European currencies which had long since fallen below face value. But, curiously enough—perhaps because of the world-wide character of the depression and the consequent cutting of prices everywhere—the suspension of gold payments and the adoption of a 'paper basis' did not have in the United Kingdom the usual inflationary effect of higher prices in the home market.

The National Government ministry decided also to abandon free trade. Since 1846 the United Kingdom and the Crown Colonies had been administered under a general system of tariffs for revenue only. There were still a few import duties, but they were levied on such goods as wine and tobacco, which did not come into competition with home-grown or home-made products, and therefore had no protective character. But hopes of general free trade throughout the world, stimulated by the British example, had come to nothing. After the 1860s the general trend of tariffs, alike in the British Dominions, in America, and in continental Europe, had been upward. The First World War had resulted in still higher rates, chiefly because each nation feared that wartime blockades might cut off essential commodities if they were not produced within its own borders. Even Great Britain protected certain key industries of outstanding military importance. The proposals of Joseph Chamberlain in the first decade of the twentieth century, and of Stanley Baldwin in the 1920s, for a general protective system, however, were not acceptable to the electorate, and it was not until after the National Government had been confirmed in office by the election of 1931 that Great Britain became a protective-tariff nation. The new British tariff, imposing a general 10 per cent rate on most imports, with further imposts up to 33 per cent on some commodities, closed the last important area in the world's free-trade market.

The Labour Chancellor of the Exchequer, Philip Snowden, balanced his budget by paring costs, but he opposed protective tariffs and resigned when they became a policy of the government. Neville Chamberlain, his successor, was a Conservative and son of the 'father of protection,' Joseph Chamberlain. He successfully refunded at 3 per cent the old 5 per cent war loan, while at the same time relieving unemployment by extension of home and road building. By the end of 1933 unemployment had sunk below the 2,000,000 mark, and by 1937 was less than 1,500,000. But the addition of a burden of rearmament, necessitated by the aggressive policy of Italy, Japan, and Germany,[4] laid new burdens on the taxpayer. It seemed alike impossible to restore the gold standard, to return to freedom of trade, or to pay the debt owed to the United States.

Prime Minister MacDonald, as the Labour head of a largely Conservative ministry, was in an even more uncomfortable position than that of Lloyd George, a decade earlier, as the Liberal head of a similar coalition. He knew that while many hailed him as the patriot who had sacrificed his party to save the nation, some of his old associates considered him a Judas who had betrayed 'socialism in our time' to the demands of the London bankers. A lifelong free trader, he had shared in the return of Great Britain to protection. A lifelong pacifist, he helplessly watched Europe slipping towards war. In his last years, enfeebled by illness, he merely presided over a government which others directed.

In 1935, for the third and last time, Stanley Baldwin became Prime Minister. His government, though essentially a partisan Conservative one, still bore the National Government label and numbered some Liberal and Labour adherents. After seeing Britain safely through the crisis created by the abdication of King Edward VIII,[5] he resigned the cares of office to his colleague Neville Chamberlain, whose administration (1937-40) was filled mainly by cares of foreign policy which he was little equipped to handle. Premier Chamberlain's real interests were national finance and social reform; his brother Austen Chamberlain, who had represented Britain at Locarno, had been the diplomat of the family. The war caused a demand for more vigorous leadership, and in 1940 Winston Churchill, a descendant of the Duke of Marlborough, the military genius of Queen Anne's day, took the helm in the midst of the greatest storm which the British ship of state has ever encountered.[6]

Though the twentieth century brought to Great Britain greater problems than Victorian statesmen had to face, the loss of the old insular national security and of the industrial leadership of the world was in some degree balanced by a more vigorous policy of reform.

[4] See Chapter XLII for the events leading up to the Second World War.
[5] See Chapter XXXIX for the abdication crisis.
[6] See Chapter XLII.

At the close of the nineteenth century, British life was still half aristocratic and almost wholly capitalistic; by the 1940s it was almost completely democratic and not far from half way to socialism. The rich were forced to pay extremely heavy 'ransom' to the nation for their wealth (under war conditions the basic income-tax rate went up to 50 per cent, but it was fully half that before war broke out) and the nation had assumed full responsibility that no one should fall into utter destitution, by such devices as old-age pensions, sickness insurance, unemployment allowances, and the like. Public education had been widely extended. Trade unionism and collective bargaining had come to be universally accepted—far more generally, it might be added, than in the United States. Ireland had been emancipated at last,[7] though she was apparently somewhat uncertain what use to make of her emancipation in an age when war respects so little the rights of small nationalities. The Empire had been transformed, so far as the Dominions were concerned, into a Commonwealth of equal partners. Because the old landmarks—Crown, Lords, and established Church—had not been removed, many people, in Britain and in foreign lands alike, failed to realize how great had been the change in the substance of British life.

There were also social and cultural changes scarcely less significant than those in politics and economics. The feminist movement, once chivalrously supported by such men as John Stuart Mill and George Meredith, had triumphed at nearly every point. Women not only had the vote but had entered every profession and almost every branch of industry and trade. They had cast aside conventions of decorum which had limited their freedom. The gay young flapper of the 1920s with her knee-length skirt and backless bathing suit, her motor car, her cigarette, her boyish bob, and her unrestrained freedom of speech, would certainly have amazed Queen Anne or Queen Victoria, though in some respects Queen Elizabeth might have understood her. Domestic ties were relaxed somewhat, though divorces were fewer and divorce laws stricter in Britain than in many other countries. Certainly the 'domestic hearth,' reverenced by Tennyson and ridiculed by Samuel Butler, was less of a magnet. The rich man was more apt to buy a motor car, a yacht, or even an air-

---

[7] See Chapter XXXIX.

plane; less apt to invest his capital in a mansion or a train of liveried servants. Even the poor now took their week-end holidays on bicycles or char-à-bancs. Motion pictures and popular periodicals introduced American colloquialisms into English speech. Continental art and literature had great and increasing influence on British culture.

There was a notable literary renaissance in the 'Celtic fringe.' In part this showed itself in a revival of Gaelic, Erse, and Welsh, but much of the best of the Scottish, Irish, and Welsh national culture was still expressed in English. The Irish found the drama a congenial mode of expression, and the plays of Bernard Shaw, John Synge, W. B. Yeats, Lord Dunsany, Lady Gregory, and others made up perhaps the most brilliant constellation of dramatic talent in one time and country since Shakespeare's England. Shaw, however, though richly endowed with Irish wit, was rather a cosmopolitan figure than a nationalist leader, and he had really more in common with Ibsen than with Yeats. Though James Barrie was as successful with his plays as with his stories of Scottish life, it is chiefly in romantic fiction that Scotland found expression, through the pens of Robert Louis Stevenson, John Buchan, and many others. If among them there was no Walter Scott, neither did England produce a new Hardy, Thackeray, or Dickens. The novels of John Galsworthy (equally distinguished as a dramatist), Hugh Walpole, Arnold Bennett, and other twentieth-century realists, however, are admirable photography if they do not always rise to portraiture.

Three names stand out, not as the greatest perhaps but certainly as the most conspicuous, of those critics of society who carried on the work of Ruskin, Carlyle, and Matthew Arnold of a previous generation. Of Bernard Shaw, genial cynic and unsocial Socialist, we have already spoken. H. G. Wells, ever dreaming of humanity's future, divided his attention among popular histories, imaginative scientific romances, realistic studies of everyday life, and arguments for internationalism and socialism. Similar in breadth of interest and in variety of medium, though very different in opinion, was G. K. Chesterton, essayist, poet, biographer, literary critic, short-story writer, and champion of a richly romantic view of life.

o XLI o

THE UNITED STATES IN OUR OWN TIME

DURING the Long Armistice of 1918-39 the United States endeavored to return to what President Harding (1921-3) called 'normalcy.' This implied a wistful, nostalgic vision of times past when Americans had no foreign problems worth mentioning and economic questions were solved by voluntary bargaining between capital and labor, with little or no intervention by the government. The attempt proved an utter failure. Old World affairs constantly thrust themselves on the reluctant American attention, and the national economic life alternated between a vast upswing of overproduction and a prolonged downswing of depression which necessitated federal regulation of private business to an extent unprecedented even in time of war.

President Harding's brief administration is remembered chiefly for a triumph and a failure. The triumph was a conference on Pacific and naval affairs held in Washington in 1921 and 1922, which postponed, though it did not avert, the rise of war clouds in the Pacific and Far East, assuring sunny weather in that quarter during the 1920s. Secretary of State Hughes (later Chief Justice of the Supreme Court) won a personal as well as a national triumph in piloting the Washington Conference to success. A Four Power Treaty engaged Britain, France, Japan, and the United States to respect each other's Pacific island possessions; a Nine Power Treaty (which included also Italy, Belgium, the Netherlands, Portugal, and China but not, it is interesting to note, Germany or Soviet Russia) [1] pledged the signatory Powers to respect the independence and integrity of China; the fortification of Pacific naval bases was suspended; a ten years' holiday in the construction of capital warships approved; and a fixed ration of naval strength among the leading Powers adopted. In

[1] Germany had lost her Pacific colonies; the Bolshevist government of Soviet Russia had not yet been recognized by other Powers.

capital ships the strength of Great Britian and of the United States was rated equal: the first time in modern history that a British Government accepted another Power as equal at sea, a reassuring evidence that the British did not regard the United States as under any circumstances a possible foe. Japan was to have a fleet three-fifths as strong as either the British or the American; France and Italy were each rated at a little more than half the strength of Japan. No agreement with respect to minor craft—light cruisers, destroyers, torpedo boats, submarines—was reached until the London Conference of 1930.

Though President Harding had little to do with the detailed work of the Washington Conference, he had assumed the official responsibility belonging to him as chief executive, and thus deserves credit for its success. On the same principle of delegated responsibility, he must be debited with the scandals which blackened his administration, though he was probably personally innocent and even ignorant of them at the time they occurred. The most notorious was the act of Albert Fall, Secretary of the Interior, who leased the Elk Hill oil reserve in California to the Doheny interests, and the Teapot Dome reserve in Wyoming to the Sinclair interests, in return for personal loans and gifts. Fall actually went to prison for his dishonesties: a unique event in American history for a politician of cabinet rank. Less famous but equally discreditable was the misbehavior of some minor appointees such as Colonel Forbes, in charge of the Veterans' Bureau, and Colonel Miller, alien property custodian, both convicted of frauds against the government. Attorney-General Harry Daugherty, the President's closest friend in the cabinet, escaped legal conviction but was involved in many discreditable dealings. President Harding, whose death saved him from learning the full extent to which his easy confidence had been betrayed, was kindly and well-intentioned, but his utter inability to tell honest men from rogues made him probably the unfittest man who has ever held the presidency.

Vice-President Calvin Coolidge, who succeeded on President Harding's death, was a native of Vermont who had been governor of Massachusetts: a reticent Yankee, thrifty and conservative. How he would have fared in more troubled times is an interesting speculation, but he had the good fortune to be in the White House during the quietest years (1923-9) that the nation had known in a century.

He was easily elected in 1924 to succeed himself against John W. Davis, the Democratic candidate, nominated as a compromise after the Democratic convention had become exhausted by a prolonged deadlock between W. G. McAdoo, advocate of prohibition, and Governor Alfred E. Smith of New York, a leading opponent of the 'drys.' Senator Robert La Follette of Wisconsin, a lifelong pacifist and progressive, ran on a third ticket, polling about five million votes and carrying his own state.

The really significant political changes of the 1920s bore little relation to the stale quadrennial tournaments between Republicans and Democrats. The adoption of the eighteenth amendment to the Federal Constitution, prohibiting the manufacture and sale of alcoholic beverages, and of the nineteenth, establishing woman suffrage, were not the work of the parties but of agitation carried on by independent 'pressure groups' such as the Anti-Saloon League and the various suffragist associations. The issue of the League of Nations played a part, though probably a minor one, in the election of 1920, but thereafter dropped out of politics as an active issue. The decision to close the open door to immigration was also a non-partisan one.

Immigration restriction was a policy long demanded by the trade unions, who feared the competition of cheaper labor from abroad. A series of laws, beginning with 1882, prohibited the immigration of Chinese laborers, and excluded contract laborers generally, as well as paupers, polygamists, anarchists, and various other undesired groups and classes. Four times Congress passed bills to exclude illiterates, but Presidents Cleveland, Taft, and Wilson all vetoed these measures on the ground that illiteracy was a test of opportunity and not of worth. In 1917, however, Congress carried over the presidential veto a measure excluding illiterates. A series of much more drastic laws in 1921, 1924, and 1929 imposed for the first time a quantitative limit on immigration. The test proposed was the ratio of immigrants to the number of persons of the same 'national origin' already present in the United States, and a fixed annual quota was assigned to each nation. Immigration from eastern Asia was excluded without quota: a step which caused deep offense to the Japanese.

Herbert Hoover, Secretary of Commerce in the Harding and Coolidge cabinets but more famous for his work as the director of Belgian relief and as wartime Food Administrator, was elected on the Republican ticket in 1928 against Alfred E. Smith, four times governor of New York. The election was notable as the first (and last) since 1876 in which any considerable portion of the Solid South deserted the Democratic ticket. Even traditional sectional prejudice against the Republican party could not overcome Smith's fourfold handicap of being a New York City man, a member of Tammany Hall (the local Democratic 'machine' in the city), a Roman Catholic, and an opponent of prohibition in the rural, intensely Protestant, and politically 'dry' South. But even without such personal handicaps no opponent could have defeated Mr. Hoover at the very crest of the wave of national prosperity; whereas almost any candidate could have defeated him four years later. The mysterious economic forces which cause national wealth to ebb and flow were even then beginning to turn.

As we have seen,[2] the wartime prosperity of 1916-20 was largely fictitious. Such as it was, it was swallowed up by the sharp reaction of 1921. But a second period of business expansion, in 1923-9, brought more genuine prosperity. To be sure, it was very partial. It extended hardly at all to the farmer, who never recovered from the post-war falling off the foreign grain market, and slighted certain branches of industry, such as the coal mines (the coal industry was in the doldrums almost everywhere in the world), the shipping interests, the railways, and the New England textile factories. But the general picture was certainly one of material well being. The average buying power of wages increased at least a third; hours of labor were generally shortened till the eight-hour day became the rule. The output per individual worker increased by 15 per cent in transportation, 18 per cent in agriculture, 33 per cent in mining, and 40 per cent in manufacturing during the brief period 1919-25.[3]

No other nation equalled the United States in mechanization. The farmer harvested his crops with power-driven machinery; the housewife began to clean the floor with a vacuum cleaner in place of a broom and to cool the groceries in an electric refrigerator instead of the old-fashioned ice box; the businessman almost everywhere insisted on typewriter, dictaphone, mimeograph, adding machine, and cash register. Amusement, too, was mechanized; favorite national

[2] See Chapter xxxviii, pp. 492-3.
[3] *Commerce Yearbook* (1928), 1, 19, 266-7.

recreations were automobile driving, the motion pictures, the radio, and the phonograph. There were almost as many automobiles as houses, and there was a telephone in nearly every prosperous home in the land.

Nevertheless, industrialists had not succeeded completely in adjusting themselves to the increasing rhythm of mechanization. Technological changes came with such frequency as to displace great masses of labor. Thus, the competition of motor trucks and passenger busses caused heavy losses to railroads and street car lines. Even in the most prosperous times there was some unemployment. Moreover, tariffs, international debts, currency fluctuations, and other political factors interfered with the natural flow of international trade and prevented the world from taking full advantage of the increased production made possible by the improvement of industrial technique.

One sign of prosperity was the unprecedented amount given by philanthropists or voted by state legislatures to the schools and colleges. The Federal Bureau of Education estimated in 1928 that both secondary and higher education were offered to almost as many students in the United States as in all the rest of the world together, though the elementary schools included less than 30 per cent of the world's pupils, and the total population was only about 6 per cent of the world's aggregate. About half the young people of high school age were in public or private secondary schools, and about one in eight of those of college age were in colleges, universities or professional schools. No other land or age had ever approached such a record.

Other evidences of national wealth appeared in the growing sums spent for travel and recreation. Down to the First World War the American people, though in every generation much given to migration, moved as a rule to places where they could work more profitably, seeking good farmland in Kentucky, Illinois, Oregon; coal fields in Pennsylvania and West Virginia; gold fields in pioneer California; oil wells in Oklahoma and Texas; commercial positions in the business districts of New York and Chicago. In our own generation millions have moved to places where they could enjoy a mild climate and year-round recreation in the open air. Southern California, southern Florida, and similar national playgrounds grew more rapidly in population than any other sections of the country.

The Federal Government opened many new national parks; states, municipalities, and universities erected athletic stadia, swimming pools, golf courses, tennis courts, and other recreational facilities. Dancing to new types of syncopated and irregular rhythms—ragtime, jazz, and swing in succession—became an almost universal custom among the younger generation. As in Great Britain, and perhaps to an even greater degree, women shared all the educational, professional, social, and recreational activities of men.

The optimistic American has a way of treating every depression as a cloud sure to pass and every transient gleam of prosperity as a 'new economic era' sure to stay. Though voices of warning were raised here and there against overspeculation, buying on long-term credits, and other bad economic habits, most economists seemed to believe that the worst punishment that would befall the gay and reckless country would be a temporary slump, like those of 1907, 1914, and 1921, not a prolonged depression like those of the 1870s and '90s. At a time when real prosperity had already, though very slowly, begun to recede, the stock market had its greatest boom. Not until the Wall Street panic of October 1929 did the public become seriously alarmed. Even then, since fear itself is the greatest danger in a fire, a run on a bank, or a flurry in the stock market, President Hoover and the leading financiers of the nation deemed it their duty to profess a cheerfulness that they did not perhaps feel and proclaim that American business was still 'fundamentally sound.' Republican congressmen pinned their faith to an upward revision of the tariff, the Hawley-Smoot bill of 1930.

The faith cure proved unsuccessful. Down to the summer of 1932 values continued to fall, business failures to multiply, prices and wages to recede, and unemployment to increase. We have no such exact figures for American unemployment as Great Britain possessed through her system of unemployment insurance, but estimates for the worst days of 1932 and 1933 placed the number of those seeking work at anywhere from twelve to sixteen millions. State and municipal aid and private charity proving unable to solve the problem of relief, the Federal Government, contrary to all precedent, was forced to assume the burden.

President Hoover, as a world citizen with a wider outlook than that of most politicians, knew that the depression was a worldwide phenomenon which could not be cured by purely domestic remedies. So he hoped to bring about a revival of trade by suspending both Germany's reparation account and the inter-allied war debts. In 1931 he succeeded in obtaining a one year's moratorium on both forms of international indebtedness. For the moment the stock market responded favorably, but it soon resumed its downward trend. In 1932 the European Powers agreed at Lausanne to cut reparations to a relatively small sum if war debts also were permanently cancelled. The United States, which would have been the heaviest loser by such an agreement, as creditor to many and debtor to none, refused to agree. But, as a matter of fact, neither reparations nor war debts were ever again revived.

For 'priming the pump' of industry within the United States President Hoover relied on the activities of the Reconstruction Finance Corporation (RFC) established in 1932 to grant loans to businesses occupying a key position in the economic system, such as banks and railroads. Its work proved so useful that it was continued and even extended in the next administration. But the market did not recover, bank failures continued, and farmers unable to meet their debts threatened violence against anyone who would attempt to foreclose mortgages against their homes.

In this atmosphere of gloom and depression the general election of 1932 took place. President Hoover was renominated by the Republicans but badly defeated by Governor Franklin Delano Roosevelt of New York, who carried every section of the country except a few northeastern states. So far as any definite issue entered the campaign it was prohibition. Roosevelt, like Alfred E. Smith four years earlier, was for repeal; his victory ensured it and the experiment of national prohibition was soon terminated. Friends of Smith, the 1928 candidate, were displeased, however, that he had not been given another chance at the presidency and from the start they formed a sullen opposition group within the Democratic party.

President Franklin Roosevelt was related, though distantly, to former President Theodore Roosevelt. Both men were of New York Dutch ancestry and moderately wealthy. Though they diverged politically, one into the Democratic and one into the Republican camp, they were personally much alike; both played the political game with skill and gusto, shifting their policies frequently to catch the favoring winds of public opinion but often defying party orthodoxy; at once opportunists and crusaders. Franklin Roosevelt had been Assistant Secretary of the Navy in the First World War,[4] and had been candidate for Vice-President in 1920; his health had been shattered by a stroke of infantile paralysis which temporarily took him from politics, but he had later recovered sufficiently to become Smith's successor as governor of New York. The Democratic platform of 1932 gave scarcely an inkling of the policies which the incoming administration was to pursue under the general designation of a 'New Deal' for the nation.

The Roosevelt program can here be only briefly summarized. It consisted, in the first line, of a number of emergency measures, such as reorganizing and strengthening the banks before they reopened, temporarily reducing federal salaries and pensions, abandoning the gold standard, and, later, reducing the gold content of the dollar. The Federal Government also extended the loans initiated by the Reconstruction Finance Corporation, which President Hoover had started, and added new credit agencies, such as the Home Owners' Loan Corporation (HOLC). A Federal Emergency Relief Administration (FERA) aided the states to carry the burden of poor relief. The problem of unemployment was partly met by undertaking public works. Thus the Civilian Conservation Corps (CCC) offered employment to healthy young men in the forestry service; the Works Projects Administration (WPA) under Harry L. Hopkins presented a diversified program of local public improvements, while the Public Works Administration (PWA), under Secretary Ickes of the Interior, specialized on wholesale construction works, such as building projects.

Other reforms were intended to outlast the emergency and bring about permanent economic reforms. Thus bank deposits were guaranteed, and the stock exchange was placed under federal regulation. General business was asked to draw up and then submit to codes of fair competition under the National Recovery Administration (NRA). A program of crop restriction, designed to raise farm prices and take out of use poor land, was supervised by the Agricultural Adjustment Administration (AAA). Tariff rates were lowered, not by any general revision but by special reciprocity treaties negotiated

---

[4] By an interesting coincidence Theodore Roosevelt, and later one of his sons, held this same position.

by Cordell Hull, the Secretary of State. A bold, though exceptional, experiment in state socialism was the sale of electric power from the nationally owned hydroelectric plant of the Tennessee Valley Authority (TVA). A Social Security Act of 1935 gave heavy subsidies to states which granted compensation, pensions, or insurance benefits to the aged, the unemployed, and other necessitous groups. The government recognized trade unionism and favored collective bargaining; it did what it could within constitutional limits to stamp out child labor.

Whether because of these measures, or in spite of them, or independently of them, there was a great measure of national recovery in 1933 and subsquently. Bank failures and commercial bankruptcies fell to less than normal figures; farm prices and industrial wages increased. Except for the major evils of continued unemployment and an unbalanced national budget, 1936-9 might be considered normal, and 1940-41, stimulated by war purchases from abroad, 'boom' years. An unpleasant symptom of recovery was the outbreak of numerous industrial strikes. Third-party radicalism failed to achieve anything in American politics because Roosevelt had rallied most of the Left-wing forces around his own administration; but in the economic field there was acute conflict between the conservative trade unions, organized by crafts, such as the American Federation of Labor, and the new industrial unions, such as the Committee for Industrial Organization (CIO). Sometimes the new unions resorted to the 'sit down strike' or occupation of a plant by strikers with the object of preventing others from taking their places.

The federal courts were in several cases asked to pass on the constitutionality of much of the New Deal legislation. The Supreme Court upheld the suspension of gold payments, the reduction of the gold content of the dollar, the Tennessee Valley enterprise, and the majority of regulatory acts. But it found unconstitutional the National Recovery codes for the regulation of competitive business, decreed that the processing tax on which the crop regulation plan of the AAA depended was illegal, and invalidated an act regulating the coal industry. Irritated at the negative decisions of the Court, President Roosevelt urged Congress to pass a law giving him the power to appoint a new judge—presumably young and progressive—for each member of the Court who was over seventy. Congress, fearing that this would amount to 'packing' the Supreme Court, refused, although both Houses had large majorities of the President's own Democratic party. There has never been a more striking demonstration of the essential conservatism of the American people and of their devotion to traditional constitutional forms. But the occurrence of several vacancies on the Court shortly afterwards enabled the President to strengthen the liberal wing by new appointments.

In spite of the failure of the President's plan for enlarging the Supreme Court, the most serious political defeat he ever experienced, in most respects he carried the majority of the nation with him. In 1936 he was re-elected against Governor Alfred Landon of Kansas, who carried only the two states of Maine and Vermont. No other President except Washington and Monroe had come so near to a unanimous vote in the Electoral College. In 1940 he had the unprecedented honor of being elected for a third term. His opponent was a successful businessman, Wendell Willkie, who had never held public office and who supported the main lines of President Roosevelt's foreign policy, though he demanded more consideration for private business. The political campaign of 1940 resembled that of 1916 in being fought to the sound of guns from across the ocean, while the chief thought in every American mind was not whether a Republican or a Democrat would occupy the White House for the next four years, but whether the United States would or would not be dragged into the vortex of a World War.[5]

The United States remained more faithful to the two-party system than did Great Britain or any of her Dominions. There were many radical movements of various types initiated during the Long Armistice, some of which enjoyed local success, but none that played a major part in national politics. The Farmers' Non-Partisan League in North Dakota, the Farmer-Labor party in Minnesota, the Progressive party of La Follette in Wisconsin represented certain discontents of the western farmers and were only of sectional importance. Father Coughlin's Union for Social Justice, Huey Long's Share-the-Wealth League, and Dr. F. E. Townsend's plan for old-age pensions (with the proviso that the recipient retire from work and spend each monthly installment before receiving the next) were

[5] See Chapter XLII for American relation to the Second World War.

eccentric remedies to cope with the depression; they merged into a Union party in 1936 with Representative Lemke of North Dakota as their presidential candidate, but did not carry a single state. The regular Socialist party, under the pacifist Norman Thomas, and the Communists, directed by Earl Browder, showed very little strength anywhere.

Certain fascist tendencies, such as anti-foreignism, may be traced in the Ku Klux Klan of the 1920s; Huey Long's powerful political machine in Louisiana, which ended with the leader's assassination and the prosecution of his chief henchmen for financial dishonesties, was almost a disguised state dictatorship; and there were several anti-Semitic groups, such as the Silver Shirts, the Christian Front, and the like. But all these movements added together scarcely ruffled the surface of national politics, and hardly included one American in a hundred. It is perhaps also significant that even these quasi-fascist groups pretended to be entirely democratic; though they violated the spirit of American liberalism they were pious in their worship of its letter. The totalitarian philosophy had probably fewer friends in the United States than in any other land under the sun.

But while the religion of Americanism, whose scriptures are the Declaration of Independence and the Bill of Rights of the Federal Constitution, was almost universally accepted, many alert critics questioned the imperfect practice of the religion by its devotees. A wide literature of national self-criticism developed during the 1920s, typified by such writers as Sinclair Lewis the novelist and Robert Lynd the sociologist, who did not content themselves with attacking the obvious abuses of business trusts and city bosses, like the reformers of the Theodore Roosevelt era, but condemned the average good citizen for materialism and provincial prejudice. Historians and biographers reviewed in a more critical spirit the American past, often incurring thereby the wrath of patriotic societies and chauvinist politicians. The depression of the 1930s, though it swept away much of the merely querulous fault-finding of the intellectuals, irritated at the placidity of bourgeois prosperity in the 1920s, introduced a deeper note of questioning. What was to become of the 'American promise,' the 'American dream,' if free individualistic enterprise failed to give bare employment, let alone the American standard of living, to hard-working toilers?

American poetry had a second blooming between 1914 and 1942, almost as brilliant as that of the generation before the War for Southern Independence. Robert Frost, Edwin A. Robinson, Vachel Lindsay, Edgar Lee Masters, Carl Sandburg and many others [6] form an impressive galaxy. Most of them followed the Walt Whitman tradition of free verse and irregular rhythms. Eugene O'Neill, Maxwell Anderson, and Robert Sherwood placed on the stage the first really important American dramas.

[6] T. S. Eliot, author of the much discussed *The Waste Land*, became a British subject. Stephen Vincent Benét's *John Brown's Body* is the nearest to a true American epic. Amy Lowell is famous for her studies of Keats as well as for her experiments in imagist verse.

THE SECOND WORLD WAR

THE failure of the world to learn from the First World War that peace, like victory, cannot be had for the mere wishing but must be earned by thought and toil and self-sacrifice is the great tragedy of modern times. In the blisteringly accurate phrase of H. G. Wells, the 'fatuous twenties' were succeeded by the 'frightened thirties' and the 'brigand forties.' The responsibility of the English-speaking nations for the return of war was real, but passive. They had no territorial ambitions to be served by war, no defeats to avenge, no harvest of laurels to be reaped for the benefit of an insecure dictatorship. But they too readily assumed that all other nations and governments were moved by the same abhorrence of the very thought of war which made their own peoples reluctant to prepare a strong military force and equally reluctant to assume the far-reaching international obligations by which war might have been averted. In the case of the United States this negative approach to international problems took the form of 'isolation'; in the case of the British Commonwealth of 'appeasement.'

After the Washington Conference of 1921-3 [1] American foreign policy was long marked by aloofness. Presidents Harding, Coolidge, Hoover, and Roosevelt, though abandoning the Wilson policy embodied in the League of Nations, all sought to bring the United States into the Court of International Justice, but the Senate remained obdurate. Individual Americans took part in every activity of the League and the Court, but not as representing their government. Not until the Roosevelt Administration did the United States join the International Labor Organization, or recognize the official existence of Soviet Russia.

On the positive side, the United States participated in the confer-

[1] See Chapter XLI.

ences for limitation of naval armaments at Washington, Geneva, and London, and the Economic Conference of 1933. American diplomacy had a share in framing the Paris Peace Pact (also known as the Briand-Kellogg Pact, to honor the American and French statesmen who helped make it) for the renunciation of war. Individual American financiers, such as Charles Dawes and Owen D. Young, acted as expert advisers in adjusting German reparation payments. But no obligations were assumed that might by any chance require American arms to enforce.

Great Britain, though unable to imitate the aloofness of the United States to the problems of continental Europe, showed signs of desiring to reduce the risk of involvement in European conflicts. When the Geneva Protocol was proposed to give a keener cutting edge to the powers of the League of Nations, the British Government stood back in doubt, though accepting the more limited obligations of the Locarno agreement. When France and Italy were zealously competing for alliances among the lesser European states, Great Britain held apart from both.

The international system, such as it was, of the 1920s went to pieces under the shock of the world depression. When Japan invaded Manchuria in 1931 Henry Stimson, President Hoover's able Secretary of State, refused to recognize the conquest. At a later stage of Japanese penetration, President Roosevelt vainly endeavored to save China by invoking a meeting of the Nine Powers that had guaranteed Chinese integrity and independence at the Washington Conference. Neither the League Powers nor the United States, however, went beyond the 'moral pressure' to which Japan seemed so insensitive. In 1933 Germany became a dictatorship, vowed to vengeance on the authors of the Treaty of Versailles, and in 1935 Italy made war on Ethiopia. The League Powers, less timid in the case of Italy than in that of Japan but still insufficiently in earnest, imposed economic sanctions on Italy. This did not save Ethiopia, but it so angered the Italian dictator Benito Mussolini that he joined Germany in an alliance, the so-called Rome-Berlin Axis, and repudiated his old wartime association with Britain and France.

The British Government continued to follow a policy of peace by conciliation or, as the phrase went, 'appeasement.' Japan was permitted to conquer Manchuria, invade China, and withdraw from the

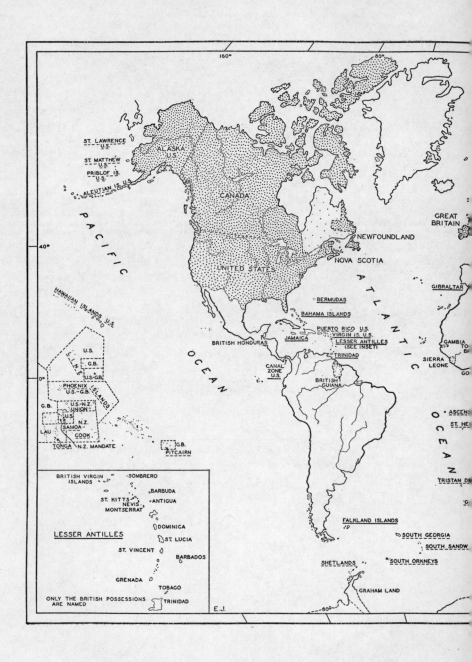

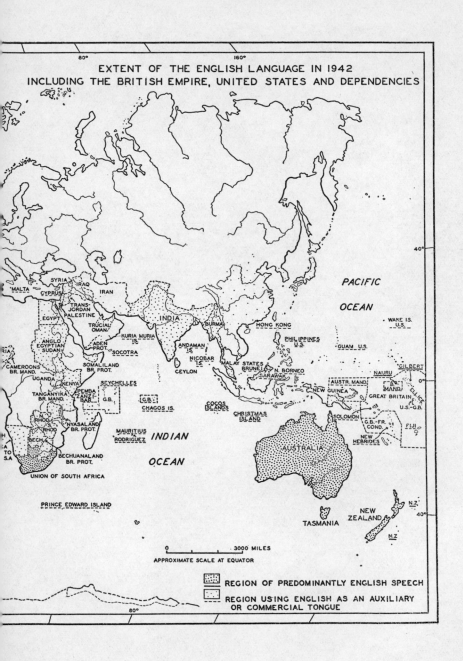

EXTENT OF THE ENGLISH LANGUAGE IN 1942
INCLUDING THE BRITISH EMPIRE, UNITED STATES AND DEPENDENCIES

::::: REGION OF PREDOMINANTLY ENGLISH SPEECH

·:·:· REGION USING ENGLISH AS AN AUXILIARY
OR COMMERCIAL TONGUE

0 _____ 3000 MILES
APPROXIMATE SCALE AT EQUATOR

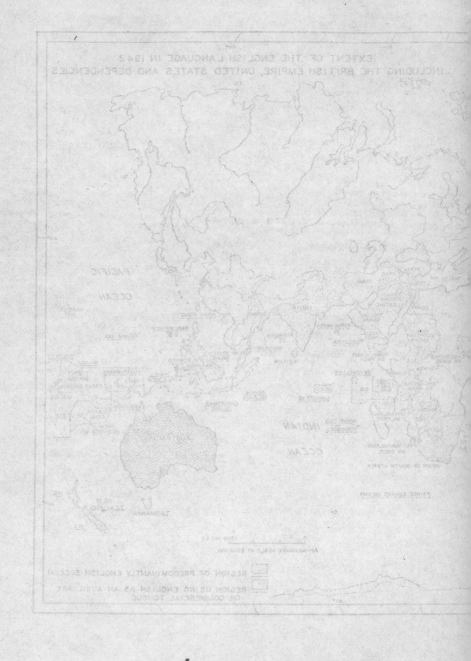

League of Nations with islands still in her possession which belonged to her only as mandates from the League. The steps taken against Italy were deprived of much of their efficacy by an ill-conceived attempt to buy off Italy by colonial concessions (the Hoare-Laval agreement). Germany was permitted to violate the Treaty of Versailles and the Locarno Pact by reoccupying the Rhineland with her armies. Though the European Powers agreed on a policy of neutrality in Spain, Italy was permitted to send soldiers into the civil conflict there and assure dictator Franco's victory. Germany's annexation of Austria passed without more than formal protest.

In 1938 Hitler insisted on the annexation of the German-speaking rim of Czechoslovakia, the 'Sudetenland.' Prime Minister Neville Chamberlain flew by airplane to Germany to assure that this transfer of territory might take place without war; he also negotiated with Germany, France, and Italy the Pact of Munich, which, so he fondly hoped, might assure the peace of western Europe 'for our time.' Though many individuals in Britain denounced this policy of unlimited concession to aggressor states as dangerous, it was not abandoned until Germany took over the Slavic remnant of Czechoslovakia in the spring of 1939.

With this clear proof in hand that Germany was seeking not national unity merely but imperial conquest and expansion, the Chamberlain Government reversed its former policy. Peacetime conscription, for the first time in modern British history, became law. Alliances with Poland and Rumania were hastily concluded; negotiations opened with Turkey and Russia. The Russian negotiations, however, broke down and the Soviet Union announced neutrality. This diplomatic revolution encouraged Germany to attack Poland, and war broke out in September 1939, twenty-five years and one month after Germany's attack on France and Belgium in 1914. The Long Armistice was at an end.

Though the fact was insufficiently recognized at the opening of the Second World War, the British Commonwealth actually stood in much greater peril in 1939 than in 1914. Britain and France could not on this occasion count on any aid from Russia, Italy, or Japan. Russia and Japan were intent on conquests of their own—Russia in Finland, Estonia, Latvia, Lithuania, eastern Poland, and the Rumanian province of Bessarabia; Japan in the Chinese Republic. Italy was waiting for the best moment to strike at France in the hope of winning a new colonial empire. Though Germany had a smaller navy than in 1914, she had a much more powerful air force than any other nation on earth. While Britain, France, and America had slept, Germany had seized the mastery of the air and Great Britain 'was no longer an island.'

.The war began with a German dash to the east and a defensive policy in the west, exactly reversing the strategy of 1914. The obliteration of Poland in a single month was the sole important campaign of 1939; neither Britain nor France was in a position to send timely aid. The chief British activity of these early months was by sea. The Germans responded, as in 1917, to the pressure of British blockade by sinking all merchant ships approaching the British coasts. A few warships on both sides were destroyed. One of the most dramatic incidents was the fight off South America between the German battleship *Graf Spee* and some British cruisers, ending in the internment of the German warship in a neutral harbor and its destruction by its own crew.

In 1940 the pace of war quickened. Germany seized Denmark and Norway without warning, partly to protect her iron trade with Sweden and partly to secure new air and submarine bases against Britain. The failure of the British to detect and intercept the German invasion of Norway led to much criticism of the government of the day and hastened the resignation of Prime Minister Chamberlain, who was succeeded by Winston Churchill. But immediately after the invasion of Norway came the heavier German stroke of the invasion of Belgium and the Netherlands. Both countries were caught unprepared and the German armies swept on to fresh triumphs in France. A British expeditionary force was isolated and trapped in Flanders. By a miracle of pluck and luck it was brought back to Britain from Dunkirk almost intact, though most of its material and equipment had to be abandoned. The nightmare of 1914-18 was now an actuality; Germany held the Channel ports and could use them against Great Britain.

Within a few weeks France capitulated. Italy struck wounded France a final blow, and then turned to a cautious war against British shipping and colonies in the Mediterranean area. Great Britain, Germany's only unconquered active adversary,[2] had to face, as in Napoleon's day, a foe who already dominated the European continent and threatened to invade the British homeland. Hitler was, to be sure, no such genius as Napoleon, but he had a far more formidable weapon than the French Emperor ever possessed, in the power to strike down cities from the sky.

The fall of France and the German air raids on Britain began the crucial phase of the war. A year of aerial bombardments failed to shake British power and actually increased British morale. The numerically inferior British air fleet inflicted greater loss than it suffered and forced the German planes to fly so high that they flung their incendiary or explosive bombs not closely at military targets but almost at random over whole cities—London, Coventry, Plymouth, Bristol, Southampton, and many others. Never before in history, so said Prime Minister Churchill, 'had so many owed so much to so few.'

Victories on sea and land followed victories in the air. The loss of the *Hood* was balanced by the sinking of the *Bismarck*. British forces drove Italian armies back from the Egyptian frontier and across half the coastline of Libya, and broke up the Italian empire of East Africa—Eritrea, Somaliland, and Ethiopia.

Germany, fearing the total collapse of her Italian ally, sent reinforcements to Libya, and began a new offensive in the Balkan region, where Greece, with British aid, was more than holding her own against the superior forces of Italy on the Albanian frontier. Having already occupied without resistance Rumania, Hungary, and Bulgaria, Germany persuaded the Regency of Yugoslavia to sign an agreement, preparatory to launching a drive against Greece. A popular revolution in Yugoslavia resulted in the repudiation of the pact with Germany; but what diplomacy had lost, mechanized warfare regained. German tanks and airplanes smashed Yugoslavia and hurled themselves successfully at the British and Greek lines of defense. A small British expeditionary force was harried from the Greek mainland and later from the island of Crete.

[2] Norway, Belgium, the Netherlands, Poland were still nominally in a state of war with Germany but their countries had been completely occupied; France had surrendered, except for a small force under General De Gaulle; Rumania offered no resistance; Greece and Yugoslavia had not yet entered the war.

The Near Eastern situation was now full of peril. The whole southeastern quarter of Europe was subject to Germany and Italy; a weak and terrified French Government permitted German planes to use bases in Syria; a hostile native government arose in Iraq; Italian armies stood once again on the frontiers of Egypt. The British, however, succeeded in reoccupying Iraq and seizing French Syria, against the resistance of the regular French forces but with the aid of independent French volunteers under De Gaulle. Then a German attack on Russia threw the whole war into new perspective. Though the Germans advanced rapidly in the summer of 1941 they did not succeed, as they had against Poland and France, in breaking the main lines of resistance by Blitzkrieg methods. At the cost of enormous losses on both sides, the Russians held out for many months against Germany's heaviest attacks while the skies over Britain remained almost free from hostile aircraft. Russia and Britain together forced German agents out of Iran (Persia).

The Far East as well as the Near East caused anxiety. Japan, Britain's ally in the First World War, was now an Axis Power, allied to Germany. Though formally neutral, and in fact much too occupied with her unsuccessful war in China to be altogether free for new enterprises, Japan gave grounds for uneasiness by seizing French Indo-China and by veiled threats against the Dutch and British East Indies, Hong-Kong, and Singapore. Australia, New Zealand, and India would all be menaced if Japanese ambition were to lead to fresh military ventures.

The United States had watched the approach of the Second World War with growing concern. President Roosevelt, though restrained by an anxious Senate from giving full rein to his concern to save the peace of the world, was personally no isolationist. Before the war broke out he had expressed a desire to 'quarantine' aggressive Powers, had assured Canada that an attack on the Dominion would be considered a threat against the United States (thus adding a useful pendant to the Monroe Doctrine), and had urged Germany to follow pacific courses in the Czechoslovak crisis. His Secretary of State, Cordell Hull, was an internationalist of the Bright and Cobden type, seeing in tariff barriers one of the chief obstacles to world peace.

There was, however, grave fear that once again, as in 1812 and in 1917, a European conflict would draw a reluctant United States into war. This resulted in a code of neutrality legislation forbidding American ships to enter danger zones, placing a similar injunction on individuals traveling on belligerent ships, prohibiting loans or sales on credit, and even a provision (until President Roosevelt secured its repeal) restricting the export of munitions. For the sake of peace, the United States had surrendered the freedom of the seas for which the nation had twice gone to war.

In both the First and Second World Wars the United States, while still technically neutral, became an arsenal and granary for the enemies of Germany. There are, however, marked differences between the two cases. In both 1914 and 1939 American sentiment was predominantly pro-British, but on the former occasion the government did not officially take sides until German attacks on American ships and lives brought the United States into war. President Roosevelt, unlike President Wilson, wore his sympathies openly on his sleeve. From the first he took every measure 'short of war' which he thought public opinion would approve to aid one belligerent group and thwart the other. Popular polls and straw votes, as well as his own re-election for the unprecedented honor of a third term, showed that his increasingly unneutral course was approved by a large majority of his fellow Americans.[3]

After the fall of France, mere sympathy with British courage or abstract antagonism to Nazi principles gave way to acute concern for American safety. National apprehension expressed itself in a huge expansion of the army, navy, and air force; in the adoption of conscription for the youth of the land; in the transfer of fifty destroyers from the American to the British fleet in return for permission to erect naval bases on British islands along the Atlantic coast; in the military occupation of Greenland and Iceland; and, most significantly of all, in the passage of a measure authorizing the President, at his

[3] 'There were those who favored the Allies because they considered this war a replica of the last, and those who favored the Allies because they thought this war was different; those who saw Hitler as the modern expression of "Kaiserism," and those who saw Germany as genuinely menacing to America—unlike the Kaiser; those who saw Germany as the recurring source of the world's troubles, and those who confined their enmity to the Germany of 1940.' H. Lavine and J. Wechsler, *War Propaganda and the United States* (1940), p. 72.

discretion, to lease or lend war materials to friendly Powers and the extension of $7,000,000,000 (£1,400,000,000) for that purpose.

The United States even broke all diplomatic precedent by joining with a belligerent Power in a joint statement of war aims. At a dramatic meeting in the waters of the North Atlantic, in August 1941, President Roosevelt and Prime Minister Churchill drew up a statement of eight points for permanent peace. In many respects they resembled Wilson's famous 'fourteen,' but they had added significance in coming not from the chief of a single Power but in the name of all the English-speaking peoples round the world.

The United States was already belligerent in sympathy and in economic aid, but not in legal form or in military action, on that fateful morning of 7 December 1941, when Japan attacked Pearl Harbor in the Hawaiian Islands. The treacherous character of this attack, in the very midst of peace negotiations at Washington, roused a resentment that ended all debate between 'interventionist' and 'isolationist' Americans. Congress forthwith declared war on Japan; Germany and Italy without delay declared war on the United States.

Owing to the drain on British resources elsewhere, the Pacific colonies of the Commonwealth were inadequately defended, and the Dutch, whose homeland had been conquered by Germany, could send no aid to their colonies at all. Japan reaped all the advantages which preparedness, surprise, and breach of faith can bring to the aggressor. Within a few months the Japanese had seized the Philippines, Guam, and Wake Islands from the United States; conquered the Malay peninsula, Hong-Kong, Singapore, Burma, and both the Dutch and British East Indies; threatened India, Australia, and Siberia, and advanced her armies farther into China. The British rescued Madagascar, weakly held by a German-dominated French government, barely in time to prevent a Japanese occupation.

Germany in the meantime pushed her campaign against Russia in the Ukraine and the Crimea, and advanced across Libyan deserts towards Egypt. The English-speaking peoples did not stand altogether alone, for they had on their side the hard-fighting Russians, the stubborn Chinese, the refugees from martyred continental Europe, and the support of most of Latin America. But so great was the driving power of the Axis tyrannies that the whole world must have succumbed to their rule if it had not been for the industrial power and enduring moral temper of the United States and the British Commonwealth. It is no flourish of rhetoric, but a simple statement of fact, to say that on them depended the salvation of all mankind.

Fortunately, the war came at the one moment in history when these lands of English speech understood each other most completely and could work together in greatest harmony. Though the United States and each British Dominion as well enjoyed absolute freedom of action, goods were made and exchanged, armies and navies intermingled, policies proclaimed and enforced, with a degree of unity rarely to be found even among the subjects of a single centralized government.

This significant trend should not be interpreted as 'colonialism,' 'Anglomania,' or a feeling that 'blood is thicker than water.' The people of the United States, as this book has repeatedly emphasized, are not even predominantly of British ancestry, and the large minority who are of British origin are only a little more inclined to favor British interests as such than those whose ancestors came from Holland, Germany, Sweden, Italy, and Poland. Indeed, in the years when the British and American people were most different in their customs and most divergent in sentiment and policy (let us say about the time of the War of 1812) the proportion of British blood in America was greater than it is today.

The real bond of union among the English-speaking peoples is not racial. It is partly one of language, but even more of similarity of institutions and ideals. Principles common to Great Britain, the Dominions, and the United States include the 'reign of law' as opposed to mere executive force, civilian control of military power, a wider range of personal and local liberty and freedom for minorities than prevails elsewhere in the world, and ethical ideals of kindliness, decency, and fair play. So long as the English-speaking nations hold their place in the world these conceptions will find a home, and so long as the language is spoken or its literature remembered they will find utterance.

SUGGESTIONS FOR FURTHER READING

As thousands of books have been written about the general history of the United States or the various parts of the British Empire-Commonwealth, and an even greater number have dealt with particular periods, men, and events, it would be obviously impossible to present a detailed bibliography without making it as disproportionate to the brevity of this volume as is the tail of a comet to its head. In this short supplementary note, therefore, we have rigidly limited ourselves to listing a few standard works in which the reader can find fuller treatment of the details of national or imperial history.

GENERAL REFERENCES

In seeking wider pastures the reader may turn first of all to some such bibliographical guide as *A Guide to Historical Literature* (1931), edited by W. A. Allison, S. B. Fay, A. H. Shearer, and H. R. Shipman, and read the brief comments on the books listed in the sections on Great Britain and Ireland, Exploration and Colonial Expansion, Asia, Africa, Oceanica, British North America, and the United States. Even the best bibliographies, however, speedily get out of date and must be supplemented by the reviews of recent books in such professional periodicals as the *American Historical Review*, the *English Historical Review*, the *Canadian Historical Review*, and others of like standing. For more detailed study, there are such comprehensive surveys of sources as Charles Gross's *Sources and Literature of English History from the Earliest Times to about* 1485.

Both the British Empire and the United States have comprehensive biographical studies of their famous dead: the *Dictionary of National Biography*, edited by Leslie Stephen and Sir Sidney Lee, and the *Dictionary of American Biography*, edited by Allen Johnson. For the living, we have the British *Who's Who, Who's Who in America, Who's Who in Canada*, and similar publications. One need scarcely mention such familiar annual compilations of factual material as *The Statesman's Year Book, The Annual Register, Whitaker's Almanac, The World Almanac, Political Handbook of the World*, and the like.

In selecting a 'Gideon's band' of a few chosen titles among many, not the least embarrassment is to choose between the great classics which are sometimes a little out of date, such as the works of Freeman, Froude,

Macaulay, and Bancroft, and more recent works which may have less literary power but enjoy the advantage of later research. In general, we have given preference to works of quite recent date and to later editions of books which have been republished. The older histories should most certainly be read, but in the spirit in which a modern biologist would read Darwin's *Origin of Species,* as a classic of his science rather than as a current factual text.

BRITISH HISTORY

General histories published in many volumes, each volume by a historian especially interested in a particular period, are inevitably somewhat uneven in treatment but they have the advantage of discussing events in considerable detail, as much as the general reader is likely to need, and of containing very full bibliographies to guide the specialist to the literature available on particular topics. Three excellent recent series for British history are *The Political History of England* (1905-10), edited by William Hunt and Reginald L. Poole, in twelve volumes; the slightly briefer *History of England* (1904-13), edited in seven volumes by Charles Oman; and, the most recent of all, *The Oxford History of England,* edited by G. N. Clark. All the books in these three series are at least competent, and some of them, in spite of their youth, are already ranked among the standard texts of British historiography. Attention may also be called to the volumes of H. D. Traill's *Social England* (1894-8), a rather encyclopedic survey of the facts of British social history.

General histories by individual authors are usually less detailed, but they are indispensable for those who have neither time nor shelf room for the great series histories. Of the older books of this type two are still widely read: J. R. Green's *Short History of the English People* (first published in 1874) for its literary power, and S. R. Gardiner's *Student's History of England* (1891), for its wealth of detail; both have been frequently republished. Many good texts, written on both sides of the Atlantic, have since appeared; among these it is hard to select the best, but it is safe to mention at least G. M. Trevelyan's very readable *History of England* (1926); A. L. Cross's detailed *Shorter History of England and Greater Britain* (1939); E. Wingfield-Stratford's philosophic *History of British Civilization* (1932); R. B. Mowat's *New History of Great Britain* (1922); W. E. Lunt's *History of England* (1938). Every reader will take pleasure also in being introduced, however briefly, to the great nineteenth-century historians in G. P. Gooch's *History and Historians of the Nineteenth Century* (1913) and in C. A. Beard's *Introduction to the*

English Historians (1906), the former an estimate of the men, the latter a series of typical extracts from their writings.

Since all the world is so greatly debtor to England's unique constitutional and legal experience, the literature on these subjects is vast. It is not possible to list all of even the major works in this field, but a few which might be mentioned are G. B. Adams, *Constitutional History of England* (1921); T. P. Taswell-Langmead, *English Constitutional History* (1929 ed.); Bishop William Stubbs, *Constitutional History of England* (3 vols., first published in 1874-8 but often republished), a standard pioneer study; A. L. Lowell, *The Government of England* (2 vols., 1910), an American view; A. B. White, *Making of the English Constitution* (1925), concerned chiefly with the later Middle Ages; F. W. Maitland, *Constitutional History of England* (1908); Sir Frederick Pollock and F. W. Maitland, *History of English Law before the Time of Edward I* (2 vols., 1899), dealing with origins; W. S. Holdsworth, *History of English Law* (9 vols., 1903-26), very comprehensive and technical; H. Potter, *Introduction to the History of English Law* (1926); A. F. Pollard, *The Evolution of Parliament* (1920); G. B. Adams and H. M. Stephens, *Select Documents of English Constitutional History* (1910).

Next to parliaments and juries, the chief British contribution to world history has been the development of power-driven machine industry. Hence it is not surprising that there have been many general economic and industrial surveys, such as A. P. Usher, *Introduction to the Industrial History of England* (1920); E. P. Cheyney, *Introduction to the Industrial and Social History of England* (1920); William Cunningham, *Growth of English Industry and Commerce* (3 vols., 1915-21); E. Lipson, *Introduction to the Economic History of England* (1915); C. M. Waters, *Economic History of England* (1925); J. H. Clapham, *Economic History of Great Britain* (2 vols., 1933); G. H. Perris, *The Industrial History of Modern England* (1914); also special studies in almost every phase of agricultural, commercial, and industrial life.

For the medieval period see Charles Oman, *England before the Norman Conquest* (1910); R. H. Hodgkin, *History of the Anglo-Saxons* (1935); J. E. A. Jolliffe, *The Constitutional History of Medieval England* (1937); C. H. Haskins, *The Normans in European History* (1915); L. F. Salzman, *English Industries of the Middle Ages* (1923) and *Henry II* (1915); J. S. McKechnie, *Magna Carta* (1914); Mary Bateson, *Medieval England* (1904); E. Jenks, *Edward Plantaganet* (1902), for the legislation of Edward I; G. M. Trevelyan, *England in the Age of Wycliffe* (1904); and, for those who have leisure and interest to study the contested problems of medieval history, the works of

Freeman on the Norman conquest and of Seebohm and Vinogradoff on the old English village community.

The Tudor and Stuart periods are very rich in historical studies. For a very brief introduction to the former one may turn to Conyers Read, *The Tudors* (1936); for a somewhat fuller account to Arthur Innes, *England under the Tudors* (1937); while no short survey of the latter is better than G. M. Trevelyan, *England under the Stuarts* (1930). In the *Political History of England* series the volumes by H. A. L. Fisher and by A. F. Pollard, covering the Tudor period, are unusually good. Of course everyone thinks of the brilliant writings of James Anthony Froude in the Tudor period, but Gladys Temperley, *Henry VII* (1915), A. F. Pollard, *Henry VIII* (1905), J. E. Neale, *Queen Elizabeth* (1934), and E. P. Cheyney, *History of England from the Defeat of the Spanish Armada to the Death of Elizabeth* (2 vols., 1914-26) are more recent and in some respects more reliable. The great student of the Stuart period was Samuel Gardiner, whose standard works on *The History of England from the Accession of James I to the Outbreak of the Civil War* (10 vols., 1901 ed.), *History of the Great Civil War* (4 vols., 1901 ed.), and *History of the Commonwealth and Protectorate* (4 vols., 1903) have not since been surpassed. C. H. Firth, *Last Years of the Protectorate* (2 vols., 1909) brings Cromwell's period to its end. Carlyle, Gardiner, Firth, Morley, and other men of ability have told and retold Cromwell's own story, but perhaps the most readable of them all is John Buchan's *Cromwell* (1934).

With the Restoration the stream of history becomes a river. Some contemporary sources are still worth reading, such as the diaries of Samuel Pepys and of John Evelyn, and Bishop Burnet's history of his own time. Of later writers Lord Macaulay's *History of England from the Accession of James II* (5 vols., 1849-61, often republished) secured the widest audience ever given to a single secular historian. O. Airy, Arthur Bryant, and David Ogg have all written recent studies of the reign of Charles II; Hilaire Belloc (somewhat too favorably) of James II; G. M. Trevelyan of the reign of Queen Anne, and Winston Churchill of his ancestor the Duke of Marlborough. W. E. H. Lecky's *History of England in the Eighteenth Century* (8 vols., 1878-90 and later editions) is the best survey of the early Hanoverian period as a whole. One may also use the briefer account of C. G. Robertson, *England under the Hanoverians* (1911). John Morley has provided us with good studies of Walpole and Burke, and Basil Williams with probably the best on Chatham. For a close understanding of British politics in the mid-eighteenth century one should consult L. B. Namier, *The Structure of Pol-*

itics at the Accession of George III (2 vols., 1929). *The Cambridge History of British Foreign Policy,* 1783-1919, edited by Sir A. W. Ward and G. P. Gooch (3 vols., 1922-3), and the various studies of Napoleon and his great enemy William Pitt the younger by J. Holland Rose, are of special value for the Napoleonic years. W. T. Laprade, *England and the French Revolution* (1909), and W. P. Hall, *British Radicalism,* 1791-97 (1912), show the ferment of revolutionary ideas in Britain.

Among the general histories of the nineteenth and twentieth centuries may be mentioned G. M. Trevelyan, *British History in the Nineteenth Century* (1922); Gilbert Slater, *The Growth of Modern England* (1933); Sir Spencer Walpole, *History of England from the Conclusion of the Great War in* 1815 (6 vols., 1910-13 ed.), and its supplement, *History of Twenty-Five Years,* 1856-1880 (4 vols., 1904-8 ed.); E. Halévy, *History of the English People* (1924 ff.), a French view; H. W. Paul, *History of Modern England* (5 vols., 1904-6); J. McCarthy, *History of Our Own Times* (2 vols., 1887 and later editions); R. H. Gretton, *Modern History of the English People,* 1880-1910 (2 vols., 1913); R. W. Seton-Watson, *Britain in Europe,* 1789-1914 (1937), a study of foreign affairs; R. C. K. Ensor, *England,* 1870-1914 (1936); C. R. Fay, *Great Britain from Adam Smith to the Present Day* (1928), stressing economic matters; A. Viton, *Great Britain, An Empire in Transition* (1940).

There are biographies for all the great nineteenth-century figures from Lytton Strachey's slightly ironic *Queen Victoria* (1921) and P. Guedalla's studies of Wellington and Palmerston to G. Wallas's able *Life of Francis Place* (1891), the emancipator of the trade unions. Gladstone and Disraeli were specially fortunate. John Morley's *Life of Gladstone* (3 vols., 1903) and W. F. Monypenny and G. E. Buckle's *Life of Benjamin Disraeli* (6 vols., 1910-20) are biographical classics, while there are many good short studies of both men, such as W. P. Hall, *Mr. Gladstone* (1931) and A. Maurois, *Disraeli* (1927), which have quarried from these longer works.

Some studies in special fields of recent history include E. Porritt, *The Unreformed House of Commons* (2 vols., 1909); G. S. Veitch, *The Genesis of Parliamentary Reform* (1913); Charles Seymour, *Electoral Reform in England and Wales* (1915); Walter Bagehot, *The English Constitution* (1872), a famous description of Victorian constitutional balance; C. J. H. Hayes, *British Social Politics* (1913), dealing with social reform in the early twentieth century; the studies of the village and town laborer by John and Barbara Hammond, and of the trade-union movement by Sidney and Beatrice Webb; the numerous memoirs brought out by the First World War, of which the most interesting are probably those by former Premier David Lloyd George, Sir Edward Grey, Winston Churchill, and Col. T. E. Lawrence; and such studies of post-war conditions as C. F. G. Masterman, *England after the War* (1923), A. Siegfried, *Post-war Britain* (1924), and W. Dibelius, *England* (1930), representing respectively an English, a French, and a German view.

There are relatively few general historical works on the individual countries of Scotland, Ireland, and Wales, though there are many pages dealing with them in practically all histories of Britain and (in spite of the slight inaccuracy of designation) in many histories of England; and particular picturesque episodes, such as the career of Queen Mary Stuart or the Jacobite rebellions, have attracted many authors. A good brief introduction to Scottish history is R. L. Mackie's *Short History of Scotland* (1931). The histories of Scotland by Peter H. Brown (3 vols., 1902-9), C. S. Terry (1920), and Andrew Lang (4 vols., 1900-07) are fuller; they all stress the period of Scottish independence more than the years since the union with England. On special topics one may mention J. Mackinnon's works on the *Constitutional History of Scotland from Early Times to the Reformation* (1924), *The Union of England and Scotland* (1896), *Social and Industrial History of Scotland* (2 vols., 1920-21); Robert S. Rait, *Parliaments of Scotland* (1924); W. L. Mathieson's studies on the interrelation of politics and religion in *Politics and Religion, a Study in Scottish History from the Reformation to the Revolution* (2 vols., 1902), *Scotland and the Union* (1905), *The Awakening of Scotland* (1910), and *Church and Reform in Scotland* (1916). Good Scottish biographies are fairly numerous; such are for example Sir H. E. Maxwell, *Robert the Bruce* (1909), the studies on Queen Mary and on the Young Pretender by Andrew Lang, and John Buchan's *Montrose* (1928).

The Irish home-rule movement in the late nineteenth and twentieth centuries called attention to the long-neglected field of Irish history, but a good deal of the recent history writing has been partisan and the reader must be watchful for bias for or against Irish nationalism. Among the better works are Stephen Gwynn's *History of Ireland* (1923) and *Ireland* (1924); E. Curtis, *A History of Ireland* (1937); G. H. Orpen, *Ireland under the Normans* (4 vols., 1911, 1920); W. O. Morris, *Ireland, 1494-1868* (1909); R. Bagwell, *Ireland under the Tudors* (3 vols., 1885-90) and *Ireland under the Stuarts* (2 vols., 1909); J. G. MacNeill, *Constitutional and Parliamentary History of Ireland till the Union* (1917); E. Barker, *Ireland in the Last Fifty Years, 1866-1916*

(1919); E. R. Turner, *England and Ireland* (1919), a popular sketch of the past relations of the two countries; R. M. Henry, *The Evolution of Sinn Fein* (1920); D. R. Gwynn, *The Irish Free State* (1928); N. Mansergh, *The Irish Free State* (1934) and *The Government of Northern Ireland* (1937).

Some good works on Wales are Sir John Rhys and Sir David Brynmor-Jones, *The Welsh People* (1900); Gilbert Stone, *Wales, Her Origins, Struggles and Later History* (1915); O. M. Edwards, *Wales* (1902); and Wm. Rees, *South Wales and the March* (1924), dealing with the period of Anglo-Welsh wars.

IMPERIAL AND COLONIAL HISTORY

The British Empire has been the subject of a number of comprehensive surveys, partly historical and partly descriptive and geographical. Among these may be mentioned *The Cambridge History of the British Empire* (1929 ff.), edited by J. H. Rose, A. P. Newton, E. A. Benians; *The Oxford Survey of the British Empire* (1914), edited by A. J. Herbertson and O. J. R. Howarth; *The Historical Geography of the British Colonies* (1888-1923), edited by Sir Charles Lucas; *The British Empire, A Survey* (1924), edited by Hugh Gunn.

There are also shorter works by individual historians, such as A. P. Hall's *A History of England and the British Empire* (1937); J. A. Williamson's *A Short History of British Expansion* (1931); J. T. Adams, *Building the British Empire* (1938), supplemented by his *Empire on the Seven Seas,* 1784-1939 (1940); H. Robinson, *The Development of the British Empire* (1936); C. F. Mullett, *The British Empire* (1938); A. F. Pollard, *The British Empire, Its Past, Present and Future* (1909); G. W. Morris and L. S. Wood, *The English-speaking Nations* (1924); H. Egerton, *A Short History of British Colonial Policy* (1897); P. Knaplund, *The British Empire,* 1815-1939 (1941).

Histories of British colonial activity date back to Richard Hakluyt's *Principall Navigations, Voyages and Discoveries of the English Nation* in Elizabeth's time, continued under the Stuarts by Samuel Purchas, and reprinted in many subsequent forms. For those who wish a modern account G. B. Parks's *Richard Hakluyt and the English Voyages* (1928) is useful. Some other works dealing wholly or mainly with early colonization are Sir C. Lucas, *Beginnings of English Overseas Enterprise* (1917); W. E. Lingelbach, *Merchant Adventurers of England* (1902); J. Hannay, *The Great Chartered Companies* (1926); John Fiske, *The Discovery of America* (3 vols., 1892); H. E. Bolton and T. M. Marshall, *The Colonization of North America* (1920); A. B. Keith, *Constitutional History of the First British Empire* (1930); L. Gipson, *The British Empire before the American Revolution* (1936), and the notable series of studies by G. L. Beer, *Origins of the British Colonial System,* 1578-1660 (1908), *The Old Colonial System,* 1660-1754 (2 vols., 1912), and *British Colonial Policy,* 1754-1765 (1922).

On the American colonies, individually and collectively, books are legion. To mention only a very few of the most important general works, the reader might well begin with Francis Parkman's distinguished series of studies, mainly dealing with the conflict of the French and English in Canada, which are still valuable after many years (centenary edition in 13 vols., 1922). Important books of more recent date include C. M. Andrews, *The Colonial Period in American History* (3 vols., 1934-7) and his *Colonial Background of the American Revolution* (1924); E. B. Greene, *Foundation of American Nationality* (1935); J. T. Adams, *The Founding of New England* (1921) and *Revolutionary New England* (1923); C. W. Alvord, *The Mississippi Valley in British Politics* (2 vols., 1917); the scholarly, if somewhat ponderous, studies by H. L. Osgood, *The American Colonies in the Seventeenth Century* (3 vols., 1904-7) and *The American Colonies in the Eighteenth Century* (4 vols., 1924-5); and such studies of social life in colonial America as Edward Eggleston's *The Transit of Civilization from England to America in the Seventeenth Century* (1901); T. J. Wertenbaker, *The First Americans,* 1607-90 (1927), and J. T. Adams, *Provincial Society,* 1690-1763 (1927). Revolutionary histories, and general American histories overlapping the colonial period, will be considered in a later section of this bibliography.

Britain has, of course, an American empire still. Its most important unit, Canada, has already a most extensive historiography. A convenient bibliographical aid is the *Review of Historical Publications Relating to Canada* (22 vols., 1896-1919), edited by G. M. Wrong, H. H. Langton, and W. S. Wallace. There are several series on Canadian history: *Chronicles of Canada* (32 vols., 1914-16), edited by G. M. Wrong and H. H. Langton; *The Makers of Canada,* a series of biographies edited by D. C. Scott and Pelham Edgar (1906-16), and *Canada and Its Provinces* (1914-17), edited by A. Shortt and A. G. Doughty. Shorter works that might be mentioned are C. Wittke, *A History of Canada* (1933); H. Egerton, *Canada under British Rule* (1917); Sir J. G. Bourinot, *Canada under British Rule* (1922); E. Porritt, *Evolution of the Dominion of Canada* (1918); J. G. Brebner, *New England's Outpost: Acadia before the Conquest of Canada* (1927); A. L. Burt, *A*

Short History of Canada for Americans (1942). Other American possessions of the British Crown are considered in J. D. Rogers, *Newfoundland* (1931); H. Wrong, *The Government of the West Indies* (1923); F. W. Pitman, *Development of the British West Indies, 1700-1763* (1917); C. Atchley, *The West Indies* (1905); L. J. Ragatz, *Fall of the Planter Class in the British Caribbean* (1929); W. L. Mathieson, *British Slavery and Its Abolition* (1926); V. F. Boyson, *Falkland Islands* (1924).

Turning to the Old World, one finds the vast Indian Empire the main center of historical study. Besides such series as the *Cambridge History of India* (6 vols., 1922), there are individual works among which might be mentioned *The Oxford History of India*, by V. A. Smith (1923); P. E. Roberts, *History of British India under the Company and the Crown* (1923); Sir Valentine Chirol, *India, Old and New* (1921) and *India* (1926); A. B. Keith, *A Constitutional History of India* (1936); A. D. Innes, *A Short History of the British in India* (1919). Farther east: A. Wright and T. Reid, *Malay Peninsula* (1912); A. Ireland, *The Far Eastern Tropics* (1905); G. H. Scholefield, *The Pacific, Its Past and Future* (1919).

For Australasia one might mention E. Jenks, *History of the Australasian Colonies* (1896); A. Jose, *History of Australasia* (1899); E. Scott, *Short History of Australia* (1916); B. R. Wise, *Commonwealth of Australia* (1913); W. P. Reeves, *State Experiments in Australia and New Zealand* (2 vols., 1923) and *New Zealand* (1925); Sir J. H. P. Murray, *Papua of Today* (1926); J. B. Condliffe, *Short History of New Zealand* (1925); G. H. Scholefield, *New Zealand in Evolution* (1909); A. Siegfried, *Democracy in New Zealand* (1914).

For Africa there is an indispensable work of reference in political geography, Sir Edward Hertslet's *Map of Africa by Treaty* (1908-9). Good general accounts of the partition of Africa include Sir H. H. Johnston's *History of the Colonization of Africa by Alien Races* (1913); Sir C. Lucas, *Partition and Colonization of Africa* (1922); N. D. Harris, *Europe and Africa* (1927); G. L. Beer, *African Questions at the Paris Peace Conference* (1923); and two hostile views, P. Moon, *Imperialism and World Politics* (1926) and L. S. Woolf, *Empire and Commerce in Africa* (1919). The European diplomatic background is well sketched in W. L. Langer, *The Diplomacy of Imperialism* (2 vols., 1935). Egypt and South Africa, in particular, have been the subject of many studies; one might instance Lord Cromer's *Modern Egypt* (2 vols., 1908); Sir Valentine Chirol, *The Egyptian Problem* (1920); G. M. Young, *Egypt* (1927); Sir Alfred Lyall, *Rise and Expansion of the*

British Dominion in Egypt (1923); R. I. Lovell, *The Struggle for South Africa* (1934); R. H. Brand, *Union of South Africa* (1909). Crown colony government in general is well discussed in Sir Charles Bruce's *The Broad Stone of Empire* (2 vols., 1910).

Some books no longer of value for current fact are still important because of the influence they had on their own time in stimulating imperialist sentiment; among them were Sir John Seeley's *Expansion of England* (1883), Sir Charles Dilke's *Greater Britain* (1868); J. A. Froude's *Oceana* (1886). This transition to greater interest in colonial affairs is recounted in C. A. Bodelson, *Studies in Mid-Victorian Imperialism* (1924), and P. Knaplund, *Gladstone and Britain's Imperial Policy* (1927).

The imperial organization of the British peoples in recent years has been the subject of much study and speculation. Important works in this field include W. P. Hall, *From Empire to Commonwealth* (1928); W. Y. Elliott, *The New British Empire* (1932); A. Zimmern, *The Third British Empire* (1926); H. D. Hall, *The British Commonwealth of Nations* (1920); A. Demangeon, *The British Empire* (1925), a French view; R. Jebb, *Studies in Colonial Nationalism* (1905) and *The Imperial Conference* (2 vols., 1911); C. M. MacInness, *The British Commonwealth and its Unsolved Problems* (1925); H. Egerton, *Federations and Unions within the British Empire* (1924); and the legal studies by A. B. Keith, *Responsible Government in the Dominions* (1928), *Dominion Home Rule in Practice* (1921), *War Government of the British Dominions* (1921) and *Selected Speeches and Documents on British Colonial Policy* (2 vols., 1918). Lionel Curtis's *Problem of the Commonwealth* (1916) is typical of a large number of works dealing with the still unsolved problem of imperial federation.

HISTORY OF THE UNITED STATES

Like Great Britain and Canada, the United States has a number of histories published in series by various authors. The best known is *The American Nation,* in 28 volumes, under the editorship of Albert B. Hart (1904-18). More recent are the *Chronicles of America,* in 50 short volumes under the editorship of Allen Johnson; *A History of American Life,* still in process of publication, edited by A. M. Schlesinger and D. R. Fox, and *The Pageant of America,* edited by R. H. Gabriel (1926 ff.). These four series do not overlap so much as one might expect; the first is standard history, factual and mainly political; the second, less academic in tone, emphasizes some picturesque by-paths of national history; the third is economic and social history, almost to the exclusion of politics; the fourth is built around pictorial illustrations.

Probably the best short treatment of the period since independence is *The Growth of the American Republic* by S. E. Morison and H. S. Commager (2 vols., 1942). For those who can give time to a longer survey by a single scholar, the standard work is E. Channing, *History of the United States* (6 vols., 1905-25), written with advanced students in mind. Other good general histories, selected from scores of almost equally meritable works, are E. B. Greene and C. R. Fish, *Short History of the American People* (1924), the first volume covering the colonial and revolutionary period, the second the years of independence; H. C. Hockett and A. M. Schlesinger, *Political and Social History of the United States* (2 vols., 1925), a similar partnership, but with the line of division coming in Jackson's time; Charles A. and Mary Beard, *The Rise of American Civilization* (2 vols., 1927), emphasizing economic and cultural history; D. S. Muzzey, *United States of America* (2 vols., 1924); J. T. Adams, *The Epic of America* (1931); J. D. Hicks, *The Federal Union* (1937) and *The American Union* (1941); S. E. Morison, *Oxford History of the United States* (2 vols., 1927); D. Dumond, *A History of the United States* (1942).

Foreign studies of America have been numerous from St. John de-Crèvecœur's *Letters of an American Farmer* (1782) and the Comte de Tocqueville's study of *Democracy in America* (1835) to the present, but far and away the most important of them was Viscount James Bryce's *The American Commonwealth* (1888 and 1910), which has been supplemented by his two volume *Modern Democracies* (1921), containing an instructive comparison of the American, Canadian, Australasian, French, and Swiss political systems.

For the American Revolution and its background, in addition to the titles already listed under imperial and colonial history, one might mention C. H. Van Tyne, *Causes of the War of Independence* (1922), *The War of Independence* (1929), and *Loyalists of the American Revolution* (1902); C. M. Andrews, *Colonial Background of the American Revolution* (1924); H. Egerton, *Causes and Character of the American Revolution* (1923); A. M. Schlesinger, *Colonial Merchants and the American Revolution* (1918); C. H. McIlwain, *The American Revolution, a Constitutional Interpretation* (1923); R. G. Adams, *Political Ideas of the American Revolution* (1922); C. L. Becker, *The Declaration of Independence* (1922); Allan Nevins, *American States during and after the Revolution* (1924); Sir Geo. O. Trevelyan, *The American Revolution* (6 vols., 1920-22), a sympathetic British point of view; L. B. Namier, *England in the Age of the American Revolution* (1930) for the parliamentary background of the struggle.

The constitution-making period, the Constitution itself, and the political methods which have grown up under its aegis have been the subject of very extensive historical treatment. *The Federalist,* a defense of the Constitution by Hamilton, Madison, and Jay, is of fresh interest after a century and a half of subsequent history. A. C. McLaughlin, *The Confederation and the Constitution,* in the American Nation series, is excellent, and John Fiske's *The Critical Period of American History,* 1783-89 (1888) still has value. One may also consult Charles Warren, *The Making of the Constitution* (1928), R. L. Schuyler, *The Constitution of the United States* (1923), Max Farrand, *The Framing of the Constitution of the United States* (1913), and C. A. Beard's iconoclastic *Economic Interpretation of the Constitution of the United States* (1913).

On American politics in general see, in addition to Bryce's books already mentioned, E. Stanwood, *History of the Presidency* (1928); H. J. Laski, *The American Presidency* (1940); Woodrow Wilson, *Congressional Government* (1925 ed.), a famous study first published in 1885; Charles Warren, *The Supreme Court in American History* (2 vols., 1926); A. C. McLaughlin, *Constitutional History of the United States* (1935); C. E. Merriam, *The American Party System* (1922); E. Robinson, *Evolution of American Political Parties* (1924) and *History of American Political Theories* (1926 ed.); E. Robinson, *Evolution of American Political Parties* (1924); M. I. Ostrogorskii, *Democracy and the Party System in the United States* (1919), a Russian view; R. H. Gabriel, *The Course of American Democratic Thought* (1940); Dexter Perkins, *The Monroe Doctrine* (1927), perhaps the best of many studies of this topic; S. F. Bemis, *The Diplomatic History of the United States* (1936); R. G. Adams, *History of the Foreign Policy of the United States* (1924); A. Nevins, *America in World Affairs* (1942).

On the early republic, the westward movement and the rise of democracy one may instance John B. McMaster, *History of the People of the United States from the Revolution to the Civil War* (8 vols., 1883-1913); Henry Adams, *History of the United States of America* (9 vols., 1889-91), covering the administrations of Jefferson and Madison; F. L. Paxson, *History of the American Frontier* (1925), and *The Last American Frontier* (1928); F. J. Turner, *The Frontier in American History* (1920); A. Henderson, *Conquest of the Old Southwest* (1920); B. Hinsdale, *Old Northwest* (1899); C. Goodwin, *The Trans-Mississippi West,* 1803-53 (1922); W. J. Ghent, *The Road to Oregon* (1929); J. Schafer, *History of the Pacific Northwest* (1905); J. H.

Smith, *The War with Mexico* (2 vols., 1919), taking a perhaps too favorable view of American expansionism; W. P. Webb, *The Great Plains* (1931); Stuart Henry, *Conquering Our Great American Plains* (1930); V. L. Parrington, *Main Currents of American Thought* (2 vols., 1927), showing American culture as a reflection of social forces; Van Wyck Brooks, *The Flowering of New England* (1936); C. R. Fish, *The Rise of the Common Man* (1927); Dixon Wecter, *The Hero in America* (1941), a study in changing national ideals.

Douglas Freeman has written not only the standard life of General Lee, the best American military biography, but has given us a bibliographical introduction to Southern history in general in his *The South to Posterity* (1939). Other good background studies to the sectional conflict are U. B. Phillips, *American Negro Slavery* (1929) and *Life and Labor in the Old South* (1929); W. E. Dodd, *The Cotton Kingdom*, and J. Macy, *The Anti-Slavery Crusade*, both in the Chronicles of America series; G. H. Barnes, *The Anti-Slavery Impulse* (1933); D. Dumond, *The Secession Movement* (1931); R. S. Henry, *The Story of the Confederacy* (1931). The standard political history of the period is J. F. Rhodes, *History of the United States from the Compromise of 1850* (8 vols., 1920 ed.), an admirable work but best in its earlier volumes. J. G. Randall, *The Civil War and Reconstruction* (1937) is also excellent. J. G. Nicolay and John Hay, *Abraham Lincoln* (10 vols., 1890, 1917) is really a history of the war as well as a biography. N. W. Stephenson has written what is probably the best short biography of Lincoln, and Carl Sandburg the best full length study. Englishmen have been greatly interested in this phase of American history; witness, for example, Sir F. Maurice's life of Lee, Colonel G. Henderson's biography of Jackson, Lord Charnwood's portrayal of Lincoln, General Fuller's study of Grant, and the historical plays on Lincoln and on Lee by John Drinkwater.

The throng of books dealing with various aspects of recent American history almost defies selection. Some of the best shorter works are in the American Nation series, such as W. A. Dunning's *Reconstruction;* in the Chronicles of America series, such as W. L. Fleming, *The Sequel of Appomatox,* S. J. Buck, *The Agrarian Crusade,* C. Seymour, *Woodrow Wilson and the World War;* in the History of American Life series, A. Nevins, *The Emergence of Modern America,* 1865-78, A. M. Schlesinger, *The Rise of the City,* and H. U. Faulkner, *The Quest for Social Justice.* There are many short histories, of the textbook type, by C. A. Beard, L. B. Shippee, F. L. Paxson, P. L. Haworth, C. R. Lingley, H. B. Parkes, J. D. Hicks, Dwight Dumond and others, which deal wholly or mainly with recent decades; and a few longer histories, such as those of Rhodes or Oberholtzer. Biography is often much more than biography; thus A. Nevins's *Hamilton Fish* (1936) is really the best account we have of the Grant administration, and C. Seymour's *Intimate Papers of Colonel House* (4 vols., 1928), B. J. Hendrick's *Life and Letters of Walter Hines Page* (3 vols., 1922) and Frederick Palmer's *Newton D. Baker* (2 vols., 1931) contribute as much to our knowledge of America in the First World War as C. Seymour's sympathetic *American Diplomacy during the World War* (1933) or W. Millis's critical *The Road to War* (1935). Some of the best surveys of American life in these latter days are labeled 'economics' or 'sociology,' but they warrant the attention of the historian; thus one of the most valuable records of average twentieth-century life is *Middletown* (1929) by Robert and Helen Lynd, and the facts of American industrial development are nowhere better summarized than in the highly statistical *Recent Social Trends in the United States* (2 vols., 1929), edited under the chairmanship of Herbert Hoover. For very recent tendencies C. A. Beard's *America in Midpassage* (1939) is a good summary of domestic problems, and H. R. Luce, *The American Century* (1941), of world perspectives.

INTERRELATIONS

Finally, there are books which concern alike the American and the British Commonwealths. Some are primarily diplomatic studies, such as Wm. A. Dunning, *The British Empire and the United States* (1914), a review of their relations during the century of peace that followed the Treaty of Ghent; R. B. Mowat, *Diplomatic Relations of Great Britain and the United States* (1925); G. M. Wrong, *The United States and Canada* (1921); J. M. Callahan, *American Foreign Policy in Canadian Relations* (1937); A. L. R. Burt, *The United States, Great Britain and British North America* (1940), for the years before 1814; E. D. Adams, *Great Britain and the American Civil War* (2 vols., 1925). Some are more broadly political, such as A. C. McLaughlin, *America and Britain* (1919); E. D. Adams, *Great Britain, America and Democracy* (1919); G. L. Beer, *The English-Speaking Peoples, Their Future Relations and Joint International Obligations* (1917); L. M. Gelber, *The Rise of Anglo-American Friendship* (1938); R. H. Heindel, *The American Impact on Great Britain, 1898-1914* (1940). Some are studies of migration, such as S. C. Johnson, *History of Emigration from the United Kingdom to North America* (1913), or H. J. Ford, *The Scotch-Irish in America* (1915). Some show the reactions of individual travellers, such as Allan Nevins, *American Social History as Recorded by British Travellers* (1924), and R. B. Mowat, *Americans in England* (1935). Some are propagandist, advocating political union in one form or another, such as S. Kennedy, *The Pan-Angles* (1915), or the more famous *Union Now with Britain* (1941) by C. K. Streit.